의미로 분류한
한국어 · 영어 학습사전

<의미로 분류한 한국어·영어 학습사전>은 한국문화사 사전개발비의 보조를 받아 개발되었음.

편집: 박상길
삽화: 임은희 · 명유경
표지 디자인: 명유경

의미로 분류한
한국어 · 영어 학습사전

신현숙
박정운
강우순
임테레사

Handbook of Korean Lexicon

Hyon-Sook Shin
Jeong-Woon Park
Woosoon Kang
Theresa Yim

한국문화사
Hankook Publishing Co.

© 2000 Hankook Publishing Company
All rights reserved
Printed in Korea

Hyon-Sook Shin (신현숙), has a Ph.D. in Korean Linguistics from Kun-Kuk University and is currently a professor of Korean Language Education at Sangmyung University.

Jeong-Woon Park (박정운), a professor of English Linguistics at Hankuk University of Foreig Studies, has a Ph.D. in Linguistics from University of California, Berkeley.

Woosoon Kang (강우순), has a Ph.D. in English Linguistics from Kyung Hee University and is currently a postdoctoral of BK 21 Linguistics at Kyung Hee University.

Theresa Yim, a graduate of University of Toronto, is currently teaching English at Hankuk University of Foreign Studies.

Address	Professor Hyon-Sook Shin Department of Korean Language Education Sangmyung University 7 Hongji-Dong, Jongro-Gu, Seoul 110-743, Korea TEL.: (02)2287-5093 (Office) FAX.: (02)395-4564 (Office) e-mail: hssh@pine.sangmyung.ac.kr
	Hankook Publisher Co. 133-112 Songdong-gu Songsu 1-ga 2 Dong 13-156 Tel.: (02)464-7708, 3409-4488 Fax.: (02)499-0846 E-mail: munhwasa@hanmail.net Registration number: 2-1276 Price ₩40,000 ISBN 89-7735-739-X

Preface

With the sudden increase in Korean language learners recently, we felt a need for an appropriate dictionary for Korean language learners. For instance, some dictionaries contain information that is even difficult for Koreans to understand, and some dictionaries carry a lot of information that is not useful for Korean learners. Consequently, this project started with an interest in developing a dictionary for English-speaking Korean language learners. Moreover, since there are no dictionaries of this kind in Korea, we had faced much difficulties from the start — from selecting words, grouping words, to defining words not found in the English language.

In *Korean Lexicon*, we took 14,020 words used in everyday life and categorized them into 43 semantic fields to effectively provide information on the Korean language to Korean learners and Korean language instructors. For example, in a short time all words related to "Education" such as *kindergarten, elementary school, middle school, high school,* and *uni* can be found under one semantic field.

The nature of this book being a dictionary made us spend an entire year proofreading and editing. However, we are sure that there is still room for improvement. With your continuous criticisms and guidance, we believe this project will become more valuable and fruitful.

We would like to thank all those who participated in developing this project. We are also grateful to Mr. Jin-Soo Kim, the president of Hankuk Publishing Company, and his editing staff. Without their support this dictionary would have been still in its draft form from 15 years ago.

A Guide to Using the Dictionary

1. Lexical Choice

1) This dictionary contains words that are most commonly used.
2) Native Korean words, Sino-Korean words, and foreign loan words have all been included here. However, what are considered to be foreign words have been excluded. In other words, words that do not have appropriate substitutes and have become common in Korean-speaking life, for example 'bus,' have been treated as entry words, although words such as 'wife' have not.
3) Words that are used daily in present-day Korean life and culture, some of which are not included in other dictionaries, have been included.
4) This dictionary focuses on words rather than on phrases and sentences.
5) Function words, such as noun particles and verb particles, have been supplemented with examples. These examples have been selected from current junior high school and high school textbooks.

2. Classification Criteria

1) Although the classification criterion of this dictionary is based on meaning, the lexical field has been divided into general categories. The categories are arranged according to the order of the Korean alphabet making the words easy to find.
2) The order of lexical fields is anthropocentric: fields related to people have been placed first.
3) Because action and state are treated within the purview of each of its own lexical field, related words can be found according to meaning. However, words concerned with action and state have been compiled and placed at the end of the dictionary so that concerned words can be found separately.

3. Symbols

- (—) (hyphen): used in front or behind the affix, noun particles, and verb particles
- · (middle dot): used in instances of the same content
- ' ' (single quotation marks): used for attributing material to another or for emphasis

Contents

1	People and Relationships	1
2	Family and Relatives	11
3	Sex and Marriage	20
4	The Body and Hygiene	26
5	Diseases and Treatments	38
6	Life and Death	51
7	Senses and Sense Organs	59
8	Thoughts and Emotions	68
9	Characters and Attitudes	84
10	Clothing Life	97
11	Diet	111
12	Domestic Life	137
13	Spoken and Written Languages	157
14	Journalism and Publishing	180
15	Information and Communication	187
16	Education	193
17	Science and Scholarship	209
18	Religions and Beliefs	222
19	Civilization and Culture	234
20	Arts	238
21	Hobbies	257
22	Games	263
23	Exercise	268
24	Names of Countries	275
25	Nation and Politics	280
26	Law and Order	298
27	National Defense	309
28	Society and Social Activities	321
29	Economy and Economic Activities	330
30	Employment	353
31	Industry	365
32	Fuel and Energy	382
33	Traffic and Transportation	386
34	Natural Phenomena	394
35	Animals	405
36	Plants	419
37	Shapes	430
38	Light and Colors	438
39	Number and Quantity	445
40	Time	458
41	Space and the Universe	472
42	States and Degrees	485
43	Action and Movement	507

Appendix: Function Words

- ▶ Indicators 557
- ▶ Connectors 567
- ▶ Particles 571
- ▶ Endings 579

Appendix: Index 591

1 인간과 인간관계
People and Relationships

This chapter contains lexical entries, describing people based on their appearance, personality, action, age, gender or class. It also contains lexical entries which name various human relationships and the roles within these relationships.

가난뱅이	① poor man ② pauper
가명	① fictitious name ② pseudonym
가정주부	housewife
각시	bride
갓난아기	newborn baby
개구쟁이	① brat ② naughty child
개척자	pioneer
거인	giant
거지	beggar
거짓말쟁이	liar
걸인	beggar
게으름뱅이	① idle fellow ② indolent person
겨레	① offspring of the same forefather ② people
계집	① girl ② one's wife
계집애	girl
고아	orphan
곰보	① pockmarked person ② person with a pitted face
곱추	hunchback
공주	princess

남자	여자
남성	여성
소년	소녀
총각	처녀
남자친구	여자친구
신랑	신부
신사	숙녀
아저씨	아주머니
할아버지	할머니

공처가	① man bossed by his wife ② henpecked husband
과부	widow
괴짜	① eccentric ② weirdo
괴한	① suspicious-looking fellow ② strange-looking guy
구경꾼	spectator
구두쇠	miser
군	Mr.
귀공자	young noble
귀머거리	deaf
귀부인	① lady ② noble woman
기형아	deformed child
깍쟁이	① tightwad ② shrewd person ③ sly dog
꼬마	① kid ② child
나그네	traveler
난쟁이	dwarf
남	① another person ② others ③ stranger ④ outsider
남녀	man and woman
남녀노소	① people of all ages and both sexes ② men and women of all ages
남성	male
남자	man
남자친구	boyfriend
남학생	male student
녀석	① guy ② chap ③ boy ④ kid
노약자	the old and the weak
노인	elderly person
노파	elderly person
놈	① fellow ② guy ③ chap ④ boy ⑤ kid
농아	mute
느림보	① laggard ② dawdler
늙은이	old person

—님	① Mr. ② Mrs. ③ Miss
달인	① expert ② master ③ masterhand
당사자	person concerned
대장부	manly man
독불장군	man of self-assertion
독신	① celibacy ② bachelorhood ③ spinsterhood ④ being single
동갑	same age
동급생	classmate
동기동창	① graduates of the same class ② classmate
동기생	① graduates of the same class ② classmate
동년배	same age bracket
동료	① colleague ② fellow worker
동무	friend
동문	alumni
동반자	① accompanist ② companion
동창	alumni
동창생	① fellow student ② schoolfellow ③ schoolmate
동포	① brothers ② brethren ③ fellow countrymen
동호인	persons sharing the same interest
두목	① boss ② captain
둔재	dull person
뚱보	① fat person ② obese person
뜨내기	① vagabond ② wanderer
말썽꾸러기	troublemaker
망나니	① rough-and-tumble man ② rascal
맹인	blind person
멋쟁이	fashionable dresser
멍청이	fool
명인	① master-hand ② expert
목격자	witness
못난이	① simpleton ② fool

미남	handsome man
미녀	beautiful woman
미망인	widow
미성년자	① minor ② juvenile
미인	beautiful woman
민간인	① private citizen ② civilian
민족	race
바보	fool
반항아	rebel
배신자	traitor
배우자	spouse
백만장자	millionaire
백수	① jobless person ② bum
백인종	the white race
벗	① friend ② crony
벙어리	① dumb ② mute
병신	① deformity ② deformed person ③ cripple
보호자	① guardian ② parent ③ benefactor
본인	① her/himself ② oneself
본토박이	① native ② aboriginal
부녀자	① woman ② women folks
부인	① woman ② lady ③ one's wife ④ married woman
부자	① rich (wealthy) person ② affluent
불청객	① self-invited guest ② uninvited guest ③ gate crasher
빈털터리	penniless
사나이	man
사내	man
사내아이	boy
사람	person
사망	death
사모님	① teacher's wife (deferential) ② your/his wife (deferential) ③ madam
사부	teacher

사생아	illegitimate child
사팔뜨기	cross-eyed person
새댁	newly married woman
새색시	bride
새침데기	① person who pretends innocence ② prude
색시	① bride ② maid
선구자	pioneer
선남선녀	① handsome man and beautiful woman ② good man and woman
선교사	missionary
선머슴	naughty (mischievous) child
선배	senior
선비	① scholar ② learned man ③ gentleman
선생님	teacher
선후배	seniors and juniors
성인	adult
소경	blind person
소녀	girl
소년	boy
소아	① young child ② infant
손아래사람	one's junior
손윗사람	one's senior
수재	① talented student ② bright person
숙녀	lady
순악질	purely evil-natured
술고래	① lush ② boozer
술주정뱅이	troublesome drunkard
스승	one's teacher
시각장애자	① eyesight-handicapped ② visually handicapped
시골뜨기	① country folk ② country bumpkin
식물인간	human vegetable
신동	① infant genius ② child prodigy ③ wonder child ④ wonder boy

신랑	bridegroom
신부	bride
신사	gentleman
신생아	① neonate ② newborn
신세대	new generation
신체장애자	① physically handicapped ② disabled person
신출내기	① greenhorn ② novice
실향민	person who couldn't go to his (her) hometown
심술쟁이	ill-natured person
씨	① Mr. ② Mrs. ③ Miss
아가	① baby ② infant
아가씨	① Miss ② husband's younger sister
아기	baby
아담	Adam
아동	child
아랫사람	one's junior
아씨	① madame ② your (good) lady
아이	child
아저씨	① uncle ② middle-aged man
아주머니	① aunt ② middle-aged lady
아줌마	middle-aged lady
아편쟁이	opium addict
악당	① scoundrel ② rascal ③ villain
악동	① bad child ② brat
악질	evil nature
안주인	landlord
앉은뱅이	cripple
알부자	really wealthy person
애늙은이	① person who looks older than his/her years ② mature person
애송이	① fledgeling ② greenhorn ③ novice
애인	lover
애주가	habitual drinker
야만인	① barbarian ② savage

약사	pharmacist
양	Miss (when you refer to somebody younger than the person who is talking)
양반	① nobility ② aristocratic class
어르신	old person (deferential)
어른	adult
어린이	① child ② children
억만장자	billionaire
여걸	heroine
여류작가	woman writer
여사	Madame
여성	① woman ② women
여왕	queen
여인	woman
여자	woman
여자친구	girlfriend
여장부	heroine
여학생	female student
연인	lover
영감	① old man ② sir
영아	infant
영재	① gifted person ② brilliant child
오른손잡이	right-handed person
오줌싸개	bed wetter
왕	king
왕비	queen
왕자	prince
외톨이	lonely person
왼손잡이	left-handed person
욕심쟁이	① avaricious person ② greedy person
욕쟁이	① foul-mouthed person ② slanderer
울보	① blubberer ② crybaby
웃어른	① senior ② elder
원시인	primitive person
원주민	① native ② aborigine
위인	① great man ② great mind

People and Relationships

윗사람	① superordinate ② senior
유망주	up-and-coming person
유목민	nomads
유명인	famous person
유명인사	celebrity
유복자	posthumous child
유아 (幼兒)	infant
유아 (乳兒)	baby
의뢰인	client
이방인	① outsider ② stranger
이브	Eve
이웃	neighbor
이웃사촌	good neighbor
이재민	① the sufferers ② the afflicted people ③ the victims
인간	human being
인류	mankind
인명	① human life ② life
인사	celebrity
인재	① capable man ② talented person
인조인간	robot
인종	race (amongst the human race)
잠꾸러기	① sleepyhead ② late riser
장난꾸러기	① menace ② rogue
장년	① prime of life ② heyday
장님	blind
장애인	① disabled person ② the handicapped
장정	man
저능아	mentally deficient child
절름발이	cripple
젊은이	young person
정박아	mentally challenged child
정부 (情夫)	paramour (of a married woman)
정부 (情婦)	① mistress ② lady love ③ paramour (of a married man)
정상인	normal person

정신박약아	psychopaedic
정신병자	① insane person ② lunatic
제삼자	① third person (party) ② outsider ③ disinterested party
제자	① one's student ② disciple ③ pupil
주동자	① promoter ② principle person
주부	housewife
중년	middle age
지진아	mentally challenged child
지체부자유자	① disabled person ② the handicapped
직장동료	co-worker
직장상사	superior official in one's workplace
책벌레	bookworm
처녀	① virgin ② maid ③ spinster
철인 (鐵人)	iron man
철인 (哲人)	① wise man ② sage
청각장애자	the hearing impaired
청년	① youth ② young man
청소년	① youth ② teenager
초보자	① novice ② beginner
촌놈	① rustic ② bumpkin
촌뜨기	① countryman ② bumpkin
총각	bachelor
추남	ugly man
추녀	ugly woman
친구	friend
키다리	① long-legged person ② tall person
태아	① embryo ② fetus
털보	hairy person
팔방미인	multi-talented person
폭군	tyrant
행운아	① child of fortune ② lucky person
허풍쟁이	① boaster ② braggart
현대인	① modern person ② person in the modern age
홀몸	① single person ② alone

홀아비	widower
홀쭉이	① skinny person ② lanky person
황인종	the yellow race
후계자	successor
후배	junior
후보자	candidate
흑인종	the black race

2 가족과 친인척
Family and Relatives

> This chapter contains lexical entries describing family relationships, family system and pedigrees, particularly lexical entries dealing with Korean family life.

가문	① one's family ② one's clan
가부장제	patriarchy
가정	① home ② family ③ household
가정환경	① home background
	② home environment
가족	family
가족계획	family planning
가족관	view of family
가족관계	family relation
가족제도	family system
결손가정	① broken family
	② single parent family
결혼	marriage
겹사돈	person doubly related by children's marriage
계모	stepmother
계부	stepfather
고모	aunt (father's sister)
고모부	uncle (father's sister's husband)
고부	mother-in-law and daughter-in-law
고조할머니	great-great grandmother

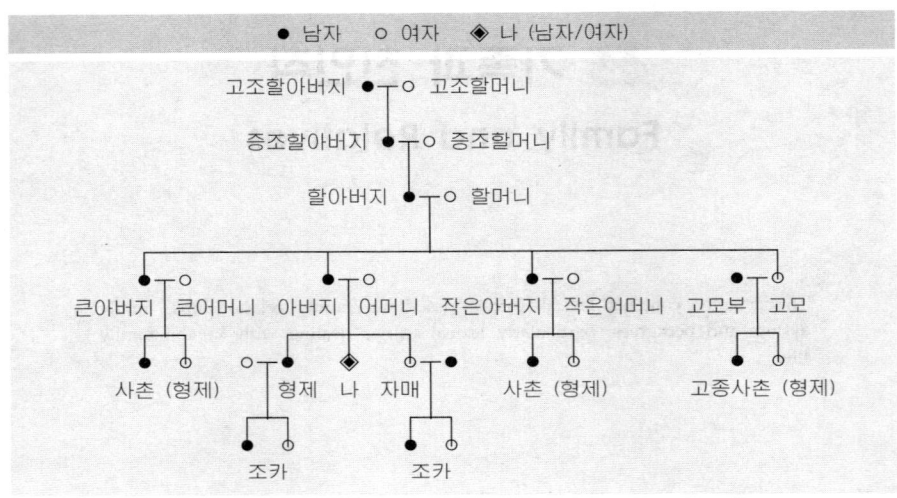

고조할아버지	great-great grandfather
고종사촌	cousin (paternal aunt's child)
남동생	younger brother
남매	brother and sister
남편	husband
누나	male's elder sister
누님	male's elder sister (honorific)
누이	sister
누이동생	younger sister
당숙	father's first male cousin
대	generation
대가족	① large family ② extended family
데릴사위	① man who marries into his wife's family ② son-in-law taken into the family
도련님	husband's younger brother
동기	siblings
동생	younger brother or sister
동서	① husband's brother's wife ② wife's sister's husband
따님	daughter (deferential)
딸	daughter

마누라	one's wife
막내	youngest child
맏딸	eldest daughter
맏아들	eldest son
맏이	eldest child
매부	male's elder sister's husband
매제	male's younger sister's husband
매형	male's elder sister's husband
며느리	daughter-in-law
모녀	mother and daughter
모성애	maternal love
모자	① mother and son ② mother and child
모친	mother
무남독녀	only one daughter without sons
바깥사돈	father-in-law of one's child
바깥양반	one's husband
방계가족	collateral family
배다른 형제	step brother or step sister (from different mother)
백모	aunt
백부	uncle
본처	① legal wife ② one's wedded wife
부군	husband
부녀	father and daughter
부모	parents
부부	husband and wife
부인	wife
부자	father and son
부친	father
불효자	unfilial son
사돈	relatives by marriage
사돈어른	father-in-law of one's child
사돈처녀	unmarried sister of daughter- or son-in-law
사돈총각	unmarried brother of daughter- or son-in-law

● 남자　○ 여자　◆ 나 (남자/여자)　■ 배우자 (남자/여자)

사돈　　나　　사돈
며느리　아들　딸　사위

사위	son-in-law
사촌	cousin
삼촌	uncle (on the father's side)
새아버지	stepfather
새어머니	① stepmother ② new mother
새언니	female's elder brother's new wife
생모	① one's real mother
	② one's biological mother
생부	① one's real father
	② one's biological father
생질	nephew
서방	① one's husband ② Mr.
서방님	① husband
	② husband's married younger brother
손녀	granddaughter
손부	① one's grandson's wife
	② one's granddaughter-in-law
손자	grandson
손주	grandson
수양딸	adopted daughter
수양아들	adopted son
숙모	aunt (father's younger brother's wife)
숙부	uncle (father's married younger brother)
시누이	husband's sister
시댁	① hunsband's family
	② the house of woman's father-in-law
시동생	husband's younger brother
시부모	① woman's parents-in-law
	② one's husband's parents

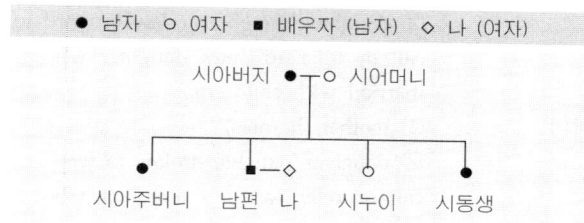

시아버지	husband's father
시아주버니	husband's brother
시어머니	husband's mother
시집	① husband's home ② husband's family
식구	family
아내	one's wife
아드님	your/his son (deferential)
아들	son
아버님	father (honorific)
아버지	father
아범	my husband (humble)
아비	father
아빠	① dad ② daddy
아우	① male's younger brother ② female's younger sister
아저씨	uncle
아주머니	aunt
아주버님	husband's older brother
안사돈	mother-in-law of one's child
안사람	one's wife
양녀	adopted daughter
양부모	stepparents
양아들	adopted son
양아버지	stepfather
양어머니	stepmother
양자	adopted son
어머니	mother
어머님	mother (honorific)
어멈	① mother (humble)

어미	② daughter/daughter-in-law (a word to call or refer to one's daughter who is married with children) ① mother (humble) ② daughter/daughter-in-law (a word to call or refer to one's daughter who is married with children)
언니	female's elder sister
엄마	① mom ② mommy
여동생	younger sister
여편네	① one's wife ② married woman
오누이	brother and sister
오라버니	female's elder brother
오빠	female's elder brother
올케	female's elder brother's wife
외가	① the house of mother's parents ② mother's maiden home
외가집	mother's family's home
외동딸	only daughter
외사촌	cousin on the mother's side
외삼촌	maternal uncle (mother's brother)
외손녀	daughter's daughter
외손자	daughter's son
외손주	daughter's son
외숙모	maternal aunt
외숙부	maternal uncle

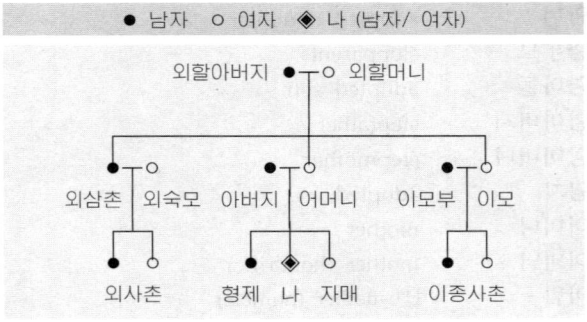

외아들	only son
외할머니	one's maternal grandmother
외할아버지	one's maternal grandfather
의붓아버지	stepfather
의붓어머니	stepmother
의붓자식	stepchild
의형제	sworn brothers
이모	maternal aunt
이모부	maternal uncle
이복형제	① half brother or sister ② half brothers and sisters
이산가족	dispersed families
이종사촌	maternal cousin (mother's sister's child)
인척	relatives
입양아	adopted child
입양하다	to adopt
자녀	children
자당	your/his mother (honorific)
자매	sisters
자손	descendents
자식	① child ② offspring
작은아버지	father's married younger brother
작은어머니	father's married younger brother's wife
작은집	father's married younger brother's house
장남	eldest son
장녀	eldest daughter
장모	wife's mother
장모님	wife's mother (honorific)
장인	wife's father

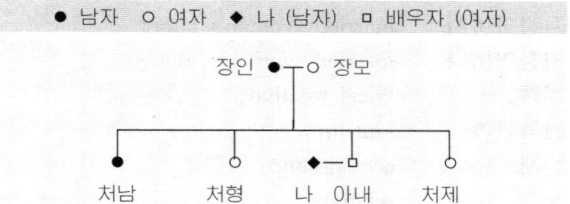

장인어른	wife's father (honorific)
전처	ex-wife
제부	wife's younger sister's husband
제수	male's younger brother's wife
조강지처	① one's wife married in poverty ② one's old life partner
조부모	grandparents
조상	ancestors
조카	nephew or niece
족보	genealogy
종갓집	head family house
종친회	meeting of the royal family
증손녀	great granddaughter
증손자	great grandson
증조할머니	great-grandmother
증조할아버지	great-grandfather
직계가족	family members in a direct line
질녀	niece
질부	nephew's wife
집사람	one's wife
집안	one's family
처가	one's wife's family
처남	wife's brother
처제	wife's younger sister
처조카	wife's nephew or niece
처형	wife's elder sister
춘부장	your/his father
친인척	relatives
친자	one's biological son
친정	married woman's home
친정아버지	married woman's father
친정어머니	married woman's mother
친족	lineal relative
친족관계	kinship
친지	acquaintance
친척	relative

친할머니	one's grandmother on father's side
친할아버지	one's grandfather on father's side
큰아버지	father's elder brother
큰어머니	father's elder brother's wife
큰집	head house
할머니	grandmother
할아버지	grandfather
항렬	generations of the clan
핵가족	nuclear family
현모양처	wise mother and good wife
혈연	blood kin
혈연관계	relationship by blood
형	elder brother
형님	elder brother (honorific)
형부	female's elder sister's husband
형수	male's elder brother's wife
형제₁	brothers and sisters
형제₂	brothers
혼인	marriage
홀어머니	① one's mother without her husband ② widow
효녀	dutiful daughter
효도	filial piety
효부	dutiful daughter-in-law
효자	dutiful son
후손	① descendant ② scion ③ posterity ④ offspring
후처	second wife

3 성과 결혼
Sex and Marriage

This chapter contains lexical entries related to sex (e.g., sexual activities, sex-related jobs, body organs, and physiological characteristics). It also contains lexical entries connected to marriage, marriage ceremonies, pregnancy/childbirth, and married life.

결혼하다	
장가가다 (남자)	시집가다 (여자)
신랑	신부
남편	아내
바깥양반	안사람

간음	adultery
간통	adultery
간통죄	① adultery ② criminal conversation
강간	rape
개가	remarriage
결혼	marriage
결혼기념일	wedding anniversary
결혼반지	wedding ring
결혼상담소	matrimonial center
결혼서약	wedding oath
결혼식	wedding ceremony
결혼식장	wedding hall
결혼하다	to marry
결혼행진곡	wedding march
과부	widow
궁합	matching the horoscopes of a prospective bride and groom
금실	conjugal harmony
금혼식	golden wedding
기혼자	the married

난산	hard delivery
난자	ovum
남성	male
낳다	① to bear (a child) ② to give birth to (a baby) ③ to be delivered of (a child) ④ to have (a baby)
노처녀	① old maid ② spinster
노총각	old bachelor
눈맞다	to fall in love with each other
동성	① same gender ② same sexuality
동성연애	homosexuality
동성연애자	homosexual
동침하다	to sleep together
득남하다	to give birth to a son
들러리	① best man ② bridesmaid
뚜쟁이	① pander ② pimp ③ matchmaker
맞선	meeting with a view to marriage
매춘	prostitution
매춘부	① prostitute ② whore
면사포	bridal veil
몸풀다	① to bear ② to give birth to a baby
미숙아	① preemie ② premature baby
미혼	① single ② unmarried
미혼모	mother (unmarried)
밀월여행	honeymoon
바람둥이	① licentious man ② wonton
바람피우다	to have an affair
배우자	spouse
백년해로	living together in happy union till parted by death
별거	separation
부부	① husband and wife ② couple
부부관계	conjugal relation
부부생활	married life
부부싸움	quarrel between husband and wife
부조	① help ② support ③ offering money

	(goods) to help (a person)(to) perform a marriage (funeral) service
부조금	congratulatory money
부케	(bride's) bouquet
분가	branch family
분만	delivery
분만실	delivery room
분만하다	to deliver
불륜	immorality
사랑	love
사랑하다	to love
사산	stillbirth
사정	ejaculation
사정하다	to ejaculate
산달	month of parturition
새댁	newly married woman
새색시	bride
새신랑	bridegroom
새신부	bride
생리	① physiology ② menstruation
생식	reproduction
생식기	genital organ
선	interview with a view to marriage
성	sex
성관계	sexual relationship
성교	sexual intercourse
성교하다	to have sexual intercourse
성기	① sexual organ ② genital organ
성생활	sex life
성욕	sexual desire
성차별	sexual discrimination
성추행	sex scandal
성폭행	sexual assault
성혼선언	declaration of marriage
성혼선언문	written declaration of marriage
성희롱	sexual harrassment

수정	insemination
순결	① chastity ② virginal purity
순산	easy labor (delivery, childbirth)
숫처녀	① pure virgin
	② innocent (immaculate) virgin
숫총각	① (male) virgin ② innocent bachelor
시댁	one's husband's family (home)
시집	husband's home
시집가다	to take a husband
시집살이	female's life in her parents-in-law's home
신랑	bridegroom
신방	bridal room
신부	bride
신생아	newborn baby
신생아실	newborn baby room (in hospital)
신접살림	living in a new home
신혼	newly-married
신혼부부	newly-married couple
신혼여행	honeymoon
애무	caress
애무하다	to caress
애정	① affection ② love
약혼	engagement
약혼녀	fiancée
약혼반지	engagement ring
약혼식	engagement ceremony
양수	amniotic fluid
연분	① fate ② destiny ③ connection
연애결혼	love marriage
연애하다	to fall in love
예단	silks offered as a wedding gift
예물	wedding gift
예식장	wedding hall
오르가즘	orgasm
원앙	mandarin duck

월경	① menstruation ② menses
웨딩드레스	wedding dress
유도분만	induced delivery
유부남	married man
유부녀	married woman
은혼식	silver wedding
음경	penis
이성	opposite sex
이혼	divorce
인공분만	artificial delivery
인공수정	artificial insemination
일부다처제	polygamy
일부일처제	monogamy
일처다부제	polyandry
임산부	pregnant woman
임신	pregnancy
임신하다	to conceive
입덧	morning sickness
잉꼬부부	happily married couple
잉태	① pregnancy ② conception
자궁	womb
자연분만	natural delivery
장가	taking a wife
장가가다	to take a wife
재혼	second marriage
전통혼례	traditional wedding
정자	sperm
제왕절개수술	Caesarean section
주례	① officiating at a wedding ② officiator
주례사	officiating speech at a wedding
중매	matchmaking
중매결혼	arranged marriage
중매쟁이	matchmaker
중성	unisex
질	vagina
짝사랑	unrequited love

〈전통혼례〉

창녀	① prostitute ② whore
처가살이	living in one's wife's home
처녀	① virgin ② young lady
첫날밤	bridal night
첫사랑	first love
청첩장	wedding invitation
청혼하다	to propose
체위	posture
초혼	first marriage
총각	① bachelor ② young man
축의금	congratulatory money
출산	delivery
키스	kiss
키스하다	to kiss
태기	signs (indications) of pregnancy
태아	① embryo ② fetus
탯줄	navel string
폐백	bride's gifts to her parents-in-law
포옹하다	to hug
피로연	wedding reception
피임	contraception
피임약	contraceptive pill
하객	congratulator
해산	delivery
해산하다	① to deliver ② to give a birth
혼담	offer of marriage
혼례	marriage (wedding) ceremony
혼수	① necessary articles for marriage ② marriage expenses
혼인	wedding
혼인신고	registration of one's marriage
홀아비	widower
화혼	others' wedding

〈폐백〉

4 신체와 생리작용
The Body and Hygiene

This chapter contains lexical entries referring to body organs and bodily characteristics and appearances, as well as those relating to health and basic physiology.

가랑이	crotch
가래	phlegm
가르마	part in one's hair
가마	hair whirl
가슴	① breast ② chest
가슴둘레	① girth ② bust
각선미	beauty of leg lines
간	liver
간니	adult tooth
갈비뼈	rib
감각기관	sensory organ
건강하다	to be healthy
검버섯	black spot on old man's skin
검지	① forefinger ② index finger
겨드랑이	armpits
고개	① nape ② head
골	brain
골격	① skeletal structure ② build
곱슬머리	curly hair
관상	physiognomic judgment of character
관자놀이	temple

관절	joint
광대뼈	cheekbone
구레나룻	whisker
구슬땀	beads of sweat
군살	① superfluous flesh ② fat
굳은살	① callosity ② callus ③ corn
궁둥이	① buttock ② hip
귀	ear
귀밑머리	hair braided behind the ears
귀지	earwax
귓가	close to one's ears
귓등	back of the ear
귓바퀴	① auricle ② pinna
귓밥	① earlobe ② earwax
귓불	earlobe
근육	muscle
금발	blonde
급소	vital part
기지개	stretching one's body
기침	cough
길몽	lucky dream
꼬르륵	with a rumble
꿈	dream
나체	① naked body ② nude body
난시	astigmatism
난청	hard of hearing
납작코	flat nose
낮잠	nap
낯	face
내장	① viscera ② internal organs
넓적다리	thigh
노폐물	waste matter
뇌	brain
누다	① to evacuate ② to let out (off) ③ to relieve nature (oneself)
눈	eye

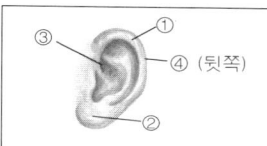

〈귀〉
① 귓바퀴
② 귓불
③ 귓구멍
④ 귓등

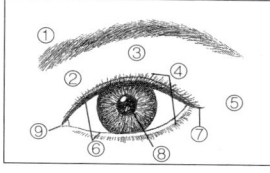

〈눈〉
① 눈썹   ② 눈꺼풀
③ 눈두덩 ④ 속눈썹
⑤ 눈가   ⑥ 눈시울
⑦ 눈꼬리 ⑧ 눈동자
⑨ 눈물샘

눈곱	eye discharge
눈꺼풀	eyelid
눈꼬리	① canthus ② corner of the eye
눈꼽	eye discharge (colloquial)
눈동자	pupil
눈두덩	protuberant part of the eyelid
눈망울	eyeball
눈매	① (cast of the) eyes
	② expression of the eyes
눈물	tear
눈물샘	lachrymal gland
눈살	wrinkles between the eyebrows
눈시울	① edge of an eyelid ② eye rims
눈썹	eyebrow
눈알	eyeball
눈자위	eyeball area
눈초리	① look ② canthus
눈총	① glare ② sharp look
늦잠	oversleeping
다리	leg
단발머리	bobbed hair
담즙	bile
대머리	baldhead
대변	feces
대장	large intestine
덧니	snaggletooth
동맥	artery
돼지코	upturned nose
두뇌	brain
뒤통수	① occiput ② back of the head
드르렁	snoring
들숨	① inhalation ② inspiration
들창코	upturned nose
등	back
따귀	face
딸기코	bulbous blotched nose

딸꾹질	hiccup
땀	① sweat ② perspiration
땀구멍	pores
땀띠	prickly heat
때	dirt
똥	① excrement ② feces
똥구멍	anus
똥배	potbelly
마렵다	to feel an urge to ease nature
매부리코	hooked nose
맥	pulse
맥박	pulsation
맹장	appendix
머리	① head ② hair
머리카락	hair
명치	pit of the stomach
모공	pore
목	neck
목덜미	nape
목젖	uvula
몸	body
몸매	① one's figure ② one's form
몸무게	weight
몸집	① stature ② build
몸통	trunk
몽고반점	Mongolian spot
무릎	knee
물렁뼈	cartilage
박동	pulsation
반점	① spot ② speck
발	foot
발가락	toe
발꿈치	heel
발등	instep
발목	ankle
발바닥	sole

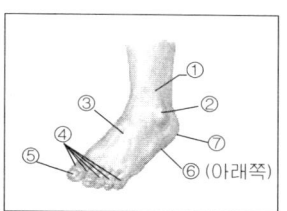

〈발〉
① 발목　② 복사뼈
③ 발등　④ 발가락
⑤ 발톱　⑥ 발바닥
⑦ 발꿈치

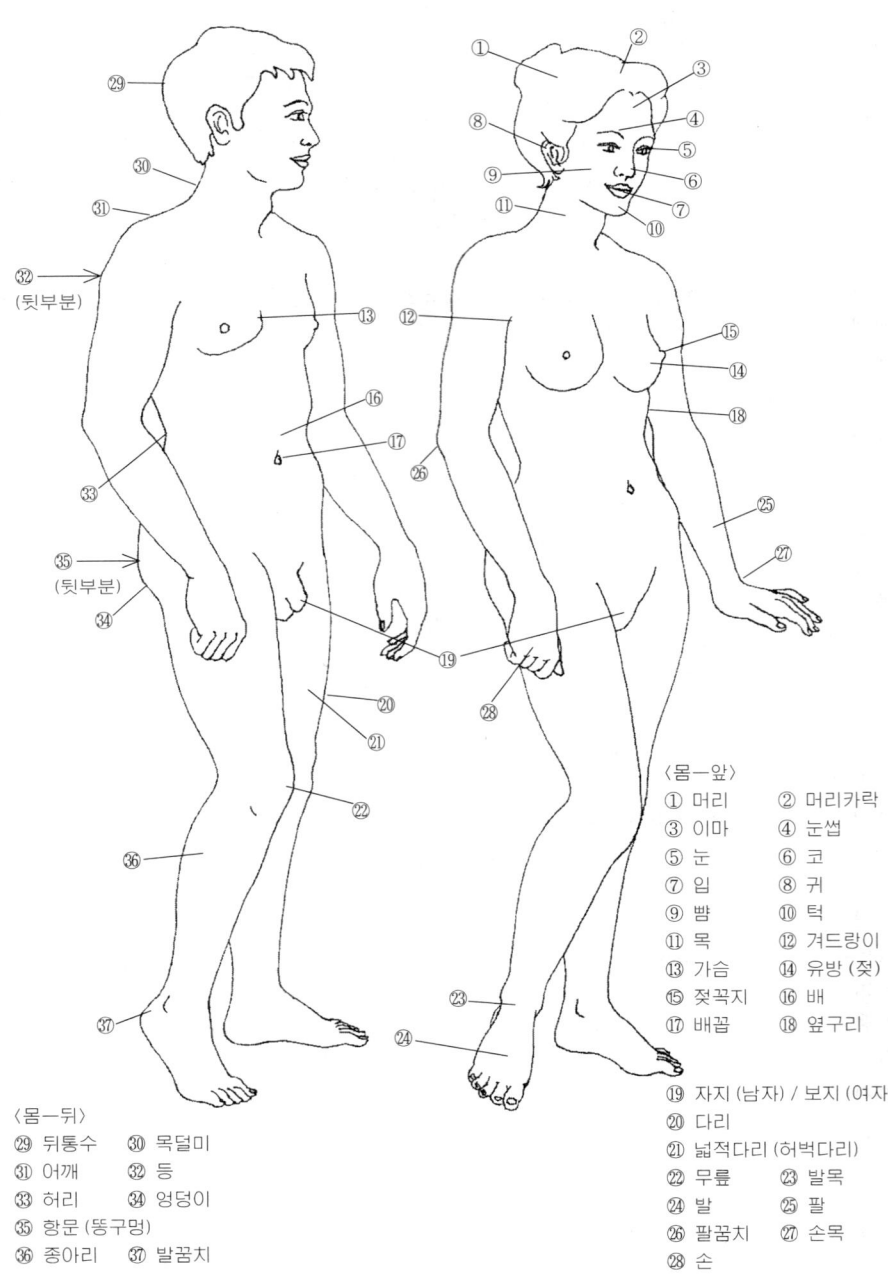

〈몸―앞〉
① 머리　② 머리카락
③ 이마　④ 눈썹
⑤ 눈　⑥ 코
⑦ 입　⑧ 귀
⑨ 뺨　⑩ 턱
⑪ 목　⑫ 겨드랑이
⑬ 가슴　⑭ 유방 (젖)
⑮ 젖꼭지　⑯ 배
⑰ 배꼽　⑱ 옆구리
⑲ 자지 (남자) / 보지 (여자)
⑳ 다리
㉑ 넓적다리 (허벅다리)
㉒ 무릎　㉓ 발목
㉔ 발　㉕ 팔
㉖ 팔꿈치　㉗ 손목
㉘ 손

〈몸―뒤〉
㉙ 뒤통수　㉚ 목덜미
㉛ 어깨　㉜ 등
㉝ 허리　㉞ 엉덩이
㉟ 항문 (똥구멍)
㊱ 종아리　㊲ 발꿈치

발톱	toenail
밥통	stomach
방귀	fart
배	① abdomen ② belly
배꼽	① navel ② bellybutton
배설	excretion
배설기관	excretory organ
백발	white (gray) hair
백혈구	white corpuscle
버짐	ringworm
변	① feces ② stool (s)
보조개	dimple
보지	vulva
복사뼈	malleolus
볼	cheek
볼기	buttock
볼우물	dimple
분비물	secretion
불알	testicle
비뇨기	urinary organs
비듬	dandruff
비지땀	heavy sweat
뺨	cheek
뻐드렁니	bucktooth
뼈	bone
뼈대	(bony) frame
뼈마디	joint
뽕	① pop ② farting sound
사랑니	wisdom tooth
사마귀	wart
사시	squint
사타구니	groin
삭발	shaving one's head
살	flesh
살갗	skin
살결	① complexion ② skin

상투	topknot
새끼손가락	little finger
생리	physiology
생머리	① uncurly hair ② unpermed hair
생식기	genital organ
선잠	① light (short) sleep ② doze ③ slumber (s) ④ dogsleep
성기	genital organ
성대	vocal cord
소름	gooseflesh
소변	urine
소장	small intestine
소화기	digestive organ
소화기관	digestive organ
속눈썹	eyelashes
손	hand
손가락	finger
손금	lines of the palm
손등	back of the hand
손목	wrist
손바닥	palm
손톱	fingernail
솜털	downy hair
송곳니	canine tooth
수면	sleep
수염	① mustache ② beard ③ whiskers
수혈	blood transfusion
숙면	sound sleep
숙변	feces contained long in the intestines
순환계	circulatory system
숨	breath
숨구멍	① windpipe ② pore
숫구멍	fontanel(le)
숱	thickness (of hair)
시력	eyesight
시신경	optic nerve

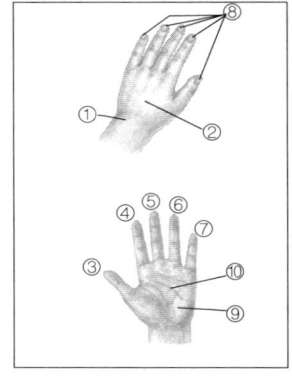

〈손〉

① 손목　② 손등
③ 엄지　④ 검지
⑤ 중지　⑥ 약지
⑦ 새끼손가락　⑧ 손톱
⑨ 손바닥　⑩ 손금

식도	gullet
식은땀	cold sweat
신경	nerve
신경계	nervous system
신장 (身長)	height
신장 (腎臟)	kidney
신진대사	① metabolism ② metastasis
신체	body
심장	heart
심전도	electrocardiogram
십이지장	duodenum
싸다	to excrete (urine, feces)
쌍꺼풀	double eyelid
쓸개	gallbladder
아랫배	lower belly
아랫입술	lower lip
악몽	nightmare
안구	eyeball
안색	① complexion ② countenance
알통	biceps
앞니	① incisor ② front teeth
애꾸눈	one-eyed
약손가락	ring finger
약지	ring finger
약체	weakling
약하다	to be weak
어금니	molar
어깨	shoulder
얼굴	face
엄지	thumb
엄지발가락	big toe
엄지손가락	thumb
엉덩이	① buttock ② hip
여드름	pimple
염통	heart
영구치	adult tooth

옆구리	flank
오금	hollow (back) of the knee
오동통	① plump ② chubby
오줌	urine
옥니	inturned tooth
요도	urethra
원시	farsightedness
월경	① menstruation ② menses
위	stomach
위산	acid in the stomach
위장	① stomach ② stomach and intestine
윗배	upper belly
윗입술	upper lip
유방	breast
유전자	DNA
유치	① milk tooth ② baby tooth
육체	body
은발	silvery hair
음경	penis
이	tooth
이마	forehead
이빨	tooth
인공호흡	artificial respiration
인대	ligament
인상	① physiognomy ② looks ③ facial features
입	mouth
입술	lip
입천장	① roof of the mouth ② palate
잇몸	gum
자궁	womb
자지	penis
작은창자	small intestine
잠	sleep
장기	① internal organ ② viscera
장지	middle finger

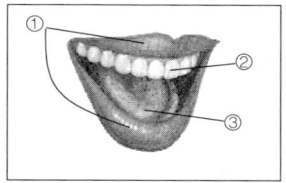

〈입〉
① 입술 ② 이 ③ 혀

재채기	sneeze
적혈구	① red corpuscle ② red blood cell
점	① spot ② speck
정강이	shin
정맥	vein
정수리	crown of the head
젖	milk
젖가슴	breast
젖꼭지	nipple
젖니	milk tooth
종아리	calf
주걱턱	protruding chin
주근깨	freckle
주름살	wrinkle
주먹	fist
주먹코	bulbous nose
중지	middle finger
지리다	to wet (soil) one's pants
지문	fingerprint
진땀	sticky sweat
집게손가락	forefinger
짱구	bulging head
쭈글쭈글	wrinkled
창자	intestine
척추	① backbone ② spine
청력	hearing ability
체온	bodily temperature
체중	weight
체중계	scale
체질	physical constitution
체취	① body smell ② body odor
체형	body type
치아	tooth
침	① spit ② saliva
침샘	saliva gland
코	nose

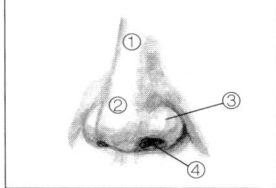

〈코〉
① 콧날
② 콧등
③ 콧방울
④ 콧구멍

코딱지	snot
코털	① nose hair ② vibrissa
콧구멍	nostril
콧날	ridge of the nose
콧대	nose bridge
콧등	nose bridge
콧물	nasal mucus
콧방울	wing of the nose
콧수염	mustache
콩팥	kidney
큰창자	large intestine
키	height
태몽	dream of forthcoming conception
턱	jaw
턱수염	beard
털	hair
토실토실	① plump ② chubby
트림	① belch ② burp
튼튼하다	① to be strong ② to be healthy
틀니	① denture ② artificial teeth
티눈	corn
파마머리	permed hair
팔	arm
팔꿈치	elbow
팔등신	well-proportioned figure
팔뚝	forearm
팔목	wrist
폐	lung
폐활량	lung capacity
포동포동	① plump ② chubby
피	blood
피부	skin
핏줄	① blood vessel ② vein
하품	yawn
항문	anus
해골	① skeleton ② skull

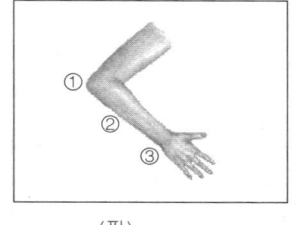

〈팔〉
① 팔꿈치
② 팔뚝
③ 팔목

허리	waist
허벅다리	upper thigh
허벅지	thigh
허우대	stature
허파	lung
혀	tongue
혈관	blood vessel
혈기	① vitality ② strength
혈색	complexion
혈압	blood pressure
혈액순환	blood circulation
혈액형	blood type
호흡	breath
호흡기관	respiratory organ
혹	① wen ② lump
흉터	scar
흰머리	gray hair
힘줄	tendon

5 병과 치료
Diseases and Treatments

This chapter contains lexical entries related to the types of diseases and symptoms that frequently afflict Koreans, and as well as physical or psychological handicaps. In addition, it contains and lists lexical entries on methods, medical devices, and medicines involved in the treatment of diseases.

가려움증	① itch ② itchiness
가루약	powdered medicine
가슴앓이	heartache
간경화증	hepatocirrhosis
간디스토마	fluke
간병인	nurse of the sick
간병하다	to nurse
간암	liver cancer
간염	① inflammation of the liver ② hepatitis
간질	epilepsy
간호사	nurse
간호하다	to nurse
감기	cold
감기약	cold medicine
감염	① infection ② contagion
개인병원	clinic
건강	health
건망증	① forgetfulness ② failure of memory ③ slip of memory
검진하다	① to examine

결리다	② to give a medical examination ① to feel a stitch ② to feel constrained ③ to be over-powered ④ to flinch from
결막염	conjunctivitis
결핵	① tubercle ② tuberculosis
경련	① convulsions ② spasm ③ cramp ④ twitch
경상	slight injury
고름	pus
고열	high fever
고통	pain
고혈압	high blood pressure
골다공증	osteoporosis
골병	internal disease
골수암	bone marrow cancer
골절	fracture
골절상	fracture of a bone
곪다	① to form pus ② to fester ③ to gather ④ to come to a head
과대망상증	megalomania
과로	① overwork ② over exertion ③ strain
관절염	① inflammation of a joint ② arthritis
교정하다	to correct
구급약	first-aid medicine
구급차	ambulance
구충제	insectifuge
구토	vomit
귓병	ear infection
근시	shortsightedness
근육통	muscular pain
급체	sudden indigestion
기관지염	bronchitis
기절	① fainting ② swoon
기침	cough
꾀병	malinger
끙끙	with groans

나병	leprosy
난소염	ovaritis
난시	astigmatism
난청	hearing difficulty
난치병	incurable disease
낫다	① to get well ② to recover
내과	① internal department ② internal medicine
내복약	internal medicine
노망	① senility ② dotage
노안	① presbyopia ② longsightedness
녹내장	glaucoma
뇌성마비	cerebral palsy
뇌염	encephalitis
뇌졸증	cerebral apoplexy
뇌진탕	concussion of the brain
뇌출혈	cerebral hemorrhage
눈병	eye disease
다래끼	sty
당뇨병	diabetes
독감	① influenza ② flu ③ bad cold
돌림병	epidemic
동맥경화증	arteriosclerosis
동상	frostbite
두드러기	① hives ② nettle rash
두통	headache
디스크	disk
딱지	scab
땀띠	① prickly heat ② heat rash
뜸	moxa cautery
류머티즘	rheumatism
마비	① paralysis ② palsy ③ monoplegia
마취	anesthesia
마취과	department of anesthesia
마취제	anesthetic
마취하다	① to put under anesthesia ② to apply

	anesthesia ③ to anesthetize
말라리아	malaria
매독	syphilis
멀미	① sickness ② nausea
멍	① bruise ② black eye
멍울	lump
면역	immunity
목발	crutch
몸살	illness from fatigue
몽유병	sleepwalking
무좀	athlete's foot
문둥병	leprosy
문병	visit to a sick person
물리치료	physical therapy
물리치료사	physical therapist
물약	liquid medicine
물집	blister
반신불수	hemiplegia
반창고	bandage
발작	① fit ② spasm
발진	eruption (on the skin)
방사선과	department of radiology
방사선치료	① irradiation ② radiation therapy
배탈	① stomach disorder ② stomach upset
백내장	cataract
백일해	whooping cough
백혈병	leukemia
버짐	ringworm
변비	constipation
병	① sickness ② illness ③ disease
병균	① pathogenic bacteria ② germ ③ virus
병동	ward
병문안	visit to a sick person
병실	① sickroom ② sick ward ③ infirmary
병약하다	① to be weak ② to be sickly ③ to be invalid ④ to be infirm

병원의 분야
내과
방사선과
비뇨기과
산부인과
성형외과
소아과
신경과
안과
외과
이비인후과
정신과
정형외과
치과
피부과
흉부외과
:

병원	hospital
병원균	① pathogenic bacteria ② germ
병치레	sickness
보약	① restorative medicine ② invigorating drug
보호자	guardian
복용하다	to take (a medicine)
복통	stomachache
볼거리	① parotitis ② mumps
부상	① injury ② wound
부스럼	① boil ② furuncle
부작용	side effect
부황	swelling from starvation
분만실	delivery room
불면증	insomnia
불치병	① incurable disease ② fatal disease
붕대	① dressing ② bandage
비뇨기과	department of urology
비만	obesity
빈혈	anemia
삐다	① to dislocate ② to sprain
사상자	casualty
산부인과	department of obstetrics and gynecology
살균	sterilization
상사병	lovesickness
상처	wound
색맹	color blindness
생리통	menstrual cramps
설사	diarrhea
성병	venereal disease
성인병	① diseases of adult people ② geriatric diseases
성형외과	plastic surgery
세균	① bacillus ② germ
소독	disinfection

소독약	① disinfectant ② antiseptic
소아과	pediatrics
소아마비	infantile paralysis
소화불량	① dyspepsia ② dyspepsy
소화제	digestive
수간호사	head nurse
수두	① chicken pox ② varicella
수면제	sleeping drug
수술	① surgical operation ② practical surgery
수술실	operating room
수술하다	to perform an operation
수포	① water blister ② resicle
수혈	blood transfusion
숙환	① chronic (an inveterate) disease ② deep-rooted disease
스트레스	stress
습진	eczema
식곤증	languor
식염수	saline solution
식중독	food poisoning
신경과	department of neurology
신경쇠약	① nervous breakdown ② nervous debility
신경통	neuralgia
신생아실	new-born baby room
신장염	nephritis
신장이식	kidney transplant
실명	loss of (eye) sight
실명하다	① to lose one's (eye) sight ② to become sightless ③ to become (go) blind
실신	① faint ② fainting fit
심근경색	myocardial infarction
심장마비	heart attack
심장병	heart disease

44 Diseases and Treatments

	약	
모양	기능	
	-약	-제
가루약	감기약	구충제
물약	구급약	수면제
알약	내복약	영양제
연고	보약	지사제
:	소독약	진정제
	안약	진통제
	양약	촉진제
	외용약	치료제
	주사약	항생제
	한약	항암제
	:	해독제
		해열제
		환각제
		:

심장이식	heart transplant
십이지궤양	duodenal ulcer
쑤시다	① to ache ② to throb with pain
쓰리다	to have a burning feeling in one's stomach
아물다	① to heal up ② to close up
아편	opium
아프다	① to be sick ② to be painful
아픔	① pain ② ache ③ sore
안과	department of ophthalmology
안약	① eyewash ② eyewater ③ medicine for the eyes ④ eyedrops
안질	① eye disease (trouble) ② sore eyes
알레르기	allergy
알약	pill
앓다	① to be ill ② to be sick
암	cancer
야맹증	night blindness
약	medicine
약국	① pharmacy ② chemist's
약물중독	medicinal poisoning
약방	① pharmacy ② drugstore ③ chemist's (shop)
약사	pharmacist
약시	① weak eyesight ② amblyopia
약재	medicinal stuff
약초	medical herb
약품	① medicines ② drugs ③ medical supplies ④ chemicals
약효	① effect of a medicine ② virtue of a medicine
양약	Western medicine
어지럼증	dizziness
에이즈	AIDS (Acquired Immune Deficiency Syndrome)
에취	achoo

여드름	pimple
연고	ointment
염증	inflammation
영양실조	① unbalanced nutrition ② malnutrition
영양제	nutrition supplement
예방주사	① preventive injection ② preventive shot
예방하다	to prevent
완치	① complete cure ② complete recovery
왕진	① (sick) visit ② home (house) call
외과	① surgery ② department of surgery
요도염	urethritis
요양원	nursing home
요양하다	① to recuperate ② to have a medical treatment
요통	lumbago
우울증	① mental depression ② melancholy ③ blues
원시	① long sight ② farsightedness
위경련	gastrospasm
위궤양	gastric ulcer
위암	gastric cancer
위염	gastritis
위통	stomachache
유방암	breast cancer
유전병	hereditary disease
유행병	epidemic
유행성출혈열	epidemic hemorrhagic fever
응급실	emergency room
응급환자	emergent patient
의료기구	medical appliance
의료보험	medical insurance
의료보험증	medical insurance book
의료원	medical center
의료진	medical team
의부증	morbid suspicion about one's husband's

	chastity
의사	doctor
의약품	medicines
의원	① hospital ② doctor's office
의처증	morbid suspicion about one's wife's chastity
이명증	tinnitus
이비인후과	① otorhinolaryngology ② department of the ear, nose, and throat
이식수술	transplantation operation
인공심장	artificial heart
일사병	sunstroke
임질	gonorrhea
입병	mouth disease
입원	hospitalization
입원실	① sickroom ② sick ward ③ infirmary
입원하다	① to enter hospital ② to be hospitalized
자궁암	uterine cancer
자폐증	autism
잔병치레	having slight (minor) sickness
장기	internal organs
장염	enteritis
장티프스	typhoid
저리다	① to be numbed (benumbed) ② to be asleep
저혈압	low blood pressure
전염	contagion
전염병	contagious disease
전치	① state of injury ② degree of injury
절다	to limp
정박아	mentally handicapped child
정신과	department of psychiatry
정신박약아	mentally handicapped child
정신병	① mental disease ② psychosis
정신병자	① insane person ② lunatic

정형외과	(department of) orthopedic surgery
제약회사	pharmaceutical cooperation
조제실	dispensary
조제하다	to dispense
졸도	① faint ② fainting fit
종기	boil
종합병원	general hospital
주사기	① injector ② syringe
주사놓다	① to inject ② to shot
주사맞다	① to be injected ② to take a shot
주사약	hypodermic
주치의	① physician in charge (of) ② one's (family) doctor
중독	① intoxication ② poisoning ③ addiction
중상	① serious wound ② serious injury
중이염	① otitis media ② ear infection
중태	① serious condition ② critical state
중환자	serious patient
중환자실	intensive care unit (ICU)
증상	symptom
증세	condition of disease
지병	① chronic (constitutional) disease ② old complaint
지사제	① diarrhea medicine ② paregoric
진단서	medical certificate
진단하다	to diagnose
진료	diagnosis and treatment
진료하다	to examine and treat
진물	watery discharge from a sore
진정제	tranquilizer
진찰실	consultation room
진찰하다	to examine
진통제	① anodyne ② balm ③ pain-killer
진폐증	pneumoconiosis
질병	disease

질환	① disease ② ailment ③ trouble
찜질	fomentation
찰과상	① abrasion ② scratch
처방	① prescription ② dispensation
처방전	prescription note
처방하다	to prescribe
천식	asthma
천연두	① smallpox ② variola
청심환	pill for cardiac fever
청진기	stethoscope
체증	indigestion
체하다	① to sit heavy on one's stomach ② to remain undigested in the stomach ③ to have an attack of indigestion
촉진제	① accelerator ② accelerant
축농증	ozena
춘곤증	lassitude of spring
충치	carious (decayed) tooth
치과	the dentist
치료제	treatment medicine
치료하다	to treat
치루	anal fistula
치매	dementia
치사량	lethal dose
치질	hemorrhoids
치통	toothache
침	acupuncture
콜레라	cholera
콜록콜록	cough
타박상	bruise
탈골	sprain
탈모증	① hair loss ② alopecia
탈진	① being utterly exhausted (fatigued) ② being dead tired
토하다	① to vomit ② to bring (fetch) up ③ to throw (cast) up

통증	pain
퇴원	discharge from hospital
퇴원하다	① to leave hospital
	② to be discharged from the hospital
투병	① fight against a disease
	② struggle against a disease
투약하다	① to prescribe a medicine
	② to administer a medicine
	③ to medicate
파상풍	tetanus
패혈증	① septicemia ② blood poisoning
편도선염	tonsils
편두통	① megrim ② migraine
폐결핵	pulmonary tuberculosis
폐렴	pneumonia
폐암	lung cancer
포진	herpes
풍진	① German measles ② rubella
풍토병	endemic disease
피곤	① fatigue ② tiredness
피로	① fatigue ② tiredness ③ exhaustion
피부과	(department of) dermatology
피부병	① skin disease ② dermatopathy
피부암	① skin cancer ② cutaneous cancer
피부염	dermatitis
학질	① malaria ② paludism ③ ague
한방	Chinese medicine
한약	Chinese herbal medicine
한약방	herbal medicine shop
한의사	herb doctor
한의원	herbal medicine clinic
항생제	antibiotic medicine
항암제	anti-cancer medicine
해독제	antidote
해열제	antifebrile
향수병	① homesickness ② nostalgia

헌혈	blood donation
현기증	dizziness
혈압	blood pressure
혈압계	hemadynamometer
협심증	① stricture of the heart ② angina pectoris ③ stenocardia ④ heart attack ⑤ breast pang
혓바늘	rash on the tongue
혹	① wen ② lump ③ tumor
혼수상태	coma
홍역	measles
화농	① suppuration ② maturation ③ purulence
화병	nervous disorder caused by one's pent-up resentment
화상	burn
화학치료	chemical therapy
환각제	hallucinogenic drug
환자	patient
회복실	convalescent ward
회복하다	① to recover ② to get well again
회진	(doctor's) round of visits
후유증	aftereffect
후천성면역결핍증	AIDS (Acquired Immune Deficiency Syndrome)
흉부외과	surgical department of thorax
흉터	scar
흑사병	① plague ② pest

6 삶과 죽음
Life and Death

This chapter contains and lists lexical entries relating to the various stages of life that Koreans go through from birth to death. For example, lexical entries relating to the way of living and life and death, and lexical entries relating to funeral, sacrificial rites, and the world after death.

감옥살이	prison life
객사	dying while staying away from home
갱년기	menopause
고아	orphan
고인	① the dead ② the deceased ③ the departed
고인돌	dolmen
고향	hometown
고희	seventy years of age
곡	wailing
공동묘지	public cemetery
관	coffin
관혼상제	① ceremonial occasions ② ceremonies of coming of age, marriage, funeral and ancestral worship
교사	① instigation ② incitement
교살	① strangulation ② strangling ③ hanging
급사	sudden death
기일	anniversary of death
나이	age

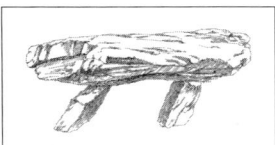
〈고인돌〉

납골당	① charnel house ② ossuary ③ cinerarium
넋	① soul ② spirit
노년기	① senescence ② old age
뇌사	brain death
대	generation
더부살이	resident servant
독살	① poisoning ② killing by poison
돌	① anniversary ② first birthday
돌아가다	① to die ② to pass away
돌연사	sudden death
동사	death from cold
두건	mourner's hempen hood
띠	zodiac sign
만장	① elegy ② funeral ode
매장	burial
매장하다	to bury
명	life
명복	heavenly bliss
목숨	life
묘	① grave ② tomb
묘지	graveyard
무덤	① grave ② tomb
무생물	inanimate object
묻다	to bury
미망인	widow
미생물	① microorganism ② microbe
발인	departure of a funeral cortege
변사체	dead body accidentally killed
변성기	age of puberty (change of voice)
별세	① death ② passing away
별세하다	① to die ② to pass away
병사	death of sickness
부검	① necroscopy ② necrosy ③ postmortem examination
부고	obituary

〈무덤〉

부음	news of (a person's) death
부의	donation for funeral expenses
비문	epitaph
비석	tombstone
빈소	mortuary
사망	death
사망률	death rate
사망하다	to die
사생활	private life
사십구재	Buddhist memorial service on the forty-ninth day after a person's death
사주	horoscopic data
사주팔자	fate
사체	dead body
사춘기	① puberty ② adolescence
사형	capital punishment
사형수	condemned criminal
사형장	execution ground
산소	grave
살	age (unit of age)
살다	to live
살림살이	housekeeping
살인	murder
살인범	murderer
살해	① killing ② homicide ③ murder
살해되다	to be murdered
살해하다	to murder
삶	life
삼우제	third memorial service after one's death
삼일장	burial on the third day after death
상	mourning
상가	① house of mourning ② family in mourning
상복	① mourning dress ② funeral garments
상석	stone altar in front of a tomb
상식	food offered to spirit

상여	hearse
상장 (喪章)	mourning badge
상장 (喪杖)	mourning stick
상제	mourner
상주	chief mourner
생기	① vitality ② vigor
생년월일	date of birth
생로병사	birth, aging, diseases and death
생명	life
생명력	power to live
생물	living thing
생신	birthday (honorific)
생애	① life ② lifetime ③ career
생일	birthday
생존	① existence ② life ③ subsistence ④ survival.
생활	life
생활화	making it part of our everyday life
생활환경	living environment
서거	death
서거하다	① to die ② to pass away
선산	ancestral graveyard
성년 (成年)	full (adult) age
성년 (盛年)	virile
성묘	visit to one's ancestral grave
세	age (unit of age) (deferential)
세상살이	① living ② way of living
셋방살이	living in a rented house
소년기	juvenescence
소복	(white) mourning clothes
송장	① corpse ② dead body
수의	shroud
순교하다	① to die a martyr for one's faith

신생아기 — 유아기 — 유년기 — 소년기 — 청소년기 / 사춘기 — 청년기 — 장년기 — 중년기 — 갱년기 — 노년기

	② to be martyred
순국하다	to die for one's country
순직하다	① to die at one's post (of duty) ② to be killed at work ③ to die in harness
숨쉬다	① to breathe ② to draw (one's) breath ③ to take breath ④ to respire
숨지다	① to die ② to breathe one's last
시집살이	married life in the husband's parents' home
시체	① corpse ② dead body
식생활	diet
신생아기	neonate period
신주	ancestral tablet
아사	death from hunger
안락사	① euthanasia ② mercy killing
암매장	secret burial
암매장하다	to bury secretly
압사	① death from pressure ② suffocation
연령	age
연세	age (honorific)
연옥	purgatory
염	① washing and shrouding a dead body ② preparing the body for burial
영결식	funeral ceremomy
영구차	hearse
영안실	mortuary
영혼	soul
오일장	burial on the fifth day after death
요절	① premature death ② early death
운명	fate
위령제	memorial service
위패	mortuary (memorial) tablet
유가족	bereaved family
유골	① ashes ② remains
유년기	① childhood ② puerility
유물	inheritance

유산	inheritance
유서	① note left behind by a dead person ② will
유아기 (乳兒期)	infanthood
유아기 (幼兒期)	babyhood
유언	will
유품	① relics ② article left behind
유해	① ashes ② bones
윤회	① metempsychosis ② transmigration of soul
의문사	mysterious death
의생활	clothing habits
이승	this world
익사	death from drowning
인명	human life
인생	life
인생살이	living
임종하다	① to be on one's deathbed ② to die
입관	encoffining
자살	suicide
자살하다	① to kill oneself ② to commit suicide
자연사	natural death
장년기	prime time of manhood
장례	funeral
장례식	funeral service
장사	funeral
장송곡	dead march
장의사	undertaker
장의차	hearse
장지	burial place
저승	① the other world ② the world of the dead
저승사자	messenger from the world of the dead
적령기	marriageable age
전사	death in battle
전생	former life

제사	① memorial service ② sacrificial rite
제주	chief mourner
조문객	caller for condolence
조물주	Creator
조위금	condolence money
조의금	condolence money
주검	① corpse ② dead body
주생활	housing life
죽다	to die
죽음	death
죽이다	to kill
즉사	① instantaneous death ② death on the spot
지방	ancestral tablet made of paper
지석	memorial stone
지석묘	dolmen
지옥	hell
진갑	61st birthday
진혼곡	requiem
진화론	evolution theory
질식사	death from suffocation
징역살이	① serving a prison term ② serving a sentence in jail
차례	ancestral memorial rites
창조론	creation theory
창조주	Creator
처가살이	married life in the wife's parents' home
처형	① punishment ② execution
천당	heaven
청년기	adolescent age
청소년기	juvenescence
청춘	① springtime of life ② youth ③ the bloom of youth
초상	mourning
초상집	house in mourning
총살	shooting to death

죽다		
관련 동사	관련 명사	
[죽다]	[죽음]	[죽임]
사망하다	객사	살해
숨지다	교사	살인
별세하다	돌연사	교살
서거하다	동사	독살
운명하다	병사	암살
타계하다	아사	자살
돌아가시다	안락사	총살
:	압사	:
	의문사	
	익사	
	전사	
	즉사	
	질식사	
	순국	
	순교	
	순직	
	:	

추도식	memorial service
추모식	cherishing memorial services
춘추	age
출산	① delivery ② childbirth ③ birth
출생	birth
출생률	birthrate
칠순	70th birthday
타계	death
타계하다	① to die ② to pass away
타살	homicide
타향살이	living away from home
탄생	① birth ② nativity
탈상	going out of mourning
태생	① birth ② origin
토정비결	Tojung's book of fortunetelling
팔순	80th birthday
평생	lifetime
피난살이	refugee life
피살	being killed
피살되다	to be killed
하관	depositing a coffin in the grave
하늘나라	heaven
하루살이	hand-to-mouth life
합장	burying together
향년	age (of a person) at death
호상	propitious mourning
혼	① soul ② spirit
혼백	① soul ② spirit
화장	cremation
화장터	crematory
화장하다	to cremate
환갑	60th birthday
황혼기	twilight age of life
회갑	60th birthday

7 감각과 감각기관
Senses and Sense Organs

This chapter contains lexical entries centering on the senses of sight, hearing, taste, smell, touch, hunch, and body. It also contains lexical entries on sense organs or entries related to sense organs.

가렵다	to be itchy
각막	cornea
간	salty taste
간간하다	to be suitably salted
간보다	to taste to see if it is well seasoned with salt
간지럽다	① to feel ticklish ② to feel a tickle
감각	sense
감각기관	sensory organ
감지하다	① to sense ② to feel
감촉	① touch ② feel
거칠거칠	rough
거칠다	to be rough
경청하다	to listen to
고막	eardrum
고소하다	① to be sweet-smelling ② to be tasty
고요하다	① to be still ② to be quiet
고통	① pain ② pang ③ anguish ④ suffering ⑤ agony
고통스럽다	to be painful
공감각	synesthesia

공명	resonance
관찰하다	to observe
구리다	to be stinking
구린내	① offensive odor ② stink
구수하다	① to be nice-smelling
	② to be pleasant tasting
귀	ear
귀머거리	deaf
귀먹다	to become deaf
귀청	eardrum
귓바퀴	pinna
귓속말	whisper
근시	nearsighted
깔깔하다	① to be tasteless ② to be rough
껄끄럽다	to be rough
꿰뚫어보다	to see through
끈끈하다	to be sticky
끈적끈적하다	to be sticky
난시	astigmatism
낭랑하다	① to be clear ② to be sonorous
	③ to be resounding
내다보다	to look out
냄새	① smell ② odor
냄새나다	to be smelly
냄새제거제	deodorizer
노려보다	to glare at
노린내	① stink ② foul smell ③ body odor
노안	presbyopia
녹내장	glaucoma
농아	deaf-mute
누린내	① scorched smell ② stench
눅눅하다	① to be damp ② to be dampish
눈	eye
눈길	look
눈동자	pupil
눈매	shape of the eyes

눈멀다	to be blind
눈병	eye disease
눈썰미	quick eye for learning things
눈알	eyeball
눈여겨보다	to observe carefully
눈초리	look
눈총	glare
눈치	① tact ② sense
느끼다	to feel
느끼하다	to be greasy
느낌	feeling
단내	① scorched smell ② burnt smell
단단하다	to be hard
단맛	sweet taste
달다	① to be sweet ② to be sugary
달착지근하다	to be somewhat sweet
달콤하다	to be sweet
달팽이관	cochlea
더듬다	to grope
덥다	to feel hot
도청기	① wiretapping device ② bug
도청하다	① to tap ② to bug
돋보기	① magnifying glass ② reading glasses
듣다	① to listen ② to hear
들리다	to hear
따갑다	① to be prickly ② to be tingling
따끔하다	to be prickly
따뜻하다	to be warm
딱딱하다	to be hard
떫다	① to be astringent ② to be puckery
뜨겁다	① to be hot ② to be heated ③ to be burning
마렵다	to feel an urge to relieve oneself
만지다	to touch
말랑말랑	① soft ② spongy
맛	taste

맛보다	to taste
맛없다	① to be unsavory ② to be unpalatable ③ to be tasteless
맛있다	① to be delicious ② to be tasty
망막	retina
맡다	to smell
매끄럽다	① to be smooth ② to be sleek
매끈하다	① to be smooth ② to be sleek
매만지다	to tidy up
매콤하다	to be spicy
맵다	to be hot
맹인	blind
맹인안내견	guide dog
멍멍하다	to be deafened
메스껍다	① to be sickening ② to be nauseating ③ to be nauseous
목격자	witness
목격하다	to witness
목마르다	to be thirsty
무감각	senselessness
무르다	① to be soft ② to be tender
물렁물렁하다	① to be soft ② to be pliant
물렁하다	to be soft
물컹하다	① to be very soft ② to be flabby
미각	sense of taste
미끄럽다	to be slippery
미끈미끈	slippery
미끈하다	to be smooth
미끌미끌	slippery
미식가	① epicure ② gourmand ③ gourmet
미지근하다	① to be tepid ② to be lukewarm
바라보다	to look at
바삭바삭	crispy
반들반들하다	to be glossy
밝다 (눈이)	① to be sharp (eyes and ears) ② to be shrewd

밥맛	appetite
방향제	aromatic
배고프다	to be hungry
배부르다	to be full
백내장	cataract
보다	to see
보들보들하다	① to be very soft ② to be silky
보송보송하다	to be soft and dry
보청기	hearing aid
본능	instinct
봉사	blind
부드럽다	to be soft
비리다	to be fishy
비린내	fishy smell
비위	① taste ② palate
뻐근하다	① to feel stiff ② to feel a dull pain
사시	squint
살펴보다	to examine
새콤달콤하다	to be sweet and sour
새콤하다	to be sourish
색맹	① color blind ② achromatopsia
소경	blind
소란스럽다	① to be noisy ② to be boisterous
소리	sound
소음	noise
손	hand
솔깃하다	① to be interested (in) ② to be enthusiastic (about)
쉰내	sour smell
시각	vision
시각장애인	visually handicapped person
시금털털하다	to be very sour
시끄럽다	① to be noisy ② to be loud
시다	to be sour
시력	eyesight
시선	glance

시신경	optic nerve
시야	one's view
시원하다	to be cool
시청하다	to look and listen
시큼하다	to be sourish
심심하다	to be not salty enough
싱겁다	to be insufficiently salted
싸늘하다	to be cold
쌀쌀하다	① to be chilly ② to be rather cold
쌉쌀하다	to be slightly bitter
쏘아보다	to glare at
쓰다	to be bitter
쓰다듬다	to stroke
씁쓸하다	to be slightly bitter
악취	bad smell
안경	eyeglasses
안과	department of ophthalmology
안구	eyeball
안압	intraocular pressure
안약	eyewash
안질	eye disease
야들야들	① velvety ② silky ③ smooth and shiny
야맹증	night blindness
약시	weak eyesight
어둡다	① to be dark ② to be gloomy ③ to be somber
어루만지다	① to stroke ② to pat
얼큰하다	to be hot-tasting
오감	five senses
올록볼록	embossed
요란하다	① to be noisy ② to be boisterous ③ to be clamorous
우렁차다	① to be sonorous ② to be rotund
울퉁불퉁	① uneven ② rough ③ jagged
원시	farsightedness
육감	intuition

육감적	sexy
음향	sound
음향기기	sound appratus
응시하다	to stare at
이비인후과	① otorhinolaryngology
	② ENT (ears, nose, throat)
입맛	appetite
장님	blind
적막하다	① to be dreary ② to be desolate
점자	braille
조용하다	① to be quiet ② to be silent
	③ to be still
주목하다	to pay attention to
주시하다	to gaze steadily
지린내	urinous stink
지켜보다	to watch intently
직감	① intuition ② hunch
직관	intuition
짜다	to be salty
짭잘하다	to be rather salty
째려보다	to glare at
쫄깃쫄깃하다	to be chewy
차갑다	to be cold
착각하다	to have an illusion
착시	optical illusion
천리안	clairvoyance
청각	① hearing ② auditory sense
청각장애인	hearing impaired
청력	hearing ability
청신경	auditory nerve
청음	musical dictation
청취	listening
청취하다	to listen to
체취	body odor
쳐다보다	to look up
촉각	sense of touch

촉감	① feel ② touch
촉촉하다	to be moist
축축하다	to be damp
출출하다	① to feel a bit hungry
	② to feel rather empty
춥다	① to be cold ② to be chilly
침침하다 (눈이)	to be dim-sighted (eyes)
칼칼하다	to feel thirsty
코	nose
퀴퀴하다	to be stinking
탄내	burnt smell
탈취제	deodorizer
통찰하다	to penetrate into
푸석푸석	① crumbly ② brittle
푹신푹신	softly
푹신하다	① to be spongy ② to be soft
향긋하다	to be fragrant
향기	fragrance
향기롭다	① to be fragrant ② to be aromatic
향내	fragrance
향수	perfume
혀	tongue
혀끝	tip of the tongue
혀뿌리	root of the tongue
혓바닥	tongue
혜안	insight
확성기	loudspeaker
환각	① hallucination ② illusion
환청	auditory hallucination
후각	sense of smell
훑어보다	to look over
흐물흐물	① too soft ② limp ③ mushy
흘겨보다	to cast a reproachful glance

감각	다섯 가지 감각				
	시각	청각	후각	미각	촉각
감각대상	모양	소리	냄새	맛	촉감/ 감촉
감각동사	보다 관찰하다 꿰뚫어보다 내다보다 노려보다 눈여겨보다 바라보다 살펴보다 지켜보다 째려보다 쳐다보다 훑어보다 흘겨보다 :	듣다 경청하다 도청하다 청취하다 :	맡다 맡아보다 :	맛보다 간보다 :	만지다 더듬다 매만지다 쓰다듬다 어루만지다 :
관련 단어	밝다 어둡다 침침하다 :	고요하다 낭랑하다 멍멍하다 소란스럽다 시끄럽다 우렁차다 적막하다 조용하다 :	구리다 퀴퀴하다 향긋하다 향기롭다 구린내 누린내 단내 비린내 쉰내 악취 탄내 체취 향기 향내 : 고소하다 구수하다 비리다 :	느끼하다 달다 떫다 맵다 시다 싱겁다 쓰다 짜다 :	가렵다 간지럽다 거칠다 끈끈하다 눅눅하다 단단하다 매끄럽다 무르다 물렁하다 미끄럽다 부드럽다 차갑다 촉촉하다 푹신하다 :

8 생각과 감정
Thoughts and Emotions

This chapter brings together lexical entries relating to and representing people's thoughts and feelings. It also contains lexical entries with connections to intelligence and value systems/ morality, as these are considered to be types of thoughts.

가다듬다	① to collect oneself
	② to brace one's spirits
가련하다	to be pitiful
가슴앓이	heartache
가엾다	to be pitiful
가정하다	to assume
가증스럽다	to be abominable
가치관	one's values
각오하다	to form a resolution
간주하다	① to consider ② to regard
갈등	① conflict ② trouble
갈망하다	to long for
감격하다	to be deeply moved
감동	impression
감동적이다	to be impressive
감동하다	① to be moved ② to be touched
감성	sensitivity
감성지수	emotional quotient
감수성	sensibility
감정	① emotion ② feelings

감지덕지	with deep gratitude
감질나다	① to feel insatiable
	② to never feel satisfied
갑갑하다	① to be stuffy ② to be stifling
강박관념	obsession
객관성	objectivity
거북하다	to be ill at ease
걱정	worry
걱정거리	source of anxiety
걱정하다	to worry about
겁	① fear ② fright
겁나다	to be frightened
겁내다	① to fear ② to dread
결심하다	to decide
결정하다	to decide
겸연쩍다	to be embarrassed
경각심	① self-consciousness ② self-awakening
경계하다	to be cautious
경이롭다	to be in awe
경험	experience
고깝다	to have a grudge

좋은 감정		나쁜 감정								
스스로 느끼는 감정	다른 사람에 대한 감정	스스로 느끼는 감정								다른 사람에 대한 감정
		화	슬픔	겁	창피함	아쉬움	불쾌함	불편함	지루함	
감격하다 감동하다 기쁘다 뿌듯하다 상쾌하다 신나다 유쾌하다 재미있다 좋다 즐겁다 편안하다 편하다 행복하다 홀가분하다 후련하다 흐뭇하다 흥겹다 :	감사하다 고맙다 반갑다 사랑하다 사모하다 :	노엽다 노하다 분노하다 분하다 성나다 악오르다 억울하다 열받다 원통하다 화나다 :	비참하다 비통하다 서글프다 서럽다 슬프다 애달프다 애통하다 우울하다 침울하다 :	겁나다 두렵다 무섭다 :	겸연쩍다 무안하다 부끄럽다 수줍다 수치스럽다 창피하다 :	감질나다 서운하다 섭섭하다 아쉽다 안타깝다 언짢다 허무하다 허전하다 허탈하다 :	넌더리나다 불쾌하다 속상하다 실망하다 언짢다 짜증나다 :	거북하다 난감하다 난처하다 답답하다 불안하다 심란하다 :	따분하다 심심하다 지겹다 지긋지긋하다 지루하다 :	고깝다 미안하다 미워하다 삐치다 시기하다 시샘하다 싫어하다 원망하다 죄송하다 증오하다 질리다 질투하다 :

고뇌	① suffering ② agony
고대하다	to eagerly look forward to
고독하다	to be lonely
고려하다	① to take into account ② to consider
고마워하다	to be grateful
고맙다	to thank
고민	agony
고민하다	① to be in agony ② to agonize ③ to be worried about ④ to be troubled with
고정관념	fixed idea
곤란하다	① to be difficult ② to be hard
골치아프다	① to be troublesome ② to be annoying
공감하다	① to sympathize with ② to feel sympathy
공경하다	① to respect ② to revere
공포	horror
관념	idea
관심	interest
괘씸하다	① to be rude ② to be insolent
괴로움	① anguish ② agony
괴로워하다	① to suffer ② to feel pain
괴롭다	to be painful
구별하다	① to distinguish ② to make a distinction
구상하다	① to map out a scheme ② to visualize a plan
궁금증	curiosity
궁금하다	to be curious
궁리하다	to think over
권태	① tedium ② ennui
귀찮다	① to be annoying ② to be bothering ③ to be harassing
그리움	① yearning ② longing ③ nostalgia
그립다	① to long for ② to miss
근심	① anxiety ② worry
근심하다	① to feel anxious ② to worry

긍지	① pride ② dignity
기대하다	to expect
기분	① sentiment ② feeling
기뻐하다	to be pleased
기쁘다	① to be pleased ② to be happy
기쁨	joy
기억	① memory ② memorization ③ recollection
기억력	memory
기억하다	to remember
긴장	tension
긴장하다	to feel strained
까먹다	to forget
깜짝	① startingly ② surprisingly
깨닫다	① to understand ② to be aware of ③ to realize
꺼리다	① to keep a distance ② to shy off
꺼림칙하다	to have a guilty conscience
꾀	wit
꿈꾸다	to dream
꿍꿍이	underhanded scheme
끔찍하다	① to be dreadful ② to be horrible ③ to be terrible
나쁘다	to be bad
난감하다	① to be beyond one's capacity ② to be unbearable ③ to be puzzled
난처하다	① to be embarrassing ② to be awkward
납득하다	to understand
낭만	romance
낯설다	① to be strange ② to be unfamiliar ③ to be not acquainted with
내키다	① to be inclined ② to feel like ③ to be willing
냉정하다	to be cold
냉철하다	① to be cool-headed

	② to be level headed
넋	① soul ② spirit
넌더리나다	to become disgusted
노발대발	① wild rage ② violent anger
노심초사	anxiousness
노여움	indignation
노여워하다	① to take offense at ② to feel hurt
노엽다	to be indignant
노하다	to get angry
놀라다	① to be surprised ② to be astonished
뉘우치다	① to regret ② to repent
느끼다	to feel
느낌	feelings
다정하다	① to be tender ② to be intimate
다짐	pledge
다짐하다	to give one's word
단념하다	① to give up ② to abandon
단정하다	to conclude
담담하다	to have no feeling
답답하다	to feel stuffy
당황하다	① to be embarrassed ② to be thrown into confusion ③ to be bewildered ④ to be taken back
대견스럽다	to be praiseworthy
독단	dogmatism
독선	self-righteousness
동정하다	① to sympathize with ② to feel pity for
동하다	① to have an itch ② to have a desire
두근거리다	① to throb ② to palpitate ③ to beat
두근대다	① to beat ② to palpitate
두려움	fear
두려워하다	① to fear ② to dread ③ to be afraid of
두렵다	to feel fear
둔하다	to be dull

뒤숭숭하다	① to be uneasy ② to be restless ③ to be distracted
따분하다	① to feel languid ② to feel weary ③ to feel bored
딱하다	to be pitiful
떨리다	to tremble
뜨끔하다	to feel sharp
마음	① heart ② mind
마음졸이다	to feel anxious
막막하다	① to be lonesome ② to be desolate
막연하다	① to be vague ② to be hazy
만만하다	to be easy to deal with
만족스럽다	to be satisfied with
만족하다	to satisfy
망각하다	to forget
맹세	oath
맹세하다	to take an oath
면목	face
모르다	to not know
몰두하다	① to be immersed in ② to concentrate
몰상식하다	① to be absurd ② to have no common sense
몰지각하다	to be senseless
못마땅하다	to be unsatisfied with
무디다	① to be dull ② to be obtuse
무서움	fear
무섭다	① to be fearful ② to be frightening
무시하다	to ignore
무식하다	to be ignorant
무심결	without intention
무안하다	to lose face
무의식	unconsciousness
무표정	lack of expression
묵념하다	to pay a silent tribute
미덥다	① to be reliable ② to be trustworthy
미련	lingering attachment

미련하다	to be dull and stupid
미소	smile
미안하다	to be sorry
미움	hate
미워하다	to hate
민망하다	to be sorry
믿다	to believe
믿음	① belief ② faith
박식하다	① to be erudite ② to be learned
반가움	gladness
반갑다	to be glad
반기다	to greet
반색	showing great joy
반성하다	to reflect on
반하다	① to fall in love ② to fall for
배신감	sense of betrayal
벼르다	① to intend ② to plan
변심	change of heart
복수심	vengefulness
부끄러움	① shame ② disgrace ③ dishonor
부끄럽다	to feel shame
부럽다	to envy
부르르	① trembling ② shivering
부아	① resentment ② indignation ③ rage
분	anger
분간하다	to differentiate
분노	① anger ② rage ③ indignation
분노하다	to get angry
분별력	discretion
분별하다	to discern
분석하다	to analyse
분하다	to feel vexatious
불만	dissatisfaction
불쌍하다	to feel pity for
불안	① uneasiness ② anxiety
불안하다	① to feel uncertain ② to feel insecure

	③ to feel anxious
불쾌감	displeasure
불쾌하다	① to be unpleasant ② to feel offended
불평	complaint
불행	unhappiness
불행하다	to be unhappy
비관하다	to be pessimistic
비애	① sorrow ② grief
비웃다	to laugh at
비참하다	① to be wretched ② to be miserable
비통하다	① to feel grievous ② to feel bitter
비판력	ability to criticize
비판하다	to criticize
비평하다	to criticize
비합리	absurdity
뿌듯하다	to be full of satisfaction
삐치다	to be cross
사고	thought
사고력	ability to think
사고하다	to think
사랑	love
사랑스럽다	to be lovable
사랑하다	to love
사려깊다	① to be very considerate ② to be thoughtful
사리분별하다	to discern with reasoning
사리판단하다	to judge with reasoning
사모하다	to love
사무치다	to pierce one's heart
사색하다	to meditate
상상력	imagination
상상하다	to imagine
상식	common sense
상쾌하다	to be fresh
샘	① jealousy ② envy
샘내다	① to be jealous ② to envy

생각	thinking
생각하다	to think
서글프다	① to be sad ② to be sorrowful
서글픔	sorrow
서러움	① sorrow ② chagrin
서럽다	① to be sorrow ② to chagrin
서먹서먹하다	① to be unfamiliar ② to be awkward
서운하다	to feel let down
설레다	① to throb ② to flutter
설움	① sorrow ② chagrin
섭섭하다	to feel let down
성가시다	to be bothersome
성나다	to get angry
세계관	outlook on the world
소감	① one's impressions ② one's opinions
소름끼치다	① to be hair-raising ② to be thrilling
속다	to be cheated
속상하다	① to feel depressed ② to be upset
속셈	① ulterior motive ② secret intention
송구스럽다	to be much obliged to a person for a thing
수줍다	to be shy
수치스럽다	① to feel shameful ② to be disgraceful
슬기	wisdom
슬기롭다	to be wise
슬퍼하다	to grieve
슬프다	to be sad
슬픔	sadness
습득하다	to acquire
시기	① jealousy ② envy
시기하다	① to be jealous ② to envy
시름	① anxiety ② worry
시샘	① jealousy ② envy
시원섭섭하다	to feel relief and sorry at the same time
시큰둥하다	to be indifferent
신	excitement

신경쓰다	① to mind ② to care
신경질	short temper
신나다	① to be excited ② to be elated
신바람	high spirits
실감나다	① to feel ② to hit
실망하다	to be disappointed
싫다	to dislike
싫어하다	to dislike
싫증나다	to be tired of
심란하다	① to be disturbed in mind ② to be agitated
심리	mentality
심사숙고하다	to think considerately
심술	ill-nature
심정	feelings
심통	ill-nature
(—고) 싶다	to like to
(—고) 싶어하다	to want to
쑥스럽다	① to be indecent ② to feel awkward
쓸쓸하다	to be lonely
아니꼽다	to feel disgusted
아쉬움	① missing ② feeling the want of
아쉽다	① to feel the lack of ② to miss (something) ③ to be in need of
아찔하다	① to be dizzy ② to feel faint
악감정	animosity
안심하다	to be relieved
안타까움	① impatience ② pity
안타깝다	① to be impatient ② to be pitiful
알다	to know
암기하다	to memorize
애달프다	to be heartbreaking
애석하다	to be sorrowful and regrettable
애절하다	to be sorrowful
애정	① love ② affection

Thoughts and Emotions

애증	love and hate
애지중지하다	to treasure
애처롭다	① to be pitiful ② to be pathetic
애타다	① to be nervous ② to be anxious
애통하다	① to grieve ② to lament
약오르다	① to feel irritated ② to get angry
양심	conscience
어떨떨하다	to be perplexed
어리둥절하다	① to be stunned ② to be puzzled
어림짐작하다	to guess
억울하다	to feel unfairly treated
억제하다	① to restrain ② to control
언짢다	① to feel bad ② to be displeased
얼떨결	① moment of confusion ② moment of bewilderment
업신여기다	to look down on
여기다	to regard
역정	anger
연상	association
연상하다	to associate
열광	① wild enthusiasm ② fever heat
열등감	inferiority complex
열받다	① to be offended ② to get angry ③ to become indignant
열정	① ardor ② passion
염려하다	to worry
염치	sense of shame
영리하다	① to be clever ② to be bright
예견하다	to foresee
예측하다	to predict
오기	① unyielding spirit ② pride ③ proud temper
오만하다	① to be arrogant ② to be haughty
오판하다	to misjudge
오해하다	to misunderstand
외롭다	to feel lonely

외우다	to memorize
욕구	desire
욕망	greed
욕심	greed
용서하다	① to pardon ② to forgive ③ to excuse
우러르다	to look up to
우려하다	to worry about
우울증	① blues ② mental depression ③ melancholy
우울하다	① to be melancholy ② to be blue ③ to be depressed
우월감	sense of superiority
울다	① to weep ② to cry
울음	① weeping ② crying
울화통	① resentment ② wrath
웃다	to laugh
웃음	laugh
원망	① bitter feeling ② grudge ③ resentment
원망하다	① to feel bitter against ② to resent
원통하다	to be lamentable
원하다	to want
유식하다	① to be learned ② to be educated
유추	analogy
유추하다	to analogize
유쾌하다	to be pleasant
의구심	① apprehension ② suspicion
의심	doubt
의심하다	to doubt
의욕	① will ② volition
이성	reason
이해하다	to understand
인상깊다	to be impressive
인상적이다	to be impressive
인식하다	to recognize
인지하다	to cognize

일체감	sense of unity
일편단심	passionate devotion
잊다	to forget
자격지심	self-reproach
자긍심	① pride ② self-admiration
자만심	conceit
자부심	① self-confidence ② self-esteem ③ pride
자신감	self-confidence
자존심	self-respect
작정하다	to make up one's mind
재미	① pleasure ② fun
재미없다	to be not interesting
재미있다	to be fun
적적하다	① to be lonely ② to be lonesome
절망	despair
절망감	feeling of despair
정	① affection ② compassion
정감	sentiment
정겹다	① to be affectionate ② to be tender
정들다	to become attached
정떨어지다	① to get disaffected ② to be sick of
정서	emotion
정신	spirit
정신력	mental strength
조바심	① nervousness ② worry ③ anxiousness
존경하다	① to respect ② to revere
좋다	① to be good ② to like
좋아하다	to like
죄송하다	① to be sorry ② to be regrettable
죄책감	guilty feeling
주관성	subjectivity
즐거움	pleasure
즐겁다	to be cheerful
즐기다	to enjoy

증오	hate
증오하다	to hate
지각하다	to perceive
지겹다	to be tired of
지긋지긋하다	to be sick and tired of
지능	intelligence
지능지수	intelligence quotient
지루하다	① to be bored ② to be boring
지혜	wisdom
지혜롭다	to be wise
진땀나다	to sweat hard
진심	sincerity
진절머리나다	to be very sick of
진정하다	to calm
질겁	① startling ② shock
질겁하다	① to be startled ② to be shocked
질리다	to be tired of
질투	① jealousy ② envy
질투하다	① to be jealous ② to envy
짐작하다	to conjecture
집중력	ability to concentrate
집중하다	to concentrate upon
짜증	① frustration ② annoyance ③ irritation
짜증나다	① to be frustrated ② to be annoyed ③ to be irritated
짝사랑	① unrequited love ② crush
착각하다	① to have an illusion ② to have a false impression ③ to have a misunderstanding
참회하다	to repent
창의력	creativity
창피하다	① to feel shameful ② to be embarrassed
책임감	responsibility
처량하다	① to feel miserable ② to be desolate
처절하다	to be extremely heartbreaking

Thoughts and Emotions

철들다	① to know better
	② to attain the age of discretion
체면	face
초조하다	① to be anxious ② to be impatient
추론	inference
추론하다	to infer
추리	reasoning
추리하다	to reason
추억	memory
추정	presumption
추측	conjecture
추측하다	to conjecture
측은하다	to be pitiful
침울하다	to feel depressed
쾌감	feeling of excitement
탐나다	① to be desirable ② to be tempting
탐내다	① to covet ② to desire
통일감	sense of unification
판단	judgment
판단력	judgment
판단하다	to judge
판별하다	to distinguish
편견	prejudice
편안하다	① to be safe ② to be peaceful
	③ to be comfortable
편애하다	to be partial
편하다	① to be comfortable ② to be convenient
평가하다	to evaluate
평온	① peace ② tranquility
평온하다	to be peaceful
학수고대하다	to wait anxiously
학습하다	to learn
한	① bitter feeling ② unsatisfied desire
	③ grudge
합리적	reasonable
해박하다	to be extensive

행복	happiness
행복하다	to be happy
허무하다	to feel empty
허영심	vanity
허전하다	① to feel something lacking ② to miss
허탈하다	to feel empty
헤아리다	to consider carefully
혐오감	hate
혐오하다	to hate
호감	good feeling
호기심	curiosity
혼동하다	to confuse
홀가분하다	to be lighthearted
화	anger
화나다	to get angry
화내다	to get mad
화목하다	to be harmonious
환상	① fantasy ② illusion ③ vision
환호하다	to cheer
황당하다	to be absurd
회상하다	to recollect
후련하다	① to be unburdened ② to feel relieved
후회	regret
후회하다	to regret
흐느끼다	to sob
흐뭇하다	① to be gratifying ② to be satisfied ③ to be pleased ④ to be delighted
흡족하다	to be satisfactory
흥겹다	① to be exciting ② to be delightful
흥미	interests
흥미롭다	to be interesting
흥분하다	to be excited
희노애락	joy, anger, sorrow, and pleasure
희망	hope
희망하다	to hope

9 성격과 태도
Characters and Attitudes

This chapter contains lexical entries relating to personal characteristics, those actions which characterize various types of people, people's capacities, and the evaluation of others. It also contains lexical entries relating to general attitudes or mental attitudes which vary among people and situations.

성격과 태도	
좋다	나쁘다
착하다	못되다
선하다	악하다
원만하다	모나다
친절하다	불친절하다
겸손하다	교만하다
공손하다	무례하다
부지런하다	게으르다
용감하다	비겁하다
공평하다	불공평하다
당당하다	비굴하다
근면하다	나태하다
점잖다	까불다
적극적이다	소극적이다
긍정적이다	부정적이다
낙관적이다	비관적이다

가식적이다	to be pretentious
가치관	values
가혹하다	to be severe
간곡하다	① to be serious ② to be earnest ③ to be sincere
간사하다	① to be sly ② to be crafty ③ to be cunning
강박관념	obsession
개성	individuality
거드름피우다	① to act proudly ② to be haughty
거만하다	① to be arrogant ② to be haughty
거칠다	to be tough
건방지다	to be insolent
게으르다	to be lazy
결벽증	① mysophobia ② obsessive-compulsive
겸손하다	to be humble
경거망동하다	① to be rash and thoughtless ② to be imprudent
경멸하다	to contempt
경솔하다	① to be rash ② to be hasty

경시하다	① to depreciate ② to disregard ③ to make little of
경의	① respect ② regard ③ homage ④ reverence
고루하다	① to be bigoted ② to be intolerant
고분고분하다	to be compliant
고집	① obstinacy ② stubbornness
고집부리다	to be obstinate
고집세다	① to be obstinate ② to be stubborn
고집스럽다	① to be obstinate ② to be stubborn
곧다	① to be straight ② to be righteous
공경하다	① to respect ② to honor ③ to revere
공명정대하다	to be righteous
공손하다	to be polite
공정하다	to be just
공평하다	to be fair
과묵하다	to be taciturn
관대하다	① to be generous ② to be broad-minded
관용	① magnanimity ② generosity
괘씸하다	① to be rude ② to be impertinent ③ to be insolent
괴팍하다	to be fastidious
교만하다	to be arrogant
교양	① courtesy ② refinement ③ culture
교활하다	to be cunning
구차하다	to be indignantly
굳세다	to be strong
굼뜨다	① to be slow ② to be sluggish
극성맞다	① to go to extremes ② to be aggressive ③ to be impetuous
극진하다	to be devoted
근면성	diligence
근면하다	to be diligent
급하다	to be hasty
긍정적이다	to be positive

기만하다	① to deceive ② to cheat
기죽다	① to lose confidence ② to feel worthless
까다롭다	to be picky
까불다	① to act carelessly ② to play a fool
깍듯하다	① to be polite ② to be couteous
깍쟁이	shrewd person
깐깐하다	to be a stickler
깔끔하다	① to be neat ② to be tidy
깔보다	① to look down on ② to belittle
꺼리다	① to avoid ② to be reluctant (to do something) ③ to hesitate (to do something) ④ to taboo
꼼꼼하다	① to be precise ② to be exact ③ to be conscientious
꿋꿋하다	① to be strong ② to be firm
끈기	① patience ② tenacity ③ perseverance
끈질기다	① to be tenacious ② to be persevering ③ to be persistent
나쁘다	to be bad
나약하다	① to be weak ② to be feeble-minded
나태하다	to be lazy
낙관적이다	to be optimistic
낙천적이다	to be optimistic
난폭하다	① to be violent ② to be wild
날뛰다	① to behave violently ② to rave
날렵하다	to be quick
날카롭다	to be over-sensitive
남자답다	① to be manly ② to be masculine
내성적이다	to be introvert
냉담하다	to be cold
냉대하다	to treat coldly
냉정하다	to be cold
냉혹하다	to be cold-blooded
너그럽다	to be generous
넉살좋다	① to have a nerve

	② to be brazenfaced
노력하다	① to endeavor ② to make an effort
눈썰미	quick eye for learning things
눈치	① tact ② sense ③ perceptiveness
느긋하다	to be relaxed
늠름하다	to be manly
다정하다	to be sweet (to people)
단호하다	① to be firm ② to be determined ③ to be resolute
담담하다	① to be indifferent ② to be disinterested
당당하다	① to be imposing ② to be grand ③ to be majestic
대담하다	① to be bold ② to be daring
대들다	① to defy ② to oppose ③ to challenge
대범하다	to be broad-minded
대접하다	to serve
덕	virtue
덕망	moral influence
덤벙거리다	① to act frivolously ② to act rashly
도도하다	① to be proud ② to be arrogant
도리	① reason ② piety
독하다	① to be tough ② to be strong ③ to be spiteful ④ to be severe
됨됨이	① one's nature ② one's character
드세다	① to be rough ② to be tough ③ to be wild
들뜨다	to grow restless
따뜻하다	to be warm
똑똑하다	① to be smart ② to be intelligent
똘똘하다	① to be clever ② to be bright
마음가짐	mental attitude
마음보	① nature ② temper
마음씀씀이	attitude
마음씨	① disposition ② nature

만용	① brute courage ② recklessness ③ foolhardiness
망설이다	to hesitate
매력	charm
맹하다	to be stupid
멋쩍다	① to be awkward ② to be embarrassed ③ to be mortified
멍청하다	to be stupid
면목	face
멸시하다	to contempt
명랑하다	to be cheerful
명쾌하다	to be clear
모나다	to be unsociable
모순되다	to be contradictory
모시다	to serve one's superior
모욕하다	to insult
모질다	to be cold-hearted
몸가짐	① bearing ② attitude
못되다	to be bad
무던하다	to be good-natured
무디다	to be dull
무뚝뚝하다	① to be blunt ② to be unsociable
무례하다	to be rude
무모하다	① to be reckless ② to be rash ③ to be thoughtless
무시하다	① to ignore ② to look down on
미덕	virtue
미련하다	to be dull and stupid
밉살맞다	to be detestable
바르다	① to be honest ② to be righteous
박하다	to be stingy
반항하다	to resist
발랄하다	to be lively
밝다	to be cheerful
방정맞다	to be rash

방정하다	to be tidy and courteous
배반하다	to betray
배신하다	to betray
배짱	① self-confidence ② boldness ③ nerve
버릇	habits
버릇없다	to be rude
변덕스럽다	to be whimsical
변함없다	to be consistent
별나다	① to be queer ② to be odd ③ to be peculiar
본성	nature
부당하다	to be unfair
부드럽다	to be gentle
부정적이다	to be negative
부지런하다	① to be diligent ② to be industrious
불공평하다	to be unfair
불손하다	to be rude
불친절하다	to be unkind
붙임성	① sociability ② amiability ③ affability
비겁하다	to be cowardly
비관적이다	to be pessimistic
비굴하다	to be servile
비난하다	to criticize
비방하다	to slander
비열하다	① to be mean ② to be base
비판적이다	to be critical
뽐내다	① to be proud ② to be pompous
사교성	sociability
사납다	① to be feisty ② to be ferocious
사회성	sociability
상냥하다	① to be sweet ② to be kind-hearted
새침데기	person of false modesty
새침하다	① to be cold ② to be standoffish
선하다	to be good
선행	good deeds

섬세하다	① to be delicate ② to be subtle
성격	① character ② personality
성깔	temper
성미	① disposition ② temperament ③ character
성실하다	to have integrity
성질	① temper ② disposition
성품	① temperament ② nature ③ disposition
세계관	world view
소극적이다	to be passive
소심하다	① to be timid ② to be narrow-minded
소질	talent
소탈하다	① to be informal ② to be unconventional
소홀하다	to be done hurriedly
속이다	① to deceive ② to cheat
솔직하다	to be honest
솜씨	① skill ② dexterity
순박하다	① to be simple and honest ② to be unsophisticated ③ to be naive
순수하다	① to be pure ② to be genuine
순진하다	① to be naive ② to be innocent
순하다	① to be gentle ② to be obedient ③ to be tame
슬기	① wisdom ② sense
슬기롭다	① to be wise ② to be sensible
습관	habit
시건방지다	① to be insolent ② to be impudent
시무룩하다	① to be sulky ② to be sullen
신경질적이다	to be ill-tempered
신중하다	① to think discreetly ② to be deliberate
심보	① temper ② disposition
심술	① cross temper ② ill nature
심술부리다	① to be ill-tempered ② to be wicked
싱겁다	to be wishy-washy

쌀쌀맞다	① to be cold ② to be blunt ③ to be curt
씩씩하다	to be courageous
아부하다	to flatter
악독하다	① to be most wicked ② to be atrocious
악하다	① to be evil ② to be wicked
안심하다	① to be relieved ② to feel relaxed
알뜰하다	① to be thrifty ② to be frugal
앙큼하다	① to be insidious ② to be sly
앙탈부리다	to whine
야무지다	to be thorough and smart
얄밉다	to be detestable
얌전하다	① to be well-behaved ② to be genteel ③ to be polite
얌체	① selfish person ② shameless fellow
양순하다	① to be gentle and obedient ② to be meek
얕보다	① to look down on ② to underestimate ③ to underrate
어리석다	to be stupid
어질다	① to be kindhearted ② to be benign
억세다	to be tough
억지부리다	① to insist on having one's own way ② to persist unduly
얼빠지다	to be absent-minded
엄격하다	① to be strict ② to be stern ③ to be rigorous
엄살부리다	① to exaggerate pain ② to make a fuss ③ to complain too much
엄하다	① to be strict ② to be rigid
업신여기다	to look down on
엉거주춤하다	① to be indecisive ② to hesitate
엉큼하다	① to be insidious ② to be sly
여자답다	① to be feminine ② to be effeminate
염치	sense of shame
염치없다	① to have no sense of honor

	② to be shameless
예민하다	to be sensitive
예의	politeness
예의범절	manners
예절	manners
오만하다	to be arrogant
온순하다	① to be docile ② to be gentle
온유하다	① to be gentle ② to be mild
온화하다	① to be gentle ② to be mild
올바르다	to be righteous
완강하다	to be strong-willed
완고하다	to be stubborn
외유내강	to be gentle in appearance, but strong in spirit
외향적이다	① to be outgoing ② to be extrovert
요사스럽다	① to be capricious ② to be wily
욕하다	to speak ill of
용감하다	to be brave
용기	courage
우기다	to insist
우유부단하다	to be indecisive
우쭐대다	① to be conceited ② to have a swelled head
원만하다	to be sociable
융통성	① flexibility ② adoptability
음란하다	① to be salacious ② to be lewd
음탕하다	① to be debauched ② to be licentious
음흉하다	① to be wicked ② to be underhanded
응용력	ability to apply
의기양양하다	to be triumphant
의젓하다	to be dignified
의지력	① will power ② volition
이해력	understanding
인간미	humanity
인간성	human nature
인간적이다	to be humane

인격	① character ② personality
인내	patience
인내력	perseverance
인내심	patience
인사성	① politeness ② courteousness
인색하다	① to be miserly ② to be stingy
인생관	view of life
인성	human nature
인심	generous heart
인정	sympathy
인품	character
일편단심	① single-hearted devotion ② sincere heart
임기응변	adaptation to circumstances
자격지심	self-reproach
자긍심	① pride ② self-admiration
자랑하다	to boast of
자만심	conceit
자부심	① self-confidence ② self-esteem ③ pride
자세	attitudes
자신감	self-confidence
자존심	self-respect
재주	talent
재치	wit
적극적이다	to be active
적성	aptitude
절약하다	① to economize ② to save ③ to be economical ④ to be frugal
점잖다	① to be well-behaved ② to be respectable
접대하다	to serve
정	① affection ② compassion
정겹다	① to be affectionate ② to be tender
정답다	① to be affectionate ② to be loving
정성	devotion

정열적이다	to be passionistic
정의감	sense of justice
정의롭다	to be righteous
정직하다	to be honest
정확성	accuracy
조급하다	to be impatient
조심성	① carefulness ② cautiousness
존경하다	to respect
존중하다	① to respect ② to esteem
좋다	to be good
주눅들다	① to feel timid ② to lose one's nerve
주책맞다	to be thoughtless
지구력	① endurance ② persistence
지도력	leadership
지독하다	① to be cruel ② to be harsh ③ to be severe
지혜	wisdom
지혜롭다	to be wise
진솔하다	① to be true and honest ② to be sincere
진실성	sincerity
진실하다	① to be true ② to be sincere
진지하다	to be serious
집중력	concentration
쩔쩔매다	to be perplexed
쩨쩨하다	① to be stingy ② to be miserly
차갑다	to be cold
차분하다	to be calm
착실하다	① to be sincere ② to be reliable ③ to be trustworthy
착하다	① to be good ② to be nice
참을성	patience
참하다	to be charming
창의력	creativeness
책임감	responsibility
처신	behavior
천성	one's nature

철없다	① to be indiscreet ② to be thoughtless ③ to behave like a child
철저하다	to be thorough
청렴결백하다	to be upright
청승떨다	to try to get sympathy
청승맞다	① to be miserable ② to be wretched ③ to be pitiful
체면	① face ② dignity ③ reputation
체신	dignity
추진력	drive
충실하다	to be faithful
치밀하다	to be precise
친절하다	to be kind
침착성	calmness
침착하다	① to be calm ② to be composed
칭찬하다	to compliment
콧대높다	to be arrogant and pushing
쾌활하다	to be cheerful
태도	attitude
태만하다	① to be negligent ② to be neglectful
통찰력	① insight ② penetration ③ vision
퉁명스럽다	① to be blunt ② to be curt ③ to be abrupt
트집잡다	to find fault
티내다	to have an air
파렴치하다	to be shameless
판단력	judgment
편애하다	to be partial
편협하다	① to be partial ② to be intolerant ③ to be narrow-minded
포악하다	① to be atrocious ② to be ruthless
포용력	tolerance
푸대접하다	to treat unkindly
품성	① nature ② character
품위	dignity

학대하다	to abuse
한결같다	to be constant
해이하다	① to slack ② to be slacken
행동거지	behavior
행동양식	mode of behavior
헐뜯다	① to revile ② to slander
	③ to speak ill of
헤프다	① to be talkative ② to be loose
화끈하다	to be impatient and direct
확고하다	to be firm
활달하다	① to be lively ② to be cheerful
활발하다	① to be active ② to be lively
후덕하다	① to be virtuous ② to be generous
흉보다	① to find fault with
	② to mention faults
흠잡다	to find fault
희롱하다	① to make fun of ② to tease

10 의생활
Clothing Life

This chapter contains lexical entries relating to clothes and attire, as well as the process of making clothes. It also contains lexical entries which refer to body decorations, such as ornaments, make-up, body decorations, and hair decorations.

가락지	ring (old usage)
가루비누	powder soap
가면	mask
가발	wig
가방	bag
가운	gown
가위	scissors
가죽	leather
가죽장갑	leather gloves
갈아입다	to change one's clothes
감다	to wash hair
감치다	to hem
갑옷	armor
갓	traditional Korean top hat
개량한복	revised comfortable Korean clothes
거울	mirror
걷다	to take down laundry
걸다	to hang up
걸치다	① to throw on ② to slip on
겉감	outer layer
겉옷	outer garment

〈가락지〉

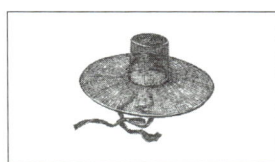

〈갓〉

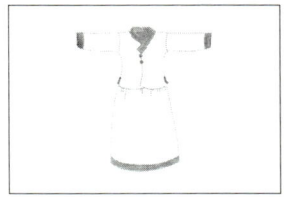

〈개량한복〉

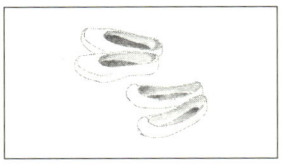
〈고무신〉

〈골무〉

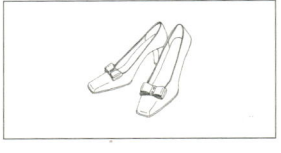
〈구두〉

〈꽃신〉

고름	breast-tie of Korean traditional clothes
고무신	rubber shoes
고무장갑	rubber gloves
곤지	rouge spot on a bride's forehead
골무	thimble
골반바지	hiphop pants
교복	school uniform
구김	wrinkle
구김가다	to be wrinkled
구두	shoes
구두약	shoe polish
구두주걱	shoehorn
구둣솔	shoe brush
구명조끼	life jacket
구슬	beads
구질구질	untidy
군복	military uniform
권투장갑	boxing gloves
귀고리	ear ring
귀금속	precious (noble) metals
금관	golden crown
기성복	ready-made clothes
기초화장	basic makeup
깁다	to patch up
깃	① collar ② lapel
꽂다	① to pin ② to stick
꽃신	flower patterned shoes
꾸미다	to decorate
꿰매다	to patch up
끄르다	to untie
끼다	to put on (items worn on hands: gloves, ring)
나들이옷	best clothes
나비넥타이	bow tie
남방셔츠	(short-sleeved) summer shirt
남성복	men's clothing

내다	to lengthen
내복	underwear
내의	underwear
널다	to hang clothes to dry
넥타이	necktie
넥타이핀	tiepin
누더기	rugged clothes
누비	quilting
누비다	to quilt
누비옷	quilted clothes
눈썹연필	eyebrow pencil
늘리다	to enlarge
다듬다	to trim up
다듬이질	fulling clothes by pounding
다리다	to iron
다림질	ironing
다림질하다	to do ironing
단	hem
단장하다	to dress
단정하다	to be neat and tidy
단추	button
단춧구멍	button hole
댕기	pigtail ribbon
덧버선	outer Korean socks
덧신	overshoes
동정	collar strip
두루마기	Korean topcoat
두르다	to encircle
드라이하다	① to dry hair using a dryer ② to dry-clean clothes
드레스	dress
등산모자	mountain-climbing hat
등산화	mountain-climbing boots
땋다	to braid
때	dirt
뜨개질	knitting

〈누비옷〉

〈다듬이질〉

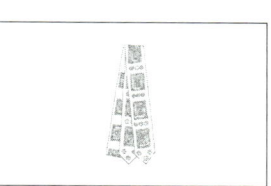
〈댕기〉

〈두루마기〉

뜨개질하다	to do knitting
뜨다	to knit
런닝셔츠	undershirt
마	① flax ② linen
마고자	Korean jacket worn over one's upper garment
마사지	massage
말리다	① to dry up ② to make dry ③ to air
망건	horsehair-woven headband worn under a traditional Korean top hat to hold one's hair in place
망토	① mantle ② cloak
맞다	to fit
맞추다	to custom-tailer
맞춤복	tailor-made
매다	to tie
매듭	knot
매만지다	① to adjust ② to tidy up
맵시	① shapeliness ② style
머리끈	hairstring
머리띠	hairband
머리방	hairshop
머리핀	hairpin
멋	① stylishness ② fashionableness ③ dandyism
멜빵	① suspenders ② braces
멜빵바지	pants with suspenders
면	cotton
면바지	cotton pants
면장갑	cotton gloves
명주	silk
모	wool
모시	ramie fabric
모자	hat
모직바지	wool pants
모피	fur

모피코트	fur coat
목걸이	necklace
목도리	muffler
무늬	pattern
무대의상	stage clothes
무대화장	stage makeup
묶다	① to tie ② to tie up
물들이다	① to dye ② to tint
미용실	beauty shop
미장원	beauty shop
밀짚모자	straw hat
밑화장	basic makeup
바느질	sewing
바늘	needle
바늘꽂이	pin cushion
바르다	to paste
바바리	trench coat
바지	① trousers ② pants
박다	to sew
반바지	① shorts ② short pants
반지	ring
반짇고리	sewing basket
발가벗다	① to strip ② to undress ③ to bare oneself
방탄조끼	bulletproof vest

〈밀짚모자〉

〈바늘과 바늘꽂이〉

〈반짇고리〉

모자		신발		장갑	양말	장신구
전통	현대	전통	현대			
갓 삿갓 :	등산모자 밀짚모자 베레모 사각모 안전모 중절모 털모자 :	고무신 꽃신 나막신 짚신 :	구두 등산화 방한화 부츠 숙녀화 슬리퍼 신사화 아동화 운동화 장화 털신 :	가죽장갑 고무장갑 권투장갑 면장갑 벙어리장갑 스키장갑 털장갑 :	덧버선 버선 스타킹 :	가락지 귀고리 넥타이핀 노리개 머리띠 머리핀 목걸이 반지 브로치 팔찌 :

방한복	snowsuit
방한화	snowshoes
배꼽티	half T-shirt
배냇저고리	new born baby's underwear
버선	Korean socks
벌	couter for suits
벗다	to take off
벙어리장갑	mittens
베레모	beret
벨트	belt
변신	① disguise ② transformation
변장	disguise
보푸라기	fluff
보풀다	① to be nappy ② to be fluffy
복식	clothing
복장	① dress ② clothes ③ attire ④ costume
볼연지	cheek rouge
볼터치	cheek blusher
부츠	boots
분	① face powder ② powder
분무기	spray

〈버선〉

옷 손질				
바느질		빨래		기타
방법	도구	방법	도구	
감치다 깁다 꿰매다 누비다 뜨개질 뜨개질하다 뜨다 박다 수놓다 시치다 자수 재봉 짜깁기 짜다 :	가위 골무 뜨개바늘 바늘 바늘꽂이 반짇고리 색실 실 재봉틀 코바늘 털실 :	개다 걷다 널다 말리다 빨다 빨래하다 세탁하다 짜다 탈수하다 헹구다 :	빨래비누 빨래집게 빨래판 빨랫줄 세제 세탁기 :	다듬이질 다리다 다림질 다림질하다 드라이클리닝 빨래방 빨래터 세탁소 :

분장	makeup
분첩	powder puff
브래지어	① brassiere ② bra
브로치	broach
블라우스	blouse
비녀	rod-like hairpin
비누	soap
비단	silk
비옷	raincoat
빗	comb
빗다	to comb
빨다	to wash
빨래	laundry
빨래건조대	laundry rack
빨래방	laundromat
빨래비누	laundry soap
빨래집게	clothespin
빨래터	clothes-washing place
빨래판	washboard
빨래하다	to wash clothes
빨랫감	laundry
빨랫줄	clothesline
빼다	to take out
사각모	mortarboard
삼베	hemp cloth
삿갓	conical bamboo rain-hat
상복	mourning garment
상의	upper clothes
상투	topknot
색동	striped cloth
색동저고리	children's striped jacket
색실	colored thread
색안경	① tinted glasses ② colored spectacles ③ sunglasses
색조화장	color makeup
생머리	① unpermed hair ② straight hair

〈비녀〉

〈비옷〉

〈빗〉

〈빨래판〉

〈색동저고리〉

설빔	New Year's best clothes
섬유	fabric
세련되다	to be refined
세제	detergent
세탁	① wash ② laundry
세탁기	washing machine
세탁소	laundry
세탁하다	① to wash ② to launder
셔츠	shirts
소매	sleeve
소복	white mourning clothes
속바지	① underpants ② drawers
속옷	underwear
속저고리	underjacket
속치마	① slip ② underskirt ③ petticoat
손가방	handbag
손거울	hand glass
손목시계	wristwatch
손수건	handkerchief
손지갑	purse
손질	mending
솔기	seam
솜	cotton
솜바지	cotton-padded trousers
숄	shawl
수놓다	to embroider
수선	mending
수수하다	① to be plain ② to be simple
수영복	swimsuit
수의	shroud
숙녀복	ladies' clothing
숙녀화	ladies' shoes
스웨터	sweater
스카프	scarf
스커트	skirt
스키장갑	ski gloves

스타킹	stockings
슬리퍼	slippers
승마복	riding suit
시치다	to tack
신	① footwear ② shoes
신다	to put on (items worn on feet: shoes, socks)
신발	① footwear ② shoes
신사복	men's suit
신사화	men's shoes
신축성	elasticity
실	thread
실내복	housedress
실내화	① slippers ② house shoes
실밥	① seam ② stitch
실크	silk
쌈지	tobacco pouch
쓰다	to put on (items worn on the head: tuque, etc)
아동복	children's clothing
아래옷	under garment
아랫도리	trousers
안감	lining cloth
안경	glasses
안전모	safety hat
앞치마	apron
양말	socks
양복	suit
양복바지	trousers
양복점	tailor's shop
양장	Western style of dress
양장점	women's shop for Western style of dress
양품점	haberdashery
어울리다	to fit
얼룩	spot

Clothing Life

옷	입다	벗다
단추	채우다	풀다
	잠그다	끄르다
윗옷·망토	걸치다	벗다
모자	쓰다	벗다
안경		
머리띠	하다	빼다
머리끈	묶다	풀다
머리핀		
비녀	꽂다	빼다
옷핀		
넥타이핀		
귀고리		
목걸이	하다	빼다
팔찌		
목도리	두르다	풀다
반지	끼다	빼다
장갑	끼다	벗다
		빼다
시계	차다	풀다
머리끈		
넥타이	매다	풀다
허리띠		끄르다
벨트		
양말	신다	벗다
신발		

여미다	① to adjust ② to arrange
여성복	women's clothing
연미복	① swallow-tailed coat ② swallowtail
연지	rouge
염색	dyeing
염색약	hairdye
염색하다	to dye
영양크림	nourishment cream
예복	full dress
옷	① clothes ② garment
옷가게	clothes shop
옷감	cloth
옷걸이	hanger
옷고름	breast tie
옷매무새	appearance of one's dress
옷솔	clothes brush
옷장	closet
옷차림	attire
옷핀	clothes pin
와이셔츠	shirt
왕관	crown
외출복	clothes worn outdoors
외투	coat

옷					옷감
기능·목적	대상	시기	장소	의식	
구명조끼	숙녀복	설빔	교복	상복	마
군복	신사복	추석빔	나들이옷	소복	면
방탄조끼	아동복	:	무대의상	연미복	명주
방한복	유아복		실내복	예복	모
비옷	임부복		외출복	원삼	모시
수영복	:		체육복	웨딩드레스	비단
승마복			:	정장	삼베
우비				활옷	섬유
운동복				:	실크
작업복					직물
잠옷					천
체육복					:
:					

우비	raincoat
운동복	sportswear
운동화	sneakers
웃옷	upper clothes
웃저고리	upper jacket
원피스	one-piece dress
월계관	laurels
웨딩드레스	wedding dress
윗도리	upper jacket
유아복	baby clothing
유연화장수	① softness wash ② soft lotion
의류	clothing
의복	① clothes ② dress
의상	① dress ② clothes
의생활	clothing habits
이발소	barber shop
이발하다	to have one's hair cut
일상복	everyday dress
임부복	maternity dress
입다	to put on (items worn on the torso: sweater, pants, etc)
입술연지	lipstick
자수	embroidery
작업복	working clothes
잠옷	① nightclothes ② nightgown
장갑	gloves
장신구	ornaments
장화	boots
재다	to measure
재단	cutting
재단하다	to cut
재봉	sewing
재봉틀	sewing machine
재킷	jacket
저고리	jacket
적삼	Korean-style unlined summer jacket

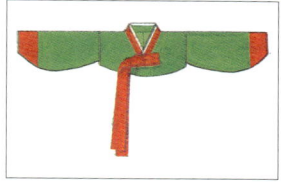

〈저고리〉

〈족두리〉

〈짚신〉

점퍼	jumper
정장	formal dress
조끼	① vest ② waistcoat
족두리	① bride's headpiece ② bridal tiara
주름	wrinkle
주름가다	to be wrinkled
주름치마	pleated skirt
주머니	pocket
줄이다	to shorten
중절모	felt hat
지갑	① wallet ② purse
지우다	to remove (one's makeup)
지퍼	zipper
직물	fabric
짚신	straw shoes
짜깁기	invisible mending
짜다$_1$	to take water out
짜다$_2$	to knit
쫄바지	tight pants
차다	① to attach ② to fasten on ③ to put on
차림	outfit
차림새	outfit
착용하다	to wear accessories
채우다	① to fasten ② to put on ③ to wear
천	cloth
청바지	blue jeans
체육복	① training attire ② sweatsuit
촌스럽다	to be boorish
추석빔	best clothes for Korean Thanksgiving Day
치렁치렁	① hanging loosely ② dangling
치마	skirt
치마바지	culottes
치장하다	① to ornate ② to decorate
칠부바지	three-quarter pants

켤레	pair (of socks or shoes)
코바늘	crochet needle
코트	coat
탈색	bleach
탈수기	① dryer ② hydroextractor
탈수하다	① to dry ② to dehydrate
탈의실	dressing room
털모자	① fur hat ② woolen cap
털신	arctic boots
털실	woolen yarn
털옷	fur robe
털장갑	① fur gloves ② woolen gloves
투피스	two-piece dress
티셔츠	T-shirt
파마머리	permed hair
파마하다	to have one's hair permed
파자마	pajamas
팔찌	bracelet
패션	fashion
팬티	panties
펴다	① to spread ② to unfold ③ to iron out
평상복	casual attire
표백제	bleach
풀다	to untie
품	width
피부관리	skin care
피부미용	skin care for beauty
핀	pin
하다	to put on (ornaments)
하의	trousers
한복	Korean clothes
핸드백	handbag
행주치마	apron
향수	perfume
허리띠	① belt ② waistband

〈한복〉

분류		현대 의복	한국 전통 의복	
겉옷 (웃옷)	외투	가운 망토 바바리 코트 모피코트	평복 두루마기	예복 원삼 활옷
	윗도리 (상의)	남방셔츠 러닝셔츠 배꼽티 블라우스 셔츠 스웨터 와이셔츠 재킷 점퍼 조끼 티셔츠	마고자 색동저고리 저고리 적삼	
	아랫도리 (하의)	골반바지 멜빵바지 면바지 모직바지 반바지 쫄바지 청바지 치마바지 칠부바지	바지	
		스커트 주름치마	치마	
속옷 내복 내의	윗도리 (상의)	러닝셔츠 브래지어	속저고리	
	아랫도리 (하의)	팬티 속치마 속바지	속치마 속바지	

헝겊	① patch ② rag ③ small piece of cloth
헹구다	① to rinse ② to wash out
호다	to sew with large stitches
호주머니	pocket
홈드레스	housedress
화려하다	① to be splendid ② to be magnificent
화장	makeup
화장대	① dresser ② dressing table
화장솔	makeup brush
화장솜	makeup cotton
화장수	astringent
화장술	art of makeup
화장지	toilet tissue
화장품	cosmetics
화장하다	to put on makeup

화장과 머리손질							
화장				머리손질			
화장법	화장품		머리 모양	손질 방법	머리장식		
	전통	현대			전통	현대	
기초화장 밑화장 무대화장 색조화장 :	곤지 볼연지 분 연지 입술연지 :	눈썹연필 립스틱 볼터치 영양크림 유연화장수 화장수 :	생머리 파마머리 :	드라이하다 땋다 묶다 빗다 염색하다 파마하다 :	댕기 비녀 족두리 :	머리끈 머리띠 머리핀 :	

11 식생활
Diet

This chapter contains and lists lexical entries closely related to the Korean people's diet, such as food names, food materials, and kitchen appliances. It also contains lexical entries describing tastes and food conditions, in addition to those relating to the processes of making foods and digesting.

가공식품	processed foods
가락국수	① wheat vermicelli ② noodles
가래떡	bar rice cake
가리다	① to be fastidious ② to be picky
가마니	straw bag
가마솥	iron pot
가물치	snakehead mullet
가스레인지	gas oven
가열하다	to heat (up)
가자미	stingray
가지	eggplant
간₁	① saltiness ② flavour
간₂	liver
간간하다	to be suitably salted
간맞추다	to season with salt
간보다	to taste to see if it is well seasoned with salt
간식	snack
간장	soy sauce
갈다	to grind

〈가마솥〉

〈갈비찜〉

〈갈비탕〉

갈비	rib
갈비찜	steamed ribs
갈비탕	beef-rib soup
갈증	thirst
갈증나다	to feel thirsty
갈치	cutlass fish
감미료	sweetener
감자	potato
감자탕	potato soup
감주	sweet rice drink
갓	mustard leaf
강냉이	corn
강정	① fried glutinous rice cake ② starch jelly
강판	grater
개고기	dog meat
개떡	pie-shaped cake made of coarse barley
개수대	sink
거르다	① to filter ② to strain
거품기	egg beater
건더기	chunks in soup
건배하다	to toast
건빵	① hardtack ② hard biscuit
건어물	stockfish
건지다	to take out of water
건포도	raisins
게	crab
겨자	mustard
경단	rice cake dumpling covered with bean paste
계란	egg
계란빵	bun made with egg
계량스푼	measuring spoon
계량컵	measuring cup
계피	cinnamon
고구마	sweet potato

고기	meat
고등어	mackerel
고량주	kaoliang wine
고명	garnish
고사리	fiddlehead
고소하다	① to be savory ② to be tasty
고추	hot pepper
고추냉이	Korean horseradish
고추장	hot pepper paste
고춧가루	ground hot pepper
곡류	① cereals ② grain
곡식	① cereals ② grain
골뱅이	snail
곯다	① to rot ② to go bad
곰국	thick beef soup
곰탕	thick beef soup
곱창	small intestine of cattle
공기	rice bowl
곶감	dried persimmon
과도	fruit knife
과식	overeating
과음	overdrinking
과일	fruit
과일쥬스	fruit juice
과자	cookie
광어	flatfish
광주리	bamboo basket
구수하다	① to be tasty ② to be savory
구이	① roast ② grill
구절판	kind of Korean fajita
국	soup
국물	① soup ② broth
국밥	boiled rice and soup
국밥집	boiled rice and soup restaurant
국수	noodles
국수전골	beef stew with noodles

〈곰탕〉

〈구절판〉

국자	① dipper ② scoop (utensil)	
국화빵	chrysanthemum shaped bun with red bean paste	
군것질	snacking between meals	
군침	saliva	
군침돌다	to be mouthwatering	
굴	oyster	
굴비	dried croaker	
굶다	① to starve ② to skip a meal	
굶주리다	to be hungry	
굽다	① to roast ② to broil ③ to toast ④ to bake	
궁중요리	royal court food	
귀리	oats	
그릇	dish	
근대	chard	
(비늘을) 긁다	to scale	
금식	fast	
금연	① prohibition of smoking ② no smoking	
금주	abstinence from drinking	
급식	① provision of meals ② feeding	
기름	oil	
기호식품	① one's favorite food ② table luxuries	
기호품	favorite food	
김	laver	
김밥	rice with various materials rolled in laver	
김장	kimchi-making for the winter	
김장철	kimchi-making season	
김치	kimchi	

〈그릇〉

〈김치〉

그릇	음식을 만드는 그릇	가마솥, 냄비, 뚝배기, 들통, 밥솥, 솥, 시루, 압력솥, 주전자, 차주전자, 프라이팬 …
	음식을 담는 그릇	공기, 다기, 대접, 식기, 접시, 종지, 주발, 찻잔, 컵 …
	음식을 보관하는 그릇	김치통, 단지, 밥통, 보온병, 수저통, 양념통, 통 …
	음식을 나르는 그릇	쟁반, 찬합 …

김치찌개	kimchi stew
김치통	kimchi container
깍두기	cubed turnip kimchi
깔대기	funnel
깡통	can
깡통따개	can opener
깨	sesame
깨물다	to bite
깻잎	perilla leaf
껌	chewing gum
꼬들꼬들	dry and chewy
꼬르륵	with a rumble
꼬리곰탕	ox tail soup
꼬치	skewered food
꼴뚜기	small squid
꽁치	mackerel pike
꽃게	blue crab
꾸역꾸역	unwillingly
꿀	honey
꿀꺽	at a gulp
꿀떡	honey rice cake
꿀맛이다	to be sweet and tasty
꿩고기	pheasant meat
끓다	to boil
끓이다	to boil
끼니	meal
끼얹다	to pour
나물	① (edible) herb ② potherb
낙지	common octopus
냄비	pot
냄비받침	pot holder
냉국	cold soup
냉동하다	to freeze
냉면	cold noodles
냉이	shepherd's purse
냉장고	① refrigerator ② fridge

〈깍두기〉

〈꽁치〉

〈꽃게〉

〈넙치〉

냉차	ice tea
냉채	cold vegetable dish
냉커피	iced coffee
냠냠	yum-yum
넙치	flounder
녹두	mung beans
녹말가루	starch powder
녹이다	to defrost
녹차	green tea
누룩	① malted wheat ② yeast
누룽지	burned rice at the bottom of the pot
누린내	unpleasant smell of fat
눌은밥	burned rice at the bottom of the pot
느끼하다	① to be greasy ② to be fatty
느타리버섯	agaric mushroom
닝닝하다	① to be watery ② to be bland
다과회	tea party
다기	tea utensils
다도	tea ceremony (cult)
다듬다	① to trim ② to clean
다시마	(sea) tangle
다이어트	diet
다지다	① to mince ② to crush
단란주점	karaoke bar
단무지	pickled turnip
단백질	protein
단술	sweet rice drink
단식	fasting
단지	① jar ② pot
단팥죽	sweet redbean soup
달걀	egg
달다	to be sweet
달래	wild rocambole
달착지근하다	to be sweetish
달콤하다	to be sweet
닭고기	chicken

〈단지〉

닭똥집	chicken stomach
담그다	to make (kimchi)
담배	tabacco
담백하다	to taste mild
당근	carrot
대구	codfish
대마초	hashish
대접	soup bowl
대파	green onion
대하	prawn
대합	clam
더덕	root (*Codonopsis lanceolata*)
덮밥	food over rice
데우다	① to warm ② to make warm
데치다	① to scald ② to parboil
도라지	Chinese bellflower root
도마	chopping board
도미	① sea bream ② red snapper
도시락	lunch box
독	jar
돌나물	① sedum ② stonecrop
동동주	unrefined rice wine
동치미	watery turnip kimchi
동태	frozen pollack
돼지갈비	pig rib
돼지고기	pork
되다 (된)	to be hard
된장	soybean paste
된장찌개	soybean paste stew
두드리다	to pound
두르다	to put around
두부	① bean curd ② tofu
두유	soy milk
드시다	to eat (deferential)
들기름	perilla oil
들깨	perilla

〈대구〉

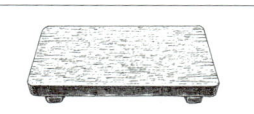

〈도마〉

〈동치미〉

들이켜다	to gulp
들통	① pail ② bucket
등심	upper part of sirloin
따르다	to pour
땅콩	peanut
떡	rice cake
떡국	rice dumpling soup
떡볶이	dish made of bars of rice cake and red pepper paste
떫다	to be astringent
뚜껑	lid
뚝배기	earthenware bowl
뜨다	to ferment
뜸들이다	to cook thoroughly
띄우다	to ferment
라면	① ramyun ② instant noodles
마가린	margarine
마늘	garlic
마른반찬	dried meat or fish side dishes
마른안주	assortment of dried meat and fish served with drinks
마시다	to drink
마요네즈	mayonnaise
막걸리	unrefined rice wine
막국수	noodles with assorted mixtures
만두	dumpling
만둣국	dumpling soup
만들다	to cook
만찬	dinner
말다	to roll up
맛	taste
맛나다	to be tasty
맛보다	① to taste ② to try
맛없다	to be tasteless
맛있다	to be tasty
매운탕	peppery pot

〈만두〉

매콤하다	① to be spicy ② to be hot
맥주	beer
맵다	① to be spicy ② to be hot
먹거리	food
먹다	to eat
멍게	sea squirt
메기	catfish
메뉴	menu
메밀	buckwheat
메밀국수	noodles made of wheat
메주	fermented soybeans
메추리알	quail egg
멸치	anchovy
명태	walleye pollack
목마르다	to be thirsty
무	① turnip (Korean) ② radish (Western)
무기질	mineral
무지개떡	many colored rice cake
무치다	to mix with seasonings
무침	mixing with seasonings
묵	jelly
문어	octopus
물	water
물렁물렁	① softly ② tenderly
물엿	starch syrup
물컹물컹	① squashily ② softly
묽다	① to be washy ② to be watery
미꾸라지	loach

〈메주〉

'먹다'	
모양	방법
꾸역꾸역 꿀꺽 냠냠 벌컥벌컥 오물오물 우물우물 쩝쩝 후루룩 :	끓다 과식 과음 굶다 굶주리다 금식 깨물다 단식 드시다 들다 들이켜다 마시다 빨다 삼키다 생식 섭취하다 소식 시식하다 식사 식사하다 씹다 잡수시다 편식 포식 폭식 핥다 :

맛						
짠맛	단맛	신맛	쓴맛	매운맛	기타	
짜다	달다	시다	쓰다	맵다	느끼하다 담백하다 떫다 상큼하다 싱겁다 :	
간간하다 짭짤하다 :	달착지근하다 달콤하다 :	새콤하다 시금털털하다 시큼하다 :	씁쓸하다 씁쓸하다 :	매콤하다 얼큰하다 칼칼하다 :		
	새콤달콤하다					

〈무지개떡〉

〈미꾸라지〉

미나리	Japanese parsley
미숫가루	powder of roast grain
미식가	① epicure ② gourmand ③ gourmet
미역	brown seaweed
미음	thin rice gruel
믹서기	mixer
밀	wheat
밀가루	flour
밀다	to roll
밀봉하다	to seal
밀폐용기	airtight container
밑반찬	pickled or salted side dish
바가지	gourd dipper
바구니	basket
바닷가재	lobster
바삭바삭	① with a crisp ② to be crispy
반주	liquor taken with a meal
반죽하다	to knead
반찬	side dish
발라내다	① to bone ② to tear off ③ to peel off
발효	fermentation
발효시키다	to ferment
발효식품	fermented food
밤참	midnight snack
밥	boiled rice
밥맛	appetite
밥상	small dining table
밥솥	rice cooker
밥통	container for boiled rice
밥풀	rice paste
배고프다	to be hungry
배부르다	to be full
배추	Chinese cabbage
배탈	stomach upset
배탈나다	to suffer from stomach trouble
백반	meal with boiled rice

밥	[재료]	감자밥, 굴밥, 무밥, 쌀밥, 콩나물밥, 콩밥 …
	[다른 음식]	쌈밥, 미역국밥, 김치볶음밥 …
	[상태]	고두밥, 눌은밥, 더운밥, 식은밥, 쉰밥 …
	[그릇/도구]	도시락밥, 솥밥, 주발밥 …
	[장소]	감옥밥, 기숙사밥, 식당밥, 절밥, 하숙밥 …
	[시간]	새벽밥, 아침밥, 저녁밥, 점심밥 …

백설기	steamed rice cake
백숙	meat boiled in water
뱅어포	dried slices of seasoned whitebait
버무리다	to mix together
버섯	mushroom
버섯전골	mushroom stew
버터	butter
벌꿀	honey
벌컥벌컥	gulpingly
벗기다	to peel
베이킹파우더	baking powder
변하다	to go bad
병따개	bottle opener
병어	pomfret
보리	barley
보리차	barley tea
보신탕	dog soup
보쌈	wrapped-up food
보쌈김치	wrapped-up kimchi
보온병	thermos bottle
복어	blowfish
볶다	① to panbroil ② to roast (beans)
볶음밥	fried rice
부대찌개	stew with various meats
부럼	nuts (eaten as superstition)
부엌가구	kitchen furniture
부엌용품	cooking utensils
부엌칼	kitchen knife
부추	leek

〈보쌈김치〉

〈복어〉

부치다	① to griddle ② to fry ③ to cook in a greased pan
부침가루	flour for frying
부침개	vegetable pancake
북어	dried walleye pollack
분식	powdered food
분식집	powdered food restaurant
분유	① dry milk ② powdered milk
불고기	bulgogi (roast beef)
불량식품	junk food
붓다	to pour
붕어빵	carp-shaped bun with red bean paste
뷔페	buffet
뷔페식당	buffet restaurant
비계	① lard ② fat
비름	amaranth
비리다	to be fishy
비린내	fishy smell
비비다	to mix
비빔밥	boiled rice with assorted mixtures
비위	① taste ② palate
비지	bean-curd dregs
비타민	vitamin
빈대떡	mung bean pancake
빚다	① to shape dough ② to roll into balls ③ to make into a shape
빨다	to suck
빨대	straw
빵	bread
빵집	bakery
빻다	① to pound up ② to grind down
빼내다	① to extract ② to pull out
뻥튀기	popped rice snack
뽑다	① to extract ② to pluck
사각사각	with a crunch
사식	prisoner's private food

〈비빔밥〉

사이다	soda pop
사탕	candy
삭히다	① to ferment ② to make ripe
산삼	mountain ginseng
살코기	① lean meat ② red meat
삶다	to boil
삼겹살	meat from side or back of a pig
삼계탕	chicken soup
삼치	Spanish mackerel
삼키다	to swallow
상추	lettuce
상하다	to go bad
새우	shrimp
새참	snack
새콤달콤	sour and sweet
새콤하다	to be sour
생강	ginger
생강차	ginger tea
생맥주	draft beer
생선	fish
생선묵	fish jelly
생선조림	fish stew seasoned with soy sauce
생선찌개	fish stew
생선회	① sashimi ② sliced raw fish
생수	spring water
생식	eating raw foods
석식	supper
쉬다	to mix
선지국	ox-blood soup
설렁탕	beef soup
설익다	to be half-cooked
설탕	sugar
섬유질	fiber

〈삼계탕〉

아침 조식 조찬	새참	점심 중식 오찬	새참	저녁 석식 만찬	밤참

섭취하다	to ingest
소고기	beef
소금	salt
소꼬리	oxtail
소라	turban shell
소식	① small meal ② eating small
소주	sojwu (Korean hard liquor)
소주방	soju-bar
소쿠리	bamboo basket
소화	digestion
소화불량	indigestion
소화제	digestive medicine
소화하다	to digest
솜사탕	cotton candy
송이버섯	mushroom (Armillaria edodes)
송편	① half-moon-shaped rice cake ② full-moon cake
솥	pot
쇠고기	beef
쇠꼬리	oxtail
수수	red sorghum
수육	boiled beef
수저	① spoon and chopsticks ② spoon (deferential)
수정과	cinnamon-flavored punch
수제비	soup with dough flakes
숙성	ripening
숙주나물	green bean sprouts
순대	sausage
순댓국	sausage soup
순두부	uncurdled bean curd
숟가락	spoon
술	① liquor ② alcohol
술떡	rice cake made with wine
숭늉	water boiled with burned rice
시금치	spinach

〈소라〉

〈수저〉
① 숟가락
② 젓가락

〈수저통〉

〈수정과〉

시금털털하다	to be very sour
시다	to be sour
시루떡	steamed rice cake
시식하다	to sample
시장	being hungry
시장기	being hungry
시장하다	to be hungry
시큼하다	to be very sour
식기	bowls
식기건조기	dish drier
식기건조대	plate-rack
식기세척기	dish washer
식단	menu
식당	restaurant
식도락	① epicurism ② gourmandism
식도락가	epicure
식량	food
식료품	foodstuff
식빵	bread
식사량	amount of a meal
식사하다	to eat a meal
식성	eating habits
식수	drinking water
식욕	appetite
식욕부진	anorexia
식용유	cooking oil
식이요법	dietary treatment
식중독	food poisoning
식초	vinegar
식칼	kitchen knife
식탁	dining table
식탁예절	table manners
식탐	gluttony
식품	food
식혜	sweet rice drink
신선하다	to be fresh

〈시루〉

〈시루떡〉

심심하다	to be insufficiently salted
싱겁다	to be insufficiently salted
싱싱하다	to be fresh
쌀	rice
쌀가루	rice flour
쌀통	rice container
쌈	boiled rice wrapped in lettuce
쌈밥	boiled rice wrapped in lettuce
쌉쌀하다	to be bitterish
썩다	① to rot ② to go bad
썰다	① to cut ② to slice
쑤다	to boil (rice into gruel)
쑥	mugwort
쑥갓	crown daisy
쓰다	to be bitter
씀바귀	lettuce (*Ixeris dentata*)
씹다	to chew
씻다	① to wash ② to clean
아이스크림	ice cream
아침	breakfast
안심	lean beef rib
안주	assortment served with drinks
알사탕	ball candy
압력솥	① pressure rice pot ② pressure rice cooker
앞치마	apron
애호박	young pumpkin
야채	vegetable
야채쥬스	vegetable juice
약과	fried cake made of wheat flour
약수	mineral water
약식	sweet rice dish
약주	rice wine
양고기	mutton
양념	① spices ② seasoning
양념장	seasoning sauce

〈약과〉

양념통	cruet
양념하다	① to season ② to flavor
양담배	cigarette made in Western countries
양배추	cabbage
양상추	lettuce
양송이	mushroom
양식 (洋食)	Western-style meal
양식 (糧食)	food
양식당	Western-style restaurant
양조장	① brewery ② brewhouse ③ winery
양주	Western hard liquor
양파	onion
어류	fishes
어묵	fish cake
어패류	fishes and shellfishes
얹다	to put (a pot) on (the fire)
얼리다	to freeze
얼큰하다	to be hot-tasting (spicy)
연어	salmon
열무	young radish
열무김치	young radish kimchi
엿	taffy
영양	nutrition
영양가	nutritive value
영양사	nutritionist
영양소	nutrient
오곡밥	boiled rice and mixed with four other staple cereals
오리고기	duck meat
오리알	duck egg
오물오물	mumblingly
오므라이스	rice omelet
오븐	oven
오이	cucumber
오이소박이	cucumber kimchi
오징어	squid

〈연어〉

〈열무김치〉

영양소

단백질
무기질
비타민
섬유질
유산균
지방
칼슘
:

〈오이소박이〉

오찬	lunch
옥수수	corn
옥수수차	corn tea
완두콩	pea
외식	dining out
요구르트	yogurt
요리	cooking
요리사	① cook ② chef
요리하다	to cook
우동	wheat noodles
우리다	to steep
우물우물	mumblingly
우유	milk
우족탕	thick beef soup made of cow foot
원두커피	filtered coffee
유산균	lactobacillus
유자차	citron tea
육개장	spicy beef soup
육류	meat
육수	① meat stock ② beef broth
육포	jerky
육회	dish of minced raw beef
율무	adlay
율무차	adlay tea
으깨다	to crush
음료	① drink ② beverage ③ soda
음료수	① drink ② beverage ③ soda
음식	food
음식점	restaurant
이스트	yeast

〈육개장〉

요리동사	일반	만들다, 요리하다, 조리하다 …
	불이 필요한 것	가열하다, 고다, 굽다, 데우다, 데치다, 뜸들이다, 볶다, 삶다, 익히다, 중탕하다, 짓다, 튀기다 …
	불이 필요하지 않은 것	무치다, 반죽하다, 버무리다, 비비다, 양념하다 …
	칼을 사용하는 것	다지다, 썰다, 채썰다, 칼질하다, 칼집내다 …
	기타	담그다 (김치·간장·된장·술 등), 빚다 (만두·떡·술 등) …

이쑤시개	toothpick
이유식	baby food
익히다	① to ripen ② to cook ③ to mature
인삼차	ginseng tea
인스턴트식품	instant food
인절미	glutinous rice cake coated with bean flour
일식	Japanese food
일식집	Japanese restaurant
일품요리	à la carte
임연수어	Atka mackerel
입맛	appetite
입맛다시다	to smack
잉어	carp
자동판매기	vending machine
자반	salted fish
자장면	noodles with black bean sauce
자판기	vending machine
잡수시다	to eat (deferential)
잡채	mung bean noodles mixed with vegetables and meat

음식물의 상태	
신선도	씹히는 느낌
신선하다 싱싱하다 부패하다 상하다 :	꼬들꼬들 물렁물렁 물컹물컹 바삭바삭 사각사각 쫀득쫀득 쫄깃쫄깃 :

〈잡채〉

음식	주식	밥	김밥, 눌은밥, 덮밥, 백반, 볶음밥, 비빔밥, 쌈밥, 약식, 오곡밥, 오므라이스, 잡곡밥, 장국밥, 주먹밥, 찬밥, 찰밥 …
		국·탕	갈비탕, 감자탕, 곰국, 곰탕, 꼬리곰탕, 냉국, 떡국, 만둣국, 매운탕, 보신탕, 삼계탕, 선짓국, 설렁탕, 순댓국, 우족탕, 육개장, 장국, 추어탕 …
		죽	단팥죽, 잣죽, 전복죽, 팥죽, 호박죽 …
		국수	냉면, 라면, 막국수, 메밀국수, 비빔국수, 우동, 자장면, 짬뽕, 칼국수 …
	부식	김치	깍두기, 동치미, 열무김치, 오이소박이, 총각김치, 파김치 …
		찌개	김치찌개, 된장찌개, 부대찌개, 생선찌개 …
		전골	곱창전골, 국수전골, 버섯전골 …
	간식	떡	가래떡, 개떡, 경단, 꿀떡, 무지개떡, 백설기, 송편, 술떡, 시루떡, 인절미, 전병, 절편, 증편, 찰떡, 찹쌀떡, 호떡 …
		빵·과자	강정, 건빵, 계란빵, 국화빵, 껌, 뻥튀기, 사탕, 솜사탕, 식빵, 알사탕, 약과, 찐빵, 케이크, 풀빵, 한과 …
	음료	음료수	감주, 과일주스, 냉차, 냉커피, 녹차, 단술, 보리차, 사이다, 생강차, 수정과, 숭늉, 식혜, 야채주스, 옥수수차, 원두커피, 유자차, 율무차, 인삼차, 커피, 콜라, 홍차, 화채 …
		술	동동주, 막걸리, 소주, 인삼주, 청주, 탁주, 고량주, 맥주, 생맥주, 양주, 포도주 …

〈장독과 장독대〉
① 장독   ② 장독대

〈전〉

〈전골〉

〈전복〉

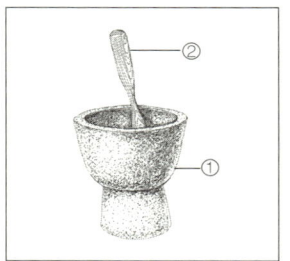

〈절구와 절굿공이〉
① 절구
② 절굿공이

잣	pine nuts
잣죽	rice and pine-nut porridge
장국	beef soup
장국밥	rice served in beef soup
장독	soy jar
장독대	soyjar terrace
장아찌	pickled vegetables
장조림	beef boiled down in soy sauce
재다	to put in layers
잼	jam
쟁반	serving tray
저녁	dinner
저미다	① to mince ② to cut into pieces
전	vegetable pancake
전골	beef stew
전병	pancake
전복	① abalone ② ear shell
전복죽	abalone portridge
전분	starch
전자레인지	microwave oven
전채요리	hors d'oeuvre
절구	stone (wood) mortar
절굿공이	pounder
절이다	① to pickle ② to salt fish/vegetables
절편	fancy rice cake
점심	lunch
접시	plate
젓가락	chopsticks
젓갈	pickled sea foods
정수기	water purifier
정식	① meal of fixed menu ② dinner
정어리	sardine
정육점	butcher shop
젓다	to stir
제과점	bakery
제기	ritual vessels

제육볶음	seasoned pork fry
조	foxtail millet
조개	shellfish
조기	croaker
조리	cooking
조리기구	cooking utensils
조리대	kitchen counter
조리하다	to cook
조미료	① seasoning ② flavoring
조식	① morning meal ② breakfast
조찬	breakfast
졸이다	to boil down
종지	small bowl
주걱	spatula
주먹밥	rice ball
주발	bowl
주방기구	kitchenware
주방용품	kitchen supplies
주식	staple food
주요리	main dish
주전자	kettle
주점	pub
죽	rice gruel
죽순	bamboo shoot
중국집	Chinese restaurant
중식₁	lunch
중식₂	Chinese food
중탕하다	to heat in boiling water
쥐치포	dried slices of seasoned filefish
주스	juice
즙	① juice ② sap
증편	steamed rice-cake
지방	fat
지지다	① to stew ② to boil
진지	meal (deferential)
질그릇	earthenware dishes

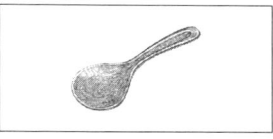

〈주걱〉

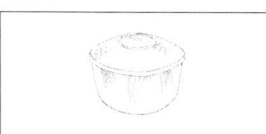

〈주발〉

질다 (진)	① to be watery ② to be soft
짓다	to cook (rice)
짜다	to be salty
짬뽕	hot and spicy noodle soup
짭짤하다	to be salty
쩝쩝	smacking
쪽파	thin onion
쫀득쫀득	stickily
쫄깃쫄깃	chewy
찌개	stew
찌다	to steam
찐빵	steamed bun filled with bean jam
찜	① smothered dish ② stew
찧다	① to pound ② to hull
차	tea
차림표	menu
차주전자	tea pot
차지다	to become sticky
찬거리	materials for making side dishes
찬밥	cold rice
찬합	picnic box
찰떡	glutinous-rice cake
참기름	sesame oil
참깨	sesame
참치	tuna
찹쌀	glutinous rice
찹쌀떡	glutinous-rice cake filled with red bean paste
찻잔	teacup
채소	vegetable
채식주의자	vegetarian

〈찬합〉

보통

싱겁다   심심하다   •   간간하다   짭짤하다   짜다

〈음식의 간〉

채썰다	to cut into shreds
채칼	① chef's knife
	② knife for shredding vegetables
청국장	fermented soybeans
청량음료	① soda ② soft drink ③ refresher
청주	refined rice wine
체₁	indigestion
체₂	sieve
체증	indigestion
체하다	to have indigestion
총각김치	radish kimchi
총각무	whole radish
추어탕	loach soup
취	aster
치즈	cheese
칠면조	turkey
카페	café
칵테일	cocktail
칼	knife
칼국수	fresh noodle soup
칼슘	calcium
칼질하다	① to cut ② to chop
칼집내다	to make a slit
칼칼하다	to feel thirsty
커피	coffee
커피메이커	coffee maker
커피전문점	coffee house
커피포트	coffee pot
컵	cup
컵받침	saucer
케이크	cake
콜라	cola
콩	bean
콩가루	soybean flour
콩고물	soybean paste
콩기름	soybean oil

〈총각김치〉

〈콩〉

〈콩나물〉

〈파김치〉

〈팥〉

콩나물	bean sprout
콩자반	boiled beans in soysauce
타다	to burn
(목이) 타다	to be thirsty
타조알	ostrich egg
탁주	makkoli (raw rice wine)
탄산음료	soda
탄수화물	carbohydrate
탕	① soup ② broth
탕수육	sweet and sour pork
토란	taro
토마토	tomato
토마토케첩	tomato ketchup
토막내다	to cut to pieces
통	① cask ② barrel
통닭	chicken cooked whole
통조림	canned food
튀기다	to deep-fry
튀김	deep-fried food
튀김옷	fried food batter
파	green onion
파김치	green onion kimchi
파래	green laver
팥	red bean
팥죽	rice and red-bean porridge
팽이버섯	nettle tree mushroom
편식	unbalanced diet
편육	slices of boiled beef
포	jerky
포도주	wine
포만감	feeling of satiety
포식	① gluttony ② satiation
포장마차	street vendor
포크	fork
폭식	① overeating ② voracious eating
표고버섯	shiitake mushroom

푸다	to scoop up
풀빵	shaped bun filled with red bean paste
풋고추	unripe hot pepper
프라이팬	frying pan
피우다	to smoke
피자	pizza
한과	Korean-style biscuit
한식	Korean food
한식집	Korean restaurant
한정식	Korean meal of fixed menu
핥다	to lick
항아리	jar
해동하다	to defrost
해산물	sea products
해삼	① sea slug ② sea cucumber
해파리	jellyfish
햅쌀	① new rice ② the year's new crop of rice
햇과일	new fruits
행주	dishcloth
향신료	① spices ② herbs
향어	Israeli carp
허기	hunger
허기지다	to be hungry
헹구다	① to rinse ② to wash out
현미	brown rice
호떡	Chinese pancake
호박	① pumpkin ② squash
호박죽	pumpkin porridge
호프집	pub
홍당무	carrot
홍어	skate
홍차	black tea
홍합	hard-shelled mussel
화채	punch
화학조미료	monosodium glutamate (MSG)

〈홍합〉

〈화채〉

회	① dish of raw fish or beef ② sashimi
효모	① yeast ② ferment
후라이팬	frying pan
후루룩	slurping
후식	dessert
후추	black pepper
흡연	smoking

12 주생활
Domestic Life

This chapter deals with lexical entries relating to houses, buildings, and facilities, as well as to their construction and furnishing. It also contains lexical entries relating to living environments and living management: i.e., lexical entries closely relating to domestic management.

가건물	temporary building
가게	① store ② shop
가겟집	① store ② shop
가구 (家具)	furniture
가구 (家口)	household
가구디자인	furniture design
가구배치	furniture arrangement
가루비누	powder soap
가리개	two-fold screen
가마니	straw bag
가방	bag
가스관	gas pipe
가습기	humidifier
가옥	① house ② residence
가위	scissors
가장	head of one's house
가전제품	home appliances
가정	home
가정환경	① home background
	② home environment

가구		
부엌가구, 신혼가구, 중고가구 …		
장	의자	탁자
문갑 벽장 붙박이장 서랍장 수납장 옷장 장롱 장식장 찬장 책장 ⋮	소파 안락의자 회전의자 흔들의자 ⋮	식탁 책상 ⋮

간판	signboard
갑	pack
개수대	kitchen sink
개조하다	to remodel
개축	reconstruction
거실	living room
거울	mirror
거주자	resident
거주지	residence
거주하다	① to live ② to reside
거처	residence
건너방	room opposite the master bedroom
건물	building
건설	construction
건설비	construction expenses
건설업체	construction company
건설하다	① to construct ② to build
건축	construction
건축가	architect
건축기사	architect
건축물	① structure ② building
건축설계사	architect
건축양식	architectural style
건축하다	① to construct ② to build
건축현장	construction site
건평	floor space
걸레	rag
게시판	notice board
경로당	senior citizens' recreation hall
경보기	alarm
경치	① scenery ② landscape
계단	① stairs ② staircase ③ stairway
고아원	orphanage
고을	county
고장	district
고층빌딩	high-rise building

고층아파트	high-rise apartment
고치다	① to fix ② to repair
골무	thimble
골방	small room attached to the main room
곳간	barn
공공건물	public building
공구	tool
공기청정기	air purifier
공동주택	co-operative housing
공부방	study
공사	① construction ② construction work
공사장	construction site
공사판	construction site
공인중개사	real estate agent
공책	notebook
과도	fruit knife
관	government
관청	government office
광	shed
광역시	megalopolis
광주리	bamboo basket
교회	church
구	district
구두약	shoe polish
구두주걱	shoehorn
구둣솔	shoe brush
구들장	stone slab for Korean traditional heating system
군	county
굴뚝	chimney
궁	palace
궁궐	palace
궁전	palace
궤	① box ② chest
궤짝	① box ② chest
귀이개	earpick

〈궁〉
① 창경궁　② 창덕궁
③ 덕수궁　④ 경복궁

〈귀이개〉

〈기와집〉

〈너와집〉

기구	① utensil ② implement
기둥	① pillar ② column
기숙사	dormitory
기와	roofing tile
기와집	tile-roofed house
기저귀	diaper
기초공사	foundation work
깔개	rug
깔대기	funnel
깡통	can
깡통따개	can opener
끈	① string ② cord
나무	tree
나사못	screw
난간	① handrail ② banister
난로	stove
난방	heating
남향	① southern exposure ② south view ③ facing south
내부공사	interior construction
내장	interior
내장재	materials for interior construction
냉방	air conditioning
냉장고	① refrigerator ② fridge
너와집	wood tile-roofed house
널빤지	① board ② plank
누추하다	to be shabby
다락방	attic
다리미	iron
다리미대	ironing stand
다리미판	ironing board
다세대주택	multi-household residence
다용도실	laundry room
단독주택	house
단열	insulation
단열재	insulating material

단층집	one-story house
단칸방	single-room house
달동네	poor mountainous neighborhood
달력	calendar
담	① wall ② fence
담요	blanket
대걸레	mop
대궐	palace
대들보	crossbeam
대리석	marble
대문	gate
대야	basin
대지	① lot ② plot of land
댁	① home ② house
덮개	cover
덮다	to cover
도	province
도끼	① axe ② hatchet
도마	chopping board
도배하다	to wallpaper
도시	city
도시락가방	lunch bag
도장	seal
독	jar
돗자리	mat
동	① sub-district ② east
동거하다	① to cohabit ② to live together
동네	neighborhood
동선	moving distance
동향	① same hometown ② eastern exposure ③ east view
두꺼비집	main fuse box
둥우리	nest
둥지	nest
뒷문	back door
드라이버	screwdriver

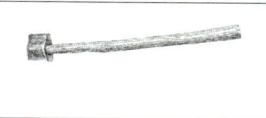

〈도끼〉

〈도장과 인주〉

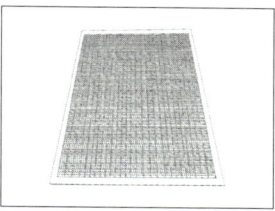

〈돗자리〉

드릴	drill
등	light
등기	① registration ② registry
등기서류	registered document
등잔	lamp
뜨개바늘	knitting needle
뜰	① yard ② garden
라디오	radio
리	*li* (subdivision of district)
마개	stopper
마당	① yard ② court ③ garden
마루	wooden floor
마을	village
막사	camp in the army
만년필	fountain pen
망치	hammer
맨션	luxury condominium
먼지떨이	duster
메모지	memo pad
면	*myun* (subdivision of a county)
면도기	razor
면도칼	razor blade
모기장	mosquito net
모래	sand
모텔	motel
목욕탕	bathroom
목재	wood
못	nail
무선전화기	cordless phone
무허가주택	house built without housing permit
묵다	① to stay ② to lodge
문	① door ② gate
문간방	room near the porch
문갑	stationery cabinet
문고리	ring-shaped door handle
문구	stationery

문
대문
뒷문
정문
창
창문
현관문
후문
:

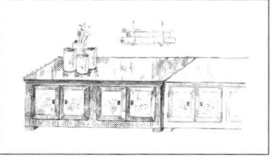

〈문갑〉

문지방	threshold
문패	① doorplate ② nameplate
물비누	liquid soap
믹서기	mixer
민박	lodging private residence to short-term period
민박집	private residence providing lodging to short-term guests
밀봉하다	to seal
밀폐용기	airtight container
바가지	gourd dipper
바구니	basket
바늘	needle
바늘꽂이	pin cushion
바닥	floor
바닥재	flooring
반	subdivision of a ward
반짇고리	sewing basket
발	screen
밥상	tray
밧줄	rope
방	room
방망이	club
방석	cushion
방수	waterproof
방음	soundproof
방충망	screen
배낭	backpack
배선	wiring
백열등	incandescent lamp
백화점	department store
번지	house number
베개	pillow
베란다	① balcony ② verandah
벽	wall
벽걸이	① wall tapestry ② wall hangings

방		
-방(房)	-실(室)	기타
건넌방	거실	광
골방	다용도실	부엌
공부방	보일러실	서재
다락방	사무실	식당
문간방	욕실	창고
부엌방	응접실	:
사랑방	집무실	
안방	침실	
어린이방	화장실	
옆방	:	
온돌방		
주방		
:		

벽난로	fireplace
벽돌	brick
벽돌집	brick house
벽시계	wall clock
벽장	closet
벽지	wallpaper
변기	toilet
변소	① washroom ② restroom
별장	villa
별채	annex
병	bottle
병따개	bottle opener
병풍	folding screen
보금자리	① nest ② home
보료	fancy mattress used as cushion
보수공사	repair works
보안장치	safety devices
보온	keeping warm
보육원	orphanage
보일러	boiler
보일러실	boiler room
보자기	cloth wrapper
보조가방	spare bag
복덕방	① real estate agency ② realtor
복도	hallway
본채	main quarters of a house
볼펜	ball point pen
봉지	bag
봉투	envelope
봉하다	to seal
부대	sack
부동산	real estate agency
부뚜막	kitchen range in Korean-style house
부수다	to demolish
부실공사	substandard construction
부엌	kitchen

〈병풍〉

〈보료〉

〈보자기: 조각보〉

부엌가구	kitchen furniture
부엌방	room attached to kitchen usually for a maid
부지	building site
부채	fan
부촌	wealthy neighborhood
북향	① northern exposure ② north view
분무기	spray
붓다	to pour
붙박이장	built-in closet
비	broom
비누	soap
비닐하우스	hothouse
비디오	VCR (video cassette recorder)
비우다	to empty
비품	① fixtures ② furnishings ③ office supplies
빈민가	slum
빌딩	building
빌라	condominium
빗	comb
빨대	straw
삐삐	① beeper ② pager
사글세	monthly rent
사다리	ladder
사랑방	room in male quarters
사랑채	male quarters
사무실	office
사진기	camera
산장	cabin
살다	① to live ② to dwell ③ to reside
살림살이	household goods
살림집	private residence
상가	shopping district
상수도	waterworks
상자	box

상점	shop	
생리대	sanitary napkin	
생활용품	daily necessities	
생활필수품	daily necessities	
서랍	drawer	
서랍장	chest (of drawers)	
서류가방	briefcase	
서재	study	
서향	① western exposure ② west view	
석재	stone	
선반	shelf	
설계	design	
설계도	① plan ② blueprint	
설계하다	to design	
성냥	match	
성당	Catholic church	
세간	household goods	
세대	household	
세대주	head of a household	
세면대	bathroom sink	
세부공사	detail work	

생활용품	가방	도시락가방, 배낭, 보조가방, 서류가방, 손가방, 손지갑, 시장가방, 신발주머니, 지갑, 책가방, 핸드백 …
	가전제품	가습기, 공기청정기, 냉장고, 다리미, 라디오, 믹서기, 비디오, 세탁기, 전축, 제습기, 청소기, 텔레비전 …
	깔개	돗자리, 방석, 보료, 양탄자, 전기장판, 화문석 …
	문구	공책, 만년필, 볼펜, 연필, 연필꽂이, 자, 지우개, 필통 …
	비누·세제	가루비누, 물비누, 빨래비누, 세숫비누, 세정제, 세척제, 표백제 …
	소품	거울, 귀이개, 달력, 면도기, 면도칼, 모기장, 병따개, 분무기, 빗, 성냥, 손톱깎이, 솔, 수건, 수세미, 액자, 열쇠, 양산, 옷솔, 옷핀, 우산, 우산꽂이, 이쑤시개, 자물쇠, 재떨이, 족집게, 지팡이, 집게, 칫솔, 파리채 …
	시계	괘종시계, 벽시계, 뻐꾸기시계, 손목시계, 자명종시계, 탁상시계 …
	연장	가위, 나사못, 도끼, 드라이버, 드릴, 망치, 못, 송곳, 압정, 장도리, 철사, 톱, 펜치 …
	조명기구	백열등, 전구, 전등, 초, 형광등 …
	청소도구	걸레, 대걸레, 먼지떨이, 비, 쓰레기통, 쓰레받기, 청소기, 총채, 휴지통 …
	침구	베개, 요, 이불, 침대보 …

세숫대야	washbasin
세우다	① to build ② to construct
세입자	tenant
세정제	detergent
세제	detergent
세척제	detergent
세탁기	washing machine
셋방	rental room
소지품	one's belongings
소쿠리	bamboo basket
소파	① sofa ② couch
소화기	fire extinguisher
손가방	handbag
손거울	hand glass
손목시계	watch
손수건	handkerchief
손지갑	wallet
손톱깎이	nail clipper
솔	brush
송곳	gimlet
쇠사슬	iron chain
수건	towel
수납장	closet organizer
수도 (首都)	capital city
수도 (水道)	water pipe
수도꼭지	tap
수리하다	to repair
수세미	scouring pad
수세식	① flush toilet ② water closet
수퍼마켓	supermarket
수화기	telephone receiver
숙박	lodging
숙박시설	① accomodations ② lodging facilities
승강기	elevator
시	city
시계	① watch ② clock

시골	country
시골집	① country house ② farm house
시공	execution
시멘트	cement
시설	facilities
시설물	facilities
시장가방	shopping bag
식기건조기	dish dryer
식기세척기	dishwasher
식당	dining room
식칼	kitchen knife
식탁	dining table
식탁보	tablecloth
신발장	shoe rack
신발주머니	shoe bag
신방	bridal room
신축	new construction
신혼가구	bridal furniture
실내	interior
실내장식	interior decoration
실외	outer
쌈지	tobacco pouch
쓰레기통	① wastebasket ② garbage can
쓰레받기	dustpan
아궁이	① fuel hole ② furnace
아랫목	warmer part of a Korean traditional room
아파트	apartment
안락의자	easy chair
안방	master bedroom
안채	inner quarters
압정	tack
액자	picture frame
약도	route map
양도세	transfer tax
양동이	① pail ② bucket

〈아궁이〉
① 아궁이
② 부뚜막
③ 가마솥

양로원	nursing home
양산	parasol
양옥	western-style house
양탄자	rug
어린이방	children's room
에스컬레이터	escalator
엘리베이터	elevator
여관	inn
여염집	middle-class home
여인숙	inn
역	station
연립주택	townhouse
연장	① tools ② instruments
연필	pencil
연필꽂이	pencil holder
열쇠	key
영세민	① destitute people ② needy people
옆방	next room
오두막	① hut ② cottage
오피스텔	studio apartment
옥상	rooftop
온돌	Korean heating system of old times
온돌방	room with Korean traditional heating system
온수	hot water
온풍기	heater
올리다	to build additional floors
옷걸이	hanger
옷솔	clothes brush
옷장	closet
옷핀	clothes pin
완공	completion
완구	toy
외장	exterior
외장재	materials for exterior construction
요	① mattress ② sleeping pad

〈양산〉

욕실	bathroom
욕조	bathtub
용기	container
우리	pen
우산	umbrella
우산꽂이	umbrella stand
우편번호	① zip code ② postal code
울타리	fence
움막	dugout
원두막	gazebo over a melon patch
월세	monthly rent
윗목	unheated side of a Korean traditional room
유리	glass
으리으리	① magnificent ② splendid
읍	town
읍내	downtown
응접세트	livingroom set
응접실	reception room
의자	chair
이민	① emigration ② immigration
이부자리	bedding
이불	quilt
이사	move
이쑤시개	toothpick
이웃	neighborhood
이웃집	neighbor
이주	migration
이층집	two-storied house
인감도장	one's registered seal
인주	vermilion ink pad
임대	lease
임대료	rent
임대주택	rental house
자	ruler
자갈	① gravel ② pebbles

〈원두막〉

물건을 담는 그릇	
전통	현대
가마니	갑
광주리	깡통
궤	대야
궤짝	밀폐용기
독	병
바가지	봉지
바구니	봉투
소쿠리	부대
쌈지	상자
양동이	자루
질그릇	주머니
함	통
항아리	:
:	

자루	sack
자명종시계	alarm clock
자물쇠	lock
자취방	rented room
자취하다	to live on one's own
작은방	small room
잠자리	bed
장	wardrobe
장난감	toy
장도리	hammer
장롱	wardrobe
장식장	china cabinet
장식품	goods (products/ materials) for decoration
장식하다	to decorate
장판	flooring
재개발	redevelopment
재건축	reconstruction
재떨이	ashtray
재봉틀	sewing machine
재산세	property tax
저울	scale
저택	mansion
전광판	electric sign
전구	light bulb
전기장판	electric mat
전등	electric lamp
전등갓	lampshade
전망	view
전선	wire
전세	lease of a house on a deposit basis
전원주택	villa
전축	record player
전화기	telephone
전화번호	telephone number
전화선	telephone wire

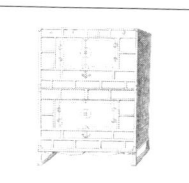

〈장롱〉

점포	① shop ② store
접착제	gummy
정문	front door
정원	garden
정화조	septic tank
제습기	dehumidifier
조감도	① bird's-eye view ② aerial view
조리대	kitchen counter
조립주택	prefabricated house
조립하다	① to assemble ② to construct
조명	lighting
조명기구	lighting apparatus
족집게	① tweezers ② nippers
종이	paper
주거	residence
주거지	area of residence
주거환경	residential environment
주머니	① pocket ② pouch
주민	resident
주민등록	resident registration
주민등록증	citizenship card
주방	kitchen
주방용품	kitchenware
주생활	domestic life
주소	address
주차장	parking lot
주춧돌	corner stone
주택	house
주택가	residential quarter
주택조합	housing association
준공	completion
준공검사	inspection of completion
줄자	measuring tape
중고가구	used furniture
중앙난방	central heating system
지갑	① wallet ② purse

지내다	① to live ② to get along
지방	① rural region ② country
지붕	roof
지우개	eraser
지팡이	cane
지하실	basement
질그릇	① pottery ② earthenware
집	① home ② house ③ case
집게	tongs
집기	① household furniture (and utensils) ② fixtures ③ fittings
집무실	office for one's duties (business)
집문서	① title deed ② house deed
집세	rent
집어넣다	to put in

집					
가옥, 저택, 주택 …					
양식		재료	용도	장소	
한옥	양옥				
궁·궁궐 기와집 너와집 초가집 오두막 :	고층아파트 다세대주택 단독주택 맨션 빌라 아파트 연립주택 오피스텔 이층집 조립주택 :	기와집 너와집 벽돌집 초가집 통나무집 판잣집 :	기숙사 민박집 별장 살림집 오피스텔 하숙집 :	산장 시골집 전원주택 :	

집	[사람]	[모양]	ㄱ자집, 단층집, 단칸집, 한옥집 …
		[재료]	기와집, 돌집, 천막집, 판잣집 …
		[위치]	고향집, 동향집, 앞집, 첫째집 …
		[구성원]	기생집, 사돈집, 친정집, 통장집 …
		[사건]	빵집, 살림집, 잔칫집, 전셋집 …
	[동물]	[인위적]	개집, 비둘기집, 새집, 토끼집 …
		[자연적]	개미집, 거미집, 제비집 …
	[무생물]	[인위적]	벼루집, 수저집, 안경집, 칼집 …
		[자연적]	닭똥집, 모래집, 몸집, 물집 …

집주인	① landlord ② landlady ③ house owner
짓다	① to build ② to construct ③ to erect
차고	garage
착공	starting construction
착공하다	to start construction
찬장	cupboard
창	window
창고	① warehouse ② storage
창문	window
창틀	window frame
채	unit for counting houses
채광	natural lighting
채우다	① to fill ② to pack
책가방	school bag
책꽂이	bookcase
책상	desk
책장	bookshelf
처마	eaves
천막	tent
천장	ceiling
철거하다	to remove
철근	reinforcing iron rod
철사	wire
청소기	vacuum cleaner
청소도구	cleaning supplies
체류하다	① to stay ② to sojourn
체육관	gymnasium
체중계	scale
초	candle
초가집	thatched house
초인종	door bell
총채	duster
층	① story ② floor
층계	① stairs ② staircase ③ stairway
치약	toothpaste

칠	paint
칠하다	to paint
침구	bedding
침대	bed
침대보	① bedspread ② bedding
침실	bedroom
칫솔	toothbrush
칼	knife
커튼	curtain
컴퓨터	computer
콘크리트	concrete
큰방	large room
타자기	typewriter
탁자	table
탈수기	dryer
탑	tower
터	① site ② lot
터전	① base ② grounds
텔레비전	television
토목공사	public works
톱	saw
통	① cask ② barrel
통나무집	log cabin
특별시	metropolitan city
파리채	fly swatter
판자촌	shanty town
판잣집	shack
페인트	paint
펜치	pinchers
평	3.954 sq. yds
평면도	① plan ② ground plan
평수	floor space
평형	apartment size based on floor space
폐가	deserted house
표백제	bleach
풀	glue

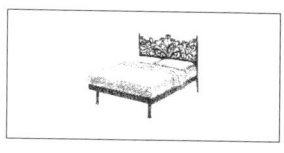

〈침대〉

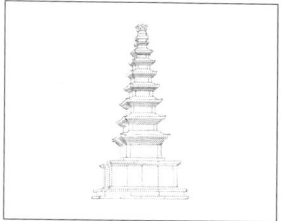

〈탑〉

피뢰침	lightning rod
필기구	writing tool
필기도구	writing tool
하수구	drain
하수도	sewer system
하숙집	boarding house
하숙하다	to board
학교	school
한옥	Korean-style house
함	chest
합숙	living together for a special purpose
항아리	jar
핸드백	handbag
행정구역	administrative district
행주	dishcloth
헐다	to take down
헛간	barn
현관	① entrance ② porch
형광등	fluorescent light
호루라기	whistle
호주	head of a family
호텔	hotel
호화롭다	to be luxurious
화문석	fancy mat
화장대	vanity table
화장실	bathroom
화재경보기	fire alarm
환기	ventilation
환풍	ventilation
환풍기	ventilation fan
회전의자	swivel chair
후문	back gate
휴지통	wastebasket
흉가	haunted house
흔들의자	rocking chair

13 말과 글
Spoken and Written Languages

This chapter contains lexical entries relating to spoken languages and written languages, particularly lexical entries and sentence markers of various actions and movements directly connected to Korean people's experience with language. It also contains basic terms and notions needed for language study.

가운뎃점 (·)	middle dot
각주	footnote
간접인용	indirect quotation
간접화법	indirect speech
간청하다	① to entreat ② to solicit
감탄사	exclamation
갑골문자	inscriptions on bones and tortoise carapaces
강독	reading
강연	① lecture ② talk
강연하다	to lecture
강요하다	① to compel ② to force
강의	lecture
강의하다	to give a lecture
거부하다	① to deny ② to refuse
거센소리	aspirated sounds
거절하다	① to refuse ② to reject
거짓말	lie
건의하다	① to propose ② to request
격	case

격려사	① keynote speech
	② words of encouragement
격언	maxim
격음	tensed sound
결론	conclusion
결론짓다	to conclude
경고하다	to warn
경어	honorific
경음	fortis
계약하다	to contract
계통론	phylogenesis
고발하다	to accuse
고백	confession
고백하다	to confess
고사성어	idiomatic phrase from an ancient story
고소하다	to sue
고유명사	proper noun
고유어	native word
고자질하다	① to tell on (someone) ② squeal
고지하다	① to notify ② to announce
공갈치다	to lie
공고	announcement
공박하다	① to refute ② to confute
공약하다	to pledge oneself (publicly)
공용어	official language
공통어	① common tongue
	② common language
공표하다	to announce
과거시제	past tense
과거완료	past perfect
과거형	past form
과묵하다	to be taciturn
관계대명사	relative pronoun
관용어	idiom
관형사	noun modifier (a part of speech)
관형어	noun modifier (lexical level)

괄호 (( ))	parenthesis
교섭하다	to negotiate
교열	editing
교정	proofreading
구	phrase
구개음화	palatalization
구두점	punctuation marks
구사하다	to express
구술하다	to state orally
구어	spoken language
구절	phrase and clause
국어	① Korean language ② native language
국어순화	purification of the Korean language
군말	redundant words
군소리	unnecessary remark
군소리하다	to make an unnecessary remark
굴곡	inflection
권고하다	to advise
권유하다	to advise
권장하다	to encourage
권하다	to recommend
귀띔하다	① to tell secretly ② to give a tip
귀머거리	deaf
귓속말	whisper
규탄하다	① to censure ② to denounce
그리스어	Greek language
그림씨	adjective
글	writing
글씨	① handwriting ② character
글씨체	style of penmanship
글자	letter
글짓기	composition
금지하다	to prohibit
금하다	① to forbid ② to prohibit
긋다	to draw a line
긍정하다	to affirm

기도하다	to pray
기록	record
기록하다	to record
기본형	base (form)
기술하다	to describe
기약하다	to promise
기원하다	① to pray ② to wish
기입하다	to fill in
기재하다	① to record ② to state
꺾쇠표 (〈 〉)	angled bracket
꼬시다	① to tempt ② to seduce ③ to lure ④ to entice
꾸밈씨	modifier
꾸중	① scolding ② rebuke
꾸중하다	① to scold ② to rebuke
꾸지람	① scolding ② rebuke
꾸짖다	① to scold ② to rebuke
나무라다	① to reprove ② reprimand
낙서	graffiti
난독증	dyslexia
난서증	writer's block
낭독하다	to read aloud
낭송하다	to recite
낮춤말	intimate (friendly) speech
낱말	word
너스레	① idle remarks ② idle talk
넋두리	① grumble ② complaint
노어	Russian language
논박하다	to argue against
논술	essay
논의하다	① to discuss ② to argue
논쟁하다	① to argue ② to dispute
논증하다	to prove
논평하다	to comment
놀리다	to make fun of
농담	joke

높임말	honorific
높임법	honorific way of saying
누설하다	① to leak ② to disclose ③ to reveal
느낌씨	① exclamation ② interjection
느낌표 (!)	exclamation mark
능동태	active voice
다그치다	to press for an answer
다독	broad reading
다의어	polysemy
다중언어화자	multi-lingual
다짐하다	① to vow ② to pledge
단락	paragraph
단어	word
단언하다	① to state ② to assert
단의어	single meaning word
단일어	monomorphemic word
단정하다	to conclude
달래다	① to soothe ② to pacify
담소	chat
담소하다	to chat
담판하다	to negotiate
담화	discourse
답례하다	to return a salute
답변하다	to answer
답하다	to reply
당부하다	① to ask ② to make a request
닿소리	consonant
대격	dative
대괄호 ([ ])	square bracket
대꾸하다	to talk back
대답	talk
대담하다	① to talk with ② to have a talk
대답하다	to answer
대들다	to challenge
대립어	① opposite word ② antonym
대명사	pronoun

대문자	capital letter
대변하다	to speak for
대사	lines
대이름씨	pronoun
대화	conversation
대화하다	to converse with
덕담	well-wishing remarks
도움말	help
독립어	independent word
독백	soliloquy
독서	reading
독어	German language
독자	reader
독촉하다	to urge
동문서답	incoherent reply
동사	verb
동시통역사	simultaneous interpreter
동음어	homophone
동음이의어	homonym
동의어	synonym
동의하다	to agree with
되받아치다	to retort
된소리	tensed sound
드러냄표 (˙˙)	emphatic marks
듣기	① hearing ② listening
듣다	① to hear ② to listen
들머리	introduction
따옴표 (" ")	quotation marks

'말하기' 동사

질문	대답	칭찬	비난	허락	거절	명령	요청	약속	기원	논의	논쟁
문의하다	답변하다	격려하다	꾸중하다	수락하다	거부하다	명령하다	간청하다	계약하다	기구하다	논의하다	담판하다
묻다	답하다	자화자찬하다	꾸짖다	승인하다	거절하다	명하다	부탁하다	공약하다	기도하다	상의하다	따지다
질문하다	대꾸하다	찬양하다	나무라다	허가하다	사양하다	분부하다	신청하다	다짐하다	기원하다	심의하다	말다툼하다
캐묻다	대답하다	치하하다	불평하다	허락하다	사절하다	시키다	요구하다	맹세하다	빌다	의논하다	반박하다
:	응답하다	칭송하다	비꼬다	허용하다	퇴짜놓다	신청하다	요청하다	서약하다	:	제의하다	언쟁하다
	:	칭찬하다	비난하다	:	:	주문하다	청구하다	선서하다		토론하다	주장하다
		:	비방하다			:	청하다	약속하다		토의하다	:
			욕하다				:	:		:	
			질책하다								
			:								

따지다	to demand an explanation
때매김	tense
떠들다	to make noise
뜻	meaning
띄어쓰기	spacing
라틴어	Latin language
마무리	① conclusion ② finishing touches
마침표 (.)	period
만년필	fountain pen
만담	① gag ② joke
말	words
말걸다	to speak to
말꼬리	end of one's words
말다툼	quarrel
말다툼하다	to quarrel
말대꾸	① retort ② back talk
말대꾸하다	to talk back
말더듬이	stammerer
말바꿈표 (−)	dash
말발	speaking skill
말버릇	manner of speaking
말솜씨	one's way of speaking
말씀	words (honorific)
말씀하시다	to speak (honorific)
말씨	① way of speaking ② speech ③ wording
말주변	ability to speak promptly and wisely
말줄임표 (……)	ellipsis
말투	style of talking
말하기	speaking
말하다	to speak
맞장구치다	to give agreeable responses
맞춤법	spelling
매김씨	noun modifier (a part of speech)
맹세하다	to make an oath
맺음말	conclusion

머리말	introduction
머무름표 (;)	semi-colon
메모	memo
메모지	note pad
면담하다	① to interview ② to talk over
명령하다	to order
명명하다	to name
명사	noun
명언	wise saying
명하다	① to order ② to command
모국어	native language
모국어화자	native speaker
모독하다	① to blaspheme ② to profane ③ to insult
모음	vowel
모음조화	vowel assimilation
목소리	voice
목적격	accusative
목적어	object
목차	table of contents
몸짓언어	body language
묘사하다	to describe
묵독	silent reading
묶음표 ([ ])	brackets
문구	① word ② phrase ③ expression
문맹	illiteracy
문법	grammar
문법론	theory of grammar
문법서	grammar book
문서	document
문어	written language
문의하다	to inquire
문자	① letters of a language ② characters of a language
문자언어	written language
문장	sentence

문장부호	punctuation
문장성분	constituent of a sentence
문책하다	to censure
문화어	① cultural language
	② official language in North Korea
묻다	to ask
물결표 (~)	swung dash
물음표 (?)	question mark
미래시제	future tense
미래형	future form
밀고하다	to inform on
반대말	① opposite word ② antonym
반대하다	to oppose
반론하다	① to counterargue ② to refute
반말	low forms of speech
반문하다	to ask a question in return
반박하다	to refute
반성문	written document of reflection
반의어	① antonym ② opposite word
반포하다	① to proclaim ② to announce publicly
반항하다	① to resist ② to defy ③ to oppose
받아쓰기	dictation
받침	consonant subjoined at the end of a Korean orthographic syllable
발령하다	① to give an order
	② to announce officially
발설하다	to disclose
발언	utterance
발의하다	① to suggest ② to propose
발표	presentation
발표자	① reader ② speaker
발표하다	① to present ② to announce
발화	utterance
밝히다	to clarify
방백	aside
방언	dialect

문장부호	
가운뎃점	·
꺾쇠표	〈 〉
느낌표	!
대괄호	[ ]
드러냄표	∴
마침표	.
말바꿈표	—
말줄임표	……
묶음표	[ ]
물결표	~
물음표	?
붙임표	-
빗금	/
빠짐표	□
소괄호	( )
숨김표	×× ○○
쉼표	,
쌍반점	;
쌍점	:
작은따옴표	' '
줄표	—
중괄호	{ }
큰따옴표	" "

방언론	dialectology
번역	translation
벙어리	deaf
베끼다	to copy
베트남어	Vietnamese language
변론하다	to argue
변명하다	to make an excuse
변호하다	to defend
보고하다	to report
보도하다	to report
보어	complement
보조동사	auxiliary verb
보조사	delimiter
보조용언	auxiliary adjective or verb
보조형용사	auxiliary adjective
보통명사	common noun
복창하다	to recite
복합어	compound
본딧말	original word
본론	body
본문	body
볼멘소리	① sullen words ② grouchy words
볼펜	ball-point pen
봉투	envelope
봉하다	to seal
부록	appendix
부르다	to call
부르짖다	to cry
부사	adverb
부사어	adverbial
부언하다	① to make an additional remark
부연하다	to expatiate on
부인하다	to deny
부정하다	to deny
부탁하다	to ask a favor
분부하다	① to direct ② to instruct

불규칙동사	irregular verb
불규칙형용사	irregular adjective
불어	French language
불임표 (-)	hyphen
불평하다	to complain
비교급	comparative
비꼬다	to be sarcastic
비난하다	① to criticize ② to censure
비방하다	① to slander ② to defame
비속어	vulgar language
비슷한말	similar word
비판하다	to criticize
비평하다	to criticize
빈말	idle talk
빌다	to pray
빗금 (/)	slash
빠짐표 (□)	omission mark
사과하다	to apologize
사동	causatives
사설	editorial
사전	dictionary
사절하다	① to decline ② to refuse
사정하다	① to beg considerations ② to entreat
사죄하다	① to apologize ② to beg pardon
사투리	dialect
사회자	presider
삼인칭	third person
상	aspect
상담	① counselling ② consultation
상소리	① coarse language ② vulgar word
상위어	meta language
상의하다	to consult
상형문자	hieroglyphics
색인	index
서론	introduction
서반아어	Spanish language

서법	mood
서술어	predicate
서술하다	① to describe ② to state
서약하다	① to swear ② to vow
서적	① books ② publications
선고하다	to sentence
선서하다	to take an oath
선어말어미	prefinal ending
선언하다	to declare
선포하다	to proclaim
설교하다	① to sermon ② to preach
설득	persuasion
설득하다	to persuade
설명	explanation
설명하다	to explain
설형문자	cuneiform
셈씨	numeral
소개하다	to introduce
소곤거리다	to whisper
소괄호 (( ))	parathensis
소리치다	to cry out
소문	rumor
소문내다	to spread a rumor
소식	news
소유격	possessive
소재	subject
소환하다	to summon
속기	shorthand
속담	proverb
속독	speed reading
속삭이다	to whisper
속어	slang
수다	chattering
수다떨다	to chat
수다스럽다	① to be talkative ② to be garrulous ③ to be loquacious

수다쟁이	chatterbox
수동태	passive voice
수락하다	to accept
수사	numeral
수식어	modifier
수정하다	① to revise ② to edit
수화	sign language
쉼표 (,)	comma
승낙하다	① to consent ② to permit
승인하다	to approve
시말서	① written explanation ② written apology
시비하다	① to dispute ② to quarrel
시어	① poetic word ② poetic diction
시인하다	to admit
시제	tense
시키다	to make (someone to do something)
신고하다	① to report ② to make a report
신음하다	to moan
신청하다	to apply
실어증	aphasia
실언하다	to make a slip of the tongue
실토하다	to confess
심문하다	to interrogate
심의하다	to deliberate
쌍반점 (;)	semi-colon
쌍점 (:)	colon
쐐기문자	cuneiform
쑥덕공론	① secret conference ② secret talks
쓰기	writing
쓰다	to write
아랍어	Arabian language
악담	curse
악담하다	① to speak ill of ② to backbite ③ to curse
안내하다	to guide

안부묻다	① to inquire about a person's health ② to ask about how someone is doing
알리다	to inform
알타이어족	Altaic language family
암송하다	to recite
애걸하다	① to beg for ② to plead for
애도하다	to mourn for
애원하다	① to implore ② to appeal
야단치다	to scold
야유하다	① to ridicule ② to hoot
약속하다	to promise
얘깃거리	① conversation topic ② conversation piece
어간	stem
어근	root of a word
어르다	to coax
어말어미	word final ending
어미	ending
어법	① usage ② wording ③ phraseology
어원	etymology
어절	phrase
어족	language family
어찌씨	adverb
어휘	vocabulary
어휘론	lexicology
어휘소	lexeme
어휘집	① wordbook ② vocabulary
언급하다	to mention
언도하다	① to sentence ② to pronounce
언약하다	to give one's word to
언어	language
언어교육	language education
언어능력	① language ability ② linguistic competence
언어사용	language use
언어사용자	language user

언어생활	language uses
언어수행	① language performance ② linguistic performance
언어순화	language purification
언어습득	language acquisition
언어예술	speech art
언어장벽	language barrier
언어장애	speech impediment
언어정책	language policy
언쟁하다	① to quarrel ② to dispute
언중	public speaking
얼버무리다	to speak vaguely
역설하다	to emphasize
연사	① speaker ② orator ③ lecturer
연설	speech
영어	English language
예고하다	to notify beforehand
예보하다	to forecast
예삿말	normal word usage
예언하다	to foretell
예찬하다	① to worship ② to adore
옹알이	babbling
외국어	foreign language
외래어	adopted word
외우다	to memorize
외치다	to shout
요구하다	① to require ② to demand
요청하다	① to demand ② to request
욕	① insult ② swear
욕설	① insult ② swear
욕하다	① to curse ② to insult
용언	verb or adjective
우기다	to insist
우랄어족	Uralic language family
우롱하다	to make a fool of
우스갯소리	joke

운소	suprasegmental feature
울부짖다	to scream
움직씨	verb
웅변가	orator
원급	positive degree
원어민	native speaker
월	sentence
유아어	baby talk
유언비어	groundless rumor
유의어	synonym
유행어	popular phrase
으름장	threat
은어	① argot ② jargon
읊다	to recite
음독	reading based on sounds
음성	① speech sound ② voice ③ phone
음성언어	oral language
음성학	phonetics
음소	phoneme
음운	phoneme
음운론	phonology
음절	syllable
응답하다	① to answer ② to reply
응하다	① to answer ② to comply with
의논하다	to consult
의문대명사	interrogative pronoun
의문문	interrogative sentence
의미론	semantics
의사소통	communication
의성어	onomatopoeia
의태어	mimic words
이력서	① resumé ② personal history
이르다	to explain
이름씨	noun
이야기	story
이야기하다	to talk with

이인칭	second-person
이중언어화자	bilingual speaker
인도유럽어족	Indo-European language family
인사하다	to greet
인용	quotation
인용하다	① to quote ② to cite
인칭	person
인칭대명사	personal pronoun
일기장	① diary ② journal
일본어	Japanese language
일상어	everyday language
일인칭	first-person narrator
일컫다	to call
읽기	reading
읽다	to read
임자씨	subject
입력하다	to input
입심	① loquacity ② talkativeness
입씨름	① dispute ② wrangle
자동사	intransitive verb
자문하다 (諮問—)	to consult
자문하다 (自問—)	to question oneself
자백하다	to confess
자음	consonant
자음동화	consonant assimilation
자청하다	to volunteer
자칭하다	to call oneself
자화자찬하다	to praise oneself
작가	writer
작문	composition
작은따옴표 (' ')	single quotation marks
잔말	① small talk ② chatter ③ nagging ④ small complaints
잔소리하다	to nag
잡담하다	① to gossip ② to chat
장담하다	to assure

재귀대명사	reflexive pronoun
재잘거리다	① to chatter ② to prattle
재촉하다	to urge
저술하다	to write a book
저자	① writer ② author
저주하다	to curse
저지하다	① to obstruct ② to hold back
적다	to write
전문용어	technical terms
전화걸다	to make a call
전화하다	to call
절	clause
점자	braille
접두사	prefix
접미사	suffix
접사	affix
접속사	conjunction
정독	perusal
정서법	orthography
제안하다	① to propose ② to suggest
제의하다	to propose
제지하다	to restrain
조동사	auxiliary verb
조롱하다	① to make a fool of ② to mock at ③ to ridicule
조르다	① to beg for ② to ask importunately
조사	postposition
조언하다	to advise
존댓말	honorific expressions
종성	coda
주격	nominative
주문하다	to order
주석	footnote
주어	subject
주의주다	to warn
주장하다	to insist

주제	topic
준말	abbreviation
줄임말	abbreviation
줄표 (—)	dash
중괄호 ({ })	curly bracket
중국어	Chinese language
중상모략하다	to slander
중성	neutral
중얼거리다	to mumble
증언	testimony
증언하다	to testify
지껄이다	① to chat ② to chatter
지시대명사	demonstrative pronoun
직접인용	direct quotation
직접화법	direct speech
진담	serious talk
진술	statement
진술하다	to state
진행형	progressive form
질문하다	① to inquire ② to ask a question
질의하다	to ask a question
질책하다	① to scold ② to reprove ③ to reproach
집필하다	to write
차례	table of contents
차용어	borrowed word
찬양하다	to praise
참견하다	① to meddle in ② to interfere
참고문헌	references
참말	① true remark ② truth ③ fact
찾아보기	index
책	book
책망하다	① to blame ② to reprimand
책벌레	bookworm
철자	spelling
청각장애자	the hearing impaired
청구하다	① to ask for ② to charge

청자	① hearer ② listener
청중	audience
체언	nominal
초성	onset
최상급	superlative
추궁하다	to press hard for an answer
축하하다	to congratulate
충고하다	to advise
치하하다	to praise
칭송하다	① to admire ② to praise
칭찬하다	① to compliment ② to praise
캐묻다	① to pry ② to press for an answer
큰따옴표 (" ")	double quotation marks
타동사	transitive verb
타이르다	to admonish
타자치다	to type
탄원하다	to plea
탐독	avid reading
탓하다	to blame
토론하다	to discuss
토박이말	native language
토씨	postposition
토의하다	to discuss
통고하다	to notify
통독	reading from cover to cover
통보하다	to report
통사론	syntax
통역사	interpreter
통역하다	to interpret
통지하다	① to inform ② to notify
퇴짜놓다	① to refuse ② to reject
투덜대다	① to grumble ② to complain
투정하다	① to grumble ② to complain
파생	derivation
파생어	derived word
판결하다	to judge

평하다	to evaluate
포고하다	① to proclaim ② to announce
폭로하다	to reveal
표	table
표기법	marking notation
표기하다	to mark
표명하다	① to state ② to express
표음문자	phonetic symbol
표의문자	ideogram
표준어	standard language
풀이씨	predicate
푸념하다	to grumble
품사	part of speech
피동문	passive sentence
핀잔주다	① to rebuke ② to reprimand
필기	taking notes
필기도구	writing tools (instruments)
필기하다	① to take a note ② to write down
필독	required reading
필독도서	required readings
필사본	① copy ② transcript
필사하다	① to copy ② to transcribe ③ to write down in longhand
핑계대다	to make an excuse
하소연	① appealing ② complaining
하소연하다	① to make an appeal ② to complain
하위어	subdivisional word
학술용어	technical term
한국어	Korean language
한글	Hangul (Korean alphabet)
한글날	Hangul Day
한자	Chinese characters
한자어	Sino-Korean word
합성어	compound word
합의하다	① to come to an agreement ② to talk over

항변하다	to make a plea
항의하다	to protest
해명하다	① to elucidate ② to explain
해설	commentary
해설하다	to explain
허가하다	to permit
허락하다	to consent
허용하다	to allow
헐뜯다	① to revile ② to slander
험담하다	to speak ill of
헛소리	nonsense
현재시제	present tense
현재완료	present perfect
현재형	present form
협박하다	to threaten
협상하다	① to negotiate ② to bargain with
협의하다	to discuss
형용사	adjective
형태론	morphology
형태소	morpheme
호소하다	to appeal
호언장담하다	① to talk big ② to boast
호출하다	① to page someone ② to call someone through a pager
호통치다	① to shout ② to roar ③ to yell
혹평하다	to criticize sharply
혼잣말	talking to oneself
홀소리	vowel
화법	speech
화술	① act of narration ② narrative skill
화용론	pragmatics
화자	speaker
화제	topic
확언하다	① to assert ② to affirm
환담하다	to have a pleasant chat
활용	① conjugation ② inflection

회담	meeting
회답하다	① to reply ② to answer
회화	conversation
훈계하다	to admonish
훈독	reading based on meaning
훈민정음	Korean alphabet in 15th century
훈시하다	① to instruct ② to admonish

14 언론과 출판
Journalism and Publishing

This chapter contains and lists lexical entries relating to press organizations and press activities in addition to publishing, publications, and the publishing process, particularly in connection with Korean people and Korean society.

간행하다	① to publish ② to issue
검열하다	① to inspect ② to survey
게재료	fee for publishing a paper
게재하다	① to publish ② to insert ③ to print
경제면	financial page
계간지	quarterly
고료	① contribution fee
	② fee for a manuscript
공개방송	open broadcasting
공영방송	public broadcasting
공저	① co-authorship ② joint authorship
광고	advertisement
광고면	advertisement page
교열기자	revised article
교육방송국	Education Broadcasting System (EBS)
교정	proofreading
교정하다	to proofread
교통방송	traffic broadcasting
구독자	subscriber
구독하다	to subscribe to
구성작가	composing writer

구인란	help-wanted section
구직란	employment section
국영방송	national broadcasting station
그림책	picture book
기독교방송	Christian broadcasting station
기사	① news ② article ③ news story
기자	① reporter ② journalist
난시청	poor reception
날씨란	weather column
녹화방송	recorded TV broadcast
녹화하다	① to record ② to videotape
논설위원	editorial writer
논평	① criticism ② comment ③ review
뉴스	news
다큐멘터리	documentary
대서특필	① feature ② cover story ③ wide news coverage
대중매체	mass media
도서	books
도서상품권	book gift certificate
독자	reader
독자투고란	reader's column
드라마	drama
라디오	radio
만평	① rambling criticism ② desultory criticism
만화	① cartoon ② comic strip
머릿글	headlines
머릿기사	headline news
무협지	martial arts novel
문화면	cultural column
문화방송국	Munhwa Broadcasting Company (MBC)
미군방송	American Forces Korea Network (AFKN)
민영방송	non-governmental broadcasting
발간하다	① to publish ② to issue
발행부수	circulation

발행인	publisher
발행하다	① to publish ② to issue
방송	① broadcasting ② broadcast
방송국	broadcasting station
방송망	broadcasting network
방송매체	broadcasting media
방송사고	broadcasting trouble
방송심의위원회	broadcasting review committee
방송작가	broadcasting writer
방송하다	to broadcast
방영하다	to televise
방청객	audience
방청석	audience seat
방청하다	① to hear ② to listen to ③ to attend
보도	① news ② report ③ information
본문	body of text
부	issue
부고란	obituary column
부수	circulation
부제	subtitle
불교방송	Buddhism broadcasting station
사설	editorial
사이비기자	reporter impersonator
사이비언론	quasi-journalism
사진기자	photo journalist
사회면	local news page

방송		
주체	방송국	종류
공영방송 국영방송 민영방송 중앙방송 지방방송 :	교육방송 (EBS) 교통방송 (TBS) 기독교방송 (CBS) 문화방송 (MBC) 미군방송 (AFKN) 불교방송 (BBS) 서울방송 (SBS) 평화방송 (PBS) 한국방송공사 (KBS) :	공개방송 녹화방송 생방송 위성방송 유선방송 재방송 :

사회자	master of ceremony (MC)
생방송	① live broadcasting ② live telecast
생중계	live relay broadcasting
생활면	life page
서울방송국	Seoul Broadcasting Station (SBS)
서적	① books ② publications
서점	bookstore
서점가	bookstore street
석간	① evening paper ② evening edition
선전	① advertisement ② propaganda ③ publicity
소식	① news ② information
속보	① prompt report ② news flash
송년호	special issue for the New Year
수신료	TV reception fee
스포츠면	sports column
시사	current events
시사지	current event magazine
시청료	TV subscription fee
시청률	① program rating ② popularity rating
시청자	① TV viewer ② televiewer ③ TV audience
시청하다	to watch
신문	① newspaper ② paper ③ journal
신문배달	newspaper delivery
신문사	newspaper publishing company
싣다	① to carry ② to record
아나운서	anchorperson
애독자	reader
애청자	fan of a certain radio program
언론	① speech ② press
언론기관	① press ② media
언론매체	media
언론사	press company
언론인	journalist
언론중재위원회	press intervention committee

여성지	women's magazine
연예면	entertainment page
연출	production
연출가	producer
연출자	producer
연출하다	to produce
원고	manuscript
원고료	① remuneration for writing ② fee for an article
월간지	monthly magazine
위성방송	satellite broadcasting
위성중계	satellite relay broadcasting
위인전	biography of famous
유선방송	cable broadcasting
인쇄	① printing ② presswork
인쇄물	① printed matter ② prints
인쇄소	① press ② printing house
인쇄하다	① to print ② to put into print
일간지	① daily newspaper ② daily press
자서전	autobiography
자유기고가	freelancer
작가	writer
잡지	magazine
잡지사	magazine company
재방송	rerun
저서	publications
저작권	① copyright ② literary property
전기	biography
정기간행물	periodical
정기구독	regular subscription
정부간행물	governmental publication
정치면	political page
제작하다	① to make ② to produce
조간	① morning paper ② morning edition
조연출	supporting producer
조판하다	to typeset

주간지	weekly magazine
주파수	frequency
중계방송	live broadcasting
중계하다	① to relay ② to rebroadcast
중앙방송	central broadcasting
지면	① space ② paper ③ sheet
지방방송	regional broadcasting
진행자	program leader
찍다	to print
채널	channel
책	book
청취율	① program rating ② popularity rating
청취자	① radio listener ② radio audience
청취하다	to listen to
촬영	① filming ② shooting
출간하다	to publish
출연료	performance fee
출연자	performer
출연하다	to perform
출판	① publication ② publishing
출판사	publishing company
출판하다	to publish
취재기자	reporter
취재하다	to collect data
텔레비전	television
통신사	news agency
투고하다	to contribute

출판		
신문	잡지	책·도서·서적
석간 일간지 조간 주간지 :	계간지 송년호 시사지 신년호 여성지 월간지 주간지 :	그림책 위인전 자서전 저서 전기 회고록 :

특보	① special report ② special news
특종기사	① exclusive news ② exclusive
특집	special edition
특파원	special correspondent
티브이편성표	TV programming chart
편집기자	editor
편집인	editor
편집장	chief editor
편집하다	to edit
편파보도	① partial reporting ② unfair report
평화방송	Peace Broadcasting Station (PBS)
표절	copy
필사본	plagiarism
표제	title
프로듀서	producer
한국방송공사	Korean Broadcasting Station (KBS)
행사란	event column
호외	special edition of a newspaper
화면	① picture ② scene
회고록	memoirs

15 정보와 통신
Information and Communication

This chapter contains lexical entries relating to information and communication: i.e., lexical entries on Korean people's methods of communication and their changes necessitated by the coming of the information age.

게시판	notice board
게시하다	to notify
고지하다	① to notify ② to announce
공고하다	to annonce
공중전화	① public phone ② pay phone
광고	advertisement
광고지	① flier ② advertising circular
광섬유	optical fiber
광통신	optical communication
교통정보	traffic information
구축하다	to install
국가기밀	national secrets
국제우편	international mail
국제전화	international call
군사우편	military mail
규격봉투	standard-sized envelope
그림엽서	picture postcard
기밀	secret
기지국	base station
누설하다	to reveal
뉴스	news

대중매체	mass media
대화방	chatting room
도청	wiretapping
도청기	① wiretapping device ② bug
도청하다	① to tap ② to bug
두절	① stoppage ② cessation
등기	registered mail
등기우편	registered mail
디스켓	diskette
라디오	radio
마우스	mouse
무선전화기	wireless phone
무선통신	wireless communication
무선호출기	① beeper ② pager
무전기	radio
발송	sending
방	notice
방송	broadcasting
방송망	broadcasting network
방송매체	broadcasting media
방송하다	to broadcast
보도	① information ② news ③ report
보통우편	regular mail
본체	main body
봉인	seal
봉화	signal fire
불통	① suspension ② interruption (of communication)
비밀	secret
비상연락망	emergency network
빠른우편	fast mail
삐삐	① beeper ② pager
사보	company news letter
산업정보	industrial information
생방송	① live broadcasting ② live telecast
생중계	live relay broadcasting

선전	① advertisement ② propaganda ③ publicity
소식	news
소식불통	suspension
소식지	news letter
소식통	① (well)informed circles ② source
소인	① postmark ② (postal) canceling ③ (cancellation) mark
소통	good communication
소포	parcel
소포우편	parcel mail
소프트웨어	software
속보	① prompt (quick) report (announcement) ② (news) falsh
송금	① remittance ② sending money
수화기	① (telephone) receiver ② earpiece
시내전화	local call
시외전화	long distance call
신문	newspaper
안내	① information ② advices
안내인	guide
안내장	circular
안내하다	① to guide ② to introduce ③ to show
안테나	antenna
알리다	to inform
언론	press
언론매체	press media
연락	① contact ② communication
연락두절	losing contact
연락망	network
연하장	① Season's greetings card ② New Year's card
엽서	postcard
우체국	postoffice
우체통	postbox
우편물	mail

우편번호	① postal code ② zip code
우편엽서	postcard
우편집배원	① postman ② mail carrier
우편함	mailbox
우표	stamp
위성방송	satellite broadcasting
위성중계	satellite relay broadcasting
위성통신	satellite communication
유선방송	cable broadcasting
이동통신	transfer communication
이메일	e-mail
인공위성	satellite
인터넷	internet
일간지	daily
입력	input
자판	keyboard
잡지	magazine
장거리전화	long distance call
전단	① leaflet ② bill
전보	telegram
전송 (傳送)	forward
전송 (電送)	transmit
전자우편	electronic mail
전파	① electric wave ② radio wave
전하다	① to convey ② to report ③ to deliver
전화	telephone
전화국	telephone office
전화기	telephone
전화번호	phone number
전화번호부	phone book
전화선	phone cord
전화카드	calling card
전화하다	① to call ② to phone
접선	① contact ② tangent
접속	connection
정보	① information ② data

정보검색	① information search ② data search
정보과학	information science
정보교환	information exchange
정보기관	secret (intelligence) service
정보망	intelligence network
정보비	information cost
정보사회	informational society
정보산업	information industry
정보수집	information collection
정보원	informer
정보지	information leaflet
정보처리	data processing
정보처리사	data processing person
정보통	① (well)informed circles ② source
정보통신부	Ministry of Information-Communication
정보화	informationization
주간지	weekly
중계기	transformer
중계방송	live broadcasting
중계하다	① to relay ② to rebroadcast
채널	channel
첩보	intelligence report
첩보망	spy network

정보 · 통신 수단			
과거	현재		
	정보	통신	
		전화 · 전송	우편
방 봉화 파발 ⋮	게시판 라디오 사보 소식지 신문 인터넷 주간지 텔레비전 ⋮	무전기 삐삐 온라인 전보 전화 컴퓨터통신 팩시밀리 핸드폰 ⋮	국제우편 군사우편 등기우편 보통우편 빠른우편 소포 연하장 엽서 편지 항공우편 ⋮

첩보원	spy
축전	congratulation telegram
출력	printing out
컴퓨터	computer
컴퓨터통신	computer communication
텔레비전	television
통고하다	to notify
통신	communication
통신사	news agency
통신시설	communication facilities
통신원	reporter
통신위성	① comsat ② news satellite
통신판매	mail order
통화	① call ② telephone conversation
통화료	phone bill
통화하다	① to speak (talk) over (upon) the telephone ② to speak by telephone
특보	① special report ② special news
특종	① exclusive news ② exclusive
파발	post station
팩스	facsimile
팩시밀리	facsimile
편지	letter
편지봉투	envelope
편지지	stationery
프린터	printer
피시통신	PC communication
하드웨어	hardware
학술정보	academic information
항공우편	airmail
호출기	① beeper ② pager
확성기	① (loud)speaker ② megaphone
휴대전화	① mobile phone ② cellular phone
휴대폰	① mobile phone ② cellular phone

16 교육
Education

This chapter contains lexical entries relating to educational organizations and facilities, and teaching/learning activities, particularly those specifically dealing with Korean education.

가르치다	① to teach ② to give lessons
가정교육	home education
가정통신문	home correspondence
가정학습	home study
간호대학	college of nursing
간호사관학교	nursing academy
강당	① auditorium ② lecture hall ③ assembly hall
강사	lecturer
강사진	faculty
강의	lecture
강의계획서	① syllabus ② lecture plan
강의실	① lecture room ② classroom
개강	opening of a course
개교기념일	school anniversary
개교하다	to open a school
개근상	① award for perfect attendance ② certificate for perfect attendance
개인교습	① individual training ② private lesson
개학	① start of school ② start of a school year

개학하다	to start the school year
객관식	multiple choice
걸상	chair
검정고시	qualification examination
견학	field trip
결석	absence
결석하다	to be absent
겸임교수	concurrent professor
경찰대학교	police academy
고등학교	① senior high school ② secondary school
고등학생	high school student
고시	① examination ② civil service examination
고시원	lodging facility for people to prepare examination
공고	technical high school
공교육	public education
공교육비	① public educational expenses ② public school expenses
공군사관학교	air-force academy
공립학교	public school
공부	① study ② learning
공부하다	to study
공업고등학교	technical high school
공책	notebook
과외	extracurricular study
과제	① homework ② assignment
과제물	① homework ② assignment
과학고등학교	high school of science
과학기술대학교	University of Science and Technology
괘도	① hanging chart ② wall chart
교감	vice principal
교과과정	① curriculum ② course of study
교과서	textbook
교구	① teaching tools

교단	② educational materials platform
교무실	office of school affairs
교문	school gate
교복	school uniform
교사	teacher
교생	① student teacher ② student practice teacher
교수	professor
교수식당	faculty cafeteria
교수요목	teaching points
교수진	faculty
교실	classroom
교원	① teacher ② instructor
교육	education
교육감	superintendent of education
교육공학	educational technology
교육과정	① educational process ② course of study
교육기관	educational organizations
교육내용	① educational contents ② teaching contents

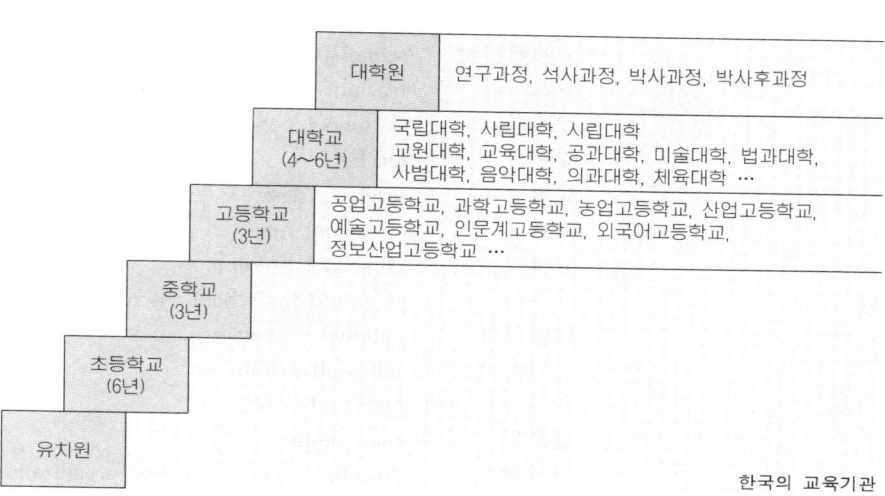

한국의 교육기관

교육대학	college of education
교육목적	① educational goals ② teaching goals
교육목표	educational goals
교육방법	① educational methods ② method of teaching
교육법	teaching method
교육부	Ministry of Education
교육비	① educational expenses ② cost of school education
교육시설	educational facilities
교육실습	teaching practice
교육열	eagerness for education
교육위원회	① board of education ② school board
교육자	① educator ② teacher
교육적	educational
교육철학	philosophy of education
교육평가	① evaluation of teaching ② educational evaluation
교육행정	educational administration
교장	principal
교장실	principal's office
교재	① teaching materials ② teaching aids
교지	school magazine
교지편집실	school paper editing room
교직	teaching profession
교직원	① school personnel ② school staff
교직자	teacher
교탁	teacher's desk
교표	① school mark ② school badge
교훈	① school precepts ② motto for school discipline
국립대학	national university
극기훈련	self-control training
근신	good behavior
급훈	class motto
기성회비	dues for school supporting organization

기숙사	dormitory
낙방하다	to fail an examination
낙제생	repeating student
낙제하다	to flunk an exam
노인대학	senior citizens' college
녹음기	tape recorder
놀이방	child care center
농고	agricultural high school
농업고등학교	agricultural high school
단과대학	college
단답형	simple answer questions
단원	① unit ② section
담당교사	teacher in charge
담임교사	homeroom teacher
답안지	answer sheet
대학교	university
대학본부	main building of a university
대학생	① college student ② university student
대학원	graduate school
대학원생	graduate student
도서관	library
도서실	library
독서실	reading room
독학사	self-educated university graduate
동아리방	club office
득점	scoring
등교하다	to attend school
등록금	tuition
등록하다	to register
등수	rank
마이크	microphone
면접	interview
명강의	famous lecture
명예교수	professor emeritus
명예박사	honorary doctor
명찰	① name plate ② identification tag

모교	① one's alma mater ② one's old school
모범생	model student
모의수업	mock class
무기정학	suspension of attendance for an indefinite period
무용실	dancing studio
문제	① problems ② questions
문제집	① workbook ② problem sets
문제학생	problematic student
미술대학	college of fine arts
미술도구	tools for fine arts
미술실	art room
박사	① doctor ② expert
발표	presentation
방송대학	correspondence university (via radio)
방송실	broadcasting room
방학	vacation
방학식	vacation ceremony
배우다	to learn
법과대학	college of law
보강	supplementary lecture
보건소	public health center
보고서	① written report ② paper
보기	example
보습학원	academy for supplementary lessons
보육원	① day nursery ② nursery school
보조가방	accessary bag
보조교사	assistant teacher
보충수업	supplementary lessons
복사기	copying machine
복수전공	double major
복습	review
복습하다	to review
복학	returning to school
복학생	returning student
본교	principal school

볼펜	ball point pen
봉사활동	volunteer work
부교수	associate professor
부전공	minor
부총장	vice-president
분교	branch school
분필	chalk
불량학생	delinquent student
비교육적	non-educational
비디오	video tape
사교육	private education
사교육비	private educational expenses
사립대학	private college
사립학교	private school
사물함	locker
사범대학	college of education
사서교사	librarian
사은회	dinner party given by the graduates in honor of their teachers
사지선다형	① multiple choice questions ② choosing among four
사회교육	social education
사회교육원	institute of social education
산업고등학교	industrial high school
산업대학	industrial college
상고	commercial high school
상급생	① upper-class student ② senior student
상담교사	guidance counsellor
상담실	counsellor's office
상아탑	ivory tower
상업고등학교	commercial high school
상장	certificate of merit
새내기	① freshman ② first-year student
생활관	place for teaching manners
생활기록부	student file
석사	① Master's degree ② Master of Arts

	(MA)
석차	① grade ② ranking
선생	teacher
선생님	teacher (deferential)
성교육	sex education
성적	① record ② score ③ result
성적증명서	certificate of school record
성적표	report card
소풍	school picnic
수능시험	Scholastic Aptitude Test
수료증	certificate of completion
수석	top student
수업	① class ② lesson
수업료	tuition
수업시간	class hour
수제자	best student
수학능력	learning capacity
수학능력시험	scholastic ability examination
수학여행	school trip
수험생	student preparing for an examination
수험표	① certificate for examination ② admission ticket for examination
숙제	① homework ② assignment
스승	① mentor ② master ③ teacher
스승의 날	Teacher's Day
슬라이드	slide
시간강사	part-time lecturer
시간표	① timetable ② schedule
시립대학	city college
시청각교육	audio-visual education
시청각교재	audio-visual aids
시청각수업	audio-visual class
시청각실	audio-visual room
시험	① examination ② test
시험감독	supervising an examination
시험감독관	proctor of an examination

시험지	examination paper
신발주머니	shoe bag
신입생	① new student ② incoming freshman
신학기	new school term
신학대학	college of theology
실물화상기	real picture projector
실습	① practice ② practical exercise
실습실	practicing room
실업학교	job training school
실험	① experimentation ② laboratory work
실험실	laboratory
아동교육	childhood education
알림장	notice book
애제자	one's favorite student
액정프로젝터	liquid projector
야외수업	outdoor class
야학	night school
약학대학	① college of pharmacy ② pharmaceutical college
양호교사	nurse teacher
양호실	nurse's office
어린이집	child care center
어학실습실	language laboratory
어학연수	language study
여고생	female high school student
여대생	female university student
여학생	female student
연구생	research student
연구소	① research institute ② research laboratory
연구수업	① research class ② test class
연구실	professor's office
연수	research study
연수원	training center
연필	pencil
열등생	slow learner

영아원	nursery
영재교육	education for gifted children
예고	high school of art
예능교육	art education
예술고등학교	high school of art
예습	lesson preview
예습하다	to preview lessons
오지선다형	① multiple choice ② choosing among five
외고	foreign language high school
외국어고등학교	foreign language high school
우등상	achievement award
우등생	honor student
운동장	① playground ② athletic field
원생	graduate student
원장	director of an institution
유급	repeating a grade
유기정학	suspension of attendance for a definite period
유아교육	early childhood education
유아원	① nursery ② preschool
유치원	kindergarten
유치원생	kindergartener
유학 (遊學)	studying away from home
유학 (留學)	studying abroad
유학생 (遊學生)	student studying away from home
유학생 (留學生)	student studying abroad
육군사관학교	Military Academy
육성회비	school supporting fees
은사	① one's former teacher ② one's respected teacher
음악대학	college of music
음악실	music room
응시자	① participant in an examination ② applicant
의과대학	college of medicine

의자	chair
이름표	identification tag
이사장	chief director
익히다	to learn
인문대학	college of humanities
인솔교사	escorting teacher
임시교사	temporary teacher
입시	entrance examination
입시생	entrance preparing student
입학	entrance into a school
입학금	entrance fee
입학생	new student
입학시험	entrance examination
입학식	entrance ceremony
입학하다	① to enter a school
	② to be admitted to a school
자	ruler
자습서	self-study workbook
자연대학	college of natural science
자율학습	self-learning
자퇴	leaving school voluntarily
장학관	school inspector
장학금	scholarship
장학사	government school inspector
장학생	① student on a scholarship
	② scholarship student
재교육	reeducation
재수생	student who failed an entrance exam and has been studyng to try again
재적	registered
재적생	registered student
재학	enrollment
재학생	enrolled student
재활교육	rehabilitation education
재활학교	rehabilitation school
전공	major

전과	change of one's major
전담교사	teacher in charge
전용강의실	lecture room for exclusive use
전인교육	holistic education
전임강사	full-time lecturer
전학	transfer of school
전학생	transferred student
점수	① marks ② grades ③ points ④ score
정근상	award for good attendance
정보산업고등학교	high school of information and industry
정학	suspension from school
제자	① student ② disciple ③ follower
제적	① removal from the register ② expulsion from school
조교	assistant
조교수	assistant professor
조기교육	early education
조기졸업	early graduation
조퇴	leaving school early for the day
조퇴하다	to leave the class before it is dismissed
조회	homeroom period
졸업	graduation
졸업생	① graduate ② alumnus
졸업식	graduation ceremony
졸업여행	graduation trip
졸업장	diploma
졸업증명서	certificate of graduation
졸업하다	to graduate
종강	last class
종례	class meeting at the end of the day
종업식	school year closing ceremony
종합대학	university
주관식	written questions
주임교사	head teacher
중퇴	dropping out of school

중학교	① middle school ② junior high school
중학생	① middle school student
	② junior-high school student
지각	lateness
지각하다	to be late
지도교수	① advisor ② supervisor
지우개	eraser
지진아	mentally challenged child
지침서	study guide
직업교육	① vocational education
	② professional education
진도표	progress chart
진학	entrance into a school of higher grade
차석	second top student
참고서	reference book
채점	grading
채점하다	to grade
책	book
책가방	book bag
책꽂이	bookshelf
책받침	celluloid board laid under writing paper
책상	desk
책장	① bookshelf ② bookcase
청소도구	cleaning tools
체벌	physical punishment
체육관	gymnasium
체육대학	college of physical education
초등학교	① elementary school ② primary school
초등학생	① primary school student
	② elementary school student
총장	president (of university)
출석	attendance
출석부	attendance list
출제	making questions for an examination
치맛바람	excessive intervention of a student's

	mother with school affairs
칠판	blackboard
컴퓨터	computer
탁아소	① nursery school ② public nursery
탁자	table
텔레비전	television
토론	① discussion ② talk ③ debate
통학	commuting to school
통학생	extern
퇴학	① leaving school
	② withdrawal from school
특강	special lecture
특별활동	extracurricular activity
특수교육	special education
특수학교	① school for the handicapped
	② special school
편입	transferring to another college
편입생	transferred student
평가	① evaluation ② assessment
평생교육	① lifelong education
	② continuing education
평생교육원	① institution for lifelong education
	② institution of continuing education
평점	examination marks
폐교	abolition/closing of a school
필기도구	writing tool
필통	pencil case
하급생	lower-grade student
학과	department
학과사무실	department office
학과장	chairperson
학교	school
학교교육	school education
학군	school group
학급	class
학급문고	class library

학급회의	class meeting
학기	① school term ② semester
학년	① school year ② grade
학력	① school career ② academic career
학령기	school age
학번	student number
학벌	① academic clique ② school ties
학보	school newspaper
학보사	school newspaper office
학부	department
학부사무실	department office
학부장	department chairperson
학부형	parents of students
학비	① school expenses ② tuition
학사 (學事)	school affairs
학사 (學士)	① Bachelor's degree ② Bachelor of Arts (BA)
학사경고	warning for poor grades less than standard points
학사일정	school calendar
학생	student
학생식당	① cafeteria ② student cafeteria
학생증	student identification card
학생회	student council
학생회관	student building
학생회비	student membership fee
학생회장	① student president ② president of student council
학술답사	field trip
학습	① learning ② study
학습서	study guide
학업	① studies ② classwork ③ schoolwork
학예회	① exhibition of student works ② school concert
학용품	school supplies
학원	① academy ② school ③ private school

〈학예회〉

〈학위수여식〉

학원생	① institute student ② academy student
학원폭력	school violence
학위	academic degree
학위논문	thesis for a degree
학위수여식	ceremony of conferment of a degree
학장	dean of a school
학적	school register
학적부	school register
학점	① credit ② unit
한국교육개발원	Education Development Institute of Korea
합격하다	to pass an examination
해군사관학교	Naval Academy
현장학습	field study
환등기	slide projector
휴강	① no lecture ② no class
휴게실	student lounge
휴교	closure of a school
휴학	leave of absence
휴학생	student on temporary leave

17 과학과 학문
Science and Scholarship

This chapter contains lexical entries indicating basic terms, theories, and notions frequently used in science and scholarship.

가능성	① possibility ② chances
가설	hypothesis
가속도	acceleration
가속도의 원리	acceleration principle
가스	gas
가정	assumption
가정하다	to assume
가치관	one's values
간주하다	① to consider ② to regard
간호학	① science of nursing
	② professional nursing
개념	① notion ② concept ③ idea
객관성	objectivity
거름종이	filter paper
건전지	battery
건축학	architecture
건축학자	architect
검증	verification
검증하다	to verify
결과	result
결론	conclusion
결정하다	to decide

경영학	business management
경영학자	scholar of business administration
경제학	economics
경제학자	economist
경험	experience
경험주의	empiricism
고고학	archaeology
고고학자	archeologist
고전주의	classicism
고체	solid matter
공동연구	joint research
공부하다	① to study ② to work
공학	engineering
공학자	engineer
과학	science
과학기술	science technology
과학실	science room
과학자	scientist
관성	inertia
관성법칙	law of inertia
관찰	observation
관찰하다	to observe
관측	observation
관측하다	to observe
교육학	education
교육학자	educator
구별하다	① to distinguish ② to make a distinction
구상하다	① to map out a scheme ② to visualize a plan
국문학	Korean literature
국문학자	scholar of Korean literature
국어학	Korean linguistics
국어학자	scholar of Korean linguistics
군사학	military science
귀결	① conclusion ② consequence

귀납법	① induction ② inductive method
규칙	rule
극관	polar cap
극성	polarity
기체	vapor
기화	vaporization
깨닫다	① to understand ② to be aware of ③ to realize
끓는점	boiling point
나트륨	natrium (Na)
납	lead
냉철하다	① to be cool-headed ② to be levelheaded
노문학	Russian literature
노문학자	scholar of Russian literature
노어학	Russian linguistics
노어학자	scholar of Russian linguistics
녹는점	melting point
논리	logic
논문	① thesis ② paper ③ dissertation
논문계획서	thesis proposal
논법	① logic ② reasoning
농도	① density ② thickness
농학	agricultural science
농학자	agriculturist
단서	① clue ② key
단정하다	to conclude
독문학	German literature
독문학자	scholar of German literature
독어학	German linguistics
독어학자	scholar of German linguistics
동기	motive
동위원소	isotope
렌즈	lens
리트머스시험지	litmus paper
마그네슘	magnesium (Mg)

마찰	friction
마찰력	friction power
만유인력의 법칙	law of gravity
망원경	telescope
매진하다	① to push on (forward) ② to dash on ③ to strive (for)
목적	① goal ② aim
목표	target
몰두하다	① to be immersed in ② to concentrate
몽골학	Mongolian studies
무역학	commerce studies
무용학	dancing studies
무조건반사	unconditional response
문학	literature
문헌정보학	library information science
문헌정보학자	scholar of library information
물	water
물레방아	water mill
물리학	physics
물리학자	physicist
미국학	American studies
미학	aesthetics
민속학	folklore
민속학자	scholar of folklore
밀도	density
바람	wind
반사	reflection
반사경	reflection mirror
반응	reaction
발표요지	handout
방법론	methodology
방사능	radio-active
방사능물질	radio-active material
방사선	① radiation ② radioactive rays
법칙	law
법학	law

변별하다	to make a distinction
변증법	dialectic
병렬	arranging in a row
본론	main body
볼록렌즈	convex lens
분간하다	to differentiate
분별력	discretion
분별하다	to discern
분석하다	to analyse
분자	molecule
분해	decomposition
분해하다	to decompose
불	fire
불꽃	① flame ② blaze
불문학	French literature
불문학자	scholar of French literature
불어학	French linguistics
불어학자	scholar of French linguistics
비판력	critical ability
비판하다	to criticize
비평	criticism
비평하다	to criticize
비합리	absurdity
빙점	freezing point
사고	thought
사고력	ability to think
사고하다	to think
사리	reason
사리분별하다	to discern with reasoning
사리판단하다	to judge with reasoning
사상	① thought ② ideology
사색하다	to meditate
사학	history
사학자	historian
사회과학	social science
사회학	sociology

사회학자	sociologist
산	acid
산성	acidity
산소	oxygen
산화	oxidation
삼단논법	syllogism
삼발이	tripod
삼투압	osmotic pressure
삼투압원리	osmotic pressure principle
상대성이론	theory of relativity
생물학	biology
생물학자	biologist
서론	introduction
서적	① books ② publications
석유	petroleum
석탄	coal
세미나	seminar
세포	cell
속도	speed
수력	hydropower
수소	hydrogen
수의학	veterinary science
수학	mathematics
수학자	mathematician
순수학문	pure sciences
숯	charcoal
숯불	charcoal fire
슬기	wisdom
습득하다	to acquire
시약	chemical reagent
시험관	test tube
식별하다	① to discern ② to distinguish
신문방송학	journalism and broadcasting
신문학	journalism
신학	theology
신학자	scholar of theology

실습실	practice room
실용주의	pragmatism
실용학문	applied sciences
실험	experiment
실험보고서	experiment report
실험실	laboratory
실험하다	to experiment
심리	① mentality ② psychology
심리학	psychology
심리학자	psychologist
심사숙고하다	to think considerately
심포지엄	symposium
아연	zinc
알칼리성	alkalinity
알코올	alcohol
알코올램프	alcohol lamp
압력	pressure
액체	liquid
액화	liquefaction
약학	pharmacy
약학자	pharmacist
양극	two poles
어는점	freezing point
어학	study of languages
언어학	linguistics
언어학자	linguist
에너지	energy
역사학	history
역사학자	historian
연구	research
연구계획서	research plan
연구발표	research presentation
연구비	research funds
연구소	① research institute ② research laboratory
연구실	① professor's office

	② researcher's office
연구원	researcher
연구하다	① to research ② to study ③ to work
연구회	society for the study of …
연료	fuel
연상	association
연상하다	to associate
연역법	① deduction ② deductive method
연탄	briquet
열량	calorie
염기성	basic
염산	hydrochloric acid
염소	chlorine
영문학	English literature
영문학자	scholar of English literature
영어학	English linguistics
영어학자	scholar of English linguistics
예견하다	to foresee
예측하다	to predict
오목렌즈	concave lens
오판하다	to misjudge
오해하다	to misunderstand
온도	temperature
용해도	solubility
원리	principle
원소	element
원소기호	element sign
원예학	horticulture
원예학자	horticulturist
원인	cause
원자	atom
원자력	① atomic energy ② nuclear power
원자로	nuclear reactor
유추	analogy
유추하다	to analogize
유학	studying abroad

유학자	student studying abroad
융해	fusion
융해열	heat of fusion
음극	negative pole
음악학	studies of music
응고점	① setting point ② freezing point
응용력	ability to apply
응용하다	① to adapt ② to apply
의학	medical science
의학자	medical scientist
이론	theory
이성	reason
이해하다	to understand
인력	① attraction ② gravitation
인류학	anthropology
인류학자	anthropologist
인문과학	cultural sciences
인식하다	to recognize
인지하다	to cognize
일문학	Japanese literature
일문학자	scholar of Japanese literature
일어학	Japanese linguistics
일어학자	scholar of Japanese linguistics
임학	forestry
입증	proof
입증하다	to prove
자극 (磁極)	magnetic pole
자극 (刺戟)	stimulus
자기장	magnetic field
자석	magnet
자연과학	natural science
작용반작용의 법칙	law of action and reaction
작용하다	to act on
저서	① literary work ② one's writings
적용하다	to apply
전공하다	to major in

전극	electrode
전기	electricity
전력	electric power
전류	electric current
전압	① voltage ② electric pressure
전자계산학	computer science
전자관	electron tube
전자석	electromagnet
전자파	electromagnetic waves
전자회로	electric circuit
전제	presupposition
전지	① electric cell ② battery
전해질	electrolyte
정보과학	information science
정설	established theory
정신	mind
정신력	mental strength
정전기	static electricity
정진하다	to devote oneself
정치학	politics
정치학자	scholar of political science
조건반사	conditioned response
조경학	landscape design
조도	luminous intensity
종교학	religious studies
주관성	subjectivity
주파수	frequency
중국문학	Chinese Literature
중력	gravity
중성	neutrality
중성자	neutron
중어학	Chinese Linguistics
증명하다	to prove
증발하다	to evaporate
지각하다	to perceive
지능	intelligence

지능지수	intelligence quotient
지리학	geography
지리학자	scholar of geography
지질학	geology
지질학자	geologist
지혜	wisdom
직렬	series
진공관	vacuum tube
진동	① oscillation ② vibration
진리	truth
진자운동	movement of a pendulum
질량	mass
질량불변의 법칙	law of constancy of mass
질산	nitric acid
질소	nitrogen
짐작하다	to conjecture
집중력	ability to concentrate
착각하다	① to have an illusion ② to have false impression ③ to misunderstand
참고문헌	① references ② bibliography
창의력	creativity
채집	collection
채취하다	① to collect ② to gather
책	book
천문대	observatory
천문학	astronomy
천문학자	astronomer
천연가스	natural gas
철학	philosophy
철학자	philosopher
체육학	physical education
초음파	supersonic (ultrasonic) waves
촉매	catalyzer
촉매제	catalytic material
추론	inference
추론하다	to infer

추리	reasoning
추리하다	to reason
추정	presumption
추측	conjecture
추측하다	to conjecture
축산학	study of animal husbandry
침전물	① deposit ② sediment
칼륨	potassium
칼슘	calcium
컴퓨터공학	computer engineering
컴퓨터공학자	computer engineer
탄소	carbon
탐구하다	① to delve ② to dig
태양열	solar heat
터득하다	① to understand ② to learn
톱밥	sawdust
통계학	statistics
통계학자	① statistician ② statist
통찰력	insight
판단	judgment
판단력	judgment
판단하다	to judge
판별하다	to distinguish
팽창	expansion
평가하다	to evaluate
표본	sample
풍차	windmill
학계	academic circles
학구적	academic
학구파	hard worker of knowledge
학문	① learning ② knowledge
학문적	① learned ② scholarly
학설	① theory ② doctrine
학술	scholarship
학술대회	① scholarly conference ② academic conference

학술원		the Academy
학습하다		to learn
학파		① school ② sect
학풍		① academic traditions
		② school character
학회		learned society
한국과학재단		Korea Science Engineering Foundation
한국학		Korean studies
한국학술진흥재단		Korea Research Foundation
한국학자		scholar of Korean studies
한문학		Chinese classics
한문학자		scholar of Chinese classics
한의학		Chinese medical science
한학		study of Chinese classics
한학자		scholar of Chinese classics
합리		rationality
합리주의		rationalism
핵		nucleus
행정학		political science
행정학자		scholar of public administration
헬륨		helium
현미경		microscope
화력		① thermal power ② heating power
화학		chemistry
화학반응		chemical reaction
화학약품		chemicals
황		sulfur
황산		sulphuric acid
휘발유		gasoline
힘		① power ② strength

학문	인문과학	교육학, 국문학, 국어학, 노문학, 노어학, 독문학, 독어학, 문학, 불문학, 불어학, 심리학, 언어학, 역사학, 영문학, 영어학, 인류학, 일문학, 일어학, 중국문학, 중어학, 철학, 한문학 …
	사회과학	경영학, 경제학, 무역학, 문헌정보학, 법학, 사회학, 신문방송학, 정치학, 행정학 …
	자연과학	간호학, 건축학, 공학, 물리학, 생물학, 수의학, 수학, 약학, 원예학, 의학, 조경학, 지리학, 지질학, 천문학, 컴퓨터과학, 통계학, 한의학, 화학 …

18 종교와 믿음
Religions and Beliefs

This chapter contains lexical entries connected with religious artifacts, rituals, groups and people of special importance to Korean people. It also contains many of the facilities and goods necessary to the religious life of the Koreans.

감리교	Methodist Church
개신교	Protestant
개종	conversion
개종하다	① to change one's religion ② to be converted
경배	worship
경외심	awe-struck
경외하다	① to stand in awe ② to dread
경전	① scriptures ② sacred books
계	commandment
고사	Shamanistic practice appeasing household spirits
고해성사	sacrament of confession
고행	① penance ② asceticism
공덕	① charity ② pious act
공양	① offering ② mass for the dead soul
공양미	① rice offering ② rice offered to Buddha
공자	Confucius
관상	① physiognomy ② phrenological interpretation

관혼상제	ceremonial occasions (coming of age, wedding, funeral and death memorial)
광신도	religious fanatic
교단	① religious order ② religious fraternity
교리	① doctrine ② dogma
교리문답	catechism
교인	believer
교조	① tenet ② dogma
교주	founder of a religion
교파	① (religious) denomination ② sect
교황	Pope
교회	church
구교	① Roman Catholicism ② Catholic Church
구세군	Salvation Army
구세주	Saviour
구약성서	Old Testament
구원	salvation
국교	national religion
굿	exorcism
굿판	spot of exorcism
굿하다	① to exorcise ② to perform an exorcism
권사	deaconess
귀신	① ghost ② spirit
귀의하다	① to become a believer ② to embrace Christianity
그리스도	Christ
그리스정교	Greek Orthodox
극락정토	① Land of Happiness ② paradise
기구	organization
기도	prayer
기도문	① prayer ② Lord's prayer
기도원	① oratory ② prayer house
기도하다	to pray
기독교	Christianity
기원	① prayer ② supplication

〈굿〉

기적	miracle
나무아미타불	Save us, merciful Buddha
낙원	paradise
넋	① soul ② spirit
논어	Analects of Confucius
다신교	polytheism
대사	① saint ② great Buddhist priest
대순진리회	Truth of Great Order
대주교	archbishop
도	① teachings ② doctrines
도교	Taoism
도깨비	① goblin ② monster
독실하다	to be faithful
돌부처	stone Buddhist image
라마교	Lamaism
마귀	① evil spirit ② devil ③ demon
마녀	① witch ② sorceress
마호메트교	Islam
목사	① pastor ② minister ③ clergyman
목탁	wood block in a Buddhist temple
몰몬교	Mormonism
무교	no religion
무당	① exorcist ② sorceress ③ female shaman
무속	Shamanism
무속신앙	Shamanism
무신론	atheism
묵주	rosary
미사	① mass ② Mass
미사드리다	to say mass
미신	① superstition ② superstitious belief
민간신앙	folk religion
믿다	to believe
믿음	① belief ② faith
박수무당	① male shaman ② sorcerer
백일기도	hundred days prayer

〈목탁〉

〈무당〉

백팔번뇌	108 passions a man is subject to
번뇌	① agony ② anxiety
법	Buddha's teaching
법사	Buddhist priest
보살	Bodhisattva
복	blessing
복사	① acolyte ② altar boy
복음	① Christian gospel ② good news
복음서	Bible
복음성가	gospel songs
복자	blessed
부목사	vice pastor
부적	① talisman ② amulet
부처	Buddha
부처님	Buddha (deferential)
부활절	Easter
불경	① Buddhist scriptures ② sutra
불교	Buddhism
불도	teachings of Buddha
불법	① Buddhism ② sacred law of Buddha ③ Buddhist canon
불사	① Buddhist temple ② Buddhist rituals and services
불상	① image of Buddha ② Buddhist image
불운	bad luck
불탑	① pagoda ② stupa ③ tope
불화	Buddhist painting
비구니	Buddhist nun
빌다	① to pray ② to wish
사교	① heretical religion ② heresy
사당	① shrine ② ancestral shrine
사도신경	Apostles' Creed
사랑	love
사리	relics of Buddha or of a Buddhist saint
사서삼경	Four Books and Three Classics
사원	① temple ② monastery

〈불상〉

사월초파일	April 8th, Buddha's birthday
사이비	① pseudo- ② quasi-
사이비종교	① false religion ② pseudoreligion
사주	horoscopic data-year, month, day, hour of birth
사주팔자	fate
사찰	Buddhist temple
산신	mountain god
산신령	guardian god (spirit) of a mountain
살	evil spirit
삼강오륜	three fundamental principles and the five moral disciplines in human relations
서낭당	shrine of a tutelary deity
서낭신	god of a tutelary deity
서방정토	① Buddhist Elysium ② Western Paradise
석가모니	① Shakyamuni ② Buddha
석가탄신일	Buddha's Birthday
선교	missionary work
선교사	missionary
설교하다	① to preach ② to preach a sermon
성가	hymnal
성가대	church choir
성결교	the Holiness Church
성경	Bible
성공회	① Protestant Episcopal Church ② Anglican Church
성균관	*Sungkyunkwan* (National University o Yi Dynasty)
성당	Catholic church
성령	Holy Spirit
성모	① Holy Mother ② Virgin Mary
성모마리아	① Virgin Mary ② Blessed Mary
성부	Holy Father
성서	Bible

〈서낭당〉

성신	Holy Spirit
성인	saint
성자 (聖子)	Son
성자 (聖者)	saint
성전	① sacred shrine ② sanctuary
성지	① sacred place ② holy place
성지순례	pilgrimage of holy places
성직자	① churchman ② minister ③ clergyman
성탄절	① Christmas ② Christmas Day
성호	holy cross
세례	① baptism ② christening
세례명	① baptismal name ② Christian name
수녀	① nun ② sister of the Catholic church
수녀원	① nunnery ② convent
수도사	monk
수도원	monastery
수도하다	① to lead an ascetic life ② to practice asceticism
순교자	martyr
숭배	① worship ② adoration ③ admiration
숭상	① respect ② veneration ③ revere
숭앙	admiration
스님	Buddhist monk
승려	Buddhist monk
시주	benefactor
신	① God ② the Almighty ③ Providence ④ the Lord
신교	Protestantism
신교도	protestant
신내리다	① to fall into trance ② to be possessed by a spirit
신당	shrine
신도	① believer ② devotee ③ adherent
신들리다	to be possessed by a spirit
신령	① divine spirit ② spirits ③ gods
신령님	① divine spirit ② god

신부	① Catholic priest ② holy father
신성하다	to be holy
신앙	① faith ② belief
신앙고백	① confession of faith ② confession
신앙생활	① life of faith ② religious life
신앙심	① faith ② belief
신앙인	believer
신약성서	New Testament
신자	① believer ② devotee
신주	mortuary tablet
신흥종교	new religion
심령술	spiritualism
심령술사	psychic
심방하다	to visit
십일조	tithes
십자가	① cross ② rood ③ crucifix
아멘	Amen
악귀	evil spirit
악마	① devil ② demon ③ fiend ④ Satan
안식교	Sabbath
안식일교	Sabbath
알라	Allah
액	disaster
액땜하다	to forestall a disaster with a lesser sacrifice
업	① karma ② one's deed as a determinant factor in one's future life
업보	effects of karma
여호와	Jehovah
여호와의 증인	Jehovah's Witness
역술가	fortune-teller
연등행사	lotus lamp parade
열반	① Nirvana ② Buddha's death ③ salvation
염라대왕	King of Hell
염불	① Amitabha ② Buddihist invocation

염불하다	① to pray to Amitabha ② to do Buddhist invocation
염주	① Buddhist rosary ② prayer beads
영성체	Holy Communion
영세	baptism
영세명	baptismal name
영혼	① soul ② spirit
예배	① worship ② adoration
예배당	① church ② chapel
예배드리다	to attend divine service
예배보다	① to worship ② to adore
예불하다	to worship before the image of Buddha
예수	Jesus
예수교	Christianity
예수님	Jesus (honorific)
우상숭배	① idol worship ② idolatry
운수	① luck ② fortune
원불교	Won Buddhism
유교	Confucianism
유대교	Judaism
유령	① ghost ② apparition ③ specter
유림	① Confucianists ② Confucian scholars
유생	Confucian
유신론	theism
유일신	the Only God
유태교	Judaism
유학	Confucianism
윤회	① rotation ② transmigration ③ cycles of life
은총	① grace ② favor
이단	① heresy ② paganism ③ heathenism
이슬람교	Islam
이승	① this life ② this world ③ this existence
인 (仁)	① perfect virtue ② benevolence ③ humanity

〈염주〉

인연	① karma ② fate ③ affinity
일신교	monotheism
자비	① mercy ② benevolence ③ compassion ④ pity
자연숭배	nature worship
자연신앙	natural religion
잡귀	minor demons
장로	church elder
장로교	Presbyterian Church
저승	world of the dead
저승사자	messenger from the world of the dead
전도	① missionary work ② evangelism
전도사	① preacher ② missionary ③ evangelist
전도하다	① to evangelize ② to propagate one's religion
절	Buddhist temple
절대자	① the Absolute ② the absolute being
점	① fortune-telling ② divination
점괘	divination sign
점보다	to have one's fortune told
점성술	astrology
점쟁이	fortune-teller
점집	fortune-teller's house
점치다	① to practice divination ② to tell fortune
정통	① legitimacy ② orthodoxy
제사	① sacrifice ② sacrificial rites ③ ancestral rites
제사상	offerings to god or ancestors
제사지내다	① to perform an ancestral rite ② to sacrifice
제삿날	memorial day of an ancestor
제주 (祭酒)	sacrificial wine
제주 (祭主)	chief mourner
조계종	one of nomination of Buddhism

〈제사상〉

조상	① ancestor ② forefather
조상신	① ancestor god ② forefather god
종교	religion
종교개혁	religion reform
종교계	religion society
종교관	view of religion
종교단체	religious organization
종교서적	religious books
종교음악	sacred music
종교의식	religious ritual
종교인	man of religion
종교전쟁	religious war
종교철학	philosophy of religion
종교탄압	religious persecution
종파	religious denomination
주교	bishop
주기도문	Lord's Prayer
주님	Lord as God and Jesus (honorific)
주문	① spell ② incantation
주술	① incantation ② magic
주일	Sunday
주지스님	chief priest of a Buddhist temple
중	① Buddhist priest ② monk
중생	living things
증산교	one of Korean new religions
지방	ancestral tablet made of paper
지옥	① hell ② inferno
집사	deacon
차례	ancestor-memorial rites
차례상	offerings to ancestors on special days
차례지내다	to perform ancestral rites
찬미	① praise ② admiration ③ glorification
찬불가	hymn to Buddha
찬송	① glorification of God ② praise to God
찬송가	① hymn ② psalm
찬송하다	to sing a hymn

〈차례상〉

찬양하다	to praise
창조자	① creator ② the Creator
천국	① kingdom of Heaven ② Heaven ③ Paradise
천당	① Heaven ② palace of Heaven ③ Paradise
천도교	Religion of the Heavenly Way
천리교	Religion of Natural Laws
천사	angel
천주교	Catholicism
천주님	① Lord of Heaven ② God
최면	hypnosis
최면술	① mesmerism ② hypnotism
추기경	cardinal
추수감사절	Thanksgiving Day
축복	blessing
출가하다	① to enter priesthood ② to become a bonze
침례	baptism
침례교	Baptist Church
카톨릭교	Catholic
코란	Koran
크리스마스	Christmas
크리스트교	Christianity
탱화	altar portrait of Buddha
토정비결	Tojung's book of fortune-telling
통과의례	passing rites
통일교	Unification Church
파계승	depraved monk
포교	① propagation of religion ② missionary work ③ propagandism
포교사	missionary temple
푸닥거리	exorcism
하나님	① God ② the Almighty ③ the Lord (Protestant)
하느님	① God ② the Almighty

	③ the Lord (Catholic)
학습	catechism
합장하다	① to join one's hands
	② to put one's hands flat together
해몽	interpretation of dreams
해탈	① deliverance of one's soul
	② emancipation ③ salvation
행운	① luck ② fortune
향교	local old-time school belonging to a Confucian temple
헌금	① collection ② offering
혼	① soul ② spirit
혼령	① spirit of a dead person
	② departed soul ③ soul
혼백	① soul ② spirit ③ ghost
회교	① Mohammedanism ② Islamism
회교도	Muslim
힌두교	Hinduism

분류	대상	이념	경전	사람	장소	의식
유교	공자님, 조상신	인 (仁)	사서삼경 (四書三經)	유림, 유생 ⋮	서원, 향교	차례, 제사 ⋮
불교	부처님, 석가모니	자비	불경	대사, 법사 승려, 스님 중, 비구니 보살 ⋮	절, 사원	예불, 염불 ⋮
기독교	하나님, 예수님	사랑	성경	목사, 전도사 장로, 권사 집사, 선교사	교회, 예배당 ⋮	예배, 세례 ⋮
천주교	천주님, 예수님 성모마리아	사랑	성경	교황, 추기경 대주교, 주교 신부, 수녀	성당, 수도원 ⋮	미사, 고해성사 세례, 영세
민간신앙	신, 자연물	복 (福)		무당, 박수무당 ⋮	서낭당, 신당 ⋮	고사, 굿, 점 ⋮

19 문명과 문화
Civilization and Culture

This chapter contains lexical entries relating to mecca of human civilization, types of cultures, and the development of culture. It also contains lexical entries relating to cultural sites and the cultural life of the Koreans.

개화기	① age of enlightenment
	② the time of blooming
개화하다	to enlighten
계승하다	to succeed
고대문명	ancient civilization
고문서	ancient document
구석기시대	stone age
국립경주박물관	Kyongju National Museum
국립광주박물관	Kwangju National Museum
국립민속박물관	Folklore National Museum
국립부여박물관	Puyo National Museum
국립중앙박물관	National Museum of Korea
국보	national treasure
기계문명	industrial civilization
기념물	monument
기능보유자	functional holder
농경문화	farming culture
대중문화	mass culture
동양문화	Eastern culture
르네상스	Renaissance
마야문명	Mayan civilization

메소포타미아문명	Mesopotamia civilization
무형문화재	intangible cultural assets
문명	civilization
문명사	history of civilization
문명사회	civilized society
문물	civilization
문물교류	civilization exchange
문예부흥	renaissance
문호개방	open-door
문화	culture
문화계	cultural world
문화관광부	Ministry of Culture & Tourism
문화교류	cultural exchange
문화권	cultural area
문화대혁명	cultural revolution
문화민족	cultural race
문화부	department of culture
문화비	cultural expenses
문화사	history of culture
문화생활	cultural life
문화수준	cultural level
문화시설	cultural facilities
문화예술	culture and arts
문화예술진흥기금	Korean Culture & Arts Fund
문화예술진흥법	Law of Korean Culture & Arts
문화유산	cultural heritage
문화융합	cultural fusion
문화의식	cultural consciousness
문화인	man of culture
문화인류학	cultural anthropology
문화재	cultural assets
문화재관리국	Public Trustee Office
문화재보호	protection of cultural properties
문화접변	cultural assimilation
문화제	cultural festival
문화창조	creation of culture

문화행사	cultural activity
문화혁명	cultural revolution
문화회관	cultural center
미개	primitive
미개인	primitive people
미케네문명	Mycenae Civilization
민속	folk customs
민속자료	folk customs data
민속촌	folk village
발달하다	to develop
발상지	① cradle ② birthplace
발전하다	① to develop ② to expand ③ to grow
발해문화	Balhae culture
보물	treasure
복식문화	① culture of dress and its ornaments ② clothing culture
불교문화권	region of Buddhist culture
비단길	silk road
사적	historic relics (remains)
생활양식	way of living
서구문명	Western civilization
서구문화	Western culture
서양문화	Western culture
선사문화	prehistoric culture
선사시대	prehistoric age
선진문명	advanced civilization
세계문화유산	world cultural assets
세시풍속	manners and customs of new year's day
세종문화회관	Sejong Cultural Center
신석기시대	neolithic age
실크로드	silk road
안데스문명	Andes civilization
야만	savageness
야만인	① barbarian ② savage
에게문명	Aegean civilization
온양민속박물관	On-Yang Folk Museum

옹기민속박물관		Pottery Folklore Museum
원시인		primitive man
유물		relic
유적		remains
음식문화		food culture
이집트문명		Egyptian civilization
인간문화재		human cultural assets
인도문명		Indian civilization
인류문명		civilization of human beings
인류문화		culture of human beings
잉카문명		Incan civilization
전래문화		traditional culture
전승문화		oral culture
전승하다		to hand down
전통문화		traditional culture
전파하다		to propagate
중국문명		Chinese civilization
철기시대		iron age
청동기시대		copper age
크레타문명		Creta civilization
트로이문명		Troy civilization
풍습		customs
한국문화예술진흥원		Korean Culture & Arts Foundation
한국자수박물관		Museum of Korean Embroidery
한국정신문화연구원		Academy of Korean Studies
한국화		Korean drawings
한글문화		Hangul culture
한자문화권		region using Chinese characters
향유하다		to enjoy
현대문명		modern civilization

문명	시대	고대문명, 현대문명 …
	지역	마야문명, 메소포타미아문명, 미케네문명, 서구문명, 아즈텍문명, 안데스문명, 에게문명, 이집트문명, 인도문명, 잉카문명, 중국문명, 크레타문명, 트로이문명 …
문화	시대	선사문화, 전래문화, 전승문화, 전통문화 …
	지역	서구문화, 서양문화, 동양문화, 발해문화 …
	종교	불교문화, 이슬람문화 …
	유형	농경문화, 복식문화, 음식문화, 한글문화 …

20 예술

Arts

This chapter contains lexical entries describing Korean people's art-related activities, creation, representation, and appreciation: i.e., basic lexical entries used in painting, music, dancing, literature, play, cinema and entertainment and lexical entries of instruments, such as painting tools and musical instruments (there are only basic items regarding musical instruments).

〈가야금〉

〈강강수월래〉

가곡	song in the classical style
가락	tune
가면극	mask play
가무단	singing and dancing group
가사 (歌辭)	traditional Korean verse
가사 (歌詞)	lyrics
가수	singer
가야금	twelve-stringed Korean harp
가요	song
가요계	singers circle
가요제	music festival
가창력	singing ability
각본	script
각색	dramatization
간주	interlude
간주곡	① interlude ② intermezzo
감독	director
감상하다	① to appreciate ② to enjoy
강강수월래	Korean traditional circle dance
개봉관	first-run movie theater

개봉박두	coming soon
개사	revising lyrics
객석	seat
거문고	six-stringed Korean lute
건반악기	keyboard instrument
건전가요	wholesome song
걸작	① masterpiece ② great work
경음악	light music
계몽문학	literature of enlightenment
고려가요	Koryo verses
고전무용	classical dance
고전문학	classical literature
고전음악	classical music
고전주의	① classicism ② classicalism
고전해학극	classical comedy
곡	① music ② piece of music
곡조	melody
공간미술	space arts
공간예술	space art
공연	performance
공연예술	performing art
공연장	place for performance
공연하다	to perform
공예	craft
공예품	craft work
관객	① audience ② spectator
관람객	① audience ② spectator
관람료	① admission fee ② admission
관람불가	rated-R
관람석	seat
관람하다	① to see ② to view
관악기	wind instrument
관현악단	orchestra
교향곡	symphony
교향악단	symphony orchestra
교회음악	church music

〈거문고〉

구도	composition
구비문학	oral literature
국민가수	people's singer
국민가요	people's song
국악	Korean classical music
국악기	Korean classical instruments
군악대	military band
궁중무용	royal court dance
그리다	to draw
그림	picture
극	play
극시	① dramatic poem ② dramatic poetry
극작가	playwright
극장	① theater ② playhouse
극적	dramatic
글짓기	① composition ② writing
금관악기	① brass ② musical instrument made of metal
금속공예	metal craftwork
기록영화	documentary film
기악	instrumental music
기악곡	piece of instrumental music
기악대	instrumental music band
꼭두각시춤	puppet dance
꽹과리	small gong
꾸밈음	decorated note
나팔	trumpet
낭만주의	romanticism
내림표	flat note
노래	song
노천극장	open-air theater
농악	farm music
농악대	farm (peasant) band
단막극	one-act play
단소	short bamboo flute
단역	① minor part ② bit ③ bit player

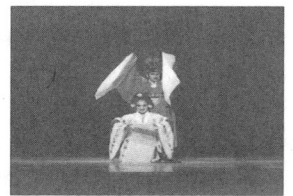
〈궁중무용〉

〈꽹과리〉

〈농악〉

	④ extra
단음계	minor mode
단조	minor key
단편소설	short story
대금	large bamboo flute
대본	① script ② play script
대사	lines
대역	① substitute ② understudy
대중가요	popular song
대중음악	popular music
대하소설	① novel ② saga
데뷔하다	to debut
도돌이표	da capo
도예	ceramic art
도자기	① ceramic ware ② pottery
도화지	drawing paper
독주	solo performance
독주회	① solo ② recital
독창	solo
독창회	solo concert
독후감	book report
동기	motif
동상	bronze statue
동시	① children's verse ② nursery rhyme
동시상영	double feature
동시상영관	double feature cinema
동양화	oriental painting
동양화가	painter of oriental paintings
동요	children's songs
동화	fairy tale
드라마	drama
등단하다	to debut as a poet or an author
등장인물	① characters ② cast
등장하다	to enter the stage
디자이너	designer
디자인	design

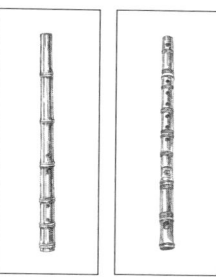

〈단소〉 〈대금〉

〈동상〉

레이아웃	layout
르네상스	renaissance
리듬	rhythm
리사이틀	recital
마당극	① open-air theater ② outdoor theater
마디	bar
막	act
만담가	stand-up comedian
만화	① comic book ② comic strip ③ cartoon
만화영화	animated movie
매표소	ticket office
먹	Chinese ink stick
멀티미디어디자인	multimedia design
명곡	famous work of music
명도	brightness
명암	light and darkness
명창	well-known singer of Korean songs
명화	masterpiece (painting)
모델	model
모음곡	collected piece
목공예	woodcraft
목관악기	musical instrument made of wood
목탄	charcoal pencil
무대	stage
무대감독	stage producer
무대예술	① stage art ② theatrical art
무대의상	stage dress
무대화장	stage makeup
무도	dance
무도복	dance costume
무도회	① ball ② dance
무성영화	silent film
무언극	pantomime
무용	dancing
무용가	dancer

무용극	ballet
무용단	① dance group ② ballet troupe
무용복	dance costume
무용음악	music for dance
무용화	dancing shoes
문단	literary world
문방사우	four writing materials (paper, brush, ink stick, and inkstone)
문예	literary art
문예반	literary club
문예부흥	renaissance
문예비평	literary criticism
문예사조	literary trend
문예지	literary magazine
문예창작	creation of literary art
문인	① literary man ② man of letters ③ writer
문체	style
문학	literature
문학도	student of literature
문학반	literary club
문학작품	work of literature
문학평론	literary criticism
물감	paint
미 (美)	beauty
미술	① art ② fine arts
미술가	artist
미술관	① art gallery ② art museum
미술사	art history
미술작품	work of art
미술품	work of art
민담	folklore
민속공예	folkcraft
민속무용	folk dance
민속음악	folk music
민요	folk song

〈무용화〉

〈바라춤〉

〈발레〉

〈부채춤〉

〈북〉

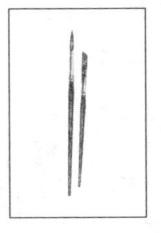

〈붓〉

민요가수	folk singer
민족문학	① national literature ② folk literature
민화	① folk picture ② folk painting
바라춤	Buddhist dance with a gong
바이올린	violin
박자	① time ② rhythm
반음	① semitone ② halftone
반주	accompaniment
반주자	accompanist
반주하다	to play an accompaniment
발레	ballet
발레리나	ballerina
발표회	① presentation ② exhibition ③ recital
밤무대	night stage
방송인	broadcaster
방송작가	broadcasting writer
배역	① cast ② role
배우	① actor ② actress
번안소설	adapted novel
번역	translation
베이스	base
벼루	inkstone
벽화	① fresco ② wall painting
변주곡	variation
병창	parallel singing with a musical instrument
부르다	to sing
부조	relief
부채춤	fan dance
북	drum
분장	makeup
분장사	makeup artist
분장실	dressing room
붓	paintbrush
붓글씨	brush writing
비극	tragedy

비디오	video
비디오아트	video art
비평가	critic
빠르기표	presto
사군자	the four gracious plants (plum, orchid, chrysanthemum and bamboo)
사극	historical drama
사물놀이	Korean musical play with four musical instruments
사생화	① sketch ② picture drawn from nature
사실주의	realism
사진예술	photography art
사진작가	photo artist
사진작품	photo work
산문	prose
산문시	prose poetry
산수화	landscape painting
산조	solo performance of a Korean musical instrument
살풀이춤	exorcist dance
삼중창	trio
삽화	illustration
상설무대	permanent stage
상영관	① cinema ② movie theater
상영하다	to run
색상	color
색연필	colored pencil
색종이	colored paper
색지	colored paper
색채	color
색칠하다	① to color ② to paint
서사시	epic
서양화	Western painting
서양화가	artist of Western painting
서예	calligraphy
서예가	calligrapher

〈사군자〉
① 매화 ② 난초
③ 국화 ④ 대나무

〈살풀이춤〉

서정시	lyric
석고상	plaster figure
선율	melody
설치미술	installation art
설치예술	installation art
설화	fable
성악	vocal music
성악가	vocalist
성악곡	piece of vocal music
성우	voice actor
성인영화	adult film
성화	① sacred picture ② picture of a sacred subject
세종문화회관	Sejong Cultural Center
셈여림표	volume indicator such as decresendo or fortissimo
소고	small drum
소극장	small theater
소리	① Korean traditional song ② sound
소리꾼	singer of Korean traditional songs
소묘	① sketch ② rough drawing
소설	① novel ② fiction
소설가	novelist
소조	① modeling ② molding
소품	stage props
소품실	property room
소프라노	soprano
쇼	show
수공예	handcraft
수묵화	Chinese ink painting
수예	handicraft
수채화	watercolor painting
수필	essay
수필가	essayist
순수음악	pure music
쉼표	rest

〈소고〉

스케치하다	to sketch
승무	Buddhist dance
시	poem
시각디자인	visual design
시각예술	visual art
시나리오	scenario
시나위	improvisational concert of musical instruments
시사회	movie preview
시인	poet
시조	three-verse Korean poem
시화전	exhibition of illustrated poems
신소설	style of fiction that emerged in the early 20th century Korea
신인	new face
신인가수	new singer
신인배우	new actor
신춘문예	new year's literary contest
신파극	melodrama prevalent in Korea during 1910s to 1940s
신화	myth
실내악단	chamber orchestra
실내음악	chamber music
실용음악	applied music
실험극	experimental play
십장생	ten animals representing longevity
아동극	children's play
아동문학	children's literature
아동문학가	writer of children's literature
아동미술	children's artwork
아역	child's role
아쟁	seven-stringed fiddle
악곡	musical piece
악기	musical instrument
악단	band
악보	sheet of music

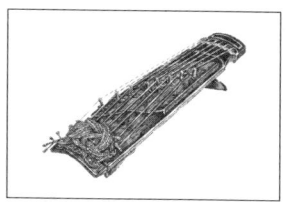

〈아쟁〉

악역	villain's part (role)
안무	choreography
안무가	choreographer
알토	alto
앙코르	encore
애니메이션	animation
야외극	outdoor play
야외극장	outdoor theater
야외무대	outdoor stage
야외음악	outdoor music
야외음악당	① outdoor auditorium ② bandstand
양각	relief
언어예술	literary art
여배우	actress
연극	① play ② drama
연극배우	① stage actor ② stage actress
연극비평	play criticism
연극인	theatrical people
연극제	① play festival ② theater festival
연극평론	play review
연기자	talent
연기하다	① to play ② to act
연속극	soap opera
연예	entertainment
연예가	entertainment circle
연예계	entertainment world
연예인	entertainer
연예지	entertainment magazine
연주	musical performance
연주자	① player ② performer
연주장	performing place
연주하다	① to play ② to perform
연주회	concert
연출자	producer
열연	impassioned performance
염료	dyes

염색공예	dye craft
영사기	movie projector
영사실	① projection room ② projection booth
영상	① image ② screen
영화	① movie ② film
영화감독	film director
영화계	film world
영화관	① cinema ② movie theater
영화배우	① actor ② actress ③ movie actor ④ movie actress
영화상	film award
영화음악	① film music ② soundtrack
영화인	people related to film industry
영화제	film festival
영화평론가	movie critic
예고편	trailer
예매하다	to reserve
예술	arts
예술가	artist
예술계	world of arts
예술공연	artistic performance
예술단체	artist organization
예술사	art history
예술사진	art picture
예술성	artistic quality
예술원	art academy
예술의 전당	Seoul Arts Center
예술작품	work of art
예술지상주의	art for art's sake
예술품	work of art
예술혼	artistic soul
오선지	music paper
오케스트라	orchestra
오페라	opera
오페라가수	opera singer
온음	whole note

문학	고전	고려가요, 고전문학, 구비문학, 민담, 설화, 시조, 판소리문학, 한문학, 향가 …
	현대 산문	극본, 단편소설, 대본, 대하소설, 독후감, 동화, 번안소설, 수필, 시나리오, 신소설, 장편소설, 전래동화, 중편소설, 평론, 희곡 …
	운문	시, 서정시, 산문시, 서사시, 극시, 동시, 시조 …
음악	곡	고전음악, 교향곡, 교회음악, 국악, 기악, 농악, 대중음악, 모음곡, 무용음악, 민속음악, 변주곡, 산조, 성악곡, 시나위, 실내음악, 실용음악, 영화음악, 재즈, 종교음악, 즉흥곡, 창작곡, 춤곡, 행진곡 …
	노래	가곡, 가요, 건전가요, 고려가요, 국민가요, 대중가요, 동요, 민요, 유행가, 자장가, 타령, 향가 …
미술	회화	동양화, 만화, 민화, 사생화, 산수화, 삽화, 서양화, 인물화, 초상화, 추상화, 탱화, 판화 …
	조소	부조, 소조, 조각, 환조 …
공예		금속공예, 도예, 목공예, 민속공예, 수공예, 염색공예 …
디자인		멀티미디어디자인, 시각디자인, 제품디자인, 컴퓨터그래픽스, 환경디자인 …
춤		강강수월래, 고전무용, 궁중무용, 꼭두각시춤, 무용, 바라춤, 발레, 부채춤, 살풀이춤, 승무, 칼춤, 탈춤, 창작무용, 현대무용 …
연극		고전해학극, 신파극, 마당극, 무언극, 무용극, 실험극, 아동극, 야외극, 오페라, 인형극, 일인극, 판소리 …

올림표	sharp
운문	verse
운율	① rhythm ② meter
원근법	perspective
원로가수	senior singer
원로배우	senior actor
유미주의	aestheticism
유행가	popular song
유화	oil painting
으뜸음	keynote
음각	intaglio
음계	musical scale
음반	① record ② compact disc
음색	tone color
음악	music
음악가	musician
음악감상실	music hall
음악계	musical world
음악관	concert hall

음악당	concert hall
음악성	musicality
음악실	music room
음악인	musician
음악제	music festival
음악회	concert
음자리표	clef
음정	interval
음표	musical note
음향	sound
응용미술	applied arts
의상	costume
이중창	duet
인기	popularity
인기가수	popular singer
인기배우	popular actor
인물화	figure painting
인형극	puppet play
일러스트레이션	illustration
일인극	monodrama
자막	subtitle
자선공연	① charity show ② charity performance
자장가	lullaby
작가	writer
작곡	composition
작곡가	composer
작곡하다	to compose
작사	① lyric making ② writing songs
작사하다	① to make lyrics ② to write songs
작품사진	art photo
장구	hourglass drum
장단	① time ② rhythm
장음계	major scale
장인	① artisan ② craftsman
장인정신	craftsmanship
장조	major key

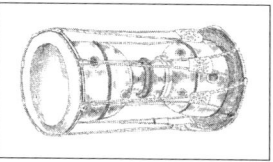

〈장구〉

장편소설	novel
재즈	jazz
전람회	exhibition
전래동화	traditional fairy tale
전설	legend
전속가수	singer under exclusive contract with a company
전시장	pavilion
전시회	① exhibition ② show
전위예술	avant-garde art
전주	prelude
전축	record player
전통가요	traditional song
정	burin
정물	inanimate objects for still lifes
정물화	still life
정밀묘사	detailed drawing
정밀화	still drawing
제자리표	natural
제작사	production company
제작자	producer
제품디자인	product design
조각	① sculpture ② carving
조각가	sculptor
조각도	graver
조각칼	chisel
조각품	① sculpture ② carving
조각하다	① to carve ② to sculpt
조감독	assistant director
조명	lighting
조명실	lighting room
조소	carving or modeling
조역	supporting role
조연	① supporting actor ② supporting actress
조율	tuning

조형예술	formative arts
종교음악	religious music
종합예술	composite art
주역	leading role
주연	① leading actor ② leading actress
주인공	① hero ② heroine ③ main character
주제가	title song
중창	part singing
중창단	part singing group
중편소설	① short novel ② novella
즉흥곡	impromptu
지휘	conducting
지휘자	conductor
징	gong
창	Korean traditional song
창작곡	original composition
창작무용	creative dance
창작예술	creative art
창작품	① creation ② original work
창작하다	to create (art work)
창조하다	to create
채도	chroma
청각예술	acoustic art
청음	musical dictation
첼로	cello
초상화	① portrait ② portrait painting
촬영하다	① to film ② to shoot
추다	to dance
추상화	abstract painting
축가	song of celebration
축음기	① gramophone ② phonograph
출연료	performance fee
출연하다	① to play ② to perform
춤	dance
춤곡	musical piece for dancing
춤꾼	dancer

〈징〉

〈칼춤〉

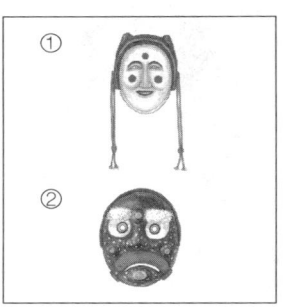

〈탈〉
① 하회탈(각시탈)
② 봉산탈

〈탈춤〉

춤동작	dance movements
춤사위	dance movements
치다	to play (piano, guitar, drum, etc.)
칠하다	to paint
칼춤	knife dance
캐드	CAD (computer-aided design)
컴퓨터그래픽스	computer graphics
컴퓨터아트	computer art
켜다	to play (violin, cello, etc.)
콧노래	humming
크레파스	crayon
타령	type of Korean traditional song
타악기	percussion instrument
탈	mask
탈춤	mask dance
탐미주의	estheticism
태평소	Korean musical instrument made of brass
탤런트	① TV actor ② TV star
탱화	altar portrait of Buddha
테너	tenor
텔레비전	television
판소리	traditional Korean long epic song
판소리문학	literature of traditional Korean long epic song
판화	woodcut print
판화가	woodblock artist
퍼포먼스	performance
편곡	arrangement
편곡하다	to arrange
평론	criticism
평론가	critic
표구	mounting
표절	plagiarism
풍경	① scenery ② landscape
풍경화	landscape painting

풍금	organ
풍악	Korean music
피리	pipe
피아노	piano
한국무용	Korean dance
한문학	Chinese classics
합주	① concert ② ensemble
합주단	① concert group ② ensemble group
합창	chorus
합창단	choir
행위예술	performing art
행진곡	march
향가	folk song of Shilla period
현대무용	modern dance
현대문학	modern literature
현대미술	① modern painting ② modern art
현대음악	modern music
현악기	stringed instrument
협주곡	concerto
화가	painter
화랑	gallery
화면	① picture ② scene
화방	art store
화백	① painter ② artist
화법	drawing technique
화선지	Chinese drawing paper
화성	① harmony ② concord ③ chord
화실	① studio ② atelier
화음	chord
화판	drawing board
환경디자인	environment-friendly design
환조	carving in the round
황금분할	golden section
회화	① pictures ② paintings ③ drawings
효과	effect
흥행사	promotional agency

흥행하다	to be a hit
희곡	① drama ② play
희극	comedy
희극인	comedian

21 취미
Hobbies

> This chapter contains lexical entries relating to climbing, fishing, travelling, photography, and other hobbies popular among Koreans. It also contains lexical entries referring to the necessary instruments and objects needed to take part in such hobbies.

가족사진	family photograph
감광지	photosensitive paper
강태공	angler
결혼사진	wedding photograph
관광	sightseeing
관광객	tourist
관광국가	nation with tourism as its main industry
관광단	tour group
관광도시	tourist city
관광버스	tour bus
관광사업	tourism
관광시설	tourist facilities
관광안내원	tour guide
관광업	tourist business
관광열차	sight-seeing train
관광유람선	cruise
관광자원	resources for tourism
관광정책	policy on tourism
관광지	tourist attraction

관광지도	tour map
관광하다	to sightsee
관광호텔	tourist hotel
국립공원	national park
국토순례	① tour around the country ② country tour
그물	net
그물낚시	net fishing
기록사진	documentary photograph
기차여행	train tour
꽃꽂이	flower arrangement
나들이	outing
낚다	to catch
낚시	fishing
낚시꾼	angler
낚시바늘	hook
낚시질	① fishing ② angling
낚시터	fishing place
낚시하다	to fish
낚싯대	fishing rod

취미					
분류	여행	낚시	사진	등산	기타
종류	기차여행 도보여행 무전여행 배낭여행 해외여행 :	민물낚시 바다낚시 밤낚시 얼음낚시 :	기록사진 보도사진 스냅사진 예술사진 작품사진 칼라사진 흑백사진 :	등반 등정 등반대회 빙벽타기 암벽타기 :	꽃꽂이 독서 바둑 영화감상 음악감상 :
관련 단어	관광지 사증 여비 여행객 여행사 :	그물 낚시 낚싯대 낚싯밥 낚싯줄 떡밥 미끼 :	사진기 사진술 사진첩 사진틀 암실 역광 인화 촬영 필름 현상 :	등산화 등산복 등산모 등산양말 등산장비 메아리 산울림 산악회 :	극장 꽃 꽃병 바둑알 바둑판 음악감상실 장기판 책

낚싯밥	bait
낚싯봉	sinker
낚싯줄	fishing line
노자	travelling expenses
단체사진	group photograph
단풍놀이	excursion for viewing scarlet maple leaves
답사	field trip
답사하다	to go on a field trip
대어	big fish
도보여행	walking tour
독사진	portrait
돌사진	first birthday picture
동호회	① club ② special interest groups
등반	climbing
등반대	climbing team
등반대회	climbing contest
등반장비	climbing equipment
등반하다	to climb
등산	mountain climbing
등산가	① mountaineer ② alpinist
등산객	mountain hiker
등산모	mountain-climbing cap
등산복	mountain-climbing outfit
등산양말	mountain-climbing socks
등산장비	mountain-climbing equipment
등산하다	to mountainclimb
등산화	mountain-climbing boots
등정	climbing to the summit
떡밥	bait
릴	reel
말	horse
메아리	echo
명함판사진	businesscard-size photograph
무전여행	travelling without money
문화관광부	Ministry of Culture & Tourism

〈바둑〉

물고기	fish
미끼	bait
민물낚시	fresh water fishing
바다낚시	ocean fishing
바둑	baduk
바둑알	baduk stone
바둑판	baduk board
반명함판사진	half-business-card-size photograph
밤낚시	night fishing
배낭여행	backpack trip
백일사진	photograph taken on the hundredth day of birth
벚꽃놀이	outing to see cherry blosoms
보도사진	news photograph
빙벽타기	ice ridge climbing
사증	visa
사진	① photograph ② picture
사진관	photo studio
사진기	camera
사진기자	photo journalist
사진사	photographer
사진술	photography
사진예술	art of photography
사진작가	photography artist
사진작품	works of photography
사진첩	photo album
사진틀	picture frame
산악인	mountaineer
산악회	mountaineers' association
산울림	mountain echo
성지순례	pilgrimage to the Holy Land
소풍	① excursion ② picnic
숙박	lodging
숙박료	accomodation fee
스냅사진	snapshot photograph
시내관광	city tour

암벽타기	rock climbing
암실	darkroom
야유회	① picnic ② outing
양화	positive picture
얼음낚시	ice fishing
여가선용	good use of leisure time
여객	passenger
여권	passport
여권사진	passport photograph
여비	travelling expenses
여행	travel
여행가	traveler
여행객	tourist
여행계획	① tour plan ② itinerary
여행기	travel journal
여행담	① account of one's travels ② travel log
여행비	tour expenses
여행사	travel agency
여행자보험	travel insurance
여행자수표	traveler's check
여행지	destination
여행하다	① to travel ② to journey ③ to take a trip
역광	backlight
연극감상	play appreciation
영정	portrait
영화감상	movie appreciation
예술사진	artistic photograph
월척	big fish
유람하다	to go sightseeing
유흥비	① entertainment expenses ② expenses for pleasures
음악감상	music appreciation
음화	negative picture
인물사진	portrait
인화	printing

인화지	printing paper
인화하다	to print
입질	biting
입질하다	to bite
작품사진	photographic work
잔챙이	small fry
장기	Korean chess
장기판	board of Korean chess
조난사고	① disaster ② accident
즉석사진	instant photograph
증명사진	identification photograph
찌	floater
찍다	to take a picture
촬영	taking pictures
촬영하다	to take a picture
취미	hobbies
취미생활	pursuing one's hobby
취미활동	hobby activities
칼라사진	color photograph
필름	film
하산	descending a mountain
한국관광공사	Korea National Tourism Organization
해외관광	overseas tour
해외여행	overseas travel
현상	developing
현상하다	to develop
확대사진	enlarged photograph
활동사진	motion film
효도관광	tour paid by one's children
휴양지	resort
흑백사진	black and white photograph

22 놀이와 게임
Games

This chapter lists various games, focusing on those games that Korean people tend to enjoy.

가위바위보	rock-scissors-paper
게임	game
게임방	video arcade
게임하다	to play a game
경마	horse racing
경마장	① racecourse ② race track
고무줄놀이	long elastic cord game
고싸움	Korean folk game
곡마단	circus troupe
곡예	acrobatics
곡예단	acrobatics troupe
곡예사	acrobat
곤지곤지	word telling a baby to point a palm with the other hand's finger
공기놀이	type of jacks game
구슬치기	marble game
그네	swing
그네뛰기	swinging on a swing
기마전	playing a mock cavalry battle
꼭두각시놀음	puppet show
끝말잇기	connecting with the last word
낱말맞추기	crossword puzzle

〈가위바위보〉
① 가위 ② 바위 ③ 보

〈고싸움〉

〈공기놀이〉

〈그네뛰기〉

〈널뛰기〉

내기	betting
내기하다	to bet
널뛰기	Korean seesaw
노름	gambling
노름꾼	gambler
노름하다	to gamble
놀다	to play
놀이	① play ② game
놀이공원	amusement park
놀이동산	amusement park
놀이터	playground
눈싸움	snowball fight
눈썰매	sled
달맞이	moon greeting
닭싸움	cock-fight
도리도리	word telling a baby to shake its head
도박	gambling

한국 전통 놀이	현대 놀이와 게임		
	유아	어린이·청소년	어른
고싸움	곤지곤지	가위바위보	마작
그네뛰기	도리도리	고무줄놀이	바둑
기마전	잼잼	공기놀이	불꽃놀이
꼭두각시놀음	짝짜꿍	끝말잇기	서양장기
널뛰기	:	낱말맞추기	장기
썰매타기		눈썰매	카드놀이
연날리기		딱지치기	투전
연싸움		딱총놀이	폭죽놀이
윷놀이		땅따먹기	화투
자치기		말뚝박기	:
제기차기		병원놀이	
줄다리기		사방제기	
줄타기		사방치기	
쥐불놀이		소꿉놀이	
팽이치기		수건돌리기	
:		숨바꼭질	
		숨은그림찾기	
		스무고개	
		인형놀이	
		전쟁놀이	
		집짓기	
		:	

도박사	gambler
도박하다	to gamble
딱지치기	playing dumps
딱총놀이	playing with firecrackers
딸랑이	noisemaker toy
땅따먹기	game of possessing lands
마술	magic
마작	majang
말뚝박기	piling
물장구	① beating ② flutter kick
미끄럼	slide
미끄럼틀	slide
민속놀이	folk games
바둑	baduk
바람개비	① vane ② weathercock
병원놀이	playing hospital
병정놀이	playing soldiers
보물찾기	treasure hunt
불꽃놀이	fireworks
사방제기	four persons shuttle cock game
사방치기	hopscotch
서양장기	chess
세발자전거	tricycle
소꿉놀이	playing house
수건돌리기	drop-the-hankerchief game
수수께끼	riddle
술래	① tagger ② 'it'
술래잡기	hide-and-seek
숨바꼭질	hide-and-seek
숨은그림찾기	hidden picture game
스무고개	game of twenty questions
시소	seesaw
썰매타기	sledding
연	kite
연날리기	kite flying
연싸움	kite fight

〈윷놀이〉

〈인형〉

〈제기차기〉

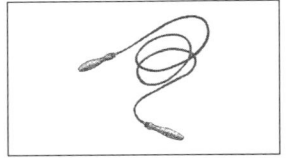

〈줄넘기〉

〈쥐불놀이〉

엿치기	taffy-breaking game
오뚝이	① tumbler ② roly-poly
오락	amusement
오락시간	time for amusement
오락실	video arcade
완구	toy
요술	magic
유원지	amusement park
윷	Korean traditional stick game
윷놀이	Korean traditional stick game
인형	doll
인형놀이	playing with doll
자전거	bicycle
자치기	tipcat
잠자리채	dragonfly net
장기	Korean chess
장기자랑	talent contest
장난	① prank ② joke
장난감	toy
장난치다	to play with
재주넘기	somersault
잼잼	word telling a baby to close and open his/her palms
전자오락	① video game ② electronic game
전자오락실	video arcade
전쟁놀이	war game
접시돌리기	plate spinning
제기차기	shuttlecock game
주사위	dice
줄넘기	jump rope
줄다리기	tug of war
줄타기	rope walking
쥐불놀이	spinning fire on fields
집짓기	building a house
짝짜꿍	baby's hand clapping
철봉	horizontal bar

카드놀이	card game
컴퓨터오락실	computer game room
투전	card gambling
팔씨름	arm wrestling
팽이	top
팽이치기	top spinning
쪽죽놀이	playing with firecrackers
풍선	balloon
화투	Korean playing cards

〈팽이치기〉

〈화투〉

23 운동
Exercise

This chapter presents a number of lexical entries describing exercises that Korean people enjoy and the devices needed for those exercises as well as words for athletes and the act of exercising.

감독	head coach
개구리헤엄	breaststroke
개인전	individual games
개헤엄	doggy paddle
검	sword
검도	kendo
겨루다	① to vie with ② to compete
격투기	fighting game
경기	① game ② match ③ competition
경기규칙	game rule
경기장	① sports ground ② stadium
경기하다	① to have a match ② to compete
경보	walkathon
경주하다	to run a race
계주	relay race
곤봉	① club ② bludgeon
골대	goalpost
골프	golf
골프채	golf club
공	ball
공격	attack

공격수	offensive player
공던지기	ball throwing
구기종목	ball games
국가대표선수	member of national team
국궁	Korean archery
국민체조	mass exercise
궁도	archery
권투	boxing
권투장갑	boxing gloves
기계체조	gymnastics using apparatus
기권	① default ② absence
농구	basketball (game)
농구공	ball (basketball)
높이뛰기	high jump
다이빙	diving
단체전	team games
달리기	run
당구	① billiards ② pool
대표선수	member of representative team
도복	uniform
등산	① hiking ② mountain climbing
뜀틀	① vaulting horse ② buck
럭비	rugby
레슬링	wrestling
리듬체조	rhythm calisthenics
마라톤	marathon
매달리기	chinning
맨손체조	free gymnastics
멀리뛰기	long jump
무술	martial arts
무승부	tie
물안경	goggles
미식축구	American football
반칙	foul
방어	defense
배구	volleyball (sports game)

〈국궁〉

배구공	ball (volleyball)
배드민턴	badminton
배영	backstroke
번지점프	bungee jumping
볼링	bowling
비기다	to end in a tie
빙상경기	ice sports
사격	marksmanship
사이클	cycle
사회체육	① sports and recreation ② sport for all
샅바	band used in Korean traditional wrestling
생활체육	① sports and recreation ② sport for all
선발하다	to select
선수	player
선수교체	player replacement
선수권	championship
선수단	team
선수촌	athletes' village
세단뛰기	triple jump
수구	water polo
수비	defense
수비수	defensive player
수상스키	water ski
수영	swimming
수영모자	swimming cap
수영복	swimming suit
수중발레	synchronized swimming
스케이트	skate
스키	ski
스키장갑	ski gloves
스포츠	sports
승리	win
승리하다	to win
승마	horse riding

〈스케이트〉

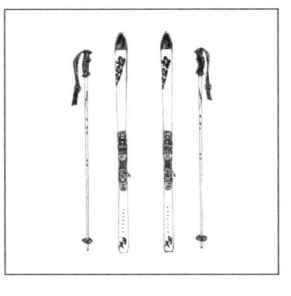

〈스키〉

승패	① victory or defeat
	② outcome of a match
시합	① match ② game
시합하다	to have a match
실내체육관	gymnasium
심판	① umpire ② referee
씨름	Korean traditional wrestling
아령	dumbbell
아시안게임	The Asian Games
아이스하키	ice hockey
안마	pommel horse
야구	baseball
야구공	ball (baseball)
야구방망이	baseball bat
야구장갑	baseball gloves
양궁	Western-style archery
에어로빅	aerobics
역기	barbell
역도	weight lifting
연승	① straight victories
	② series of victories
올림픽	Olympics
요가	yoga
요트	yacht
우승	① victory ② championship
운동	① exercise ② sports ③ fitness
운동감각	athletic ability
운동경기	sports
운동기구	① sporting goods ② gym equipment
운동량	amount of exercise
운동모자	sports cap
운동복	sportswear
운동부	athletic club
운동선수	athlete
운동신경	motor nerve
운동장	playground

〈씨름〉

운동정신	sportsmanship
운동종목	sports categories
운동하다	to exercise
운동화	① sneakers ② running shoes
운동회	athletic meeting
원반	disc
원반던지기	discus
원정경기	out match
월계관	laurel crown
월드컵축구	Worldcup football
윗몸일으키기	sit-up
유도	judo
육상경기	track and field
응원가	rooter's song
응원단	cheering squad
응원하다	① to support ② to cheer
이기다	to win
이어달리기	relay run
자유형	free-style
자전거	bicycle
장대높이뛰기	high jump
전국체전	national athletic meet
전지훈련	field training
접영	butterfly
정구	tennis
주전선수	ace player
준비운동	warm-up excercise
줄	rope
줄넘기	jump rope
지다	to lose
창	javelin
창던지기	javelin throw
천하장사	champion of Korean traditional wrestling match
철봉	horizontal bar
체력	physical strength

〈유도〉

체력단련	physical strength training
체육	physical education
체육관	gymnasium
체육복	① sweat suit ② gym clothes ③ exercise attire
체육부	athletic club
체육회	athletics association
체조	gymnastics
총	gun
축구	soccer
축구공	soccer ball
출전선수	participating athlete
출전하다	① to participate ② to play
카누	canoe
코치	coach
쿵푸	Kung Fu
타자	hitter
탁구	① table tennis ② ping pong
탁구공	table tennis ball
태권도	tae-kwon-do (representative Korean martial art)
택견	kind of Korean martial arts
턱걸이	chin-up
테니스	tennis
투수	pitcher
투원반	discus throw
투포환	shot-put
판정승	outpoint
판정하다	to judge
팔굽혀펴기	push-up
패자부활전	repechage
패하다	to lose
펜싱	fencing
평균대	balance beam
평영	breaststroke
평행봉	parallel bars

〈축구〉

〈태권도〉

폐활량	lung (breathing) capacity
포수	catcher
포환	cannonball
포환던지기	shot put
피구	type of dodgeball
하키	hockey
합기도	kind of Korean martial arts
핸드볼	handball
헤엄	swimming
호신술	art of self-defense
혼영	medley race
화살	arrow
활	bow
후보선수	substitute player
훈련	training
훌라후프	hula hoop

운동				
공을 가지고 하는 운동	육상	두 사람이 겨루는 운동	체조	수영
농구	높이뛰기	검도	곤봉	다이빙
당구	달리기	권투	뜀틀	배영
럭비	장대높이뛰기	레슬링	리듬체조	자유형
배구	마라톤	씨름	평균대	접영
볼링	멀리뛰기	유도	평행봉	평영
수구	원반던지기	콩푸	:	혼영
미식축구	세단뛰기	태권도		:
야구	이어달리기	택견		
축구	창던지기	펜싱		
탁구	포환던지기	합기도		
테니스	:	:		
피구				
핸드볼				
:				

24 나라 이름
Names of Countries

This chapter contains lexical entries of countries' names related to Korean history and names of other countries closely related to Korea, in addition to the names of the continents.

가나	Ghana
가봉	Gabon
가야	Kaya
고구려	Koguryo
고려	Koryo
고조선	Kochoson
과테말라	Guatemala
그리스	Greece
나이지리아	Nigeria
남미	South America
남아메리카	South America
남아프리카공화국	Republic of South Africa
남한	South Korea
네델란드	Netherlands
네팔	Nepal
노르웨이	Norway
뉴질랜드	New Zealand
니카라과	Nicaragua
대만	Taiwan
대영제국	Great Britain
대한민국	Republic of Korea (South Korea)

한국의 역사적 이름	
고조선	서기전 2333 ~ 108
삼한	서기전 3-4세기경
부여	서기전 1세기경
신라	서기전 57 ~ 935
고구려	서기전 37 ~ 668
백제	서기전 18 ~ 660
동예	1세기 초
가야	42 ~ 6세기 중엽
통일신라	676 ~ 918
발해	698 ~ 926
고려	918 ~ 1392
조선	1392 ~ 1910
대한민국	1948 ~ 현재

덴마크	Denmark
도미니카 공화국	Dominican Republic
독일	Germany
동남아	Southeast Asia
동예	Dongyeh
라오스	Laos
러시아	Russia
레바논	Lebanon
루마니아	Romania
룩셈부르크	Luxembourg
리비아	Libya
마한	Mahan
말레이시아	Malaysia
멕시코	Mexico
모나코	Monaco
모로코	Morocco
모잠비크	Mozambique
몽골	Mongolia
미국	USA (United States of America)
미얀마	Myanmar
미합중국	United States of America
바레인	Bahrain
바티칸	Vatican City
발해	Palhae
방글라데시	Bangladesh
백제	Baekje
베네수엘라	Venezuela
베트남	Vietnam
벨기에	Belgium
변한	Byuhan
보스니아	Bosnia
볼리비아	Bolivia
부여	Byuyo
부탄	Bhutan
북미	North America
북아메리카	North America

북한	North Korea
불가리아	Bulgaria
불란서	France
브라질	Brazil
사우디아라비아	Saudi Arabia
삼한	Three Han States
소말리아	Somalia
수단	Sudan
스리랑카	Sri Lanka
스웨덴	Sweden
스위스	Switzerland
스페인	Spain
슬로바키아	Slovakia
슬로베니아	Slovenia
시리아	Syria
신라	Shilla
싱가포르	Singapore
아르헨티나	Argentina
아시아	Asia
아이슬란드	Iceland
아일랜드	Ireland
아프가니스탄	Afghanistan
아프리카	Africa
알바니아	Albania
알제리	Algeria
에스파냐	Estonia
에콰도르	Ecuador
에티오피아	Ethiopia
엘살바도르	El Salvador
영국	England
오세아니아	Oceania
오스트레일리아	Australia
오스트리아	Austria
옥저	Okjeo
온두라스	Honduras
요르단	Jordan

우간다	Uganda
우루과이	Uruguay
우크라이나	Ukraine
유고슬라비아	Yugoslavia
유라시아	Eurasia
유럽	Europe
이라크	Iraq
이란	Iran
이스라엘	Israel
이집트	Egypt
이탈리아	Italy
이태리	Italy
인도	India
인도네시아	Indonesia
일본	Japan
자메이카	Jamaica
잠비아	Zambia
조선	Chosun
중국	China
중남미	Mid-South America
중동	Middle East
진한	Jinhan
체코	Czechoslovakia
칠레	Chile
카메룬	Cameroon
캄보디아	Cambodia
캐나다	Canada
케냐	Kenya
코스타리카	Costa Rica
콜롬비아	Colombia
콩고	Congo
콩고민주공화국	Republic of Congo
쿠바	Cuba
쿠웨이트	Kuwait
크로아티아	Croatia
탄자니아	Tanzania

태국	Thailand
터키	Turkey
통일신라	United Silla
파나마	Panama
파라과이	Paraguay
파키스탄	Pakistan
파푸아뉴기니	Papua New Guinea
페루	Peru
포루투칼	Portugal
폴란드	Poland
프랑스	France
핀란드	Finland
필리핀	Philippines
한국	Korea (South Korea)
한반도	Korean peninsula
헝가리	Hungary
호주	Australia
화란	Netherlands

25 국가와 정치
Nation and Politics

This chapter contains lexical entries connected to factors involved in forming a nation (e.g., territory, people and rights) and to national organizations and services. It also contains lexical entries relating to politics and international relations.

간첩	spy
감사원	Board of Audit & Inspection
강대국	country in power
개각	reorganizing the Cabinet
개각하다	to reorganize the Cabinet
개발도상국	developing nation
개천절	National Foundation Day of Korea
개편하다	to reorganize
개표	ballot counting
개표소	ballot-counting office
개표참관인	ballot-counting witness
개표하다	to open the ballot boxes
개헌	constitutional amendment
건국	founding of a nation
건설교통부	Ministry of Construction & Transportation
검찰청	Public Prosecutions Administration
겨레	① people ② race
경찰서	police station
경찰청	National Police Administration
경호실	guard office

계엄	guarding against danger
계엄령	martial law
고국	homeland
고대국가	ancient country
공공기관	public institution
공공단체	public organization
공공시설	public facilities
공권력	government power
공명선거	① clean election ② fair election
공무원	① public service personnel ② civil servant
공보실	Public Information Office
공산주의	communism
공산주의국가	communist country
공약	① (public) pledge ② public promise (commitment)
공정거래위원회	Fair Trade Commission
공주	princess
공직	① public office ② official position
공직자	① public officer ② civil servant
공천	nomination
공천자	official candidate
공천하다	to nominate
공화국	republic
과학기술부	Ministry of Science and Technology
관공서	government and public offices
관세청	Customs Administration
관직	government post
관청	government office
광복절	Independence Day of Korea
광역시	megalopolis
교육부	Ministry of Education
교포	overseas Korean
구	district
구의원	district assemblyman
구의회	district assembly

구청	district office
구청장	① chief of district ② alderman
국가	① nation ② country
국가과학기술자문회의	Advisory Committee of National Science and Technology
국가관	spirit of nationalism
국가론	theory of the state
국가명	name of country
국가보훈처	Ministry of Patriots and Veterans Affairs
국가안전기획부	Agency for National Security Planning
국가안전보장회의	National Security Council
국가정보원	national informant
국경	national boundary
국경선	national borderline
국경일	national holiday
국교 (國交)	national relation
국교 (國敎)	national religion
국군	national army
국권	national rights
국기	national flag
국내	domestic
국내외	inside and outside of the country
국내정세	domestic political situation
국내정치	domestic politics
국력	national power
국립	national
국무	① affairs (matters) of state ② state affairs
국무조정실	Department of State Affairs
국무총리	Prime Minister
국무총리비서실	Prime Minister's Secretariat
국무회의	① State Council ② State Council meeting
국문	country's written language
국민	① nation ② people
국민경제	national economy

국경일

개천절 (10월3일)
광복절 (8월15일)
제헌절 (7월17일)

국민교육헌장	National Charter of Education
국민문화	national culture
국민복지	national welfare
국민성	① character of a nation ② nationality
국민소득	national income
국민의례	national ceremony
국민의식	national consciousness
국민자본	national capital
국민투표	① plebiscite ② national referendum
국방	national defense
국방부	Ministry of National Defense
국법	national law
국사 (國事)	national affairs
국사 (國史)	national history
국산	made in one's country
국세청	National Tax Administration
국수주의	① ultranationalism
	② extreme patriotism
국어	one's mother tongue
국왕	king
국외	abroad
국외정세	international political situation
국적	nationality
국정 (國定)	national decision
국정 (國政)	① national administration
	② state affairs ③ government
국정감사	inspection of the administration
국제	international
국제기구	international organization
국제연합	United Nations
국제정세	international political affairs
국제정치	international politics
국제화	globalization
국토	national territory
국토방위	national defense
국호	name of a country

국화 (國花)	national flower
국회	National Assembly
국회법	National Assembly Law
국회사무처	Secretariat of the National Assembly
국회안건	bill of the National Assembly
국회의사당	National Assembly Building
국회의원	① assemblyman
	② member of the National Assembly
국회의장	Speaker of the National Assembly
국회해산	dissolution of the National Assembly
국회회기	session of the National Assembly
군	county
군수	chief of county
군주	① monarch ② sovereign ③ king
군주국가	monarchy
군주정치	monarchy
군주제	monarchism
군중	crowd
군청	county office
권력	① power ② authority
권한	rights
귀화	naturalization
기권	abstention from voting
기권하다	to abstain from voting
기상청	① Meteorological Administration
	② weather bureau
기획예산처	Department of Planning and Budget
나라	① country ② nation
낙선	being defeated in an election
내각	cabinet
내국인	native
노동부	Ministry of Labor
농림부	Ministry of Agriculture and Forestry
농촌진흥청	Rural Development Administration
다수당	① majority party ② dominant party
다스리다	to govern

단일민족	homogeneous race
당권	party hegemony
당대표	party representative
당리당략	party interests and tactics
당선	① being elected ② winning an election
당선되다	to be elected
당선자	elected candidate
당원	member of party
당쟁	① party strife ② faction
당파	party
대권	① supreme power ② prerogative
대변인	spokesman
대사	ambassador
대사관	embassy
대선	major election
대의명분	just cause
대통령	President
대통령제	presidential government
대통령중심제	presidential government
데모	demonstration
도	province
도시국가	city state
도지사	① governor ② provincial governor
독재국가	① autocratic state ② despotic state
독재자	dictator
독재정치	① dictatorship ② autocracy
동	dong (sub-district)
동맹	① alliance ② union
동맹국	alliance
동사무소	sub-district office

구역	행정구역								자치구역		
	도(道)	특별시 (特別市)	광역시 (廣域市)	시(市)	군(郡)	구(區)	읍(邑)	면(面)	동(洞)	통(統)	반(班)	리(里)
책임자	도지사	시장	시장	시장	군수	구청장	읍장	면장	동장	통장	반장	이장
관할 관청	도청	시청	시청	시청	군청	구청	읍사무소	면사무소	동사무소			

동장	chief of sub-district
동족	same race
동포	① fellow countrymen ② compatriots
득표	pole
득표율	polling rate
득표하다	to poll
리	town
만국기	flags of all nations
망국	national ruin
망명	flight from one's own country
매국노	traitor
면	township
면사무소	(township) office
면장	chief of township
모국	① mother country ② homeland
문화관광부	Ministry of Culture & Tourism
문화원	cultural center
문화재관리국	Cultural Properties Preservation Bureau
문화재관리청	Cultural Properties Preservation Bureau
문화체육부	Ministry of Culture and Sports
민심	public sentiment
민족	① race ② people
민족성	racial characteristics
민족의식	racial consciousness
민족주의	nationalism
민주국가	democratic state
민주정치	democratic government
민주주의	democracy
민주주의국가	democratic state
민주평화통일자문회의	Advisory Council on Democratic and Peaceful Unification
민중	① the people ② the masses
반	squad
반장	head of squad
백성	① the people ② subjects
백악관	White House

법무부	Ministry of Justice
법제처	Ministry of Legislation
법치국가	constitutional state
벼슬	① government post ② official rank
병무청	Military Manpower Administration
보건복지부	Ministry of Health and Welfare
보궐선거	special election
보좌관	presidential aide
복지국가	welfare state
본국	one's own country
봉건제도	feudalism
봉건주의	feudalism
부동표	floating votes
부재자투표	absentee voting
부정선거	① rigged election ② unfair election
부총리	① deputy prime minister ② vice-premier
부총재	vice-president (of a party)
부통령	① vice-president ② vice-president (of a nation)
분단	division
분단국가	divided nation
불법체류자	① illegal ② illegal alien
비상	emergency
비상기획위원회	Emergency Planning Committee
비서관	secretary
비서실	secretary's office
비자	visa
뽑다	to elect
사무관	assistant junior official
사상범	political offender arrested on the charge of harboring dangerous ideas
사증	visa
사회주의	socialism
사회주의국가	socialist state
산림청	Forestry Administration

산업자원부	Ministry of Industrial Resources
삼권분립	separation of the three powers (of administration, legislation, and judiciary)
삼선	election for third term
서기관	① section-chief-grade official ② secretary
서리	① deputy ② acting director
서민	① (common) people ② populace ③ masses
선거	election
선거공약	election pledges
선거관리위원회	Election Administration Committee
선거구	① electoral district ② precinct
선거권	right to vote
선거법	election (electoral) law
선거운동	① election campaign ② canvassing ③ electioneering
선거운동원	election campaigner
선거유세	election campaign
선거일	day of election
선거자금	election campaign fund
선거재판	election trial
선거전	election campaign (fight)
선거전략	election strategy
선거철	election season
선거하다	to vote for
선진국	advanced country
선출	election
선출하다	to elect
세계	world
세계인	cosmopolitan
세계적	international
세계주의	cosmopolitanism
세계화	globalization
소방서	fire station
소수당	minority party

소수민족	minor people
속국	① subject state ② tributary state
수교	friendly relationship
수교하다	to form a friendly relationship
수도	capital
수상	prime minister
수호하다	① to protect ② to guard
순방하다	to make a round of calls
시	city
시민	citizen
시민권	citizenship
시위	demonstration
시의원	① city councilor ② alderman ③ municipal assemblyman
시의회	① municipal assembly ② city council
시장	mayor
시청	city hall
식민지	colony
식품의약품안전청	Food and Drug Administration
심의기관	① council ② inquiry commission
압력단체	pressure group
애국	① love of (for) one's country ② patriotism
애국가	Korean national anthem
애국심	patriotism
애국자	patriot
야권	power of opposition party
야당	opposition party
약소국	powerless country
여권 (旅券)	passport
여권 (與圈)	power of ruling party
여당	ruling party
여론	public opinion
여성특별위원회	Women's Special Committee
여왕	queen
연방국	① federal nation ② confederate nation

	③ commonwealth
연합국	① allied powers ② allied nations
연합하다	to ally
영공	① territorial sky ② airspace
영사	① consul ② consular representative
영사관	consulate
영주권	permanent residentship
영토	territory
영해	territorial waters
예산청	Budget Office
왕	king
왕국	kingdom
왕비	queen
왕세자	crown prince
왕손	① grandchild of a king
	② royal descendant
왕자	prince
왕조	dynasty
왕족	① royal family ② royal blood
왕후	queen
외교	diplomacy
외교관	diplomat
외교통상부	Ministry of Diplomacy and Commerce
외국	foreign country
외국인	foreigner
우리나라	our country
우방	① friendly nation ② ally
	③ allied nation
우방국	allied nation
우체국	post office
원내총무	① leader of the House ② floor leader
유권자	eligible voter
유세	political campaign
유세장	place for political campaign
읍	town
읍사무소	(town) office

읍장	chief of town
의결기관	legislative organ
의석	parliamentary seat
의석수	number of parliamentary seats
의원	① member of an assembly ② assemblyman
의원내각제	parliamentary government system
의회	① assembly ② Parliament (England) ③ Congress (USA)
의회정치	① parliamentarism ② parliamentary politics
이민	① emigration ② immigration
이민국	① emigration office ② immigration office
이민족	different race
이장	head of town
이중국적	dual nationality
인민	the people
인민공화국	people's republic
임금	① king ② ruler ③ sovereign ④ monarch
임시국회	special session of the National Assembly
입국사증	entry visa
입법기관	① lawmaking organ ② legislature
입법부	① legislative body ② legislature
입헌군주국	constitutional monarchy
입헌주의	constitutionalism
입후보	candidate
입후보자	candidate
자문기관	advisory organization
자본주의	capitalism
자본주의국가	capitalist state
자유주의	liberalism
자유주의국가	liberal state
자치령	self-governing dominion

장관	minister
재미교포	① Korean-American ② Korean living in the U.S.A.
재선	being reelected
재선거	reelection
재일동포	Korean living in Japan
재정경제부	Ministry of Finance and Economy
적국	① hostile country ② enemy state
적대국	① hostile country ② enemy state
전국	whole country (land)
전국구	national constituency
전당대회	national convention (of a party)
전체주의	totalitarianism
전화국	telephone office
정견	one's political views (opinions)
정경	politics and economics
정계	world of politics
정권	political power
정권교체	change of regime
정기국회	regular session of the National Assembly
정당	party
정보통신부	Ministry of Information-Communication
정부	① government ② administration
정부종합청사	① (Integrated) Government Office Building ② Government Complex
정세	state of things (affairs)
정족수	quorum
정책	policy
정치	① government ② politics
정치가	① statesman ② politician
정치개혁	political reform
정치계	world of politics
정치관	one's political view
정치구조	political structure
정치권	political sector

정치기구	political organization
정치노선	political line
정치단체	political group
정치도덕	political morality
정치범	① political offense ② political offender
정치비리	political corruption
정치사상	① political idea ② political thought
정치유세	political campaign
정치윤리	political ethics
정치이념	political ideology
정치인	politician
정치일정	political schedule
정치자금	political funds
정치체제	political structure
정치하다	to engage in politics
정치협상	political negotiation
제국	empire
제국주의	imperialism
제헌절	Constitution Day
조국	① homeland ② mother country
조달청	Supply Administration
조선족	Korean living in China
조약	treaty
족벌체제	clan system
종족	① race ② tribe
주권	① sovereignty ② sovereign power
주권국가	sovereign nation (power)
주변국	neighbor country
중립국	neutral state
중소기업청	Small & Medium Business Administration
중소기업특별위원회	Special Committee of Small & Medium Business
중앙집권제	centralism
중진국	developing (semideveloped) country (nation)

지구당	party chapter
지구촌	global community
지명	nomination
지명하다	to nominate
지방자치단체	local autonomy organization
지방자치제	local autonomy system
지방행정	local administration
지배하다	① to rule ② to govern
지역구	local constituency
지원유세	campaign speech for a candidate
집권당	ruling party
집권하다	to take power
찍다	to vote for
차관	① vice-minister ② deputy secretary
참전국	country participated in a war
철도청	National Railroad Administration
첩보	intelligence report
첩자	spy
청문회	hearing
청와대	Blue House
초선	first election
총리	prime minister
총선	general election
총선거	general election
총재	president (of a party)
출마	candidacy
출마자	candidate
출마하다	to run for
침략하다	to invade
침범하다	to invade
쿠데타	coup d'état
타국	foreign country
태극기	Korean national flag
통	the second-lowest city administrative unit
통계청	National Statistical Office

〈청와대〉

〈태극기〉

통일	unification
통일국가	unified country
통일부	Ministry of National Unification
통장	head of second-lowest city administrative unit
통치자	① ruler ② sovereign
통치하다	① to govern ② to rule
투표	vote
투표권	① right to vote ② voting power
투표소	① polling place ② voting booth
투표용지	ballot paper
투표율	① turnout rate ② voting rate
투표자	voter
투표하다	① to ballot ② to vote
투표함	ballot box
특별시	metropolitan city
특허청	① Korean Industrial Property Office ② Patent Office
파벌	① faction ② clan
파출소	police box
평민	commoner
폭동	riot
표밭	favorable voting constituency
한민족	Korean people
합중국	federation
해양경찰청	National Maritime Police Agency
해양수산부	Ministry of Maritime Products
해외	overseas
행정	administration
행정가	administrator
행정고시	civil service examination
행정기관	administrative organ
행정부	The Administration
행정소송	administrative litigation
행정요원	administrative personnel
행정자치부	administrative autonomy department

혁명	revolution
협약	agreement
협정	① convention ② treaty
혼혈	mixed blood
혼혈아	half-breed
화교	overseas Chinese
환경	① environment ② surroundings ③ circumstances
환경부	Ministry of Environment
황제	emperor
황태자	crown prince
황후	empress

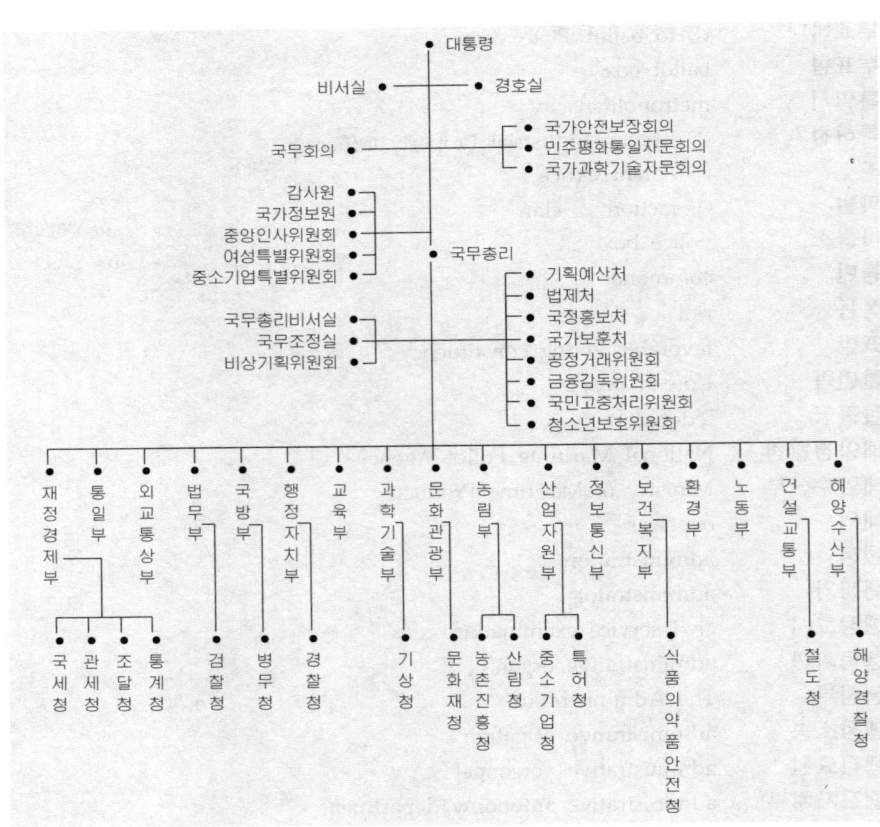

회담	① talk ② conference
회의	① conference ② meeting
후진국	underdeveloped country
휴전선	armistice line
흑색선전	① malicious propaganda ② mud slinging

26 법과 질서
Law and Order

This chapter contains lexical entries relating to the creation and observation of laws and to the judicial and executive branches of government, including names of official posts and words connected to crimes, trials, and punishment.

가석방	release on parole
가정법원	family court
가해자	① assailant ② offender
감금하다	① to imprison ② to confine
감방	cell
감옥	prison
감옥살이	① prison life ② imprisonment
강도	① burglar ② robber
강력계	section in charge of violent crimes
강력범	criminal of violence
검거하다	to arrest
검문	① inspection ② examination ③ checkup
검문소	checkpoint
검문하다	① to inspect ② to examine ③ to checkup
검사	prosecutor
검찰	investigation and prosecution
검찰청	public prosecutor's office
경범죄	minor offence
경제법	law of economics

경찰	police
경찰관	police officer
경찰대학	police academy
경찰서	police station
경찰청	National Police Administration
경호원	① bodyguard ② security guard
경호하다	to guard
고등법원	high court
고문	torture
고발	prosecution
고소	① accusation ② legal action
고소장	written accusation
공개수배	public wanted notice
공공질서	public order
공범	accomplice
공법	public law
공소	prosecution
공소시효	prosecution prescription
공익근무요원	public service worker
공판	① trial ② hearing
과태료	① negligence fine ② penalty
관습법	costom law
교도관	prison guard
교도소	① prison ② correctional institution
교수형	death by hanging
교통경찰	traffic police
교통계	traffic division
구금	① detention ② custody ③ imprisonment
구류	① detention ② custody
구속	arrest
구속영장	warrant of arrest
구속하다	to arrest
구치소	detention house
국내법	national law
국법	national law

국제법	international law
국제변호사	international lawyer
규정	① rule ② regulation ③ law ④ prescription ⑤ ordinance
규칙	① rule ② regulations
기각	dismissal
기소	① prosecution ② indictment ③ accusation
깡패	① rough ② hooligan ③ gangster
노동법	labor law
누명	① false charge ② being framed
단서	clue
단속하다	① to crackdown ② to control ③ to supervise
대법관	justice of the Supreme Court
대법원	Supreme Court
대법원장	Chief Justice of the Supreme Court
대통령령	presidential order
도굴꾼	snatcher
도굴하다	to rob a grave
도덕	moral
도둑	thief
도둑질	① theft ② stealing
딱지	ticket for a fine
목격자	witness
몰수	① confiscation ② seizure
무기수	life prisoner
무기징역	life imprisonment
무법자	outlaw
무죄	innocence
무질서	disorder
묵비권	right of silence
미수	attempted
민법	civil law
민사소송	civil suit
방범	crime prevention

방범대원	① security guard ② watchman
방화범	arsonist
방화죄	arson
배심원	jury
벌	① punishment ② penalty
벌금	① fine ② penalty
벌금형	punishment with (by) a fine
벌칙	penal regulations
범법	① breaking the law
	② violation of the law
범법자	lawbreaker
범법행위	illegal act
범인	criminal
범죄	① offense ② crime
범죄율	crime rate
범죄자	① offender ② criminal
범칙	infringement of regulations
범칙금	fine
범행	crime
법	law
법관	① judge ② justice
법규	laws and regulations
법규정	laws and regulations
법령	law

법					
효력	종류			기관	
	공법	사법	사회법		
헌법 ↑ 법률 ↑ 조례 ↑ 규칙 ↑ 명령	헌법 형법 행정법	민법 상법	경제법 노동법 사회보장법	대법원	
^ ^ ^ ^ ^ ^ ^ ^ ^				↑ 상고 · 재항고 ↑	
				고등법원	지방법원 본원 합의부(항소부)
				↑ 항소 · 항고 ↑	
				지방법원 및 지원합의부	지밥법원 및 지원단독판사

법령집	① book of statutes ② complete collection of laws and regulations
법률	① law ② legislation
법률위반	violation of the law
법안	bill
법원	court
법전	① code of law ② statute
법정	court
법조계	legal profession circle
법조인	person of the legal profession
법치주의	① constitutionalism ② legalism
변론	① proceedings ② pleadings
변호사	lawyer
변호인	① counsel ② defender
보석	① bail ② bailment
보석금	bail money
복권	reinstatement
복역하다	to serve a prison term
부도덕	immorality
부장검사	superintendent public prosecutor
부장판사	superintendent judge
불량배	blackguard
불법	① unlawfulness ② illegality
불심검문	① questioning of a suspicious person by a patrolman ② police questioning
사건	case
사기	① fraud ② fraudulence
사기꾼	① imposter ② swindler ③ shark
사면	① pardon ② remission
사무장	head clerk
사법 (私法)	private law
사법 (司法)	① administration of justice ② judicature
사법고시	judicature examination
사법기관	organ of the judicature
사법부	judicature

사법서사	① judicial scrivener ② copyist
사상범	political offender arrested on the charge of harboring dangerous ideas
사형	capital punishment
사형수	prisoner under death sentence
사형하다	① to execute a death sentence ② to put to death
사회법	social law
상고	final appeal
상법	commercial law
상소	appeal
상속재판	trial on inheritance
석방	release
선거사범	election-related crime
선거소송	election lawsuit
선고	① sentence ② verdict
선도	guidance
선례	precedent
소년원	reformatory
소매치기	pickpocket
소송	lawsuit
소송비	litigation costs
소송인	① plaintiff ② litigator
소송장	statement of a lawsuit
송장	invoice
수감	① confinement ② imprisonment
수감자	prisoner
수갑	handcuffs
수배	search instruction
수배자	① person wanted by the police ② wanted criminal
수배하다	to search
수사	investigation
수사관	investigator
수사기관	investigation office
수사대	criminalinvestigation squad

수사망	police dragnet
수사본부	investigating headquarter
수사하다	① to investigate
	② to conduct an investigation
수색	search
수색영장	search warrant
수임료	acceptance of appointment fee
순경	police officer
순찰대	patrol squad
순찰차	patrol car
순찰하다	to patrol
승소	winning a lawsuit
신문	① questioning ② (cross-)examination
	③ inquest
심리	① trial ② examination ③ inquiry
심문	① questioning ② cross-examination
	③ inquest
심사	① investigation ② judgment
압수	① seizure ② confiscation
양심	concience
양심수	prisoner of conscience
영장	warrant
완전범죄	perfect crime
용의자	suspect
원고	plaintiff
위반	violation
위법	illegality
위헌	unconstitutionality
유괴	① kidnap(ping) ② abduction
유괴범	kidnapper
유도신문	leading question
유죄	guilty
유치장	① detention room ② police cell
윤리	① ethics ② morals
의무경찰	obliged police officer
이감	transferring to another prison

이의신청	formal objection
이혼소송	divorce suit
인권변호사	human rights lawyer
인륜	① humanity ② morality
일당	① ring ② gang ③ conspirators
입법부	legislature
입정	admission to the courtroom
입헌	constitution
입헌주의	constitutionalism
자격정지	suspension of qualifications
자백	confession
장물	stolen goods (articles)
장물아비	seller of stolen goods
재범	① repetition of offense ② second conviction
재판	① trial ② justice
재판관	judge
재판소	trial court
재판정	trial court
적법	legality
전과자	ex-convict
전투경찰	riot police
정치범	political criminal
조례	① regulations ② rules
좀도둑	① sneak thief ② petty thief ③ pilferer
종신형	life sentence
죄	① crime ② sin
죄수	prisoner
죄수복	① prisoner's clothes ② stripe
죄악	① crime ② sin ③ vice
죄인	① criminal ② convict
주차단속원	parking inspector
중죄	① felony ② grave offense
증거	① evidence ② proof
증언하다	to testify
증인	witness

지방법원	district court
지서	① police substation ② branch station
진범	real culprit
진술	statement
진술서	written statement
진술하다	to state
진정	① petition ② appeal
진정서	written petition
질서	order
집행유예	① probation ② suspended sentence
집행하다	to execute
징계	① disciplinary punishment ② official reprimand
징계하다	① to punish for delinquency ② to reprimand
징역	① penal servitude ② imprisonment
징역살이	① prison life ② imprisonment
참고인	① witness ② informant
처벌	① punishment ② penalty
처벌하다	① to punish ② to inflict a penalty on
처형	① punishment ② execution
처형하다	① to punish ② to execute
천벌	divine punishment
청소년범죄	juvenile delinquency
청원경찰	policeman on special guard assignment
체포	arrest
체포하다	to arrest
초범	first offense
출감	release from prison
출옥	release from prison
치안	public security
탄원	petition
탄원서	written petition
탄핵	impeachment
탈옥	jailbreak

탈옥수	① jail-breaker ② escaped prisoner
퇴정	withdrawal from the court
특별사면	special amnesty
특별수사대	special criminal investigation squad
파출소	police station
판결	① judicial decision ② decision of the court
판결문	decision
판례	① precedent ② case
판사	judge
패륜아	immoral person
패소	① losing a suit ② lost case
폭력배	① hoodlums ② gangsters
피고	① defendant ② accused
피고인	accused
피의자	suspect
피해자	victim
합법	① lawfulness ② legality
합헌	constitutionality
항고	complaint
항소	appeal
행정법	administrative law
행정소송	administrative litigation
헌법	constitution
현행범	criminal caught in act of crime
혐의	suspicion
혐의자	① criminal suspect ② suspect
형구	implement of punishment
형기	① term of imprisonment ② prison term
형무소	prison
형벌	① punishment ② penalty
형법	criminal law
형사	detective
형사소송	criminal suit
형장	place of execution
훔치다	to steal

휴정	① court recess
	② adjourning the court
흉악범	heinous criminal

27 국방
National Defense

This chapter contains lexical entries related to battle, the military, and national defense.

가스전	gas war	
간첩	① spy ② espionage agent ③ secret agent	
간호사관학교	military academy of nursing	
간호장교	officer in charge of nursing	
강적	formidable enemy	
개선	improvement	
개선하다	to improve	
게릴라전	guerrilla war	
격전	fierce battle	
격전지	battleground	
결투	① duel ② mortal combat	
계급	rank	
계급장	① badge of rank ② insignia	
공격	① attack ② assault ③ raid	
공격개시	opening an attack	
공군	air force	
공군사관학교	air-force academy	
공병	military engineers	
공수부대	airborne unit	
공습 (攻襲)	① raid ② attack	
공습 (空襲)	① air raid ② aerial attack	

군인계급			
장교	장관		대장
			중장
			소장
			준장
	영관		대령
			중령
			소령
	위관		대위
			중위
			소위
하사관			준위
			상사
			중사
			하사
사병			병장
			상병
			일등병
			이등병

공습하다	① to make an air raid
	② to make an air strike
공익근무요원	public service personnel
국군	national army
국군병원	national army hospital
국방	national defense
국방부	Ministry of National Defense
국방부장관	minister of National Defense
국지전	① localized warfare
	② limited warfare
국토방위	① defense of the country
	② national defense
군가	① army song ② marching song
군기 (軍氣)	military spirit
군기 (軍紀)	military discipline
군대	① troops ② army
군대행진곡	military march
군목	chaplain
군무원	military service personnel
군번	soldier identification number
군법	martial law
군법무관	military judicial officials
군법회의	court-martial
군복	military uniform
군복무	military service
군비제한	arms limitation
군사 (軍事)	military affairs
군사 (軍士)	group of soldiers
군사개입	military intervention
군사고문	military advisor
군사고문단	military advisory board
군사교육	military education
군사기밀	military secrets
군사기지	① military post ② military base
군사도시	military city
군사동맹	military alliance

군사력	① military power ② armaments
군사법원	military court
군사분계선	Military Demarcation Line
군사비	military expenses
군사시설	military facilities
군사우편	military post
군사위성	military satellite
군사재판	① military trial ② court-martial
군사정책	military policy
군사지도	military map
군사지역	military zone
군수뇌부	military chief executives
군수물자	war supplies
군수품	military supplies
군악대	military band
군용	military use (purposes)
군용기	① warplane ② military plane
군용도로	military road
군용지	military area
군용차	troop vehicle
군의관	army surgeon
군인	soldier
군장	military uniform
군장비	military equipment
군함	① warship ② war vessel ③ man-of-war
군항	military port
군화	① military shoes ② combat boots
굴복하다	① submit ② surrender ③ yield
권총	① pistol ② handgun
기관총	machine gun
기병	cavalry soldier
기병대	cavalry
기지	base
낙하산	① parachute ② chute
내무반	(living) quarters

냉전	cold war
단검	dagger
단기사병	short-term cavalry soldier
대령	colonel
대위	lieutenant
대장	① general ② admiral
대포	cannon
돌격	① charge ② sudden attack
돌격대	① attack team ② raider
따발총	machine gun
매복하다	① to lie in ambush ② to ambush
무기	① weapon ② arms ③ weaponry
무기산업	arms business
무장하다	to arm
무장해제	① disarmament ② demilitarization
물자전	resources war
미사일	missile
민방위대	civil defense unit
박격포	① trench mortar ② mine thrower
발사하다	to fire
방독면	① gas mask ② gas helmet
방아쇠	trigger
방어	① defense ② protection
방위	defense
방패	① shield ② buckler
배수진	background base
병력	① military force ② force of arms
병무청	Military Manpower Administration
병사	soldier
병역	military service
병영	barracks
병장	sergeant
보급품	impedimenta
보병	① infantry ② foot soldier
복무	service
복무연한	term of service

복역하다	to serve in the army
부관	adjutant
부대	① military unit ② corps
부상병	① injured soldier ② wounded soldier
부하	subordinate
분쟁	① dispute ② trouble
불명예제대	dishonorable discharge
불침번	night watch
비무장지대	demilitarized zone
사격	① firing ② shooting ③ gunshot
사격하다	① to fire ② to shoot
사관	commissioned officer
사관생도	① officer ② cadet
사관학교	Military Academy
사관후보생	cadet
사령관	commander
사령부	headquarters
사병	① private soldier ② enlisted man
사수	desperate (stubborn) defense
사수하다	① to defend to the last ② to defend desperately
상관	senior officer
상등병	corporal
상병	corporal
상사 (上司)	① higher officer ② one's superior
상사 (上士)	sergeant
생포하다	to capture alive
생화학전	biochemical war
석사장교	master officer
세계대전	World War
소령	① major ② lieutenant commander
소위	second lieutenant
소장	major general
수류탄	grenade
수비	① defense ② garrisoning
수비군	① garrison ② guards

수비대	① garrison ② guards
수비망	defensive net
수비하다	① to defend ② to guard ③ to garrison
습격	① attack ② assault ③ raid
습격하다	① to attack ② to assault ③ to raid
승리	① victory ② triumph ③ win
승리하다	① to win the victory ② to triumph ③ to prevail
승전	① successful battle ② victory
승전국	victorious country
시한폭탄	time bomb
싸우다	to fight
싸움	fight
싸움터	battlefield
쏘다	to shoot
아군	① our forces ② our army
여군	women army
영관	field officer
예비군	reserve forces
예비역	service in the first reserve
요새	① fortress ② stronghold ③ fortifications
용감무쌍하다	to be brave and unrivaled
용맹하다	① to be dauntless ② to be brave
용사	brave warrior
운전병	soldier whose duty is driving
원수	① (field) marshal ② general of the army
위관	company officer
위생병	hospital orderly
유격대	① guerilla unit ② mobile forces
유격전	guerilla war
육군	army
육군사관학교	Military Academy
육탄전	① suicidal raid

	② hand-to-hand struggle
의무병 (醫務兵)	medical soldier
의무병 (義務兵)	obliged soldier
의용군	volunteer army
이기다	① to win ② to gain victory
이등병	second class private
인해전술	① human sea tactics ② strategy of throwing waves of men into action
일등병	first class private
일선	① front line ② first fighting line
임관	appointment (to an office)
입대	joining the army
입대하다	to join the army
작전	① tactics ② strategy ③ military operations
잠수정	submarine
잠수함	submarine
장갑차	armored motorcar
장관급	general (officer) class
장교	officer
장군	general
장성	generals
저항	resistance
저항하다	to resist
적	enemy
적국	① hostile country (power) ② enemy
적군	① hostile army ② enemy troops
적지	enemy's territory
적진	① enemy('s) camp ② enemy's position ③ enemy line
전략	① strategy ② stratagem
전략가	strategist
전방	the front
전범	war criminal
전사	death in battle
전사하다	① to die in battle ② to fall in action

전선	war front
전술	① tactics ② strategy
전술가	tactician
전승	① victory ② triumph
전역	discharge from military service
전우	comrade
전우애	comradeship
전장	① battlefield ② the front
전쟁	war
전쟁고아	war orphan
전쟁터	battlefield
전차	tank
전투	① battle ② combat ③ fight
전투기	fighter
전투력	fighting strength
전투복	① combat uniform ② battle jacket
전투부대	① combat unit ② combat forces
전투적이다	to be militant
전투하다	to fight a battle
전투함	battleship
정규군	regular army
정비병	soldier whose duty is maintenance
정찰	① reconnaissance ② scouting
제대	discharge from military service
제대하다	① to leave the army ② to be discharged from military service
제독	admiral
졸병	private
주둔지	① post ② army post
준위	warrant officer
준장	brigadier general
중령	lieutenant colonel
중사	sergeant
중위	first lieutenant
중장	lieutenant general
지다	① to be defeated ② to suffer a defeat

	③ to be beaten
지략	strategy
지뢰	land mine
지역전	regional war
지원군	support army
지원병	volunteer
지원부대	backup (support) forces
지키다	① to defend ② to guard
지휘관	commander
진	① camp ② position
진격	① attack ② charge
진격하다	① to attack ② to make an attack
진급	promotion
진급하다	to be promoted
진영	① camp ② encampment
진지	① position ② encampment
징병	① conscription ② enlistment
징집	① enlistment ② enrollment
징집되다	to be conscripted
참모총장	Chief of the General Staff
참전	① participation in a war
	② entry into a war
참전국	country participated in a war
참전용사	① soldier participating in a war
	② war veteran
참호	① trench ② dugout
창	spear
천하무적	person without a rival in the world
철모	steel helmet
첩보	① secret information
	② intelligence report
쳐들어가다	① to invade ② to attack ③ to raid into
초소병	soldier whose duty is to guard post
총	① gun ② rifle
총검	firearms and swords
총사령관	supreme commander

총알	bullet
총알받이	receiving bullets
최루탄	tear gas
취사병	soldier whose duty is kitchen work
침공	① invasion ② raid ③ attack
침공하다	to invade
침략	① aggression ② invasion
침투	infiltration
카투사	KATUSA (Korean Augmentation Troops to US Army)
칼	sword
탄환	projectile
탈영	① desertion from barracks ② decampment
탈영병	deserted solider from barracks
탈영하다	to desert from barracks
탈환	① recapture ② recovery
탈환하다	① to recapture ② to win back
탱크	tank
통신병	signalman
퇴각	retreat
퇴각하다	① to retreat ② to beat a retreat
투쟁	① fight ② combat
투항	surrender
투항하다	to surrender
특공대	special attack unit
특수부대	special forces
패배	defeat
패배하다	① to be defeated ② to fail
패잔병	① remnants (of a defeated troop) ② stragglers
패전	① lost battle ② defeat
패전국	defeated nation
패전하다	① to lose a war ② to be defeated in a battle
포로	prisoner of war

포로수용소	① prison camp ② POW camp ③ concentration camp
포병	artilleryman
폭격	① aerial bombing ② bombing attack
폭격하다	① to bomb ② to drop bombs
폭발	explosion
폭약	① detonator ② explosive compound
폭탄	bomb
폭파	① blasting ② blowup ③ explosion
피난	① refuge ② shelter
피난민	① refugees ② evacuees
하사	staff sergeant
하사관	① noncommissioned officer ② petty officer
하사관학교	school for noncommissioned officers
학군단	Students' Defense Corps
학도병	student soldier
학사장교	Reserve Officers' Training Corps (ROTC)
함락	① depression ② collapse ③ cave-in
항복	① surrender ② submission ③ yielding
항복하다	① to surrender ② to capitulate ③ to submit
해군	navy
해군사관학교	Naval Academy
해병대	Marine Corps
핵무기	nuclear weapon
핵전쟁	nuclear war
핵폭탄	nuclear bomb
행군	① march ② marching
행군하다	to march
행정병	soldier whose duty is administration
헌병	military policeman
헌병대	military police
헬기	helicopter
화생방전	biochemical and radiological warfare
화약	gunpowder

화염방사기	① flame thrower ② flame projector
화포	gun
후방	① home front ② the rear
후퇴	① backdown ② retreat ③ regress
후퇴하다	① to retreat ② to go back ③ to go back away
훈련	① training ② drill ③ practice
훈련병	soldier trainee
훈련생	student trainee
훈련소	training school
훈련조교	drillmaster
훈장	① order ② medal
휴전	① armistice ② truce ③ cease-fire
휴전선	① cease-fire line ② armistice line
흉기	murder weapon

28 사회와 사회활동
Society and Social Activities

This chapter contains lexical entries describing social activities and groups. It focuses especially on Korean people's social activities, the development of Korean society and Korean social classes and social problems.

가명	① fictitious name ② pseudonym
가부장제도	patriarchal system
가족제도	family system
개인	individual
개인주의	individualism
개인행동	acting individually
개혁	reform
개화	enlightenment
개회식	① opening ceremony ② inaugural meeting
겨레	① offspring of the same forefather ② people
경례	① salutation ② salute ③ bow
경례하다	① to salute ② to give (mark) a salute ③ to bow
경의	① respect ② regard ③ homage ④ reverence
경조사	birthdays, weddings and funerals
계급사회	class society
계몽운동	enlightenment campaign
계층	class

계층이동	class migration
고소득층	upper-income bracket
고용인	employee
고용주	employer
공경하다	① to respect ② to honor ③ to revere
공공사업	public works
공공질서	public order
공동사회	community
공동체	community
공동체의식	community consciousness
공립	public institution
공산주의	communism
공중도덕	public morality
공청회	public (open) hearing
관례	custom
관습	① custom ② convention
교통문제	traffic matters
구민	district residents
구성원	constituent
국립	national institution
국민	citizen
군민	county residents
군중	crowd
권력	① power ② authority
권리	right
규범	① standard ② norm
규율	① order ② discipline
규제	① regulation ② control ③ restriction
기념식	ceremony
기념품	souvenir
기념하다	to celebrate
기득권층	class of vested rights
노인문제	senior citizen's issues
농경사회	agricultural society
농민	farmer
농성	sit-down strike

농어민	farmers and fishermen
농촌봉사활동	volunteer service for rural communities
다과회	tea party
단체	① party ② group
단체생활	group life
단체의식	group consciousness
단체장	head of a group
단체행동	acting collectively
단체행동권	right to collective action
대중	① masses ② multitude ③ general public
대중화	popularization
대표자	representative
데모	demonstration
도덕	moral
도민	province residents
도시빈민	poor urban people
동맹	① alliance ② league ③ union
동문회	alumni association
동아리	club
동창회	① alumni association ② alumni meeting
동포	① fellow countrymen ② compatriots
동호회	① club ② special interest groups
뒤풀이	end party
막역하다	to be intimate
맞절	bow to each other
면허증	license
명찰	① name plate (tag) ② identification tag
명함	① name card ② business card
모임	① meeting ② gathering
무질서	disorder
문명사회	civilized society
미래사회	future society
미풍양속	good manners and customs
민족	race

모임		
누가	언제	왜
동문회		공청회
동창회		박람회
동호회	송년회	송별회
반상회	신년회	친목회
부녀회	뒤풀이	자치회
청년회	:	집회
학생회		학회
:		:

사회	
시기	유형
원시사회	농경사회
전통사회	봉건사회
현대사회	복지사회
미래사회	문명사회
:	산업사회
	선진사회
	정보사회
	조직사회
	:

민족주의	nationalism
민주사회	democratic society
민주주의	democracy
민중	people
박람회	exhibition
반상회	neighborhood meeting
방명록	guest book
법인	corporation
별명	nick name
복지사회	welfare society
본명	one's real name
봉건사회	feudal society
봉사활동	volunteer work
부녀회	women's meeting
부유층	wealthy class
부자	wealthy person
빈곤층	the needy
빈민	the poor
빈민가	slum
빈민사회	the poor
빈민층	the poor
사귀다	① to make friends with
	② to get acquainted with
사랑하다	to love
사립	private institution
사망률	mortality rate
사회	society
사회계층	social class
사회공동체	social community
사회구성원	social constituent
사회구조	social structure
사회규범	social code
사회규약	social covenant
사회단체	① social group ② social party
사회문제	social problem
사회발전	social development

사회변동	① social change ② social shift
사회보장제도	social security system
사회복지	social welfare
사회봉사	① social service ② public service
사회부조리	social absurdities
사회비리	corruption in society
사회사업	social work
사회생활	social life
사회성	sociability
사회심리	social psychology
사회악	social evil
사회운동	social movement
사회윤리	social ethics
사회적	social
사회정의	social justice
사회제도	social system
사회조직	social organization
사회주의	socialism
사회질서	social order
사회집단	social group
사회체계	social system
사회체제	social system
사회통념	generally accepted idea
사회현상	social phenomena
사회협약	① social agreement ② social convention
사회화	socialization
사회활동	social activities
산업사회	industrial society
상류사회	high society
상류층	upper class
서명	signature
서민	common people
서민층	common class
선진사회	advanced society
성	① family name ② surname

	③ last name
성명	name
성함	name
세력	power
소수집단	minority group
소외계층	alienated class
송년회	year-end party
송별회	farewell party
시무식	resumption of office business after the New Year recess
시민	citizen
시민단체	citizens' group
시위	demonstration
신년하례식	congratulatory ceremony of the New Year
신년회	New Year meeting
신분	status
신분제도	caste system
신분증	identification card
실명	one's real name
아동문제	children's issues
악수하다	to shake hands
악습	bad habit
안내	① guide ② instruction
약속	① promise ② engagement ③ appointment
양반	① the nobility ② the aristocratic class
어민	fishermen
여성문제	women's issues
연하장	New Year's card
영세민	① needy person ② destitute person
예명	stage (screen) name
예식	ceremony
우두머리	head
원시사회	primitive society
유명인사	celebrity

윤리	ethics
의무	① duty ② obligation
이름	name
이름표	name tag
이웃	neighbor
인구	population
인구동향	population trend
인구문제	population problems
인구밀도	population density
인구분포	population distribution
인구이동	population movement
인구정책	population policy
인구조사	census
인구폭발	population explosion
인권	human rights
인권보호	protection of human rights
인권선언	declaration of human rights
인권유린	infringement upon human rights
인맥	relationship with the same social class
인사	celebrity
인사하다	to greet
인솔	① lead ② guide
인습	① custom ② convention
자격증	certificate of qualifications
자본주의	capitalism
자치단체	self-governing community
자치활동	autonomous activity
자치회	autonomous association
작명하다	to name
잔치	party
장본인	ringleader
쟁의	① dispute ② strife
저명인사	celebrity
저소득층	small income
적십자사	Red Cross Society
전통	tradition

전통사회	traditional society
절친하다	① to be intimate ② to be familiar ③ to be close
절하다	to bow
정보사회	informational society
정의사회	justice society
정책	policy
제도	① system ② institution
조직	organization
조직사회	organized society
존경하다	to respect
주민	resident
주민등록증	resident registration card
주택문제	housing problem
중류사회	middle-class society
중류층	middle-class
중산층	middle class
증명서	certificate
지도자	leader
지도층	ruling class
지도층인사	leader
지방자치단체	local self-governing community
지배자	ruler
지역감정	regional grudge
지역사회	community
지연	territorially related
질서	order
집단	group
집단생활	group life
집단의식	group consciousness
집단이기주의	group egoism
집단행동	collective action
집회	① meeting ② gathering
책임	responsibility
책임자	person in charge
천민	low-class people

철야농성	overnight sit-in demonstration
청년회	youth association
청소년문제	① youth problems ② juvenile problems
초대장	① letter of invitation ② invitation card
초청장	① letter of invitation ② invitation card
축가	song of congratulation
축배	toast
축의금	congratulation money
축제	festival
출생률	birthrate
친교	fellowship
친목회	get-together
친하다	① to be close ② to be intimate
탁아문제	day-care problems
통솔하다	to lead
특권층	privileged class
폐회식	closing ceremony
폭동	riot
표어	① slogan ② motto
풍속	customs
풍습	① customs ② practices
학생회	student council
학연	school ties
학회	academic society
현대사회	modern society
환경문제	environmental problems
환경오염	environmental pollution
회담	① talk ② conference
회원	member
회의	① conference ② meeting

29 경제와 경제활동
Economy and Economic Activities

This chapter contains lexical entries related to the economy and economic activities related to money, taxation, and finances, in addition to those related to market transaction and consumer activities.

가게	store
가격	price
가격인상	markup
가격인하	markdown
가격표	price tag
가계	① household economy
	② family finances
가계부	account book
가계소득	family income
가계수표	personal check
가계지출	family outcome
가공무역	processing trade
가구점	furniture shop
가난하다	to be poor
가맹점	① franchise store ② chain store
가불하다	① to get an advance
	② to pay in advance
가스요금	① gas rate ② gas charge
간접세	indirect tax
갑근세	acronym of grade A income tax
갑종근로소득세	grade A income tax

값·가격

고가
공장도가격
권장소비자가격
도매가
매매가
분양가
소매가
시가
액면가
원가
저가
정가
정찰가
주가
중저가
할인가
:

값	price
값어치	① value ② worth
강세	① emphasis ② stress
갚다	① to pay back ② to repay
개방경제	open economy
개시	first sale of the day
개업	opening of a business
개점	① opening of a shop
	② opening of business
거금	large (big) sum (of money)
거래	transactions
거래처	① business connection ② customer
	③ business acquaintance
거스름돈	change
거시경제	macroeconomy
거액	① large sum of money ② lot of money
검소하다	to be frugal
격려금	cash reward to encourage a person
견본품	sample
결산	settlement of accounts
결재	① authorization ② approval
	③ decision
결재일	① authorization date ② approval date
경기	① business ② prosperity
경기변동	business fluctuations
경리	accounting
경매	auction
경매인	auctioneer
경비	① expense(s) ② cost(s)
경상수지	current account
경상지출	operating expense
경영	management
경영자	manager
경제	economy
경제계	economic world
경제공황	Depression

경제권 (經濟權)	economic power
경제권 (經濟圈)	economic sector
경제발전	economic development
경제성	economic condition
경제성장	① growth of economy ② economic growth
경제원리	economic principle
경제인	economist
경제적	economical
경제지표	economic indicator
경품	free bonus gift
경품권	gift coupon
계 (計)	sum total
계 (契·楔)	① fraternity ② mutual aid (financing) association
계산	calculation
계산대	counter
계산서	bill
계산하다	to calculate
계약	contract
계약금	deposit
계좌	account
계획경제	planned economy
곗돈	money for the mutual financing association
고가	high price
고가품	① expensive goods ② high priced goods
고객	customer
고급품	high quality goods
고리대금업	usurious loan
고리대금업자	① usurious loaner ② loan shark
고액권	large denomination notes
고정환율제도	fixed exchange system
골동품	antique
공공요금	public utilities charge
공과금	① public imposts (charges) ② taxes

공금	public fund
공급	supply
공급자	① supplier ② provider
공납금	regular school payments
공돈	① windfall income ② easy money
공산품	industrial products
공수표	blank check
공장도가격	factory price
공짜	free of charge
공채	① public loan ② public bond
공탁금	security deposit
공탁하다	① to deposit ② to place on deposit
과세	taxation
과소비	over-consumption
과용	overspending
과점	oligopoly
과태료	① default charges ② negligence fine
관리비	management expenses
관세	customs
관세청	Customs Administration
교역	① trade ② commerce
교육세	educational tax
교환	exchange
구매	purchase
구매자	buyer
구매하다	to purchase
구멍가게	small store
구입	① purchase ② buying
구입하다	to buy
국가경제	national economy
국내경제	domestic economy
국내시장	domestic market
국민소득	national income
국민자본	national capital
국민총생산	gross national product (GNP)
국세	national tax

국세청	National Tax Administration
국제경제	international economy
국제수지	balance of international payments
국제시장	international market
국채	① national loan ② government bonds
권리금	key money
권장소비자가격	suggested retail price
귀중품	valuables
규격품	standardized goods
근로소득	income
금고	safe
금리	interest
금액	amount
금융	① circulation of money ② finance
금융가	financial world
금융기관	① banking organ ② financial agency
금융시장	financial market
금융실명제	financial real name system
금융자산	financial property
금일봉	gift of money
금전	① money ② cash
금전출납부	account book
금화	gold coin
급여	① pay ② salary
기금	① fund ② foundation
기념주화	commemorative coin
기념품	souvenir
기부금	donation
기업	enterprise
기업가	entrepreneur
기업인	man of enterprise
기업주	owner of enterprise
기업체	conglomerate
기탁금	trust money
기탁하다	to intrust
기호품	favorite food

기획상품	promotional item
긴축정책	curtailment policy
깎다	① to cut down the price
	② to get a discount
꽃시장	flower market
꽃집	flower shop
꾸다	to borrow
꾸어주다	to lend
낙찰	successful bid
난방비	heating expenses
날리다	① to lose ② to waste
납부하다	to pay
납세	payment of taxes
납세자	taxpayer
납입금	① money paid ② money due
납입액	amount due
납품하다	① to deliver goods ② to supply goods
낭비하다	① to waste ② to be wasteful
내국세	inland revenue
내림세	downward trend
내수시장	domestic market
넉넉하다	① to be enough ② to be plenty
	③ to be well-off
노점	street stall
노점상	street vendor
농산물시장	agricultural products market
농지세	farmland tax
뇌물	bribe
단골	regular customer
단골손님	regular customer
단란주점	karaoke bar
달러	dollar
달러화	dollar
담보	① mortgage ② security
당좌수표	check
당좌예금	current account

내거나 받는 돈

격려금
계약금
곗돈
권리금
급료
급여
기부금
납부금
등록금
배당금
벌금
보너스
보상금
보조금
보증금
보험금
보험료
봉급
봉사료
비상금
비자금
사례금
상금
상여금
성금
세뱃돈
수수료
수업료
수익금
위자료
이익금
임대료
자금
자본금
장려금
집세
찬조금
축의금
포상금
할부금
：

한국의 돈	
단위	모양
1원	
5원	
10원	
50원	
100원	
500원	
1,000원	
5,000원	
10,000원	

대금	① cost ② price
대기업	conglomerate
대리점	agency
대부	loaning
대부금	loan
대부하다	① to lend ② to make a loan
대여	lease
대여하다	to lease
대용품	substitute
대차대조표	balance sheet
대출	① lending ② loan
대출금	loaned money
대출하다	to make a loan
대형할인매장	big-sized discount market
덤	① extra ② bonus
덤핑판매	dumping sale
도깨비시장	① illegal market ② black market
도매	wholesale
도매가	wholesale price
도매상	① wholesale store ② wholesaler
도매시장	wholesale market
도산	bankruptcy
독과점	monopoly and oligopoly
독점	monopoly
돈	money
돈놀이	① money lending ② usury
동전	coin
뒷거래	① backdoor dealing ② illegal business
등록금	tuition
떡값	bribe
떡집	rice cake store
떨이	① goods for clearance sale ② articles offered at marked-down prices
떼돈	lot of money
마수걸이	first sale (transaction) of the day
마진	margin

만물상	general shop
맡기다	to deposit
매기다	① to set ② to fix
매도율	selling rate
매매	① buying and selling
	② purchase and sale
매상	① sales ② selling
매상고	① amount sold ② sales
매입	① purchase ② buying
매입율	buying rate
매장	shop
매점	① stand ② stall ③ booth
면세점	duty free store
면허세	license tax
명품	famous product or work
모으다	to save
모조품	imitation
목돈	sizeable sum of money
무료	① free ② no charge
무역	trade
무역센터	trade center
무역수지	balance of payments
문구점	stationary shop
문방구	stationary
문화비	cultural expense
물가	price
물가지수	retail price index
물건	thing
물물교환	barter
물품	goods
미시경제	microeconomy
미화	American dollar
밑지다	to lose on the cost price
바가지쓰다	① to be charged extravagantly
	② to be ripped-off
	③ to be overcharged

바겐세일	bargain sale
바자회	bazaar
반품	returned item
방앗간	mill
배당금	① dividend ② share
배상금	① indemnity ② compensation
백화점	department store
버스카드	bus card
벌금	fine
벌다	to earn
벌이	moneymaking
법인세	corporation tax
벼룩시장	flea market
보관소	depository
보너스	bonus
보따리	① bundle ② pack
보물	treasure
보배	treasure
보상금 (報償金)	remuneration
보상금 (補償金)	① indemnity ② compensation
보석상	jeweller
보수	pay
보조금	subsidy
보증	① guarantee ② security
보증금	security deposit
보증서다	to guarantee
보증인	guarantor
보통예금	regular deposit
보합세	prices of stocks
보험	insurance
보험금	insurance money
보험료	insurance bill
보험회사	insurance company
복제품	① reproduction ② duplicate
본사	① head office of a firm ② main office
본전	① principle sum ② capital

	③ cost price
본점	① head office ② main store
봉급	salary
봉사료	service charge
부가가치	value added
부가가치세	value added tax
부가세	surtax
부과하다	to charge
부담금	one's share (in expenses)
부담하다	to bear
부도	① dishonor ② nonpayment
부도수표	dishonored bill
부동산중개업소	real estate agent
부르다	to make a bid
부속물	belongings
부속품	① accessory ② fittings
부유하다	to be rich
부족하다	to be insufficient
부채	① debt ② liabilities
부품	① parts ② spare parts ③ components
분양	① sale in lots ② lot sale
분양가	price of a lot
분점	branch store
불경기	① depression ② recession
불입금	money (to be) paid
불입액	amount paid
불입하다	① to deposit ② to pay
불황	① depression ② bad business ③ recession
비과세	tax exemption
비매품	goods not for sale
비상금	emergency fund
비수기	low-demand season
비싸다	to be expensive
비용	expenses
비자금	slush fund

빌려주다	to lend
빌리다	① to borrow ② to loan
빚	debt
빚쟁이	creditor
빚지다	to fall into debt
빵집	bakery
사다	to buy
사례금	honorarium
사비	private money
사업	business
사업자	businessman
사은품	bonus gift
사장	president
사채 (社債)	① (corporation) debenture ② bond
사채 (私債)	① private loan ② private debt
사채업자	① private loaner ② private moneylender
삯	① wage ② pay
상가	shopping district
상금	prize money
상사	trading company
상설할인매장	discount store
상속세	inheritance tax
상술	knack (trick) of the trade
상업	commerce
상업성	commercial
상여금	bonus
상인	merchant
상점	shop
상표	① trademark ② brand
상품 (賞品)	① prize ② trophy
상품 (上品)	① first-class article ② article of superior quality
상품 (商品)	goods for sale
상품권	gift certificate
새마을금고	Saemaul (New Community) fund

새벽시장	wholesale market that opens early in the morning
생산	production
생산구조	production structure
생산자	producer
생활비	living expenses
서점	bookstore
선물	① present ② gift
선불	advance payment
성과급	① result (profit) based payment ② payment based on result
성금	① contribution ② donation
성수기	high-demand season
세	tax
세계시장	① world market ② global market
세금	tax
세놓다	to rent out
세무사	licensed tax accountant
세무서	tax office
세뱃돈	New Year's cash gift
세일	sale
세주다	to let out
소득	income
소득세	income tax
소매	retail
소매가	retail price
소매상	① retail store ② retailer
소매시장	retail market
소모품	expendables
소비	consumption
소비구조	consumption structure
소비생활	consumption life
소비자	consumer
소비자경제	consumer economy
소비하다	to consume
손님	customer

시장	상점
금융시장	노점
꽃시장	도매상
농산물시장	매점
벼룩시장	면세점
새벽시장	백화점
세계시장	소매상
수산시장	슈퍼마켓
야시장	편의점
인력시장	할인매장
:	:

손익계산서	statement of profit and loss
손해	loss
손해배상	compensation for damage
수금	① collection of money ② bill collecting
수당	allowance
수도요금	water rate
수산시장	fish market
수수료	commission
수신	receipt of credit
수업료	tuition
수요	demand
수요자	consumer
수익	① earnings ② gains ③ profit
수익금	① earnings ② gains ③ proceeds
수익률	① earning rate ② rate of yield
수입 (輸入)	import
수입 (收入)	income
수입품	① imports ② imported goods
수출	export
수출품	① export goods ② exports
수표	check
술집	① tavern ② pub
슈퍼마켓	supermarket
시가	current price
시세 (時勢)	① market price ② current price
시세 (市勢)	balanced degree of demand and supply
시장	market
시장가격	market price
시장경제	market economy
시장성	marketability
시장점유율	market occupancy rate
시장조사	market research
식비	food expenses
신상품	new items
신용금고	credit union
신용보증기금	trust guarantee funds

신용장	letter of credit
신용카드	credit card
신장개업	opening of a business
신탁	trust
실명제	real name system (when one opens a bank account)
실물경제	spot economy
실물자산	real property
실업	unemployment
실업가	businessman
실용품	utility goods
싸구려	① cheap article ② bargain
싸다	to be cheap
쌀집	rice store
쌈지돈	pocket money
쓰다	to spend
아끼다	① to spare ② to economize ③ to be frugal
알뜰살뜰	thrift and frugal
알뜰하다	① to be thrifty ② to be frugal
액면가	nominal value
액수	① sum ② amount
야시장	night market
약국	pharmacy
약세	weak
약속어음	promissory note
어음	note
에누리	overcharge
엔	yen
엔화	yen currency
엥겔계수	Engel's coefficient
여비	traveling expenses
여신	extending credit
여유있다	to be able to afford
여행자수표	traveller's check (TC)
연금	pension

연말정산	year-end tax adjustment
연봉	annual salary
연체료	arrearage charge
엽전	brass coin
영수증	receipt
영업	business
영업사원	salesman
영치금	provisional holding money
예금	deposit
예금주	depositor
예금하다	to deposit
예비비	preparation fee
예산	budget
예치	deposit
오르다	① to rise ② to go up
오름세	upward tendency
완구점	toy store
완성품	finished product
완제품	finished goods
외상	① credit ② trust
외채	foreign loan
외판원	salesman
외화	foreign currency
외환	foreign exchange
외환보유고	foreign exchange holdings
외환시장	foreign exchange market
요금	① charge ② rate ③ fee
용돈	① pocket money ② allowance
원	won
원가	cost price
원금	principal
원료시장	raw material market
원화	won currency
월급	monthly salary
월부	monthly installment
월부금	monthly payment

위문품	care package
위약금	① damages for breach of contract ② penalty
위자료	solatium
위조지폐	counterfeit money
위탁금	① money in trust ② trust money
위탁판매	commission sale
유가증권	① securities ② stocks and bonds
유로화	making currencies into euro
유료	① charged ② pay
유사품	imitation
유통	circulation
유통경로	distribution channels
유통구조	distribution structure
유통마진	distribution interests
유통망	distribution net
융자	financing
은행	bank
은행가	banker
은행대출	bank loan
은행원	bank clerk
은행장	president of a bank
은화	silver coin
음식점	restaurant
이월금	balance brought forward
이윤	① interests ② profits ③ returns
이익	① profit ② gain
이익금	① profit ② gains
이자	interest
이자율	interest rate
이체	transfer
인건비	labor cost
인력시장	labor market
인상	raise
인하	reduction
일당	daily wages

일시불	payment in a lump sum
임금	① wages ② pay
임대	lease
임대가	rental fee
임대가격	rental price
임대료	rent
임대하다	to lease
임차료	rent
입금	① money received ② credit
입찰	bidding
자금	funds
자기앞수표	① cashier's check ② certified check
자동차세	automobile tax
자매품	① companion item ② sister goods
자본	① capital ② fund
자본가	capitalist
자본금	capital
자비	one's own expense (charge)
자선바자회	charity bazaar
자영업	independent enterprise
잔고	① balance ② remainder
잔금	balance
잔돈	① change ② small money
잔액	① balance ② remainder
잡비	general expenses
잡화상	general store
잡화점	general store
장	market
장려금	bounty
장보기	grocery shopping
장부	account book
장사	① trade ② business
장사꾼	① merchant ② dealer
장사하다	to sell
장터	market place
장학금	scholarship

재고	in stock
재고정리	clearance sale
재고품	goods in stock
재래시장	① traditional market ② outdoor market ③ open air market
재무	financial affairs
재물	property
재벌	① business conglomerate ② chaebol
재산	① property ② assets
재산세	property tax
재정	① public finance ② finances
재화	① money and property ② wealth
재활용	recycled
재활용품	recycled product
저가	low price
저금	savings
저금하다	to save money
저당	mortgage
저렴하다	① to be cheap ② to be low in price
저축	savings
저축하다	to save money
적금	installment savings
적금하다	to save in installments
적립	① reserving ② accumulation
적립금	accumulated money
적자	deficit
전기요금	electricity bill
전당포	pawnshop
전화요금	① telephone bill ② telephone charges
전화카드	telephone card
절약하다	to economize
점원	clerk
점포	shop
정가	fixed price
정기예금	time deposit
정기적금	fixed period installment savings

정미소	rice mill
정액권	prepaid card
정찰가	tag price
정찰제	fixed price system
정치자금	money for political activities
제과점	bakery
제조하다	① to manufacture ② to produce
제품	product
제품시장	manufactured goods market
조달하다	to supply
조세	taxes
조폐공사	Mint Bureau
조합	association
조합원	union member
종합금융사	finance corporation
주가	price of a stock
주가지수	price index of stocks
주거비	housing expenses
주급	weekly payment
주머닛돈	pocket money
주문	order
주문생산	ordered production
주문서	order form
주문하다	to order
주민세	resident tax
주식	stocks
주식시장	stock market
주유소	gas station
주주	stockholder
주화	① minting ② coinage ③ coin
중간상인	broker
중개업자	① broker ② agent
중개인	agent
중계무역	transit trade
중고품	① used article ② secondhand goods
중소기업	small and medium sized enterprise

중앙시장	central market
중앙은행	central bank
중저가	low price
증권	① securities ② bond
증권거래소	bond market
증권시장	① bond market ② securities market
증권회사	securities company
증여세	donation tax
지급	payment
지급하다	① to provide ② to pay
지대	rent on land
지물포	paper goods store
지방세	local taxes
지불	payment
지불하다	to pay
지역시장	regional market
지점	branch
지출	expenditure
지출하다	① to expend ② to disburse
지폐	① paper money ② bill
직거래	direct transaction
직불	direct payment
직불카드	direct payment card
직원	① employee ② personnel
직장	place of work
직접세	direct tax
진열대	display rack
진열장	① showcase ② display rack
진열하다	to display
진품 (眞品)	genuine article
진품 (珍品)	rare article
집세	house rent
징수	collection
징수하다	① to collect ② to impose ③ to charge
차용	① borrowing ② loan
차용증서	I.O.U.

차용하다	① to borrow ② to loan ③ to get a loan
찬조금	contribution
찻집	① teahouse ② coffee shop
창구	window
채권 (債券)	① debenture ② bond
채권 (債權)	credit
채권자	creditor
채무	debt
채무자	debtor
책방	bookstore
청과시장	vegetable and fruit market
청구	① demand ② claim
청구서	bill
청구하다	① to ask for ② to claim
체납하다	① to fail to pay ② to default
최상품	article of the best quality
축의금	congratulation money
출금	payment
출납	① receipts and disbursements ② revenue and expenditure
출자	① investment ② financing
치다	① to put a price on ② to value
치르다	to pay off
카드	card
카드빚	credit card debt
토산품	local produce
토지세	land tax
통상	① commerce ② trade
통신판매	mail order
통장	bankbook
통화	currency
통화팽창	currency inflation
투기	① speculative trading ② land speculation
투기꾼	speculator
투자	investment

투자가	investor
투자신탁	investment trust
투자자	investor
특별소비세	special consumption tax
특산물	special product
판돈	stakes
판매	sale
판매고	sale price
판매액	sale amount
판매업자	sales agent
판매원	salesperson
판매하다	to sell
팔다	to sell
편의점	convenience store
평가절상	① revaluation ② appreciation
평가절하	devaluation
폐업 (閉業)	closing business
폐업 (廢業)	discontinuance of business
폐점	① closing a shop ② closing down business
폐품	① waste material ② junk
포상금	① prize money ② reward money
폭리	excessive profits
푼돈	small sum of money
품목	item
품삯	① wages ② pay
품질	quality
품질관리	quality control
품팔이	① day laborer ② wage-worker
풍부하다	to be abundant
풍족하다	to be affluent
학비	school expenses
학용품	school supplies
한국은행	Bank of Korea
할부	installment payment
할부금	allotment

화폐	
현금	수표
금화	가계수표
동전	여행자수표
은화	자기앞수표
주화	:
지폐	
:	

할인	discount
할인가	discount off the price
할인매장	discount store
할인품목	discount item
할증료	① extra charge ② premium
합계	① sum total ② total amount
허비하다	to be wasteful
현금	cash
현금지급기	cash machine
현금카드	cash card
현찰	cash
호황	① prosperous condition ② prosperity
화폐	① money ② currency
화폐가치	value of money
화훼시장	flowering plant market
환불 (換拂)	exchange
환불 (還拂)	refund
환산	① conversion ② change
환율	exchange rate
환전	exchange
회비	membership fee
회사	company
회수금	money collected
회장	chairperson
후불	deferred payment
휴업	① suspension of business ② closure
흑자	① profit ② in the black
흥정	① dealings ② bargain
흥정하다	to make a deal

30 직업
Employment

This chapter contains lexical entries related to employment, particularly jobs Korean people typically have.

가사	housekeeping
가수	singer
가정부	housemaid
간부사원	executive (of a company)
간호사	nurse
감독	director
갑판장	boatswain
강사	lecturer
개그맨	gagman
건달	① idler ② lazybones
건설업	building business
건설업자	builder
건축가	architect
건축기사	① architect ② bum
검사	prosecutor
결근	absence
경력사원	experienced employee
경비원	guard
경영인	manager
경영진	management team
경영하다	to manage
고용	employment

고용인	employee
고용주	employer
고용하다	to employ
고참	senior
공무원	government official
공업	industry
공예가	craftsman
공원	factory worker
공장장	factory manager
과학자	scientist
관리자	manager
관리직	managerial job
광대	crown
광부	miner
광업	mining
교수	professor
교원	teaching staff
교황	pope
구두닦이	shoeshine
구성작가	drama (show) writer
국무총리	prime minister
국회의원	congressman
군수	magistrate of a county
군인	soldier
극작가	play writer
근로자	worker
근무	① duty ② work
근무자	① men in service ② men on duty ③ workers
근무지	① one's place of employment ② one's place of business ③ one's place of work
근무처	① one's place of employment ② one's place of business ③ one's office ④ one's place of work
근무하다	① to work ② to serve

금융업	financial business
급여	① pay ② salary
기관사	[locomotive] engineer
기관장	① chief engineer ② head of an organ
기능사	technician
기사 (技師)	professional
기사 (技士)	engineer
기사 (棋士)	chess professional
기술사	technician
기술직	technical job
기업인	man of enterprise
기자	journalist
기장	plane captain
낙농업	dairy farming
노동	labor
노동자	laborer
농부	farmer
농업	agriculture
능력	ability
능률	efficiency
당직	day (night) duty
대기업	① conglomerate ② large enterprise
대통령	president (country)
대표	① representative ② leader
대표이사	president (company)
도예가	potter
도지사	governor
동시통역사	simultaneous interpreter
동장	chief of 동 (sub-district)
디자이너	designer
리포터	reporter
마담	bar hostess
마술사	magician
막노동	① rough work ② hard manual labor
막노동꾼	hard manual laborer
막일	rough work

맞벌이	husband and wife both working
매니저	manager
면장	chief of 면 (township)
면접	interview
명예퇴직	honorary retirement
모델	model
목사	① minister ② pastor
무당	female shaman
무용가	dancer
무직	① joblessness ② unemployment
미용사	hairdresser
미장이	plasterer
반장	① foreman ② head of a neighborhood association
반주자	accompanist
발령	giving an official order
발명가	inventor
방송인	broadcaster
방송작가	script writer
배관공	plumber
배달부	deliverer
배달원	deliveryman
배우	① actor ② actress
백수	unemployed
법관	① judge ② justice
변리사	patent attorney
변호사	lawyer
보너스	bonus
보모	nurse
보일러공	boilermaker
복무하다	to serve
복부인	real estate lady
복직하다	to resume office
본봉	① regular salary ② base pay
본업	one's regular work (occupation)
봉급	① salary ② pay

봉급쟁이	salary man
부랑자	bum
부업	part-time job
부하직원	subordinate personnel
분장사	make-up artist
비구니	Buddhist nun
비행사	pilot
사냥꾼	hunter
사무직	office job
사업	business
사업가	businessman
사업자	businessman
사원	employee of a company
사장	president of a company
사직서	letter of resignation
사진사	photographer
사표	letter of resignation
산업	industry
상사	superior officer
상업	commerce
상여금	bonus
상인	merchant
생계수단	means of living
생산직	production job
생업	① vocation ② calling ③ occupation
서비스업	service business
서예가	calligrapher
선교사	missionary
선생님	teacher
선원	sailer
선임	predecessor
선장	captain (of a ship)
설계사	designer
성악가	vocalist
세무사	licensed tax accountant
소매치기	pickpocket

소설가	novelist
수공업	handicraft
수녀	nun
수당	① allowance ② compensation
수산업	fishery
수상	prime minister
수습	apprenticeship probation
수위	janitor
수의사	① veterinary surgeon ② veterinarian
수필가	essayist
숙직	① night duty ② night watch
스님	Buddhist priest
스튜어디스	① stewardess ② flight attendant
승려	Buddhist priest
승무원	crew
승진	promotion
시말서	written explanation
시인	poet
시장	mayor
신문배달원	newspaper boy
신문판매원	news vendor
신부	Catholic priest
신입사원	new employee
신참	newcomer
실업	unemployment
실업가	man of enterprise
실업자	unemployed person
실직	losing one's job
실직자	one who has lost his job
실직하다	to lose one's job
아나운서	announcer
안무가	choreographer
야근	night duty
약사	pharmacist
양돈업	hog raising industry
양봉업	① beekeeping industry ② apiculture

양식업	cultivating (breeding) industry
양잠업	sericulture
어부	fisherman
어업	fishery
업무	business
연구원	researcher
연극인	theatrical people
연금	pension
연기자	① actor ② performer
연봉	annual salary
연예인	public entertainer
연주가	performer (of an instrument)
연출자	① producer ② director
영양사	① dietitian ② nutritionist
영업	business
영업사원	① salesman ② salesperson
영업직	sales position
영업하다	to sell
영화감독	film director
영화인	cinema person
예술가	artist
예언가	① prophet ② predictor
외교관	diplomat
외근	outside duty (service)
외판원	salesman
요리사	cook
용역	service
우편배달부	postman
운동선수	athlete
운영하다	to manage
운전기사	driver
원예업	horticulture
월급	monthly salary
월급쟁이	salary man
은행원	bank employee
은행장	president of a bank

음악가	musician
읍장	chief of 읍 (town)
의사	(medical) doctor
이력서	resume
이발사	barber
이사	① director ② trustee
인사발령	placement of personnel
인사이동	personnel changes
인쇄업	printing business
인턴사원	intern
일	① work ② job
일거리	① piece of work ② job ③ work to do
일꾼	worker
일당	① daily allowance ② daily pay
일자리	① employment ② job
일직	day duty
일터	workplace
일하다	to work
임금	① wages ② pay
임시직	temporary position
임시직원	temporary staff
임업	forestry
임원	executive
입사하다	to join a company
자영업	self-management business
자유기고가	freelancer
작가	writer
작곡가	composer
작사가	song writer
잡역부	handy man
장관	minister
장사꾼	① merchant ② trader ③ dealer
장의사	undertaker
재단사	cutter
재봉사	tailer
전기기사	electric engineer

전도사	evangelist
전문가	specialist
전문직	professional job
전업	professional job or business
점원	clerk
점쟁이	① fortuneteller ② psychic
접대부	barmaid
정년퇴임	retirement
정원사	gardener
제조업	manufacturing industry
조각가	sculptor
조리사	cook
조종사	pilot
조퇴	leaving work (office, school) early
종사하다	to work on
종업원	employee
좌천	relegation
좌천되다	to be relegated
주급	weekly pay
주방장	chef
주부	housewife
주차관리인	parking manager
중소기업	small and medium sized enterprise
중장비기사	heavy equipment engineer
지관	geomancer
지배인	manager
지휘관	commander
지휘자	conductor
직공	① workman ② worker ③ factory hand
직급	level of one's position
직업	① occupation ② job
직업관	vocational view
직업병	occupational disease
직업윤리	vocational ethics
직업의식	professionalism
직원	staff

직업

법
- 검사
- 법관
- 변호사
- 판사
- :

교육·연구
- 교수
- 교사
- 교원
- 강사
- 선생님
- 연구원
- 학자
- :

생산
- 근로자
- 노동자
- 광부
- 농부
- 어부
- :

믿음과 종교
- 목사
- 수녀
- 스님
- 신부
- 예언가
- 전도사
- 점쟁이
- :

병과 치료
- 간병인
- 간호사
- 약사
- 의사
- 한의사
- :

공직
- 공무원
- 국무총리
- 국회의원
- 군수
- 대통령
- 도지사
- 동장
- 면장
- 외교관
- 읍장
- 장관
- 총재
- :

서비스
- 가정부
- 구두닦이
- 미용사
- 신문배달원
- 요리사
- 은행원
- 이발사
- 장의사
- 접대부
- 정원사
- 파출부
- 피부관리사
- :

건설·수리
- 건설업자
- 건축가
- 미장이
- 배관공
- 보일러공
- 설계사
- 전기기사
- 중장비기사
- :

관리
- 감독
- 경비원
- 관리자
- 기업인
- 수위
- 실업가
- 회사원
- :

언론·출판
- 기자
- 리포터
- 방송인
- 방송작가
- 아나운서
- 프로듀서
- 편집인
- :

교통
- 기관사
- 기관장
- 비행사
- 선원
- 선장
- 스튜어디스
- 승무원
- 운전기사
- 조종사
- 주차관리인
- :

연예
- 가수
- 개그맨
- 모델
- 배우
- 연기자
- 연예인
- 연출가
- 영화감독
- 코메디언
- 탤런트
- :

예술
- 공예가
- 도예가
- 디자이너
- 무용가
- 사진사
- 소설가
- 시인
- 연주가
- 작곡가
- 작가
- 조각가
- 화가
- :

직장	workplace
직장동료	co-worker
직장상사	superior official in one's workplace
직장생활	work life
직장인	employee
직종	① type of occupation
	② occupational category
창녀	① prostitute ② whore
창업	① inauguration of an enterprise

	② foundation ③ establishment
채용하다	to employ
책임자	person in charge
청소부 (淸掃婦)	cleaning woman
청소부 (淸掃夫)	cleaning man
총리	prime minister
총재	president (political party)
촬영기사	cameraman
축산업	stock farming
출근	attendance
출장	business trip
출판인	publisher
취직	getting a job
취직하다	to find employment
카메라맨	cameraman
코미디언	comedian
태업	work slow-down strike
탤런트	talent
통신사	news agency
통장	head of 통 (town section)
퇴근	leaving one's office
퇴직	retirement
퇴직금	retirement allowance
퇴직하다	to retire
퇴출	walking out
파업	strike
파출부	cleaning person
판매직	sales job
판사	judge
편집인	editor
폐업	discontinuance of business
프로듀서	producer
피부관리사	beautician
하청업자	subcontractor
학생	student
학자	scholar

한의사	doctor of oriental medicine
항해사	mate
해고하다	to fire
행정직	administrative job
화가	painter
환경미화원	① street cleaner ② garbage collector
회계사	accountant
회사	company
회사원	employee of a company
회장	① president ② chairperson
효율	efficiency
후임	① successor ② replacement
휴가	leave
휴업	① business suspension ② closure ③ shutdown
휴직	temporary retirement from office

31 산업
Industry

> This chapter contains lexical entries connected to farming, fishery, rearing, mining, and other industries and services which are considered important in Korea.

가공업	processing industry
가공하다	① to process ② to manufacture
가내수공업	cottage industry
가동하다	① to operate ② to work ③ to run
가래	① shovel ② spade
가마	① kiln ② stove ③ oven
가마니	straw bag
가을걷이	autumn reaping
가축	① livestock ② cattle
간척지	① reclaimed land ② innings
갈다	① to plow ② to cultivate
갈퀴	bamboo rake
개간지	cultivated land
개간하다	to bring under cultivation
개량종	improved variety (breed)
개량하다	① to improve ② to reform
개펄	mud flat
개항	opening of a port
갱	① pit ② shaft
갱도	① mine ② tunnel ③ pit
거두다	① to harvest ② to reap

거름	① manure ② fertilizer
거름주다	to fertilize
건어물	① dried fish ② stock-fish
건조시키다	① to dry up ② to desiccate
건조장	drying place
경운기	cultivator
경작지	cultivated land
경작하다	① to cultivate ② to farm
경지	arable land
경지정리	readjustment of arable land
고기잡이	① fishing ② fishery
고기잡이철	fishing season
고깃배	fishing boat
고랑	① furrow ② trough
고랭지	highlands
고랭지농업	highlands agriculture
곡괭이	① pick ② pickaxe
곡물	① grain ② cereals ③ corn
곡식	① grain ② cereals
공구	① tool ② implement
공단	industrial complex
공산품	industrial products
공업	industry
공업국	industrial nation
공업단지	industrial complex
공업도시	industrial city
공업연료	industrial fuel
공업용	industrial use
공업용수	industrial water
공업지대	① industrial area ② manufacturing district
공업화	industrialization
공원	① factory worker ② factory hand ③ machine operator
공장	factory
공장장	① factory manager ② supervisor

	③ plant-superintendent
공장주	factory owner
공장폐수	① industrial sewage ② industrial waste ③ factory waste
공정	① amount of work ② process of work
과수원	orchard
과일	fruit
관개	irrigation
관개수	water for irrigation
관광업	tourism
광맥	① mineral vein ② deposit
광물	mineral
광물질	mineral
광부	① miner ② digger
광산	mine
광산업	mine business
광산촌	miners' town
광석	① ore ② crystal ③ mineral
광업	① mining ② mining industry
괭이	① pick ② pickaxe
교배하다	① to hybridize ② to crossbreed ③ to mate
구리	copper
구유	① manger ② trough
귀금속	precious metals
귀농	returning to the farm
귀농현상	returning to the farm phenomenon
그루갈이	① double-cropping ② two crops a year
그물	① net ② netting
극장	① theater ② playhouse
근해어업	inshore fishery
금	gold
금강석	diamond
금광	① gold ore ② gold mine
금괴	① lump (nugget) of gold ② gold bar ③ gold ingot

광물

구리
금강석
납
동
망간
사금
석영
석유
석탄
석회석
천연가스
원유
철
흑연
:

보석

금
다이아몬드
백금
수정
옥
은
자수정
:

금속	metal
금융업	① financial sector ② banking business
기간산업	① basic industries ② key industries
기계	machine
기계공업	machine industry
기계화	mechanization
기관	① boiler ② steam generator
기르다	① to rear ② to raise
기름지다	to be fertile
기반시설	① basic equipment ② basic facilities
기술	technology
김매기	weeding
김매다	to weed
꼴	① pasture ② fodder ③ forage
낙농업	dairy farming
낙농업자	dairy farmer
낚다	① to fish ② to catch
낚시	fishing hook
낚시꾼	① fisherman ② angler
낚시질	fishing
낚시터	fishing place
낚시하다	to fish
낚싯대	fishing rod
낚싯밥	bait
낚싯줄	fishing line
난류	warm current
낟가리	stack of grain stalks
납	lead
낫	sickle
노	① oar ② paddle
노다지	① bonanza ② rich vein ③ rich mine ② killing
노동자	① laborer ② worker ③ labor
노래방	karaoke room
논	① rice field ② rice paddy
논두렁	levee of a rice paddy

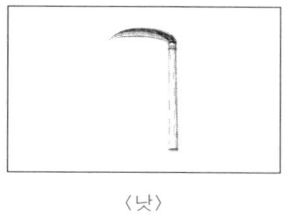

〈낫〉

논둑	raised border between individual rice fields
농가	farmhouse
농경지	farmland
농기계	farm machines
농기구	farm machines and implements
농림부	Ministry of Agriculture and Forestry
농민	farmer
농번기	① farmer's busy season ② farming season
농부	farmer
농사	① agriculture ② farming ③ agricultural affairs
농사꾼	farmer
농사일	farm work
농사짓다	① to engage in farming ② to do farming
농사철	farming season
농산물	① agricultural products ② farm produce
농악	① farmers' instrumental music ② farm music
농악놀이	farm music play
농약	agricultural chemicals
농어민	farmers and fishermen
농어촌	fishing and farming villages
농업	① agriculture ② farming ③ agricultural industry
농업국	agricultural (farming) country
농업용수	agricultural (farming) water
농업협동조합	agricultural cooperative
농원	① farm ② plantation
농작물	① crops ② farm produce
농장	① farm ② plantation
농지	① farmland ② agricultural land ③ cropland

농지정리	adjustment of farmland
농촌	① farm village ② rural community
농촌진흥청	Rural Development Administration
농축산물	farm (agricultural) and stock raising products
농토	① farmland ② agricultural land ③ cropland
농한기	leisure season for farmers
농협	agricultural cooperative
누에치기	① sericulture ② silk-farming
다방	coffee shop
다이아몬드	diamond
단란주점	① bar ② pub
닻	anchor
대량생산	mass production
대어	big fish
대여료	rental fee
덕장	place for drying fish
도살	① slaughter ② butchery
도살장	slaughterhouse
도정	hulling
도정하다	to hull
동	copper
두둑	① bank ② ridge ③ path between fields
두엄	① compost ② barnyard manure
마구간	① stable ② barn
마지기	Korean measure of farmland (approximately 5 acres)
만선	full boat
만화방	comic book store
망	net
망간	manganese
매다	to weed out
멍석	straw mat
모내기	① rice-planting ② rice transplantation

모이	feed
모자리	rice-planting spot
모종	① seedling ② seedbed
모종삽	garden trowel
모텔	motel
모판	seedbed
목공소	woodworking shop
목동	① herdboy ② shepherd boy
목욕관리사	public bathhouse worker
목욕탕	public bathhouse
목장	① stock farm ② ranch ③ pasture
목초지	① pasture ② meadow
목축	① stock-farming ② cattle breeding
목축업	stock farming
못자리	rice seedbed
묘목	① sapling ② seedling
물고기	fish
물꼬	① sluice ② irrigation gate
물대기	① irrigation ② water supply
물질	(woman diver's) diving
미끼	bait
미용사	① hairdresser ② hairstylist
미용업	beauty business
미장원	hair salon
민물낚시	freshwater fishing
바다낚시	sea fishing
반도체	semiconductor
발동기	① motor ② engine
방목	grazing
방아	① mill ② mortar
방앗간	① rice mill ② mill
밭	① vegetable patch ② dry field
밭농사	dry-field farming
밭두렁	ridge in a dry field
밭둑	ridge in a dry field
배달부	delivery person

배달원	delivery person
백금	① white gold ② platinum
뱃사람	① sailor ② seaman
번식	① breeding ② reproduction ③ propagation ④ multiplication
벼농사	rice farming
볍씨	seed rice
병충해	damage by blight and noxious insects
보석	① jewel ② precious stone ③ gem
봉사료	service charge
부치다	① to cultivate ② to farm ③ to grow
분업	① division of labor ② specialization
불량율	percentage of defectives
불량품	① inferior goods ② defective goods
비닐하우스	plastic hothouse
비디오가게	video shop
비디오방	video room
비료	① fertilizer ② manure ③ compost
비옥하다	to be fertile
빨래방	laundromat
사금	① gold dust ② alluvial gold
사료	① livestock feed ② provender ③ fodder
사용료	rental fee
사육장	① farm ② feedlot
사육지	breeding ground
사육하다	① to breed ② to raise
산업	industry
산업구조	industrial structure
산업용	industrial use
산업재해	industrial disaster
산업전선	industrial front
산업정책	industrial policy
산업체	manufacturing company
산업혁명	industrial revolution
산업화	industrialization

살충제	insecticide
삼모작	three crops a year
삼차산업	tertiary industry
삽	① shovel ② spade ③ scoop
새마을운동	Saemaul Movement
생산	production
생산물	product
생산하다	to produce
서비스	service
서비스업	① service industry ② service work
석영	quartz
석유	oil
석탄	coal
석회석	limestone
설비	① equipment ② production
섬	bushel
세차장	car wash
세탁소	dry cleaners
세탁업	laundry business
소극장	① small theater ② small playhouse
소작농	① tenant farmer ② tenantry
소작인	① tenant farmer ② tenantry
솎다	① to thin out ② to weed out
수고비	① labor fee ② wages
수공업	① manual industry ② handicraft
수리공	repairman
수매하다	① to purchase ② to buy
수산물	marine products
수산시장	fish market
수산업	fisheries
수산업협동조합	fisheries cooperative
수정	① crystal ② crystallized quartz
수족관	aquarium
수협	fisheries cooperative
수확	① harvest ② harvesting ③ crop ④ yield

수확량	① the yield ② the crop
수확하다	to harvest
숙련공	① skilled worker ② master mechanic
숙박료	① lodging fee ② accomodation fee
숙박업	① lodging business ② hotel industry
식당	restraunt
신토불이	Things from one's own land are the best (Lit., Body and land are one).
알곡	grain
야근	① night duty ② night shift
양계업	① poultry farming ② chicken raising
양계장	poultry farm
양곡	① grain ② cereals ③ corn
양돈업	hog raising industry
양봉	① beekeeping ② apiculture
양봉업	① beekeeping industry ② apiculture
양수기	water pump
양식	① raising ② culture ③ cultivation
양식업	cultivating industry
양식장	① nursery ② farm
양식하다	① to rear ② to raise ③ to breed
양어장	fish farm
양잠업	sericulture
양치기	shepherd
어류	fishes
어망	fishing net
어민	fishermen
어부	① fisherman ② fisher
어선	fishing boat
어시장	fish market
어업	① fishery ② fishing industry
어장	fishing ground
어촌	fishing village
어패류	fish and shells
어항 (魚缸)	fish basin
어항 (漁港)	fishing port

어휘	
어획	① fishery ② fishing
어획고	① haul of fish ② fish catch
어획량	① haul of fish ② fish catch
어획물	① haul ② catch
얼레	① reel ② spool
여공	① factory girl ② female worker
여관	inn
여물	① chaff ② fodder ③ forage
여인숙	① inn ② lodging house
여행사	travel agency
여행업	① travel business ② travel industry
염전	① salt farm ② salt pans
영농	farming
영농법	① agricultural management ② farming method
영농인	farming person
영농후계자	agricultural management successor
옥	jade
옥토	fertile soil
외식산업	restaurant industry
외양간	① stable ② barn
요식업	restaurant business
용역	service
우리	① cage ② hutch ③ coop
우시장	cow market
운송업	① transport industry ② transport business
운수업	transportation business
원료	① raw material ② materials
원산지	① place of origin ② home
원양어선	deep-sea fishing vessel
원양어업	deep-sea fishery
원유	crude petroleum (oil)
원자재	raw material
월척	big fish
유가공	milk processing

유기농업	organic agriculture
유전	oil field
유흥가	entertainment section
유흥업	entertainment industry
유흥업소	entertaining place
육가공	meat processing
은	silver
은광	silver mine
은행	bank
음식점	restaurant
이농	giving up farming
이농현상	giving up farming phenomenon
이랑	① furrow ② ridge in a field
이모작	double-cropping
이발사	① barber ② haircutter
이발소	barbershop
이삭	① ear ② head ③ spike
이삿짐센터	moving company
이앙기	rice-planting season
이앙법	method of rice-planting
이용료	price of haircut
이용업	hairstyling business
이차산업	secondary industry
인건비	labor cost
인력	manpower
일구다	to bring under cultivation
일차산업	primary industry
임산물	forestry products
임업	forestry
자동화	automation
자수정	amethyst
자영농	self-management farming
자작농	one's own farming
자재	materials
작두	straw cutter
작물	① crops ② products

작살	fish spear
작업	work
작업대	work stand
작업반장	foreman
작업복	working clothes
작업시간	working hours
작업실	work room
작업장	workplace
작황	① harvest ② crop ③ yield
잠업	① sericulture ② sericultural industry
잡곡	cereals
잡다	① to catch ② to hold
장치	① equipment ② installation
재배	① cultivation ② growing ③ raising
재배하다	① to cultivate ② to grow
쟁기	plow
전동기	① electric motor ② motor
접대부	① waitress ② barmaid
정	① chisel ② gad
정미소	rice mill
정미하다	to polish rice
제작	① production ② work
제작하다	① to produce ② to work
조립	① constructing ② fabrication
조립하다	① to construct ② to fabricate
조업	① operation ② work
종묘	① seeds and saplings ② seedlings
종자	seed
중장비	heavy equipment
지게	A-frame carrier
지주	① landlord ② landowner ③ landholder
지하자원	underground resources
직공	① workman ② worker ③ factory hand
쭉정이	empty heads of grain
찌	① float ② quill

채굴하다	to mine
채소	① vegetables ② greens
채취하다	① to pick ② to gather
척박하다	to be arid
천연가스	natural gas
천연수지	natural resin
철	iron
철광	iron mine
철야작업	overnight work
청소부 (淸掃夫)	cleaning man
청소부 (淸掃婦)	cleaning woman
청소업	janitorial services
청소원	janitor
청정해역	① uncontaminated waters ② clean sea area
추곡	purchase of autumn grain
추곡수매	government purchase of autumn grain
추수	① harvesting ② harvest
추수하다	to harvest
축사	① cattle shed ② barn
축산업	① livestock industry ② stockbreeding
축산업자	livestock raiser
축산업협동조합	National Livestock Cooperative
축산폐수	livestock sewage
축협	National Livestock Cooperative
치다	① to raise ② to breed
치어	① fry ② fingerling
캐다	① to dig up ② to grub ③ to unearth
콤바인	① combine ② combine harvester
타작	① thresh ② thrashing
타작하다	① to thresh ② to thrash
탄광	coal mine
탄광촌	coal miners' town
탄전	coalfield
탈곡	threshing
탈곡기	① thresher ② thrasher

〈타작〉

탈곡하다	① to thresh ② to thrash
태업	work slow-down strike
택배	delivery to one's home
텃밭	vegetable garden
토양	soil
토질	fertility of soil
퇴비	① compost ② barnyard manure
트랙터	tractor
특송	fast delivery
특용작물	crop for a special use
파업	① strike ② walkout
파출부	cleaning lady
패류	shellfish
평	3.954 sq. yds.
평년작	normal crop
폐광	abandoned mine
폐업	discontinuance of business
포경선	① whaling ship ② whaler
품앗이	exchange of work
품종	① kind ② sort
품종개량	improvement of breed
품질검사	quality inspection
풍년	① year of abundance ② fruitful year
풍작	① good harvest ② heavy crop
한류	cold current
합성수지	① synthetic resins ② plastics
해녀	woman diver
해류	① ocean current ② current
해산물	① maritime products ② sea products
해역	① waters ② sea area
해조류	seafoods
해초	seaweed
허수아비	scarecrow
호미	weeding hoe
호텔	hotel
화학처리	chemical treatment

〈트랙터〉

〈호미〉

분류	농업	수산업	축산업	광업	공업	서비스업
유형	고랭지농업 밭농사 벼농사 유기농업 :	근해어업 민물낚시 바다낚시 원양어업 양식업 :	낙농업 목축업 양계업 양돈업	광산업 :	가공업 가내수공업 기계공업 수공업	관광업 금융업 미용업 세탁업 숙박업 여행업 요식업 운송업 운수업 유흥업 청소업 :
사람	농민 농부 농사꾼 영농후계자	뱃사람 어민 어부 :	낙농업자 목동	광부 :	공장장 공원 수리공 직공	미용사 배달원 접대부 청소부 파출부 :
재료	관개수 농약 거름 비료 퇴비 :	낚싯밥 미끼	꼴 모이 사료 여물		공업용수 원료 원자재 자재	
도구	가래 갈퀴 경운기 낫 양수기 이앙기 쟁기 탈곡기	고깃배 그물 낚시 낚싯대 낚싯줄 어망 어선 원양어선 포경선	구유 작두	곡괭이 정 :	공구 기계 기관 기반시설 발동기 전동기 중장비	
생산물	곡물 곡식 과일 농산물 양곡 작물 잡곡 채소 특용작물	건어물 수산물 어류 어획물 패류 해산물 해조류	고기 계란 우유	광석 광물 금속 보석 지하자원	공산품 기계	
장소	과수원 경작지 논 농경지 농토 밭 :	건조장 덕장 양식장 양어장 어장	마구간 목장 목초지 사육장 양계장 외양간 축사	광산 갱 금광 유전 은광 철광 탄광 탄전	공단 공장 공업지대 :	
행위	경작하다 농사짓다	낚다 물질하다	기르다 사육하다 치다 :	캐다 채굴하다 채취하다	생산하다 제작하다 조립하다	

〈산업〉

화훼단지	flowers and plants complex
환경미화원	① street sweeper ② sanitary engineer
황금어장	① rich fishing ground ② golden fishing ground
훑다	① to thrash ② to thresh
휴업	① suspension of business ② shutdown
흉년	① bad year ② lean year ③ year of bad harvest
흉작	① bad harvest ② scanty harvest ③ failure of crops
흑연	① black lead ② graphite

32 연료와 에너지
Fuel and Energy

> This chapter contains names for various fuels and energies and other related words.

가마	iron pot
가스	gas
가스레인지	gas oven
가열하다	to heat
건전지	battery
경유	① light oil ② gasoline
고체연료	solid fuel
굴뚝	chimney
기름	oil
끄다	① to turn off ② to put out
난로	stove
난방	heating
누전	electric leak(age)
도시가스	city gas
동력	electric power
등유	① kerosene ② lamp oil
때다	① to burn ② to make a fire
땔감	① fuel ② firewood
땔나무	firewood
라이터	lighter
물	water
물레방아	water mill

바람	wind
발전	generation of electric power
발전기	① dynamo ② (power) generator
방사능	radio-active
방사능물질	radio-active material
방전	electric discharge
방화	setting or extinguishing fire
방화사	fire prevention sand
방화수	fire prevention water
버너	burner
번개탄	lighting coal
벽난로	fireplace
변압기	transformer
보일러	boiler
부뚜막	kitchen range (traditional)
부싯돌	firestone
부탄가스	butane
불	fire
불길	① flame ② ablaze
불꽃	① flame ② blaze
불똥	sparks (of fire)
석유	petroleum
석유곤로	oilstove
석탄	coal
성냥	match
성냥개비	matchstick
소화	extinguishing fire
소화기	fire extinguisher
소화전	hydrant
수력	hydropower
숯	charcoal
아궁이	fuel (fire) hole
알코올	alcohol
알코올램프	alcohol lamp
에너지	energy
엘엔지	LNG (Liquified Natural Gas)

〈숯〉

엘피지		LPG (Liquefied Petroleum Gas)
연료		fuel
연소		combustion
연탄		briquet
열		heat
열량		calorie
열효율		heat efficiency
온돌		ondol, hot floor
원동력		① motive power ② generation power ③ driving force
원유		crude oil
원자력		① atomic energy ② nuclear power
원자로		nuclear reactor
자기력		self-magnetic power
자력		magnetic power
장작		① firewood ② wood (for fuel)
장작개비		firewood stick
전기		electricity
전동기		① electromotor ② electric motor
전력		electric power
전류		electric flow
전열기		electric heater
전지		① electric cell ② battery
점화		① ignition ② lighting
조개탄		oval (egg-shaped) briquette
주유소		gas station
지피다		① to make (a fire) ② to put (fuel on fire) ③ to feed (a fire with coal)
진화		extinguishing

연료	고체	고체연료, 석탄, 숯, 연탄, 장작, 조개탄, 톱밥 …
	기체	가스, 도시가스, 천연가스 …
	액화	부탄가스, 엘엔지 (LNG), 엘피지 (LPG) …
	액체	경유, 등유, 석유, 알코올, 원유, 휘발유 …
에너지	자연에너지	바람, 수력, 풍력, 태양에너지 …
	인공에너지	건전지, 방사능, 원자력, 전기, 핵 …

질화로	① earthenware (charcoal) brazier
	② earthenware fire pot
천연가스	natural gas
충전기	charger
충전하다	to charge
켜다	① to light ② to turn (switch) on
	③ to kindle
태양에너지	solar energy
태양열	solar heat
태양열발전	solar heat electric power
태양열주택	solar heat house
톱밥	sawdust
폭발물	explosive
폭발하다	to explode
풍력	① velocity (force) of the wind
	② wind force
풍로	① portable cooking stove
	② handy charcoal stove
풍차	windmill
피우다	to make a fire
합선	short circuit
핵	nuclear
화덕	① (charcoal) brazier ② oven
화력	① thermal power ② heating power
화로	① (charcoal) brazier ② fire pot
화재	① fire ② conflagration
휘발유	gasoline
힘	power

33 도로와 교통
Traffic and Transportation

This chapter lists various means of transportation, in addition to words involved in transportation (e.g., streets, shipping ways) and traffic laws.

가로등	① street lamp ② road lamp
가로수	roadside tree
가마	① palanquin ② sedan chair
가속	acceleration
갑판	deck
갑판장	boatswain
개항	opening a port
객실	guest room
거마비	transportation allowance
거북선	turtle-shaped ship
건널목	① crosswalk ② railroad crossing
견인차	tow truck
경비선	guardship
경비행기	private plane
경찰차	police car
고가도로	overpass
고깃배	fishing boat
고속도로	① freeway ② highway
고속버스	express bus
공항	airport
과속	speeding
관광버스	tour bus

〈거북선〉

관제탑	control tower
교통	traffic
교통경찰	traffic police
교통법규	traffic regulations
교통비	transportation expenses
교통사고	traffic accident
교통수단	transportation means
교통지도	traffic map
교통질서	traffic order
교통체증	traffic jam
구급차	ambulance
구명보트	lifeboat
구명정	lifeboat
국도	local highway
국민차	national automobile (public automobile)
군용기	military plane
기관사	engineer
기관차	① engine ② locomotive engine
기장	(plane) captain
기차	train
기차표	train ticket
나루	dock

길	하늘	항로	
	물	선로, 수로, 항로, 해로 …	
	땅	고가도로, 고속도로, 국도, 도로, 신작로, 일방통행로, 전용도로, 지하도, 징검다리, 육교, 차도, 찻길, 철길, 철도, 활주로, 횡단보도 …	
교통수단	하늘	경비행기, 군용기, 기구, 비행기, 수송기, 여객기, 우주선, 전투기, 제트기, 항공기, 헬리콥터 …	
	물	거북선, 경비선, 고깃배, 구명보트, 나룻배, 낚싯배, 돛단배, 뗏목, 바지선, 배, 보트, 선박, 어선, 여객선, 연락선, 요트, 운반선, 원양어선, 유람선, 유조선, 잠수함, 통통배, 함정, 항공모함, 화물선 …	
	땅	전통	가마, 수레 …
		현대	견인차, 경찰차, 고속버스, 관광버스, 구급차, 국민차, 기관차, 기차, 마을버스, 버스, 불자동차, 소방차, 승용차, 시내버스, 시외버스, 열차, 오토바이, 우등고속버스, 유조차, 자가용, 자동차, 자전거, 장갑차, 장의차, 전차, 전철, 좌석버스, 지게차, 직행버스, 차, 택시, 통근버스, 통학버스, 트럭, 화물열차, 화물차 …

나루터	dock
나룻배	ferry
나침반	compass
낙하산	parachute
낚싯배	fishing boat
날다	to fly
내리다	to get off
노	oar
닻	anchor
대합실	waiting room
도로	① road ② way ③ street
도로교통	street traffic
돛단배	sailboat
등대	lighthouse
뗏목	raft
마을버스	neighborhood bus
마중	going out to meet (greet)
막히다	to be jammed
바지선	barge
바퀴	wheel
반도	peninsula
배	ship
배웅	seeing off
배표	ticket
버스	bus
버스카드	bus pass
병목현상	bottle-neck phenomenon
보트	boat
부기장	assistant captain
부두	wharf
불법주차	illegal parking
불자동차	fire engine (truck)
비행기	airplane
비행기표	plane ticket
비행사	pilot
비행장	airport

비행하다	to fly
사고	accident
사공	① boatman ② ferryman
상선	merchant ship
선로	railroad track
선박	vessel
선실	passenger's quarters
선장	(ship) captain
선착장	harbor
선창	pier
소방차	fire engine
속도	speed
속도측정기	speedometer
속력	velocity
수레	① wagon ② cart ③ carriage
수로	waterway
수송기	transport plane
스튜어드	① steward ② flight attendant
스튜어디스	① stewardess ② flight attendant
승객	passenger
승무원	crew
승선하다	to go on board
승조원	crew
승차	getting on
승차권	ticket
승하차	getting on and off
시내버스	local bus
시외버스	inter-city bus
신작로	newly constructed road
신호등	traffic light
안전	safety
안전띠	seatbelt
어선	fishing boat
여객	passenger
여객기	passenger plane
여객선	passenger ship

역	station
연락선	ferry
열차	train
예매하다	① to book ② to reserve
오르다	to get on
오토바이	motorcycle
왕래하다	to come and go
요트	yacht
우등고속버스	deluxe express bus
우주선	spaceship
우회전	right turn
운반	transport
운반비	transporting expenses
운반선	transport ship
운송	transport by vehicle
운송비	transporting expenses
운송수단	means of transport
운수업	① transport industry ② transportation business
운임	① fare ② freight
운전	driving
운전기사	driver
운전면허시험	driving test
운전면허증	driver's license
운전사	driver
운전석	driver's seat
운전하다	to drive
운항하다	to operate
운행	operation
원양어선	deep-sea fishing boat
유람선	excursion steamer
유조선	oiler
유조차	tank car
육교	overpass
음주운전	drinking and driving
음주측정기	breathalyzer

이동	movement
이륙하다	to take off
인도	sidewalk
일방통행로	one-way
임시열차	temporary train
자가용	car
자동차	automobile
자동차등록증	registration book
자전거	bicycle
잠수함	submarine
장갑차	armored car
장의차	hearse
전용도로	road for exclusive use
전용차로	driveway for exclusive use
전용차선	traffic lane for exclusive use
전진	forward movement
전차	streetcar
전철	subway
전철표	subway ticket
전투기	combat aircraft
접촉사고	car crash
정거장	station
정류장	bus stop
정비사	mechanic
정액권	① transit pass ② pre-paid card/ticket
제트기	jet plane
좌석버스	deluxe bus
좌회전	left turn
주차	parking
주차관리인	parking attendant
주차권	parking ticket
주차기	ticket machine
주차장	parking lot
지게차	① A-frame (carrier) ② coolie rack
지도	map
지하도	① underpass ② underground passage

지하철	subway
직진	going straight
직행버스	① non-stop bus ② direct bus
질서	order
징검다리	stepping stones
차	wheeled vehicle
차도	road
차량	vehicle
차로	road
차선	traffic lane
차표	ticket
착륙하다	to land
찻길	① roadway ② driveway
철길	railroad
철도	railroad
초보운전	novice driving
출항하다	to start on a voyage
키	① rudder ② helm ③ (steering) wheel
타다	① to ride ② to take ③ to get on
탑승	boarding
탑승구	boarding entrance
탑승수속	boarding procedure
택시	taxi
터널	tunnel
터미널	terminal station
통근버스	commuter bus
통통배	motorboat
통학버스	school bus
통행료	toll fee
트럭	truck
패스	pass
하선하다	to get off the ship
하차	getting off
한국도로공사	Korea Highway Corporation
할증료	① extra charge ② surcharge
함정	① war (naval) vessels ② warships

〈징검다리〉

항공권	plane ticket
항공기	aeroplane
항공모함	aircraft carrier
항공사	airline
항공운항	airline service
항구	① port ② harbor
항로	airway
항로	sea route
항만	harbor
항해사	① mate ② navigation officer
항해지도	navigating map
항해하다	to navigate
해로	sea route
해상교통	marine traffic
헬리콥터	helicopter
혼잡통행료	rush hour traffic toll
혼잡하다	① to be crowed ② to be congested
화물	freight
화물선	cargo ship
화물열차	freight train
화물차	freight truck
활주로	① runway ② airstrip
회수권	booklet of tickets
회전	rotation
횡단보도	crosswalk
후진	backward movement

34 자연현상
Natural Phenomena

This chapter contains words for natural phenomena such as clouds, mist, rain, snow, and wind, as well as more general words for weather and climate.

가랑비	drizzle
가물가물	glimmeringly
가물다	to be arid
가뭄	drought
가시광선	visible ray
가을바람	autumn wind
강바람	river wind
강수	precipitation
강수량	(the amount of) precipitation
강우	rainfall
강우량	(the amount of) rainfall
강추위	① dry cold weather ② (cold) snap
개다	① to clear up ② to become clear
건조주의보	dry weather alert
건조하다	to be dry
걷히다	① to be lifted ② to clear off
겨우살이	winter clothes and food
겨울바람	winter wind
계절풍	① monsoon ② periodic wind
고기압	high (atmospheric) pressure
고드름	icicle
광풍	gale

구름	clouds
궂다	① to be cloudy ② to be rainy ③ to be snowy
그림자	shadow
그치다	① to stop ② to subside
기상	weather conditions
기상관측	meteorological observation
기상청	weather bureau
기상통보	① weather news ② weather report
기상특보	special weather report
기압	air pressure
기압계	barometer
기온	temperature
기후	climate
꽃샘추위	① cold snap in the flowering season ② spring cold
끼다	① to be foggy ② to cloud up
나쁘다	to be bad
난류	warm current
날	day
날씨	weather
남풍	south wind
낮다	to be low
내려가다	① to go down ② to fall ③ to drop
내리다	to fall (snow, dew etc.)
냉기	① cold ② chill
노을	glow in the sky
녹다	to melt
높다	to be high
높새바람	foehn
눅눅하다	to be damp

보통

{매우 춥다} {춥다} {쌀쌀하다} {시원하다}　　{따뜻하다}　{덥다}　{무덥다}

〈기온〉

눈	snow
눈꽃	snowflake
눈발	① streaks of snow ② snow flakes
눈보라	snowstorm
눈사람	snowman
눈사태	① snowslide ② avalanche
눈송이	snowflake
눈싸움	① snowball fight ② snowballing
눈썰매	① sleigh ② sled
늦더위	late summer heat
단비	① welcome rain ② long-waited rain
달그림자	moon shadow
달무리	halo around the moon
달빛	moon light
대기오염	air pollution
대설경보	heavy snow alarm
대설주의보	heavy snow warning
대자연	Mother Nature
더위	heat
덜덜	shiveringly
덥다	to be hot
동풍	east wind
두둥실	buoyantly
두리둥실	buoyantly
둥실둥실	buoyantly
따갑다	① to be stinging ② to be prickly
따뜻하다	to be warm
땅거미	① dusk ② twilight ③ nightfall
땡볕	scorching sun
떨다	to shiver
뜨겁다	to be hot
뜨다	to rise
마파람	south wind
만년설	perpetual snow
맑다	to be clear
맺히다	to form (dew)

먹구름	black cloud
먼지	dust
멎다	to stop
무더위	sultriness
무덥다	to be sultry
무역풍	monsoon
무지개	rainbow
물결	wave
물안개	wet fog
뭉게구름	cumulus
뭉게뭉게	like clouds
미지근하다	to be tepid
밀물	inflow of the tide
바람	wind
발령하다	to issue
밤안개	night fog
백야	white night
백엽상	instrument shelter
번개	lightning
번쩍	flashing
범람하다	to flood
벼락	① thunderbolt ② thunderstroke
볕	① sunshine ② sunlight
보슬보슬	drizzling
보슬비	drizzle
봄바람	spring wind
부슬부슬	drizzling
북풍	north wind
불다	to blow
불볕	burning hot
불쾌지수	discomfort index
비	rain
비구름	rain cloud
비바람	① wind and rain ② rainy wind
빗방울	raindrop
빗줄기	streak of rain

뿌옇다	to be foggy
산들바람	gentle breeze
산들산들	gently
산바람	mountain wind
산불	forest (wood) fire
산사태	① landslide ② land slip ③ landfall
산성비	acid rain
살랑살랑	rustlingly
삼복더위	midsummer heat
삼한사온	cycle of three cold days and four warm days
상온	high temperature
새다	to dawn
새벽안개	morning fog
새털구름	cirrus
샛바람	north wind
생태계	ecosystem
서늘하다	to be cool
서리	frost
서풍	west wind
설경	① snow scene ② snowscape
섭씨	Celsius
성에	frost
소나기	shower
소나기구름	shower cloud
솔솔	gently
수심	depth of water
수온	water temperature
수은주	mercurial column
수질	quality of water
수질오염	water pollution
수해	flood damage
습기	① moisture ② humidity ③ damp
습도	humidity
습도계	hygrometer
습하다	to be humid

시리다	to be (painfully) cold
시원하다	① to be cool ② to be refreshing
실바람	light breeze
실온	① temperature of a room ② room temperature
싸늘하다	to be chilly
싸락눈	① snow grains ② snow pellets
쌓이다	to pile up
쌩쌩	① whistlingly ② whizzingly
썰렁하다	to be chilly
썰물	ebb tide
아지랑이	haze
악천후	① foul (bad) weather ② rough (inclement) weather
안개	fog
안개경보	fog alarm
안개구름	stratus
안개비	misty rain
안개주의보	fog warning
양떼구름	cumulus
얼다	to freeze
얼음	ice
엄동설한	rigorous (hard) winter
여우비	sprinkling rain while the sun shines
열	fever
열기	① hot air ② heat
열대야	tropical night
열리다	to form (icicle)
영상	above zero
영하	below zero
오다	to fall (rain)
오들오들	shiveringly
오로라	aurora
오존주의보	ozone warning report
온기	warmth
온난전선	warm front

〈용암〉

온도	temperature
온도계	thermometer
올라가다	① to go up ② to rise (temperature)
용암	lava
우량계	① hyetometer ② rain gauge
우레	thunder
우르르쾅쾅	rumblingly
우박	hail
운량	cloudiness
월식	lunar eclipse
월출	moonrise
육풍	land breeze
이글이글	burning aglow
이슬	dew
이슬비	① drizzle ② fine rain ③ mist
일기	weather
일기예보	weather forecast
일다	① to rise ② to get up ③ to spring up
일몰	sunset
일사병	sunstroke
일식	solar eclipse
일출	sunrise
자연	nature
자연과학	natural science
자연법칙	natural law
자연보호	conservation of nature
자연숭배	nature worship
자연식품	natural foods
자연재해	natural disaster
자연주의	naturalism
자연파괴	destruction of nature

보통

←──── {차다/ 차갑다} {싸늘하다} {시원하다}　　{미지근하다} {따뜻하다} {따끈하다} {뜨겁다} ────→

〈온도〉

자연현상	natural phenomena
자연환경	natural environment
자외선	ultraviolet rays
자욱하다	to be dense, foggy, thick
잔잔하다	① to be still ② to be quiet ③ to be calm ④ to be tranquil
장마	rainy season
장마전선	seasonal rainy front
저기압	low (atmospheric) pressure
저물다	to grow dark
적설량	snowfall
적외선	infrared rays
젖다	to get wet
제설기	snowplow
제설작업	snow removing work
조류	① tide ② (tidal) current
좋다	to be good
주룩주룩	sprinklingly
지다$_1$	to come to be
지다$_2$	to set (sun, moon, etc.)
지열	earth heat
지진	earthquake
지진대	earthquake zone (belt)

☀	☁	☂	☃	≈				≡
해	구름	비	눈	바람				안개
				방향	세기	계절	불어오는 곳	
태양	먹구름 뭉게구름 비구름 새털구름 안개구름 양떼구름 :	가랑비 단비 보슬비 산성비 소나기 안개비 여우비 이슬비 폭우 폭풍우 호우 :	만년설 싸락눈 진눈깨비 첫눈 폭설 함박눈 :	남풍 높새바람 동풍 마파람 무역풍 북풍 샛바람 서풍 편동풍 편서풍 하늬바람 :	광풍 산들바람 실바람 태풍 황소바람 회오리바람 :	가을바람 겨울바람 계절풍 봄바람 :	강바람 산바람 육풍 해풍 :	물안개 밤안개 새벽안개 :

지질	geology
직사광선	direct ray of light
진눈깨비	sleet
쨍쨍	① glaringly ② blazingly ③ brightly
찌다	to be sultry
차갑다	① to be cold ② to be chilly
차다	to be cold
천둥	thunder
천재지변	① natural disaster (calamity) ② disturbances of the elements
첫눈	first snowfall of the season
청명하다	① to be clear and bright ② to be fair
체감온도	perceived temperature
촉촉하다	to be moist
총총	starry
추위	cold
축축하다	to be damp
출렁거리다	① to surge ② to roll ③ to wave
춥다	to be cold
치다	① to strike ② to roll
태양광선	solar ray
태양열	solar heat
태풍	typhoon
통풍	ventilation
파도	① waves ② billows ③ surges
펄펄	flutteringly
펑펑	thickly
편동풍	prevailing easterlies
편서풍	prevailing westerlies
폐수	waste water
폭설	very heavy snowfall
폭우	heavy rain
폭풍	storm
폭풍경보	storm alarm
폭풍우	rainstorm
폭풍주의보	storm warning

푹푹	sultrily
풍속	wind velocity
풍속계	① anemometer ② wind gauge
풍향	① direction of the wind
	② wind direction
풍향계	anemoscope
피어오르다	to curl up
하늬바람	west wind
한기	① cold ② chill
한더위	midsummer heat
한들한들	swayingly
한랭전선	cold front
한류	cold current
한파	cold wave (snap)
한파주의보	cold wave (snap) warning report
함박눈	large snowflakes
해	sun
해돋이	sunrise
해류	① ocean current ② current
해오름	sunrise (younger generation use)
해일	tidal (storm) wave
해제하다	① to call off ② to clear
해풍	sea wind
햇볕	sunshine
햇빛	sunlight
햇살	sunray
호우	heavy rain
호우경보	heavy rain alarm
호우주의보	heavy rain warning
홍수	flood
화산	volcano
화산대	volcanic zone
화씨	Fahrenheit
화창하다	① to be sunny ② to be bright
환경오염	environmental pollution
환기	ventilation

환절기	turning of seasons
활화산	active volcano
황사현상	sandy dust phenomena
황소바람	heavy draft
황혼	① dusk ② (evening) twilight
회오리바람	whirlwind
휴화산	dormant volcano
흐르다	to flow
흐리다	to be cloudy

35 동물
Animals

This chapter contains names of various animals, from miniscule insects to fish, amphibia, reptiles, birds and mammals. It also contains words for animals' organs and cries as well as those related to the growth and development of animals.

가리비	scallop
가물치	snakehead mullet
가슴	① breast ② chest ③ bosom
가오리	stingray
가자미	flatfish
가재	crawfish
가죽	① skin ② leather
가축	① livestock ② cattle
갈기	mane
갈매기	sea gull
갈치	cutlass fish
강아지	puppy
개	dog
개구리	frog
개굴개굴	croaking
개똥벌레	firefly
개미	ant
거머리	leech
거미	spider
거미줄	spider web
거북이	turtle

거위	goose
게	crab
겨울잠	hibernation
계란	egg
고니	swan
고둥	spiral shellfish
고등어	mackerel
고래	whale
고릴라	gorilla
고슴도치	① hedgehog ② porcupine
고양이	cat
고치	cocoon
곤충	insect
곤충류	insects
골뱅이	snail
곰	bear
곰팡이	mold
공룡	dinosaur
공작	peacock
관상어	aquarium fish
광어	flatfish
괴물	monster
교미하다	① to mate ② to copulate ③ to couple
구관조	mynah
구구구	① cluck-cluck (chicken) ② coo-coo (pigeon)
구더기	maggot
구렁이	yellowish brown serpent
굴	oyster
귀	ear
귀뚜라미	cricket
귀뚤귀뚤	chirr
균	① germ ② fungus
금붕어	goldfish
기러기	wild goose
기르다	to breed

기린	giraffe
기생충	① parasite ② parasitic insect
기생하다	to be parasitic
길들이다	① to tame ② to domesticate
깃털	feather
까나리	launce
까마귀	① crow ② raven
까악까악	caw-caw
까치	Korean magpie
까투리	hen pheasant
깡충깡충	hop
껍데기	① shell ② skin
껍질	skin
꼬꼬댁	cackle-cackle
꼬끼오	cock-a-doodle-doo
꼬리	tail
꼴뚜기	small squid
꽁무니	rear end
꽁지	bird tail
꽁치	① mackerel ② pike
꽃게	blue crab
꽃사슴	deer (spotted)
꽥꽥	quack-quack
꾀꼬리	oriole
꾀꼴꾀꼴	oriole warbling
꿀꿀	oink-oink
꿀벌	honey-bee
꿩	pheasant
끼룩끼룩	honking
나방	moth
나비	butterfly
낙지	common octopus
낙타	camel
난생	oviparity
날개	wing
날다	to fly

〈까마귀〉

〈까치〉

〈까투리〉

동물	내는 소리
개	멍멍
갈매기·기러기	끼룩끼룩
개구리	개굴개굴
고양이	야옹
까마귀	까악까악
꾀꼬리	꾀꼴꾀꼴
닭	꼬끼오·꼬꼬댁
돼지	꿀꿀
말	히잉
맹꽁이	맹꽁맹꽁
병아리	삐악삐악
부엉이	부엉부엉
비둘기	구구구
뻐꾸기	뻐꾹뻐꾹
사자·호랑이	어흥
소·염소	음매
오리·거위	꽥꽥
쥐	찍찍
참새	짹짹

날짐승	① fowls ② birds
날파리	① ephemera ② dayfly
낳다	① to breed ② to lay (egg)
냉혈동물	cold-blooded animal
너구리	raccoon
넙치	flounder
노루	roe deer
노새	mule
누에	silkworm
눈	eye
늑대	wolf
다람쥐	squirrel
다랑어	① tunny ② tuna
다리	leg
다슬기	marsh snail
달걀	egg
달팽이	snail
닭	chicken
담비	marten
담수어	fresh water fish
당나귀	donkey
대가리	head
대구	codfish
대장균	colon bacillus
대하	prawn
대합	clam
더듬이	① feeler ② tentacle ③ antenna
도루묵	sandfish
도마뱀	lizard
도미	① sea bream ② porgy
독	poison
독거미	tarantula
독사	viper
독수리	eagle
돌고래	dolphin
동면	hibernation

동물	animal
동물원	zoo
돼지	pig
두견새	cuckoo
두꺼비	toad
두더지	mole
두루미	crane
뒤뚱뒤뚱	totteringly
들소	① wild ox ② bison
들쥐	field mouse
들짐승	wild animal
등	back
등에	horsefly
딱따구리	woodpecker
떼	① group ② herd ③ flock
똥개	mongrel
똥파리	bottle-green fly
마디	joint
마리	counter for animals
말	horse
말미잘	sea anemone
망둥이	goby
망아지	pony
매	falcon
매미	cicada
맴맴	droning of a cicada
맹꽁맹꽁	croaking
맹꽁이	small round frog
맹수	fierce beast
머리	head
먹이	① food ② prey
먹이사슬	food chain
먹이연쇄	food chain
멍게	ascidian
멍멍	bowwow
메기	catfish

〈두루미〉

〈매미〉

〈메뚜기〉

〈무당벌레〉

메뚜기	grasshopper
메추라기	quail
메추리	quail
메추리알	quail egg
멧돼지	wild boar
면양	sheep
멸치	anchovy
명태	walleye pollack
모기	mosquito
모래주머니	gizzard
모이	feed
몸통	① trunk ② body
무당벌레	ladybug
무리	group (herd, flock, swarm, etc.)
무척추동물	nonvertebrate animal
문어	octopus
물갈퀴	webfoot
물개	fur seal
물고기	fish
물방개	diving beetle
물소	buffalo
미꾸라지	loach
미생물	microorganism
민물고기	freshwater fish
민어	① sciaenoid fish ② croaker
바구미	weevil
바다물고기	sea fish
바다사자	Steller's sea lion
바다표범	seal
바닷가재	lobster
바이러스	virus
바퀴벌레	cockroach
박쥐	bat
반달곰	Asian bear
반디	firefly
발굽	hoof

방아깨비	Oriental longheaded locust
방울뱀	rattlesnake
배다	to bear
백곰	white bear
백로	snowy heron
백사	white snake
백조	swan
뱀	snake
뱀장어	eel
뱁새	chickadee
번데기	pupa
번식하다	① to breed ② to multiply
벌	bee
벌레	① bug ② insect
범	tiger
베짱이	① katydid ② long-horned grasshopper
벼룩	flea
변온동물	cold-blooded animal
변태	metamorphosis
병아리	chick
병어	pomfret
보호색	protective color
복어	blowfish
봉황	Chinese phoenix
부레	bladder
부리	beak
부엉부엉	tu-whit tu-whoo
부엉이	owl
부화	hatch
북극곰	polar bear
불가사리	starfish
불사조	phoenix
붕어	crucian carp
붕장어	① conger (eel) ② sea eel
비늘	scale

〈백로〉

〈봉황〉

비둘기	pigeon
빈대	bedbug
뻐꾸기	cuckoo
뻐꾹뻐꾹	cuckoo
뼈	bone
뿔	horn
삐악삐악	cheep-cheep
사마귀	wart
사슴	deer
사육장	breeding place
사육하다	① to breed ② to rear
사자	lion
산돼지	wild boar
산양	antelope
산짐승	mountain animal
산토끼	① hare ② wild rabbit
산호	coral
살	flesh
살모사	viper
삵쾡이	wildcat
삼치	Spanish mackerel
상어	shark
새	bird
새끼	young (animal)
새끼치다	to breed
새알	bird's egg
새우	① shrimp ② prawn
생쥐	house mouse
생태계	ecosystem
서식지	habitat
서식하다	to inhabit
성게	① sea chestnut ② sea urchin
성충	imago
세균	bacterium
세포	cell
소	① cattle ② cow ③ bull

〈성게〉

소금쟁이	water strider
소라	① conch ② top shell
소쩍새	Chinese scops owl
솔개	hawk
송사리	① cyprinodont ② top minnow
송아지	calf
송어	trout
송충이	worm
수놈	male (animal)
수달	otter
수컷	male (animal)
순록	reindeer
순종	full blood
숭어	grey mullet
실뱀	small thin snake
십자매	finch
쌀벌레	rice weevil
쓰르라미	clear-toned (green-colored) cicada
아가미	gill
악어	① crocodile ② alligator
알	egg
암놈	female (animal)
암컷	female (animal)
애벌레	larva
애완동물	pet
앵무새	parrot
야생동물	wild animal
야수	beast
야옹	meow
약육강식	① survival of the fittest ② law of the jungle
양	sheep
양서류	amphibia
어류	fishes
어미	mother
어패류	fishes and shellfishes

어미	새끼
개	강아지
개구리	올챙이
닭	병아리
말	망아지
소	송아지

어흥	roar
얼굴	face
얼룩말	zebra
여왕벌	queen bee
여우	fox
여치	katydid
연어	salmon
열대어	tropical fish
염소	goat
옆줄	lateral line
오리	duck
오리알	duck's egg
오징어	① cuttlefish ② squid
올빼미	owl
올챙이	tadpole
용	dragon
우렁쉥이	ascidian
우렁이	mud (pond) snail
우리	① cage ② hutch ③ coop
울다	① to sing ② to chirp
원숭이	monkey
원앙	mandarin duck
유산균	lactobacillus
유인원	anthropoid
유전	heredity
유전자	gene
유충	larva
육식동물	carnivorous animal
은어	sweetfish
음매	moo
이	lice
이리	wolf
이무기	anaconda
인어	mermaid
일벌	worker bee
임연수어	Atka mackerel

〈원앙〉

입	mouth
잉꼬	① parakeet ② macaw
잉어	carp
자라	terrapin
자연법칙	natural law
잠자리	dragon-fly
잡식동물	polyphagous animal
잡종	hybrid
장구벌레	wiggler
장끼	cock pheasant
장수하늘소	long-horned beetle
장어	eel
재두루미	white-naped (-necked) crane
적자생존	survival of the fittest
전복	① ear shell ② omer
정어리	sardine
젖소	dairy cattle
제비	swallow
조개	shellfish
조기	yellow corbina
조랑말	pony
조류	birds
족제비	weasel
좀벌레	bookworm
종달새	skylark
주둥이	① muzzle ② mouth
쥐	mouse
쥐치	filefish
지네	centipede
지느러미	fin
지렁이	earthworm
지저귀다	① to chirp ② to twitter ③ to warble
진돗개	dog indigenous to Jindo region
진드기	tick
진딧물	① plant louse ② aphid ③ aphis
진화론	evolution theory

〈장끼〉

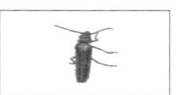

〈장수하늘소〉

〈제비〉

416 Animals

짐승	① animal ② beast
집게벌레	earwig
집짐승	domestic animal
짖다	① to bark ② to cry
짹짹	chirping
쪼다	to peck
찌르레기	gray starling
찌르르르	chirping
찍찍	squeak
참새	sparrow
참치	tuna
창조론	creation theory
척추	① backbone ② spine
척추동물	vertebrate animal
천연기념물	natural monument
천적	natural enemy
철새	migratory bird
청개구리	tree frog
청둥오리	wild duck
청어	herring
초식동물	herbivorous animal
칠면조	turkey
침팬지	chimpanzee
카나리아	canary
코	nose
코끼리	elephant
코뿔소	rhinoceros
크낙새	Korean redheaded woodpecker
키우다	① to breed ② to rear
타조	ostrich
타조알	ostrich's egg
탄생	① birth ② nativity
태생	viviparity
태어나다	to be born
털	① hair ② fur
텃새	① native bird ② home bird

〈참새〉

토끼	rabbit
토종	indigenous animal
파리	fly
파충류	reptilia
패류	shellfish
펭귄	penguin
포유류	mammals
표범	leopard
풍뎅이	gold beetle
풍산개	dog indigenous to Poongsan region
플랑크톤	plankton
피라미	minnow
하늘소	long-horned beetle
하루살이	① dayfly ② ephemera
하마	hippopotamus
학	crane
항온동물	constant-temperature animal
해달	sea otter
해마₁	sea horse
해마₂	walrus
해삼	① trepang ② sea cucumber
해오라기	night heron
해충	harmful insect
해파리	jellyfish
핵	nucleus
향어	Israeli carp

〈풍뎅이〉

포유류	개, 고래, 고양이, 곰, 기린, 낙타, 노루, 돼지, 말, 물개, 박쥐, 사슴, 사자, 소, 양, 여우, 염소, 원숭이, 쥐, 토끼, 하마 …
조류	갈매기, 거위, 공작, 까마귀, 까치, 꿩, 닭, 독수리, 두견새, 두루미, 매, 메추라기, 백로, 백조, 부엉이, 뻐꾸기, 오리, 참새, 학 …
파충류	거북이, 구렁이, 뱀, 악어, 자라 …
양서류	개구리, 두꺼비, 맹꽁이 …
어류	가자미, 갈치, 고등어, 금붕어, 멸치, 붕어, 삼치, 상어, 송어, 숭어, 연어, 임연수어, 장어, 잉어, 조기, 청어, 향어 …
조개류	가리비, 골뱅이, 굴, 대합, 소라, 우렁이, 전복, 조개, 홍합 …
곤충류	개똥벌레, 개미, 거미, 귀뚜라미, 벌, 나방, 나비, 등에, 매미, 메뚜기, 모기, 무당벌레, 방아깨비, 베짱이, 사마귀, 송충이, 잠자리, 풍뎅이, 하루살이 …

혀	tongue
호랑이	tiger
홍어	skate
홍학	flamingo
홍합	hard-shelled mussel
황새	stork
황소	bull
황소개구리	bullfrog
훨훨	fluttering
흑염소	black goat
히잉	① hee-haw ② bray

36 식물
Plants

This chapter lists the names of various plants from the lower plants and fungi to weeds, flowers, trees, fruits, vegetables, and marine algae (plants).

가꾸다	① to grow ② to cultivate
가로수	roadside tree
가시	thorn
가시나무	thorn tree
가지₁	branch
가지₂	eggplant
갈대	reed
갈래꽃	fork flower
감	persimmon
감나무	persimmon tree
감자	potato
갓	leaf mustard
강낭콩	kidney bean
강아지풀	foxtail
개나리	forsythia
개화기	time of blooming
개화하다	to bloom
거두다	① to harvest ② to reap
거름	fertilizer
거목	great (large, big) tree
고구마	sweet potato
고목	old tree

〈개나리〉

고비	flowering fern
고사리	fiddlehead
고추	pepper
곡식	① cereals ② grain
과수원	orchard
과실	fruit
과일	fruit
광합성	photosynthesis
구기자	Chinese matrimony vine
국화 (菊花)	chrysanthemum
국화 (國花)	national flower
귀리	oat
귤	tangerine
그루	stump
근대	chard
금귤	kumquat
금잔화	marigold
기장	Chinese millet
김	laver
깨	sesame
깻잎	sesame leaf
꺾다	to break
껍데기	skin
껍질	① skin ② bark ③ husk
꼭지	① stem ② stalk

과일나무

감나무
대추나무
밤나무
배나무
복숭아나무
사과나무
살구나무
앵두나무
잣나무
호두나무
:

식물	풀	갈대, 강아지풀, 억새, 엉겅퀴, 잔디, 질경이, 토끼풀 …
	꽃	개나리, 국화, 장미, 나팔꽃, 매화, 맨드라미, 모란, 목련, 무궁화, 민들레, 백일홍, 백합, 봉숭아, 수국, 수선화, 안개꽃, 유채꽃, 진달래, 채송화, 철쭉, 할미꽃, 해바라기 …
	나무	느티나무, 단풍나무, 대나무, 떡갈나무, 미루나무, 버드나무, 사철나무, 소나무, 오동나무, 은행나무, 전나무, 참나무, 행운목, 회양목 …
	과일	감, 귤, 다래, 딸기, 머루, 모과, 배, 버찌, 복숭아, 사과, 살구, 수박, 앵두, 자두, 참외, 포도 …
	곡식	강낭콩, 귀리, 기장, 녹두, 메밀, 모, 밀, 벼, 보리, 수수, 완두콩, 조, 콩, 팥 …
	채소	가지, 감자, 고구마, 고추, 깻잎, 당근, 도라지, 무, 미나리, 배추, 상추, 시금치, 쑥갓, 양파, 오이, 파, 호박 …
	해초	김, 다시마, 미역, 톳, 파래 …

꽃	flower
꽃가루	pollen
꽃꽂이	flower arrangement
꽃눈	flower bud
꽃다발	① bunch of flowers ② bouquet
꽃대	flower stalk
꽃받침	calyx
꽃봉오리	bud
꽃씨	flower seed
꽃향기	flower fragrance
꽈리	ground cherry
나리	lily
나무	tree
나물	vegetable
나뭇가지	branch
나뭇잎	leaf
나이테	annual ring
나팔꽃	morning glory
낙엽	fallen leaves
난초	orchid
냉이	shepherd's purse
넝쿨	vine
노송나무	① Japanese cypress ② white cedar
녹두	① mung bean ② green gram
논	① paddy field ② rice field
눈	bud
느타리버섯	agaric mushroom
느티나무	zelkova tree
늦—	late
다년생	perennial
다래	Actinidia arguta fruit
다시마	kelp
닥나무	paper mulberry
단	bundle
단풍	red leaves
단풍나무	maple tree

〈나팔꽃〉

달래	wild rocambole
달리아	dahlia
담배	tabacco
담쟁이덩굴	ivy
당근	carrot
대나무	bamboo
대마	hemp
대추나무	jujube tree
더덕	Codonopsis lanceolata
덩굴	① bine ② vine ③ runner
도라지	Chinese bellflower root
도라지꽃	Chinese bellflower
독버섯	① poisonous mushroom ② toadstool
돋다	① to grow ② to bud ③ to sprout
돋아나다	① to grow ② to bud ③ to sprout
돌나물	① sedum ② stonecrop
동백꽃	camellia
동백나무	camellia tree
두엄	① compost ② barnyard manure
두해살이	biannual crops
들국화	wild chrysanthemum
들꽃	wild flower
등꽃	wisteria flower
등나무	wisteria tree
따다	① to pick ② to pluck
딸기	strawberry
떡갈나무	oak tree
떡잎	① seed leaf ② cotyledon
떨기	① bunch ② cluster
라일락	lilac
레몬	lemon
마늘	garlic
망고	mango
매실	Japanese apricot
매화	plum flower
맨드라미	cockscomb

맺다	to bear
머루	wild grapes
메밀	buckwheat
메밀꽃	buckwheat flower
멜론	melon
모	① rice sprouts ② rice seedling
모과	quince
모란	peony
모종	① seedling ② sapling ③ young plant
목단	(tree) peony
목련	magnolia
목이버섯	Kind of mushroom
목화	cotton flower
묘목	① seedling ② sapling
무	① radish ② turnip
무궁화	rose of Sharon
무화과	fig
물망초	forget-me-not
물이끼	bog moss
미나리	① dropwort ② Japanese parsley
미루나무	popular tree
미역	brown seaweed
민들레	dandelion
밀	wheat
밀감	① mandarin orange ② tangerine
밀림	jungle
바닷말	① seaweed ② marine algae
밤나무	chestnut tree
밭	① field ② patch
배	pear
배나무	pear tree
배추	Chinese cabbage
백일홍	crape myrtle
백합	lily
버드나무	willow tree
버섯	mushroom

〈목련〉

〈무궁화〉

버섯
송이버섯
느타리버섯
목이버섯
양송이
팽이버섯
싸리버섯
영지버섯
독버섯
:

버찌	cherry
벚꽃	cherry blossom
벚나무	cherry tree
베다	① to cut ② to reap
벼	rice
보리	barley
복숭아	peach
복숭아나무	peach tree
봉선화	① balsam ② touch-me-not
부추	leek
분꽃	① marvel-of-Peru ② four-o'clock ③ afternoon lady
분재	planting in a pot
붓꽃	① iris ② blue flag
비닐하우스	plastic hothouse
비름	amaranth
뽕나무	mulberry tree
뿌리	root
사과	apple
사과나무	apple tree
사철나무	spindle tree
산딸기	wild berries
산림	forest on a mountain
산삼	mountain ginseng
살구	apricot
살구나무	apricot tree
살다	to live
삼나무	① cedar ② cryptomeria
삼림	① forest ② wood
상록수	evergreen tree
상추	lettuce
생강	ginger
생화	natural (fresh) flower
석류	pomegranate
선인장	cactus
설익다	to get half-ripen

〈분재〉

〈붓꽃〉

소나무	pine tree
속	inside
솎다	to thin out
송이	① blossom ② bunch ③ cluster
송이버섯	Kind of mushroom (*Armillaria edodes*)
수국	hydrangea
수목원	① tree garden ② arboretum
수박	watermelon
수선화	daffodil
수세미외	sponge gourd
수수	African millet
수술	stamen
수풀	① wood ② forest ③ grove
수확하다	① to harvest ② to crop
숙주나물	mung-bean sprouts
숲	① forest ② wood
시금치	spinach
시들다	① to wither ② to droop
식목일	Arbor Day
식물	plant
식물원	botanical garden
식용식물	edible plants
심다	to plant
싸리버섯	Kind of mushroom (*Clavaria botrytis*)
싹	① sprout ② bud ③ shoot
싹트다	① to bud ② to sprout
쑥	mugwort
쑥갓	crown daisy
씀바귀	Kind of lettuce (*Ixeris dentata*)
씨	seed
씨방	seed room
씨앗	seed
아열대림	subtropical forest
아욱	mallow
아카시아	acacia
아카시아나무	acacia tree

〈소나무〉

안개꽃	baby's breath
암술	pistil
앵두	cherry
앵두나무	cherry tree
야생화	wild flower
야자	coconut
야자수	palm tree
야채	vegetables
약용식물	medicine plants
약초	(medicinal) herb
양귀비	poppy
양배추	cabbage
양상추	lettuce
양송이	mushroom
양파	onion
억새	kind of plant (*Miscanthus purpurascens*)
엉겅퀴	thistle
여러해살이	perennial
여물다	① to corn ② to grow ripe ③ to ripen
연근	lotus root
연꽃	lotus flower
열다	to bear
열대림	tropical forest
열리다	to bear
열매	fruit
열무	young radish
영산홍	azalea
영지버섯	kind of mushroom (*Ganoderma lucidum*)
오동나무	paulownia tree
오디	mulberry
오렌지	orange
오미자	Maximowiczia typica
오이	cucumber

고유어	한해살이	두해살이	여러해살이
한자어	일년생	이년생	다년생

옥수수	corn
온대림	Temperate forest
온실	greenhouse
올—	early (harvest)
옻나무	lacquer tree
완두콩	pea
우엉	burdock
움트다	① to sprout ② to shoot ③ to bud
월계수	laurel tree
유자	citron
유채꽃	① rape (plant) flower ② cole flower
은방울꽃	lily of the valley
은행나무	ginkgo tree
이끼	moss
익다	① to ripen ② to mature
인삼	ginseng
일년생	annual
임야	① forests and fields ② forest land
잎	leaf
잎사귀	leaf
잎새	leaf
자두	plum
자라다	to grow
자몽	grapefruit
작약	peony
잔디	① lawn ② turf
잡초	weed
잣나무	pine tree
장미	rose
전나무	fir tree
접붙이다	to graft
접시꽃	hollyhock
정원	garden
제비꽃	violet
조	foxtail millet
조화	artificial (imitation) flower

〈유채꽃〉

〈제비꽃〉

종묘	① seeds and saplings ② seedlings
종자	seed
죽순	bamboo shoot (sprout)
줄기	① trunk ② stem ③ stalk
지다	to fall
진달래	azalea
질경이	plantain
찔레꽃	wild rose
차조	glutinous millet
참-	① genuine ② prototypical
참나무	oak tree
참외	melon
창포	sweet flag
채소	vegetable
채송화	① sun plant ② rose moss
천연기념물	natural monument
철쭉	royal azalea
초롱꽃	bellflower
총각무	whole radish
취	aster
치자나무	gardenia
칡	arrowroot
카네이션	carnation
코스모스	cosmos
콩	bean
콩나물	bean sprout
토끼풀	clover
토란	taro
톳	100-sheet bundle of laver
통꽃	floret
퇴비	① compost ② barnyard manure
튤립	tulip
파	Welsh onion
파래	green laver
팥	red bean
패다	① to come into ears ② to ear (up)

〈채송화〉

〈코스모스〉

패랭이꽃	pink
팽이버섯	nettle tree mushroom
포기	① head (of cabage) ② clump (of grass)
포도	grape
표고버섯	shiitake mushroom
푸성귀	① greens ② greenstuff
풀	grass
풀밭	① grassy place ② glassland
풋—	① unripe ② green
플라타너스	① platan tree ② sycamore tree
피다	to blossom
한해살이	annual
할미꽃	pasqueflower
해당화	sweet brier
해바라기	sunflower
해조류	① seaweed ② marine algae (plants) ③ kelp
해초	① seaweed ② marine algae (plants)
햇—	new
행운목	① fortune tree ② lucky tree
향나무	Chinese juniper tree
호두나무	walnut tree
호박	pumpkin
호박꽃	pumpkin flower
홍당무	carrot
화단	flower-bed
화분	flowerpot
화초	flowering plant
화환	① wreath ② garland (of flowers)
화훼	flowering plant
활짝	in full bloom
회양목	box tree
효모	fungus
후추	black pepper

〈할미꽃〉

37 모양
Shapes

This chapter contains the names of two-dimensional and three-dimensional shapes. It also contains lexical entries related to size, width, length, height, and thickness.

가느다랗다	to be thin
가늘다	① to be thin ② to be slim
가득하다	to be full
가루	powder
가지가지	various
각	angle
각도	angle
각도기	protractor
각양각색	every shape and color
같다	to be same
거대하다	① to be huge ② to be gigantic
고도	altitude
고르다	① to be even ② to be uniform
고저	high and low
곡선	curve
곧다	① to be straight ② to be upright
광대하다	① to be vast ② to be extensive ③ to be immense
광활하다	to be extensive
구	globe
구부러지다	to bend

굵기	thickness
굵다	to be thick
굵다랗다	to be thickish
굵직하다	to be thickish
굽다	to bend
기다랗다	to be long
기울다	① to incline ② to slope
길다	to be long
길이	length
길쭉하다	to be longish
깊다	to be deep
깊숙하다	to be deep
깊이	depth
꼬이다	to get tangled
꼭지점	apex
꼴	shape
나란히	① in a line ② side by side
나선형	① spiral ② helical
나지막하다	to be on the low side
나직하다	to be on the low side
날카롭다	to be sharp
납작하다	to be flat
낮다	to be low
너비	width
널따랗다	① to be wide ② to be extensive ③ to be broad
널찍하다	① to be extensive ② to be open ③ to be wide
넓다	to be wide
넓이	width
넓적하다	to be broad and flat
넓히다	to widen
네모	square
네모나다	to be square
네모지다	to be squared
높낮이	high and low

높다	to be high
높다랗다	to be rather high
높이	height
다각형	polygon
다르다	to be different
다면체	polyhedron
달걀형	oval
닮다	to resemble
닮은꼴	similar shape
대각선	diagonal line
대소	large and small
대형	large size
덩어리	① lump ② mass
덩이	① lump ② mass
덩치	① bulk ② build ③ size
도톰하다	to be thick
도형	① figure ② shape
동그라미	circle
동그랗다	to be round
동글납작하다	to be round and flat
동글동글	roundish
동일하다	① to be equal ② to be the same ③ to be identical
두껍다	to be thick
두께	thickness
두둑하다	to be thick
두리뭉실하다	to be nondescript
두툼하다	to be thick
둔각	obtuse angle
둥그스름하다	to be roundish
둥글넓적하다	to be round and broad
둥글다	to be round
둥글둥글	roundish
드넓다	① to be vast ② to be large ③ to be wide
똑같다	to be identical

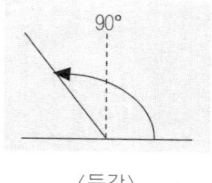

〈둔각〉

똑바르다	to be dead straight
마름모	diamond
면	① face ② surface
면적	① area ② square measure ③ size
모나다	to be angled
모서리	① corner ② angle
모습	figure
모양	shape
모양자	shape ruler
모형	model
무늬	pattern
무형	① formless ② shapeless
문형	pattern
뭉뚝하다	to be blunt
밑면	base
밑변	base
반듯하다	to be straight
변	side
볼록하다	① to be protuberant ② to be bulging
부스러기	crumbs
부채꼴	fan shape
비대하다	to be fat
비뚤다	① to be crooked ② to be awry
비스듬하다	① to be slanting ② to be sloping ③ to be inclined
비슷하다	to be similar
비좁다	① to be narrow ② to be confined ③ to be cramped
빗변	hypotenuse
빠듯하다	to be tight
뾰족뾰족	sharp
뾰족하다	to be sharp
사각형	quadrilateral
사다리꼴	trapezoid
사면체	tetrahedron
사선	oblique line

삼각형	triangle
생김새	① shape ② form
선	line
선분	segment (of a line)
세모	triangle
세모나다	to be triangular
세모지다	to be triangular
소복하다	① to be heaped up ② to be heaping
소형	small size
수북하다	① to be heaped up ② to be heaping
수직	perpendicularity
수직선	perpendicular line
수평	horizontality
수형도	tree diagram
신장	height
실선	solid line
십이면체	dodecahedron
쌍곡선	hyperbola
쌍둥이	twin
아담하다	① to be snug ② to be cozy
야트막하다	to be shallow
얄팍하다	to be thin
얇다	to be thin
얕다	to be shallow
얕으막하다	to be shallowish
어중간하다	to be in between
역삼각형	reversed triangle
옆면	side
예각	acute angle
오각형	pentagon
오똑하다	① to be high ② to be lofty
오목하다	to be hollow
오밀조밀	① intricate ② elaborate
올록볼록	① uneven ② bumpy
올망졸망	in clusters
완만하다	to be gently-sloping

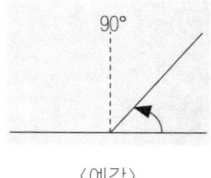

〈예각〉

우람하다	① to be imposing ② to be commanding
울퉁불퉁	① uneven ② rough
움푹하다	to be sunken
웅대하다	① to be grand ② to be magnificent
웅장하다	① to be grandeur ② to be magnificent ③ to be splendor
원	circle
원기둥	(circular) cylinder
원뿔형	cone
원통형	cylinder
원형	circle
유사하다	to be similar
유형	type
육각형	hexagon
육면체	hexahedron
으리으리하다	① to be majestic ② to be magnificent ③ to be imposing
이등변삼각형	isosceles
자	ruler
자잘하다	① to be small ② to be tiny ③ to be minute
작다	to be small
잘다	① to be small ② to be fine
잘록하다	① be narrow ② to be slender
장단	long and short
장방형	rectangle
점	dot
점선	dotted line
정사각형	square
정삼각형	equilateral triangle
정형	fixed form
조그맣다	to be tiny
좁다	to be narrow
중형	medium
직각	right angle
직사각형	rectangle

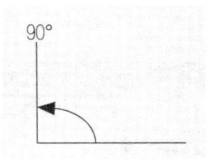

〈직각〉

직선	straight line	
짤막하다	① to be short ② to be rather short	
짧다	to be short	
초대형	extra large	
초소형	extra small	
축소하다	to reduce	
측면	side	
커다랗다	to be huge	
크기	size	
크다	to be big	
큼직하다	to be fairly big	
키	height	
타원	oval	
타원형	oval form	
토실토실	① plump ② chubby ③ fat	
틀	frame	
판판하다	to be flat	
팔각형	octagon	
팔면체	octahedron	
펑퍼짐하다	to be flat and round	
평	3.954 sq. yds.	
평각	straight angle	
평평하다	to be flat	
평행	parallel	
평행사변형	parallelogram	
평행선	parallel line	
포동포동	① plump ② fleshy	
포물선	parabola	
폭	width	
푹	① deep ② deeply	
합동	congruence	

〈평각〉

분류	크기	길이	굵기	깊이	높이	두께	너비	넓이
↑	크다	길다	굵다	깊다	높다	두껍다	넓다	넓다
↓	작다	짧다	가늘다	얕다	낮다	얇다	좁다	좁다

〈사물의 모양을 가리키는 단어〉

협소하다	to be narrow
형	① shape ② form
형상	① form ② shape
형태	① form ② shape
형형색색	various shapes and colors
확대하다	to magnify
휘다	to bend
흡사하다	to be very much alike

평면도형	
원	○
타원형	⬭
삼각형	△
사각형	□
오각형	⬠
육각형	⬡
팔각형	⯃
평행사변형	▱
마름모	◇
사다리꼴	⏢
부채꼴	⌔

38 빛과 색채
Light and Colors

This chapter contains and lists types of lights and colors that Korean people frequently use. It also contains lexical entries expressing light and colors.

사물 이름을 따서 만든 색 이름	
—색	—빛
국방색	구릿빛
금색	금빛
똥색	살구빛
미색	앵두빛
밤색	우유빛
병아리색	은빛
산호색	잿빛
살색	쪽빛
상아색	:
쑥색	
옥색	
와인색	
은색	
재색	
쥐색	
진달래색	
풀색	
하늘색	
황토색	
회색	
:	

가지각색	all kinds of colors
각양각색	every shape and color
갈색	brown
감색	dark blue
거무스름하다	to be blackish
거무죽죽하다	to be blackish
거무튀튀하다	to be blackish
검다	to be black
검은색	black
검정	black
검정색	black
고동색	brown
광선	① light ② beam ③ ray
광채	luster
구릿빛	copper color
국방색	khaki
군청색	① ultramarine ② sea blue
굴절	refraction
그림자	shadow
금빛	golden (color)
금색	gold (color)
까만색	black

까망	black
까맣다	to be black
까뭇까뭇	blackish
깜깜하다	to be pitch-dark
꽃분홍색	dark pink
남빛	indigo
남색	indigo
노란색	yellow
노랑	yellow
노랗다	to be yellow
노르스름하다	to be yellowish
노릇노릇	yellowish
녹두색	dark green
녹색	green
다채롭다	to be colorful
달빛	moonlight
똥색	dung color
명도	brightness
명암	light and darkness
무색	colorless
무지개색	rainbow color
무채색	achromatic color
미색	① beige ② pale yellow
바래다	to fade away
바탕색	background color
반사	reflection
반짝반짝	glittering
밝기	brightness
밝다	to be bright
밤색	① chestnut color ② brown
배색	color scheme
백색	white
백옥같다	to be like white jade

무지개색

| 빨강 | 주황 | 노랑 | 녹색 | 파랑 | 남색 | 보라 |

변색	change of color
병아리색	light yellow
보라	violet
보랏빛	violet
보색	complementary color
보호색	protective color
분광기	spectroscope
분홍	pink
불그스름하다	to be reddish
불긋불긋	reddish
불빛	light
붉다	to be red
붉으락푸르락	red (the state of being angry)
비추다	to shine on
비치다	to shine
빛	light
빛깔	color
빛나다	① to shine ② to beam
빨간색	red
빨강	red
빨갛다	to be red
산호색	coral color
살구빛	apricot color
살색	① flesh color ② skin color
삼원색	three primary colors
상아색	ivory
새—	① deep ② vivid ③ intense
색	color
색감	color sense
색깔	color
색도	chromaticity
색동	(cloth with) five stripes of colors
색맹	① color blind ② achromatopsia
색상	color tone
색상지	color tone paper
색소	① pigment ② coloring

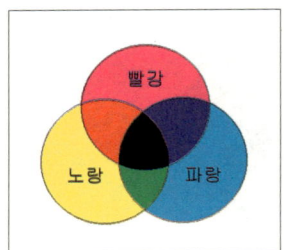

〈색의 삼원색〉

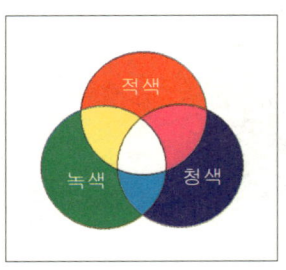

〈빛의 삼원색〉

색연필	color pencil
색조	① tone of color ② shade
색종이	colored paper
색지	colored paper
색채	color
색채감각	sense of color
색칠	coloring
색칠하다	① to paint ② to color
색환도	color graph
선명하다	① to be vivid ② to be clear
선홍색	deep pink
쑥색	① mugwort color ② dark green
알록달록	colorful
암갈색	① dark brown ② umber
앵두빛	cherry color
야광	luminous glow
어둡다	to be dark
연-	light
연두색	yellow green
연하다	to be light
염색	dye

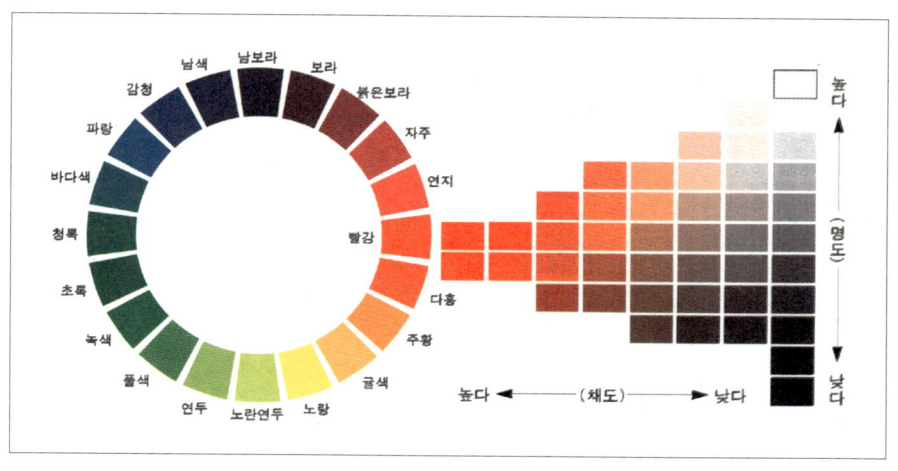

〈색환도〉

염색하다	to dye
옅다	① to be light ② to be pale
오색	five colors
오색찬란하다	to be glistening
옥색	jade color
와인색	wine color
우유빛	milk color
울긋불긋	in various colors
원색	primary color
유채색	color
은빛	silver (color)
은색	silver (color)
은은하다	to be subtle
음영	① shadow ② shade
자연색	natural color
자주	purple
자주색	purple
재색	ash grey
잿빛	ash color
적색	red
조명	lighting
주홍	vermilion
주황	orange
쥐색	grey
진—	dark
진달래색	azalea color (deep pink)
진하다	to be dark
짙다	to be dark
쪽빛	indigo blue
채도	chroma
채색	① coloring ② painting
천연색	natural color
청록	bluish green color
청색	blue
초록	green
총천연색	all natural colors

칠하다	to paint
컴컴하다	to be dark
탈색	bleaching
탈색하다	to bleach
투명하다	to be transparent
파랑	① blue ② green
파랗다	① to be blue ② to be green
파릇파릇	vividly green
파란색	blue
표백하다	to bleach
푸르다	① to be blue ② to be green
푸르스름하다	① to be bluish ② to be greenish
풀색	grass color
하늘색	sky blue
하얀색	white
하양	white
하얗다	to be white
허여멀걸다	to be whitish
형광	fluorescence
형광색	fluorescent color
형형색색	various shapes and colors
홍색	red
화사하다	to be colorful
환하다	to be bright
황색	yellow
황토색	reddish brown
회색	grey
후광	halo

하양	까망	빨강	노랑	파랑
백옥같다 하얗다 허여멀걸다 희끗희끗 희다 :	거무스름하다 거무죽죽하다 검다 까맣다 까뭇까뭇 :	불그스름하다 불긋불긋 붉다 빨갛다 :	노랗다 노르스름하다 노릇노릇 누렇다 :	파랗다 파릇파릇 푸르다 푸르스름하다 :

〈한국의 다섯 가지 색깔〉

훤하다	to be light
휘황찬란하다	to be radiant
흑백	black and white
흑색	black
희끗희끗	spotted with white
희다	to be white
흰색	white

39 수와 수량
Number and Quantity

This chapter contains lexical entries related to numbers and its orders in Korean. It also contains lexical entries of various units of counting and terms frequently used in calculation and mathematics.

가감승제	+	더하다	더하기	덧셈
	−	빼다	빼기	뺄셈
	×	곱하다	곱하기	곱셈
	÷	나누다	나누기	나눗셈

⟨기본적인 계산법⟩

가감승제	addition, subtraction, multiplication and division
가감하다	to add and subtract
가구 (집)	counting unit for houses
가닥 (실)	strand (of thread)
가마 (쌀)	sack (of rice)
가산점	markup points
가지	① kind ② sort
각도	angle
각도기	protractor
갑 (담배)	pack (of cigarette)
갑절	① double ② twice
값	value
개 (물건)	piece (of things)
개비 (담배)	counter for cigarettes
거리	distance
검산하다	to verify the accounts
겹 (종이)	layer (of paper)
경	ten quadrillion
계	total
계량	weighing

계량하다	to weigh
계산	calculation
계산기	calculator
계산서	① check ② bill
계산하다	to calculate
계측하다	to measure
곡 (노래)	piece (of songs)
곱	double
곱셈	multiplication
곱절	① times ② double
곱하기	multiplying
곱하다	to multiply
공배수	common multiple
공약수	common measure (divisor)
공통분모	common denominator
과반수	① majority ② greater part [number] (of)
관 (과일)	3.75kg: quantifier for fruit
구	nine
구구단	multiplication table
굵기	thickness
권 (책)	volume (of book)
그램 (무게)	gram
그루 (나무)	counter for trees
그릇 (밥)	bowl (of steamed rice)
근 (고기)	600g: quantifier for meat
기수	cardinal number
기압계	barometer
길이	length
깊이	depth
꼽다	to count
꾸러미 (달걀)	batch of ten eggs
끼 (밥)	meal
나누기	dividing
나누다	to divide
나눗셈	division

나머지 (나누고 남은 수)		remainder
나이		age
내다		to yield
냥 (금)		37.5g: quantifier for gold
넉		four
넓이		① width ② area
네		four
네댓		four or five
넷		four
넷째		fourth
놈 (동물, 사람)		counter for animal or person (guy, detestable fellow, boy, etc)
높이		height
누계		① total ② total amount
눈금		division of a scale
닢 (돈)		old Korean unit of money
다		all
다발 (꽃)		① bunch (of flowers) ② bouquet
다섯		five
다섯째		fifth
다스 (연필)		dozen (of pencil)
단 (야채, 나무)		bunch (of vegetable or sticks)
단수		one digit
단위		① unit ② denomination
달다		to weigh
대 (기계)		counter for large machines
대수		algebra
대수학		algebra
대여섯		five or six

재는 단위	길이	리, 미터, 밀리미터, 발, 뼘, 센티미터, 자, 치, 킬로미터 …
	넓이	마지기, 제곱미터, 제곱센티미터, 제곱킬로미터, 평 …
	무게	관, 그램, 근, 냥, 돈, 킬로그램, 톤 …
	분량	모금, 섬, 아름, 움큼, 줌, 홉 …
		용기에 따라 · 그릇, 되, 말, 병, 봉, 봉지, 상자, 술, 접시, 통 …

〈한국에서 재는 단위〉

댓	about five
더하기	adding
더하다	to add
덧셈	addition
도 (각도)	degree (of angle)
도막 (생선)	piece (of fish)
돈 (금)	3.75g: quantifier for gold
동 (건물)	counter for buildings
되 (소금)	0.477 U.S. gallons
되다	to weigh (corns, powders, liquids, etc)
두	two
두께	thickness
두름 (생선)	string (of fish)
두서너	two or three
둘	two
둘레	circumference
둘째	second
땀 (바늘)	stitch (of needle)
량 (기차)	car (of train)
리	0.4km
리터	liter
마 (옷감, 종이)	91.44cm: quantifier for clothing or paper
마리 (소)	head (of cow)
마지기 (논)	about 500 sq. meters of paddy land
마흔	forty
만	ten thousand
많다	① to be many ② to be numerous ③ to be much ④ to be plentiful ⑤ to be rich
말 (콩)	4.765 U.S. gallons
면적	① area ② square measure
명 (사람)	counter for people
모 (두부)	counter for tofu
모금 (물)	gulp (of water)
모두	① all ② every

모조리	① all ② without exception ③ to the very last
몫	quotient
무게	weight
무리수	irrational number
무한대	infinity
묶음	bundle
미터	meter
밀도	density
밀리미터	millimeter
반올림	rounding off
반올림하다	to round off
반지름	radius
발	① fathom ② length of outstretched arms
방울	drop
방정식	equation
배	double
백	hundred
백분율	percentage
버금	① the second in order ② the next
버리다	to throw away
번	times
번지	house number
번호	number
벌 (양복)	counter for suits
병	bottle
복수	plural
봉 (약)	packet (of medicine)
봉지 (과자)	package (of snack)
부분집합	subset
부피	volume
분 (각도)	degree (of angle)
분 (사람)	honorific counter for people
분수	fraction
분자	numerator
비율	ratio

빼기	subtracting
빼다	to subtract
뺄셈	subtraction
뼘	span
뿌리	counter for roots
사	four
사람 (사람)	counter for people
산수	arithmetic
산술	arithmetic
살 (나이)	counter for age
삼	three
상자	box
서너	three or four
서른	thirty
서수	ordinal number
석	three
섬 (곡식)	47.65 U.S. gallons: quantifier for grains
세 (歲)	counter for age
세	three
세다	to count
셈	calculation
셈하다	to calculate
셋	three
셋째	third
소계	subtotal
소수 (小數)	decimal fraction
소수 (素數)	prime number
소수점	decimal point
손 (생선)	2 fish: quantifier for fish
송이 (꽃)	counter for flowers
수	number
수두룩하다	① to be a lot of ② to be plentiful
수량	quantity of something
수치	numerical value
술 (밥)	spoon (of steamed rice)
숫자	number

쉰	fifty
스물	twenty
습도계	hygrometer
실수	real number
십	ten
십진법	decimal system
십진수	decimal number
쌍	pair
아름	armful
아홉	nine
아홉째	ninth
아흔	ninety
알 (콩)	counter for beans
암산	mental calculation

```
                    ┌ 양수: 자연수 (1, 2, 3, …)
            ┌ 정수 ┤ 0
      ┌ 유리수 ┤    └ 음수 (-1, -2, -3, …4)
      │       │
수 ┬ 실수 ┤    └ 정수 아닌 수: 분수 (½, ⅓, ¼, …), 소수 (0.1, 1.2, 10.5, …)
   │   │
   │   └ 무리수
   └ 허수
```

아라비아 숫자	1	2	3	4	5	6	7	8	9	10
한자어	일 (一)	이 (二)	삼 (三)	사 (四)	오 (五)	육 (六)	칠 (七)	팔 (八)	구 (九)	십 (十)
고유어	하나	둘	셋	넷	다섯	여섯	일곱	여덟	아홉	열
순서	첫째	둘째	셋째	넷째	다섯째	여섯째	일곱째	여덟째	아홉째	열째
아라비아 숫자	10	20	30	40	50	60	70	80	90	100
한자어	십 (十)	이십 (二十)	삼십 (三十)	사십 (四十)	오십 (五十)	육십 (六十)	칠십 (七十)	팔십 (八十)	구십 (九十)	백 (百)
고유어	열	스물	서른	마흔	쉰	예순	일흔	여든	아흔	온

아라비아 숫자	100	1,000	10,000	100,000	1,000,000	10,000,000	100,000,000	1,000,000,000,000
한자어	백 (百)	천 (千)	만 (萬)	십만 (十萬)	백만 (百萬)	천만 (千萬)	억 (億)	조 (兆)

〈한국에서 많이 쓰는 숫자와 순서〉

약분	reduction (of a fraction) to its lowest terms
약수	divisor
양	quantity
양수	natural number
어림잡다	① to estimate roughly
	② to make a rough estimate (of)
억	hundred million
여남은	ten or just over ten
여덟	eight
여덟째	eighth
여든	eighty
여러	many
여섯	six
여섯째	sixth
연령	age
연배	similar age
연상	senior (in age)
연세	age (deferential)
연하	junior (in age)
열	ten
열댓	about fifteen
열째	tenth
영	zero
예닐곱	six or seven
예순	sixty
오	five
온도계	thermometer
올 (실)	strand (of thread)
우량계	rain gauge
움큼	handful
원 (돈)	won (unit of Korean money)
원소	element
원주율	ratio of the circumference of a circle to its diameter
유리수	rational number

육	six
으뜸	① the first ② number one
음수	negative number
이	two
이진법	① binary system ② dyadic system
인	person
인분 (음식)	serving
일	one
일곱	seven
일곱째	seventh
일흔	seventy
자	ruler
자 (길이)	30.3 cm
자루 (연필)	counter for long thin objects
자연수	natural number
작다	to be small
장 (종이)	piece (of paper)
재다	to measure
저울	① balance ② (weigh) scale
적다	① to be few ② to be little ③ to be small ④ to be scarce
절대값	absolute value
점 (고기)	piece (of chopped meat)
접 (마늘)	hundred (bulbs of garlic)
접시 (반찬)	plate (of side dishes)
정량	fixed quantity
정수	① integral number ② whole number
제 (한약)	bundle of 20 packets (of Chinese medicine)
제―	e.g. 제2: ① number 2 ② the second
제곱	square (a number)
조	trillion
주먹구구	rough estimate
주산	abacus calculation
주판	abacus
줄	row

줄자	tape measure
줌	handful
지름	diameter
지수	① index number ② exponent
지진계	seismometer
질 (책)	set (of books)
질량	mass
집	house
집합	set
짝 (신)	pair (footwear)
짝수	even number
—째	e.g. 두 (2) 번째 (the second)
쪽 (사과)	slice (of apple)
차	difference
채 (집)	counter for houses
쳑 (길이)	0.994 feet
천	thousand
첩 (한약)	packet (of Chinese medicine)
첫	① beginning ② first
첫—	first
첫째	first
총계	total
최소공배수	least common multiple
최소공약수	least common measure
축 (오징어)	ten (squids)
측량	① measurement ② measuring
측량하다	to measure
측정	measurement
측정하다	to measure
층 (건물)	floor (building)
치 (길이)	1.193 inches
칠	seven
칸 (방)	counter for rooms
켤레 (양말, 신)	pair (of socks or shoes)
크기	① size ② dimensions
크다	to be large

킬로그램	kilogram
킬로미터	kilometer
톤	ton
톨	counter for grains and nuts
톳 (김)	100-sheet bundle (of laver)
통	counter for watermelon, cabbages, etc.
통 (편지)	counter for letters
통계	statistics
통분	reduction (of fractions) to a common denominator
판₁	box (egg or tofu)
판₂	① round ② game
팔	eight
퍼센트	percent
편 (저작)	counter for literary work
평 (땅)	3.954 sq. yd
평균치	average value
포기 (배추)	head (of cabbage)
쪽	width
푼₁	0.375g: quantifier for gold
푼₂	percentage (less than 0.1)
푼 (돈)	old Korean unit of money
필₁ (匹)(말)	head (of horse)
필₂ (疋)(비단)	roll (of silk)
하나	one
한	one
한두	one or two
할	percentage (0.1 or greater)
합	sum
합계	total
합산	adding up
합산하다	to add up
합집합	union
해	hundred quintillion
허수	imaginary number
홀수	odd number

| 홉 | 0.381 U.S. pint |
| 확률 | probability |

사람	높임	분	
	예사	명	
	낮춤	놈	
동물	말	필	마리
	생선	손 (두 마리)	
	조기	두름 (스무 마리)	
	오징어	축 (열 마리)	
	알	알, 꾸러미 (열 알)	
식물	과일	개, 알	
	꽃	송이	
	나무	그루	
	마늘	접 (100개)	
	밤·쌀알	톨	
	포도	송이	
	풀·채소	뿌리, 포기, 다발, 단	
사물	개수	개, 쌍 (두 개)	
	건물	동	
	노래	곡	
	담배·매	대	
	돈	원, 닢, 푼	
	두부·묵	모	
	문학작품	편	
	배	척	
	식사	끼	
	신발·양말·장갑	켤레	
	실·끈	가닥, 올	
	액체	방울	
	연필	자루, 다스 (열두 자루)	
	열차	량 (따로 떨어진 낱개)	
	옷	벌	
	옷감	마 (길이), 필 (묶음)	
	종이	장	
	집	집, 채	
	차량·악기·전자제품	대	
	책	권, 질 (여러 권)	
	편지	통	
	한약	첩, 제	
	횟수	번, 회	
	사물의 상태에 따라	길고 가는 것	가지, 가락
		넓고 평평한 것	판
		조각·부분	도막, 점, 쪽, 짝

〈한국에서 많이 쓰는 수량을 세는 단위〉

40 시간
Time

This chapter contains lexical entries referring to the seasons and their 24 Korean divisions as well as those indicating year, month, day and time. It also contains the names of national holidays and festive days in Korea, and also a number of lexical entries concerned with temporal order and speed.

가끔	sometimes
가다	① to pass ② to fly
가을	① fall ② autumn
간격	interval
간혹	① occasionally ② at times
갑자기	suddenly
갓	① fresh from ② newly
개천절	National Foundation Day (October 3rd)
개화기 (開化期)	age of enlightenment
개화기 (開花期)	time of blooming
겨를	spare moments
겨우내	throughout the winter
겨울	winter
격월	every other month
격일	every other day
격주	every other week
결혼기념일	wedding anniversary
—경	around
경축일	national holiday
경칩	"end of hibernation" (about 5th of

	March)
계속	continuously
계절	season
고대	ancient times
곡우	"rainfall for seeding" (20th or 21st of April)
곧	① soon ② immediately ③ at once
곧장	right away
공휴일	holiday
과거	past
광복절	Independence Day (August 15th)
구정	① lunar New Year's Day ② New Year by the lunar calendar
국경일	national holiday
그끄저께	three days ago
그글피	four days from now
그때	at that time
그때그때	every occasion
그믐	end of the month
그믐날	last day of the month
그저께	day before yesterday
그전	in the past
그제	day before yesterday
근대	modern times
글피	three days from now
금년	this year
금방	right now
금번	this time
금세	right now
금요일	Friday
금일	today
기간	① term ② period
기념일	anniversary
기원전	before Christ
기일	date of a person's death
긴급하다	to be urgent

긴박하다	to be tense
길다	to be long
길일	① propitious day ② lucky day
김장철	kimchi-making season
꼭두새벽	early at dawn
끝	end
나날이	everyday
나중	later
나흘	① four days ② fourth day of the month
날	day
날마다	every day
날짜	date
낮	day
내내	throughout
내년	next year
내달	next month
내일	tomorrow
내후년	three years hence
—녘	around
년	year
느리다	to be slow
늘	always
늦—	late
늦게	late
늦다	to be late
다달이	every month
다음	next
다음달	next month
다음번	next time
다음해	next year
단기	Tangun Era
단숨에	in one breath
단시일	short time

	일 년				
···	봄	여름	가을	겨울	···

단옷날	5th of May in the lunar Calendar
달	month
달력	calendar
닷새	① five days ② 5th day of the month
당대	those days
당분간	for a while
당시	at that time
당일	that day
당장	① at once ② right away
당초	the beginning
대보름	15th of January according to the lunar calendar
대서	"intense heat" (about 24th of July)
대설	"heavy snowfall" (about 8th of December)
대한	"intense cold" (about 21st of January)
더디다	① to be late ② to be behind time
돌	anniversary
동시	at the same time
동안	① during ② while
동지	"winter solstice" (about 22nd or 23rd of December)
동짓달	November in the lunar Calendar
뒤	after
때	time
때때로	sometimes
때마침	at the right time
뜸하다	to be infrequent
마지막	last
마침	at the right moment
마침내	at last
막	① just ② right at the moment
막간	intermission
—말	end
말미	end
말복	the last of the three days of summer

	slump
망종	"barley harvesting" (about 5th of June)
매—	every
매년	every year
매월	every month
매일	everyday
맨날	everyday
먼저	first
며칠	① how many days ② a few days
명	life
명절	festive day
몇	① some ② several
모레	day after tomorrow
목요일	Thursday
무렵	around
미래	future
미리	in advance
바뀌다	to change
바야흐로	① now ② at the height
반나절	half day
반세기	half century
밤	night
밤중	middle of the night
방금	① right now ② just now
백로	first dew of the year (about 8th or 9th of September)
백일	one hundredth day after birth
벌써	already
별안간	① on all of a sudden ② unexpectedly
보름	15th day of the month
보름날	15th day of a month
봄	spring
분	minute
분기	term
불기	Buddhist Era
빈번하다	to be frequent

빠르다	to be fast
빨리	quickly
사계절	four seasons
사시사철	all year round
사이	① between ② while
사흘	① three days ② 3rd day of the month
삼일절	Independence Movement Day (March 1st)
삽시간	① in no time ② in a flash
상강	"frost-falling" (about 23rd or 24th of September)
상순	first ten days of the month
새	① between ② while
새벽	dawn
새해	new year
생일	birthday
서기	*Anno Domini* (A.D.)
서력기원	origin of the Christian Era
선사시대	prehistoric age
섣달	12th lunar month
설날	New Year's Day
세기	century
세모	end of the year
세밑	year-end
세월	time
소만	the 8th *julgi* that falls on about 21st of May
소서	"beginning of summer heat" (about 7th or 8th of July)
소설	"light snowfall" (about 22nd or 23rd of November)
소한	"beginning of the severest cold" (about 6th of January)
수요일	Wednesday
순간	moment
순식간	① in no time ② in a flash

십이지 (十二支)	동물	띠	해
자 (子)	쥐	쥐띠	1996
축 (丑)	소	소띠	1997
인 (寅)	호랑이	호랑이띠	1998
묘 (卯)	토끼	토끼띠	1999
진 (辰)	용	용띠	2000
사 (巳)	뱀	뱀띠	2001
오 (午)	말	말띠	2002
미 (未)	양	양띠	2003
신 (申)	원숭이	원숭이띠	2004
유 (酉)	닭	닭띠	2005
술 (戌)	개	개띠	2006
해 (亥)	돼지	돼지띠	2007

스승의 날	Teachers' Day (May 15th)
시	hour
시각	time
시간	① time ② hour
시기	① time ② season
시나브로	① little by little ② bit by bit
시대	age
시일	① date ② time
시속	speed per hour
시절	① season ② the times
시점	point of time
시초	beginning
식목일	Arbor Day (April 5th)
신년	new year
신정	New Year's Day
십이지	the twelve horary signs
쏜살같다	to be as swift as an arrow
아까	some time ago
아직	yet
아침	morning
아흐레	① nine days ② 9th day of the month
앞	① future ② past
앞날	① days ahead ② future
앞서	previously
애초	beginning
야간	night time
양력	solar calendar
어느덧	before one knows it
어느새	before one knows it
어린이날	Children's Day (May 5th)
어버이날	Parents' Day (May 8th)
어저께	yesterday
어제	yesterday
언제	when
언제나	whenever
언제든지	anytime

얼른	quickly
여드레	① eight days ② 8th day of the month
여름	summer
여름내	throughout the summer
여태	up to now
역대	successive generations (up to now)
연간	for one year
연대	① age ② period
연도	fiscal year
연말	end of the year
연말연시	end of the year and the beginning of the following year
연중	all year round
연초	beginning of the year
열흘	① ten days ② 10th day of the month
엿새	① six days ② 6th day of the month
영원	eternity
영원히	① eternally ② forever
예전	old days
옛날	in the past
옛날옛적	a long, long time ago
오늘	today
오전	in the morning
오후	in the afternoon
온종일	whole day
올	this
올해	this year
왕년	years gone by
왕왕	① so often ② now and then

1 년 (양력)											
일월	이월	삼월	사월	오월	유월	칠월	팔월	구월	시월	십일월	십이월

1 년 (음력)											
정월	이월	삼월	사월	오월	유월	칠월	팔월	구월	시월	동짓달	섣달

〈한국의 1년〉

요새	these days
요일	day
요즘	nowadays
우수	first rainfall of the year (about 18th of February)
원년	first year of an era
원시시대	primitive ages
월	month
월요일	Monday
유수같다	to be like flowing water
윤년	leap year
윤달	leap month
윤일	leap day
음력	lunar calendar
이날이때	now
이내	① within ② at once
이듬해	following year
이따가	a little later
이따금	once in a while
이때	this time
이레	① seven days ② 7th day of the month
이르다	to be early
이미	already
이번	this time
이번달	this month
이십사절기	the 24 divisions of the year in the lunar Calendar
이전	before
이제	now
이틀	① two days ② 2nd day of the month
인제	now
일	date

…	그그저께	그제 그저께	어제	오늘	내일	모레	글피	그글피	…
…	재작년	작년		올해	내년	후년		내후년	…

일간	① in the near future ② one of these days
일광절약시간	daylight savings time
일요일	Sunday
일전	days ago
일찌감치	early
임박하다	① to be imminent ② to be close
입동	first day of winter (around the 8th of November)
입추	first day of autumn (around 6th to 9th of August)
입춘	first day of spring (about the 4th of February)
입하	first day of summer (about 5th of May)
자꾸	① frequently ② repeatedly
자정	midnight
자주	frequently
작년	last year
작은달	month with 30 or less days
잠깐	for a moment
잠시	for a little while
장차	in the future
잦다	① to be frequent ② to be incessant
재작년	year before last

이 십 사 절 기 (1년)

입춘	우수	경칩	춘분	청명	곡우	입하	소만	망종	하지	소서	대서	입추	처서	백로	추분	한로	상강	입동	소설	대설	동지	소한	대한
立春	雨水	驚蟄	春分	清明	穀雨	立夏	小滿	芒種	夏至	小暑	大暑	立秋	處暑	白露	秋分	寒露	霜降	立冬	小雪	大雪	冬至	小寒	大寒

10일 (고유어)

하루	이틀	사흘	나흘	닷새	엿새	이레	여드레	아흐레	열흘

일 주 일

월요일	화요일	수요일	목요일	금요일	토요일	일요일

저녁	evening
저번	① last time ② the other day
전	before
전성기	① period of prosperity ② golden age
전성시대	① period of prosperity ② golden age
절기	each of the 24 divisions of the year in the lunar Calendar
점심	lunch time
정각	o'clock
정오	noon
정월	the first lunar month (January)
정월대보름	15th of January in the lunar Calendar
정초	first ten days of January
제삿날	memorial day of an ancestor
제헌절	Constitution Day (July 17th)
종일	① all day long ② whole day
종종	① often ② frequently
주	week
주간	week
주말	weekend
주일 (主日)	Sunday
주일 (週日)	weekdays
주중	weekdays
주초	early in the week
줄곧	① all the time ② all through ③ throughout
중복	the second of the three days of summer slump
중세	the Middle Ages
중순	middle ten days of the month
즈음	about
즉시	immediately
지금	now
지나다	to pass
지난날	bygone days
지난달	last month

지난번	last time
지난해	last year
진작	earlier
짧다	to be short
짬	① interval ② time
—쯤	about
차일피일	procrastinatingly
찰나	① moment ② instant
처서	the end of summer (about 23rd of August)
처음	first time
천천히	slowly
철	season
청명	"clear and bright" (about 5th or 6th of April)
초	second
초—	beginning
—초	① beginning ② early
초복	the first of the three days of summer slump
초순	first ten days of the month
초저녁	early in the evening
초하루	first day of the month
촉박하다	to be urgent
최초	first
최종	① last ② end
최후	① final ② last
추분	autumnal equinox
추석	Korean Thanksgiving Day
춘분	vernal equinox
춘하추동	spring, summer, fall, and winter
큰달	month with 31 days
태양력	solar calendar
태음력	lunar calendar
태초	the beginning of the world
태평성대	peaceful reign

터울	difference of age between siblings
토요일	Saturday
틈	① time ② interval
평년	normal year
평일	weekday
풍년	year of abundance
하루	one day
하루종일	all day long
하순	last ten days of the month
하오	afternoon
하지	summer solstice
한—	mid-
한글날	Hangul Day (October 9th)
한나절	① whole afternoon ② half day
한동안	for a while
한로	"cold dew" (about October 8th)
한밤중	① around midnight ② middle of the night
한참	for a while
한창	① climax ② peak
항상	always
해	year
현대	modern times

			하 루			
…	새벽	아침	낮 / 대낮·한낮	저녁	밤 / 한밤중	…

	하 루		
…	오전 (A.M.)	오후 (P.M.)	…
자정 0시	정오 12시	자정 0시	

하 루																							
0시	1시	2시	3시	4시	5시	6시	7시	8시	9시	10시	11시	12시	13시	14시	15시	16시	17시	18시	19시	20시	21시	22시	23시
자정	오전 (A.M.)											정오	오후 (P.M.)										

현재	present
현충일	Memorial Day (June 6th)
혼삿날	wedding day
화요일	Tuesday
환절기	time of changing seasons
후	after
후년	year after next
후대	next generation
훗날	days ahead
휴일	holiday
흉년	bad year
흐르다	① to pass ② to elapse ③ to go by

41 공간과 우주
Space and the Universe

This chapter contains lexical entries related to the space and direction or compass directions, including geographical spaces such as mountains, rivers, and oceans. Further, it contains names of objects in the universe such as sun, moon, and stars.

가	① brink ② edge
가깝다	to be near
가로	width
가운데	middle
가장자리	edges
간격	space
갓길	shoulder
강	river
강가	riverside
강변	riverside
강어귀	mouth of a river
개울	① brook ② creek
개펄	mud flat
거기	(over) there
거리 (距離)	distance
거리	street
거문고자리	Lyra
건너편	opposite side
겉	① outer ② surface ③ outside
경계	boundary
경계선	boundary

경도	longitude
경사	① slant ② slope
경사지다	① to incline ② to slant
곁	beside
계곡	① gorge ② valley
고개	① hill ② mountain pass
고갯마루	ridge of a mountain
고원	plateau
고을	county
고장	district
고지대	highland
고향	hometown
골목	① side street ② lane ③ alleyway
골짜기	valley
곳	place
곳곳	everywhere
공간	space
공기	air
공백	empty space
공전	revolution
공중	midair
—곶	cape
광년	light-year
광속	light-speed
광야	wild plain
광활하다	① to be spacious ② to be vast
구간	① section ② block
구릉	hill
구부러지다	to bend
구불구불	serpentine
구석	corner
구석구석	① every corner ② every nook and cranny ③ all the corners
구역	district
군데	① place ② spot
군데군데	① here and there ② sparsely

군도	① group of islands ② archipelago
굴	cave
궤도	orbit
귀퉁이	① corner ② edge
그곳	① the place ② place closer to the hearer
그리	there
그쪽	that way
그믐달	waning moon
근방	① neighborhood ② vicinity
근접하다	to be adjacent
근처	near
금성	Venus
기울기	degree of slant
길	① street ② road
길거리	① street ② road
길모퉁이	street corner
길목	① street corner ② bend of a road
꼬불꼬불	winding
꼭대기	top
끄트머리	① end ② tip ③ tail end
나침반	compass
남극	south pole
남쪽	south
낭떠러지	① cliff ② precipice
내	① stream ② brook
내리막	① slope ② downward path ③ downhill
내부	inside
넓다	to be wide
논	① rice field ② paddy field
논밭	rice paddies and vegetable patches
농촌	farmland
누리	world
늪	① swamp ② marsh
달	moon
달나라	moon

달동네	poor hilly neighborhood
대기	atmosphere
대기권	atmosphere
대도시	big city
대륙	continent
대륙붕	continental shelf
대지	① earth ② ground
댐	dam
데	① place ② spot
도랑	ditch
도로	road
도시	city
도심	downtown
돌	stone
동굴	cave
동네	① neighborhood ② town
동네방네	all over the neighborhood
동산	neighborhood hill
동서남북	east, west, north, and south
동쪽	east
두메	① remote countryside ② backwoods
둑	bank
둔치	waterfront
둘레	circumference
뒤	① back ② behind
뒷면	backside
들	field
들판	plain
등지다	to be against
땅	① earth ② soil ③ ground
땅굴	tunnel

달				
초승달	반달 (상현달)	보름달	반달 (하현달)	그믐달

떠돌이별	planet
마을	town
마주하다	to face each other
만	bay
맞은편	opposite side
맨	very
멀다	① to be far ② to be distant ③ to be remote
면	side
면적	① area ② square measure
명당	① propitious site for a grave ② very good place
명소	① place of scenic interest ② noted place
명왕성	Pluto
모래	sand
모서리	edge
모퉁이	corner
목동자리	① Boötes ② Herdsman
목성	Jupiter
못	pond
무인도	uninhabited island
물고기자리	① Pisces ② Fishes
물병자리	① Aquarius ② Water Bearer
뭍	land
미리내	Milky Way
미확인비행물체	UFO (Unidentified Flying Object)
민물	fresh water
민속촌	Folk Village
밀림	jungle
밑	bottom
바깥	outside
바다	① sea ② ocean
바닥	① floor ② bottom
바닷가	seashore
바닷물	① seawater ② saltwater
바른쪽	right

바위	rock
밖	outside
반달	half moon
반대편	opposite side
반도	peninsula
반짝반짝	twinkling
방면	① direction ② side
방방곡곡	every nook and corner of the country
방위	① point of the compass ② compass direction ③ direction
방향	direction
밭	vegetable field
벌판	① field ② plain
범위	scope
벼랑	cliff
변두리	① outer edge ② outskirts
별	star
별똥별	shooting star
별자리	constellation
보름	① fifteen days ② 15th day of the (lunar) month
보름달	full moon
본토	mainland
부근	① neighborhood ② vicinity
북극	north pole
북극성	① North Star ② polar star
북두칠성	Great Bear
북쪽	north
분지	basin
붙박이별	sun (fixed star)
비다	to be empty
비탈	① slope ② incline
비탈길	sloping road
비행접시	flying saucer
사거리	intersection
사막	desert

별자리	날짜
물병자리	1월 20일 ～ 2월 18일 생
물고기자리	2월 19일 ～ 3월 20일 생
산양자리	3월 21일 ～ 4월 20일 생
황소자리	4월 21일 ～ 5월 20일 생
쌍둥이자리	5월 21일 ～ 6월 21일 생
게자리	6월 22일 ～ 7월 22일 생
사자자리	7월 23일 ～ 8월 22일 생
처녀자리	8월 23일 ～ 9월 22일 생
저울자리	9월 23일 ～ 10월 21일 생
전갈자리	10월 22일 ～ 11월 21일 생
사수자리	11월 22일 ～ 12월 21일 생
염소자리	12월 22일 ～ 1월 19일 생

사방	all directions
사방팔방	① every direction ② everywhere
사수자리	① Sagittarius ② Archer
사이	① space ② gap
사자자리	① Leo ② Lion
사차원	four-dimension(al)
산	mountain
산골	mountain district
산골짜기	ravine
산기슭	foot of a mountain
산꼭대기	summit of a mountain
산동네	mountainous neighborhood
산등성이	mountain ridge
산림	mountain forest
산마루	top of a mountain ridge
산맥	① mountain range ② range
산모롱이	spur of a mountain
산모퉁이	corner of a mountain foot
산봉우리	mountain peak
산비탈	mountain slope
산지	mountainous region
산촌	mountain village
산허리	mountainside
삼각주	delta
삼거리	three-way junction
삼차원	three-dimension(al)
상단	① upper row ② highest place
상현달	half moon (moon on the 7-8th day of the lunar month)
샘	① spring ② fountain
샘터	fountain place
샛길	side street
샛별	Morning Star
서쪽	west
섬	island
세계	world

세계지도	world map
세로	length
세상	world
소재지	whereabouts
속	① inner ② inside
수렁	slough
수성	Mercury
수평선	horizon
수풀	woods
숲	forest
습지	① swampy place ② damp ground
시골	country
시공	space-time
시내₁	downtown
시내₂	stream
시냇가	stream bank
쌍둥이자리	① Gemini ② Twins
아래	① below ② lower
아래쪽	lower part
안	inside
안팎	inside and outside
앞	front
앞뒤	front and back
앞면	front side
약도	route map
양달	sunny place
양자리	① Aries ② Ram
양지	sunny place
어디	where
어귀	entrance
어촌	fishing village
언덕	hill
언덕길	slope
언저리	periphery
여기	here
여기저기	here and there

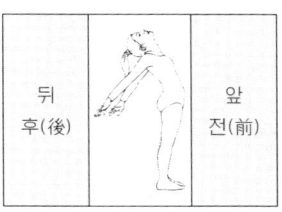

여백	① blank ② margin
여울	rapids
여울목	neck of rapids
연못	pond
열도	archipelago
염소자리	① Capricon ② Goat
영역	area
옆	side
오르막	① ascent ② acclivity ③ upward slope
오른쪽	right
오솔길	① narrow path ② trail
옥토	① fertile soil ② fertile land
온누리	all the world
온천	① hot spring ② spa
옹달샘	small spring
완만하다	to be gently-sloping
외계	outer space
외계인	alien
외부	outer part
왼쪽	left
우물	well
우주	① universe ② cosmos ③ (outer) space
우주개발	space development
우주먼지	space dust
우주복	space suit
우주비행사	astronaut
우주선	spaceship
우주여행	space travel
우주인	spaceman
우주정거장	space station
우주탐사	space exploration
우측	right side
운석	① meteor (small one) ② meteorite (big one)
운하	canal
웅덩이	pool

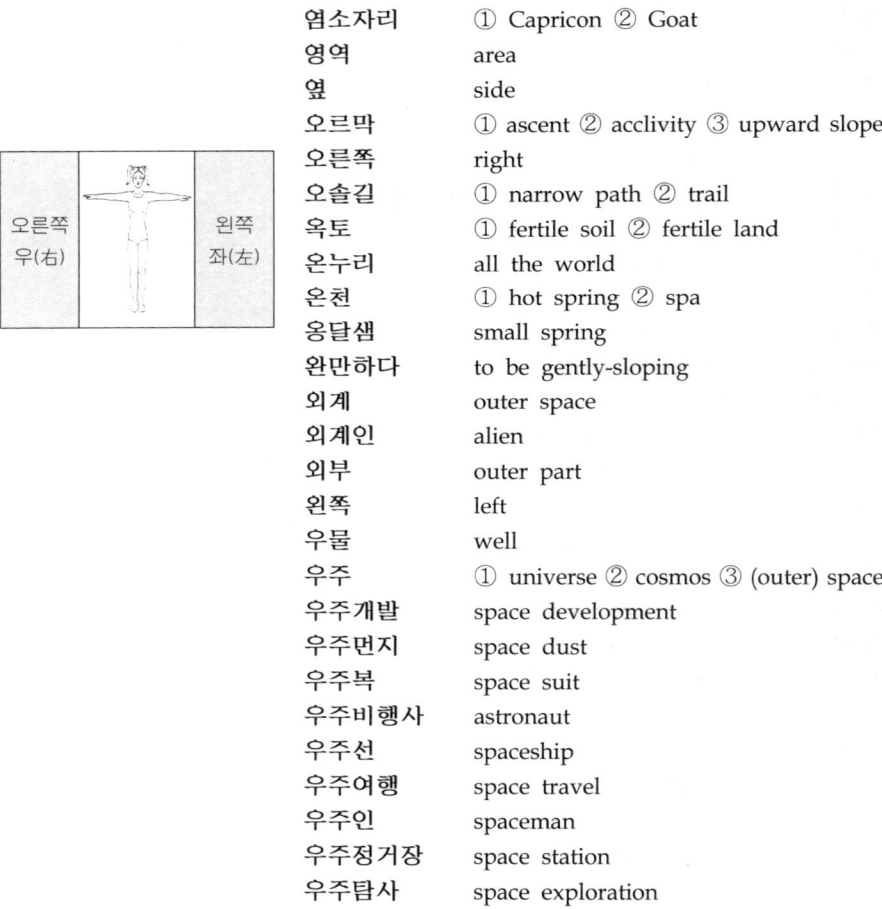

월식	lunar eclipse
위	① above ② upper
위도	latitude
위성	satellite
위쪽	upper part
위치	location
위치하다	to be located
유성 (流星)	① shooting star ② meteor
유성 (遊星)	planet
육지	land
은하계	Galaxy
은하수	Milky Way
음지	shaded lot
응달	shaded lot
이곳	this place
이곳저곳	here and there
이리	here
이리저리	this way and that way
이쪽	here
이쪽저쪽	here and there
이차원	two-dimension(al)
이웃	neighbor
인공위성	satellite
인근	① neighborhood ② vicinity
인접하다	① to be close by ② to be adjacent
일차원	one-dimension(al)
입구	entrance
자갈	① gravel ② pebbles
자리	place
자전	rotation
작은곰자리	Little Bear
장소	place
저곳	that place over there
저기	(over) there
저리	that way
저울자리	① Libra ② Scale

저지대	lowland
저쪽	① that side ② other side
적도	equator
전갈자리	① Scorpio ② Scorpion
전면	front side
전방	① front ② forward
절벽	cliff
정면	① front ② front part
제방	bank
좁다	to be narrow
좌측	left side
주변	① surroundings ② periphery
주위	surroundings
중간	middle
중력	gravity
중턱	① mid-slope of a mountain ② hillside
지구	earth
지구본	globe
지구의	globe
지대	① zone ② belt
지도	map
지동설	heliocentric theory
지름길	shortcut
지리	geography
지방	① region ② countryside
지역	region
지축	earth's axis
지평선	horizon
지하수	subterranean (underground) water
지형	topography
지형도	topographical map
진흙	mud
쭉	① in a row ② without ceasing
차다	① to become full ② to be filled
차원	dimension
찰흙	clay

창공	blue sky
처녀자리	① Virgo ② Virgin
천동설	Ptolemaic theory
천문대	astronomical observatory
천왕성	Uranus
천지	heaven and earth
천체	celestial body
천체망원경	astronomical telescope
청정해역	uncontaminated waters
초승달	crescent
촌	village
출구	exit
출입구	① entrance ② door ③ gate
측면	side
큰곰자리	Great Bear
태양	sun
태양계	solar system
터	① site ② lot ③ land
터전	① base ② grounds
테두리	① frame ② border
토성	Saturn
토지	① land ② estate
통과하다	to pass
통로	① passage ② path
틈	① room ② space ③ gap
편	① direction ② way
평야	plain
평원	prairie
평평하다	① to be flat ② to be even
폭포	waterfall
표면	surface
풍랑	wind and waves
하구	mouth of a river
하구언	bank of a rivermouth
하늘	sky
하단	lowest row

하천	stream
하현달	half moon (moon on the 22nd-23rd day of the lunar month
한가운데	① middle ② center
한복판	① middle ② heart
항성	sun (fixed star)
해	sun
해변	seashore
해수욕장	beach
해안	coast
해왕성	Neptune
해저	① bottom of the sea ② ocean floor
해협	strait
행성	planet
허공	air
허허벌판	wild plain
협곡	gorge
혜성	comet
화성	Mars
황무지	wasteland
황소자리	① Taurus ② Bull
황야	① wilderness ② the wild
후면	backside
후미지다	to be deeply indented
후방	backward
흑점	sunspot
흙	① earth ② soil

42 상태와 정도
States and Degrees

This chapter mostly contains lexical entries related to states or degrees of shape and qualities of things: intensity, density, frequency, strength, humidity, quantity and weight.

가까스로	① just ② barely
가난하다	to be poor
가냘프다	to be slim
가느다랗다	to be thin
가늘다	① to be thin ② to be slim
가능	possibility
가능하다	to be possible
가득	full
가득차다	to get filled
가득하다	to be full
가루	powder
가물다	to be droughty
가볍다	to be light
가뿐하다	to be rather light
가장	① most ② to the extreme
가지런하다	to be arranged neatly
가짜	① imitation ② fake
간결하다	to be simple
간단하다	to be simple
간편하다	to be simple and convenient
갈기갈기	① to pieces ② to shreds

가치	
긍정	부정
진짜	가짜
진실	거짓
좋은점	나쁜점
장점	단점
합격	불합격
성공	실패
우세	열세
맞다	틀리다

강도	
높다	낮다
강하다	약하다
단단하다	무르다
질기다	연하다
딱딱하다	물렁물렁하다

강도	① strength ② intensity
강력하다	to be strong
강인하다	to be strong
강하다	① to be powerful ② to be strong
강화	reinforcement
같다	to be the same
거대하다	① to be huge ② to be gigantic
거룩하다	to be holy
거세다	to be tough
거의	almost
거짓	① falsehood ② lie
거짓되다	to be false
거창하다	① to be immense ② to be gigantic
거칠다	to be rough
건강하다	to be healthy
건실하다	① to be steady ② to be sound
건전하다	① to be healthy ② to be wholesome
건조하다	to be dry
걸맞다	① to be well-balanced ② to be well-matched
걸쭉하다	to be thick
겨우	barely
견고하다	to be steadfast
결백하다	to be innocent
결점	demerit
결함	defect
계속되다	to be continued
고루	evenly
고르다	① to be even ② to be uniform
고상하다	① to be lofty ② to be noble
고소하다	① to be tasty ② to be savory
고약하다	① to be wicked ② to be ill-natured
고체	solid
곤경	① distressed circumstances ② dilemma
곤란하다	① to be hard ② to be difficult
과하다	to be excessive

광대하다	① to be vast ② to be extensive ③ to be immense
광활하다	to be extensive
괜찮다	to be all right
괴상하다	to be strange
구부러지다	to bend
구불구불	winding
구불텅구불텅	winding
구수하다	① to be tasty ② to be savory
구식	old-fashioned
굳다	① to become hard ② to harden
굵기	thickness
굵다	to be thick
굵다랗다	to be thickish
굵직하다	to be thickish
굽다	to bend
궁상맞다	to be miserable-looking
궂다	① to be bad ② to be nasty
귀엽다	① to be cute ② to be adorable
귀하다	① to be uncommon ② to be rare
규칙적	regular
균형	balance
급변	sudden change
기다랗다	to be long
기어코	① by all means ② at any cost
기운없다	① to be spiritless ② to have no energy
기운있다	to be energetic
기운차다	to be vigorous
기울다	① to incline ② to slope
기절하다	to faint
기체	① gas ② vapor
기필코	① certainly ② without fail
기화	vaporization
길다	to be long
길이	length
길쭉하다	to be long

깊다	to be deep
깊숙하다	to be deep
깊이	depth
까맣다	to be black
까무러치다	to go faint
까칠하다	to be rough
깔깔하다	① to be rough ② to be coarse
깔끔하다	① to be neat ② to be tidy
깜깜하다	to be pitch-dark
깨끗하다	to be clean
껄끄럽다	to be rough
꼬깃꼬깃	wrinkled
꼬질꼬질	① to be dirty ② to be filthy ③ to be foul
꼭	① exactly ② precisely
꼿꼿하다	① to be stiff ② to be hard
꽁꽁	frozen hard
꽉	fully
꽉꽉	① firmly ② tightly
꽤	quite
꾸준하다	to be steady
끈끈하다	to be sticky
나른하다	to be languid
나쁘다	to be bad
나지막하다	① to be rather low ② to be lowish
나직하다	to be on the low side
난국	crisis
날씬하다	to be slim
날카롭다	to be sharp
낡다	to be worn out
남루하다	① to be ragged ② to be shabby
납작하다	to be flat
낫다	to be better
낮다	to be low
너무하다	to be too hard
너비	width

너저분하다	① to be shabby ② to be untidy
너절하다	① to be shabby ② to be worn out
넉넉하다	to be sufficient
널따랗다	① to be wide ② to be broad
널리	widely
널찍하다	① to be extensive ② to be open ③ to be wide
넓다	to be wide
넓이	width
넓적하다	to be broad and flat
넘치다	① to overflow ② to run over
네모나다	to be square
네모지다	to be squared
노련하다	to be experienced
녹다	to melt
농도	① density ② thickness
농후하다	① to be thick ② to be strong
높다	to be high
높다랗다	to be rather high
높이	height
뇌사상태	state of being brain dead
눅눅하다	to be damp
느슨하다	to be loose
늘다	to increase
늘씬하다	to be tall and stylish
늙다	to get old
능숙하다	to be skillful
다	all
다르다	to be different
다만	① only ② simply
다소	① some ② somewhat
다정하다	to be affectionate
닥지닥지	① thickly ② heavily
단단하다	to be hard
단순하다	to be simple
단점	① defect ② fault ③ weakness

농도	
높다	낮다
진하다	묽다
되다	질다
탁하다	맑다

	④ demerit
단조롭다	to be monotonous
달다	① to be sweet ② to be sugary
닮다	① to resemble ② to take after
담백하다	to be mild tasting
대개	generally
대단하다	to be great
대부분	most
대체로	generally
대체적	general
더	more
더럽다	to be dirty
더부룩하다	to be heavy on the stomach
더욱	① even ② more
덜	less
덥다	to be hot
덩어리	lump
도막	① chop ② chip
도톰하다	to be thick
독특하다	① to be unique ② to be original
돋다	① to break out ② to come out
돌연변이	mutation
동강	piece
동그랗다	to be round
동등하다	to be equal
동일하다	to be identical
되다	to be thick
두둑하다	to be thick
두드러지다	① to be prominent ② to be notable ③ to be distinct
두루뭉실하다	to be round all around
두툼하다	to be thick
둔탁하다	to be dull
둔하다	to be dull
둥그스름하다	to be roundish
둥글넓적하다	to be round and flat

둥글다	to be round
뒤범벅되다	① to be mixed up ② to be jumbled
뒤죽박죽	① in disorder ② mixed up
드넓다	① to be spacious ② to be extensive
드문드문	sparsely
드물다	to be rare
드세다	to be tough
들쭉날쭉	① notched ② jagged ③ indented
따갑다	① to be stinging ② to be prickly
따끈하다	to be hot
따뜻하다	to be warm
딱딱하다	to be hard
똑같다	to be identical
똑똑하다	① to be smart ② to be bright
똑바르다	to be dead straight
뚜렷하다	① to be clear ② to be explicit
뚫리다	to be pierced
뚱뚱하다	to be fat
뜨겁다	to be hot
뜸하다	to be infrequent
띄엄띄엄	sparsely
마르다	① to dry up ② to run dry
마비	paralysis
마취상태	anesthesia
막히다	to be blocked
만족	satisfaction
많다	to be many/ much
많이	① many ② much
말끔하다	to be neat and tidy
말랑말랑	very soft
맑다	to be clear
맞다	to be right
매우	very
맥없이	① weakly ② spiritlessly ③ in low spirits
맵다	① to be spicy ② to be hot

수량	
많다	적다
넉넉하다 넘치다 풍부하다 풍족하다 :	모자라다 부족하다 :

맺히다	to form
먼지	dust
멀겋다	① to be weak ② to be thin
멀다	① to be far ② to be distant
	③ to be remote
멍청하다	to be stupid
메마르다	to be dried up
메스껍다	① to be sickening ② to be nauseating
명료하다	① to be clear ② to be obvious
명백하다	① to be obvious ② to be clear
명쾌하다	① to be clear ② to be explicit
명확하다	to be clear
모나다	to be angled
모두	all
모르다	to be ignorant of
모자라다	① to be not enough ② to lack
	③ to be insufficient
모조리	① without exception ② all
	③ to the very last
몹시	very
못	cannot
못하다	to be inferior to
몽땅	everything
무겁다	to be heavy
무기력하다	① to be spiritless ② to be enervated
무능하다	to be incompetent
무던하다	to be good-natured
무디다	① to be dull ② to be obtuse
무럭무럭	① (grow) rapidly ② well
무력하다	to be helpless
무르다	to be soft
무의미하다	to be meaningless
무익하다	to be useless
무조건	unconditionally
무척	greatly
무효	invalid

무게	
무겁다	가볍다
묵직하다	가뿐하다
:	:

묵다	to beome old
묵직하다	to be rather heavy
물렁물렁하다	to be soft and tender
물컹하다	to be pulpy
묽다	to be weak
뭉뚝하다	to be blunt
뭉치다	① to unite ② to lump
미끄럽다	to be slippery
미달	① shortage ② deficiency
미만	less than
미숙하다	① to be immature
	② to be inexperienced
미완성	incompletion
미치다	① to go mad ② to be insane
밀도	density
밀집	crowdedness
밉다	① to dislike ② to hate
바래다	to fade away
바르다	① to be erect ② to be upright
바쁘다	to be busy
바싹바싹	dry as bone
반드시	surely
반들반들하다	to be glossy
반듯하다	to be straight
반짝반짝	twinkling
밝다	to be bright
배고프다	to be hungry
배배	① winding ② twisted
배부르다	to be full
번들거리다	to be glossy
번잡하다	to be complex
번쩍번쩍	① flashing in rapid succession
	② glittering
변동	change
변하다	to be changed
변함없다	to be constant

밀도	
높다	낮다
닥지닥지 붐비다 빼곡하다 빽빽하다 오밀조밀 우글우글 촘촘하다 :	느슨하다 드문드문 띄엄띄엄 성글다 얼기설기 :

변형	transformation
변화	change
별나다	to be peculiar
병들다	① to fall ill ② to have an illness
보들보들하다	① to be very soft ② to be silky
보송보송하다	to be soft and dry
보통	normally
보편적	general
복스럽다	to be round and healthy looking
복잡하다	to be complicated
볼록하다	① to be protuberant ② to be bulging
볼품없다	① to be poor-looking ② to be unattractive
부당하다	to be unfair
부드럽다	to be soft
부분적	partial
부조화	disharmony
부족하다	to be insufficient
부쩍	rapidly
부패하다	① to rot ② to become rotten
분명하다	to be clear
분명히	clearly
분산	dispersion
분주하다	to be busy
붇다	① to swell up ② to increase
불가능	impossibility
불가능하다	to be impossible
불규칙	irregularity
불균형	unbalance
불명확하다	to be unclear
불분명하다	① to be obscure ② to be ambiguous
불안정하다	to be instable
불안하다	① to be anxious ② to be troubled
불완전	incompleteness
불일치	discordance
불편하다	① to be inconvenient

	② to feel uncomfortable
불합격	failure
불확실하다	to be uncertain
붐비다	to be crowded
붓다	to be swollen
비교적	comparatively
비다	to be empty
비대하다	to be fat
비뚤다	to be crooked
비로소	for the first time
비슷하다	to be similar
비싸다	to be expensive
비좁다	to be narrow
비치다	to be shined
비형식	informal
빈도	frequency
빈번하다	to be frequent
빈약하다	① to be poor ② to be scanty
빠듯하다	to be tight
빽빽하다	to be dense
뻣뻣하다	to be rigid
빼곡하다	to be compact
빽빽하다	to be full
뻣뻣하다	to be stiff
뽀얗다	to be milk-white
뾰족하다	to be pointed
삐뚤삐뚤	① wobbling ② shaking
사정	state of things
사태	circumstances
삭다	① to be worn out ② to calm down
산뜻하다	to be clean and refreshing
살살	① softly ② gently
상대적	relative
상승하다	① to rise ② to go up
상태	state
상하다	to get damaged or rotten

빈도	
높다	낮다
흔하다	귀하다
빈번하다	뜸하다
자주	이따금

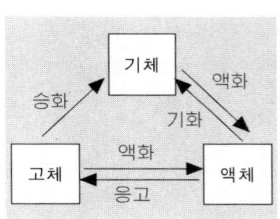

〈상태 변화〉

상황	situation
새다₁	① to leak ② to come through
새다₂	① to dawn ② to break
새롭다	① to be new ② to be fresh
색다르다	① to be unusual ② to be uncommon
생소하다	① to be unfamiliar
	② to be unaccustomed
서툴다	① to be unskilled ② to be clumsy
선명하다	① to be vivid ② to be clear
설익다	to be half-ripen
섬세하다	① to be delicate ② to be subtle
성공	success
성공하다	to succeed
성글다	to be sparse
성질	character
세다₁	to be strong
세다₂	to turn white
세모나다	to be triangular
세모지다	to be triangular
세차다	to be strong
소박하다	① to be simple
	② to be unsophisticated
속성	property
손쉽다	to be easy
솔솔	① gently ② smoothly
쇠하다	to become weak
수상하다	① to be strange ② to be doubtful
수월하다	① to be easy ② to be simple
수직	verticality
수평	horizontality
순결하다	① to be pure ② to be chaste
순수하다	to be pure
순조롭다	to be smooth
순진하다	① to be naive ② to be innocent
숭숭	(chop) into small pieces
쉬다	① to go bad ② to turn sour

쉽다	to be easy
슬기롭다	to be wise
습하다	to be humid
승화	sublimation
시다	to be sour
시들다	to get withered
시원하다	to be cool
신선하다	to be fresh
신식	modern
실상	actuality
실신하다	① to faint ② to fall unconscious
실재	real existence
실제	reality
실존	existence
실패	failure
실패하다	to fail
십중팔구	① nine out of ten ② mostly
싱겁다	to be insufficiently salted
싱싱하다	to be fresh
싸늘하다	to be chilly
싸다	to be cheap
쌀쌀하다	to be rather cold
썩다	to rot
쑥	① with a jerk ② with a vigorous pull
쏠리다	① to lean ② to incline
쓰다	to be bitter
쓰러지다	① to fall down ② to collapse
쓰리다	① to be sore ② to be burning
쓸데없다	① to be useless ② to be unnecessary
쓸모없다	to be useless
쓸모있다	to be useful
아깝다	① to be precious ② to be valuable
아득하다	① to be far-off ② to be vague
아롱다롱	① spotted ② mottled
아른아른	flickering
아름답다	to be beautiful

아물다	to be healed up
아주	very
아프다	① to be sick ② to be ill
안전하다	① to be safe ② to be secure
안정	rest
알다	to know
알맞다	① to be fit ② to be suitable
앙증맞다	to be cute and tiny
액상	liquid state
액체	liquid
액화	liquefaction
야트막하다	to be rather shallow
야하다	① to be showy ② to be gaudy ③ to be sexy
약간	① little ② bit
약하다	to be weak
약화	weakening
얄팍하다	to be thin
얇다	to be thin
양호	good
양호하다	① to be good ② to be satisfactory
얕다	to be thin
어둡다	to be dark
어려움	difficulty
어렵다	to be difficult
어수선하다	① to be disordered ② to be disarranged
어슷어슷	slant
어지럽다	to be dizzy
억세다	to be tough
얼기설기	in a disorderly way
얼다	to freeze
엄청나다	① to be exorbitant ② to be enormous
없다	to do not exist
엉기다	① to coagulate ② to congeal
엉성하다	① to be sparse ② to be loose

엉키다	① to tangle ② to get tangled
엉터리	① fake ② quack
여물다	to ripen
여위다	to lose weight
연약하다	to be feeble
연하다	① to be weak ② to be soft ③ to be tender
열세	inferiority
영리하다	to be clever
영원하다	to be eternal
예리하다	① to be sharp ② to be keen
예쁘다	to be pretty
오글오글	full of wrinkles
오똑하다	to be high
오래되다	① to be antiquated ② to have been a long time
오로지	solely
오밀조밀	minutely and intricately
오직	only
옮다	to transfer
옳다	to be right
옹기종기	in a small, closely gathered group
와르르	clattering
완만하다	to be gently-sloping
완벽하다	to be perfect
완성	completion
완전	perfection
완전하다	① to be perfect ② to be complete
용액	solution
용해	① melting ② fusion
우글우글	in swarms
우람하다	① to be imposing ② to be commanding
우세	superiority
우세하다	to be superior
우수	superiority
우수하다	to be superior

울창하다	to be dense
움푹하다	to be sunken
웅대하다	① to be grand ② to be magnificent
원숙하다	to be mature
원형	prototype
위험하다	to be dangerous
유난히	exceptionally
유능하다	to be capable
유달리	exceptionally
유력하다	to be influential
유별나다	to be peculiar
유사하다	to be similar
유익하다	to be beneficial
유일하다	to be unique
유효하다	to be valid
육중하다	to be bulky and heavy
응고	① solidification ② congealment
응고하다	① to solidify ② to congeal
이글이글	burning aglow
이따금	once in a while
이롭다	to be profitable
이상 (以上)	not less than
이상 (異常)	abnormality
이상하다	① to be abnormal ② to be strange
이하	not more than
익다₁	to ripen
익다₂	to be accustomed
익숙하다	to be accustomed to
인공	artificial
인조	artificial
일치	agreement
입자	particle
있다	to exist
자그마치	as much/many as
자연	nature
자욱하다	① to be dense ② to be thick

자잘하다	① to be small ② to be tiny ③ to be minute
자주	frequently
작다	to be small
잔뜩	① full ② to the full
잘	well
잘다	to be thin and small
잘록하다	① to be narrow ② to be slender
장점	merit
저물다	to grow dark
적다	① to be small ② to be little
적당하다	to be appropriate
적막하다	① to be dreary ② to be desolate
전반적	general
전부	all
전적으로	mainly
전체적	overall
절대	absoluteness
젊다	to be young
정갈하다	to be clean and neat
정당하다	to be just
정세	state of things
정황	circumstances
젖다	to get wet
제법	① fairly ② pretty
제일	① first ② number one
조각	fragment
조그맣다	to be tiny
조금	① small ② little
조밀하다	① to be dense ② to be crowded
조용하다	① to be quiet ② to be silent ③ to be still
조화	harmony
존재하다	to exist
좁다	to be narrow
줄다	① to become smaller ② to diminish

중간	middle
즐비하다	to stand closely in a row
증발	evaporation
지나치다	to exceed
지다	to fall
지저분하다	① to be filthy ② to be foul
지치다	① to be tired ② to be fatigued
지혜롭다	① to be wise ② to be sagacious
진실	truth
진실하다	to be honest
진짜	genuine
진하다	① to be thick ② to be strong
질기다	① to be durable ② to be tough ③ to be lasting
질다	to be soft
짙다	to be dark
짜다	to be salty
짤막하다	① to be short ② to be rather short
짧다	to be short
쪼글쪼글	① crumpled ② wrinkled
쪼들리다	① to be in needy circumstances ② to be strapped for money
찌들다	to get dirty
차다	to fill
차다	to be cold
찬란하다	① to be shining ② to be radiant ③ to be glittering
참	really
참되다	to be true
참신하다	to be original
천연	nature
천진난만하다	to be innocent
철철	overflowing
청결하다	① to be clean ② to be pure
청순하다	to be pure and fresh
청초하다	to be clean and fresh

체하다	to have an attack of indigestion
초과	excess
촉촉하다	① to be wet ② to be moist
촘촘하다	to be compact
총명하다	① to be clever ② to be smart ③ to be bright
추세	tendency
추하다	to be ugly
축축하다	to be damp
충만하다	to be full
취하다	to be drunk
치렁치렁	① hanging loosely ② dangling
친숙하다	to be familiar
친하다	① to be intimate ② to be close
침침하다	① to be dim ② to be dim-sighted
커다랗다	to be huge
크다	to be big
큼직하다	to be fairly big
타다	① to burn ② to be sunburned
탁하다	① to be thick ② to be impure
탄탄하다	to be sturdy
탱탱하다	① to be taut ② to be tight ③ to be inflated
토막	① block ② piece
통통하다	① to be round ② to be plump ③ to be chubby
투명하다	to be transparent
투박하다	① to be rough ② to be crude
트다	① to sprout ② to break ③ to open ④ to be chapped
특성	characteristic
특수하다	to be special
특이하다	to be peculiar
특질	property
특징	distinctive feature
튼튼하다	① to be sturdy ② to be healthy

틀리다	to be wrong
틀림없이	without a doubt
티끌	dust
판판하다	to be flat
패다	to come out
팽팽하다	① to be tight ② to be stretched to the full
퍼지다	to spread out
퍽	considerably
펑퍼짐하다	① to be flat and round ② to be broad and roundish
편리하다	to be convenient
편안하다	to feel comfortable
편하다	to be comfortable
평균	average
평범하다	to be common
평평하다	to be flat
평형	equilibrium
폭	width
표본	sample
푸짐하다	① to be plentiful ② to be abundant
푹신하다	① to be spongy ② to be soft
풍기다	① to give out an ordor ② to smell
풍만하다	to be plump
풍부하다	to be abundant
풍성하다	to be plentiful
풍요롭다	to be rich
풍족하다	to be affluent
피곤하다	to feel tired
피다	① to bloom ② to come out
필요하다	① to be necessary ② to be required
하강하다	to descend
하늘하늘	lightly
하도	too much
하찮다	to be trivial
한가하다	① to be free ② to be disengaged

한결	markedly
한결같다	① to be constant ② to be unchanging
합격	passing an examination
해롭다	① to be harmful ② to be injurious
허구	fiction
허기지다	to be exhausted with hunger
허름하다	① to be shabby ② to be worn-out
허물	fault
허상	virtual image
허술하다	to be negligent
허약하다	to be weak
허점	① blind spot ② weak point
헐겁다	① to be baggy ② to be too large
헐렁하다	to be baggy
험상궂다	① to look horrible ② to look threatening
헤프다	to be uneconomical
현명하다	to be wise
현실	reality
협소하다	to be narrow and small
형식	form
형편	condition
형평	equity
혼수상태	coma
혼잡하다	to be crowded
홀쭉하다	to be skinny
화목하다	to be in harmony
확고하다	to be determined
확실하다	to be certain
확실히	certainly
확연하다	to be definite
활기차다	① to be active ② to be energetic ③ to be lively ④ to be vigorous
훌륭하다	① to be nice ② to be excellent ③ to be magnificent
훨씬	far

휑하다	to be hollow
휘다	to bend
흉악하다	① to be atrocious ② to be heinous
흐리다	① to be weak ② to be thin
흔하다	to be common
흠	① crack ② scratch ③ defect
흠집	① crack ② flaw ③ scratch
흡사하다	to be very much like
흥건하다	to be full of water
희귀하다	to be rare
희박하다	to be rare
힘들다	① to be laborious ② to be arduous
힘없다	① to be powerless ② to have no energy
힘있다	① to be powerful ② to be strong

43 동작

Action and Movement

This chapter contains lexical entries related to people's actions: i.e., moving, appearing, disappearing, contacting, combining, separating, wearing, cooking, producing, and performing speech acts. In addition, it lists lexical entries describing people's psychological activities and functions.

가공하다	① to process ② to manufacture
가꾸다	① to grow ② to decorate
가누다	to control
가다	to go
가다듬다	① to collect oneself
	② to brace one's spirits
가동하다	① to operate ② to work ③ to run
가두다	① to shut in ② to lock in
가라앉다	to sink
가로젓다	to shake one's head
가로지르다	to cross
가르다	to separate
가르치다	to teach
가리다$_1$	① to cover ② to hide
가리다$_2$	to sort out
가리키다	to point to
가불하다	① to get an advance
	② to pay in advance
가시다	① to wash ② to rinse
가열하다	to heat

가지다	① to have ② to possess
가출하다	to run away from home
각성하다	to come to one's senses
각오하다	to be ready for (hardship)
간맞추다	to season with salt
간병하다	to nurse
간보다	to taste to see how it is seasoned with salt
간섭하다	① to interfere ② to meddle
간청하다	① to entreat ② to solicit
간추리다	① to sum up ② to summarise
간행하다	① to publish ② to issue
간호하다	to nurse
갈다₁	to change
갈다₂	to grind
갈라놓다	to divide
갈라서다	① to stand apart ② to get a divorce
갈라지다	to split
갈망하다	to long for
갈아입다	to change one's clothes
갉다	to gnaw
감다₁	to close (eyes)
감다₂	to wash (hair)
감다₃	to wind (thread)
감독하다	① to superintend ② to supervise ③ to direct
감동하다	① to be impressed ② to be moved
감사하다	to thank
감상하다	① to appreciate ② to enjoy
감소하다	① to decrease ② to diminish ③ to lessen
감시하다	to watch
감싸다	to wrap
감지하다	① to perceive ② to sense
감추다	to hide
감치다	to hem

감퇴하다	to decline
강연하다	to lecture
강요하다	① to compel ② to force
강의하다	to give a lecture
갖추다	to equip
갚다	to pay back
개간하다	to bring under cultivation
개다₁	to soften with water
개다₂	to fold
개발하다	to develop
개방하다	to open
개선하다	to improve
개시하다	to begin
개입하다	to intervene
개조하다	to remodel
개척하다	to pioneer
갸웃하다	to tilt one's head
거느리다	① to head ② to command
거동하다	① to act ② to behave ③ to move
거두다	① to harvest ② to reap
거들다	① to help ② to assist
거르다	to filter
거부하다	① to deny ② to refuse
거스르다	to give or receive change
거절하다	① to refuse ② to reject
거주하다	① to live ② to reside
거치다	① to stop by ② to go by way of
걱정하다	to worry about
건너다	to cross
건드리다	to touch
건배하다	to toast
건설하다	to build
건의하다	① to propose ② to request
건지다	to take out of water
건축하다	① to construct ② to build
걷다₁	to collect

걷다₂	to walk
걸다	to hang
걸치다	① to throw on ② to slip on
걸터앉다	to sit (on a chair)
검거하다	to arrest
검문하다	① to inspect ② to examine ③ to checkup
검사하다	to inspect
검산하다	to verify the accounts
검열하다	① to inspect ② to survey
검증하다	to verify
검진하다	to give a medical examination
검침하다	to check a meter
검토하다	to examine
겁나다	① to be frightened ② to be seized with fear
겁내다	① to fear ② to dread
게시하다	to post a notice
게우다	① to vomit ② to throw up
게임하다	to play a game
게재하다	① to publish ② to insert ③ to print
겨누다	to aim
겨루다	to vie with
격려하다	to encourage
격리시키다	to isolate
겪다	to experience
견디다	① to endure ② to bear
견주다	to compare with
결단하다	to determine
결론짓다	to conclude
결박하다	① to bind ② to tie up ③ to shackle
결별하다	to part with
결석하다	to be absent
결성하다	① to form ② to organize
결속하다	① to band together ② to unite
결심하다	① to determine ② to resolve

결정하다	to decide
결판내다	① to settle ② to finish
결합하다	① to unite ② to combine
결혼하다	to marry
경계하다	to be cautious
경고하다	to warn
경례하다	① to salute ② to make a salutation ③ to bow
경멸하다	to despise
경사지다	① to incline ② to slant
경영하다	to manage
경유하다	to go by way of
경작하다	① to cultivate ② to farm
경청하다	to listen
경험하다	to experience
계량하다	① to measure ② to weigh
계산하다	to calculate
계약하다	to contract
계측하다	to measure
계획하다	to plan
고꾸라지다	to fall forward
고다	① to boil ② to simmer
고려하다	to consider
고르다	① to choose ② to select
고립하다	to be isolated
고민하다	to be in agony
고발하다	to accuse
고백하다	to confess
고생하다	① to have a hard time ② to suffer hardships
고소하다	to sue
고안하다	to devise
고자질하다	① to tell on (someone) ② to squeal
고지하다	① to notify ② to announce
고집부리다	① to have one's own way ② to be stubborn

결합	분리
결합하다	분리하다
달다	떼다
만나다	헤어지다
매다	끄르다
묶다	풀다
붙다	떨어지다
엮다	풀다
잇다	끊다
잠그다	열다 · 풀다
합치다	나누다

고치다	① to fix ② to repair
골다	to snore
골라내다	to sort out
곯다	① to be hungry ② to go bad
공감하다	① to sympathize with ② to feel sympathy
공격하다	to attack
공경하다	to respect
공고하다	to notify
공그르다	to blindstitch
공박하다	① to refute ② to confute
공부하다	to study
공약하다	to pledge oneself (publicly)
공표하다	to announce
관광하다	to tour
관람하다	to see
관찰하다	to observe
관통하다	to pass through
괴다₁	to stagnate
괴다₂	① to prop ② to support
괴로워하다	① to suffer ② to feel pain
교대하다	to take turns
교류하다	to exchange
교섭하다	to negotiate
교제하다	to date
교체하다	to replace
교환하다	to exchange
구경하다	① to watch ② to go sightseeing
구기다	to crumple
구르다	to tumble
구박하다	to be hard on
구별하다	① to make a distinction ② to distinguish
구부러지다	to bend
구부리다	to bend down
구성하다	① to make ② to compose

	③ to constitute
구속하다	① to restrict ② to restrain
구술하다	to state orally
구출하다	to rescue
구타하다	to beat
구하다₁	to ask for
구하다₂	to save
군소리하다	to make an unnecessary remark
굴리다	to roll
굶다	① to skip a meal ② to starve
굶주리다	to starve
굽다	① to bake ② to roast ③ to broil
굽히다	① to bend ② to stoop
권고하다	to advise
권유하다	to advise
권장하다	to encourage
권하다	to recommend
귀가하다	① to come home ② to return home
귀띔하다	① to tell secretly ② to give a tip
귀순하다	to defect
귀향하다	to make a homeward voyage
귀화하다	to be naturalized
귀환하다	to return home
규명하다	① to examine closely ② to reveal
규제하다	to restrict
규탄하다	① to censure ② to denounce
그리다	① to draw ② to picture ③ to paint
그리워하다	to long for
그만두다	to quit
그치다	to stop
극복하다	to overcome
근무하다	to be on duty
근절하다	to exterminate
근접하다	to draw near
근접하다	to be adjacent
긁다	to scratch

금지하다	to prohibit
금하다	① to forbid ② to prohibit
긋다	to draw a line
긍정하다	to affirm
기다	to crawl
기다리다	to wait for
기대다	to lean against
기대하다	to expect
기도하다	to pray
기록하다	to record
기르다	① to breed ② to raise
기뻐하다	to be pleased
기술하다	to describe
기약하다	to promise
기어가다	to crawl
기억하다	to remember
기원하다	① to pray ② to wish
기입하다	to record
기재하다	① to record ② to state
기획하다	① to plan ② to make a plan
긴장하다	to be tense
긷다	to draw
길들이다	to tame
깁다	① to saw ② to stitch
까다	to peel
까불다	① to act carelessly ② to play a fool
깎다	to cut
깔다	to spread out
깨다	to break
깨뜨리다	to break
깨물다	to bite
깨우다	to wake (someone) up
깨우치다	① to teach ② to enlighten
꺼리다	① to keep at a distance ② to shy off
꺼지다	① to go out ② to blow out ③ to be extinguished

꺾다	① to break off ② to break
껴안다	① to embrace ② to hug
꼬다	to twist
꼬시다	① to tempt ② to seduce ③ to lure ④ to entice
꼬이다	to be entangled
꼬집다	to pinch
꼽다	to count with one's fingers
꽂다	① to insert ② to put in ③ to pierce
꾀다	① to swamp ② to lure
꾸다	to borrow
꾸리다	to pack
꾸미다	to decorate
꾸어주다	to lend
꾸중하다	① to scold ② to rebuke
꾸짖다	① to scold ② to rebuke
꿇다	to kneel down
꿈꾸다	to dream
꿈틀하다	to wriggle
꿰다	to sew
꿰뚫어보다	to see through
꿰매다	① to saw ② to stitch
끄다	① to put out ② to switch off ③ to turn off
끄덕이다	to nod
끄르다	① to untie ② to undo
끊다	① to sever ② to cut
끌다	① to pull ② to drag
끓이다	to boil
끝내다	to finish
끝마치다	to finish
끼얹다	to sprinkle
나가다	to go out
나누다	to divide
나르다	to carry
나무라다	① to blame ② to reprove

대상이동	
꾸다	↔ 갚다
넣다 · 담다	↔ 빼다 · 쏟다
밀다	↔ 당기다 · 끌다
사다	↔ 팔다
주다 · 보내다	↔ 받다 · 얻다

Action and Movement

앞으로 이동	뒤로 이동
나아가다	물러가다
전진하다	물러나다
추진하다	물러서다
행진하다	후진하다
:	후퇴하다
	:

나서다	to come forward
나아가다	to go forward
나열하다	① to enumerate ② to arrange in a row
나오다	to come out
나타나다	to appear
낙하하다	① to fall ② to come down
낚다	to fish
낚시하다	to fish
날다	to fly
날뛰다	to rave
날리다	to fly
날아가다	to fly away
날조하다	① to fabricate ② to forge
남다	to remain
납득하다	to understand
납부하다	to pay
납치하다	① to kidnap ② to hijack
낫다	to get well
낭비하다	to waste
낭송하다	to recite
낮추다	to lower
낳다	to give birth
내기하다	to bet
내놓다	to take out
내다	to set up
내려가다	to go down
내려오다	to come down
내리다	to get off
내밀다	to put forth
내보내다	to send out
내세우다	to make stand
내쫓다	to expel
내키다	to feel like (doing something)
냉대하다	to treat coldly
냉동하다	to freeze
널다	① to spread out ② to hang out

넓히다	to widen
넘기다	to pass over
넘다	to go over
넘보다	① to look down on
	② to look with greed
넘어지다	to fall down
넣다	to put in
노래하다	to sing
노려보다	to stare at
노리다	① to have an eye on ② to aim
노여워하다	to take offense at
노출하다	to expose
녹이다	to melt
녹화하다	① to record ② to videotape
논박하다	to argue against
논의하다	① to discuss ② to argue
논쟁하다	① to argue ② to dispute
논증하다	to prove
논평하다	to comment
놀다	to play
놀라다	to be surprised
놀러가다	to go somewhere to enjoy
놀러오다	to come over for pleasure
놀리다	to make fun of
농담하다	to joke
농사짓다	① to engage in farming
	② to do farming
높이다	to raise
놓다	① to release ② to place
놓아주다	① to let go ② to release
놓치다	① to miss one's hold ② to drop
	③ to lose ④ to let escape
누다	① to excrete ② to let out
누르다	① to press down ② to hold down
누리다	to enjoy
누비다	to quilt

Action and Movement

그대로 ㄱ	
길게	
나란히	
모로	눕다
몸져	
반듯이	
벌렁	
병들어	
앓아 ㅡ	
:	

누설하다	① to leak ② to disclose ③ to reveal
눈여겨보다	to take a good look
눈웃음치다	to smile with one's eyes
눕다	to lie down
뉘우치다	to regret
느끼다	to feel
늑장부리다	① to dawdle ② to linger
늘리다	① to increase ② to extend
늘어놓다	① to scatter ② to spread out
다가가다	to go near
다가서다	to get near
다가오다	to come up to
다그치다	to press for an answer
다녀가다	to drop in for a short visit
다니다	① to pass by ② to go to and from
다다르다	① to reach ② to get to
다듬다	① to trim off ② to prune
다루다	to treat
다리다	① to iron ② to press
다림질하다	to iron
다물다	① to shut ② to close
다스리다	to govern
다시다	to smack one's lips
다지다	① to mince ② to chop up
다짐하다	① to vow ② to pledge
다치다	to be hurt
다투다	① to dispute ② to argue
닦다	① to polish ② to wipe
단념하다	to give up
단속하다	① to keep under control ② to crack down on
단언하다	① to state ② to assert
단장하다	① to make up ② to decorate
단절하다	① to sever the relations ② to cut off
단정하다	to conclude
단축하다	to shorten

닫다₁	to close
달다₂	① to hang ② to suspend
달다₃	to weigh
달라붙다	① to stick ② to adhere
달래다	① to soothe ② to pacify
달려가다	to run
달려들다	to rush at
달리다	to run
달아나다	to run away
달이다	to boil down
담그다	① to make ② to pickle
담다	to put in
담소하다	to chat
담판하다	to negotiate
답례하다	to return a salute
답변하다	to answer
당기다	to pull
당부하다	① to ask ② to make a request
대꾸하다	to talk back
대다	to bring into contact
대담하다	① to talk with ② to have a talk
대답하다	to answer
대들다	to challenge
대립하다	to be opposed to
대변하다	to speak for
대응하다	to confront each other
대접하다	to serve
대출하다	to loan
대화하다	to converse with
더듬다	to grope
던지다	to throw
덜다	① to subtract ② to take off from
덤벙거리다	to act frivolously
덤비다	to attack
덮다	to cover
덮치다	to throw one's body over

데다	to be burnt
데우다	① to warm ② to make warm
데치다	① to scald ② to parboil
도려내다	① to scoop out ② to cut out
도망가다	to run away
도망오다	to run away from
도망치다	to run away
도박하다	to gamble
도배하다	to wall paper
도사리다	to sit cross-legged
도안하다	to design
도착하다	to arrive
도청하다	to tap
도피하다	① to escape ② to flee
독촉하다	to urge
돌다	to turn
돌보다	to take care of
돌아가시다	to pass away (deferential)
돌아다니다	to walk around
돌아보다	to look back
돌아서다	to turn one's back on
돕다	to help
동여매다	to tie to
동요하다	① to be disturbed ② to stir ③ to shake
동의하다	to agree with
동이다	① to bind ② to tie up ③ to cord
동작	movement
동정하다	① to sympathize with ② to feel pity for
동행하다	to accompany
되다	to measure
되돌리다	to put back
되돌아가다	to turn back
되묻다	to ask back
되받아치다	to retort
두근거리다	① to throb ② to palpitate ③ to beat

두근대다	① to beat ② to palpitate
두다	① to place ② to put ③ to keep
두드리다	to pound
두들기다	to beat
두려워하다	① to fear ② to dread ③ to be afraid of
두르다	① to gird ② to wrap ③ to pour around
두리번거리다	to look around
둘러보다	to look around
둘러앉다	to sit around
뒤따르다	to follow
뒤지다	to ransack
뒤집다	to turn inside out
뒤쫓다	① to chase ② to follow
뒹굴다	to roll about
드나들다	to go in and out
드러나다	to reveal itself
드러내다	to expose
드리다₁	to give (honorific)
드리다₂	to tie a braid
드시다	to eat (deferential)
듣다	to hear
들다₁	to eat (deferentail)
들다₂	to go into
들락날락하다	to go in and out frequently
들르다	① to drop by ② to stop by
들어가다	to go in
들어오다	to come in
들여다보다	to look in
들이대다	to thrust before
들이밀다	to push in
들이받다	to dash against
들이켜다	to gulp
들추다	to disclose
들키다	to be caught

등교하다	to attend school
등록하다	to register
등반하다	to climb up
등산하다	to climb a mountain
등장하다	① to come on the stage ② to appear
등지다	to lean against
디디다	to step on
딛다	to put a foot on
따다	① to pick ② to open
따돌리다	to leave out
따라가다	to follow
따라오다	to follow
따르다$_1$	to pour
따르다$_2$	to follow
따지다	to demand an explanation
땋다	to braid
때다	① to burn ② to make a fire
때리다$_1$	to beat
때리다$_2$	① to hit ② to beat
때우다	to solder
떠나다	to leave
떠돌다	to wander
떠들다	to make noise
떠보다	to fathom
떨다	① to tremble ② to sweep off
떨리다	to shiver
떨어뜨리다	to drop

출발	경유	도착
나다	가로지르다	내리다
떠나다	거치다	다다르다
이륙하다	건너다	닿다
출발하다	경유하다	도착하다
:	들르다	들다
	지나다	착륙하다
	통과하다	:
	:	

다니다, 돌아다니다, 오락가락하다, 왕래하다, 이동하다, 출입하다 …

떨어지다	to fall
떼다	① to take off ② to remove
뚫다	① to drill ② to build
뛰다	① to jump ② to leap ③ to run
뜨개질하다	to knit
뜨다₁	to float
뜨다₂	to knit
뜨다₃	to leave
뜨다₄	to open
뜨다₅	to scoop
뜯다	① to pluck ② to tear off
뜸들이다	to steam
띄우다	① to ferment
	② to make something afloat
마르다₁	to cut out
마르다₂	① to dry up ② to run dry
마무리짓다	to finish
마시다	to drink
마주보다	to look at each other
마중하다	to go out to meet
마치다	to finish
막다	to block
만나다	to meet
만들다	to make
만족하다	to satisfy
만지다	to touch
말걸다	to speak to
말다₁	to put into soup
말다₂	to roll
말다₃	① to stop ② Don't (do something)
말다툼하다	to quarrel
말대꾸하다	to talk back
말썽부리다	to cause trouble
말씀하시다	to speak (honorific)
말하다	to speak
맛보다	to taste

위로 이동	아래로 이동
뜨다	낙하하다
상승하다	내려오다
솟다	내리다
오르다	떨어지다
올라가다	추락하다
올라오다	침몰하다
:	하강하다
	하락하다
	:

오르내리다, 오르락내리락

Action and Movement

망각하다	to forget
망보다	① to look out ② to keep a watch
망설이다	to hesitate
맞다	① to greet ② to be exposed to
맞이하다	① to meet ② to go out to meet
맞잡다	to hold hands together
맞장구치다	to make agreeable responses
맞추다	① to assemble ② to join ③ to fit
맞히다	to hit
맡기다	to deposit
맡다	to smell
매다$_1$	① to bind ② to tie (up) ③ to fasten ④ to do up
매다$_2$	to weed out
매어두다	to tie (something) up
매진하다	to push on
맹세하다	to make an oath
맺다	① to bear ② to produce ③ to knot
머금다	to hold something in one's mouth
머무르다	to stay
머뭇거리다	to hesitate
먹다	to eat
먹이다	to feed
멀다	① to be far ② to be distant ③ to be remote
멈추다	① to stop ② to halt
멎다	to stop
메다	to strap something on the shoulder
메우다	to fill up
면담하다	① to interview ② to talk over
면제하다	to exempt
면하다	to be exempt from
면회하다	① to see ② to meet
명령하다	to order
명명하다	to name
명하다	① to order ② to command

모독하다	① to blaspheme ② to profane ③ to insult
모르다	to not know
모방하다	to imitate
모색하다	① to grope ② to brainstorm
모시다	① to attend to ② to serve
모욕하다	to insult
모으다	① to collect ② to gather
모이다	① to gather ② to collect
목격하다	to witness
몰다	① to drive ② to herd
몰두하다	to be absorbed in
몸풀다	to give birth to
못하다	to be poor
묘사하다	to describe
무너뜨리다	to break down
무르다	to refund
무서워하다	to fear
무시하다	to ignore
무장하다	to arm
무찌르다	to wipe out
무치다	to mix
묵다	① to stay ② to lodge
묶다	to bind
문안드리다	to inquire about the health of one's superior
문의하다	to inquire
문지르다	to rub
문책하다	to censure
묻다$_1$	to bury
묻다$_2$	to ask
물다	to bite
물들이다	to dye
물러가다	① to retreat ② to move back
물러나다	① to retreat ② to move back
물러서다	to step back

뭉개다	to crush
뭉치다	① to unite ② to make a lump
미끄러지다	to slide
미루다	to postpone
미워하다	to hate
미치다	to reach
믿다	to believe
밀고하다	to inform on
밀다	① to knead ② to push
바꾸다	to change
바라다	① to hope ② to wish
바라보다	to look at
바래다	① to discolor ② to fade away
바로잡다	① to straighten ② to correct
바르다₁	to split off
바르다₂	① to paste ② to smear ③ to put on ④ to spread
바치다	to offer (honorific)
박다	to drive in
반기다	to greet
반대하다	to oppose
반론하다	① to counter argue ② to refute
반문하다	to ask a question in return
반박하다	to refute
반발하다	① to oppose ② to defy
반성하다	to examine oneself
반주하다	to accompany for someone playing a musical instrument
반죽하다	to knead
반포하다	① to proclaim ② to announce publicly
반하다	① to fall in love ② to fall for
반항하다	① to resist ② to defy ③ to oppose
받다	to receive
받아쓰다	① to write down ② to take down a dictation

발가벗다	① to strip ② to undress ③ to bare oneself
발견하다	to discover
발라내다	① to shell ② to pare ③ to hull
발령하다	① to give an order ② to announce officially
발명하다	to invent
발버둥치다	to struggle
발사하다	① to shoot ② to launch
발생하다	① to occur ② to happen
발설하다	to disclose
발의하다	① to suggest ② to propose
발포하다	to fire
발표하다	① to present ② to announce
발휘하다	① to display ② to exhibit
밝히다	to clarify
밟다	to step on
방문하다	to visit
방송하다	to broadcast
방영하다	to televise
방청하다	① to hear ② to atttend
방해하다	① to disturb ② to interrupt
배기다	to bear up
배다	to bear
배반하다	to betray
배설하다	to excrete
배열하다	to arrange
배우다	to learn
배웅하다	to see off
배출하다₁	to produce
배출하다₂	to discharge
배치하다	① to place ② to deploy ③ to arrange
뱉다	to spit
버리다	to throw away
버무리다	to mix together
버티다	① to bear with ② to endure

번지다	to spread
벌다	to earn
벌름거리다	to flare (one's nose)
벌리다	to open
법석대다	to make a fuss
벗기다	① to peel ② to pare ③ to skin off ④ to tear off
벗다	to take off
베끼다	to copy
베다	to cut
베풀다	to give alms
벼르다	① to intend ② to plan
변론하다	to argue
변명하다	to make an excuse
변별하다	to distinguish
변형시키다	to transform
변호하다	to defend
변화시키다	to change
변화하다	① to change ② to undergo a change
보고하다	to report
보관하다	to take custody of
보내다	to send
보다	to see
보도하다	to report
보류하다	to hold
보살피다	① to take care of ② to care for
보유하다	to possess
보이다	to be seen
보존하다	to preserve
보채다	to beg for
보태다	to add
보호하다	to protect
복사하다	to copy
복습하다	to review
복창하다	to recite
볶다	① to parch ② to roast (beans)

가 / 누워 / 돌아 / 뛰어 / 마주 / 만나 / 먹어 / 써 / 앉아 / 자 / 해 / :] 보다

	③ to fry ④ to sautée
본뜨다	to cut out a pattern
봉하다	to seal up
부담하다	to bear the expense
부딪다	to crash into
부딪히다	① to bump into ② to crash into
부러뜨리다	to break
부르다	to call
부르짖다	to cry
부리다	① to manage ② to employ
부서지다	to be broken
부수다	① to break down ② to destroy
부언하다	① to add
	② to make an additional remark
부연하다	to expatiate on
부인하다	to deny
부정하다	to deny
부치다₁	to be beyond one's capacity
부치다₂	① to griddle ② to fry
부치다₃	to send
부탁하다	to ask a favor
분간하다	to distinguish
분노하다	to get into rage
분리하다	to separate
분만하다	to deliver a baby
분배하다	to distribute
분부하다	① to direct ② to instruct
분석하다	to analyse
분쇄하다	to reduce to powder
분실하다	① to lose ② to miss
분해하다	① to dissolve ② to decompose
불다	to blow
불리다	to soak
불참하다	to do not participate
불평하다	to complain
붓다	to pour

붕괴하다	① to collapse ② to break down ③ to fall ④ to cave in
붙다	to stick
붙들다	to hold
붙이다	to attach
붙잡다	① to seize ② to catch
비난하다	① to criticize ② to censure
비방하다	① to slander ② to defame
비비다	① to rub ② to mix
비우다	to empty
비웃다	to sneer
비집다	to split open
비추다	to light on
비키다	to get out of the way
비판하다	to criticize
비평하다	to criticize
비행하다	to fly
빈정거리다	to tease
빌다	to pray
빌려주다	to lend
빌리다	to borrow
빗다	to comb
빚다	① to shape dough for ② to roll into balls ③ to make
빠지다	① to fall into ② to loose weight ③ to omit
빨다₁	to wash
빨다₂	to suck
빻다	① to pound up ② to grind down
빼다	to take out
빼앗다	to take by force
뺑소니치다	① to run away ② to hit-and-run
뻗다	to stretch
뻗치다	to stretch out
뽐내다	to be arrogant
뽑다	to draw out

삐다	① to dislocate ② to sprain
삐치다	to become sulky
사격하다	① to shoot ② to fire at
사과하다	to apologize
사귀다	to make friends
사다	to buy
사라지다	to disappear
사랑하다	to love
사로잡다	to capture alive
사르다	to burn
사리다	to coil
사리분별하다	to discern with reasoning
사리판단하다	to judge with reasoning
사망하다	to die
사모하다	to love dearly
사무치다	to pierce one's heart
사색하다	to meditate
사양하다	to decline
사용하다	to use
사육하다	① to breed ② to rear ③ to raise
사절하다	to refuse
사정하다	① to beg considerations ② to entreat
사죄하다	① to apologize ② to beg pardon
사형하다	① to execute a death sentence ② to put to death
삭히다	to ferment
살다	to live
살림하다	① to keep house ② to manage a household
살펴보다	to examine
살피다	to make observation
살해하다	① to kill ② to murder
삶다	to boil
삼가다	to restrain oneself
삼다	to make a person one's daughter-in-law/son-in-law

삼키다	to swallow
상경하다	to come up to the capital
상기하다	to recollect
상상하다	to imagine
상실하다	① to lose ② to be deprived
상영하다	to show (on screen)
상의하다	to consult
새기다	① to engrave ② to inscribe
색칠하다	to color
샘내다	to be jealous
생각하다	① to think ② to consider
생기다	① to come into being ② to form
생산하다	to produce
생색내다	to take credit to oneself
생포하다	to capture alive
서거하다	① to die ② to pass away
서다	① to stand ② to stop
서두르다	to hurry
서성거리다	to walk up and down restlessly
서술하다	① to describe ② to state
서약하다	① to swear ② to vow
섞다	to mix
선거하다	to elect
선고하다	to sentence
선동하다	① to instigate ② to stir up
선발하다	to select
선서하다	to take an oath
선언하다	to declare
선포하다	to proclaim
설계하다	to design
설교하다	① to sermon ② to preach
설득하다	to persuade
설립하다	to found
설명하다	to explain
설치다	to run wild
설치하다	to install

서다 [갈라 / 나란히 / 둘러 / 멈추어 / 버티고 / 우뚝 / 일어 :]

섬기다	to serve
섭취하다	to ingest
성공하다	to succeed
성취하다	① to accomplish ② to achieve
세다	to count
세우다	to build
세탁하다	to wash
셈하다	① to count ② to calculate
소개하다	to introduce
소곤거리다	to whisper
소리치다	to cry out
소문내다	to spread a rumor
소비하다	to consume
소환하다	to summon
속다	to be deceived
속삭이다	to whisper
속상하다	① to feel vexatious ② to get disappointed
속이다	to cheat
솎다	to thin out
손떼다	to be through with (something)
손질하다	① to care ② to trim
솟다	to soar
쇠다	to celebrate
수놓다	to embroider
수다떨다	to chat
수락하다	to accept
수리하다	to repair
수배하다	to search
수사하다	to investigate
수색하다	to search
수선하다	to mend
수술하다	to operate
수정하다	① to revise ② to edit
수행하다	to perform
수호하다	to protect

수확하다	① to harvest ② to reap
숙이다	to hang down one's head
순교하다	to become a martyr
순국하다	to die for one's country
순방하다	to visit one after another
순시하다	to make a tour of inspection
순직하다	to die at one's post
순찰하다	to make one's round
숨기다	to hide
숨다	to hide
숨쉬다	to breathe
숨지다	to die
쉬다	to rest
스미다	to soak in
스치다	to brush past
스케치하다	to sketch
습득하다	to acquire
승낙하다	① to consent ② to permit
승리하다	to win a victory
승선하다	to go on board
승인하다	to approve
시기하다	to be jealous
시도하다	to try
시비하다	① to dispute ② to quarrel
시식하다	① to taste ② to try
시음하다	① to try ② to sample drink
시인하다	to admit
시작하다	① to start ② to begin
시중들다	① to attend on ② to wait on
시집가다	to take a husband
시찰하다	to inspect
시치다	to tack
시키다	to make (someone do something)
시행하다	to enforce
식다	① to get cold ② to subside
식별하다	to discern

식사하다	to eat a meal
신경쓰다	① to worry ② to be worried
신고하다	① to report ② to make a report
신다	to put on (something on the feet)
신음하다	to moan
신임하다	to trust
신청하다	to apply
싣다	to load
실룩거리다	to twitch
실망하다	① to be disappointed ② to be discouraged
실언하다	to make a slip of the tongue
실직하다	to loose one's employment
실천하다	to practice
실토하다	to confess
실패하다	to fail
실행하다	① to perform ② to operate ③ to execute
실험하다	to experiment
싫어하다	to dislike
심다	to plant
심문하다	to interrogate
심사숙고하다	to comtemplate
심사하다	① to examine ② to screen
심술부리다	① to act cross ② to do something nasty
심의하다	to deliberate
싸다	to excrete
싸우다	to fight
쌓다	to pile up
썩다	① to go bad ② to rot ③ to decay
썰다	to cut
쏘다	to shoot
쏘아보다	to scowl at
쏟다	① to pour ② to spill
쏠다	① to gnaw ② to nibble
쐬다	to be exposed to

Action and Movement

쑤다	to make gruel
쑤시다	to pick
쓰다₁	to use
쓰다₂	to put on (something on the head)
쓰다₃	to write
쓰다듬다	to stroke
쓸다	to sweep
씹다	to chew
씻다	to wash
아끼다	① to prize ② to value
아물다	to heal up
아부하다	to flatter
악담하다	① to speak ill of ② to backbite ③ to curse
악수하다	to shake hands
안내하다	to guide
안다	to hug
앉다	to sit
알다	to know
알리다	to inform
앓다	to suffer from
암기하다	to memorize
암송하다	to recite
압박하다	to press
앗다	to take by force
앙탈부리다	① to nag ② to whine
앞당기다	to advance a date
애걸하다	① to beg for ② to plead for
애도하다	to mourn for
애무하다	to caress
애쓰다	to make efforts
애원하다	① to implore ② to appeal
애지중지하다	to treasure
야단치다	to scold
야유하다	① to ridicule ② to hoot
약속하다	to promise

$$\left[\begin{array}{c} \text{가라} \\ \text{가만히} \\ \text{나란히} \\ \text{내려} \\ \text{둘러} \\ \text{마주} \\ \text{모여} \\ \text{일어나} \\ \text{주저} \\ \text{쪼그리고} \\ : \end{array}\right] \text{앉다}$$

양념하다	to season
양보하다	to concede
얕보다	to look down upon
어기다	to violate
어루만지다	① to stroke ② to pat
어르다	to coax
어림잡다	to estimate roughly
어림짐작하다	① to guess ② to make a shot
어우르다	to put together
어울리다	① to become match ② to fit
억누르다	to press down
억지부리다	to insist on having one's own way
언급하다	to mention
언도하다	① to sentence ② to pronounce
언약하다	to give one's word to
언쟁하다	① to quarrel ② to dispute
얹다	① to place on ② to put over
얻다	to get for free
얼리다	to freeze
얼버무리다	to speak vaguely
얽다	to weave
엄살부리다	to exaggerate pain
업다	to piggyback
업신여기다	to ignore
없애다	to remove
없어지다	① to be lost ② to be missing ③ to disappear
엎다	to turn over
엎드리다	① to lie on one's stomach ② to bend over
엎어지다	to fall on one's face
여기다	① to think ② to consider ③ to regard
여미다	① to adjust ② to arrange
여의다	① to be bereaved of ② to lose
여쭈다	① to tell (deferential) ② to ask (deferential)

Action and Movement

가다	오다
거쳐 가다	거쳐 오다
기어가다	기어오다
끌려가다	끌려오다
나가다	나오다
내려가다	내려오다
놀러 가다	놀러 오다
다가가다	다가오다
달려가다	달려오다
도망가다	도망오다
돌아가다	돌아오다
들어가다	들어오다
따 가다	따 오다
따라가다	따라오다
떠 가다	떠 오다
뛰어가다	뛰어오다
만나러 가다	만나러 오다
먹으러 가다	먹으러 오다
보러 가다	보러 오다
사러 가다	사러 오다
쉬러 가다	쉬러 오다
신고 가다	신고 오다
올라가다	올라오다
이사가다	이사오다
입고 가다	입고 오다
자러 가다	자러 오다
잡아 가다	잡아 오다
지나가다	지나오다
집어 가다	집어 오다
쫓아 가다	쫓아 오다
타고 가다	타고 오다
팔러 가다	팔러 오다
⋮	⋮

여행하다	① to travel ② to journey ③ to take a trip
역설하다	to emphasize
엮다	to weave
연결하다	① to connect ② to join
연구하다	① to research ② to study ③ to work
연기하다₁	to play a role
연기하다₂	to postpone
연상하다	to mind of
연주하다	to play music
연착하다	① to arrive late ② to be delayed
연출하다	① to direct ② to produce
열다₁	to bear (fruit)
열다₂	to open (door)
염색하다	to dye
엿듣다	to eavesdrop
엿보다	to steal a glance
영업하다	to do business
예견하다	to foresee
예고하다	to notify beforehand
예금하다	to deposit
예매하다	to buy in advance
예방하다	to prevent
예보하다	to forecast
예습하다	to prepare one's lessons
예언하다	to foretell
예찬하다	① to worship ② to adore
오다	to come
오락가락하다	to come and go
오르내리다	to walk up and down
오르다	① to rise ② to mount
오리다	to cut
오해하다	to misunderstand
올라가다	to go up
올라오다	to come up
올리다	to raise

옭다	to tie up
옭매다	to tie in a square knot
옮기다	① to move ② to transfer
옮다	to transfer
옹알거리다	① to mutter ② to murmur
완료하다	① to complete ② to finish
완만하다	to be gentlysloping
완성하다	to complete
왕래하다	to come and go
외다	to memorize
외우다	to memorize
외치다	to shout
요구하다	① to require ② to demand
요리하다	to cook
요양하다	to memorize
요청하다	① to demand ② to request
욕하다	① to curse ② to insult
용서하다	to forgive
우기다	to insist
우러러보다	to look up to
우러르다	① to respect ② to revere
우롱하다	to make a fool of
우쭐대다	① to be conceited
	② to have a swelled head
운동하다	to exercise
운명하시다	① to die (honorific)
	② to pass away (honorific)
운송하다	to transport
운영하다	① to run ② to manage
운전하다	to drive
운항하다	① to operate ② to run
울다	① to cry ② to weep
울먹이다	to be close to tears
울부짖다	to scream
움직이다	to move
움츠리다	to curl oneself up

웃다	to laugh
웅성거리다	to be in commotion
웅크리다	to crouch
원하다	to want
위조하다	① to forge ② to counterfeit
유도하다	① to induce ② to guide
유람하다	to go sightseeing
유발하다	to cause to happen
유보하다	to hold
유의하다	to keep in mind
유지하다	① to keep ② to maintain
유혹하다	① to tempt ② to entice ③ to lure
으깨다	to smash
윽박지르다	to put down with threats
읊다	① to chant ② to recite
응답하다	① to answer ② to reply
응시하다	to stare at
응원하다	① to support ② to back up
응하다	① to answer ② to comply with
의논하다	to consult
의존하다	to rely on
의지하다	to depend on
이기다	to win
이끌다	to lead
이다	to carry on the head
이동하다	to move
이루다	to accomplish
이륙하다	to take off
이르다$_1$	to arrive
이르다$_2$	to explain
이발하다	to have one's hair cut
이별하다	to separate
이사가다	to move to
이사오다	to move in
이야기하다	to tell a story
이용하다	to use

이행하다	① to fulfill ② to carry out
익히다₁	to make oneself familiar with
익히다₂	① to boil ② to cook
인사하다	① to greet ② to salute
인솔하다	to lead
인식하다	to recognize
인용하다	① to quote ② to cite
인접하다	① to be close by ② to be adjacent
일구다	to bring under cultivation
일깨우다	to awaken
일다	to wash
일어나다	① to get up ② to rise
일어서다	to stand up
일으키다	to set upright
일컫다	to call
일하다	to work
읽다	to read
잃다	to lose
잃어버리다	① to miss ② to lose
입다	① to put on (something on the body) ② to dress
입대하다	to join the army
입방아찧다	to gossip
입장하다	to enter
잇다	to connect
잊다	to forget
자다	to sleep
자라다	to grow
자랑하다	to brag
자르다	to cut
자문하다₁	to consult
자문하다₂	to question oneself
자백하다	to confess
자빠지다	to fall on one's back
자청하다	to volunteer
자칭하다	to call oneself

자화자찬하다	to praise oneself
작곡하다	to compose
작동하다	① to function ② to operate
작별하다	① to bid farewell ② to say good-bye
작사하다	to write the lyrics
작성하다	to draw up
작용하다	to act on
작정하다	to decide to
잔소리하다	to nag
잘못하다	① to make a mistake ② to do wrong
잠그다	to lock
잠들다	to fall asleep
잡다	① to grasp ② to grip
잡담하다	① to gossip ② to chat
잡수시다	to eat (deferential)
잡아내다	to pick out
잡아매다	to bind up
잣다	to spin
장가가다	to take a bride
장담하다	to assure
장사하다	to trade in
장식하다	to decorate
재다₁	① to measure ② to gauge
재다₂	to marinate
재단하다	to cut
재배하다	① to cultivate ② to grow
재잘거리다	① to chatter ② to prattle
재주부리다	to perform a trick
재촉하다	to urge
저금하다	to save
저리다	to become numb
저미다	① to mince ② to cut into pieces
저술하다	to write
저주하다	to curse
저지르다	① to commit ② to do a bad act
저지하다	① to obstruct ② to hold back

저축하다	to save
적다	to write
적발하다	to expose
전달하다	to deliver
전시하다	① to display ② to exhibit
전진하다	to go forward
전투하다	to fight a battle
전하다	① to report ② to deliver
전화하다	to make a call
절다	① to limp ② to hobble
절단하다	to cut off
절뚝거리다	to limp
절약하다	to save
절이다	① to pickle
	② to salt fish/vegetables
절하다	to bow
접대하다	to entertain
접속하다	to connect
접촉하다	to contact
젓다	to stir
정복하다	to conquer
정정하다	to correct
정지하다	to stop
정진하다	to devote oneself to
정하다	to decide
제끼다	to open
제안하다	① to propose ② to suggest
제의하다	to propose
제작하다	to produce
제조하다	to manufacture
제지하다	to restrain
제출하다	① to present ② to submit
조각하다	to carve
조롱하다	① to make a fool of ② to mock at
	③ to ridicule
조르다	① to beg for ② to ask importunately

조리하다	to cook
조립하다	to assemble
조사하다	to investigate
조언하다	to advise
조이다	to tighten
조작하다	to manipulate
조절하다	① to regulate ② to control
조정하다	to adjust
존경하다	to respect
졸다	to doze
졸이다	to boil down
좁히다	to make narrow
좇다	to follow
좋아하다	to like
죄다	to tighten
주다	to give
주먹질하다	to strike with a fist
주무르다	① to massage ② to knead
주문하다	to order
주시하다	to gaze steadily
주의하다	to pay attention to
주장하다	to insist
주저앉다	to drop on one's knees
주춤하다	to hesitate
죽다	to die
준비하다	to prepare
줄이다	to shorten
줍다	to pick up
중단하다	① to stop ② to suspend
중상모략하다	to slander
중얼거리다	to mumble
중탕하다	to heat in a water bath
쥐다	to clasp
즐기다	to enjoy
증언하다	to testify
증오하다	to hate

지껄이다	① to chat ② to chatter
지나가다	to pass
지나다	to pass
지나오다	to pass
지나치다	to go past
지니다	① to carry ② to possess
지다	to loose
지리다	to wet one's pants
지적하다	to point out
지지다	① to fry in a hot pan ② to frizzle
지지하다	to support
지켜보다	to watch intently
지키다	① to watch ② to keep
지피다	to make a fire
지휘하다	① to command ② to direct
진단하다	to diagnose
진땀난다	to break out in cold sweat
진료하다	to examine and treat
진보하다	to progress
진술하다	to state
진열하다	① to exhibit ② to display
진찰하다	to examine
진행하다	① to advance ② to progress
진화하다	to evolve
질문하다	① to inquire ② to ask a question
질의하다	to ask a question
질책하다	① to scold ② to reprove ③ to reproach
질투하다	to be jealous
짐작하다	to conjecture
집다	to pick up
집중하다	to concentrate
집필하다	to write
짓다	① to boil ② to cook (rice) ③ to prepare
짓밟다	to trample underfoot

짓이기다	① to beat to a pulp
	② to knead to a mash
징검다리	stepping stones
징계하다	to reprimand
짚다	to use an instrument to support oneself
짜다₁	to wring
짜다₂	to knit
째다	to rip
쩨려보다	to stare at
쩔쩔매다	to fluster oneself
쪼개다	① to split ② to cleave
쪼그리다	to crouch
쫓다	① to drive out ② to chase
쬐다	to be exposed to heat
찌그러지다	to crush
찌다	① to steam ② to heat with steam
찌르다	① to pierce ② to stab ③ to thrust
찌푸리다	to frown
찍다	① to cut down ② to take a picture ③ to print ④ to put in print
찡긋하다₁	to knit one's eyebrows
찡긋하다₂	to twitch
찢다	to tear
찧다	to pound
차다₁	to kick
차다₂	① to attach ② to fasten on ③ to wear (something mainly around the waist and wrist)
차단하다	to intercept
차리다	to set the table
차비하다	to prepare
차용하다	① to borrow ② to get a loan
착각하다	to have an illusion (false impression, misunderstanding)
착륙하다	to land
착복하다	to wear clothes

착수하다	to start
착용하다	to wear accessories
찬양하다	to praise
참가하다	to participate
참견하다	① to meddle in ② to interfere
참다	to bear
참회하다	to repent
창작하다	to create
창조하다	to create
찾다	① to search ② to look for
찾아가다	to visit
찾아오다	to visit
채다	① to carry off ② to snatch
채우다	to fasten
책망하다	① to blame ② to reprimand
챙기다	to gather all together
처리하다	① to handle ② to manage
처방하다	to prescribe
처벌하다	① to punish ② to inflict a penalty on
철거하다	to demolish
청구하다	① to ask for ② to charge
청취하다	to listen to
청하다	① to ask ② to request ③ to beg
청혼하다	to propose
체포하다	to arrest
쳐다보다	to look up
쳐부수다	① to break down ② to beat
촐랑거리다	to act frivolous
촬영하다	① to film ② to shoot
추궁하다	to press hard for an answer
추다₁	to dance
추다₂	to pick out
추락하다	① to fall ② to crash
추론하다	to infer
추리하다	to reason
추수하다	to harvest

추측하다	to conjecture
추키다	to hold up
축소하다	① to reduce ② to cut down
축하하다	to congratulate
출간하다	to publish
출발하다	to start
출산하다	to give birth to
출석하다	to attend
출세하다	to rise in the world
출연하다 (出演―)	to appear on the stage
출연하다 (出捐―)	to contribute
출입하다	to go in and out
출전하다	① to participate ② to play
출판하다	to publish
출항하다	to start on a voyage
출현하다	to appear
충고하다	to advise
충돌하다	to collide
취급하다	① to treat ② to handle
취재하다	① to collect news materials ② to collect data
취직하다	to find employment
측량하다	to measure
측정하다	① to weigh ② to measure
치다	① to strike ② to hit
치료하다	to treat
치르다	to pay
치우다	to clear
치하하다	to praise
칠하다	① to paint ② to color
침몰하다	to sink
칭송하다	① to admire ② to praise
칭찬하다	① to compliment ② to praise
캐내다	to dig up
캐다	to dig up
캐묻다	① to pry ② to press for an answer

켜다₁	to saw
켜다₂	to turn on
킁킁거리다	to sniff
키스하다	to kiss
키우다	① to breed ② to rear
타다₁	to get on
타다₂	to add (liquid or powder) to
타다₃	① to be scorched ② to be burnt
타이르다	to admonish
탄원하다	to plea
탈수하다	to dry
탈출하다	to escape
탈환하다	① to recapture ② to win back
탐구하다	① to explore ② to investigate
탐사하다	to explore
탐색하다	to search for
탑승하다	to board
탓하다	to blame
태우다	① to burn ② to scorch
터뜨리다	to burst
털다	to shake off
토론하다	to discuss
토의하다	to discuss
토하다	① to vomit ② to throw up
통고하다	to notify
통곡하다	① to weep bitterly ② to wail
통과하다	to pass
통보하다	to report
통솔하다	to command
통지하다	① to inform ② to notify
통찰하다	to penetrate into
통합하다	① to integrate ② to unify
퇴장하다	① to leave ② to go away ③ to exit
퇴짜놓다	① to refuse ② to reject
투덜대다	① to grumble ② to complain
투정하다	① to grumble ② to complain

둥기다	① to flip ② to flick
튀기다₁	to flip
튀기다₂	to fry
뛰다	① to bound ② to spark
트집잡다	to find fault
틀다	to twist
티내다	to have an air
파견하다	① to dispatch ② to send
파괴하다	to destroy
파다	to dig
파마하다	to get a perm
파멸하다	to be ruined
파산하다	to become bankrupt
파손하다	to damage
파열하다	to explode
판결하다	to judge
판단하다	to judge
판매하다	to sell
판별하다	to distinguish
판정하다	to decide (by an umpire)
팔다	to sell
패다	to beat
팽개치다	to throw forcefully
퍼붓다	to heap upon
펴다	① to spread ② to unfold
편입하다	to transfer
편집하다	to edit
평평하다	① to be flat ② to be even
평하다	to evaluate
폐쇄하다	to block
포개다	to put one upon another
포기하다	to give up
포박하다	to tie up
포옹하다	to hug
폭로하다	to reveal
폭파하다	① to blast ② to blow up

표기하다	to mark
표명하다	① to state ② to express
표백하다	to bleach
푸다	to scoop up
풀다₁	to blow one's nose
풀다₂	to untie
품다	to hold in one's arms
피우다	to smoke
핀잔주다	① to rebuke ② to reprimand
필기하다	to write a note
핑계대다	to make an excuse
하다	to do
하소연하다	① to make an appeal ② to complain
하품하다	to yawn
학습하다	to learn
한눈팔다	to look somewhere else
할퀴다	to scratch
핥다	to lick
합격하다	to pass an examination
합병하다	to merge
합산하다	to add up
합의하다	① to come to an agreement ② to talk over
합치다	① to put together ② to combine
합하다	to put together
항변하다	to make a plea
항의하다	to protest
항해하다	to navigate
해결하다	to solve
해고하다	to fire
해동하다	to thaw
해명하다	① to make clear ② to explain ③ to clarify
해부하다	to dissect
해산하다	to give birth to
해설하다	to explain

해치다	① to injure ② to harm
행군하다	to march
행진하다	to march
허가하다	to permit
허덕이다	to pant
허둥대다	to fluster oneself
허락하다	to consent
허물다	to tear down
허비하다	to be wasteful
허용하다	to allow
허우적대다	to struggle
헐다	to take down
헐뜯다	① to revile ② to slander
험담하다	to speak ill of
헛구역질나다	① to retch ② to be nauseous
헛기침하다	to have a dry cough
헤매다	① to wander about ② to roam about
헤아리다	to consider carefully
헹구다	to rinse
현상하다	to develope
협동하다	① to work together ② to collaborate
협력하다	① to cooperate ② to work together ③ to collaborate
협박하다	to threaten
협상하다	① to negotiate ② to bargain with
협심하다	① to unite ② to be of one accord
협의하다	to discuss
호다	to sew with large stitches
호소하다	to appeal
호언장담하다	① to talk big ② to boast
호출하다	to page
호통치다	① to shout ② to roar ③ to yell
혹평하다	to criticize sharply
혼동하다	to be confused
혼합하다	① to mix ② to blend
홀리다	to be obsessed

홀짝거리다	to keep sipping
화나다	to be angered
화내다	to get angry
화장하다 (化粧—)	to put on makeup
화장하다 (火葬—)	to cremate
화해하다	① to make up ② to come to terms
확대하다	to magnify
확언하다	① to assert ② to affirm
확장하다	to expand
환담하다	to have a pleasant chat
환송하다	to send back
환영하다	to welcome
환호하다	① to cheer ② to give cheers
활개치다	to strut
활동하다	① to play an active part ② to be active
활용하다	to put to practical use
회답하다	① to reply ② to answer
회복하다	to recover
회상하다	① to recollect ② to recall
후미지다	to be deeply indented
후비다	to pick
후진하다	to go backward
후퇴하다	to retreat
후회하다	to regret
훈계하다	to admonish
훈시하다	① to instruct ② to admonish
훑다	to thrash
훑어보다	to look over
훔치다	to steal
훼방놓다	to interrupt
휘감다	to twine round
휘어잡다	① to have someone/something under control ② to keep a firm grip
흉내내다	to mimic
흉보다	① to find fault with

	② to mention faults
흐느끼다	to sob
흐리다	to make something muddy
흔들다	① to shake one's head
	② to wave ③ to shake
흘기다	to cast a reproachful glance
흘리다	to spill
흠잡다	to find fault
흥분하다	to be excited
흥정하다	to make a deal
흥청대다	to indulge in merrymaking
흩다	to scatter
흩어지다	to disperse
희롱하다	① to make fun of ② to tease
희망하다	to hope
희생하다	to sacrifice
힘쓰다	① to exert oneself ② to make efforts

Appendix: Function Words

This book classifies the Korean lexicon into 43 categories and provides a range of information about its semantics. However, knowledge of lexical items alone is not sufficient for true communication. Attention must also be paid to the particular characteristics of the Korean language. To this end this appendix provides a table of the 4 types of functional words and attempts to explain and demonstrate their proper usage as clearly as possible.

▶ Indicator: A functional word or semi-functional word used for indicating or modifying a person, place or thing.

▶ Connector: A functional word used to connect words, sentences, or conversations.

▶ Particle: A functional word used to indicate the function of or add meanings to the combined words in a sentence or conversation.

▶ Ending: A functional word used to connect, enumerate, or end sentences or conversations.

▶ Indicators

Indicator	Meaning	Usage
걔	[he/ she] ▶ Colloquial use to mean 'the child' or 'that person' ▶ Used when the person referred to is the same age as or younger than the speaker	◦ 영수야, 걔 좀 만나러 가자. ◦ 어제 순이를 봤는데, 걔 멋있어졌더라.
거기	[there/ over there] ▶ Place	◦ 너 거기서 무얼 하고 있니? ◦ 거기 도착하면 바로 연락해.
그	[he/ that/ it/ the] ▶ Determiner indicating a person or thing near the listener or shared by the speaker and listener	◦ 그 꽃 참 예쁘구나. ◦ 그 노인 오늘도 운동하러 나오셨어.
	[he/ that/ it] ▶ Person(usually man) or thing known to both speaker and listener	◦ 그는 미소를 지으며 달려왔다. ◦ 그보다 좋은 일이 어디 있겠어요?
그거	[that thing] ▶ Abbreviation of 그것 (that thing) ▶ Colloquial	◦ 그거 무슨 책이니? ◦ 그거라면 나한테 맡겨.
그것	[that thing] ▶ Object/ state of affairs known to both the speaker and listener or already introduced in the conversation	◦ 그것은 영국으로 수출할 컴퓨터라고 하였다. ◦ 그것이 바로 우리의 행복이 아닐까요?
그곳	[there] ▶ Location of the speaker or a distant place which is already in the conversation	◦ 그곳 날씨는 요즘 어떠니? ◦ 우리 내일 그곳에 가서 사진 좀 찍고 오자.
그네들	[they] ▶ Mainly in written contexts, this indicates people whose identities are known to both the speaker and listener	◦ 그네들의 애국심은 대단하였다. ◦ 그네들은 막 떠나려던 참이었다.

그녀	[she] ▸ Mainly used in written contexts	◦ <u>그녀</u>의 지극한 효성에 어머니 병환이 나으셨다. ◦ <u>그녀</u>의 생활은 늘 차 한잔으로 시작된다.
그놈	[the guy] ▸ Derogatory word for 'the man' ▸ 3rd person pronoun referring to a man known to both the speaker and listener or to a man already in the conversation	◦ <u>그놈</u>은 늘 지각이야. ◦ 다시 가서 <u>그놈</u>을 잡아 와라.
그대	[you] ▸ Intimately or honorifically addressing the listener ▸ Mainly used in poems and love letters	◦ 외딴 곳에서 우는 <u>그대</u>는 누구인고. ◦ <u>그대</u>를 언제 만날 수 있을까요?
그대들	[you (plural)] ▸ Intimately or honorifically addressing several listeners ▸ Mainly used in written contexts	◦ 젊은이여, <u>그대들</u>의 꿈을 이루라. ◦ <u>그대들</u>은 이 땅의 소중한 청년들이다.
그들	[they] ▸ Mainly in written contexts ▸ Used when the speaker and listener both know or are aware of the people referred to	◦ 농부는 고개를 돌려 <u>그들</u>을 바라보고 있었다. ◦ <u>그들</u>이 바로 우리의 조상이다.
그러한	▸ Adjectival determiner meaning 'like that' or 'as mentioned above' ▸ Mainly used in written contexts	◦ 이 일의 모든 책임은 나에게 있다. 우리는 늘 <u>그러한</u> 자세로 이 일에 임하자. ◦ <u>그러한</u> 지적만 일삼고 있을 때가 아니다.
그런	Abbreviation of 그러한	◦ 아니요, <u>그런</u> 뜻으로 말한 건 아니었어요. ◦ <u>그런</u> 사람을 누가 좋아하겠어?
그렇게	▸ Abbreviation of 그러하게 ▸ Adverb meaning 'as mentioned above' or 'like something we both know about'	◦ <u>그렇게</u> 말씀하시니 저도 죄송하네요. ◦ <u>그렇게</u> 좋은 일을 왜 아직 몰랐을까.

그리	► Noun or adverb meaning 'toward that place' or 'in that direction'	○ 내가 이따가 <u>그리</u>로 갈까? ○ 길이 안 좋으니 <u>그리</u> 가지 말아요.
그분	[he/ she] ► Honorific form	○ <u>그분</u>은 저희 할머니이십니다. ○ <u>그분</u>은 훌륭한 예술가였어.
그애	[that guy/ that child] ► Abbreviation of 'the child' ► Indicates a child near the listener, a child known to both the speaker and listener, or a child already in the conversation ► Refers to someone of the same age as the speaker or someone younger	○ <u>그애</u> 좀 잘 보살펴 줘라. ○ <u>그애</u>는 정말 좋은 친구였다.
그이	[he/ my husband] ► Indicates one's husband or when an adult refers to someone younger or in the same age group ► Used when speaker and listener know the person and/ or when the person is already in the conversation	○ 우리 <u>그이</u>가 요즘 부쩍 피곤해 하네. ○ 홍선생하고 같이 일했는데, <u>그이</u> 보기보다 괜찮은 사람이던데.
그자 (一者)	[that fellow] ► Derogatory reference to a younger or the same aged person whom both the speaker and listener know	○ 그런 일을 벌일 사람은 <u>그자</u>밖에 없어. ○ <u>그자</u> 생각에는 그렇게 하면 일이 다 해결될 줄 알았겠지만 천만의 말씀.
나	[I/ me] ► Used when the listener is younger or is in the same age group	○ <u>나</u>도 너와 친해지고 싶어. ○ <u>나</u>의 발걸음은 한결 가벼웠다.
남	[other person/ people]	○ <u>남</u>보다 부지런해야 잘 살 수 있다. ○ <u>남</u>을 배려하는 마음을 갖자.
너	[you] ► Used when the listener is younger than or in the same age group as the speaker	○ <u>너</u>를 만나서 기쁘다. ○ <u>너</u>도 잘 할 수 있다.

너희	[you (plural)] ▶ Used when listeners are younger than or in the same age group as the speaker	○ 너희도 우리와 함께 갈거니? ○ 너희는 늘 함께 다니는구나.
누구	[who/ whom/ somebody/ anybody]	○ 죄송하지만 전화거신 분은 누구십니까? ○ 누구라도 가끔씩은 훌쩍 여행을 떠나고 싶을 때가 있을 것이다.
당신	[you] ▶ Honorific of 너 ▶ Used between married couples or among adults	○ 여보, 당신이 사 준 책 재미있게 읽었어요. ○ 박선생, 당신 언제 차 바꿨어?
	▶ Honorific of 자기 ▶ Reflexive pronoun meaning 'the very person indicated'	○ 어머니 당신은 늘 자식 걱정으로 평생을 사셨다. ○ 그분은 당신을 언제라도 조국에 바치겠노라 다짐하셨다.
당신들	[you (plural)]	○ 당신들 오늘 내 덕에 잘 논 줄 알아. ○ 당신들이 그 모양으로 처신하니 무슨 일이 되겠어?
댁 (宅)	[you] ▶ 2nd person pronoun used to honor the listener ▶ Mainly used on formal occasions	○ 댁의 따님은 여전히 잘하지요? ○ 댁이 누구시더라?
몇	[how many]	○ 이 수를 합하면 모두 몇이지? ○ 떡을 몇 개 먹었는지 모르겠네.
무슨	[what/ what kind of] ▶ Adjectival determiner asking about the content or the characteristics of something unspecified	○ 이 냄새가 무슨 냄새니? ○ 무슨 음악인지는 몰라도 참 좋군요.
무엇	[what]	○ 이 문제 답은 무엇이니? ○ 할 일이 하도 많아서 무엇을 먼저 해야 할 지 모르겠네.
뭐	[what] ▶ Abbreviation of 무엇 mainly used in spoken contexts	○ 이게 뭐니? ○ 뭐라도 좋으니 빨리 가져오거나 해.

본인 (本人)	▶ Noun used to refer to oneself or another person himself/ herself	○ 오늘 본인은 여러분 앞에서 다음과 같은 약속을 드리고자 합니다. ○ 잘못이 있다면 본인이 책임져야지.
스스로	▶ Adverb meaning 'by himself/ herself', 'by his/ her own will/ power'	○ 스스로 알아서 할 일을 하니 참 기특하다. ○ 살아가며 스스로를 돌아보는 시간도 가져야지.
아무	[anyone/ no one] ▶ Pronoun [any] ▶ Adjectival determiner	○ 거기 아무도 없어요? ○ 아무도 찾지 않는 깊은 산 속. ○ 아무 곳에서나 잠을 자면 어떡하니? ○ 아무 대책도 세우지 못했다.
애	▶ Abbreviation of 이 아이 (this child) used mainly in spoken contexts ▶ 3rd person pronoun indicating or calling a younger or same age person near the speaker	○ 애가 내 딸아이요. ○ 애, 너 정말 오랜만이다.
어느	[which] ▶ Adjectival determiner	○ 어느 책이 클까? ○ 다음 학회가 어느 나라에서 개최되는지 모르겠어요.
어디	[where/ somewhere/ anywhere/ nowhere]	○ 할머니, 어디 가세요? ○ 어디선가 찬바람이 불어왔다.
어떤	[what kind of/ any kind] ▶ Adjectival determiner	○ 그 친구는 어떤 사람인가? ○ 어떤 이야기든 좋습니다.
어떻게	[how/ somehow] ▶ Adverb used when asking about the direction or about how something is done	○ 어떻게 그 집을 찾아가지? ○ 우리 사회는 어떻게 될까요?
어르신	[sir] ▶ Noun honoring another person's father, or other elderly person ▶ Honorific	○ 어르신께서는 안녕하신가? ○ 어르신, 그럼 이만 가보겠습니다.

어르신네	[sir] ▶ Same meaning as 어르신, only less direct ▶ Honorific	○ 어르신네께서는 안에 계십니까? ○ 어르신네, 요즘 건강은 어떠십니까?
언제	[when/ what time/ some time] ▶ Adverb or a pronoun	○ 너희들 언제 만나기로 했니? ○ 우리 언제 영화 보러 가자. ○ 우리나라의 민화가 언제부터 생겼는지 정확히 알 수 없다.
얼마	[how much/ what quantity/ how long]	○ 이거 얼마예요? ○ 우리는 한글에 대해 과연 얼마나 알고 있는가?
여기	[here] ▶ 3rd person pronoun indicating the speaker's location	○ 나는 그냥 여기 있을 게요. ○ 여기는 지금 비가 와요.
왜	[why/ what for]	○ 할머니는 왜 웃고 계실까? ○ 왜 벌써 가니?
우리	[we] ▶ Used when the listener is younger than or in the same age group as the speaker	○ 우리 내일 뭐 할 건지 의논하자. ○ 그러면 우리는 어떤 일을 맡을까?
이	[this/ these] ▶ Adjectival determiner indicating a person/ place/ thing near the speaker, or a state of affairs which the speaker knows	○ 이 과자 정말 맛있다. ○ 이 계획대로라면 지금쯤 일이 끝나 있어야 하는 거지.
	▶ 3rd person pronoun indicating a state of affairs mentioned just previously by the speaker	○ 그림을 이처럼 잘 그린 사람은 없었다. ○ 어제 거리에서 행사가 있었는데 이를 본 아이들은 모두 즐거워했다.
이거	[this thing] ▶ Abbreviation of 이것 used mainly in spoken contexts	○ 이거 누구 사진이니? ○ 이거 사야지.

이것	[this thing] ▶ 3rd person pronoun indicating a thing near the speaker, or a state of affairs about which the speaker knows	◦ 아버지, <u>이것</u> 좀 잡숴 보세요. ◦ 자녀와 늘 친하게 지내는 일, <u>이것</u>은 현대의 가정 교육에서 정말 중요한 일이다.
이곳	[this place] ▶ Pronoun indicating place which the speaker knows	◦ <u>이곳</u>에 오는 사람들은 꼭 여기를 들리지요. ◦ <u>이곳</u> 날씨는 참 맑다.
이놈	[this guy] ▶ Derogatory word of 이 남자 (this man)	◦ <u>이놈</u>을 어떻게 혼내줘야 되나? ◦ <u>이놈</u> 저놈 하지 마세요.
이들	[these people] ▶ Mainly used in written contexts ▶ 3rd person pronoun indicating several people mentioned just previously by the speaker	◦ 열심히 공부하는 학생들, <u>이들</u>은 나라의 미래이자 희망이다. ◦ 누가 <u>이들</u>에게 돌을 던지랴.
이런	[like this/ like these] ▶ Abbreviation of 이러한 ▶ Adjectval determiner	◦ 둥글고 하얀 얼굴, 커다란 눈, 누가 <u>이런</u> 사람 못 보셨나요? ◦ <u>이런</u> 일은 미리 의논하고 해야지.
이러한	[like this/ like these] ▶ Adjectival determiner meaning 'like this' or 'as the speaker mentioned'	◦ <u>이러한</u> 생각은 하지 말자. ◦ 김수장의 사설시조에서 발견되는 <u>이러한</u> 세 가지 유형은 이미 널리 알려져 있다.
이렇게	[like this/ this way] ▶ Adverb meaning 'like this (like what the speaker just said or will say next, or like a current state of affairs)'	◦ <u>이렇게</u> 예쁜 가방을 어디서 샀니? ◦ <u>이렇게</u> 해 보고 안 되면 다른 방법을 생각해 보자.
이리	[this way/ this direction]	◦ <u>이리</u> 오시오. ◦ <u>이리</u>로 곧장 가면 큰 길이 나올거야.
이분	▶ 3rd person pronoun indicating a person near the speaker with respect	◦ <u>이분</u>은 정말 훌륭한 시민이오. ◦ <u>이분</u>이 제 선생님이십니다.

이이	[this person] ▶ 3rd person pronoun used when an adult refers to another adult who is younger or of the same age ▶ Used to indicate a person near the speaker	○ 이이가 왜 이러시나. ○ 그 일이라면 이이가 전문이야.
이자 (—者)	[this fellow] ▶ Derogatory word for 이 사람 (this person) ▶ 3rd person pronoun indicating a nearby person or a person who is younger or in the same age group	○ 이자는 사람도 아니구먼. ○ 이자가 사람을 쳐?
임자	[you] ▶ 2nd person pronoun used between an old couple or among intimate old people	○ 임자도 이젠 많이 늙었구려. ○ 임자, 내 다녀오리다.
자기 (自己)	[himself/ herself/ he/ she/ own]	○ 민수는 자기만 아는 얘야. ○ 영이는 왜 그렇게 자기 동생을 미워하니?
자기자신 (自己自身)	[himself/ herself and no other]	○ 사람은 자기자신의 허물을 잘 못 본다.
자네	[you] ▶ 2nd person pronoun used by adults to address a person who is younger or of the same age	○ 자네가 그 일 좀 해 주게. ○ 자네도 많이 변했네.
자신 (自身)	[himself/ herself and no other]	○ 너 자신을 알라. ○ 훈이는 자신이 가장 잘났다고 생각한다.
자체 (自體)	[itself] ▶ Noun meaning 'by its own power' or 'the very thing indicated'	○ 그 회사는 비디오를 자체 개발하였다. ○ 그것 자체가 하나의 훌륭한 대중 문화이다.

쟤	▸ Abbreviation of 저 아이 or 저 애 used mainly in spoken contexts ▸ 3rd person pronoun referring to a person at a far distance who is younger or of the same age as the speaker	◦ 얘, 쟤 좀 봐. 참 예쁘게 생겼지? ◦ 우리 쟤한테 물어 보자.
저	[that]	◦ 저 사람 어디 아픈가 봐. ◦ 저 꽃 참 예쁘지? ◦ 저 소리가 안 들려요? ◦ 저 쪽에 앉아 계셔요.
	[I (to an elder)] ▸ Humble 1st person pronoun	◦ 안녕하세요? 저는 새로 들어온 김 혁입니다. ◦ 그럼 저는 이만 나가 보겠습니다.
저거	[that thing/ that one] ▸ Abbreviation of 저것 used mainly in spoken contexts	◦ 저거 좀 깨끗이 치워라. ◦ 저거 한 번 먹어볼까?
저것	[that thing/ that one]	◦ 일어나서 저것 좀 보렴. ◦ 저것은 연기가 아니고 수증기란다.
저곳	[that place/ over there]	◦ 저곳에는 누가 사나요? ◦ 어디가지 말고 저곳 그늘에서 기다려라.
저기	[that place/ over there]	◦ 저기 화장실이 있네. ◦ 저기 서 있는 사람이 누구니?
저놈	▸ Derogatory version of 저 남자 (that man) ▸ 3rd person pronoun, indicating a distant man seen by both the speaker and listener	◦ 저놈 잡아라. ◦ 저놈 아주 싱거운 놈이야.
저런	[like that]	◦ 저런 모양은 처음 봤다. ◦ 뭐 저런 사람이 다 있니?
저렇게	[like that/ in that way]	◦ 저렇게 즐거울 수가 있을까? ◦ 쟤는 운전을 왜 저렇게 하니?

저리	[toward that place/ in that direction/ over there]	∘ 이리 <u>저리</u> 다녀 봐도 집이 제일 좋다. ∘ <u>저리</u>로 가서 앉아 주세요.
저분	[that person] ▶ Honorific 3rd person pronoun indicating a person far from the speaker and listener but seen by both	∘ <u>저분</u>이 바로 우리 할아버지셔. ∘ <u>저분</u> 참 대단하신 분이야.
저애	▶ Abbreviation of 저 아이 (that child) ▶ 3rd person pronoun referring to a person far from the speaker and listener but seen by both of them ▶ Person referred to is younger than or of the same age as the speaker	∘ 얼른 가서 <u>저애</u> 좀 도와주자. ∘ <u>저애</u> 얼굴도 크다.
저이	[that person] ▶ 3rd person pronoun referring to a person far from the speaker and listener but seen by both of them ▶ Used by an adult to refer to a person who is younger or of the same age	∘ <u>저이</u>한테 물어보자. ∘ <u>저이</u>가 사람은 좋은데.
저자 (一者)	▶ Derogatory version of 저 사람 (that person) ▶ 3rd person pronoun referring to a person(younger or same age) far from the speaker and listener but seen by both	∘ <u>저자</u>의 집은 아무도 모른다. ∘ <u>저자</u>가 바로 도둑이다.
저희	[we] ▶ Humble form of 우리 (we)	∘ 늘 <u>저희</u>를 돌보아 주셔서 감사합니다. ∘ <u>저희</u> 가족을 소개하겠습니다.
제	[I/my] ▶ Humble form	∘ 이곳이 <u>제</u>가 다니는 학교입니다. ∘ <u>제</u> 생각을 말해 볼까요?

▶ Connectors

Connector	Meaning	Usage
게다가	[besides] ▶ Adding to and focusing on what was said previously	○ 너는 씩씩하고, 명랑하고, <u>게다가</u> 공부까지 잘 하는구나.
곧	[that is] ▶ Elaborating on something said previously	○ 어진 정치를 하세요. 곧 백성을 으뜸으로 생각하는 정치말이예요.
그래도	[though/ but/ yet/ nevertheless/ still/ however/ all the same/ for all that/ at any rate]	○ 나는 공부를 하지 않았다. <u>그래도</u> 늘 1등만 했다.
그래서	[so/ thus] ▶ Same meaning as 그러하여서 (thus), 그렇게 해서 (so)	○ 송이는 숙제를 안 했다. <u>그래서</u> 야단을 맞았다.
그래야	[only so] A word, meaning 'only so; unless so; only if one does [says] that.'	○ 감기 약 먹어. <u>그래야</u> 감기가 빨리 낫지.
그러기에	[that's why/ because of that]	○ 교육에서 사랑의 필요성은 아무리 강조해도 지나치지 않다. <u>그러기에</u> 진정한 교육자가 되기가 또한 어려운 것이다.
그러길래	[beacuse of that] ▶ Mainly used in spoken contexts	○ 아이: 엄마, 숙제 다 못했어요. 엄마: <u>그러길래</u> 놀기 전에 숙제부터 했어야지.
그러나	[but/ however]	○ 언니는 자신 있게 대답하였습니다. <u>그러나</u> 나는 고개를 숙인 채 아무 말도 못하였습니다.
그러느라고	[that's why] ▶ Meaning 'doing so'	○ 어제는 친구를 만나서 신나게 놀았어요. <u>그러느라고</u> 할 일도 다 못했네요.
그러니	[so] ▶ Mainly used in spoken contexts	○ 모두가 한 마음으로 일을 했어. <u>그러니</u> 일이 안 될 리가 있겠어?

그러니까	[consequently/ therefore]	◦ 내가 그를 미워하면 그도 나를 미워하게 마련이다. 그러니까 내가 사랑을 받고 싶으면 내가 먼저 그 사람을 사랑해야 한다.
그러다가	[by doing so]	◦ 강아지 자꾸 못살게 굴지 마. 그러다가 물릴 지도 몰라.
그러면	[if so/ then/ in that case]	◦ 독서를 마음의 양식이라고 한다. 그러면 우리는 책을 통하여 무엇을 얻을 수 있을까?
그러면서	[and at the same time] ▶ Used in suggesting that the following fact has some connection to the preceding fact	◦ 정호는 열두 살이 되면서부터 기차에서 과일과 신문을 팔았다. 그러면서 틈틈이 책을 읽으며 열심히 공부하였다.
그러므로	[therefore/ since/ hence]	◦ 사람은 평등하다. 그러므로 모든 사람을 존중해야 한다.
그런데	[by the way/ but/ however]	◦ 이제는 돌아갈 일이 걱정이었습니다. 그런데 바로 그때였습니다.
그럴수록	[as far as the situation goes] ▶ Emphasizes the degree or intensity of the preceding fact	◦ 동생이 요새 왜 자꾸 심술을 부리지? 그럴수록 동생에게 잘 해 줘라.
그럴지라도	[nevertheless/ even though]	◦ 내가 좀 살기는 어려웠지. 그럴지라도 네가 나를 그렇게 무시하는 게 아니지.
그럴지언정	[nevertheless/ still]	◦ 어렸을 때는 배도 많이 곯았다. 그러나 그럴지언정 남의 것을 훔치지는 않았다.
그럴더라도	[even so/ even though] ▶ Focuses on the following content	◦ 요즘 무척 바빠서 만나기는 어려울 것 같애. 그럴더라도 연락은 좀 하면서 살자.
그럴지만	[but/ however/ still]	◦ 뙤약볕 때문에 무척 더웠다. 그럴지만 철이는 꾹 참고 계속 올라갔다.

그리고	[and] ▸ Connects words, phrases, clauses or sentences in parallel ▸ Focuses on the following content	◦ 현수는 연필과 공책, <u>그리고</u> 책을 들고 꽃밭으로 갔습니다. ◦ 어머니는 안타까운 마음으로 딸의 손을 잡았습니다. <u>그리고</u> 간절히 기도를 하였습니다.
그리하여	[thus/ therefore] ▸ Used in formal writing	◦ 이런 사람은 천재라는 이름을 얻는다. <u>그리하여</u> 한평생 한문으로 글자살이를 하고 산다.
더구나	[moreover/ in addition] ▸ Means 'on top of the already stated fact' ▸ Emphasizes the following content	◦ 퉁명스러운 말은 사람의 마음을 언짢게 한다. <u>더구나</u> 욕설이나 거친 말은 감정까지 몹시 상하게 한다.
더욱이	[besides] ▸ Means 'on top of this/ that'	◦ 예람이는 착하다. <u>더욱이</u> 얼굴도 예쁘다.
따라서	[therefore/ thus]	◦ 땅값이 올랐다. <u>따라서</u> 집값도 올랐다.
또	[and] ▸ Means 'in addition to the previous statements'	◦ 어제는 비가 오더니 오늘은 <u>또</u> 눈이 오네.
또는	[or] ▸ Connects words, phrases or sentences	◦ 제비꽃은 '오랑캐꽃' <u>또는</u> '반지꽃'이라고 한다.
또한	[moreover/ also]	◦ 소영이는 노래를 잘 한다. <u>또한</u> 피아노도 잘 친다.
왜냐하면	[the reason it is so] ▸ Used when the following words are a cause or a reason for the previous words	◦ 나는 지금 기분이 너무 좋다. <u>왜냐하면</u> 시험이 다 끝났기 때문이다.
즉 (卽)	[that is]	◦ 언어학은 과학이다. <u>즉</u> 언어에 대하여 과학적으로 연구하는 학문이다.

하물며	[much more/ let alone/ not to mention] ▸ Makes the following content more obvious in relation to the previous content	◦ 어른도 하기 어려운 일인데, <u>하물며</u> 열 살짜리가 그 일을 할 수 있을까?
하지만	[yet/ but/ however/ though] ▸ Contrasts something with the preceding content or adds clues to the preceding content	◦ 시험에 합격했다. <u>하지만</u> 등록하지 않았다.
한편	[while]	◦ 중부지방은 날씨가 맑다. <u>한편</u> 남부지방에는 비가 많이 온다.

▶ Particles

★ Things in ( ) can be deleted, or are affected by the final sound of the preceding word.

Particle	Meaning	Example
-가	▶ Subject marker for vowel endings ▶ Used before 되다 (become), 아니다 (not)	○ 효빈이가 마당에서 공을 차며 논다. ○ 나는 천재가 아니다.
-같이	[like/ similarly as/ alike] ▶ Object marker for words with the same properties or characteristics	○ 얼음같이 차가운 바람이 뺨을 스칩니다. ○ 종서는 새벽같이 일어나서 나를 깨웠다.
-(이)고	[and] ▶ Particle linking two or more things or concepts	○ 술이고 뭐고 다 귀찮다. ○ 어른이고 아이고 다 모였어.
-과	[and] ▶ Links (attached to a word ending in a consonant) two or more parallel words	○ 하늘과 땅 ○ 동물과 식물
	[with] ▶ Meaning 'together', attached to consonant endings ▶ Marks compared object before 같다 (be the same), 다르다 (be different)	○ 철수는 친구들과 여행을 떠났다. ○ 인생은 긴 여행과 같다.
-까지	[until/ by/ till/ as far as] ▶ Limits the point of time, space, object or scope	○ 떠나는 날까지 약속을 잘 지켜줘서 고맙다. ○ 이 열차는 청량리에서 인천까지 운행합니다.
-깨나	Colloquial use of 'to some degree or amount' of a certain object	○ 돈깨나 있는 사람이 왜 그리 인색하게 굴까? ○ 우람이는 힘깨나 쓴다고 잘난 척한다.
-께	[to address (to an elder)] ▶ Honorific form of 에게	○ 사랑하는 어머님께 ○ 선생님께 인사를 드렸습니다.

-께서	Honorific form of 이/ 가	◦ 아버지께서 걱정하지 말라고 하셨어요. ◦ 이 옷은 할머니께서 사 주신 것이다.
-(이)ㄴ들	[even though]	◦ 난들 뾰족한 수가 있겠니? ◦ 내 고향을 꿈엔들 잊으리요.
-(이)나	[or/ just] ► Indicates choice between two alternatives, or when there is no choice	◦ 철수나 진아 중 한 사람만 보내자. ◦ 보채지 말고 이 과일이나 먹어.
	[or/ whether..or] ► Used when there is no particular object to be decided and when any number will do ('written like ⋯(이)나 ⋯(이)나)	◦ 너나 나나 바쁘긴 마찬가지구나. ◦ 버스나 지하철이나 되는대로 타 보자.
-(이)나마	[at least] ► Means 'insufficient but somewhat satisfactory'	◦ 그나마 어머니가 건강하셔서 다행이다. ◦ 이 집이나마 있어서 다행이군.
-는	► Subject marker for words ending in vowels ► Used to contrast words with other words	◦ 지구는 둥글다. ◦ 너만 좋은 데 가고 우리는 좋은 데 가면 안 되니?
-(이)니	Enumerates examples	◦ 뭐니 뭐니 해도 형만한 아우 없다. ◦ 팔자니 운명이니 하는 말을 믿니?
-(이)다	[to be (copula)]	◦ 우리는 멋쟁이다. ◦ 이것은 연필이다.
	Enumerates examples	◦ 갈비다 잡채다 온갖 진수성찬이 다 차려져 있었다. ◦ 그 집에는 닭이다 돼지다 안 기르는 동물이 없다.
-에다가	[in/ on] ► Place marker	◦ 차에다가 지갑을 두고 내렸어. ◦ 여기에다가 놓고 가렴.
-대로	[according to]	◦ 약속대로 신발을 사 주겠다.
	[on its own]	◦ 장미는 장미대로 들꽃은 들꽃대로 예쁘다.

-더러	[to] ▶ Used with verbs of telling	◦ 누가 너더러 그런 거 하랬니? ◦ 나더러 반장을 하라고?
-도	[too/ also/ even] ▶ Shows that something is an increment to another ▶ Used when continuing to talk about something or adding to list of similar things	◦ 이제 나도 가고 너도 가야지. ◦ 오라는 데도 없고 갈 데도 없다.
-(이)든(지)	[(what)ever/ any at all]	◦ 연필이든 볼펜이든 뭐든 줘 봐. ◦ 누구든지 노력하면 성공할 수 있다.
-(이)라	[it is ..., so]	◦ 부자라 역시 다르다. ◦ 가을이라 날씨가 좋다.
	Abbreviation of (이)라고 used for direct quotations	◦ 노래도 못 부르면서 어떻게 가수라 할 수 있겠니?
-(이)라고	Quotes another person's words directly	◦ 독서를 '마음의 양식'이라고 합니다. ◦ 그 친구가 뭐라고 하더라.
	[just because]	◦ 부자라고 반드시 행복한 것은 아니다. ◦ 아들이라고 별 수 있겠어?
-(이)라도	[even/ even though/ even if]	◦ 이거라도 가지고 가자. ◦ 지금이라도 가보는 게 좋겠어.
-(이)라든가	[such as]	◦ 시라든가 소설이라든가 하는 분야에 관심이 있다. ◦ 옷이라든가 차라든가 차림새로 보아 부자가 틀림없다.
-(이)라든지	[whether/ or/ such as]	◦ 휴대폰이라든지 삐삐라든지 연락할 방법이 없어? ◦ 숟가락이든지 젓가락이든지 하나만 줘 봐.
-(이)라면	[if] ▶ Abbreviation of (이)라고 하면	◦ 이럴 때 너희들이라면 어떻게 하겠니? ◦ 이 몸이 새라면 날아가리.

-(이)라야	[only/ not..until]	◦ 그 일은 영숙이라야 할 수 있을 걸. ◦ 그 옷에는 파란 모자라야 어울리겠어.
-(이)란	[as for]	◦ 사랑이란 왠지 모른 척 해도 관심이 있는 게 사랑이야. ◦ 사람의 마음이란 다 그런 거야.
-(이)랑	Compares something with other objects or links several things in parallel	◦ 영수는 나랑 키가 같다. ◦ 밖에서 친구들이랑 공을 차다보면 어느새 하루해가 저문다.
-(으)로	[with/ by]	◦ 그건 가위로 잘라야지. ◦ 물감으로 예쁘게 색칠을 하자.
-(으)로부터	[from]	◦ 예로부터 우리 민족은 밥을 주식으로 했다. ◦ 마음으로부터 우러나오는 자발적인 행동이 필요하다.
-(으)로서	[as/ in the capacity of]	◦ 나는 형으로서 동생의 좋은 거울이 되기로 다짐하였다. ◦ 나는 한국인으로서 자부심을 느낀다.
-(으)로써	[with]	◦ 이것으로써 오늘 행사를 마치겠습니다. ◦ 오늘로써 만난 지 100일이 되었다.
-를	Object marker attached to vowel endings	◦ 나는 저녁에 칼국수를 먹었다. ◦ 우리는 함께 공놀이를 하였다.
-마냥	[like]	◦ 나는 바보마냥 웃기만 했다. ◦ 내 마음은 새털마냥 가볍기만 하다.
-마는	Admitting the preceding content but asking for permission to say something different	◦ 네 말도 맞다마는 어쩔 수가 없구나. ◦ 나도 가고 싶지마는 못 가.
-마다	[every/ each]	◦ 너를 볼 때마다 네 엄마가 생각난다. ◦ 나는 아침마다 산책을 한다.

-마따나	[as said] ▶ Attached only to 말 (word)	◦ 네 말마따나 영이가 오늘도 소식이 없으려나 보다. ◦ 걔 말마따나 그 사람 재미있더라.
-마저	[even/ also]	◦ 너마저 내 말을 안 믿는구나. ◦ 막내딸마저 시집 보내고 나면 적적하시겠네요.
-만	[only/ just]	◦ 청춘은 어디 가고 백발만 남았는가. ◦ 왜 밥은 안 먹고 물만 마시니?
-만큼	[as much as]	◦ 나만큼 복이 많은 사람도 없는 것 같애. ◦ 장미가 사람 키만큼 자랐다.
-말고	[not/ other than] ▶ Meaning ~가 아니고 (is not), ~ 외에(other than)	◦ 커피말고 다른 차 없니? ◦ 도서관에는 나말고 두 사람이 더 있었다.
-(이)며	[and]	◦ 내가 살던 집이며 학교며 모두 그대로 남아 있었다. ◦ 눈이며 코며 예쁘지 않은 데가 없다.
-밖에	[only] ▶ 'except that, or other than that' ▶ Followed by negative ending	◦ 사람이 너밖에 없니? ◦ 자리가 하나밖에 안 남았다.
-보고	[toward] ▶ Same as 에게 (to) and 더러 ▶ Attached to a word representing a person	◦ 사람들이 저보고 천재래요. ◦ 보람이가 우리보고 빨리 오라고 손짓했다.
-보다	[than] ▶ Comparative	◦ 내가 너보다 두 살 더 많다. ◦ 꿈보다 해몽이 좋다.
-부터	[from] ▶ Starting point of an action or a state	◦ 그날부터 두 아이는 열심히 일을 하였다. ◦ 숙제부터 하고 놀아라.

-뿐	[only]	◦ 그렇게 생각하는 사람은 나<u>뿐</u>이다. ◦ 머리 속에는 온통 엄마 생각<u>뿐</u> 다른 생각은 없다.
-(이)시여	Honorific form of (이)여	◦ 하늘<u>이시여</u>. ◦ 신<u>이시여</u>, 부디 저를 용서하소서.
-아	[Hey] ► Used when calling an animal or a person who is younger or of the same age ► Attached to consonant endings	◦ 영란<u>아</u>, 이리 와. ◦ 바둑<u>아</u>, 밥 먹어라.
-야	► Used in calling an animal or a person who is younger or of the same age ► Attached to vowel endings	◦ 승우<u>야</u>, 너 참 부지런하구나. ◦ 앵무새<u>야</u>, 오늘은 왜 말이 없니?
-(이)야	[when it comes to/ indeed]	◦ 예람<u>이야</u> 잘 할거야. ◦ 달리기<u>야</u> 자신 있지.
-(이)야말로	[precisely/ exactly/ really/ none other than]	◦ 대자연<u>이야말로</u> 인간의 영원한 보금자리이다. ◦ 너<u>야말로</u> 나의 진정한 친구다.
-에	Place marker	◦ 언제 서울<u>에</u> 오거든 연락해라. ◦ 주머니<u>에</u> 돈이 하나도 없었다. ◦ 한규는 대학에 합격했다
-에게	[to/ at/ for/ by someone] ► Person affected by an action or process	◦ 이 편지를 언니<u>에게</u> 전해라. ◦ 나<u>에게</u> 소원이 있다면, 조국이 통일되는 것이다.
-에서	[at/ in/ on/ from] ► Place where an action happens or a state holds	◦ 길<u>에서</u> 영하를 만났다. ◦ 나는 이 세상<u>에서</u> 오빠가 제일 좋아.
-(이)여	► Vocative marker used as a polite address and as an exclamation ► Generally used in prayers.	◦ 소년들<u>이여</u>, 꿈을 가져라. ◦ 주<u>여</u>, 저를 용서하소서.

-와	[and] ▸ Links two or more things ending in vowels [with] ▸ Indicates a contrasting object before 같다 (be the same), 다르다 (be different) ▸ Attached to vowel endings	◦ 남자<u>와</u> 여자 ◦ 노래<u>와</u> 춤 ◦ 나는 오늘 친구<u>와</u> 함께 여행을 떠난다. ◦ 이론은 실제<u>와</u> 다르다.
-요	▸ Shows respect to a listener ▸ Attached to a word, phrase or sentence	◦ 저<u>요</u>, 다음 주에 결혼해<u>요</u>. ◦ 아버지와 함께 체조를 해<u>요</u>.
-은	▸ Topic marker ▸ Indicates point of contrast ▸ Attached to consonant endings	◦ 백두산<u>은</u> 우리나라에서 가장 높은 산이다. ◦ 미역국<u>은</u> 싫어하지만 콩나물국<u>은</u> 잘 먹어요.
-을	▸ Marks an object of a predicate ▸ Attached to consonant endings	◦ 어제는 좋은 꿈<u>을</u> 꾸었다. ◦ 운동장에서 선생님<u>을</u> 만났다.
-의	Possessive marker	◦ 하늘<u>의</u> 구름처럼 두둥실 떠 가리. ◦ 동화 속<u>의</u> 나라 같지?
-이	▸ Subject marker of a predicate attached to consonant endings ▸ Used with 되다 (become) or 아니다 (is not)	◦ 숲 속에 작은 연못<u>이</u> 있습니다. ◦ 사랑은 받는 것<u>이</u> 아니다.
-일랑	▸ Used when a certain object is particularly focused on	◦ 무거운 짐<u>일랑</u> 가져오지 마셔요. ◦ 그런 걱정<u>일랑</u> 하지 마세요.
-조차	[even]	◦ 너무 지쳐서 말하는 것<u>조차</u> 힘들었다. ◦ 암기는커녕 생각<u>조차</u> 나지 않았다.
-처럼	[like/ as if] ▸ Comparative marker	◦ 우리도 개미<u>처럼</u> 부지런히 살자. ◦ 나도 미란이<u>처럼</u> 예뻤으면 좋겠어.

-치고	[with no exceptions]	○ 어느 부모치고 자식 못 되길 바랄까. ○ 게으른 사람치고 성공한 사람 못 봤다.
-커녕	[anything but/ not at all/ far from] ► Emphasizes the negative	○ 아이들은커녕 개미새끼 한 마리 없었다. ○ 선물은커녕 인사도 제대로 못 했다.
-하고	[and] ► Links two or more objects	○ 동생하고 재미있게 놀았어요. ○ 아빠하고 나하고 만든 꽃밭
-하며	[and] ► Enumerates objects sharing something in common	○ 오빠는 연필하며 공책하며 온갖 것을 다 사주었다. ○ 수미는 말투하며 걸음걸이하며 꼭 어른 같다.
-한테	[toward (an animate object)] ► Same as 에게 (to)	○ 친구한테 편지를 보냈다. ○ 왜 나한테 오라고 하셨을까?
-한테서	[from (a person)] ► Same as 에게서 (from) ► Used in spoken contexts.	○ 나는 아내한테서 선물을 받았다. ○ 오늘은 형님한테서 전화가 왔다.

▶ Endings

★ Things in ( ) can be deleted, or are affected by the final sound of the preceding word.

Ending	Meaning	Usage
-(ㄴ)가	Asking about the present facts to a person of the same age or younger	◦ 만나서 즐거운 사람은 어떤 사람<u>인가</u>? ◦ 아버님께서는 지금 뭐하고 계<u>신가</u>?
-거나	Enumerating two or more facts or when choosing among several things	◦ 남이 보<u>거나</u> 말<u>거나</u> 막 떠든다. ◦ 내일은 비가 오<u>거나</u> 눈이 내리겠습니다.
-거늘	Reason or a cause marker	◦ 언덕도 힘들<u>거늘</u> 절벽까지야. ◦ 다 똑같은 친구이<u>거늘</u> 너는 왜 개를 미워하니?
-거니	Action or a state marker which is repeated	◦ 주거니 받<u>거니</u> 하면서 잘 논다. ◦ 두 사람이 앞서<u>거니</u> 뒤서<u>거니</u> 하면서 달려간다.
-거든	Elaborating on preceding content	◦ 아까 나 많이 먹었<u>거든</u>. ◦ 나는 바다를 좋아하<u>거든</u>.
	Condition marker	◦ 도착하<u>거든</u> 바로 연락해라. ◦ 비가 오<u>거든</u> 빨래를 걷어라.
-거라	Command marker	◦ 아침에 일찍 일어나<u>거라</u>. ◦ 이제 그만 가<u>거라</u>.
-게	Giving a mild command or asking a favor	◦ 이것 좀 잡아주<u>게</u>. ◦ 어서 집에 가 보<u>게</u>.
	Intention or purpose marker	◦ 책 좀 사<u>게</u> 돈 좀 주세요. ◦ 공부 좀 하<u>게</u> 조용히 해.
	▶ Modifies the following words ▶ Attached to adjectival roots	◦ 그렇게 곱<u>게</u> 단장하고 어디가세요? ◦ 방을 새롭<u>게</u> 꾸며 봅시다.
-게끔	[so as to] ▶ Presenting an intention or purpose	◦ 일이 되<u>게끔</u> 힘 좀 쓰자. ◦ 알아듣<u>게끔</u> 다시 얘기해 봐.

-겠-	▶ Used when a change of action or state is going to happen ▶ Attached to verbal roots	◦ 저녁 비행기로 떠나<u>겠</u>어요. ◦ 다음 사람이 힘들<u>겠</u>네요. ◦ 해가 곧 지<u>겠</u>군.
-고	[and] ▶ Enumerating or connecting content	◦ 손뼉 치<u>고</u> 노래하며 즐겁게 놀았다. ◦ 아침밥을 꼭 먹<u>고</u> 학교에 가거라.
-고서	[and then] ▶ Used when a preceding fact or event is a presupposition of the following fact or event	◦ 큰 가방을 들<u>고서</u> 여행을 떠났다. ◦ 잠자리를 손가락으로 잡<u>고서</u> 자세히 살펴보았다.
-고자	[in order to] ▶ Used to express an intention	◦ 의논을 드리<u>고자</u> 왔습니다. ◦ 이 사전을 쓰<u>고자</u> 합니다.
-구나	Used to express a confirmation	◦ 나 때문에 네가 고생이 많<u>구나</u>. ◦ 아파도 잘 참는<u>구나</u>.
-구려	Exclamation or a command marker	◦ 저 집 참 멋있<u>구려</u>. ◦ 당신 마음대로 하시<u>구려</u>.
-군	Abbreviation of 구나 has a more decisive meaning	◦ 음, 이 연필 참 좋<u>군</u>. ◦ 잘 했<u>군</u>, 잘 했어.
-군요	Honorific form of 군	◦ 영수는 또 결석을 했<u>군요</u>. ◦ 날씨가 참 좋<u>군요</u>.
-기	▶ Making a word with a conjugated ending into a noun form ▶ Attached to 이다 or a root	◦ 한 마디로 대답하<u>기</u>는 어렵다. ◦ 윤희는 신문기자이<u>기</u> 때문에 무척 바빠.
-기로	Cause or reason marker	◦ 축구 선수가 되<u>기로</u> 마음먹었다. ◦ 그럼 이렇게 하<u>기로</u> 하자.
-기로서니	[because something or someone is so and so] ▶ Stronger form of 아무리, ~다 하더라도	◦ 내가 아무리 못났<u>기로서니</u> 그 정도쯤이야 못 해주겠니? ◦ 농담 좀 했<u>기로서니</u> 왜 그렇게 화를 내고 그래?
-기에	Direct cause or reason marker	◦ 뭘 찾<u>기에</u> 그렇게 두리번거리니? ◦ 사랑하<u>기에</u> 떠나신다는 그 말 나는 믿을 수 없어.

Endings 581

-길래	▶ Direct cause or reason marker ▶ Used in spoken contexts	○ 네가 온다길래 기다리고 있었지. ○ 아기가 울길래 우유를 주었다.
-(으)ㄴ	Adjectival ending used to modify the following word	○ 예쁜 집, 맑은 하늘. ○ 식은 밥은 데워 먹어라.
-ㄴ-/-는-	Event or state marker which is happening in the present	○ 아이들이 개울에서 물고기를 잡는다. ○ 날이 점점 어두워진다.
-(으/느)ㄴ데	Used in talking about a related matter first in order to set the state for the following words	○ 품질은 좋은데 값이 좀 비싸. ○ 내가 어제 집에 가는데 길이 많이 막히더라. ○ 마음씨는 착한데 좀 게을러.
	Used in asking about or expressing awe over an unexpected fact	○ 잘 생겼는데. ○ 돈이 얼마나 있는데?
-(으)ㄴ들	Same as 라고 할 지라도 (even though) and is used to disagree with the following words	○ 밥을 먹은들 그게 살로 가겠니? ○ 화를 낸들 별 수 있어?
-(으)ㄴ지	Doubt and conjecture marker	○ 왜 그렇게 값이 비싼지 몰라. ○ 좋은지 나쁜지 잘 모르겠어.
-나	Asking a question to a person of the same age or younger	○ 요새 뭐하고 지내나? ○ 청소는 다 끝났나?
-(으)나	Linking content with preceding words	○ 뜻은 좋으나 방법이 문제야. ○ 계획은 세우나 지킬 일이 걱정이네.
	Enumerating facts (written as -(으)나)	○ 미우나 고우나 마누라가 최고지. ○ 길을 걸으나 음악을 들으나 오직 그 사람 생각뿐이다.
-(으/느)냐	Asking a question to a person of the same age or younger	○ 무슨 일이야 있겠느냐? ○ 그게 그리도 좋으냐? ○ 그것도 일이라고 하냐?
-너라	Giving commands or asking something of a person of the same age or younger to do	○ 이리 오너라. ○ 저 책 좀 가져오너라.

-네	Confirming a piece of information with a person of the same age or younger	◦ 어? 비가 오네! ◦ 그 일은 잘 한 것 같네.
-느라고	[because something or someone is in the midst of doing something] ▶ Same meaning as 하는 일로 말미암아 (because of the work)	◦ 영화 보느라고 늦게 잤지. ◦ 자느라고 전화를 못 받았어.
-는	Used to make a verbal stem into an adjectival form indicating a present tense	◦ 지금 집에 가는 중이야. ◦ 하늘에 떠 가는 저 구름.
-(으)니	Used when asking a question to a person of the same age or younger	◦ 좋은 생각 없으니? ◦ 그 집 마당이 그렇게 넓으니?
	Indicating the previous content as a cause or a reason for the following content	◦ 비옷을 입으니 덥다. ◦ 집에 와 보니 소포가 와 있었다.
-(으)니까	[since/ given that/ now that] ▶ Strong version of -(으)니	◦ 야단 맞으니까 정신이 없다. ◦ 비가 오니까 부침개가 더 맛있다.
-다	Stating a fact or an event	◦ 하늘이 높다. ◦ 산새들이 노래한다.
	[like this like that]	◦ 차들이 가다 서다 한다. ◦ 많다 적다 말들이 많다.
-다(가)	[while someone or something was doing something] ▶ Marking a change from a state or action to another	◦ 밥을 급하게 먹다 체했어. ◦ 음악을 듣다가 책을 보다가 한가한 시간을 보냈다.
-다고	Quoting words of others or to elucidate a cause or reason	◦ 수미는 인호가 좋다고 하였다. ◦ 내가 아무리 너를 야단쳤다고 네가 이럴 수 있어?
-(ㄴ/는)다면	Abbreviation of (ㄴ/는)다고 하면 and marks an assumption of a future event	◦ 네가 그곳에 간다면 아이들이 참 좋아할거야. ◦ 우리가 손을 잡는다면 일이 아주 잘 될거야. ◦ 네가 좋다면 나도 좋아.

-더-	Presenting what has been directly seen, heard or experienced	◦ 그 집 짜장면 맛있<u>더</u>라. ◦ 어제 집에 갔<u>더</u>니 민이가 울고 있<u>더</u>라.
-더니	[as a consequence of something being done] ▶ Used when the previous fact is a cause or a reason of the following fact	◦ 날이 흐리<u>더니</u> 비가 내렸다. ◦ 그 얘기를 듣<u>더니</u> 인표가 울기 시작했다.
-더라	▶ Presenting a fact which the speaker has discovered or experienced ▶ Used when the speaker is surprised by a certain fact or event	◦ 그 집 냉면 맛있<u>더라</u>. ◦ 수미는 내일 여행 간다<u>더라</u>.
-더라도	Stating a strong assumption with a distant feeling	◦ 좀 잘 못하<u>더라도</u> 너그럽게 가르쳐 주세요. ◦ 놀 때는 놀<u>더라도</u> 일할 때는 잘 하자.
-더라면	▶ Marking an assumption of a fact that did not actually happen in the past ▶ Expressing a hope that a certain situation would occur	◦ 내가 조금만 더 참았<u>더라면</u> 좋았을걸. ◦ 미리 알았<u>더라면</u> 도와주었을텐데.
-던	Marking a past action that is not yet completed	◦ 하<u>던</u> 일을 멈추고 여기를 보세요. ◦ 이 인형은 내가 어렸을 적에 가지고 놀<u>던</u> 것이다.
-던들	▶ Marking an assumption or a fact that did not actually happen in the past ▶ Expressing hope that a certain situation would occur	◦ 내가 조금만 신경을 썼<u>던들</u> 그런 사고가 안 일어났을텐데. ◦ 내가 알았<u>던들</u> 달라질 게 뭐 있었겠어?
-(어/아)도	Acknowledging a fact but express doubt over its relevance	◦ 아무리 보<u>아도</u> 알 수가 없군. ◦ 늦게 가<u>도</u> 할 수 없지.

-도록	▸ Eexpressing the reaching of a certain state ▸ Directing the conversation/ narrative	∘ 이렇게 밤늦<u>도록</u> 어딜 돌아다니니? ∘ 넘어지지 않<u>도록</u> 손잡이를 잘 잡아.
-되	[although] ▸ Used to link contrastive contents	∘ 함께 가<u>되</u> 가서는 혼자 해야한다. ∘ 우물을 파<u>되</u> 한 우물을 파라.
-든(지)	[no matter what (someone or something does)/ either/ whether] ▸ Representing an arbitrary choice	∘ 나는 네가 무엇을 하<u>든지</u> 다 이해할 수 있어. ∘ 가<u>든지</u> 말<u>든지</u> 마음대로 해. ∘ 나는 무엇을 먹<u>든</u> 괜찮아.
-(으)ㄹ	Adjectival ending marking a general fact, a guess or a future state of affairs	∘ 갈 사람은 가고 남아 있<u>을</u> 사람은 이곳을 정리하자. ∘ 시간을 잘 지키는 사람은 믿<u>을</u> 만한 사람이다.
-(으)ㄹ게	Promise marker	∘ 내일 전화로 알려 줄<u>게</u>. ∘ 종이배는 내가 접<u>을게</u>.
-(으)ㄹ게요	Promise marker to an elder person	∘ 엄마, 편지 자주 할<u>게요</u>. ∘ 이 배추 제가 다듬<u>을게요</u>.
-(으)ㄹ까	Doubt, guess or surmise marker	∘ 이제 슬슬 가볼<u>까</u>? ∘ 우리 언제 이 일을 다 마칠 수 있<u>을까</u>?
-(으)ㄹ까요	Doubt, guess or surmise marker expressed to an elder person	∘ 그럼 지금 시작할<u>까요</u>? ∘ 점심이나 같이 먹<u>을까요</u>?
-(으)ㄹ라	▸ Concern or worry marker ▸ Used with a person of the same age or younger	∘ 다칠<u>라</u> 조심해라. ∘ 그렇게 꾸물거리다가 늦<u>을라</u>.
-(으)ㄹ락	Presenting a state of being almost done or something about to happen	∘ 손이 나무 끝에 닿<u>을락</u> 말<u>락</u> 하였다. ∘ 비가 올<u>락</u> 말<u>락</u> 하네.
-(으)ㄹ래요	Telling an elder person about one's thought or intentions or to ask another person about his/ her thoughts or intentions	∘ 저는 오늘 학교에 갈<u>래요</u>. ∘ 지금 나가<u>실래요</u>?

-(으)ㄹ망정	[even though] ▶ Same as -다 하더라도 (even though)	○ 굶어 죽을망정 도둑질은 안 하겠다. ○ 가다가 쓰러질망정 여기서 그만두지는 않겠다.
-(으)ㄹ수록	[the more something happens or is done] ▶ Indicating state of affairs which is progressing	○ 갈수록 태산이다. ○ 공부는 하면 할수록 어렵다.
-(으)ㄹ지라도	[even though] ▶ Marking an assumption in order to focus on the following words	○ 비록 목숨이 위태로울지라도 옳은 것은 옳고 그른 것은 그르다. ○ 천재일지라도 노력 없이 성공할 수 없다.
-(으)ㄹ지언정	Marking an assumption in order to focus on the following words	○ 욕을 먹을지언정 할 말은 해야겠다. ○ 죽을지언정 이 일은 못하겠다.
-(어/아)라	▶ Commands (attached to verbal stems), and expresses admiration (attached to adjectival stems) marker ▶ Used with a person of the same age or younger	○ 어서 와서 밥 먹어라. ○ 아, 좋아라.
-(으)라고	Quoting a sentence or a content of a conversation indirectly	○ 아리스토텔레스는 인간이 사회적 동물이라고 말했다.
	Used when the preceding words are a cause of or a reason for the following words	○ 친구들이랑 맛있는 거 사 먹으라고 돈을 주셨다.
	Confirming or repeating another's words	○ 이걸 나 혼자 다 먹으라고?
-(으)라니	Used when confirming or expressing surprise at an unexpected fact	○ 30년 전이라니, 정말 까마득한 옛날이다. ○ 갑자기 웃으라니 웃음이 나오니?
-라도	[even if]	○ 구슬이 서말이라도 꿰어야 보배다. ○ 너 아니라도 올 사람 많아.

-(으)라든가	[such as]	◦ 옷이라든가 보석이라든가 하는 것에는 관심이 없다. ◦ 먹으라든가 말라든가 무슨 말이 있어야지.
-(으)라면	Abbreviation of (으)라고 하면 used to quote another's words indirectly	◦ 죽으라면 죽는 시늉이라도 한다. ◦ 가라면 가야지.
-(으)라면서	Confirming an already known or overheard fact, or when asking something teasingly	◦ 너 학생이라면서? ◦ 여기에 있으라면서?
-라서	▶ Marking the preceding words as a cause of or reason for the following words ▶ Attached to the stem of 이다, 아니다	◦ 출퇴근 시간이라서 길이 막힌다. ◦ 진짜가 아니라서 실망했나?
-라야	▶ Necessary condition marker ▶ Attached to the stem of 이다, 아니다	◦ 내 것이라야 내 맘대로 하지. ◦ 그게 사실이 아니라야 안심을 하지.
-란다	▶ Used to speak affectionately of a certain fact ▶ Attached to the stem of 이다, 아니다	◦ 이분은 엄마 친구분이시란다. ◦ 여기는 정말 멋진 곳이란다.
-(으)랍니다	Indirectly conveying information (such as a third person's command) to an elderly person or to a person one is not fully comfortable with	◦ 빨리 오시랍니다. ◦ 식후 30분에 이 약을 먹으랍니다. ◦ 우리 아이는 중학생이랍니다.
-(으)랴	[very much so] [doing this and that without exception]	◦ 오랜만에 만났으니 얼마나 좋으랴. ◦ 이거 하랴 저거 하랴 너무 바쁘다.
-(으)러	[(in order) to do (something)] ▶ Purpose or rationale marker is attached to verbal stems	◦ 고기를 잡으러 바다로 갈까요? ◦ 오빠는 김을 매러 밭에 가셨어요.

-(으)려고	Used when the subject expresses an intention to do something or when a certain incident is going to happen	○ 아기를 업으려고 하였다. ○ 구름이 많이 끼더니 비가 오려고 한다.
-(으)려면	Presupposition or a condition marker	○ 토끼를 잡으려면 어디로 가야 할까? ○ 어른이 되려면 한참 있어야 돼.
-(으)려무나	[may] ▶ Used when giving permission to a person of the same age or younger	○ 어디 가서 잘못했다고 빌으려무나. ○ 정 못 믿겠으면 네가 가서 보려무나.
-(으)렴	Abbreviation of (으)려무나	○ 국수 먹고 싶으면 먹으렴. ○ 무슨 일인지 말해 보렴.
-로구나	▶ Expressing surprise at learning a new fact ▶ Attached to a stem of 이, 아니	○ 꽃이 피고 새가 우니 정말 봄이로구나! ○ 어렵다더니 별거 아니로구나!
-(으)리다	Used by elderly people to express their intentions	○ 언제 한 번 들르리다. ○ 그럼 다녀오리다.
-(으)ㅁ	Used in making a word with a conjugated ending into a noun	○ 해당사항 없음. ○ 빨리 집에 오기 바람.
-(으)마	Indicating a promise made to a person of the same age or younger	○ 내일은 어린이대공원에 데리고 가마. ○ 내가 풀을 뜯으마.
-(으)며	Indicating repeating or linking actions	○ 언니는 나에게 웃으며 물었다. ○ 오며 가며 정이 들었다.
-(으)면	Hypothetical condition marker	○ 바둑이를 찾으면 빨리 연락해 줘. ○ 한국에 가면 경복궁에 꼭 가 봐.
-(으)면서	Represent two or more simultaneous states	○ 화학실험을 하면서 신문도 만들었다. ○ 이 빵은 맛있으면서 배부르다.
-(으)므로	[since (something or someone is so and so)] ▶ Indicating a reason or cause	○ 내일은 수돗물이 안 나오므로 물을 미리 받아 놓으시기 바랍니다. ○ 사랑하였으므로 행복하였노라.

-ㅂ니까/습니까	Asking a question to or confirm something with an elderly person or a person who is to be treated with deference	○ 아주머니 집에 계<u>십니까</u>? ○ 영화가 재미있<u>습니까</u>?
-ㅂ니다/습니다	Describing an action or a state to an elderly person or a person who is to be treated with deference	○ 이렇게 비싼 옷은 처음 <u>봅니다</u>. ○ 저는 잘 지내고 있<u>습니다</u>.
-(으)ㅂ시다	Expressing a demand or suggestion made to a person of the same age or younger	○ 잘 생각해 <u>봅시다</u>. ○ 자, 들어가<u>십시다</u>.
-(어/아)서	Cause or a reason indicator	○ 시간이 다 되어<u>서</u> 문을 닫았다. ○ 눈이 녹<u>아서</u> 길이 지저분하다.
-(으)세	[let's do (something) together] ▶ Used with a person of the same age or younger	○ 그럼 같이 가 보<u>세</u>. ○ 비가 오니 얼른 장독 뚜껑을 덮으<u>세</u>.
-(으)세요	[do (something)/ is something or someone so and so] ▶ Explaining something or to ask a question of an elderly person in a tender manner	○ 제 손을 꼭 잡으<u>세요</u>. ○ 안녕하<u>세요</u>?
-(으)셔요	Abbreviation of 시어요 and is an honorific way to explain something or ask a question	○ 아버지, 넥타이가 잘 어울리<u>셔요</u>. ○ 여기에 주워 답으<u>셔요</u>.
-(으)소	Old-fashioned style of speech used to express an exclamation or question	○ 수고 많았<u>소</u>. ○ 그곳 날씨는 어떻<u>소</u>? ○ 어서 이 줄을 잡으<u>소</u>.
-(으)시-	Used to honor a subject or an agent	○ 선생님께서 노래를 하<u>시</u>니 아이들이 모두 좋아하였다. ○ 아버지께서 회사에 다니<u>시</u>다가 그만 두셨어요.
-(으)시오	Formal command marker	○ 다음 문제에 답하<u>시오</u>. ○ 여기를 보<u>시오</u>. ○ 설탕이 다 녹을 때까지 저<u>으시오</u>.

-(으)십시오	[let's/ please do so and so] ▶ Asking a favor or demanding something of an elderly person or a person who is to be treated with deference	◦ 창 쪽으로 앉으십시오. ◦ 너무 염려 마십시오.
-았/었-	▶ Indicating an action or state which happened in the past or just previously ▶ No connection with the present is assumed	◦ 어제 재미있는 영화 한 편 보았지. ◦ 여기 놓아 둔 빵, 네가 먹었니?
-었었/았었-	▶ Indicating an action or state which happened in the past or just previously ▶ No connection with the present is assumed	◦ 그때는 놀러도 참 많이 다녔었다. ◦ 이 강에는 물이 많았었는데….
-야	Asking a question or present a fact to a person of the same age or younger	◦ 그 말이 맞을거야. ◦ 다시 해 볼거야?
-(어/아)야	Necessary condition indicator	◦ 좀 쉬어야 감기가 낫지. ◦ 비가 좀더 와야 곡식이 잘 자랄텐데.
-어/아	Narration, a question, a suggestion or an exclamation marker	◦ 수영 끝났어? ◦ 거기 가면 맛있는 게 많아.
	Reason, a cause or a sequential relation indicator	◦ 차례가 되어 물을 떠 마셨습니다. ◦ 얼마 가지 않아 쌀이 다 떨어졌다.
-옵-	▶ Politeness marker ▶ Used in an old style of writing or written prayers	◦ 그 일은 사실이 아니옵니다. ◦ 주님께 간절히 기도드리옵나이다.
-(어/아)요	Affectionately explain something to or ask a question of an elderly person or a person of the same age	◦ 우리 함께 놀아요. ◦ 머리 아파요?

-자	Indicating suggestion to do something together directed at a person of the same age or younger	◦ 차 마시러 가<u>자</u>. ◦ 우리 모두 나무를 가꾸<u>자</u>.
	Two movements or states in temporal sequence connector	◦ 공연이 끝나<u>자</u> 사람들이 모두 일어서서 박수를 쳤다. ◦ 해가 지<u>자</u> 어둠이 깔렸다.
-자꾸나	[let's do (something) together] ▶ Used with a person of the same age or younger	◦ 얘들아, 간식 먹<u>자꾸나</u>. ◦ 우리 잘 해 보<u>자꾸나</u>.
-자마자	[as soon as (something) has finished]	◦ 해가 지<u>자마자</u> 산 속에는 칠흑 같은 어둠이 깔렸다. ◦ 물건을 갖다 놓<u>자마자</u> 다 팔렸다.
-지	▶ Confirming something tenderly or suggesting something to a person of the same age or younger ▶ Used in a range of sentence types, including statements, suggestions, questions and so on.	◦ 어제 경기는 한국이 이겼<u>지</u>. ◦ 우유 많이 먹어야<u>지</u>. ◦ 너 어제 속상했<u>지</u>?
	Contrasting two different facts	◦ 현재가 중요하<u>지</u> 과거가 중요합니까? ◦ 독도는 한국 땅이<u>지</u> 일본 땅이 아니다.
	▶ Negating the preceding content ▶ Used with negation	◦ 나무를 꺾<u>지</u> 마시오. ◦ 나는 그것을 믿<u>지</u> 않아요.
-지요	▶ Confirming a fact or talking intimately to an elderly person or someone of the same age ▶ Used in statements or questions	◦ 오늘은 날씨가 무척 좋<u>지요</u>? ◦ 제가 그 사실을 모를 리가 없<u>지요</u>.

Appendix: Index

가	593
나	609
다	613
라	620
마	620
바	627
사	636
아	649
자	665
차	677
카	681
타	682
파	685
하	688

가

가	472
가감승제	445
가감하다	445
가건물	137
가게	137, 330
가겟집	137
가격	330
가격인상	330
가격인하	330
가격표	330
가계	330
가계부	330
가계소득	330
가계수표	330
가계지출	330
가곡	238
가공무역	330
가공식품	111
가공업	365
가공하다	365, 507
가구	137, 445
가구디자인	137
가구배치	137
가구점	330
가까스로	485
가깝다	472
가꾸다	419, 507
가끔	458
가나	275
가난뱅이	1
가난하다	330, 485
가내수공업	365
가냘프다	485
가누다	507
가느다랗다	430, 485
가늘다	430, 485
가능	485
가능성	209
가능하다	485
가다	458, 507
가다듬다	68, 507
가닥	445
가동하다	365, 507
가두다	507
가득	485
가득차다	485
가득하다	430, 485
가라앉다	507
가락	238
가락국수	111
가락지	97
가랑비	394
가랑이	26
가래	26, 365
가래떡	111
가려움증	38
가련하다	68
가렵다	59
가로	472
가로등	386
가로수	386, 419
가로젓다	507
가로지르다	507
가루	430, 485
가루비누	97, 137
가루약	38
가르다	507
가르마	26
가르치다	193, 507
가리개	137
가리다	111, 507
가리비	405
가리키다	507
가마	26, 365, 382, 386, 445
가마니	111, 137, 365
가마솥	111
가맹점	330
가면	97
가면극	238
가명	1, 321
가무단	238
가문	11
가물가물	394
가물다	394, 485
가물치	111, 405
가뭄	394
가발	97
가방	97, 137
가볍다	485
가봉	275
가부장제	11
가부장제도	321
가불하다	330, 507
가뿐하다	485
가사	238, 353
가산점	445
가석방	298
가설	209
가속	386
가속도	209
가속도의 원리	209
가수	238, 353
가스	209, 382
가스관	137
가스레인지	111, 382
가스요금	330
가스전	309
가슴	26, 405
가슴둘레	26
가슴앓이	38, 68
가습기	137
가시	419
가시광선	394
가시나무	419
가시다	507
가식적이다	84
가야	275
가야금	238
가열하다	111, 382, 507
가엾다	68
가오리	405
가옥	137
가요	238
가요계	238
가요제	238
가운	97
가운데	472
가운뎃점	157
가위	97, 137
가위바위보	263
가을	458
가을걷이	365
가을바람	394
가자미	111, 405

가장 137, 485	간 26, 59, 111	갈기 405
가장자리 472	간간하다 59, 111	갈기갈기 485
가재 405	간격 458, 472	갈다 111, 365, 508
가전제품 137	간결하다 485	갈대 419
가정 11, 137, 209	간경화증 38	갈등 68
가정교육 193	간곡하다 84	갈라놓다 508
가정법원 298	간니 26	갈라서다 508
가정부 353	간단하다 485	갈라지다 508
가정주부 1	간디스토마 38	갈래꽃 419
가정통신문 193	간맞추다 111	갈망하다 68, 508
가정하다 68, 209	간맞추다 508	갈매기 405
가정학습 193	간병인 38	갈비 112
가정환경 11, 137	간병하다 38, 508	갈비뼈 26
가족 11	간보다 59, 111, 508	갈비찜 112
가족계획 11	간부사원 353	갈비탕 112
가족관 11	간사하다 84	갈색 438
가족관계 11	간섭하다 508	갈아입다 97, 508
가족사진 257	간식 111	갈증 112
가족제도 11, 321	간암 38	갈증나다 112
가죽 97, 405	간염 38	갈치 112, 405
가죽장갑 97	간음 20	갈퀴 365
가증스럽다 68	간장 111	갉다 508
가지 111, 419, 445	간접세 330	감 419
가지가지 430	간접인용 157	감각 59
가지각색 438	간접화법 157	감각기관 26, 59
가지다 508	간주 238	감격하다 68
가지런하다 485	간주곡 238	감광지 257
가짜 485	간주하다 68, 209	감금하다 298
가창력 238	간지럽다 59	감기 38
가축 365, 405	간질 38	감기약 38
가출하다 508	간척지 365	감나무 419
가치관 68, 84, 209	간첩 280, 309	감다 97, 508
가해자 298	간청하다 157, 508	감독 238, 268, 353
가혹하다 84	간추리다 508	감독하다 508
각 430	간통 20	감동 68
각도 430, 445	간통죄 20	감동적이다 68
각도기 430, 445	간판 138	감동하다 68, 508
각막 59	간편하다 485	감리교 222
각본 238	간행하다 180, 508	감미료 112
각색 238	간호대학 193	감방 298
각선미 26	간호사 38, 353	감사원 280
각성하다 508	간호사관학교 193, 309	감사하다 508
각시 1	간호장교 309	감상하다 238, 508
각양각색 430, 438	간호하다 38, 508	감색 438
각오하다 68, 508	간호학 209	감성 68
각주 157	간혹 458	감성지수 68

감소하다 … 508	강력하다 … 486	개그맨 … 353
감수성 … 68	강바람 … 394	개근상 … 193
감시하다 … 508	강박관념 … 69, 84	개나리 … 419
감싸다 … 508	강변 … 472	개념 … 209
감염 … 38	강사 … 193, 353	개다 … 394, 509
감옥 … 298	강사진 … 193	개떡 … 112
감옥살이 … 51, 298	강세 … 331	개똥벌레 … 405
감자 … 112, 419	강수 … 394	개량종 … 365
감자탕 … 112	강수량 … 394	개량하다 … 365
감정 … 68	강아지 … 405	개량한복 … 97
감주 … 112	강아지풀 … 419	개미 … 405
감지덕지 … 69	강어귀 … 472	개발도상국 … 280
감지하다 … 59, 508	강연 … 157	개발하다 … 509
감질나다 … 69	강연하다 … 157, 509	개방경제 … 331
감촉 … 59	강요하다 … 157, 509	개방하다 … 509
감추다 … 508	강우 … 394	개봉관 … 238
감치다 … 97, 508	강우량 … 394	개봉박두 … 239
감탄사 … 157	강의 … 157, 193	개비 … 445
감퇴하다 … 509	강의계획서 … 193	개사 … 239
갑 … 138, 445	강의실 … 193	개선 … 309
갑갑하다 … 69	강의하다 … 157, 509	개선하다 … 309, 509
갑골문자 … 157	강인하다 … 486	개성 … 84
갑근세 … 330	강적 … 309	개수대 … 112, 138
갑옷 … 97	강정 … 112	개시 … 331
갑자기 … 458	강추위 … 394	개시하다 … 509
갑절 … 445	강태공 … 257	개신교 … 222
갑종근로소득세 … 330	강판 … 112	개업 … 331
갑판 … 386	강하다 … 486	개울 … 472
갑판장 … 353, 386	강화 … 486	개인 … 321
값 … 331, 445	갖추다 … 509	개인교습 … 193
값어치 … 331	같다 … 430, 486	개인병원 … 38
갓 … 97, 112, 419, 458	갚다 … 331, 509	개인전 … 268
갓길 … 472	개 … 405, 445	개인주의 … 321
갓난아기 … 1	개가 … 20	개인행동 … 321
강 … 472	개각 … 280	개입하다 … 509
강가 … 472	개각하다 … 280	개점 … 331
강간 … 20	개간지 … 365	개조하다 … 138, 509
강강수월래 … 238	개간하다 … 365, 509	개종 … 222
강낭콩 … 419	개강 … 193	개종하다 … 222
강냉이 … 112	개고기 … 112	개척자 … 1
강당 … 193	개교기념일 … 193	개척하다 … 509
강대국 … 280	개교하다 … 193	개천절 … 280, 458
강도 … 298, 486	개구리 … 405	개축 … 138
강독 … 157	개구리헤엄 … 268	개펄 … 365, 472
강력계 … 298	개구쟁이 … 1	개편하다 … 280
강력범 … 298	개굴개굴 … 405	개표 … 280

개표소 280
개표참관인 280
개표하다 280
개학 193
개학하다 194
개항 365, 386
개헌 280
개헤엄 268
개혁 321
개화 321
개화기 234, 419, 458
개화하다 234, 419
개회식 321
객관성 69, 209
객관식 194
객사 51
객석 239
객실 386
갱 365
갱년기 51
갱도 365
갸웃하다 509
거금 331
거기 472
거느리다 509
거대하다 430, 486
거동하다 509
거두다 365, 419, 509
거드름피우다 84
거들다 509
거래 331
거래처 331
거룩하다 486
거르다 112, 509
거름 366, 419
거름종이 209
거름주다 366
거리 445, 472
거마비 386
거만하다 84
거머리 405
거목 419
거무스름하다 438
거무죽죽하다 438
거무튀튀하다 438
거문고 239

거문고자리 472
거미 405
거미줄 405
거부하다 157, 509
거북선 386
거북이 405
거북하다 69
거세다 486
거센소리 157
거스르다 509
거스름돈 331
거시경제 331
거실 138
거액 331
거울 97, 138
거위 406
거의 486
거인 1
거절하다 157, 509
거주자 138
거주지 138
거주하다 138, 509
거지 1
거짓 486
거짓되다 486
거짓말 157
거짓말쟁이 1
거창하다 486
거처 138
거치다 509
거칠거칠 59
거칠다 59, 84, 486
거품기 112
걱정 69
걱정거리 69
걱정하다 69, 509
건강 38
건강하다 26, 486
건국 280
건너다 509
건너방 138
건너편 472
건널목 386
건달 353
건더기 112
건드리다 509

건망증 38
건물 138
건반악기 239
건방지다 84
건배하다 112, 509
건빵 112
건설 138
건설교통부 280
건설비 138
건설업 353
건설업자 353
건설업체 138
건설하다 138, 509
건실하다 486
건어물 112, 366
건의하다 157, 509
건전가요 239
건전지 209, 382
건전하다 486
건조시키다 366
건조장 366
건조주의보 394
건조하다 394, 486
건지다 112, 509
건축 138
건축가 138, 353
건축기사 138, 353
건축물 138
건축설계사 138
건축양식 138
건축하다 138, 509
건축학 209
건축학자 209
건축현장 138
건평 138
건포도 112
걷다 97, 509, 510
걷히다 394
걸다 97, 510
걸레 138
걸맞다 486
걸상 194
걸인 1
걸작 239
걸쭉하다 486
걸치다 97, 510

걸터앉다 ················· 510	겨레 ····················· 1, 280, 321	결심하다 ··············· 69, 510
검 ························· 268	겨루다 ····················· 268, 510	결재 ···························· 331
검거하다 ·············· 298, 510	겨를 ································· 458	결재일 ························· 331
검다 ··························· 438	겨우 ································ 486	결점 ··························· 486
검도 ··························· 268	겨우내 ····························· 458	결정하다 ········· 69, 209, 511
검문 ··························· 298	겨우살이 ·························· 394	결투 ·························· 309
검문소 ························· 298	겨울 ······························· 458	결판내다 ······················ 511
검문하다 ·············· 298, 510	겨울바람 ·························· 394	결함 ··························· 486
검버섯 ···························· 26	겨울잠 ···························· 406	결합하다 ······················ 511
검사 ····················· 298, 353	겨자 ································· 112	결핵 ····························· 39
검사하다 ······················ 510	격 ··································· 157	결혼 ······················ 11, 20
검산하다 ················ 445, 510	격려금 ···························· 331	결혼기념일 ·············· 20, 458
검소하다 ······················ 331	격려사 ···························· 158	결혼반지 ······················· 20
검열하다 ················ 180, 510	격려하다 ·························· 510	결혼사진 ···················· 257
검은색 ························· 438	격리시키다 ······················· 510	결혼상담소 ···················· 20
검정 ··························· 438	격언 ······························· 158	결혼서약 ······················· 20
검정고시 ······················ 194	격월 ······························· 458	결혼식 ·························· 20
검정색 ························· 438	격음 ······························ 158	결혼식장 ························ 20
검증 ··························· 209	격일 ······························ 458	결혼하다 ······················ 511
검증하다 ·············· 209, 510	격전 ······························· 309	결혼행진곡 ···················· 20
검지 ····························· 26	격전지 ···························· 309	겸손하다 ······················· 84
검진하다 ················ 38, 510	격주 ······························ 458	겸연쩍다 ························ 69
검찰 ··························· 298	격투기 ···························· 268	겸임교수 ····················· 194
검찰청 ···················· 280, 298	겪다 ······························· 510	겹 ····························· 445
검침하다 ······················· 510	견고하다 ·························· 486	겹사돈 ························· 11
검토하다 ······················· 510	견디다 ···························· 510	경 ····························· 445
겁 ····························· 69	견본품 ···························· 331	경각심 ·························· 69
겁나다 ··················· 69, 510	견인차 ···························· 386	경거망동하다 ·················· 84
겁내다 ··················· 69, 510	견주다 ···························· 510	경계 ···························· 472
겉 ····························· 472	견학 ······························· 194	경계선 ························· 472
겉감 ····························· 97	결과 ······························ 209	경계하다 ················ 69, 511
겉옷 ····························· 97	결근 ······························ 353	경고하다 ················ 158, 511
게 ······················· 112, 406	결단하다 ·························· 510	경기 ···················· 268, 331
게릴라전 ······················· 309	결론 ························· 158, 209	경기규칙 ······················ 268
게시판 ···················· 138, 187	결론짓다 ···················· 158, 510	경기변동 ······················ 331
게시하다 ················ 187, 510	결리다 ····························· 39	경기장 ························ 268
게우다 ·························· 510	결막염 ····························· 39	경기하다 ····················· 268
게으르다 ························ 84	결박하다 ···················· 510, 486	경단 ···························· 112
게으름뱅이 ······················· 1	결벽증 ···························· 84	경도 ···························· 473
게임 ··························· 263	결별하다 ·························· 510	경력사원 ····················· 353
게임방 ························· 263	결산 ······························ 331	경련 ···························· 39
게임하다 ················ 263, 510	결석 ······························ 194	경례 ··························· 321
게재료 ·························· 180	결석하다 ···················· 194, 510	경례하다 ················ 321, 511
게재하다 ················ 180, 510	결성하다 ·························· 510	경로당 ························· 138
겨누다 ·························· 510	결속하다 ·························· 510	경리 ···························· 331
겨드랑이 ························· 26	결손가정 ··························· 11	경마 ··························· 263

경마장 263	경제성 332	계몽문학 239
경매 331	경제성장 332	계몽운동 321
경매인 331	경제원리 332	계부 11
경멸하다 84, 511	경제인 332	계산 332, 446
경배 222	경제적 332	계산기 446
경범죄 298	경제지표 332	계산대 332
경보 268	경제학 210	계산서 332, 446
경보기 138	경제학자 210	계산하다 332, 446, 511
경비 331	경조사 321	계속 459
경비선 386	경주하다 268	계속되다 486
경비원 353	경지 366	계승하다 234
경비행기 386	경지정리 366	계약 332
경사 473	경찰 299	계약금 332
경사지다 473, 511	경찰관 299	계약하다 158, 511
경상 39	경찰대학 299	계엄 281
경상수지 331	경찰대학교 194	계엄령 281
경상지출 331	경찰서 280, 299	계절 459
경솔하다 84	경찰차 386	계절풍 394
경시하다 85	경찰청 280, 299	계좌 332
경어 158	경청하다 59, 511	계주 268
경영 331	경축일 458	계집 1
경영인 353	경치 138	계집애 1
경영자 331	경칩 458	계측하다 446, 511
경영진 353	경품 332	계층 321
경영하다 353, 511	경품권 332	계층이동 322
경영학 210	경험 69, 210	계통론 158
경영학자 210	경험주의 210	계피 112
경외심 222	경험하다 511	계획경제 332
경외하다 222	경호실 280	계획하다 511
경운기 366	경호원 299	곗돈 332
경유 382	경호하다 299	고가 332
경유하다 511	곁 473	고가도로 386
경음 158	계 222, 332, 445	고가품 332
경음악 239	계간지 180	고개 26, 473
경의 85, 321	계곡 473	고객 332
경이롭다 69	계급 309	고갯마루 473
경작지 366	계급사회 321	고고학 210
경작하다 366, 511	계급장 309	고고학자 210
경전 222	계단 138	고구려 275
경제 331	계란 112, 406	고구마 112, 419
경제계 331	계란빵 112	고국 281
경제공황 331	계량 445	고급품 332
경제권 332	계량스푼 112	고기 113
경제면 180	계량컵 112	고기압 394
경제발전 332	계량하다 446, 511	고기잡이 366
경제법 298	계모 11	고기잡이철 366

고깃배 ······················· 366, 386	고문 ································· 299	고저 ································· 430
고갑다 ······························· 69	고문서 ····························· 234	고전무용 ························· 239
고꾸라지다 ······················ 511	고민 ································· 70	고전문학 ························· 239
고뇌 ································· 70	고민하다 ···················· 70, 511	고전음악 ························· 239
고니 ································ 406	고발 ································· 299	고전주의 ··················· 210, 239
고다 ································ 511	고발하다 ···················· 158, 511	고전해학극 ······················ 239
고대 ································ 459	고백 ································· 158	고정관념 ··························· 70
고대국가 ·························· 281	고백하다 ···················· 158, 511	고정환율제도 ··················· 332
고대문명 ·························· 234	고부 ··································· 11	고조선 ····························· 275
고대하다 ···························· 70	고분고분하다 ······················ 85	고조할머니 ························ 11
고도 ································ 430	고비 ································· 420	고조할아버지 ····················· 12
고독하다 ···························· 70	고사 ································· 222	고종사촌 ··························· 12
고동색 ····························· 438	고사리 ······················ 113, 420	고지대 ····························· 473
고둥 ································ 406	고사성어 ·························· 158	고지하다 ············· 158, 187, 511
고드름 ····························· 394	고상하다 ·························· 486	고집 ·································· 85
고등법원 ·························· 299	고생하다 ·························· 511	고집부리다 ···················· 85, 511
고등어 ······················ 113, 406	고소 ································· 299	고집세다 ··························· 85
고등학교 ·························· 194	고소득층 ·························· 322	고집스럽다 ························ 85
고등학생 ·························· 194	고소장 ····························· 299	고참 ································ 354
고랑 ································ 366	고소하다 ····· 59, 113, 158, 486, 511	고체 ··························· 210, 486
고래 ································ 406	고속도로 ·························· 386	고체연료 ·························· 382
고랭지 ····························· 366	고속버스 ·························· 386	고추 ······················· 113, 420
고랭지농업 ······················· 366	고슴도치 ·························· 406	고추냉이 ·························· 113
고량주 ····························· 113	고시 ································· 194	고추장 ····························· 113
고려 ································ 275	고시원 ····························· 194	고춧가루 ·························· 113
고려가요 ·························· 239	고싸움 ····························· 263	고층빌딩 ·························· 138
고려하다 ···················· 70, 511	고아 ································ 1, 51	고층아파트 ······················ 139
고료 ································ 180	고아원 ····························· 138	고치 ································ 406
고루 ································ 486	고안하다 ·························· 511	고치다 ······················ 139, 512
고루하다 ···························· 85	고액권 ····························· 332	고통 ··························· 39, 59
고르다 ················· 430, 486, 511	고약하다 ·························· 486	고통스럽다 ························ 59
고름 ·························· 39, 98	고양이 ····························· 406	고해성사 ·························· 222
고리대금업 ······················· 332	고열 ··································· 39	고행 ································ 222
고리대금업자 ···················· 332	고요하다 ···························· 59	고향 ···························· 51, 473
고릴라 ····························· 406	고용 ································ 353	고혈압 ······························· 39
고립하다 ·························· 511	고용인 ······················ 322, 354	고희 ··································· 51
고마워하다 ························ 70	고용주 ······················ 322, 354	곡 ···················· 51, 239, 446
고막 ································· 59	고용하다 ·························· 354	곡괭이 ····························· 366
고맙다 ······························· 70	고원 ································· 473	곡류 ································ 113
고명 ································ 113	고유명사 ·························· 158	곡마단 ····························· 263
고모 ·································· 11	고유어 ····························· 158	곡물 ································ 366
고모부 ······························· 11	고을 ························· 138, 473	곡선 ································ 430
고목 ································ 419	고인 ··································· 51	곡식 ································ 113
고무신 ······························ 98	고인돌 ······························ 51	곡식 ··························· 366, 420
고무장갑 ···························· 98	고자질하다 ················· 158, 511	곡예 ································ 263
고무줄놀이 ······················ 263	고장 ························· 138, 473	곡예단 ····························· 263

곡예사 263	곱하기 446	공돈 333
곡우 459	곱하다 446	공동묘지 51
곡조 239	곳 473	공동사회 322
곤경 486	곳간 139	공동연구 210
곤란하다 70, 486	곳곳 473	공동주택 139
곤봉 268	공 268	공동체 322
곤지 98	공간 473	공동체의식 322
곤지곤지 263	공간미술 239	공룡 406
곤충 406	공간예술 239	공립 322
곤충류 406	공갈치다 158	공립학교 194
곧 459	공감각 59	공명 60
곧다 85, 430	공감하다 70, 512	공명선거 281
곧장 459	공개방송 180	공명정대하다 85
골 26	공개수배 299	공무원 281, 354
골격 26	공격 268, 309	공박하다 158, 512
골다 512	공격개시 309	공배수 446
골다공증 39	공격수 269	공백 473
골대 268	공격하다 512	공범 299
골동품 332	공경하다 70, 85, 322, 512	공법 299
골라내다 512	공고 158, 194	공병 309
골목 473	공고하다 187, 512	공보실 281
골무 98, 139	공공건물 139	공부 194
골반바지 98	공공기관 281	공부방 139
골방 139	공공단체 281	공부하다 194, 210, 512
골뱅이 113, 406	공공사업 322	공사 139
골병 39	공공시설 281	공사장 139
골수암 39	공공요금 332	공사판 139
골절 39	공공질서 299, 322	공산주의 281, 322
골절상 39	공과금 332	공산주의국가 281
골짜기 473	공교육 194	공산품 333, 366
골치아프다 70	공교육비 194	공소 299
골프 268	공구 139, 366	공소시효 299
골프채 268	공군 309	공손하다 85
곪다 39	공군사관학교 194, 309	공수부대 309
곯다 113, 512	공권력 281	공수표 333
곰 406	공그르다 512	공습 309
곰국 113	공금 333	공습하다 310
곰보 1	공급 333	공약 281
곰탕 113	공급자 333	공약수 446
곰팡이 406	공기 113, 473	공약하다 158, 512
곱 446	공기놀이 263	공양 222
곱셈 446	공기청정기 139	공양미 222
곱슬머리 26	공납금 333	공업 354, 366
곱절 446	공단 366	공업고등학교 194
곱창 113	공덕 222	공업국 366
곱추 1	공던지기 269	공업단지 366

공업도시 366
공업연료 366
공업용 366
공업용수 366
공업지대 366
공업화 366
공연 239
공연예술 239
공연장 239
공연하다 239
공영방송 180
공예 239
공예가 354
공예품 239
공용어 158
공원 354, 366
공익근무요원 299, 310
공인중개사 139
공자 222
공작 406
공장 366
공장도가격 333
공장장 354, 366
공장주 367
공장폐수 367
공저 180
공전 473
공정 367
공정거래위원회 281
공정하다 85
공주 1, 281
공중 473
공중도덕 322
공중전화 187
공직 281
공직자 281
공짜 333
공채 333
공책 139, 194
공처가 2
공천 281
공천자 281
공천하다 281
공청회 322
공탁금 333
공탁하다 333

공통분모 446
공통어 158
공판 299
공평하다 85
공포 70
공표하다 158, 512
공학 210
공학자 210
공항 386
공화국 281
공휴일 459
곶감 113
과거 459
과거시제 158
과거완료 158
과거형 158
과대망상증 39
과도 113, 139
과로 39
과묵하다 85, 158
과반수 446
과부 2, 20
과세 333
과소비 333
과속 386
과수원 367, 420
과식 113
과실 420
과외 194
과용 333
과음 113
과일 113, 367, 420
과일쥬스 113
과자 113
과점 333
과제 194
과제물 194
과태료 299, 333
과테말라 275
과하다 486
과학 210
과학고등학교 194
과학기술 210
과학기술대학교 194
과학기술부 281
과학실 210

과학자 210, 354
관 51, 139, 446
관개 367
관개수 367
관객 239
관계대명사 158
관공서 281
관광 257
관광객 257
관광국가 257
관광단 257
관광도시 257
관광버스 257, 386
관광사업 257
관광시설 257
관광안내원 257
관광업 257, 367
관광열차 257
관광유람선 257
관광자원 257
관광정책 257
관광지 257
관광지도 258
관광하다 258, 512
관광호텔 258
관념 70
관대하다 85
관람객 239
관람료 239
관람불가 239
관람석 239
관람하다 239, 512
관례 322
관리비 333
관리자 354
관리직 354
관상 26, 222
관상어 406
관성 210
관성법칙 210
관세 333
관세청 281, 333
관습 322
관습법 299
관심 70
관악기 239

관용 ……………………………… 85	광풍 ……………………………… 394	교열기자 ……………………… 180
관용어 ………………………… 158	광합성 ………………………… 420	교원 …………………… 195, 354
관자놀이 ………………………… 26	광활하다 …………… 430, 473, 487	교육 …………………………… 195
관절 ……………………………… 27	쾌도 …………………………… 194	교육감 ………………………… 195
관절염 …………………………… 39	쾌씸하다 …………………… 70, 85	교육공학 ……………………… 195
관제탑 ………………………… 387	괜찮다 ………………………… 487	교육과정 ……………………… 195
관직 …………………………… 281	괭이 …………………………… 367	교육기관 ……………………… 195
관찰 …………………………… 210	괴다 …………………………… 512	교육내용 ……………………… 195
관찰하다 ……………… 60, 210, 512	괴로움 ………………………… 70	교육대학 ……………………… 196
관청 …………………… 139, 281	괴로워하다 ………………… 70, 512	교육목적 ……………………… 196
관측 …………………………… 210	괴롭다 ………………………… 70	교육목표 ……………………… 196
관측하다 ……………………… 210	괴물 …………………………… 406	교육방법 ……………………… 196
관통하다 ……………………… 512	괴상하다 ……………………… 487	교육방송국 …………………… 180
관현악단 ……………………… 239	괴짜 ……………………………… 2	교육법 ………………………… 196
관형사 ………………………… 158	괴팍하다 ……………………… 85	교육부 ………………… 196, 281
관형어 ………………………… 158	괴한 ……………………………… 2	교육비 ………………………… 196
관혼상제 ……………… 51, 223	교감 …………………………… 194	교육세 ………………………… 333
괄호 …………………………… 159	교과과정 ……………………… 194	교육시설 ……………………… 196
광 ……………………………… 139	교과서 ………………………… 194	교육실습 ……………………… 196
광고 …………………… 180, 187	교구 …………………………… 194	교육열 ………………………… 196
광고면 ………………………… 180	교단 …………………… 195, 223	교육위원회 …………………… 196
광고지 ………………………… 187	교대하다 ……………………… 512	교육자 ………………………… 196
광년 …………………………… 473	교도관 ………………………… 299	교육적 ………………………… 196
광대 …………………………… 354	교도소 ………………………… 299	교육철학 ……………………… 196
광대뼈 …………………………… 27	교류하다 ……………………… 512	교육평가 ……………………… 196
광대하다 ……………… 430, 487	교리 …………………………… 223	교육학 ………………………… 210
광맥 …………………………… 367	교리문답 ……………………… 223	교육학자 ……………………… 210
광물 …………………………… 367	교만하다 ……………………… 85	교육행정 ……………………… 196
광물질 ………………………… 367	교무실 ………………………… 195	교인 …………………………… 223
광복절 ………………… 281, 459	교문 …………………………… 195	교장 …………………………… 196
광부 …………………… 354, 367	교미하다 ……………………… 406	교장실 ………………………… 196
광산 …………………………… 367	교배하다 ……………………… 367	교재 …………………………… 196
광산업 ………………………… 367	교복 …………………… 98, 195	교정 …………………… 159, 180
광산촌 ………………………… 367	교사 …………………… 51, 195	교정하다 ………………… 39, 180
광석 …………………………… 367	교살 …………………………… 51	교제하다 ……………………… 512
광선 …………………………… 438	교생 …………………………… 195	교조 …………………………… 223
광섬유 ………………………… 187	교섭하다 ……………… 159, 512	교주 …………………………… 223
광속 …………………………… 473	교수 …………………… 195, 354	교지 …………………………… 196
광신도 ………………………… 223	교수식당 ……………………… 195	교지편집실 …………………… 196
광야 …………………………… 473	교수요목 ……………………… 195	교직 …………………………… 196
광어 …………………… 113, 406	교수진 ………………………… 195	교직원 ………………………… 196
광업 …………………… 354, 367	교수형 ………………………… 299	교직자 ………………………… 196
광역시 ………………… 139, 281	교실 …………………………… 195	교체하다 ……………………… 512
광주리 ………………… 113, 139	교양 …………………………… 85	교탁 …………………………… 196
광채 …………………………… 438	교역 …………………………… 333	교통 …………………………… 387
광통신 ………………………… 187	교열 …………………………… 159	교통경찰 ……………… 299, 387

교통계 603

교통계 299	구두쇠 2	구슬 98
교통문제 322	구두약 98, 139	구슬땀 27
교통방송 180	구두점 159	구슬치기 263
교통법규 387	구두주걱 98, 139	구식 487
교통비 387	구둣솔 98, 139	구약성서 223
교통사고 387	구들장 139	구어 159
교통수단 387	구렁이 406	구역 473
교통정보 187	구레나룻 27	구원 223
교통지도 387	구류 299	구유 367
교통질서 387	구르다 512	구의원 281
교통체증 387	구름 395	구의회 281
교파 223	구릉 473	구이 113
교포 281	구리 367	구인란 181
교표 196	구리다 60	구입 333
교향곡 239	구린내 60	구입하다 333
교향악단 239	구릿빛 438	구절 159
교환 333	구매 333	구절판 113
교환하다 512	구매자 333	구정 459
교활하다 85	구매하다 333	구직란 181
교황 223, 354	구명가게 333	구질구질 98
교회 139, 223	구명보트 387	구차하다 85
교회음악 239	구명정 387	구청 282
교훈 196	구명조끼 98	구청장 282
구 139, 159, 281, 430, 446	구민 322	구축하다 187
구간 473	구박하다 512	구출하다 513
구개음화 159	구별하다 70, 210, 512	구충제 39
구경꾼 2	구부러지다 430, 473, 487, 512	구치소 299
구경하다 512	구부리다 512	구타하다 513
구관조 406	구불구불 473, 487	구토 39
구교 223	구불텅구불텅 487	구하다 513
구구구 406	구비문학 240	국 113
구구단 446	구사하다 159	국가 282
구급 299	구상하다 70, 210	국가경제 333
구급약 39	구석 473	국가과학기술자문회의 282
구급차 39, 387	구석구석 473	국가관 282
구기다 512	구석기시대 234	국가기밀 187
구기자 420	구성원 322	국가대표선수 269
구기종목 269	구성작가 180, 354	국가론 282
구김 98	구성하다 512	국가명 282
구김가다 98	구세군 223	국가보훈처 282
구더기 406	구세주 223	국가안전기획부 282
구도 240	구속 299	국가안전보장회의 282
구독자 180	구속영장 299	국가정보원 282
구독하다 180	구속하다 299, 513	국경 282
구두 98	구수하다 60, 113, 487	국경선 282
구두닦이 354	구술하다 159, 513	국경일 282, 459

국교 223, 282
국군 282, 310
국군병원 310
국궁 269
국권 282
국기 282
국내 282
국내경제 333
국내법 299
국내시장 333
국내외 282
국내정세 282
국내정치 282
국도 387
국력 282
국립 282, 322
국립경주박물관 234
국립공원 258
국립광주박물관 234
국립대학 196
국립민속박물관 234
국립부여박물관 234
국립중앙박물관 234
국무 282
국무조정실 282
국무총리 282, 354
국무총리비서실 282
국무회의 282
국문 282
국문학 210
국문학자 210
국물 113
국민 282, 322
국민가수 240
국민가요 240
국민경제 282
국민교육헌장 283
국민문화 283
국민복지 283
국민성 283
국민소득 283, 333
국민의례 283
국민의식 283
국민자본 283, 333
국민차 387
국민체조 269

국민총생산 333
국민투표 283
국밥 113
국밥집 113
국방 283, 310
국방부 283, 310
국방부장관 310
국방색 438
국법 283, 299
국보 234
국사 283
국산 283
국세 333
국세청 283, 334
국수 113
국수전골 113
국수주의 283
국악 240
국악기 240
국어 159, 283
국어순화 159
국어학 210
국어학자 210
국영방송 181
국왕 283
국외 283
국외정세 283
국자 114
국적 283
국정 283
국정감사 283
국제 283
국제경제 334
국제기구 283
국제법 300
국제변호사 300
국제수지 334
국제시장 334
국제연합 283
국제우편 187
국제전화 187
국제정세 283
국제정치 283
국제화 283
국지전 310
국채 334

국토 283
국토방위 283, 310
국토순례 258
국호 283
국화 284, 420
국화빵 114
국회 284
국회법 284
국회사무처 284
국회안건 284
국회의사당 284
국회의원 284, 354
국회의장 284
국회해산 284
국회회기 284
군 2, 139, 284
군가 310
군것질 114
군기 310
군대 310
군대행진곡 310
군데 473
군데군데 473
군도 474
군말 159
군목 310
군무원 310
군민 322
군번 310
군법 310
군법무관 310
군법회의 310
군복 98, 310
군복무 310
군비제한 310
군사 310
군사개입 310
군사고문 310
군사고문단 310
군사교육 310
군사기밀 310
군사기지 310
군사도시 310
군사동맹 310
군사력 311
군사법원 311

군사분계선 ·············· 311	굴복하다 ··············· 311	귀 ················· 27, 60, 406
군사비 ···················· 311	굴비 ······················ 114	귀가하다 ················ 513
군사시설 ················ 311	굴절 ······················ 438	귀결 ······················ 210
군사우편 ········· 187, 311	굵기 ············ 431, 446, 487	귀고리 ····················· 98
군사위성 ················ 311	굵다 ················ 431, 487	귀공자 ······················· 2
군사재판 ················ 311	굵다랗다 ··········· 431, 487	귀금속 ············· 98, 367
군사정책 ················ 311	굵직하다 ··········· 431, 487	귀납법 ··················· 211
군사지도 ················ 311	굶다 ················ 114, 513	귀농 ······················ 367
군사지역 ················ 311	굶주리다 ··········· 114, 513	귀농현상 ················ 367
군사학 ··················· 210	굼뜨다 ····················· 85	귀뚜라미 ················ 406
군살 ······················· 27	굽다 ········ 114, 431, 487, 513	귀뚤귀뚤 ················ 406
군소리 ··················· 159	굽히다 ··················· 513	귀띔하다 ········· 159, 513
군소리하다 ······· 159, 513	굿 ·························· 223	귀리 ················ 114, 420
군수 ··············· 284, 354	굿판 ······················ 223	귀머거리 ······· 2, 60, 159
군수뇌부 ················ 311	굿하다 ··················· 223	귀먹다 ····················· 60
군수물자 ················ 311	궁 ·························· 139	귀밑머리 ················· 27
군수품 ··················· 311	궁궐 ······················ 139	귀부인 ······················· 2
군악대 ············· 240, 311	궁금증 ····················· 70	귀순하다 ················ 513
군용 ······················ 311	궁금하다 ··················· 70	귀신 ······················ 223
군용기 ············· 311, 387	궁도 ······················ 269	귀엽다 ··················· 487
군용도로 ················ 311	궁둥이 ····················· 27	귀의하다 ················ 223
군용지 ··················· 311	궁리하다 ··················· 70	귀이개 ··················· 139
군용차 ··················· 311	궁상맞다 ················ 487	귀중품 ··················· 334
군의관 ··················· 311	궁전 ······················ 139	귀지 ························ 27
군인 ··············· 311, 354	궁중무용 ················ 240	귀찮다 ····················· 70
군장 ······················ 311	궁중요리 ················ 114	귀청 ······················· 60
군장비 ··················· 311	궁합 ······················· 20	귀퉁이 ··················· 474
군주 ······················ 284	궂다 ················ 395, 487	귀하다 ··················· 487
군주국가 ················ 284	권 ·························· 446	귀향하다 ················ 513
군주정치 ················ 284	권고하다 ··········· 159, 513	귀화 ······················ 284
군주제 ··················· 284	권력 ··············· 284, 322	귀화하다 ················ 513
군중 ··············· 284, 322	권리 ······················ 322	귀환하다 ················ 513
군청 ······················ 284	권리금 ··················· 334	귓가 ······················· 27
군청색 ··················· 438	권사 ······················ 223	귓등 ······················· 27
군침 ······················ 114	권유하다 ··········· 159, 513	귓바퀴 ················ 27, 60
군침돌다 ················ 114	권장소비자가격 ······· 334	귓밥 ······················· 27
군함 ······················ 311	권장하다 ··········· 159, 513	귓병 ······················· 39
군항 ······················ 311	권총 ······················ 311	귓불 ······················· 27
군화 ······················ 311	권태 ······················· 70	귓속말 ············· 60, 159
굳다 ······················ 487	권투 ······················ 269	규격봉투 ················ 187
굳세다 ····················· 85	권투장갑 ··········· 98, 269	규격품 ··················· 334
굳은살 ····················· 27	권하다 ··················· 284	규명하다 ················ 513
굴 ··············· 114, 406, 474	권한 ······················ 284	규범 ······················ 322
굴곡 ······················ 159	궤 ·························· 139	규율 ······················ 322
굴뚝 ················ 139, 382	궤도 ······················ 474	규정 ······················ 300
굴리다 ··················· 513	궤짝 ······················ 139	규제 ······················ 322

규제하다 ······· 513	극락정토 ······· 223	금년 ······· 459
규칙 ······· 211, 300	극복하다 ······· 513	금리 ······· 334
규칙적 ······· 487	극성 ······· 211	금발 ······· 27
규탄하다 ······· 159, 513	극성맞다 ······· 85	금방 ······· 459
균 ······· 406	극시 ······· 240	금번 ······· 459
균형 ······· 487	극작가 ······· 240, 354	금붕어 ······· 406
귤 ······· 420	극장 ······· 240, 367	금빛 ······· 438
그곳 ······· 474	극적 ······· 240	금색 ······· 438
그글피 ······· 459	극진하다 ······· 85	금성 ······· 474
그끄저께 ······· 459	근 ······· 446	금세 ······· 459
그네 ······· 263	근대 ······· 114, 420, 459	금속 ······· 368
그네뛰기 ······· 263	근로소득 ······· 334	금속공예 ······· 240
그때 ······· 459	근로자 ······· 354	금식 ······· 114
그때그때 ······· 459	근면성 ······· 85	금실 ······· 20
그램 ······· 446	근면하다 ······· 85	금액 ······· 334
그루 ······· 420, 446	근무 ······· 354	금연 ······· 114
그루갈이 ······· 367	근무자 ······· 354	금요일 ······· 459
그릇 ······· 114, 446	근무지 ······· 354	금융 ······· 334
그리 ······· 474	근무처 ······· 354	금융가 ······· 334
그리다 ······· 240, 513	근무하다 ······· 354, 513	금융기관 ······· 334
그리스 ······· 275	근방 ······· 474	금융시장 ······· 334
그리스도 ······· 223	근시 ······· 39, 60	금융실명제 ······· 334
그리스어 ······· 159	근신 ······· 196	금융업 ······· 355, 368
그리스정교 ······· 223	근심 ······· 70	금융자산 ······· 334
그리움 ······· 70	근심하다 ······· 70	금일 ······· 459
그리워하다 ······· 513	근육 ······· 27	금일봉 ······· 334
그림 ······· 240	근육통 ······· 39	금잔화 ······· 420
그림씨 ······· 159	근절하다 ······· 513	금전 ······· 334
그림엽서 ······· 187	근접하다 ······· 474, 513	금전출납부 ······· 334
그림자 ······· 395, 438	근처 ······· 474	금주 ······· 114
그림책 ······· 181	근해어업 ······· 367	금지하다 ······· 159, 514
그립다 ······· 70	글 ······· 159	금하다 ······· 159, 514
그만두다 ······· 513	글씨 ······· 159	금혼식 ······· 20
그물 ······· 258, 367	글씨체 ······· 159	금화 ······· 334
그물낚시 ······· 258	글자 ······· 159	급변 ······· 487
그믐 ······· 459	글짓기 ······· 159, 240	급사 ······· 51
그믐날 ······· 459	글피 ······· 459	급소 ······· 27
그믐달 ······· 474	긁다 ······· 513	급식 ······· 114
그저께 ······· 459	금 ······· 367	급여 ······· 334, 355
그전 ······· 459	금강석 ······· 367	급체 ······· 39
그제 ······· 459	금고 ······· 334	급하다 ······· 85
그쪽 ······· 474	금관 ······· 98	급훈 ······· 196
그치다 ······· 395, 513	금관악기 ······· 240	긋다 ······· 159, 514
극 ······· 240	금광 ······· 367	긍정적이다 ······· 85
극관 ······· 211	금괴 ······· 367	긍정하다 ······· 159, 514
극기훈련 ······· 196	금귤 ······· 420	긍지 ······· 71

기각 ······ 300	기름지다 ······ 368	기업체 ······ 334
기간 ······ 459	기린 ······ 407	기온 ······ 395
기간산업 ······ 368	기마전 ······ 263	기와 ······ 140
기계 ······ 368	기만하다 ······ 86	기와집 ······ 140
기계공업 ······ 368	기밀 ······ 187	기운없다 ······ 487
기계문명 ······ 234	기반시설 ······ 368	기운있다 ······ 487
기계체조 ······ 269	기병 ······ 311	기운차다 ······ 487
기계화 ······ 368	기병대 ······ 311	기울기 ······ 474
기관 ······ 368	기본형 ······ 160	기울다 ······ 431, 487
기관사 ······ 355, 387	기부금 ······ 334	기원 ······ 223
기관장 ······ 355	기분 ······ 71	기원전 ······ 459
기관지염 ······ 39	기뻐하다 ······ 71, 514	기원하다 ······ 160, 514
기관차 ······ 387	기쁘다 ······ 71	기일 ······ 51, 459
기관총 ······ 311	기쁨 ······ 71	기입하다 ······ 160, 514
기구 ······ 140, 223	기사 ······ 181, 355	기자 ······ 181, 355
기권 ······ 269, 284	기상 ······ 395	기장 ······ 355, 387, 420
기권하다 ······ 284	기상관측 ······ 395	기재하다 ······ 160, 514
기금 ······ 334	기상청 ······ 284, 395	기저귀 ······ 140
기념물 ······ 234	기상통보 ······ 395	기적 ······ 224
기념식 ······ 322	기상특보 ······ 395	기절 ······ 39
기념일 ······ 459	기생충 ······ 407	기절하다 ······ 487
기념주화 ······ 334	기생하다 ······ 407	기죽다 ······ 86
기념품 ······ 322, 334	기성복 ······ 98	기지 ······ 311
기념하다 ······ 322	기성회비 ······ 196	기지개 ······ 27
기능보유자 ······ 234	기소 ······ 300	기지국 ······ 187
기능사 ······ 355	기수 ······ 446	기차 ······ 387
기다 ······ 514	기숙사 ······ 140, 197	기차여행 ······ 258
기다랗다 ······ 431, 487	기술 ······ 368	기차표 ······ 387
기다리다 ······ 514	기술사 ······ 355	기체 ······ 211, 487
기대다 ······ 514	기술직 ······ 355	기초공사 ······ 140
기대하다 ······ 71, 514	기술하다 ······ 160, 514	기초화장 ······ 98
기도 ······ 223	기악 ······ 240	기침 ······ 27, 39
기도문 ······ 223	기악곡 ······ 240	기탁금 ······ 334
기도원 ······ 223	기악대 ······ 240	기탁하다 ······ 334
기도하다 ······ 160, 223, 514	기압 ······ 395	기필코 ······ 487
기독교 ······ 223	기압계 ······ 395, 446	기형아 ······ 2
기독교방송 ······ 181	기약하다 ······ 160, 514	기호식품 ······ 114
기둥 ······ 140	기어가다 ······ 514	기호품 ······ 114, 334
기득권층 ······ 322	기어코 ······ 487	기혼자 ······ 20
기러기 ······ 406	기억 ······ 71	기화 ······ 211, 487
기록 ······ 160	기억력 ······ 71	기획상품 ······ 335
기록사진 ······ 258	기억하다 ······ 71, 514	기획예산처 ······ 284
기록영화 ······ 340	기업 ······ 334	기획하다 ······ 514
기록하다 ······ 160, 514	기업가 ······ 334	기후 ······ 395
기르다 ······ 368, 406, 514	기업인 ······ 334, 355	긴급하다 ······ 459
기름 ······ 114, 382	기업주 ······ 334	긴박하다 ······ 460

긴장 ... 71	깍쟁이 ... 2, 86	꼬질꼬질 ... 488
긴장하다 ... 71, 514	깎다 ... 335, 514	꼬집다 ... 515
긴축정책 ... 335	간간하다 ... 86	꼬치 ... 115
긷다 ... 514	갈개 ... 140	꼭 ... 488
길 ... 474	갈갈하다 ... 60, 488	꼭대기 ... 474
길거리 ... 474	갈끔하다 ... 86, 488	꼭두각시놀음 ... 263
길다 ... 431, 460, 487	갈다 ... 514	꼭두각시춤 ... 240
길들이다 ... 407, 514	갈대기 ... 115, 140	꼭두새벽 ... 460
길모퉁이 ... 474	갈보다 ... 86	꼭지 ... 420
길목 ... 474	깜깜하다 ... 439, 488	꼭지점 ... 431
길몽 ... 27	깜짝 ... 71	꼴 ... 368, 431
길이 ... 431, 446, 487	깡충깡충 ... 407	꼴뚜기 ... 115, 407
길일 ... 460	깡통 ... 115, 140	꼼꼼하다 ... 86
길쭉하다 ... 431, 487	깡통따개 ... 115, 140	꼽다 ... 446, 515
김 ... 114, 420	깡패 ... 300	꼿꼿하다 ... 488
김매기 ... 368	깨 ... 115, 420	꽁꽁 ... 488
김매다 ... 368	깨끗하다 ... 488	꽁무니 ... 407
김밥 ... 114	깨다 ... 514	꽁지 ... 407
김장 ... 114	깨닫다 ... 71, 211	꽁치 ... 115, 407
김장철 ... 114, 460	깨뜨리다 ... 514	꽂다 ... 98, 515
김치 ... 114	깨물다 ... 115, 514	꽃 ... 421
김치찌개 ... 115	깨우다 ... 514	꽃가루 ... 421
김치통 ... 115	깨우치다 ... 514	꽃게 ... 115, 407
깁다 ... 98, 514	깻잎 ... 115, 420	꽃꽂이 ... 258, 421
깃 ... 98	꺼리다 ... 71, 86, 514	꽃눈 ... 421
깃털 ... 407	꺼림칙하다 ... 71	꽃다발 ... 421
깊다 ... 431, 488	꺼지다 ... 514	꽃대 ... 421
깊숙하다 ... 431, 488	꺾다 ... 420, 515	꽃받침 ... 421
깊이 ... 431, 446, 488	꺾쇠표 ... 160	꽃봉오리 ... 421
까나리 ... 407	껄끄럽다 ... 60, 488	꽃분홍색 ... 439
까다 ... 514	껌 ... 115	꽃사슴 ... 407
까다롭다 ... 86	껍데기 ... 407, 420	꽃샘추위 ... 395
까마귀 ... 407	껍질 ... 407, 420	꽃시장 ... 335
까만색 ... 438	껴안다 ... 515	꽃신 ... 98
까망 ... 439	꼬깃꼬깃 ... 488	꽃씨 ... 421
까맣다 ... 439, 488	꼬꼬댁 ... 407	꽃집 ... 335
까먹다 ... 71	꼬끼오 ... 407	꽃향기 ... 421
까무러치다 ... 488	꼬다 ... 515	꽈리 ... 421
까뭇까뭇 ... 439	꼬들꼬들 ... 115	꽉 ... 488
까불다 ... 86, 514	꼬르륵 ... 27, 115	꽉꽉 ... 488
까악까악 ... 407	꼬리 ... 407	꽤 ... 488
까치 ... 407	꼬리곰탕 ... 115	꽥꽥 ... 407
까칠하다 ... 488	꼬마 ... 2	꽹과리 ... 240
까투리 ... 407	꼬불꼬불 ... 474	꾀 ... 71
깍두기 ... 115	꼬시다 ... 160, 515	꾀꼬리 ... 407
깍듯하다 ... 86	꼬이다 ... 431, 515	꾀꼴꾀꼴 ... 407

꾀다	515
꾀병	39
꾸다	335, 515
꾸러미	446
꾸리다	515
꾸미다	98, 515
꾸밈씨	160
꾸밈음	240
꾸어주다	335, 515
꾸역꾸역	115
꾸준하다	488
꾸중	160
꾸중하다	160, 515
꾸지람	160
꾸짖다	160, 515
꿀	115
꿀꺽	115
꿀꿀	407
꿀떡	115
꿀맛이다	115
꿀벌	407
꿇다	515
꿈	27
꿈꾸다	71, 515
꿈틀하다	515
꿋꿋하다	86
꿍꿍이	71
꿩	407
꿩고기	115
꿰다	515
꿰뚫어보다	60, 515
꿰매다	98, 515
끄다	382, 515
끄덕이다	515
끄르다	98, 515
끄트머리	474
끈	140
끈기	86
끈끈하다	60, 488
끈적끈적하다	60
끈질기다	86
끊다	515
끌다	515
끓는점	211
끓다	115
끓이다	115, 515
끔찍하다	71
끙끙	39
끝	460
끝내다	515
끝마치다	515
끝말잇기	263
끼	446
끼니	115
끼다	98, 395
끼룩끼룩	407
끼얹다	115, 515
(비늘을) 긁다	114
—경	458
—곳	473

나

나가다	515
나그네	2
나날이	460
나누기	446
나누다	446, 515
나눗셈	446
나들이	258
나들이옷	98
나라	284
나란히	431
나루	387
나루터	388
나룻배	388
나르다	515
나른하다	488
나리	421
나머지	447
나무	140, 421
나무라다	160, 515
나무아미타불	224
나물	115, 421
나뭇가지	421
나뭇잎	421
나방	407
나병	40
나비	407
나비넥타이	98
나쁘다	71, 86, 395, 488
나사못	140
나서다	516
나선형	431
나아가다	516
나약하다	86
나열하다	516
나오다	516
나이	51, 447
나이지리아	275
나이테	421
나중	460
나지막하다	431, 488
나직하다	431, 488
나체	27
나침반	388, 474
나타나다	516
나태하다	86
나트륨	211
나팔	240
나팔꽃	421
나흘	460
낙관적이다	86
낙농업	355, 368
낙농업자	368
낙방하다	197
낙서	160
낙선	284
낙엽	421
낙원	224
낙제생	197
낙제하다	197
낙지	115, 407
낙찰	335
낙천적이다	86
낙타	407
낙하산	311, 388
낙하하다	516
낚다	258, 368, 516
낚시	258, 368
낚시꾼	258, 368
낚시바늘	258
낚시질	258, 368
낚시터	258, 368
낚시하다	258, 368, 516

낚싯대 ……………………… 258, 368	남녀 ………………………………… 2	낮잠 ………………………………… 27
낚싯밥 ……………………… 259, 368	남녀노소 …………………………… 2	낮추다 …………………………… 516
낚싯배 …………………………… 388	남다 ……………………………… 516	낮춤말 …………………………… 160
낚싯봉 …………………………… 259	남동생 ……………………………… 12	낯 …………………………………… 27
낚싯줄 ……………………… 259, 368	남루하다 ………………………… 488	낯설다 ……………………………… 71
난간 ……………………………… 140	남매 ………………………………… 12	낱말 ……………………………… 160
난감하다 …………………………… 71	남미 ……………………………… 275	낱말맞추기 ……………………… 263
난국 ……………………………… 488	남방셔츠 ………………………… 98	낳다 ……………………… 21, 408, 516
난독증 …………………………… 160	남빛 ……………………………… 439	내 ………………………………… 474
난로 ……………………… 140, 382	남색 ……………………………… 439	내각 ……………………………… 284
난류 ……………………… 368, 395	남성 ……………………………… 2, 21	내과 ………………………………… 40
난방 ……………………… 140, 382	남성복 …………………………… 98	내국세 …………………………… 335
난방비 …………………………… 335	남아메리카 ……………………… 275	내국인 …………………………… 284
난산 ………………………………… 21	남아프리카공화국 ……………… 275	내기 ……………………………… 264
난생 ……………………………… 407	남자 ………………………………… 2	내기하다 ………………… 264, 516
난서증 …………………………… 160	남자답다 ………………………… 86	내내 ……………………………… 460
난소염 …………………………… 40	남자친구 …………………………… 2	내년 ……………………………… 460
난시 ……………………… 27, 40, 60	남쪽 ……………………………… 474	내놓다 …………………………… 516
난시청 …………………………… 181	남편 ……………………………… 12	내다 ……………………… 99, 447, 516
난자 ………………………………… 21	남풍 ……………………………… 395	내다보다 ………………………… 60
난쟁이 ……………………………… 2	남학생 ……………………………… 2	내달 ……………………………… 460
난처하다 …………………………… 71	남한 ……………………………… 275	내려가다 ………………… 395, 516
난청 ……………………………… 27, 40	남향 ……………………………… 140	내려오다 ………………………… 516
난초 ……………………………… 421	납 ………………………… 211, 368	내리다 ……………… 388, 395, 516
난치병 ……………………………… 40	납골당 ……………………………… 52	내리막 …………………………… 474
난폭하다 ………………………… 86	납득하다 ………………… 71, 516	내림세 …………………………… 335
날가리 …………………………… 368	납부하다 ………………… 335, 516	내림표 …………………………… 240
날 ………………………… 395, 460	납세 ……………………………… 335	내무반 …………………………… 311
날개 ……………………………… 407	납세자 …………………………… 335	내밀다 …………………………… 516
날다 ……………………… 388, 407, 516	납입금 …………………………… 335	내보내다 ………………………… 516
날뛰다 ……………………… 86, 516	납입액 …………………………… 335	내복 ……………………………… 99
날렵하다 ………………………… 86	납작코 ……………………………… 27	내복약 ……………………………… 40
날리다 ……………………… 335, 516	납작하다 ………………… 431, 488	내부 ……………………………… 474
날마다 …………………………… 460	납치하다 ………………………… 516	내부공사 ………………………… 140
날씨 ……………………………… 395	납품하다 ………………………… 335	내성적이다 ……………………… 86
날씨란 …………………………… 181	낫 ………………………………… 368	내세우다 ………………………… 516
날씬하다 ………………………… 488	낫다 ……………………… 40, 488, 516	내수시장 ………………………… 335
날아가다 ………………………… 516	낭독하다 ………………………… 160	내의 ……………………………… 99
날조하다 ………………………… 516	낭떠러지 ………………………… 474	내일 ……………………………… 460
날짐승 …………………………… 408	낭랑하다 ………………………… 60	내장 ……………………… 27, 140
날짜 ……………………………… 460	낭만 ……………………………… 71	내장재 …………………………… 140
날카롭다 ………………… 86, 431, 488	낭만주의 ………………………… 240	내쫓다 …………………………… 516
날파리 …………………………… 408	낭비하다 ………………… 335, 516	내키다 ……………………… 71, 516
낡다 ……………………………… 488	낭송하다 ………………… 160, 516	내후년 …………………………… 460
남 …………………………………… 2	낮 ……………………………… 460	냄비 ……………………………… 115
남극 ……………………………… 474	낮다 ……………………… 395, 431, 488	냄비받침 ………………………… 115

냄새 ········· 60
냄새나다 ········· 60
냄새제거제 ········· 60
냉국 ········· 115
냉기 ········· 395
냉담하다 ········· 86
냉대하다 ········· 86, 516
냉동하다 ········· 115, 516
냉면 ········· 115
냉방 ········· 140
냉이 ········· 115, 421
냉장고 ········· 115, 140
냉전 ········· 312
냉정하다 ········· 71, 86
냉차 ········· 116
냉채 ········· 116
냉철하다 ········· 71, 211
냉커피 ········· 116
냉혈동물 ········· 408
냉혹하다 ········· 86
냠냠 ········· 116
냥 ········· 447
너구리 ········· 408
너그럽다 ········· 86
너무하다 ········· 488
너비 ········· 431, 488
너스레 ········· 160
너와집 ········· 140
너저분하다 ········· 489
너절하다 ········· 489
넉 ········· 447
넉넉하다 ········· 335, 489
넉살좋다 ········· 86
넋 ········· 52, 72, 224
넋두리 ········· 160
넌더리나다 ········· 72
널다 ········· 99, 516
널따랗다 ········· 431, 489
널뛰기 ········· 264
널리 ········· 489
널빤지 ········· 140
널찍하다 ········· 431, 489
넓다 ········· 431, 474, 489
넓이 ········· 431, 447, 489
넓적다리 ········· 27
넓적하다 ········· 431, 489

넓히다 ········· 431, 517
넘기다 ········· 517
넘다 ········· 517
넘보다 ········· 517
넘어지다 ········· 517
넘치다 ········· 489
넙치 ········· 116, 408
넝쿨 ········· 421
넣다 ········· 517
네 ········· 447
네댓 ········· 447
네델란드 ········· 275
네모 ········· 431
네모나다 ········· 431, 489
네모지다 ········· 431, 489
네팔 ········· 275
넥타이 ········· 99
넥타이핀 ········· 99
넷 ········· 447
넷째 ········· 447
녀석 ········· 2
년 ········· 460
노 ········· 368, 388
노년기 ········· 52
노다지 ········· 368
노동 ········· 355
노동법 ········· 300
노동부 ········· 284
노동자 ········· 355, 368
노란색 ········· 439
노랑 ········· 439
노랗다 ········· 439
노래 ········· 240
노래방 ········· 368
노래하다 ········· 517
노려보다 ········· 60, 517
노력하다 ········· 87, 489
노루 ········· 408
노르스름하다 ········· 439
노르웨이 ········· 275
노름 ········· 264
노름꾼 ········· 264
노름하다 ········· 264
노릇노릇 ········· 439
노리다 ········· 517
노린내 ········· 60

노망 ········· 40
노문학 ········· 211
노문학자 ········· 211
노발대발 ········· 72
노새 ········· 408
노송나무 ········· 421
노심초사 ········· 72
노안 ········· 40, 60
노약자 ········· 2
노어 ········· 160
노어학 ········· 211
노어학자 ········· 211
노여움 ········· 72
노여워하다 ········· 72, 517
노엽다 ········· 72
노을 ········· 395
노인 ········· 2
노인대학 ········· 197
노인문제 ········· 322
노자 ········· 259
노점 ········· 335
노점상 ········· 335
노처녀 ········· 21
노천극장 ········· 240
노총각 ········· 21
노출하다 ········· 517
노파 ········· 2
노폐물 ········· 27
노하다 ········· 72
녹내장 ········· 40, 60
녹는점 ········· 211
녹다 ········· 395, 489
녹두 ········· 116, 421
녹두색 ········· 439
녹말가루 ········· 116
녹색 ········· 439
녹음기 ········· 197
녹이다 ········· 116, 517
녹차 ········· 116
녹화방송 ········· 181
녹화하다 ········· 181, 517
논 ········· 368, 421, 474
논두렁 ········· 368
논둑 ········· 369
논리 ········· 211
논문 ········· 211

논문계획서 … 211	농성 … 322	뇌염 … 40
논박하다 … 160, 517	농아 … 2, 60	뇌졸중 … 40
논밭 … 474	농악 … 240, 369	뇌진탕 … 40
논법 … 211	농악놀이 … 369	뇌출혈 … 40
논설위원 … 181	농악대 … 240	누계 … 447
논술 … 160	농약 … 369	누나 … 12
논어 … 224	농어민 … 323, 369	누님 … 12
논의하다 … 160, 517	농어촌 … 369	누다 … 27, 517
논쟁하다 … 160, 517	농업 … 355, 369	누더기 … 99
논증하다 … 160, 517	농업고등학교 … 197	누룩 … 116
논평 … 181	농업국 … 369	누룽지 … 116
논평하다 … 160, 517	농업용수 … 369	누르다 … 517
놀다 … 264, 517	농업협동조합 … 369	누리 … 474
놀라다 … 72, 517	농원 … 369	누리다 … 517
놀러가다 … 517	농작물 … 369	누린내 … 60, 116
놀러오다 … 517	농장 … 369	누명 … 300
놀리다 … 160, 517	농지 … 369	누비 … 99
놀이 … 264	농지세 … 335	누비다 … 99, 517
놀이공원 … 264	농지정리 … 370	누비옷 … 99
놀이동산 … 264	농촌 … 370, 474	누설하다 … 161, 187, 518
놀이방 … 197	농촌봉사활동 … 323	누에 … 408
놀이터 … 264	농촌진흥청 … 284, 370	누에치기 … 370
놈 … 2, 447	농축산물 … 370	누이 … 12
농가 … 369	농토 … 370	누이동생 … 12
농경문화 … 234	농학 … 211	누전 … 382
농경사회 … 322	농학자 … 211	누추하다 … 140
농경지 … 369	농한기 … 370	눅눅하다 … 60, 395, 489
농고 … 197	농협 … 370	눈 … 27, 60, 396, 408, 421
농구 … 269	농후하다 … 489	눈곱 … 28
농구공 … 269	높낮이 … 431	눈금 … 447
농기계 … 369	높다 … 395, 432, 489	눈길 … 60
농기구 … 369	높다랗다 … 432, 489	눈꺼풀 … 28
농담 … 160	높새바람 … 395	눈꼬리 … 28
농담하다 … 517	높이 … 432, 447, 489	눈꼽 … 28
농도 … 211, 489	높이다 … 517	눈꽃 … 396
농림부 … 284, 369	높이뛰기 … 269	눈동자 … 28, 60
농민 … 322, 369	높임말 … 161	눈두덩 … 28
농번기 … 369	높임법 … 161	눈망울 … 28
농부 … 355, 369	놓다 … 517	눈맞추다 … 21
농사 … 369	놓아주다 … 517	눈매 … 28, 60
농사꾼 … 369	놓치다 … 517	눈멀다 … 61
농사일 … 369	뇌 … 27	눈물 … 28
농사짓다 … 369, 517	뇌물 … 335	눈물샘 … 28
농사철 … 369	뇌사 … 52	눈발 … 396
농산물 … 369	뇌사상태 … 489	눈병 … 40, 61
농산물시장 … 335	뇌성마비 … 40	눈보라 … 396

눈사람 396	능숙하다 489	다리미판 140
눈사태 396	늦— 421, 460	다림질 99
눈살 28	늦게 460	다림질하다 99, 518
눈송이 396	늦다 460	다만 489
눈시울 28	늦더위 396	다면체 432
눈싸움 264, 396	늦잠 28	다물다 518
눈썰매 264, 396	늪 474	다발 447
눈썰미 61, 87	니카라과 275	다방 370
눈썹 28	닝닝하다 116	다섯 447
눈썹연필 99	닢 447	다섯째 447
눈알 28, 61	—녘 460	다세대주택 140
눈여겨보다 61, 518	—님 3	다소 489
눈웃음치다 518		다수당 284
눈자위 28		다스 447
눈초리 28, 61	**다**	다스리다 284, 518
눈총 28, 61		다슬기 408
눈치 61, 87		다시다 518
눌은밥 116	다 447, 489	다시마 116, 421
눕다 518	다가가다 518	다신교 224
뉘우치다 72, 518	다가서다 518	다용도실 140
뉴스 181, 187	다가오다 518	다음 460
뉴질랜드 275	다각형 432	다음달 460
느긋하다 87	다과회 116, 323	다음번 460
느끼다 61, 72, 518	다그치다 161, 518	다음해 460
느끼하다 61, 116	다기 116	다의어 161
느낌 61, 72	다녀가다 518	다이빙 269
느낌씨 161	다년생 421	다이아몬드 370
느낌표 161	다니다 518	다이어트 116
느리다 460	다다르다 518	다정하다 72, 87, 489
느림보 2	다달이 460	다중언어화자 161
느슨하다 489	다도 116	다지다 116, 518
느타리버섯 116, 421	다독 161	다짐 72
느티나무 421	다듬다 99, 116, 518	다짐하다 72, 161, 518
늑대 408	다듬이질 99	다채롭다 439
늑장부리다 518	다락방 140	다치다 518
늘 460	다람쥐 408	다큐멘터리 181
늘다 489	다랑어 408	다투다 518
늘리다 99, 518	다래 421	닥나무 421
늘씬하다 489	다래끼 40	닥지닥지 489
늘어놓다 518	다루다 518	닦다 518
늙다 489	다르다 432, 489	단 99, 421, 447
늙은이 2	다리 28, 408	단검 312
늠름하다 87	다리다 99, 518	단골 335
능동태 161	다리미 140	단골손님 335
능력 355	다리미대 140	단과대학 197
능률 355		단기 460

단기사병 312	단체장 323	닭똥집 117
단내 61	단체전 269	닭싸움 264
단념하다 72, 518	단체행동 323	닮다 432, 490
단단하다 61, 489	단체행동권 323	닮은꼴 432
단답형 197	단추 99	담 141
단독주택 140	단축하다 518	담그다 117, 519
단락 161	단춧구멍 99	담다 519
단란주점 116, 335, 370	단층집 141	담담하다 72, 87
단막극 240	단칸방 141	담당교사 197
단맛 61	단팥죽 116	담배 117, 422
단무지 116	단편소설 241	담백하다 117, 490
단발머리 28	단풍 421	담보 335
단백질 116	단풍나무 421	담비 408
단비 396	단풍놀이 259	담소 161
단서 211, 300	단호하다 87	담소하다 161, 519
단소 240	닫다 519	담수어 408
단속하다 300, 518	달 461, 474	담요 141
단수 447	달걀 116, 408	담임교사 197
단순하다 489	달걀형 432	담쟁이덩굴 422
단술 116	달그림자 396	담즙 28
단숨에 460	달나라 474	담판하다 161, 519
단시일 460	달다 61, 116, 447, 490, 519	담화 161
단식 116	달동네 141, 475	답답하다 72
단어 161	달라붙다 519	답례하다 161, 519
단언하다 161, 518	달래 116, 422	답변하다 161, 519
단역 240	달래다 161, 519	답사 259
단열 140	달러 335	답사하다 259
단열재 140	달러화 335	답안지 197
단옷날 461	달려가다 519	답하다 161
단원 197	달려들다 519	닷새 461
단위 447	달력 141, 461	당구 269
단음계 241	달리기 269	당권 285
단의어 161	달리다 519	당근 117, 422
단일민족 285	달리아 422	당기다 519
단일어 161	달맞이 264	당나귀 408
단장하다 99, 518	달무리 396	당뇨병 40
단절하다 518	달빛 396, 439	당당하다 87
단점 489	달아나다 519	당대 461
단정하다 72, 99, 161, 211, 518	달이다 519	당대표 285
단조 241	달인 3	당리당략 285
단조롭다 490	달착지근하다 61, 116	당부하다 161, 519
단지 116	달콤하다 61, 116	당분간 461
단체 323	달팽이 408	당사자 3
단체사진 259	달팽이관 61	당선 285
단체생활 323	닭 408	당선되다 285
단체의식 323	닭고기 116	당선자 285

당숙 ····· 12	대리점 ····· 336	대의명분 ····· 285
당시 ····· 461	대립어 ····· 161	대이름씨 ····· 162
당원 ····· 285	대립하다 ····· 519	대자연 ····· 396
당일 ····· 461	대마 ····· 422	대장 ····· 28, 312
당장 ····· 461	대마초 ····· 117	대장균 ····· 408
당쟁 ····· 285	대만 ····· 275	대장부 ····· 3
당좌수표 ····· 335	대머리 ····· 28	대접 ····· 117
당좌예금 ····· 335	대명사 ····· 161	대접하다 ····· 87, 519
당직 ····· 355	대문 ····· 141	대주교 ····· 224
당초 ····· 461	대문자 ····· 162	대중 ····· 323
당파 ····· 285	대범하다 ····· 87	대중가요 ····· 241
당황하다 ····· 72	대법관 ····· 300	대중매체 ····· 181, 188
닻 ····· 370, 388	대법원 ····· 300	대중문화 ····· 234
닿소리 ····· 161	대법원장 ····· 300	대중음악 ····· 241
대 ····· 12, 52, 447	대변 ····· 28	대중화 ····· 323
대가리 ····· 408	대변인 ····· 285	대지 ····· 141, 475
대가족 ····· 12	대변하다 ····· 162, 519	대차대조표 ····· 336
대각선 ····· 432	대보름 ····· 461	대체로 ····· 490
대개 ····· 490	대본 ····· 241	대체적 ····· 490
대걸레 ····· 141	대부 ····· 336	대추나무 ····· 422
대격 ····· 161	대부금 ····· 336	대출 ····· 336
대견스럽다 ····· 72	대부분 ····· 490	대출금 ····· 336
대괄호 ····· 161	대부하다 ····· 336	대출하다 ····· 336, 519
대구 ····· 117, 408	대사 ····· 162, 224, 241, 285	대통령 ····· 285, 355
대권 ····· 285	대사관 ····· 285	대통령령 ····· 300
대궐 ····· 141	대서 ····· 461	대통령제 ····· 285
대금 ····· 241, 336	대서특필 ····· 181	대통령중심제 ····· 285
대기 ····· 475	대선 ····· 285	대파 ····· 117
대기권 ····· 475	대설 ····· 461	대포 ····· 312
대기업 ····· 336, 355	대설경보 ····· 396	대표 ····· 355
대기오염 ····· 396	대설주의보 ····· 396	대표선수 ····· 269
대꾸하다 ····· 161, 519	대소 ····· 432	대표이사 ····· 355
대나무 ····· 422	대수 ····· 447	대표자 ····· 323
대다 ····· 519	대수학 ····· 447	대하 ····· 117, 408
대단하다 ····· 490	대순진리회 ····· 224	대하소설 ····· 241
대담 ····· 161	대야 ····· 141	대학교 ····· 197
대답하다 ····· 87, 161, 519	대어 ····· 259, 370	대학본부 ····· 197
대답하다 ····· 161, 519	대여 ····· 336	대학생 ····· 197
대도시 ····· 475	대여료 ····· 370	대학원 ····· 197
대들다 ····· 87, 161, 519	대여섯 ····· 447	대학원생 ····· 197
대들보 ····· 141	대여하다 ····· 336	대한 ····· 461
대량생산 ····· 370	대역 ····· 241	대한민국 ····· 275
대령 ····· 312	대영제국 ····· 275	대합 ····· 117, 408
대륙 ····· 475	대용품 ····· 336	대합실 ····· 388
대륙붕 ····· 475	대위 ····· 312	대형 ····· 432
대리석 ····· 141	대응하다 ····· 519	대형할인매장 ····· 336

대화 162	데릴사위 12	도복 269
대화방 188	데모 285, 323	도사리다 520
대화하다 162, 519	데뷔하다 241	도산 336
댁 141	데우다 117, 520	도살 370
댐 475	데치다 117, 520	도살장 370
댓 448	덴마크 276	도서 181
댕기 99	도 141, 224, 285, 448	도서관 197
더 490	도교 224	도서상품권 181
더덕 117, 422	도굴꾼 300	도서실 197
더듬다 61, 519	도굴하다 300	도시 141, 475
더듬이 408	도깨비 224	도시가스 382
더디다 461	도깨비시장 336	도시국가 285
더럽다 490	도끼 141	도시락 117
더부룩하다 490	도덕 300, 323	도시락가방 141
더부살이 52	도도하다 87	도시빈민 323
더욱 490	도돌이표 241	도심 475
더위 396	도둑 300	도안하다 520
더하기 448	도둑질 300	도예 241
더하다 448	도라지 117, 422	도예가 355
덕 87	도라지꽃 422	도움말 162
덕담 162	도랑 475	도자기 241
덕망 87	도려내다 520	도장 141
덕장 370	도련님 12	도정 370
던지다 519	도로 388, 475	도정하다 370
덜 490	도로교통 388	도지사 285, 355
덜다 519	도루묵 408	도착하다 520
덜덜 396	도리 87	도청 188
덤 336	도리도리 264	도청기 61, 188
덤벙거리다 87, 519	도마 117, 141	도청하다 61, 188, 520
덤비다 519	도마뱀 408	도톰하다 432, 490
덤핑판매 336	도막 448, 490	도피하다 520
덥다 61, 396, 490	도망가다 520	도형 432
덧니 28	도망오다 520	도화지 241
덧버선 99	도망치다 520	독 117, 141, 408
덧셈 448	도매 336	독감 40
덧신 99	도매가 336	독거미 408
덩굴 422	도매상 336	독과점 336
덩어리 432, 490	도매시장 336	독단 72
덩이 432	도미 117, 408	독립어 162
덩치 432	도미니카 공화국 276	독문학 211
덮개 141	도민 323	독문학자 211
덮다 141, 519	도박 264	독백 162
덮밥 117	도박사 265	독버섯 422
덮치다 519	도박하다 265, 520	독불장군 3
데 475	도배하다 141, 520	독사 408
데다 520	도보여행 259	독사진 259

독살 ································· 52
독서 ································ 162
독서실 ····························· 197
독선 ································· 72
독수리 ····························· 408
독신 ·································· 3
독실하다 ·························· 224
독어 ································ 162
독어학 ····························· 211
독어학자 ·························· 211
독일 ································ 276
독자 ·························· 162, 181
독자투고란 ······················ 181
독재국가 ·························· 285
독재자 ····························· 285
독재정치 ·························· 285
독점 ································ 336
독주 ································ 241
독주회 ····························· 241
독창 ································ 241
독창회 ····························· 241
독촉하다 ···················· 162, 520
독특하다 ·························· 490
독하다 ······························ 87
독학사 ····························· 197
독후감 ····························· 241
돈 ···························· 336, 448
돈놀이 ····························· 336
돈다 ························· 422, 490
돋보기 ······························ 61
돌아나다 ·························· 422
돌 ······················ 52, 461, 475
돌격 ································ 312
돌격대 ····························· 312
돌고래 ····························· 408
돌나물 ······················· 117, 422
돌다 ································ 520
돌림병 ······························ 40
돌보다 ····························· 520
돌부처 ····························· 224
돌사진 ····························· 259
돌아가다 ··························· 52
돌아가시다 ······················ 520
돌아다니다 ······················ 520
돌아보다 ·························· 520
돌아서다 ·························· 520

돌연변이 ·························· 490
돌연사 ······························ 52
돕다 ································ 520
돗자리 ····························· 141
동 ················ 141, 285, 370, 448
동갑 ·································· 3
동강 ································ 490
동거하다 ·························· 141
동굴 ································ 475
동그라미 ·························· 432
동그랗다 ···················· 432, 490
동글납작하다 ··················· 432
동글동글 ·························· 432
동급생 ······························· 3
동기 ······················ 12, 211, 241
동기동창 ···························· 3
동기생 ······························· 3
동남아 ····························· 276
동네 ························· 141, 475
동네방네 ·························· 475
동년배 ······························· 3
동동주 ····························· 117
동등하다 ·························· 490
동력 ································ 382
동료 ·································· 3
동맥 ································ 28
동맥경화증 ························ 40
동맹 ························· 285, 323
동맹국 ····························· 285
동면 ································ 408
동무 ·································· 3
동문 ·································· 3
동문서답 ·························· 162
동문회 ····························· 323
동물 ································ 409
동물원 ····························· 409
동반자 ······························· 3
동백꽃 ····························· 422
동백나무 ·························· 422
동사 ························· 52, 162
동사무소 ·························· 285
동산 ································ 475
동상 ··························· 40, 241
동생 ································· 12
동서 ································· 12
동서남북 ·························· 475

동선 ································ 141
동성 ································· 21
동성연애 ··························· 21
동성연애자 ······················· 21
동시 ························· 241, 461
동시상영 ·························· 241
동시상영관 ······················ 241
동시통역사 ················ 162, 355
동아리 ····························· 323
동아리방 ·························· 197
동안 ································ 461
동양문화 ·························· 234
동양화 ····························· 241
동양화가 ·························· 241
동여매다 ·························· 520
동예 ································ 276
동요 ································ 241
동요하다 ·························· 520
동위원소 ·························· 211
동음어 ····························· 162
동음이의어 ······················ 162
동의어 ····························· 162
동의하다 ···················· 162, 520
동이다 ····························· 520
동일하다 ···················· 432, 490
동작 ································ 520
동장 ························· 286, 355
동전 ································ 336
동정 ································· 99
동정하다 ····················· 72, 520
동족 ································ 286
동지 ································ 461
동짓달 ····························· 461
동쪽 ································ 475
동창 ·································· 3
동창생 ······························· 3
동창회 ····························· 323
동치미 ····························· 117
동침하다 ··························· 21
동태 ································ 117
동포 ···················· 3, 286, 323
동풍 ································ 396
동하다 ······························ 72
동행하다 ·························· 520
동향 ································ 141
동호인 ······························· 3

동호회 259, 323	두리번거리다 521	드라마 181, 241
동화 241	두메 475	드라이버 141
돛단배 388	두목 3	드라이하다 99
돼지 409	두부 117	드러나다 521
돼지갈비 117	두서너 448	드러내다 521
돼지고기 117	두엄 370, 422	드러냄표 162
돼지코 28	두유 117	드레스 99
되 448	두절 188	드르렁 28
되다 117, 448, 490, 520	두통 40	드리다 521
되돌리다 520	두툼하다 432, 490	드릴 142
되돌아가다 520	두해살이 422	드문드문 491
되묻다 520	둑 475	드물다 491
되받아치다 162, 520	둔각 432	드세다 87, 491
된소리 162	둔재 3	드시다 117, 521
된장 117	둔치 475	득남하다 21
된장찌개 117	둔탁하다 490	득점 197
됨됨이 87	둔하다 72, 490	득표 286
두 448	둘 448	득표율 286
두건 52	둘러보다 521	득표하다 286
두견새 409	둘러앉다 521	듣기 162
두근거리다 72, 520	둘레 448, 475	듣다 61, 162, 521
두근대다 72, 521	둘째 448	들 475
두꺼비 409	둥그스름하다 432, 490	들국화 422
두꺼비집 141	둥글넓적하다 432, 490	들기름 117
두껍다 432	둥글다 432, 491	들깨 117
두께 432, 448	둥글둥글 432	들꽃 422
두뇌 28	둥실둥실 396	들다 521
두다 521	둥우리 141	들뜨다 87
두더지 409	둥지 141	들락날락하다 521
두둑 370	뒤 461, 475	들러리 21
두둑하다 432, 490	뒤따르다 521	들르다 521
두둥실 396	뒤뚱뒤뚱 409	들리다 61
두드러기 40	뒤범벅되다 491	들머리 162
두드러지다 490	뒤숭숭하다 73	들소 409
두드리다 117, 521	뒤죽박죽 491	들숨 28
두들기다 521	뒤지다 521	들어가다 521
두려움 72	뒤집다 521	들어오다 521
두려워하다 72, 521	뒤쫓다 521	들여다보다 521
두렵다 72	뒤통수 28	들이대다 521
두루마기 99	뒤풀이 323	들이밀다 521
두루뭉실하다 490	뒷거래 336	들이받다 521
두루미 409	뒷면 475	들이켜다 118, 521
두르다 99, 117, 521	뒷문 141	들쥐 409
두름 448	뙷굴다 521	들짐승 409
두리둥실 396	드나들다 521	들쭉날쭉 491
두루뭉실하다 432	드넓다 432, 491	들창코 28

들추다 ……………………… 521	따귀 ………………………… 28	떠돌이별 …………………… 476
들키다 ……………………… 521	따끈하다 …………………… 491	떠들다 ………………… 163, 522
들통 ………………………… 118	따끔하다 …………………… 61	떠보다 ……………………… 522
들판 ………………………… 475	따님 ………………………… 12	떡 …………………………… 118
등 ………………… 28, 142, 409	따다 …………………… 422, 522	떡갈나무 …………………… 422
등교하다 ……………… 197, 522	따돌리다 …………………… 522	떡값 ………………………… 336
등기 …………………… 142, 188	따뜻하다 ………… 61, 87, 396, 491	떡국 ………………………… 118
등기서류 …………………… 142	따라가다 …………………… 522	떡밥 ………………………… 259
등기우편 …………………… 188	따라오다 …………………… 522	떡볶이 ……………………… 118
등꽃 ………………………… 422	따르다 ………………… 118, 522	떡잎 ………………………… 422
등나무 ……………………… 422	따발총 ……………………… 312	떡집 ………………………… 336
등단하다 …………………… 241	따분하다 …………………… 73	떨기 ………………………… 422
등대 ………………………… 388	따옴표 ……………………… 162	떨다 …………………… 396, 522
등록금 ………………… 197, 336	따지다 ………………… 163, 522	떨리다 ………………… 73, 522
등록하다 ……………… 197, 522	딱따구리 …………………… 409	떨어뜨리다 ………………… 522
등반 ………………………… 259	딱딱하다 ……………… 61, 491	떨어지다 …………………… 523
등반대 ……………………… 259	딱지 …………………… 40, 300	떨이 ………………………… 336
등반대회 …………………… 259	딱지치기 …………………… 265	떫다 …………………… 61, 118
등반장비 …………………… 259	딱총놀이 …………………… 265	떼 …………………………… 409
등반하다 ……………… 259, 522	딱하다 ……………………… 73	떼다 ………………………… 523
등산 …………………… 259, 269	딸 …………………………… 12	떼돈 ………………………… 336
등산가 ……………………… 259	딸기 ………………………… 422	뗏목 ………………………… 388
등산객 ……………………… 259	딸기코 ……………………… 28	똑같다 ………………… 432, 491
등산모 ……………………… 259	딸꾹질 ……………………… 29	똑똑하다 ……………… 87, 491
등산모자 …………………… 99	딸랑이 ……………………… 265	똑바르다 ……………… 433, 491
등산복 ……………………… 259	땀 …………………… 29, 448	똘똘하다 …………………… 87
등산양말 …………………… 259	땀구멍 ……………………… 29	똥 …………………………… 29
등산장비 …………………… 259	땀띠 …………………… 29, 40	똥개 ………………………… 409
등산하다 ……………… 259, 522	땅 …………………………… 475	똥구멍 ……………………… 29
등산화 ………………… 99, 259	땅거미 ……………………… 396	똥배 ………………………… 29
등수 ………………………… 197	땅굴 ………………………… 475	똥색 ………………………… 439
등심 ………………………… 118	땅따먹기 …………………… 265	똥파리 ……………………… 409
등에 ………………………… 409	땅콩 ………………………… 118	뚜껑 ………………………… 118
등유 ………………………… 382	닿다 …………………… 99, 522	뚜렷하다 …………………… 491
등잔 ………………………… 142	때 ………………… 29, 99, 461	뚜쟁이 ……………………… 21
등장인물 …………………… 241	때다 …………………… 382, 522	뚝배기 ……………………… 118
등장하다 ……………… 241, 522	때때로 ……………………… 461	뚫다 ………………………… 523
등정 ………………………… 259	때리다 ……………………… 522	뚫리다 ……………………… 491
등지다 ………………… 475, 522	때마침 ……………………… 461	뚱뚱하다 …………………… 491
디디다 ……………………… 522	때매김 ……………………… 163	뚱보 ………………………… 3
디스켓 ……………………… 188	때우다 ……………………… 522	뛰다 ………………………… 523
디스크 ……………………… 40	땔감 ………………………… 382	뜀틀 ………………………… 269
디자이너 ……………… 241, 355	땔나무 ……………………… 382	뜨개바늘 …………………… 142
디자인 ……………………… 241	땡볕 ………………………… 396	뜨개질 ……………………… 99
딛다 ………………………… 522	떠나다 ……………………… 522	뜨개질하다 …………… 100, 523
따갑다 ……………… 61, 396, 491	떠돌다 ……………………… 522	뜨겁다 ……………… 61, 396, 491

뜨끔하다 ·································· 73
뜨내기 ······································· 3
뜨다 ················· 100, 118, 396, 523
뜯다 ····································· 523
뜰 ·· 142
뜸 ·· 40
뜸들이다 ························· 118, 523
뜸하다 ····························· 461, 491
뜻 ·· 163
띄어쓰기 ································ 163
띄엄띄엄 ······························· 491
띄우다 ······························ 118, 523
띠 ·· 52

라

라디오 ······················ 142, 181, 188
라마교 ·································· 224
라면 ····································· 118
라오스 ·································· 276
라이터 ·································· 382
라일락 ·································· 422
라틴어 ·································· 163
량 ·· 448
러시아 ·································· 276
럭비 ····································· 269
러닝셔츠 ······························· 100
레몬 ····································· 422
레바논 ·································· 276
레슬링 ·································· 269
레이아웃 ······························· 242
렌즈 ····································· 211
루마니아 ······························· 276
룩셈부르크 ··························· 276
류머티즘 ································ 40
르네상스 ······················· 234, 242
리 ······················· 142, 286, 448
리듬 ····································· 242
리듬체조 ······························· 269
리비아 ·································· 276
리사이틀 ······························· 242
리터 ····································· 448
리트머스시험지 ······················ 211

리포터 ·································· 355
릴 ·· 259

마

마 ································· 100, 448
마가린 ·································· 118
마개 ····································· 142
마고자 ·································· 100
마구간 ·································· 370
마귀 ····································· 224
마그네슘 ······························· 211
마녀 ····································· 224
마누라 ···································· 13
마늘 ······························ 118, 422
마담 ····································· 355
마당 ····································· 142
마당극 ·································· 242
마디 ······························ 242, 409
마라톤 ·································· 269
마렵다 ······························ 29, 61
마루 ····································· 142
마르다 ······························ 491, 523
마른반찬 ······························· 118
마른안주 ······························· 118
마름모 ·································· 433
마리 ······························ 409, 448
마무리 ·································· 163
마무리짓다 ··························· 523
마비 ······························· 40, 491
마사지 ·································· 100
마수걸이 ······························· 336
마술 ····································· 265
마술사 ·································· 355
마시다 ······························ 118, 523
마야문명 ······························· 234
마요네즈 ······························· 118
마우스 ·································· 188
마을 ······························ 142, 476
마을버스 ······························· 388
마음 ······································ 73
마음가짐 ································ 87
마음보 ···································· 87

마음씀씀이 ···························· 87
마음씨 ···································· 87
마음졸이다 ···························· 73
마이크 ·································· 197
마작 ····································· 265
마주보다 ······························ 523
마주하다 ······························ 476
마중 ····································· 388
마중하다 ······························ 523
마지기 ·························· 370, 448
마지막 ·································· 461
마진 ····································· 336
마찰 ····································· 212
마찰력 ·································· 212
마취 ······································ 40
마취과 ···································· 40
마취상태 ······························ 491
마취제 ···································· 40
마취하다 ································ 40
마치다 ·································· 523
마침 ····································· 461
마침내 ·································· 461
마침표 ·································· 163
마파람 ·································· 396
마한 ····································· 276
마호메트교 ··························· 224
마흔 ····································· 448
막 ································· 242, 461
막간 ····································· 461
막걸리 ·································· 118
막국수 ·································· 118
막내 ······································ 13
막노동 ·································· 355
막노동꾼 ······························ 355
막다 ····································· 523
막막하다 ······························ 73
막사 ····································· 142
막역하다 ······························ 323
막연하다 ································ 73
막일 ····································· 355
막히다 ······························ 388, 491
만 ······························ 448, 476
만국기 ·································· 286
만나다 ·································· 523
만년설 ·································· 396
만년필 ······················· 142, 163

만담 163	말솜씨 163	맡기다 337, 524
만담가 242	말썽꾸러기 3	맡다 62, 524
만두 118	말썽부리다 523	매 409
만둣국 118	말씀 163	매— 462
만들다 118, 523	말씀하시다 163, 523	매국노 286
만만하다 73	말씨 163	매기다 337
만물상 337	말주변 163	매김씨 163
만선 370	말줄임표 163	매끄럽다 62
만용 88	말투 163	매끈하다 62
만유인력의 법칙 212	말하기 163	매년 462
만장 52	말하다 163, 523	매니저 356
만족 491	맑다 396, 491	매다 100, 370, 524
만족스럽다 73	맛 61, 118	매달리기 269
만족하다 73, 523	맛나다 118	매도율 337
만지다 61, 523	맛보다 62, 118, 523	매독 41
만찬 118	맛없다 62, 118	매듭 100
만평 181	맛있다 62, 118	매력 88
만화 181, 242	망 370	매만지다 62, 100
만화방 370	망각하다 73, 524	매매 337
만화영화 242	망간 370	매미 409
많다 448, 491	망건 100	매복하다 312
많이 491	망고 422	매부 13
맏딸 13	망국 286	매부리코 29
맏아들 13	망나니 3	매상 337
맏이 13	망둥이 409	매상고 337
말 163, 259, 409, 448	망막 62	매실 422
말걸다 163, 523	망명 286	매어두다 524
말꼬리 163	망보다 524	매우 491
말끔하다 491	망설이다 88, 524	매운탕 118
말다 118, 523	망아지 409	매월 462
말다툼 163	망원경 212	매일 462
말다툼하다 163, 523	망종 462	매입 337
말대꾸 163	망치 142	매입율 337
말대꾸하다 163, 523	망토 100	매장 52, 337
말더듬이 163	맞다 100, 491, 524	매장하다 52
말뚝박기 265	맞벌이 356	매점 337
말라리아 41	맞선 21	매제 13
말랑말랑 61, 491	맞은편 476	매진하다 212, 524
말레이시아 276	맞이하다 524	매춘 21
말리다 100	맞잡다 524	매춘부 21
말미 461	맞장구치다 163, 524	매콥하다 62, 119
말미잘 409	맞절 323	매표소 242
말바꿈표 163	맞추다 100, 524	매형 13
말발 163	맞춤법 163	매화 422
말버릇 163	맞춤복 100	맥 29
말복 461	맞히다 524	맥박 29

맥없이 ………………………… 491	먼지떨이 ………………………… 142	면도기 ………………………… 142
맥주 ………………………… 119	멀겋다 ………………………… 492	면도칼 ………………………… 142
맨 ………………………… 476	멀다 ………………… 476, 492, 524	면목 ………………………… 73, 88
맨날 ………………………… 462	멀리뛰기 ………………………… 269	면바지 ………………………… 100
맨드라미 ………………………… 422	멀미 ………………………… 41	면사무소 ………………………… 286
맨션 ………………………… 142	멀티미디어디자인 ………………… 242	면사포 ………………………… 21
맨손체조 ………………………… 269	멈추다 ………………………… 524	면세점 ………………………… 337
맴맴 ………………………… 409	멋 ………………………… 100	면양 ………………………… 410
맵다 ………………… 62, 119, 491	멋쟁이 ………………………… 3	면역 ………………………… 41
맵시 ………………………… 100	멋쩍다 ………………………… 88	면장 ………………………… 286, 356
맹꽁맹꽁 ………………………… 409	명 ………………………… 41	면장갑 ………………………… 100
맹꽁이 ………………………… 409	명계 ………………………… 119, 409	면적 ………………… 433, 448, 476
맹세 ………………………… 73	명명 ………………………… 409	면접 ………………………… 197, 356
맹세하다 ………………… 73, 163, 524	멍멍하다 ………………………… 62	면제하다 ………………………… 524
맹수 ………………………… 409	명석 ………………………… 370	면하다 ………………………… 524
맹인 ………………………… 3, 62	명울 ………………………… 41	면허세 ………………………… 337
맹인안내견 ………………………… 62	명청이 ………………………… 3	면허증 ………………………… 323
맹장 ………………………… 29	명청하다 ………………………… 88, 492	면회하다 ………………………… 524
맹하다 ………………………… 88	맺다 ………………………… 397, 524	멸시하다 ………………………… 88
맺다 ………………………… 423, 524	메기 ………………………… 119, 409	멸치 ………………………… 119, 410
맺음말 ………………………… 163	메뉴 ………………………… 119	명 ………………… 52, 448, 462
맺히다 ………………………… 396, 492	메다 ………………………… 524	명강의 ………………………… 197
머금다 ………………………… 524	메뚜기 ………………………… 410	명곡 ………………………… 242
머루 ………………………… 423	메마르다 ………………………… 492	명당 ………………………… 476
머리 ………………………… 29, 409	메모 ………………………… 164	명도 ………………………… 242, 439
머리끈 ………………………… 100	메모지 ………………………… 142, 164	명랑하다 ………………………… 88
머리띠 ………………………… 100	메밀 ………………………… 119, 423	명령하다 ………………………… 164, 524
머리말 ………………………… 164	메밀국수 ………………………… 119	명료하다 ………………………… 492
머리방 ………………………… 100	메밀꽃 ………………………… 423	명명하다 ………………………… 164, 524
머리카락 ………………………… 29	메소포타미아문명 ……………… 235	명백하다 ………………………… 492
머리핀 ………………………… 100	메스껍다 ………………………… 62, 492	명복 ………………………… 52
머릿글 ………………………… 181	메아리 ………………………… 259	명사 ………………………… 164
머릿기사 ………………………… 181	메우다 ………………………… 524	명소 ………………………… 476
머무르다 ………………………… 524	메주 ………………………… 119	명암 ………………………… 242, 439
머무름표 ………………………… 164	메추라기 ………………………… 410	명언 ………………………… 164
머뭇거리다 ………………………… 524	메추리 ………………………… 410	명예교수 ………………………… 197
먹 ………………………… 242	메추리알 ………………………… 119, 410	명예박사 ………………………… 197
먹거리 ………………………… 119	멕시코 ………………………… 276	명예퇴직 ………………………… 356
먹구름 ………………………… 397	멜론 ………………………… 423	명왕성 ………………………… 476
먹다 ………………………… 119, 524	멜빵 ………………………… 100	명인 ………………………… 3
먹이 ………………………… 409	멜빵바지 ………………………… 100	명절 ………………………… 462
먹이다 ………………………… 524	멧돼지 ………………………… 410	명주 ………………………… 100
먹이사슬 ………………………… 409	며느리 ………………………… 13	명찰 ………………………… 197, 323
먹이연쇄 ………………………… 409	며칠 ………………………… 462	명창 ………………………… 242
먼저 ………………………… 462	면 ………………… 100, 142, 286, 433, 476	명치 ………………………… 29
먼지 ………………………… 397, 492	면담하다 ………………………… 164, 524	명쾌하다 ………………………… 88, 492

명태 ····· 119, 410	모음조화 ····· 164	목장 ····· 371
명품 ····· 337	모의수업 ····· 198	목재 ····· 142
명하다 ····· 164, 524	모이 ····· 371, 410	목적 ····· 212
명함 ····· 323	모이다 ····· 525	목적격 ····· 164
명함판사진 ····· 259	모임 ····· 323	목적어 ····· 164
명화 ····· 242	모자 ····· 13, 100	목젖 ····· 29
명확하다 ····· 492	모자라다 ····· 492	목차 ····· 164
몇 ····· 462	모자리 ····· 371	목초지 ····· 371
모 ····· 100, 423, 448	모잠비크 ····· 276	목축 ····· 371
모공 ····· 29	모조리 ····· 449, 492	목축업 ····· 371
모과 ····· 423	모조품 ····· 337	목탁 ····· 224
모교 ····· 198	모종 ····· 371, 423	목탄 ····· 242
모국 ····· 286	모종삽 ····· 371	목표 ····· 212
모국어 ····· 164	모직바지 ····· 100	목화 ····· 423
모국어화자 ····· 164	모질다 ····· 88	몫 ····· 449
모금 ····· 448	모친 ····· 13	몰다 ····· 525
모기 ····· 410	모텔 ····· 142, 371	몰두하다 ····· 73, 212, 525
모기장 ····· 142	모퉁이 ····· 476	몰몬교 ····· 224
모나다 ····· 88, 433, 492	모판 ····· 371	몰상식하다 ····· 73
모나코 ····· 276	모피 ····· 100	몰수 ····· 300
모내기 ····· 370	모피코트 ····· 101	몰지각하다 ····· 73
모녀 ····· 13	모형 ····· 433	몸 ····· 29
모델 ····· 242, 356	목 ····· 29	몸가짐 ····· 88
모독하다 ····· 164, 525	목걸이 ····· 101	몸매 ····· 29
모두 ····· 448, 492	목격자 ····· 3, 62, 300	몸무게 ····· 29
모란 ····· 423	목격하다 ····· 62, 525	몸살 ····· 41
모래 ····· 142, 476	목공소 ····· 371	몸집 ····· 29
모래주머니 ····· 410	목공예 ····· 242	몸짓언어 ····· 164
모레 ····· 462	목관악기 ····· 242	몸통 ····· 29, 410
모로코 ····· 276	목단 ····· 423	몸풀다 ····· 21, 525
모르다 ····· 73, 492, 525	목덜미 ····· 29	몹시 ····· 492
모방하다 ····· 525	목도리 ····· 101	못 ····· 142, 476, 492
모범생 ····· 198	목돈 ····· 337	못난이 ····· 3
모색하다 ····· 525	목동 ····· 371	못되다 ····· 88
모서리 ····· 433, 476	목동자리 ····· 476	못마땅하다 ····· 73
모성애 ····· 13	목련 ····· 423	못자리 ····· 371
모순되다 ····· 88	목마르다 ····· 62, 119	못하다 ····· 492, 525
모습 ····· 433	목발 ····· 41	몽고반점 ····· 29
모시 ····· 100	목사 ····· 224, 356	몽골 ····· 276
모시다 ····· 88, 525	목성 ····· 476	몽골학 ····· 212
모양 ····· 433	목소리 ····· 164	몽땅 ····· 492
모양자 ····· 433	목숨 ····· 52	몽유병 ····· 41
모욕하다 ····· 88, 525	목요일 ····· 462	묘 ····· 52
모으다 ····· 337, 525	목욕관리사 ····· 371	묘목 ····· 371, 423
모음 ····· 164	목욕탕 ····· 142, 371	묘사하다 ····· 164, 525
모음곡 ····· 242	목이버섯 ····· 423	묘지 ····· 52

무 119, 410, 423	무서워하다 525	무질서 300, 323
무감각 62	무선전화기 142, 188	무찌르다 525
무겁다 492	무선통신 188	무채색 439
무게 449	무선호출기 188	무척 492
무교 224	무섭다 73	무척추동물 410
무궁화 423	무성영화 242	무치다 119, 525
무기 312	무속 224	무침 119
무기력하다 492	무속신앙 224	무표정 73
무기산업 312	무술 269	무한대 449
무기수 300	무승부 269	무허가주택 142
무기정학 198	무시하다 73, 88, 525	무협지 181
무기질 119	무식하다 73	무형 433
무기징역 300	무신론 224	무형문화재 235
무남독녀 13	무심결 73	무화과 423
무너뜨리다 525	무안하다 73	무효 492
무능하다 492	무언극 242	묵 119
무늬 101, 433	무역 337	묵념하다 73
무당 224, 356	무역센터 337	묵다 142, 493, 525
무대 242	무역수지 337	묵독 164
무대감독 242	무역풍 397	묵비권 300
무대예술 242	무역학 212	묵주 224
무대의상 101, 242	무용 242	묵직하다 493
무대화장 101, 242	무용가 242, 356	묶다 101, 525
무더위 397	무용극 243	묶음 449
무던하다 88, 492	무용단 243	묶음표 164
무덤 52	무용복 243	문 142
무덥다 397	무용실 198	문간방 142
무도 242	무용음악 243	문갑 142
무도복 242	무용학 212	문고리 142
무도회 242	무용화 243	문구 142, 164
무디다 73, 88, 492	무의미하다 492	문구점 337
무뚝뚝하다 88	무의식 73	문단 243
무럭무럭 492	무익하다 492	문둥병 41
무력하다 492	무인도 476	문맹 164
무렵 462	무장하다 312, 525	문명 235
무례하다 88	무장해제 312	문명사 235
무료 337	무전기 188	문명사회 235, 323
무르다 62, 492, 525	무전여행 259	문물 235
무릎 29	무조건 492	문물교류 235
무리 410	무조건반사 212	문방사우 337
무리수 449	무좀 41	문법 164
무모하다 88	무죄 300	문법론 164
무법자 300	무지개 397	문법서 164
무색 439	무지개떡 119	문병 41
무생물 52	무지개색 439	문서 164
무서움 73	무직 356	

문안드리다 ······················· 525	문화수준 ······················· 235	물레방아 ······················· 212
문어 ····················· 119, 164, 410	문화시설 ······················· 235	물레방아 ······················· 382
문예 ···································· 243	문화어 ··························· 165	물리치료 ························· 41
문예반 ··························· 243	문화예술 ······················· 235	물리치료사 ····················· 41
문예부흥 ················· 235, 243	문화예술진흥기금 ········· 235	물리학 ··························· 212
문예비평 ······················· 243	문화예술진흥법 ············· 235	물리학자 ······················· 212
문예사조 ······················· 243	문화원 ··························· 286	물망초 ··························· 423
문예지 ··························· 243	문화유산 ······················· 235	물물교환 ······················· 337
문예창작 ······················· 243	문화융합 ······················· 235	물방개 ··························· 410
문의하다 ················· 164, 525	문화의식 ······················· 235	물병자리 ······················· 476
문인 ······························ 243	문화인 ··························· 235	물비누 ··························· 143
문자 ······························ 164	문화인류학 ···················· 235	물소 ······························ 410
문자언어 ······················· 164	문화재 ··························· 235	물안개 ··························· 397
문장 ······························ 164	문화재관리국 ········· 235, 286	물안경 ··························· 269
문장부호 ······················· 165	문화재관리청 ················· 286	물약 ································ 41
문장성분 ······················· 165	문화재보호 ···················· 235	물엿 ······························ 119
문제 ······························ 198	문화접변 ······················· 235	물음표 ··························· 165
문제집 ··························· 198	문화제 ··························· 235	물이끼 ··························· 423
문제학생 ······················· 198	문화창조 ······················· 235	물자전 ··························· 312
문지르다 ······················· 525	문화체육부 ···················· 286	물장구 ··························· 265
문지방 ··························· 143	문화행사 ······················· 236	물질 ······························ 371
문책하다 ················· 165, 525	문화혁명 ······················· 236	물집 ································ 41
문체 ······························ 243	문화회관 ······················· 236	물컹물컹 ······················· 119
문패 ······························ 143	묻다 ····················· 52, 165, 525	물컹하다 ················· 62, 493
문학 ······················ 212, 243	물 ························· 119, 212, 382	물품 ······························ 337
문학도 ··························· 243	물가 ······························ 337	묽다 ······················· 119, 493
문학반 ··························· 243	물가지수 ······················· 337	뭉개다 ··························· 526
문학작품 ······················· 243	물갈퀴 ··························· 410	뭉게구름 ······················· 397
문학평론 ······················· 243	물감 ······························ 243	뭉게뭉게 ······················· 397
문헌정보학 ···················· 212	물개 ······························ 410	뭉뚝하다 ················ 433, 493
문헌정보학자 ················· 212	물건 ······························ 337	뭉치다 ··················· 493, 526
문형 ······························ 433	물결 ······························ 397	뭍 ·································· 476
문호개방 ······················· 235	물결표 ··························· 165	미 ·································· 243
문화 ······························ 235	물고기 ··············· 260, 371, 410	미각 ································ 62
문화계 ··························· 235	물고기자리 ···················· 476	미개 ······························ 236
문화관광부 ········· 235, 259, 286	물꼬 ······························ 371	미개인 ··························· 236
문화교류 ······················· 235	물다 ······························ 525	미국 ······························ 276
문화권 ··························· 235	물대기 ··························· 371	미국학 ··························· 212
문화대혁명 ···················· 235	물들이다 ················ 101, 525	미군방송 ······················· 181
문화면 ··························· 181	물러가다 ······················· 525	미꾸라지 ················ 119, 410
문화민족 ······················· 235	물러나다 ······················· 525	미끄러지다 ···················· 526
문화방송국 ···················· 181	물러서다 ······················· 525	미끄럼 ··························· 265
문화부 ··························· 235	물렁물렁 ······················· 119	미끄럼틀 ······················· 265
문화비 ···················· 235, 337	물렁물렁하다 ··········· 62, 493	미끄럽다 ················· 62, 493
문화사 ··························· 235	물렁뼈 ····························· 29	미끈미끈 ························· 62
문화생활 ······················· 235	물렁하다 ························· 62	미끈하다 ························· 62

미끌미끌	62
미끼	260, 371
미나리	120, 423
미남	4
미녀	4
미달	493
미덕	88
미덥다	73
미래	462
미래사회	323
미래시제	165
미래형	165
미련	73
미련하다	74, 88
미루나무	423
미루다	526
미리	462
미리내	476
미만	493
미망인	4, 52
미사	224
미사드리다	224
미사일	312
미색	439
미생물	52, 410
미성년자	4
미소	74
미수	300
미숙아	21
미숙하다	493
미술	243
미술가	243
미술관	243
미술대학	198
미술도구	198
미술사	243
미술실	198
미술작품	243
미술품	243
미숫가루	120
미시경제	337
미식가	62, 120
미식축구	269
미신	224
미안하다	74
미얀마	276

미역	120, 423
미완성	493
미용사	356, 371
미용실	101
미용업	371
미움	74
미워하다	74, 526
미음	120
미인	4
미장원	101, 371
미장이	356
미지근하다	62, 397
미치다	493, 526
미케네문명	236
미터	449
미풍양속	323
미학	212
미합중국	276
미혼	21
미혼모	21
미화	337
미확인비행물체	476
믹서기	120, 143
민간신앙	224
민간인	4
민담	243
민들레	423
민망하다	74
민물	476
민물고기	410
민물낚시	260, 371
민박	143
민박집	143
민방위대	312
민법	300
민사소송	300
민속	236
민속공예	243
민속놀이	265
민속무용	243
민속음악	243
민속자료	236
민속촌	236, 476
민속학	212
민속학자	212
민심	286

민어	410
민영방송	181
민요	243
민요가수	244
민족	4, 286, 323
민족문학	244
민족성	286
민족의식	286
민족주의	286, 324
민주국가	286
민주사회	324
민주정치	286
민주주의	286, 324
민주주의국가	286
민주평화통일자문회의	286
민중	286, 324
민화	244
믿다	74, 224, 526
믿음	74, 224
밀	120, 423
밀가루	120
밀감	423
밀고하다	165, 526
밀다	120, 526
밀도	212, 449, 493
밀리미터	449
밀림	423, 476
밀물	397
밀봉하다	120, 143
밀월여행	21
밀집	493
밀짚모자	101
밀폐용기	120, 143
밉다	493
밉살맞다	88
밑	476
밑면	433
밑반찬	120
밑변	433
밑지다	337
밑화장	101
―말	461

바

바가지	120, 143
바가지쓰다	337
바겐세일	338
바구니	120, 143
바구미	410
바깥	476
바깥사돈	13
바깥양반	13
바꾸다	526
바뀌다	462
바느질	101
바늘	101, 143
바늘꽂이	101, 143
바다	476
바다낚시	260, 371
바닷물고기	410
바다사자	410
바다표범	410
바닥	143, 476
바닥재	143
바닷가	476
바닷가재	120, 410
바닷말	423
바닷물	476
바둑	260, 265
바둑알	260
바둑판	260
바라다	526
바라보다	62, 526
바라춤	244
바람	212, 383, 397
바람개비	265
바람둥이	21
바람피우다	21
바래다	439, 493, 526
바레인	276
바로잡다	526
바르다	88, 101, 493, 526
바른쪽	476
바바리	101
바보	4
바쁘다	493
바삭바삭	62, 120
바싹바싹	493
바야흐로	462
바위	477
바이러스	410
바이올린	244
바자회	338
바지	101
바지선	388
바치다	526
바퀴	388
바퀴벌레	410
바탕색	439
바티칸	276
박격포	312
박다	101, 526
박동	29
박람회	324
박사	198
박수무당	224
박식하다	74
박자	244
박쥐	410
박하다	88
밖	477
반	143, 286
반가움	74
반갑다	74
반기다	74, 526
반나절	462
반달	477
반달곰	410
반대말	165
반대편	477
반대하다	165, 526
반도	388, 477
반도체	371
반드시	493
반들반들하다	62, 493
반듯하다	433, 493
반디	410
반론하다	165, 526
반말	165
반명함판사진	260
반문하다	165, 526
반바지	101
반박하다	165, 526
반발하다	526
반사	212, 439
반사경	212
반상회	324
반색	74
반성문	165
반성하다	74, 526
반세기	462
반신불수	41
반올림	449
반올림하다	449
반음	244
반응	212
반의어	165
반장	286, 356
반점	29
반주	120, 244
반주자	244, 356
반주하다	244, 526
반죽하다	120, 526
반지	101
반지름	449
반짇고리	101, 143
반짝반짝	439, 477, 493
반찬	120
반창고	41
반치	269
반포하다	165, 526
반품	338
반하다	74, 526
반항아	4
반항하다	88, 165, 526
받다	526
받아쓰기	165
받아쓰다	526
받침	165
발	29, 143, 449
발가락	29
발가벗다	101, 527
발간하다	181
발견하다	527
발굽	410
발꿈치	29
발달하다	236
발동기	371

발등 29	밤 462	방송작가 182, 244, 356
발라내다 120, 527	밤나무 423	방송하다 182, 188, 527
발탈하다 88	밤낚시 260	방수 143
발레 244	밤무대 244	방아 371
발레리나 244	밤색 439	방아깨비 411
발령 356	밤안개 397	방아쇠 312
발령하다 165, 397, 527	밤중 462	방앗간 338, 371
발명가 356	밤참 120	방어 269, 312
발명하다 527	밥 120	방언 165
발목 29	밥맛 63, 120	방언론 166
발바닥 29	밥상 120, 143	방영하다 182, 527
발버둥치다 527	밥솥 120	방울 449
발사하다 312, 527	밥통 31, 120	방울뱀 411
발상지 236	밥풀 120	방위 312
발생하다 527	밧줄 143	방위 477
발설하다 165, 527	방 143, 188	방음 143
발송 188	방계가족 13	방전 383
발언 165	방귀 31	방정맞다 88
발의하다 165, 527	방글라데시 276	방정식 449
발인 52	방금 462	방정하다 89
발작 41	방독면 312	방청객 182
발전 383	방망이 143	방청석 182
발전기 383	방면 477	방청하다 182, 527
발전하다 236	방명록 324	방충망 143
발진 41	방목 371	방탄조끼 101
발톱 31	방문하다 527	방패 312
발포하다 527	방방곡곡 477	방학 198
발표 165, 198	방백 165	방학식 198
발표요지 212	방범 300	방한복 102
발표자 165	방범대원 301	방한화 102
발표하다 165, 527	방법론 212	방해하다 527
발표회 244	방사능 212, 383	방향 477
발해 276	방사능물질 212, 383	방향제 63
발해문화 236	방사선 212	방화 383
발행부수 181	방사선과 41	방화범 301
발행인 182	방사선치료 41	방화사 383
발행하다 182	방석 143	방화수 383
발화 165	방송 182, 188	방화죄 301
발효 120	방송국 182	밭 371, 423, 477
발효시키다 120	방송대학 198	밭농사 371
발효식품 120	방송망 182, 188	밭두렁 371
발휘하다 527	방송매체 182, 188	밭둑 371
밝기 439	방송사고 182	배 31, 388, 423, 449
밝다 62, 88, 439, 493	방송실 198	배고프다 63, 120, 493
밝히다 165, 527	방송심의위원회 182	배관공 356
밟다 527	방송인 244, 356	배구 269

배구공 270	백내장 41, 63	버선 102
배기다 527	백년해로 21	버섯 121, 423
배꼽 31	백로 411, 462	버섯전골 121
배꼽티 102	백만장자 4	버스 388
배나무 423	백모 13	버스카드 338, 388
배낭 143	백반 120	버짐 31, 41
배낭여행 260	백발 31	버찌 424
배냇저고리 102	백부 13	버터 121
배다 411, 527	백분율 449	버티다 527
배다른 13	백사 411	번 449
배달부 356, 371	백색 439	번개 397
배달원 356, 372	백설기 121	번개탄 383
배당금 338	백성 286	번뇌 225
배드민턴 270	백수 4, 356	번데기 411
배반하다 89, 527	백숙 121	번들거리다 493
배배 493	백악관 286	번식 372
배부르다 63, 120, 493	백야 397	번식하다 411
배상금 338	백열등 143	번안소설 244
배색 439	백엽상 397	번역 166, 244
배선 143	백옥같다 439	번잡하다 493
배설 31	백인종 4	번지 143, 449
배설기관 31	백일 462	번지다 528
배설하다 527	백일기도 224	번지점프 270
배수진 312	백일사진 260	번쩍 397
배신감 74	백일해 41	번쩍번쩍 493
배신자 4	백일홍 423	번호 449
배신하다 89	백제 276	벌 102, 301, 411, 449
배심원 301	백조 411	벌금 301, 338
배역 244	백팔번뇌 225	벌금형 301
배열하다 527	백합 423	벌꿀 121
배영 270	백혈구 31	벌다 338, 528
배우 244, 356	백혈병 41	벌레 411
배우다 198, 527	백화점 143, 338	벌름거리다 528
배우자 4, 21	뱀 411	벌리다 528
배웅 388	뱀장어 411	벌써 462
배웅하다 527	뱁새 411	벌이 338
배짱 89	뱃사람 372	벌칙 301
배추 120, 423	뱅어포 121	벌컥벌컥 121
배출하다 527	빻다 527	벌판 477
배치하다 527	버금 449	범 411
배탈 41, 120	버너 383	범람하다 397
배탈나다 120	버드나무 423	범법 301
배표 388	버릇 89	범법자 301
백 449	버릇없다 89	범법행위 301
백곰 411	버리다 449, 527	범위 477
백금 372	버무리다 121, 527	범인 301

범죄	301
범죄율	301
범죄자	301
범칙	301
범칙금	301
범행	301
법	225, 301
법과대학	198
법관	301, 356
법규	301
법규정	301
법령	301
법령집	302
법률	302
법률위반	302
법무부	287
법사	225
법석대다	528
법안	302
법원	302
법인	324
법인세	338
법전	302
법정	302
법제처	287
법조계	302
법조인	302
법치국가	287
법치주의	302
법칙	212
법학	212
벗	4
벗기다	121, 528
벗다	102, 528
벙어리	4, 166
벙어리장갑	102
벚꽃	424
벚꽃놀이	260
벚나무	424
베개	143
베끼다	166, 528
베네수엘라	276
베다	424, 528
베란다	143
베레모	102
베이스	244

베이킹파우더	121
베짱이	411
베트남	276
베트남어	166
베풀다	528
벨기에	276
벨트	102
벼	424
벼농사	372
벼락	397
벼랑	477
벼루	244
벼룩	411
벼룩시장	338
벼르다	74, 528
벼슬	287
벽	143, 144
벽걸이	143
벽난로	144, 383
벽돌	144
벽돌집	144
벽시계	144
벽지	144
벽화	244
변	31, 433
변기	144
변덕스럽다	89
변동	493
변두리	477
변론	302
변론하다	166, 528
변리사	356
변명하다	166, 528
변별하다	213, 528
변비	41
변사체	52
변색	440
변성기	52
변소	144
변신	102
변심	74
변압기	383
변온동물	411
변장	102
변주곡	244
변증법	213

변태	411
변하다	121, 493
변한	276
변함없다	89, 493
변형	494
변형시키다	528
변호사	302, 356
변호인	302
변호하다	166, 528
변화	494
변화시키다	528
변화하다	528
별	477
별거	21
별나다	89, 494
별똥별	477
별명	324
별세	52
별세하다	52
별안간	462
별자리	477
별장	144
별채	144
별씨	372
병	41, 144, 449
병균	41
병동	41
병들다	494
병따개	121, 144
병력	312
병렬	213
병목현상	388
병무청	287, 312
병문안	41
병사	52, 312
병신	4
병실	41
병아리	411
병아리색	440
병약하다	41
병어	121, 411
병역	312
병영	312
병원	42
병원균	42
병원놀이	265

병장 312	보석상 338	보편적 494
병정놀이 265	보송보송하다 63, 494	보푸라기 102
병창 244	보수 338	보풀다 102
병충해 372	보수공사 144	보합세 338
병치레 42	보스니아 276	보험 338
병풍 144	보슬보슬 397	보험금 338
별 397	보슬비 397	보험료 338
보 144	보습학원 198	보험회사 338
보강 198	보신탕 121	보호색 411, 440
보건복지부 287	보쌈 121	보호자 4, 42
보건소 198	보안장치 144	보호하다 528
보고서 198	보약 42	복 225
보고하다 166, 528	보어 166	복권 302
보관소 338	보온 144	복덕방 144
보관하다 528	보온병 121	복도 144
보궐선거 287	보유하다 528	복무 312
보금자리 144	보육원 144, 198	복무연한 312
보급품 312	보이다 528	복무하다 356
보기 198	보일러 144, 383	복부 312
보내다 528	보일러공 356	복부인 356
보너스 338, 356	보일러실 144	복사 225
보다 63, 528	보자기 144	복사기 198
보도 182, 188	보조가방 144, 198	복사뼈 31
보도사진 260	보조개 31	복사하다 528
보도하다 166, 528	보조교사 198	복수 449
보들보들하다 63, 494	보조금 338	복수심 74
보따리 338	보조동사 166	복수전공 198
보라 440	보조사 166	복숭아 424
보랏빛 440	보조용언 166	복숭아나무 424
보류하다 528	보조형용사 166	복스럽다 494
보름 462, 477	보존하다 528	복습 198
보름날 462	보좌관 287	복습하다 198, 528
보름달 477	보증 338	복식 102
보리 121, 424	보증금 338	복식문화 236
보리차 121	보증서다 338	복어 121, 411
보모 356	보증인 338	복역하다 302, 313
보물 236, 338	보지 31	복용하다 42
보물찾기 265	보채다 528	복음 225
보배 338	보청기 63	복음서 225
보병 312	보충수업 198	복음성가 225
보살 225	보태다 528	복자 225
보살피다 528	보통 494	복잡하다 494
보상금 338	보통명사 166	복장 102
보색 440	보통예금 338	복제품 338
보석 302, 372	보통우편 188	복지국가 287
보석금 302	보트 388	복지사회 324
		복직하다 356

복창하다 166, 528	봉급 339, 356	부랑자 357
복통 42	봉급쟁이 357	부러뜨리다 529
복학 198	봉사 63	부럼 121
복학생 198	봉사료 339, 372	부럽다 74
복합어 166	봉사활동 199, 324	부레 411
볶다 121, 528	봉선화 424	부록 166
볶음밥 121	봉인 188	부르다 166, 244, 339, 529
본교 198	봉지 144, 449	부르르 74
본국 287	봉투 144, 166	부르짖다 166, 529
본능 63	봉하다 144, 166, 529	부리 411
본딧말 166	봉화 188	부리다 529
본뜨다 529	봉황 411	부모 13
본론 166, 213	부 182	부목사 225
본명 324	부가가치 339	부부 13, 21
본문 166, 182	부가가치세 339	부부관계 21
본봉 356	부가세 339	부부생활 21
본사 338	부검 52	부부싸움 21
본성 89	부고 52	부분적 494
본업 356	부고란 182	부분집합 449
본인 4	부과하다 339	부사 166
본전 338	부관 313	부사어 166
본점 339	부교수 199	부상 42
본채 144	부군 13	부상병 313
본처 13	부근 477	부서지다 529
본체 188	부기장 388	부속물 339
본토 477	부끄러움 74	부속품 339
본토박이 4	부끄럽다 74	부수 182
볼 31	부녀 13	부수다 144, 529
볼거리 42	부녀자 4	부스러기 433
볼기 31	부녀회 324	부스럼 42
볼록렌즈 213	부담금 339	부슬부슬 397
볼록하다 433, 494	부담하다 339, 529	부실공사 144
볼리비아 276	부당하다 89, 494	부싯돌 383
볼링 270	부대 144, 313	부아 74
볼멘소리 166	부대찌개 121	부언하다 166, 529
볼연지 102	부도 339	부업 357
볼우물 31	부도덕 302	부엉부엉 411
볼터치 102	부도수표 339	부엉이 411
볼펜 144, 166, 199	부동산 144	부엌 144
볼품없다 494	부동산중개업소 339	부엌가구 121, 145
봄 462	부동표 287	부엌방 145
봄바람 397	부두 388	부엌용품 121
봉 449	부드럽다 63, 89, 494	부엌칼 121
봉건사회 324	부딪다 529	부여 276
봉건제도 287	부딪히다 529	부연하다 166, 529
봉건주의 287	부뚜막 144, 383	부유층 324

부유하다 ... 339	부하 ... 313	분실하다 ... 529
부음 ... 53	부하직원 ... 357	분양 ... 339
부의 ... 53	부화 ... 411	분양가 ... 339
부인 ... 4, 13	부활절 ... 225	분업 ... 372
부인하다 ... 166, 529	부황 ... 42	분유 ... 122
부자 ... 4, 13, 324	북 ... 244	분자 ... 213, 449
부작용 ... 42	북극 ... 477	분장 ... 103, 244
부장검사 ... 302	북극곰 ... 411	분장사 ... 244, 357
부장판사 ... 302	북극성 ... 477	분장실 ... 244
부재자투표 ... 287	북두칠성 ... 477	분재 ... 424
부적 ... 225	북미 ... 276	분쟁 ... 313
부전공 ... 199	북아메리카 ... 276	분점 ... 339
부정선거 ... 287	북어 ... 122	분주하다 ... 494
부정적이다 ... 89	북쪽 ... 477	분지 ... 477
부정하다 ... 166, 529	북풍 ... 397	분첩 ... 103
부제 ... 182	북한 ... 277	분필 ... 199
부조 ... 21, 244	북향 ... 145	분하다 ... 74
부조금 ... 22	분 ... 74, 102, 449, 462	분해 ... 213
부조화 ... 494	분가 ... 22	분해하다 ... 213, 529
부족하다 ... 339, 494	분간하다 ... 74, 213, 529	분홍 ... 440
부지 ... 145	분광기 ... 440	붇다 ... 494
부지런하다 ... 89	분교 ... 199	불 ... 213, 383
부쩍 ... 494	분기 ... 462	불가능 ... 494
부채 ... 145, 339	분꽃 ... 424	불가능하다 ... 494
부채꼴 ... 433	분노 ... 74	불가리아 ... 277
부채춤 ... 244	분노하다 ... 74, 529	불가사리 ... 411
부처 ... 225	분단 ... 287	불경 ... 225
부처님 ... 225	분단국가 ... 287	불경기 ... 339
부촌 ... 145	분리하다 ... 529	불고기 ... 122
부총리 ... 287	분만 ... 22	불공평하다 ... 89
부총장 ... 199	분만실 ... 22, 42	불교 ... 225
부총재 ... 287	분만하다 ... 22, 529	불교문화권 ... 236
부추 ... 121, 424	분명하다 ... 494	불교방송 ... 182
부츠 ... 102	분명히 ... 494	불규칙 ... 494
부치다 ... 122, 372, 529	분무기 ... 102, 145	불규칙동사 ... 167
부친 ... 13	분배하다 ... 529	불규칙형용사 ... 167
부침가루 ... 122	분별력 ... 74, 213	불균형 ... 494
부침개 ... 122	분별하다 ... 74, 213	불그스름하다 ... 440
부케 ... 22	분부하다 ... 166, 529	불긋불긋 ... 440
부탁하다 ... 166, 529	분비물 ... 31	불기 ... 462
부탄 ... 276	분산 ... 494	불길 ... 383
부탄가스 ... 383	분석하다 ... 74, 213, 529	불꽃 ... 213, 383
부통령 ... 287	분쇄하다 ... 529	불꽃놀이 ... 265
부패하다 ... 494	분수 ... 449	불다 ... 397, 529
부품 ... 339	분식 ... 122	불도 ... 225
부피 ... 449	분식집 ... 122	불똥 ... 383

불란서 277	불쾌감 75	비고급 167
불량배 302	불쾌지수 397	비교육적 199
불량식품 122	불쾌하다 75	비교적 495
불량률 372	불탑 225	비구니 225, 357
불량품 372	불통 188	비구름 397
불량학생 199	불편하다 494	비굴하다 89
불류 22	불평 75	비극 244
불리다 529	불평하다 167, 529	비기다 270
불만 74	불합격 495	비꼬다 167
불면증 42	불행 75	비난하다 89, 167, 530
불명예제대 313	불행하다 75	비녀 103
불명확하다 494	불화 225	비뇨기 31
불문학 213	불확실하다 495	비뇨기과 42
불문학자 213	불황 339	비누 103, 145
불법 225, 302	불효자 13	비늘 411
불법주차 388	붉다 440	비닐하우스 145, 372, 424
불법체류자 287	붉으락푸르락 440	비다 477, 495
불별 397	븕바다 495	비단 103
불분명하다 494	붓 244	비단길 236
불빛 440	붓글씨 244	비대하다 433, 495
불사 225	붓꽃 424	비둘기 412
불사조 411	붓다 122, 145, 495, 529	비듬 31
불상 225	붕괴하다 530	비디오 145, 199, 245
불손하다 89	붕대 42	비디오가게 372
불심검문 302	붕어 411	비디오방 372
불쌍하다 74	붕어빵 122	비디오아트 245
불안 74	붕장어 411	비뚤다 433, 495
불안정하다 494	붙다 530	비로소 495
불안하다 74, 494	붙들다 530	비료 372
불알 31	붙박이별 477	비름 122, 424
불어 167	붙박이장 145	비리다 63, 122
불어학 213	붙이다 530	비린내 63, 122
불어학자 213	붙임성 89	비만 42
불완전 494	붙잡다 530	비매품 339
불운 225	뷔페 122	비무장지대 313
불일치 494	뷔페식당 122	비문 53
불임표 167	브라질 277	비밀 188
불입금 339	브래지어 103	비바람 397
불입액 339	브로치 103	비방하다 89, 167, 530
불입하다 339	블라우스 103	비비다 122, 530
불자동차 388	비 145, 397	비빔밥 122
불참하다 529	비겁하다 89	비상 287
불청객 4	비계 122	비상금 339
불치병 42	비과세 339	비상기획위원회 287
불친절하다 89	비관적이다 89	비상연락망 188
불침번 313	비관하다 75	비서관 287

비서실 ······ 287	빈곤층 ······ 324	빨다 ······ 103, 122, 530
비석 ······ 53	빈대 ······ 412	빨대 ······ 122, 145
비속어 ······ 167	빈대떡 ······ 122	빨래 ······ 103
비수기 ······ 339	빈도 ······ 495	빨래건조대 ······ 103
비스듬하다 ······ 433	빈말 ······ 167	빨래방 ······ 103, 372
비슷하다 ······ 433, 495	빈민 ······ 324	빨래비누 ······ 103
비슷한말 ······ 167	빈민가 ······ 145, 324	빨래집게 ······ 103
비싸다 ······ 339, 495	빈민사회 ······ 324	빨래터 ······ 103
비애 ······ 75	빈민층 ······ 324	빨래판 ······ 103
비열하다 ······ 89	빈번하다 ······ 462, 495	빨래하다 ······ 103
비옥하다 ······ 372	빈소 ······ 53	빨랫감 ······ 103
비옷 ······ 103	빈약하다 ······ 495	빨랫줄 ······ 103
비용 ······ 339	빈정거리다 ······ 530	빨리 ······ 463
비우다 ······ 145, 530	빈털터리 ······ 4	빳빳하다 ······ 495
비웃다 ······ 75, 530	빈혈 ······ 42	빵 ······ 122
비위 ······ 63, 122	빌다 ······ 167, 225, 530	빵집 ······ 122, 340
비율 ······ 449	빌딩 ······ 145	빻다 ······ 122, 530
비자 ······ 287	빌라 ······ 145	빼곡하다 ······ 495
비자금 ······ 339	빌려주다 ······ 340, 530	빼기 ······ 450
비좁다 ······ 433, 495	빌리다 ······ 340, 530	빼내다 ······ 122
비지 ······ 122	빗 ······ 103, 145	빼다 ······ 103, 450, 530
비지땀 ······ 31	빗금 ······ 167	빼앗다 ······ 530
비집다 ······ 530	빗다 ······ 103, 530	빽빽하다 ······ 495
비참하다 ······ 75	빗방울 ······ 397	뺄셈 ······ 450
비추다 ······ 440, 530	빗변 ······ 433	뺑소니치다 ······ 530
비치다 ······ 440, 495	빗줄기 ······ 397	뺨 ······ 31
비키다 ······ 530	빙벽타기 ······ 260	뻐근하다 ······ 63
비타민 ······ 122	빙상경기 ······ 270	뻐꾸기 ······ 412
비탈 ······ 477	빙점 ······ 213	뻐꾹뻐꾹 ······ 412
비탈길 ······ 477	빚 ······ 340	뻐드렁니 ······ 31
비통하다 ······ 75	빚다 ······ 122, 530	뻗다 ······ 530
비판력 ······ 75, 213	빚쟁이 ······ 340	뻗치다 ······ 530
비판적이다 ······ 89	빚지다 ······ 340	뻣뻣하다 ······ 495
비판하다 ······ 75, 167, 213, 530	빛 ······ 440	뻥튀기 ······ 122
비평 ······ 213	빛깔 ······ 440	뼈 ······ 31, 412
비평가 ······ 245	빛나다 ······ 440	뼈대 ······ 31
비평하다 ······ 75, 167, 213, 530	빠듯하다 ······ 433, 495	뼈마디 ······ 31
비품 ······ 145	빠르기표 ······ 245	뺨 ······ 450
비합리 ······ 75, 213	빠르다 ······ 463	뽀얗다 ······ 495
비행기 ······ 388	빠른우편 ······ 188	뽐내다 ······ 89, 530
비행기표 ······ 388	빠지다 ······ 530	뽑다 ······ 122, 287, 530
비행사 ······ 357, 388	빠짐표 ······ 167	뽕 ······ 31
비행장 ······ 388	빡빡하다 ······ 495	뽕나무 ······ 424
비행접시 ······ 477	빨간색 ······ 440	뾰족뾰족 ······ 433
비행하다 ······ 389, 530	빨강 ······ 440	뾰족하다 ······ 433, 495
비형식 ······ 495	빨갛다 ······ 440	뿌듯하다 ······ 75

뿌리 424, 450
뿌옇다 398
뿔 412
삐다 42, 531
삐뚤삐뚤 495
삐삐 145, 188
삐악삐악 412
삐치다 75, 531

사

사 450
사각모 103
사각사각 122
사각형 433
사거리 477
사건 302
사격 270, 313
사격하다 313, 531
사계절 463
사고 75, 213, 389
사고력 75, 213
사고하다 75, 213
사공 389
사과 424
사과나무 424
사과하다 167, 531
사관 313
사관생도 313
사관학교 313
사관후보생 313
사교 225
사교성 89
사교육 199
사교육비 199
사군자 245
사귀다 324
사귀다 531
사극 245
사글세 145
사금 372
사기 302
사기꾼 302

사나이 4
사납다 89
사내 4
사내아이 4
사냥꾼 357
사다 340, 531
사다리 145
사다리꼴 433
사당 225
사도신경 225
사돈 13
사돈어른 13
사돈처녀 13
사돈총각 13
사동 167
사라지다 531
사람 4, 450
사랑 22, 75, 225
사랑니 31
사랑방 145
사랑스럽다 75
사랑채 145
사랑하다 22, 75, 324, 531
사려깊다 75
사령관 313
사령부 313
사례금 340
사로잡다 531
사료 372
사르다 531
사리 213, 225
사리다 531
사리분별하다 75, 213, 531
사리판단하다 75, 213, 531
사립 324
사립대학 199
사립학교 199
사마귀 31, 412
사막 477
사망 4, 53
사망률 53, 324
사망하다 53, 531
사면 302
사면체 433
사모님 4
사모하다 75, 531

사무관 287
사무실 145
사무장 302
사무직 357
사무치다 75, 531
사물놀이 245
사물함 199
사방 478
사방제기 265
사방치기 265
사방팔방 478
사범대학 199
사법 302
사법고시 302
사법기관 302
사법부 302
사법서사 303
사병 313
사보 188
사부 4
사비 340
사산 22
사상 213
사상범 287, 303
사상자 42
사색하다 75, 213, 531
사생아 5
사생화 245
사생활 53
사서교사 199
사서삼경 225
사선 433
사설 167, 182
사수 313
사수자리 478
사수하다 313
사슴 412
사시 31, 63
사시사철 463
사식 122
사실주의 245
사십구재 53
사양하다 531
사업 340, 357
사업가 357
사업자 340, 357

사용료 372	사채업자 340	사회정의 325
사용하다 531	사철나무 424	사회제도 325
사우디아라비아 277	사체 53	사회조직 325
사원 225, 357	사촌 14	사회주의 287, 325
사월초파일 226	사춘기 53	사회주의국가 287
사위 14	사타구니 31	사회질서 325
사육장 372, 412	사탕 123	사회집단 325
사육지 372	사태 495	사회체계 325
사육하다 372, 412, 531	사투리 167	사회체육 270
사은품 340	사팔뜨기 5	사회체제 325
사은회 199	사표 357	사회통념 325
사이 463, 478	사학 213	사회학 213
사이다 123	사학자 213	사회학자 214
사이비 226	사형 53, 303	사회현상 325
사이비기자 182	사형수 53, 303	사회협약 325
사이비언론 182	사형장 53	사회화 325
사이비종교 226	사형하다 303, 531	사회활동 325
사이클 270	사회 324	사흘 463
사자 412	사회공동체 324	삭다 495
사자자리 478	사회과학 213	삭발 31
사장 340, 357	사회교육 199	삭히다 123, 531
사적 236	사회교육원 199	삯 340
사전 167	사회구성원 324	산 214, 478
사절하다 167, 531	사회구조 324	산골 478
사정 22, 495	사회규범 324	산골짜기 478
사정하다 22, 167, 531	사회규약 324	산기슭 478
사죄하다 167, 531	사회단체 324	산꼭대기 478
사주 53, 226	사회면 182	산달 22
사주팔자 53, 226	사회문제 324	산동네 478
사증 260, 287	사회발전 324	산돼지 412
사지선다형 199	사회법 303	산들바람 398
사직서 357	사회변동 325	산들산들 398
사진 260	사회보장제도 325	산등성이 478
사진관 260	사회복지 325	산딸기 424
사진기 145, 260	사회봉사 325	산뜻하다 495
사진기자 182, 260	사회부조리 325	산림 424, 478
사진사 260, 357	사회비리 325	산림청 287
사진술 260	사회사업 325	산마루 478
사진예술 245, 260	사회생활 325	산맥 478
사진작가 245, 260	사회성 89, 325	산모롱이 478
사진작품 245, 260	사회심리 325	산모퉁이 478
사진첩 260	사회악 325	산문 245
사진틀 260	사회운동 325	산문시 245
사차원 478	사회윤리 325	산바람 398
사찰 226	사회자 167, 183	산봉우리 478
사채 340	사회적 325	산부인과 42

산불 …………………………… 398	살균 …………………………… 42	삼차산업 …………………… 373
산비탈 ……………………… 478	살다 ………… 53, 145, 424, 531	삼차원 ……………………… 478
산사태 ……………………… 398	살랑살랑 …………………… 398	삼촌 …………………………… 14
산삼 ………………… 123, 424	살림살이 ………………… 53, 145	삼치 ………………… 123, 412
산성 …………………………… 214	살림집 ……………………… 145	삼키다 ……………… 123, 532
산성비 ……………………… 398	살림하다 …………………… 531	삼투압 ……………………… 214
산소 …………………… 53, 214	살모사 ……………………… 412	삼투압원리 ………………… 214
산수 …………………………… 450	살살 ………………………… 495	삼한 ………………………… 277
산수화 ……………………… 245	살색 ………………………… 440	삼한사온 …………………… 398
산술 ………………………… 450	살인 …………………………… 53	삽 …………………………… 373
산신 ………………………… 226	살인범 ………………………… 53	삽시간 ……………………… 463
산신령 ……………………… 226	살충제 ……………………… 373	삽화 ………………………… 245
산악인 ……………………… 260	살코기 ……………………… 123	삿갓 ………………………… 103
산악회 ……………………… 260	살펴보다 ………………… 63, 531	상 …………………………… 53, 167
산양 ………………………… 412	살풀이춤 …………………… 245	상가 ………………… 53, 145, 340
산업 ………………… 357, 372	살피다 ……………………… 531	상강 ………………………… 463
산업고등학교 ……………… 199	살해 …………………………… 53	상경하다 …………………… 532
산업구조 …………………… 372	살해되다 ……………………… 53	상고 ………………… 199, 303
산업대학 …………………… 199	살해하다 ………………… 53, 531	상관 ………………………… 313
산업사회 …………………… 325	삵괭이 ……………………… 412	상금 ………………………… 340
산업용 ……………………… 372	삶 …………………………… 53	상급생 ……………………… 199
산업자원부 ………………… 288	삶다 ………………… 123, 531	상기하다 …………………… 532
산업재해 …………………… 372	삼 …………………………… 450	상냥하다 ……………………… 89
산업전선 …………………… 372	삼가다 ……………………… 531	상단 ………………………… 478
산업정보 …………………… 188	삼각주 ……………………… 478	상담 ………………………… 167
산업정책 …………………… 372	삼각형 ……………………… 434	상담교사 …………………… 199
산업체 ……………………… 372	삼강오륜 …………………… 226	상담실 ……………………… 199
산업혁명 …………………… 372	삼거리 ……………………… 478	상대성이론 ………………… 214
산업화 ……………………… 372	삼겹살 ……………………… 123	상대적 ……………………… 495
산울림 ……………………… 260	삼계탕 ……………………… 123	상등병 ……………………… 313
산장 ………………………… 145	삼권분립 …………………… 288	상록수 ……………………… 424
산조 ………………………… 245	삼나무 ……………………… 424	상류사회 …………………… 325
산지 ………………………… 478	삼다 ………………………… 531	상류층 ……………………… 325
산짐승 ……………………… 412	삼단논법 …………………… 214	상법 ………………………… 303
산촌 ………………………… 478	삼림 ………………………… 424	상병 ………………………… 313
산토끼 ……………………… 412	삼모작 ……………………… 373	상복 ………………………… 53, 103
산허리 ……………………… 478	삼발이 ……………………… 214	상사 ………………… 313, 340, 357
산호 ………………………… 412	삼베 ………………………… 103	상사병 ………………………… 42
산호색 ……………………… 440	삼복더위 …………………… 398	상상력 ………………………… 75
산화 ………………………… 214	삼선 ………………………… 288	상상하다 ………………… 75, 532
살 …………… 31, 53, 226, 412, 450	삼우제 ………………………… 53	상석 …………………………… 53
살갗 …………………………… 31	삼원색 ……………………… 440	상선 ………………………… 389
살결 …………………………… 31	삼인칭 ……………………… 167	상설무대 …………………… 245
살구 ………………………… 424	삼일장 ………………………… 53	상설할인매장 ……………… 340
살구나무 …………………… 424	삼일절 ……………………… 463	상소 ………………………… 303
살구빛 ……………………… 440	삼중창 ……………………… 245	상소리 ……………………… 167

상속세 ⋯⋯⋯⋯⋯⋯⋯⋯⋯⋯ 340	새끼치다 ⋯⋯⋯⋯⋯⋯⋯⋯⋯ 412	색채 ⋯⋯⋯⋯⋯⋯⋯⋯ 245, 441
상속재판 ⋯⋯⋯⋯⋯⋯⋯⋯⋯ 303	새내기 ⋯⋯⋯⋯⋯⋯⋯⋯⋯⋯ 199	색채감각 ⋯⋯⋯⋯⋯⋯⋯⋯⋯ 441
상수도 ⋯⋯⋯⋯⋯⋯⋯⋯⋯⋯ 145	새다 ⋯⋯⋯⋯⋯⋯⋯⋯ 398, 496	색칠 ⋯⋯⋯⋯⋯⋯⋯⋯⋯⋯⋯ 441
상순 ⋯⋯⋯⋯⋯⋯⋯⋯⋯⋯⋯ 463	새댁 ⋯⋯⋯⋯⋯⋯⋯⋯⋯⋯ 5, 22	색칠하다 ⋯⋯⋯⋯ 245, 441, 532
상술 ⋯⋯⋯⋯⋯⋯⋯⋯⋯⋯⋯ 340	새롭다 ⋯⋯⋯⋯⋯⋯⋯⋯⋯⋯ 496	색환도 ⋯⋯⋯⋯⋯⋯⋯⋯⋯⋯ 441
상승하다 ⋯⋯⋯⋯⋯⋯⋯⋯⋯ 495	새마을금고 ⋯⋯⋯⋯⋯⋯⋯⋯ 340	샘 ⋯⋯⋯⋯⋯⋯⋯⋯⋯ 75, 478
상식 ⋯⋯⋯⋯⋯⋯⋯⋯⋯ 53, 75	새마을운동 ⋯⋯⋯⋯⋯⋯⋯⋯ 373	샘내다 ⋯⋯⋯⋯⋯⋯⋯ 75, 532
상실하다 ⋯⋯⋯⋯⋯⋯⋯⋯⋯ 532	새벽 ⋯⋯⋯⋯⋯⋯⋯⋯⋯⋯⋯ 463	샘터 ⋯⋯⋯⋯⋯⋯⋯⋯⋯⋯⋯ 478
상아색 ⋯⋯⋯⋯⋯⋯⋯⋯⋯⋯ 440	새벽시장 ⋯⋯⋯⋯⋯⋯⋯⋯⋯ 341	샛길 ⋯⋯⋯⋯⋯⋯⋯⋯⋯⋯⋯ 478
상아탑 ⋯⋯⋯⋯⋯⋯⋯⋯⋯⋯ 199	새벽안개 ⋯⋯⋯⋯⋯⋯⋯⋯⋯ 398	샛바람 ⋯⋯⋯⋯⋯⋯⋯⋯⋯⋯ 398
상어 ⋯⋯⋯⋯⋯⋯⋯⋯⋯⋯⋯ 412	새색시 ⋯⋯⋯⋯⋯⋯⋯⋯⋯ 5, 22	샛별 ⋯⋯⋯⋯⋯⋯⋯⋯⋯⋯⋯ 478
상업 ⋯⋯⋯⋯⋯⋯⋯⋯⋯ 340, 357	새신랑 ⋯⋯⋯⋯⋯⋯⋯⋯⋯⋯ 22	생각 ⋯⋯⋯⋯⋯⋯⋯⋯⋯⋯⋯ 76
상업고등학교 ⋯⋯⋯⋯⋯⋯⋯ 199	새신부 ⋯⋯⋯⋯⋯⋯⋯⋯⋯⋯ 22	생각하다 ⋯⋯⋯⋯⋯⋯⋯ 76, 532
상업성 ⋯⋯⋯⋯⋯⋯⋯⋯⋯⋯ 340	새아버지 ⋯⋯⋯⋯⋯⋯⋯⋯⋯ 14	생강 ⋯⋯⋯⋯⋯⋯⋯⋯ 123, 424
상여 ⋯⋯⋯⋯⋯⋯⋯⋯⋯⋯⋯ 54	새알 ⋯⋯⋯⋯⋯⋯⋯⋯⋯⋯⋯ 412	생강차 ⋯⋯⋯⋯⋯⋯⋯⋯⋯⋯ 123
상여금 ⋯⋯⋯⋯⋯⋯⋯⋯ 340, 357	새어머니 ⋯⋯⋯⋯⋯⋯⋯⋯⋯ 14	생계수단 ⋯⋯⋯⋯⋯⋯⋯⋯⋯ 357
상영관 ⋯⋯⋯⋯⋯⋯⋯⋯⋯⋯ 245	새언니 ⋯⋯⋯⋯⋯⋯⋯⋯⋯⋯ 14	생기 ⋯⋯⋯⋯⋯⋯⋯⋯⋯⋯⋯ 54
상영하다 ⋯⋯⋯⋯⋯⋯ 245, 532	새우 ⋯⋯⋯⋯⋯⋯⋯⋯ 123, 412	생기다 ⋯⋯⋯⋯⋯⋯⋯⋯⋯⋯ 532
상온 ⋯⋯⋯⋯⋯⋯⋯⋯⋯⋯⋯ 398	새참 ⋯⋯⋯⋯⋯⋯⋯⋯⋯⋯⋯ 123	생김새 ⋯⋯⋯⋯⋯⋯⋯⋯⋯⋯ 434
상위어 ⋯⋯⋯⋯⋯⋯⋯⋯⋯⋯ 167	새침데기 ⋯⋯⋯⋯⋯⋯⋯⋯ 5, 89	생년월일 ⋯⋯⋯⋯⋯⋯⋯⋯⋯ 54
상의 ⋯⋯⋯⋯⋯⋯⋯⋯⋯⋯⋯ 103	새침하다 ⋯⋯⋯⋯⋯⋯⋯⋯⋯ 89	생로병사 ⋯⋯⋯⋯⋯⋯⋯⋯⋯ 54
상의하다 ⋯⋯⋯⋯⋯⋯ 167, 532	새콤달콤 ⋯⋯⋯⋯⋯⋯⋯⋯⋯ 123	생리 ⋯⋯⋯⋯⋯⋯⋯⋯⋯ 22, 32
상인 ⋯⋯⋯⋯⋯⋯⋯⋯⋯ 340, 357	새콤달콤하다 ⋯⋯⋯⋯⋯⋯⋯ 63	생리대 ⋯⋯⋯⋯⋯⋯⋯⋯⋯⋯ 146
상자 ⋯⋯⋯⋯⋯⋯⋯⋯⋯ 145, 450	새콤하다 ⋯⋯⋯⋯⋯⋯⋯ 63, 123	생리통 ⋯⋯⋯⋯⋯⋯⋯⋯⋯⋯ 42
상장 ⋯⋯⋯⋯⋯⋯⋯⋯⋯ 54, 199	새털구름 ⋯⋯⋯⋯⋯⋯⋯⋯⋯ 398	생맥주 ⋯⋯⋯⋯⋯⋯⋯⋯⋯⋯ 123
상점 ⋯⋯⋯⋯⋯⋯⋯⋯⋯ 146, 340	새해 ⋯⋯⋯⋯⋯⋯⋯⋯⋯⋯⋯ 463	생머리 ⋯⋯⋯⋯⋯⋯⋯⋯ 32, 103
상제 ⋯⋯⋯⋯⋯⋯⋯⋯⋯⋯⋯ 54	색 ⋯⋯⋯⋯⋯⋯⋯⋯⋯⋯⋯ 440	생명 ⋯⋯⋯⋯⋯⋯⋯⋯⋯⋯⋯ 54
상주 ⋯⋯⋯⋯⋯⋯⋯⋯⋯⋯⋯ 54	색감 ⋯⋯⋯⋯⋯⋯⋯⋯⋯⋯⋯ 440	생명력 ⋯⋯⋯⋯⋯⋯⋯⋯⋯⋯ 54
상처 ⋯⋯⋯⋯⋯⋯⋯⋯⋯⋯⋯ 42	색깔 ⋯⋯⋯⋯⋯⋯⋯⋯⋯⋯⋯ 440	생모 ⋯⋯⋯⋯⋯⋯⋯⋯⋯⋯⋯ 14
상추 ⋯⋯⋯⋯⋯⋯⋯⋯ 123, 424	색다르다 ⋯⋯⋯⋯⋯⋯⋯⋯⋯ 496	생물 ⋯⋯⋯⋯⋯⋯⋯⋯⋯⋯⋯ 54
상쾌하다 ⋯⋯⋯⋯⋯⋯⋯⋯⋯ 75	색도 ⋯⋯⋯⋯⋯⋯⋯⋯⋯⋯⋯ 440	생물학 ⋯⋯⋯⋯⋯⋯⋯⋯⋯⋯ 214
상태 ⋯⋯⋯⋯⋯⋯⋯⋯⋯⋯⋯ 495	색동 ⋯⋯⋯⋯⋯⋯⋯⋯⋯ 103, 440	생물학자 ⋯⋯⋯⋯⋯⋯⋯⋯⋯ 214
상투 ⋯⋯⋯⋯⋯⋯⋯⋯⋯ 32, 103	색동저고리 ⋯⋯⋯⋯⋯⋯⋯⋯ 103	생방송 ⋯⋯⋯⋯⋯⋯⋯⋯ 183, 188
상표 ⋯⋯⋯⋯⋯⋯⋯⋯⋯⋯⋯ 340	색맹 ⋯⋯⋯⋯⋯⋯⋯⋯ 42, 63, 440	생부 ⋯⋯⋯⋯⋯⋯⋯⋯⋯⋯⋯ 14
상품 ⋯⋯⋯⋯⋯⋯⋯⋯⋯⋯⋯ 340	색상 ⋯⋯⋯⋯⋯⋯⋯⋯⋯ 245, 440	생산 ⋯⋯⋯⋯⋯⋯⋯⋯ 341, 373
상품권 ⋯⋯⋯⋯⋯⋯⋯⋯⋯⋯ 340	색상지 ⋯⋯⋯⋯⋯⋯⋯⋯⋯⋯ 440	생산구조 ⋯⋯⋯⋯⋯⋯⋯⋯⋯ 341
상하다 ⋯⋯⋯⋯⋯⋯⋯⋯ 123, 495	색소 ⋯⋯⋯⋯⋯⋯⋯⋯⋯⋯⋯ 440	생산물 ⋯⋯⋯⋯⋯⋯⋯⋯⋯⋯ 373
상현달 ⋯⋯⋯⋯⋯⋯⋯⋯⋯⋯ 478	색시 ⋯⋯⋯⋯⋯⋯⋯⋯⋯⋯⋯ 5	생산자 ⋯⋯⋯⋯⋯⋯⋯⋯⋯⋯ 341
상형문자 ⋯⋯⋯⋯⋯⋯⋯⋯⋯ 167	색실 ⋯⋯⋯⋯⋯⋯⋯⋯⋯⋯⋯ 103	생산직 ⋯⋯⋯⋯⋯⋯⋯⋯⋯⋯ 357
상황 ⋯⋯⋯⋯⋯⋯⋯⋯⋯⋯⋯ 496	색안경 ⋯⋯⋯⋯⋯⋯⋯⋯⋯⋯ 103	생산하다 ⋯⋯⋯⋯⋯⋯ 373, 532
샅바 ⋯⋯⋯⋯⋯⋯⋯⋯⋯⋯⋯ 270	색연필 ⋯⋯⋯⋯⋯⋯⋯⋯ 245, 441	생색내다 ⋯⋯⋯⋯⋯⋯⋯⋯⋯ 532
새 ⋯⋯⋯⋯⋯⋯⋯⋯⋯ 412, 463	색인 ⋯⋯⋯⋯⋯⋯⋯⋯⋯⋯⋯ 167	생선 ⋯⋯⋯⋯⋯⋯⋯⋯⋯⋯⋯ 123
새— ⋯⋯⋯⋯⋯⋯⋯⋯⋯⋯⋯ 440	색조 ⋯⋯⋯⋯⋯⋯⋯⋯⋯⋯⋯ 441	생선묵 ⋯⋯⋯⋯⋯⋯⋯⋯⋯⋯ 123
새기다 ⋯⋯⋯⋯⋯⋯⋯⋯⋯⋯ 532	색조화장 ⋯⋯⋯⋯⋯⋯⋯⋯⋯ 103	생선조림 ⋯⋯⋯⋯⋯⋯⋯⋯⋯ 123
새끼 ⋯⋯⋯⋯⋯⋯⋯⋯⋯⋯⋯ 412	색종이 ⋯⋯⋯⋯⋯⋯⋯⋯ 245, 441	생선찌개 ⋯⋯⋯⋯⋯⋯⋯⋯⋯ 123
새끼손가락 ⋯⋯⋯⋯⋯⋯⋯⋯ 32	색지 ⋯⋯⋯⋯⋯⋯⋯⋯⋯ 245, 441	생선회 ⋯⋯⋯⋯⋯⋯⋯⋯⋯⋯ 123

생소하다 496	서론 167, 214	석방 303
생수 123	서류가방 146	석사 199
생식 22, 123	서른 450	석사장교 313
생식기 22, 32	서리 288, 398	석식 123
생신 54	서먹서먹하다 76	석영 373
생애 54	서명 325	석유 214, 373, 383
생업 357	서민 288, 325	석유곤로 383
생일 54, 463	서민층 325	석재 146
생존 54	서반아어 167	석차 200
생중계 183, 188	서방 14	석탄 214, 373, 383
생쥐 412	서방님 14	석회석 373
생질 14	서방정토 226	섞다 123, 532
생태계 398, 412	서법 168	선 22, 434
생포하다 313, 532	서비스 373	선거 288
생화 424	서비스업 357, 373	선거공약 288
생화학전 313	서사시 245	선거관리위원회 288
생활 54	서성거리다 532	선거구 288
생활관 199	서수 450	선거권 288
생활기록부 199	서술어 168	선거법 288
생활면 183	서술하다 168, 532	선거사범 303
생활비 341	서식지 412	선거소송 303
생활양식 236	서식하다 412	선거운동 288
생활용품 146	서약하다 168, 532	선거운동원 288
생활체육 270	서양문화 236	선거유세 288
생활필수품 146	서양장기 265	선거일 288
생활화 54	서양화 245	선거자금 288
생활환경 54	서양화가 245	선거재판 288
서거 54	서예 245	선거전 288
서거하다 54, 532	서예가 245, 357	선거전략 288
서구문명 236	서운하다 76	선거철 288
서구문화 236	서울방송국 183	선거하다 288, 532
서글프다 76	서재 146	선고 303
서글픔 76	서적 168, 183, 214	선고하다 168, 532
서기 463	서점 183, 341	선교 226
서기관 288	서점가 183	선교사 5, 226, 357
서낭당 226	서정시 246	선구자 5
서낭신 226	서쪽 478	선남선녀 5
서너 450	서툴다 496	선도 303
서늘하다 398	서풍 398	선동하다 532
서다 532	서향 146	선례 303
서두르다 532	석 450	선로 389
서랍 146	석가모니 226	선머슴 5
서랍장 146	석가탄신일 226	선명하다 441, 496
서러움 76	석간 183	선물 341
서럽다 76	석고상 246	선박 389
서력기원 463	석류 424	선반 146

선발하다 270, 532	설날 463	성금 341
선배 5	설득 168	성기 22, 32
선분 434	설득하다 168, 532	성깔 90
선불 341	설렁탕 123	성나다 76
선비 5	설레다 76	성냥 146, 383
선사문화 236	설립하다 532	성냥개비 383
선사시대 236, 463	설명 168	성년 54
선산 54	설명하다 168, 532	성당 146, 226
선생 200	설비 373	성대 32
선생님 5, 200, 357	설빔 104	성령 226
선서하다 168, 532	설사 42	성명 326
선수 270	설움 76	성모 226
선수교체 270	설익다 123, 424, 496	성모마리아 226
선수권 270	설치다 532	성묘 54
선수단 270	설치미술 246	성미 90
선수촌 270	설치예술 246	성병 42
선실 389	설치하다 532	성부 226
선어말어미 168	설탕 123	성생활 22
선언하다 168, 532	설형문자 168	성서 226
선원 357	설화 246	성수기 341
선율 246	섬 373, 450, 478	성신 227
선인장 424	섬기다 533	성실하다 90
선임 357	섬세하다 90, 496	성악 246
선잠 32	섬유 104	성악가 246, 357
선장 357, 389	섬유질 123	성악곡 246
선전 183, 189	섭섭하다 76	성에 398
선지국 123	섭씨 398	성욕 22
선진국 288	섭취하다 124, 533	성우 246
선진문명 236	성 22, 325	성인 5, 227
선진사회 325	성가 226	성인병 42
선착장 389	성가대 226	성인영화 246
선창 389	성가시다 76	성자 227
선출 288	성게 412	성적 200
선출하다 288	성격 90	성적증명서 200
선포하다 168, 532	성결교 226	성적표 200
선하다 89	성경 226	성전 227
선행 89	성공 496	성지 227
선홍색 441	성공하다 496, 533	성지순례 227, 260
선후배 5	성공회 226	성직자 227
섣달 463	성과급 341	성질 90, 496
설경 398	성관계 22	성차별 22
설계 146	성교 22	성추행 22
설계도 146	성교육 200	성충 412
설계사 357	성교하다 22	성취하다 533
설계하다 146, 532	성균관 226	성탄절 227
설교하다 168, 226, 532	성글다 496	성폭행 22

성품 90	세숫대야 147	소녀 5
성함 326	세시풍속 236	소년 5
성형외과 42	세우다 147, 533	소년기 54
성호 227	세월 463	소년원 303
성혼선언 22	세일 341	소독 42
성혼선언문 22	세입자 147	소독약 43
성화 246	세정제 147	소득 341
성희롱 22	세제 104, 147	소득세 341
세 54, 341, 450	세종문화회관 236, 246	소라 124, 413
세간 146	세주다 341	소란스럽다 63
세계 288, 478	세차다 496	소령 313
세계관 76, 90	세차장 373	소름 32
세계대전 313	세척제 147	소름끼치다 76
세계문화유산 236	세탁 104	소리 63, 246
세계시장 341	세탁기 104, 147	소리꾼 246
세계인 288	세탁소 104, 373	소리치다 168, 533
세계적 288	세탁업 373	소만 463
세계주의 288	세탁하다 104, 533	소말리아 277
세계지도 479	세포 214, 412	소매 104, 341
세계화 288	셈 450	소매가 341
세균 42, 412	셈씨 168	소매상 341
세금 341	셈여림표 246	소매시장 341
세기 463	셈하다 450, 533	소매치기 303, 357
세놓다 341	셋 450	소모품 341
세다 450, 496, 533	셋방 147	소묘 246
세단뛰기 270	셋방살이 54	소문 168
세대 146	셋째 450	소문내다 168, 533
세대주 146	셔츠 104	소박하다 496
세력 326	소 412	소방서 288
세련되다 104	소감 76	소방차 389
세례 227	소개하다 168, 533	소변 32
세례명 227	소경 5, 63	소복 54, 104
세로 479	소계 450	소복하다 434
세면대 146	소고 246	소비 341
세모 434, 463	소고기 124	소비구조 341
세모나다 434, 496	소곤거리다 168, 533	소비생활 341
세모지다 434, 496	소괄호 168	소비자 341
세무사 341, 357	소극장 246, 373	소비자경제 341
세무서 341	소극적이다 90	소비하다 341, 533
세미나 214	소금 124	소서 463
세밀 463	소금쟁이 413	소설 246, 463
세발자전거 265	소꼬리 124	소설가 246, 358
세뱃돈 341	소꿉놀이 265	소송 303
세부공사 146	소나기 398	소송비 303
세상 479	소나기구름 398	소송인 303
세상살이 54	소나무 425	소송장 303

소수 450	소화불량 43, 124	손주 14
소수당 288	소화전 383	손지갑 104, 147
소수민족 289	소화제 43, 124	손질 104
소수점 450	소화하다 124	손질하다 533
소수집단 326	소환하다 168, 533	손톱 32
소식 124, 168, 183, 189	속 425, 479	손톱깎이 147
소식불통 189	속국 289	손해 342
소식지 189	속기 168	손해배상 342
소식통 189	속눈썹 32	솔 147
소심하다 90	속다 76, 533	솔개 413
소아 5	속담 168	솔기 104
소아과 43	속도 214, 389	솔깃하다 63
소아마비 43	속도측정기 389	솔솔 398, 496
소외계층 326	속독 168	솔직하다 90
소위 313	속력 389	솜 104
소유격 168	속바지 104	솜바지 104
소음 63	속보 183, 189	솜사탕 124
소인 189	속삭이다 168, 533	솜씨 90
소작농 373	속상하다 76, 533	솜털 32
소작인 373	속성 496	솟다 533
소장 32, 313	속셈 76	송곳 147
소재 168	속어 168	송곳니 32
소재지 479	속옷 104	송구스럽다 76
소조 246	속이다 533, 90	송금 189
소주 124	속저고리 104	송년호 183
소주방 124	속치마 104	송년회 326
소지품 147	숙다 373, 425, 533	송별회 326
소질 90	손 32, 63, 450	송사리 413
소쩍새 413	손가락 32	송아지 413
소쿠리 124, 147	손가방 104, 147	송어 413
소탈하다 90	손거울 104, 147	송이 425, 450
소통 189	손금 32	송이버섯 124, 425
소파 147	손녀 14	송장 54, 303
소포 189	손님 341	송충이 413
소포우편 189	손등 32	송편 124
소품 246	손떼다 533	솥 124
소품실 246	손목 32	쇠고기 124
소풍 200, 260	손목시계 104, 147	쇠꼬리 124
소프라노 246	손바닥 32	쇠다 533
소프트웨어 189	손부 14	쇠사슬 147
소한 463	손수건 104, 147	쇠하다 496
소형 434	손쉽다 496	쇼 246
소홀하다 90	손아래사람 5	숄 104
소화 124, 383	손윗사람 5	수 450
소화기 32, 147, 383	손익계산서 342	수간호사 43
소화기관 32	손자 14	수감 303

수감자 ... 303	수면제 ... 43	수술실 ... 43
수갑 ... 303	수목원 ... 425	수술하다 ... 43, 533
수건 ... 147	수묵화 ... 246	수습 ... 358
수건돌리기 ... 265	수박 ... 425	수식어 ... 169
수고비 ... 373	수배 ... 303	수신 ... 342
수공업 ... 358, 373	수배자 ... 303	수신료 ... 183
수공예 ... 246	수배하다 ... 303, 533	수심 ... 398
수교 ... 289	수북하다 ... 434	수양딸 ... 14
수교하다 ... 289	수비 ... 270, 313	수양아들 ... 14
수구 ... 270	수비군 ... 313	수업 ... 200
수국 ... 425	수비대 ... 314	수업료 ... 200, 342
수금 ... 342	수비망 ... 314	수업시간 ... 200
수납장 ... 147	수비수 ... 270	수염 ... 32
수녀 ... 227, 358	수비하다 ... 314	수영 ... 270
수녀원 ... 227	수사 ... 169, 303	수영모자 ... 270
수놈 ... 413	수사관 ... 303	수영복 ... 104, 270
수놓다 ... 104, 533	수사기관 ... 303	수예 ... 246
수능시험 ... 200	수사대 ... 303	수온 ... 398
수다 ... 168	수사망 ... 304	수요 ... 342
수다떨다 ... 168, 533	수사본부 ... 304	수요일 ... 463
수다스럽다 ... 168	수사하다 ... 304, 533	수요자 ... 342
수다쟁이 ... 169	수산물 ... 373	수월하다 ... 496
수단 ... 277	수산시장 ... 342, 373	수위 ... 358
수달 ... 413	수산업 ... 358, 373	수육 ... 124
수당 ... 342, 358	수산업협동조합 ... 373	수은주 ... 398
수도 ... 147, 289	수상 ... 289, 358	수의 ... 54, 104
수도꼭지 ... 147	수상스키 ... 270	수의사 ... 358
수도사 ... 227	수상하다 ... 496	수의학 ... 214
수도요금 ... 342	수색 ... 304	수익 ... 342
수도원 ... 227	수색영장 ... 304	수익금 ... 342
수도하다 ... 227	수색하다 ... 533	수익률 ... 342
수동태 ... 169	수석 ... 200	수임료 ... 304
수두 ... 43	수선 ... 104	수입 ... 342
수두룩하다 ... 450	수선하다 ... 533	수입품 ... 342
수락하다 ... 169, 533	수선화 ... 425	수재 ... 5
수량 ... 450	수성 ... 479	수저 ... 124
수령 ... 479	수세미 ... 147	수정 ... 23, 373
수레 ... 389	수세미외 ... 425	수정과 ... 124
수력 ... 214, 383	수세식 ... 147	수정하다 ... 169, 533
수로 ... 389	수소 ... 214	수제비 ... 124
수료증 ... 200	수송기 ... 389	수제자 ... 200
수류탄 ... 313	수수 ... 124, 425	수족관 ... 373
수리공 ... 373	수수께끼 ... 265	수줍다 ... 76
수리하다 ... 147, 533	수수료 ... 342	수중발레 ... 270
수매하다 ... 373	수수하다 ... 104	수직 ... 434, 496
수면 ... 32	수술 ... 43, 425	수직선 ... 434

수질 ············· 398	숙성 ············· 124	숨기다 ············· 534
수질오염 ············· 398	숙이다 ············· 534	숨다 ············· 534
수채화 ············· 246	숙제 ············· 200	숨바꼭질 ············· 265
수출 ············· 342	숙주나물 ············· 124	숨쉬다 ············· 55, 534
수출품 ············· 342	숙주나물 ············· 425	숨은그림찾기 ············· 265
수치 ············· 450	숙직 ············· 358	숨지다 ············· 55, 534
수치스럽다 ············· 76	숙환 ············· 43	숫구멍 ············· 32
수컷 ············· 413	순간 ············· 463	숫자 ············· 450
수퍼마켓 ············· 147	순결 ············· 23	숫처녀 ············· 23
수평 ············· 434, 496	순결하다 ············· 496	숫총각 ············· 23
수평선 ············· 479	순경 ············· 304	숭늉 ············· 124
수포 ············· 43	순교자 ············· 227	숭배 ············· 227
수표 ············· 342	순교하다 ············· 54, 534	숭상 ············· 227
수풀 ············· 425, 479	순국하다 ············· 55, 534	숭숭 ············· 496
수필 ············· 246	순대 ············· 124	숭앙 ············· 227
수필가 ············· 246, 358	순댓국 ············· 124	숭어 ············· 413
수학 ············· 214	순두부 ············· 124	숯 ············· 214, 383
수학능력 ············· 200	순록 ············· 413	숯불 ············· 214
수학능력시험 ············· 200	순박하다 ············· 90	숱 ············· 32
수학여행 ············· 200	순방하다 ············· 289, 534	숲 ············· 425, 479
수학자 ············· 214	순산 ············· 23	쉬다 ············· 496, 534
수해 ············· 398	순수음악 ············· 246	쉰 ············· 451
수행하다 ············· 533	순수하다 ············· 90, 496	쉰내 ············· 63
수험생 ············· 200	순수학문 ············· 214	쉼표 ············· 169, 246
수험표 ············· 200	순시하다 ············· 534	쉽다 ············· 497
수혈 ············· 32, 43	순식간 ············· 463	슈퍼마켓 ············· 342
수협 ············· 373	순악질 ············· 5	스냅사진 ············· 260
수형도 ············· 434	순조롭다 ············· 496	스님 ············· 227, 358
수호하다 ············· 289, 533	순종 ············· 413	스리랑카 ············· 277
수화 ············· 169	순직하다 ············· 55, 534	스무고개 ············· 265
수화기 ············· 147, 189	순진하다 ············· 90, 496	스물 ············· 451
수확 ············· 373	순찰대 ············· 304	스미다 ············· 534
수확량 ············· 374	순찰차 ············· 304	스승 ············· 5, 200
수확하다 ············· 374, 425, 534	순찰하다 ············· 304, 534	스승의 날 ············· 200, 464
숙녀 ············· 5	순하다 ············· 90	스웨덴 ············· 277
숙녀복 ············· 104	순환계 ············· 32	스웨터 ············· 104
숙녀화 ············· 104	숟가락 ············· 124	스위스 ············· 277
숙련공 ············· 374	술 ············· 124, 450	스치다 ············· 534
숙면 ············· 32	술고래 ············· 5	스카프 ············· 104
숙모 ············· 14	술떡 ············· 124	스커트 ············· 104
숙박 ············· 147, 260	술래 ············· 265	스케이트 ············· 270
숙박료 ············· 260, 374	술래잡기 ············· 265	스케치하다 ············· 247, 534
숙박시설 ············· 147	술주정뱅이 ············· 5	스키 ············· 270
숙박업 ············· 374	술집 ············· 342	스키장갑 ············· 104, 270
숙변 ············· 32	숨 ············· 32	스타킹 ············· 105
숙부 ············· 14	숨구멍 ············· 32	스튜어드 ············· 389

스튜어디스 358, 389
스트레스 43
스페인 277
스포츠 270
스포츠면 183
슬기 76, 90, 214
슬기롭다 76, 90, 497
슬라이드 200
슬로바키아 277
슬로베니아 277
슬리퍼 105
슬퍼하다 76
슬프다 76
슬픔 76
습격 314
습격하다 314
습관 90
습기 398
습도 398
습도계 398, 451
습득하다 76, 214, 534
습지 479
습진 43
습하다 398, 497
승강기 147
승객 389
승낙하다 169, 534
승려 227, 358
승리 270, 314
승리하다 270, 314, 534
승마 270
승마복 105
승무 247
승무원 358, 389
승선하다 389, 534
승소 304
승인하다 169, 534
승전 314
승전국 314
승조원 389
승진 358
승차 389
승차권 389
승패 271
승하차 389
승화 497

시 147, 247, 289, 464
시가 342
시각 63, 464
시각디자인 247
시각예술 247
시각장애인 63
시각장애자 5
시간 464
시간강사 200
시간표 200
시건방지다 90
시계 147
시골 148, 479
시골뜨기 5
시골집 148
시공 148, 479
시금치 124, 425
시금털털하다 63, 125
시기 76, 464
시기하다 76, 534
시끄럽다 63
시나리오 247
시나브로 464
시나위 247
시내 479
시내관광 260
시내버스 389
시내전화 189
시냇가 479
시누이 14
시다 63, 125, 497
시대 464
시댁 14, 23
시도하다 534
시동생 14
시들다 425, 497
시력 32, 63
시루떡 125
시름 76
시리다 399
시리아 277
시립대학 200
시말서 169, 358
시멘트 148
시무룩하다 90
시무식 326

시민 289, 326
시민권 289
시민단체 326
시부모 14
시비하다 169, 534
시사 183
시사지 183
시사회 247
시샘 76
시선 63
시설 148
시설물 148
시세 342
시소 265
시속 464
시식하다 125, 534
시신경 32, 64
시아버지 15
시아주버니 15
시야 64
시약 214
시어 169
시어머니 15
시외버스 389
시외전화 189
시원섭섭하다 76
시원하다 64, 399, 497
시위 289, 326
시음하다 534
시의원 289
시의회 289
시인 247, 358
시인하다 169, 534
시일 464
시작하다 534
시장 125, 289, 342, 358
시장가격 342
시장가방 148
시장경제 342
시장기 125
시장성 342
시장점유율 342
시장조사 342
시장하다 125
시절 464
시점 464

시제 169	식료품 125	신년하례식 326
시조 247	식목일 425, 464	신년회 326
시주 227	식물 425	신다 105, 535
시중들다 534	식물원 425	신당 227
시집 15, 23	식물인간 5	신도 227
시집가다 23, 534	식민지 289	신동 5
시집살이 23, 55	식별하다 214, 534	신들리다 227
시찰하다 534	식비 342	신라 277
시청 289	식빵 125	신랑 6, 23
시청각교육 200	식사량 125	신령 227
시청각교재 200	식사하다 125, 535	신령님 227
시청각수업 200	식생활 55	신문 183, 189, 304
시청각실 200	식성 125	신문방송학 214
시청료 183	식수 125	신문배달 183
시청률 183	식염수 43	신문배달원 358
시청자 183	식욕 125	신문사 183
시청하다 64, 183	식욕부진 125	신문판매원 358
시체 55	식용식물 425	신문학 214
시초 464	식용유 125	신바람 77
시치다 105, 534	식은땀 33	신발 105
시큰둥하다 76	식이요법 125	신발장 148
시큼하다 64, 125	식중독 43, 125	신발주머니 148, 201
시키다 169, 534	식초 125	신방 23, 148
시한폭탄 314	식칼 125, 148	신부 6, 23, 228, 358
시합 271	식탁 125, 148	신분 326
시합하다 271	식탁보 148	신분제도 326
시행하다 534	식탁예절 125	신분증 326
시험 200	식탐 125	신사 6
시험감독 200	식품 125	신사복 105
시험감독관 200	식품의약품안전청 289	신사화 105
시험관 214	식혜 125	신상품 342
시험지 201	신 76, 105, 227	신생아 6, 23
시화전 247	신경 33	신생아기 55
식곤증 43	신경계 33	신생아실 23, 43
식구 15	신경과 43	신석기시대 236
식기 125	신경쇠약 43	신선하다 125, 497
식기건조기 125, 148	신경쓰다 77, 535	신성하다 228
식기건조대 125	신경질 77	신세대 6
식기세척기 125, 148	신경질적이다 90	신소설 247
식다 534	신경통 43	신식 497
식단 125	신고하다 169, 535	신앙 228
식당 125, 148, 374	신교 227	신앙고백 228
식도 33	신교도 227	신앙생활 228
식도락 125	신나다 77	신앙심 228
식도락가 125	신내리다 227	신앙인 228
식량 125	신년 464	신약성서 228

신용금고 342	실감나다 77	실크로드 236
신용보증기금 342	실내 148	실토하다 169, 535
신용장 343	실내복 105	실패 497
신용카드 343	실내악단 247	실패하다 497, 535
신음하다 169, 535	실내음악 247	실행하다 535
신인 247	실내장식 148	실향민 6
신인가수 247	실내체육관 271	실험 201, 215
신인배우 247	실내화 105	실험극 247
신임하다 535	실룩거리다 535	실험보고서 215
신입사원 358	실망하다 77, 535	실험실 201, 215
신입생 201	실명 43, 326	실험하다 215, 535
신자 228	실명제 343	싫다 77
신작로 389	실명하다 43	싫어하다 77, 535
신장 33, 434	실물경제 343	싫증나다 77
신장개업 343	실물자산 343	심근경색 43
신장염 43	실물화상기 201	심다 425, 535
신장이식 43	실바람 399	심란하다 77
신접살림 23	실밥 105	심령술 228
신정 464	실뱀 413	심령술사 228
신주 55, 228	실상 497	심리 77, 215, 304
신중하다 90	실선 434	심리학 215
신진대사 33	실수 451	심리학자 215
신참 358	실습 201	심문 304
신청하다 169, 535	실습실 201, 215	심문하다 169, 535
신체 33	실신 43	심방하다 228
신체장애자 6	실신하다 497	심보 90
신축 148	실어증 169	심사 304
신축성 105	실언하다 169, 535	심사숙고하다 77, 215, 535
신춘문예 247	실업 343, 358	심사하다 535
신출내기 6	실업가 343, 358	심술 77, 90
신탁 343	실업자 358	심술부리다 90, 535
신토불이 374	실업학교 201	심술쟁이 6
신파극 247	실온 399	심심하다 64, 126
신학 214	실외 148	심의기관 289
신학기 201	실용음악 247	심의하다 169, 535
신학대학 201	실용주의 215	심장 33
신학자 214	실용품 343	심장마비 43
신호등 389	실용학문 215	심장병 43
신혼 23	실재 497	심장이식 44
신혼가구 148	실제 497	심전도 33
신혼부부 23	실존 497	심정 77
신혼여행 23	실직 358	심통 77
신화 247	실직자 358	심판 271
신흥종교 228	실직하다 358, 535	심포지엄 215
싣다 183, 535	실천하다 535	십 451
실 105	실크 105	십이면체 434

십이지궤양 44	썰렁하다 399	(—고) 싫어하다 77
십이지장 33	썰매타기 265	
십일조 228	썰물 399	
십자가 228	쏘다 314, 535	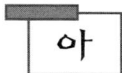
십자매 413	쏘아보다 64, 535	
십장생 247	쏙 497	
십중팔구 497	쏜살같다 464	
십진법 451	쏟다 535	아가 6
십진수 451	쏠다 535	아가미 413
싱가포르 277	쏠리다 497	아가씨 6
싱겁다 64, 90, 126, 497	쐐기문자 169	아군 314
싱싱하다 126, 497	쐬다 535	아궁이 148, 383
싸구려 343	쑤다 126, 536	아기 6
싸늘하다 64, 399, 497	쑤시다 44, 536	아까 464
싸다 33, 343, 497, 535	쑥 126, 425	아깝다 497
싸락눈 399	쑥갓 126, 425	아끼다 343, 536
싸리버섯 425	쑥덕공론 169	아나운서 183, 358
싸우다 314, 535	쑥색 441	아내 15
싸움 314	쑥스럽다 77	아니꼽다 77
싸움터 314	쓰기 169	아담 6
싹 425	쓰다 497, 536	아담하다 434
싹트다 425	쓰다 64, 105, 126, 169, 343,	아동 6
쌀 126	497, 536	아동교육 201
쌀가루 126	쓰다듬다 536	아동극 247
쌀벌레 413	쓰다듬다 64	아동문제 326
쌀쌀맞다 91	쓰러지다 497	아동문학 247
쌀쌀하다 64, 497	쓰레기통 148	아동문학가 247
쌀집 343	쓰레받기 148	아동미술 247
쌀통 126	쓰르라미 413	아동복 105
쌈 126	쓰리다 44, 497	아드님 15
쌈밥 126	쓸개 33	아득하다 497
쌈지 105, 148	쓸다 536	아들 15
쌈지돈 343	쓸데없다 497	아랍어 169
쌉쌀하다 64, 126	쓸모없다 497	아래 479
쌍 451	쓸모있다 497	아래옷 105
쌍곡선 434	쓸쓸하다 77	아래쪽 479
쌍꺼풀 33	씀바귀 126, 425	아랫도리 105
쌍둥이 434	씁쓸하다 64	아랫목 148
쌍둥이자리 479	씨 6, 425	아랫배 33
쌍반점 169	씨름 271	아랫사람 6
쌍점 169	씨방 425	아랫입술 33
쌓다 535	씨앗 425	아령 271
쌓이다 399	씩씩하다 91	아롱다롱 497
쌩쌩 399	씹다 126, 536	아르헨티나 277
썩다 126, 497, 535	씻다 126, 536	아른아른 497
썰다 126, 535	(—고) 싶다 77	아름 451

아름답다 497	아흐레 464	안부묻다 170
아멘 228	아흔 451	안사돈 15
아물다 44, 498, 536	악감정 77	안사람 15
아버님 15	악곡 247	안색 33
아버지 15	악귀 228	안식교 228
아범 15	악기 247	안식일교 228
아부하다 91, 536	악단 247	안심 126
아비 15	악담 169	안심하다 77, 91
아빠 15	악담하다 169, 536	안압 64
아사 55	악당 6	안약 44, 64
아쉬움 77	악독하다 91	안전 389
아쉽다 77	악동 6	안전띠 389
아시아 277	악마 228	안전모 105
아시안게임 271	악몽 33	안전하다 498
아씨 6	악보 247	안정 498
아역 247	악수하다 326, 536	안주 126
아연 215	악습 326	안주인 6
아열대림 425	악어 413	안질 44, 64
아우 15	악역 248	안채 148
아욱 425	악질 6	안타까움 77
아이 6	악천후 399	안타깝다 77
아이스크림 126	악취 64	안테나 189
아이스하키 271	악하다 91	안팎 479
아이슬란드 277	안 479	앉다 536
아일랜드 277	안감 105	앉은뱅이 6
아쟁 247	안개 399	알 413, 451
아저씨 6, 15	안개경보 399	알곡 374
아주 498	안개구름 399	알다 77, 498, 536
아주머니 6, 15	안개꽃 426	알뜰살뜰 343
아주버님 15	안개비 399	알뜰하다 91, 343
아줌마 6	안개주의보 399	알라 228
아지랑이 399	안경 64, 105	알레르기 44
아직 464	안과 44, 64	알록달록 441
아찔하다 77	안구 33, 64	알리다 170, 189, 536
아침 126, 464	안내 189, 326	알림장 201
아카시아 425	안내인 189	알맞다 498
아카시아나무 425	안내장 189	알바니아 277
아파트 148	안내하다 169, 189, 536	알부자 6
아편 44	안다 536	알사탕 126
아편쟁이 6	안데스문명 236	알약 44
아프가니스탄 277	안락사 55	알제리 277
아프다 44, 498	안락의자 148	알칼리성 215
아프리카 277	안마 271	알코올 215, 383
아픔 44	안무 248	알코올램프 215, 383
아홉 451	안무가 248, 358	알타이어족 170
아홉째 451	안방 148	알토 248

알통	33
앓다	44, 536
암	44
암갈색	441
암기하다	77, 536
암놈	413
암매장	55
암매장하다	55
암벽타기	261
암산	451
암송하다	170, 536
암술	426
암실	261
암컷	413
압력	215
압력단체	289
압력솥	126
압박하다	536
압사	55
압수	304
압정	148
앗다	536
앙증맞다	498
앙코르	248
앙큼하다	91
앙탈부리다	536
앙탈부리다	91
앞	464, 479
앞날	464
앞니	33
앞당기다	536
앞뒤	479
앞면	479
앞서	464
앞치마	105, 126
애걸하다	170, 536
애국	289
애국가	289
애국심	289
애국자	289
애꾸눈	33
애늙은이	6
애니메이션	248
애달프다	77
애도하다	170, 536
애독자	183

애무	23
애무하다	23, 536
애벌레	413
애석하다	77
애송이	6
애쓰다	536
애완동물	413
애원하다	170, 536
애인	6
애절하다	77
애정	23, 77
애제자	201
애주가	6
애증	78
애지중지하다	78, 536
애처롭다	78
애청자	183
애초	464
애타다	78
애통하다	78
애호박	126
액	228
액땜하다	228
액면가	343
액상	498
액수	343
액자	148
액정프로젝터	201
액체	215, 498
액화	215, 498
앵두	426
앵두나무	426
앵두빛	441
앵무새	413
야간	464
야광	441
야구	271
야구공	271
야구방망이	271
야구장갑	271
야권	289
야근	358, 374
야단치다	170, 536
야당	289
야들야들	64
야만	236

야만인	6, 236
야맹증	44, 64
야무지다	91
야생동물	413
야생화	426
야수	413
야시장	343
야옹	413
야외극	248
야외극장	248
야외무대	248
야외수업	201
야외음악	248
야외음악당	248
야유하다	170, 536
야유회	261
야자	426
야자수	426
야채	126, 426
야채쥬스	126
야트막하다	434, 498
야하다	498
야학	201
약	44
약간	498
약과	126
약국	44, 343
약도	148, 479
약물중독	44
약방	44
약분	452
약사	7, 44, 358
약세	343
약소국	289
약속	326
약속어음	343
약속하다	170, 536
약손가락	33
약수	126, 452
약시	44, 64
약식	126
약오르다	78
약용식물	426
약육강식	413
약재	44
약주	126

약지 33	양복바지 105	어간 170
약체 33	양복점 105	어귀 479
약초 44, 426	양봉 374	어근 170
약품 44	양봉업 358, 374	어금니 33
약하다 33, 498	양부모 15	어기다 537
약학 215	양산 149	어깨 33
약학대학 201	양상추 127, 426	어느덧 464
약학자 215	양서류 413	어느새 464
약혼 23	양송이 127, 426	어느점 215
약혼녀 23	양수 23, 452	어둡다 64, 441, 498
약혼반지 23	양수기 374	어디 479
약혼식 23	양순하다 91	어떨떨하다 78
약화 498	양식 127, 374	어려움 498
약효 44	양식당 127	어렵다 498
얇립다 91	양식업 359, 374	어루만지다 64, 537
얄팍하다 434, 498	양식장 374	어류 127, 374, 413
얇다 434, 498	양식하다 374	어르다 170, 537
얌전하다 91	양심 78, 304	어르신 7
얌체 91	양심수 304	어른 7
양 7, 413, 452	양아들 15	어리둥절하다 78
양각 248	양아버지 15	어리석다 91
양계업 374	양약 44	어린이 7
양계장 374	양어머니 15	어린이날 464
양고기 126	양어장 374	어린이방 149
양곡 374	양옥 149	어린이집 201
양궁 271	양자 15	어림잡다 452, 537
양귀비 426	양자리 479	어림짐작하다 78, 537
양극 215	양잠업 359, 374	어말어미 170
양녀 15	양장 105	어망 374
양념 126	양장점 105	어머니 15
양념장 126	양조장 127	어머님 15
양념통 127	양주 127	어멈 15
양념하다 127, 537	양지 479	어묵 127
양달 479	양치기 374	어미 16, 170, 413
양담배 127	양탄자 149	어민 326
양도세 148	양파 127, 426	어민 374
양돈업 358, 374	양품점 105	어버이날 464
양동이 148	양호 498	어법 170
양떼구름 399	양호교사 201	어부 359, 374
양력 464	양호실 201	어선 374, 389
양로원 149	양호하다 498	어수선하다 498
양말 105	양화 261	어숫어숫 498
양반 7, 326	얕다 434, 498	어시장 374
양배추 127, 426	얕보다 91, 537	어업 359, 374
양보하다 537	야트막하다 434	어우르다 537
양복 105	얘깃거리 170	어울리다 105, 537

어원 ······ 170	언약하다 ······ 170, 537	엄지손가락 ······ 33
어음 ······ 343	언어 ······ 170	엄청나다 ······ 498
어장 ······ 374	언어교육 ······ 170	엄하다 ······ 91
어저께 ······ 464	언어능력 ······ 170	업 ······ 228
어절 ······ 170	언어사용 ······ 170	업다 ······ 537
어제 ······ 464	언어사용자 ······ 170	업무 ······ 359
어족 ······ 170	언어생활 ······ 171	업보 ······ 228
어중간하다 ······ 434	언어수행 ······ 171	업신여기다 ······ 78, 91, 537
어지럼증 ······ 44	언어순화 ······ 171	없다 ······ 498
어지럽다 ······ 498	언어습득 ······ 171	없애다 ······ 537
어질다 ······ 91	언어예술 ······ 171, 248	없어지다 ······ 537
어찌씨 ······ 170	언어장벽 ······ 171	엉거주춤하다 ······ 91
어촌 ······ 374, 479	언어장애 ······ 171	엉겅퀴 ······ 426
어패류 ······ 127, 374, 413	언어정책 ······ 171	엉기다 ······ 498
어학 ······ 215	언어학 ······ 215	엉덩이 ······ 33
어학실습실 ······ 201	언어학자 ······ 215	엉성하다 ······ 498
어학연수 ······ 201	언쟁하다 ······ 171, 537	엉큼하다 ······ 91
어항 ······ 374	언저리 ······ 479	엉키다 ······ 499
어획 ······ 375	언제 ······ 464	엉터리 ······ 499
어획고 ······ 375	언제나 ······ 464	엎다 ······ 537
어획량 ······ 375	언제든지 ······ 464	엎드리다 ······ 537
어획물 ······ 375	언중 ······ 171	엎어지다 ······ 537
어휘 ······ 170	언짢다 ······ 78	에게문명 ······ 236
어휘론 ······ 170	얹다 ······ 127, 537	에너지 ······ 215, 383
어휘소 ······ 170	얻다 ······ 537	에누리 ······ 343
어휘집 ······ 170	얼굴 ······ 33, 414	에스컬레이터 ······ 149
어흥 ······ 414	얼기설기 ······ 498	에스파냐 ······ 277
억 ······ 452	얼다 ······ 399, 498	에어로빅 ······ 271
억누르다 ······ 537	얼떨결 ······ 78	에이즈 ······ 44
억만장자 ······ 7	얼레 ······ 375	에취 ······ 44
억새 ······ 426	얼룩 ······ 105	에콰도르 ······ 277
억세다 ······ 91, 498	얼룩말 ······ 414	에티오피아 ······ 277
억울하다 ······ 78	얼른 ······ 465	엔 ······ 343
억제하다 ······ 78	얼리다 ······ 127, 537	엔화 ······ 343
억지부리다 ······ 91, 537	얼버무리다 ······ 171, 537	엘리베이터 ······ 149
언급하다 ······ 170, 537	얼빠지다 ······ 91	엘살바도르 ······ 277
언니 ······ 16	얼음 ······ 399	엘엔지 ······ 383
언덕 ······ 479	얼음낚시 ······ 261	엘피지 ······ 384
언덕길 ······ 479	얼큰하다 ······ 64, 127	엥겔계수 ······ 343
언도하다 ······ 170, 537	얽다 ······ 537	여가선용 ······ 261
언론 ······ 183, 189	엄격하다 ······ 91	여객 ······ 261, 389
언론기관 ······ 183	엄동설한 ······ 399	여객기 ······ 389
언론매체 ······ 183, 189	엄마 ······ 16	여객선 ······ 389
언론사 ······ 183	엄살부리다 ······ 91, 537	여걸 ······ 7
언론인 ······ 183	엄지 ······ 33	여고생 ······ 201
언론중재위원회 ······ 183	엄지발가락 ······ 33	여공 ······ 375

여관 149, 375	여의다 537	연구발표 215
여군 314	여인 7	연구비 215
여권 261, 289	여인숙 149, 375	연구생 201
여권사진 261	여자 7	연구소 201, 215
여기 479	여자답다 91	연구수업 201
여기다 78, 537	여자친구 7	연구실 201, 215
여기저기 479	여장부 7	연구원 216, 359
여남은 452	여쭈다 537	연구하다 216, 538
여당 289	여치 414	연구회 216
여대생 201	여태 465	연극 248
여덟 452	여편네 16	연극감상 261
여덟째 452	여학생 7, 201	연극배우 248
여동생 16	여행 261	연극비평 248
여드레 465	여행가 261	연극인 248, 359
여드름 33, 45	여행객 261	연극제 248
여든 452	여행계획 261	연극평론 248
여러 452	여행기 261	연근 426
여러해살이 426	여행담 261	연금 343, 359
여론 289	여행비 261	연기자 248, 359
여류작가 7	여행사 261, 375	연기하다 248, 538
여름 465	여행업 375	연꽃 426
여름내 465	여행자보험 261	연날리기 265
여물 375	여행자수표 261, 343	연대 465
여물다 426, 499	여행지 261	연도 465
여미다 106, 537	여행하다 261, 538	연두색 441
여배우 248	여호와 228	연등행사 228
여백 480	여호와의 증인 228	연락 189
여비 261, 343	역 149, 390	연락두절 189
여사 7	역광 261	연락망 189
여섯 452	역기 271	연락선 390
여섯째 452	역대 465	연령 55, 452
여성 7	역도 271	연료 216, 384
여성문제 326	역사학 215	연립주택 149
여성복 106	역사학자 215	연말 465
여성지 184	역삼각형 434	연말연시 465
여성특별위원회 289	역설하다 171, 538	연말정산 344
여신 343	역술가 228	연못 480
여염집 149	역정 78	연미복 106
여왕 7, 289	엮다 538	연방국 289
여왕벌 414	연 265	연배 452
여우 414	연— 441	연봉 344, 359
여우비 399	연간 465	연분 23
여울 480	연결하다 538	연사 171
여울목 480	연고 45	연상 78, 216, 452
여위다 499	연구 215	연상하다 78, 216, 538
여유있다 343	연구계획서 215	연설 171

연세 55, 452	열기 399	엿 127
연소 384	열다 426, 538	엿듣다 538
연속극 248	열대림 426	엿보다 538
연수 201	열대야 399	엿새 465
연수원 201	열대어 414	엿치기 266
연승 271	열댓 452	영 452
연싸움 265	열도 480	영감 7
연애결혼 23	열등감 78	영결식 55
연애하다 23	열등생 201	영공 290
연약하다 499	열량 216, 384	영관 314
연어 127, 414	열리다 399, 426	영구차 55
연역법 216	열매 426	영구치 33
연예 248	열무 127, 426	영국 277
연예가 248	열무김치 127	영농 375
연예계 248	열반 228	영농법 375
연예면 184	열받다 78	영농인 375
연예인 248, 359	열세 499	영농후계자 375
연예지 248	열쇠 149	영리하다 78, 499
연옥 55	열연 248	영문학 216
연인 7	열정 78	영문학자 216
연장 149	열째 452	영사 290
연주 248	열차 390	영사관 290
연주가 359	열효율 384	영사기 249
연주자 248	열흘 465	영사실 249
연주장 248	염 55	영산홍 426
연주하다 248, 538	염기성 216	영상 249, 399
연주회 248	염라대왕 228	영성체 229
연중 465	염려하다 78	영세 229
연지 106	염료 248	영세명 229
연착하다 538	염불 228	영세민 149, 326
연체료 344	염불하다 229	영수증 344
연초 465	염산 216	영아 7
연출 184	염색 106, 441	영아원 202
연출가 184	염색공예 249	영안실 55
연출자 184, 248, 359	염색약 106	영양 127
연출하다 184, 538	염색하다 106, 442, 538	영양가 127
연탄 216, 384	염소 216, 414	영양사 127, 359
연필 149, 201	염소자리 480	영양소 127
연필꽂이 149	염전 375	영양실조 45
연하 452	염주 229	영양제 45
연하다 441, 499	염증 45	영양크림 106
연하장 189, 326	염치 78, 91	영어 171
연합국 290	염치없다 91	영어학 216
연합하다 290	염통 33	영어학자 216
열 384, 399, 452	엽서 189	영업 344, 359
열광 78	엽전 344	영업사원 344, 359

영업직 359	예리하다 499	예의 92
영업하다 359, 538	예매하다 249, 390, 538	예의범절 92
영역 480	예명 326	예전 465
영원 465	예물 23	예절 92
영원하다 499	예민하다 92	예찬하다 171, 538
영원히 465	예방주사 45	예측하다 78, 216
영장 304	예방하다 45, 538	예치 344
영재 7	예배 229	옛날 465
영재교육 202	예배당 229	옛날옛적 465
영정 261	예배드리다 229	오 452
영주권 290	예배보다 229	오각형 434
영지버섯 426	예보하다 171, 538	오감 64
영치금 344	예복 106	오곡밥 127
영토 290	예불하다 229	오글오글 499
영하 399	예비군 314	오금 34
영해 290	예비비 344	오기 78
영혼 55, 229	예비역 314	오누이 16
영화 249	예쁘다 499	오늘 465
영화감독 249, 359	예산 344	오다 399, 538
영화감상 261	예산청 290	오동나무 426
영화계 249	예삿말 171	오동통 34
영화관 249	예수 229	오두막 149
영화배우 249	예수교 229	오들오들 399
영화상 249	예수님 229	오디 426
영화음악 249	예순 452	오뚝하다 434
영화인 249, 359	예술 249	오뚝이 266
영화제 249	예술가 249, 359	오뚝하다 499
영화평론가 249	예술계 249	오라버니 16
옅다 442	예술고등학교 202	오락 266
옆 480	예술공연 249	오락가락하다 538
옆구리 34	예술단체 249	오락시간 266
옆면 434	예술사 249	오락실 266
옆방 149	예술사진 249, 261	오래되다 499
옆줄 414	예술성 249	오렌지 426
예각 434	예술원 249	오로라 399
예견하다 538	예술의 전당 249	오로지 499
예견하다 78, 216, 538	예술작품 249	오르가즘 23
예고 202	예술지상주의 249	오르내리다 538
예고편 249	예술품 249	오르다 344, 390, 538
예고하다 171, 538	예술혼 249	오르막 480
예금 344	예습 202	오른손잡이 7
예금주 344	예습하다 202, 538	오른쪽 480
예금하다 344, 538	예식 326	오름세 344
예능교육 202	예식장 23	오리 414
예닐곱 452	예언가 359	오리고기 127
예단 23	예언하다 171, 538	오리다 538

오리알 ······ 127, 414	온누리 ······ 480	옹기민속박물관 ······ 237
오만하다 ······ 78, 92	온대림 ······ 427	옹기종기 ······ 499
오목렌즈 ······ 216	온도 ······ 216, 400	옹달샘 ······ 480
오목하다 ······ 434	온도계 ······ 400, 452	옹알거리다 ······ 539
오물오물 ······ 127	온돌 ······ 149, 384	옹알이 ······ 171
오므라이스 ······ 127	온돌방 ······ 149	옻나무 ······ 427
오미자 ······ 426	온두라스 ······ 277	와르르 ······ 499
오밀조밀 ······ 434, 499	온수 ······ 149	와이셔츠 ······ 106
오븐 ······ 127	온순하다 ······ 92	와인색 ······ 442
오빠 ······ 16	온실 ······ 427	완강하다 ······ 92
오색 ······ 442	온양민속박물관 ······ 236	완고하다 ······ 92
오색찬란하다 ······ 442	온유하다 ······ 92	완공 ······ 149
오선지 ······ 249	온음 ······ 249	완구 ······ 149, 266
오세아니아 ······ 277	온종일 ······ 465	완구점 ······ 344
오솔길 ······ 480	온천 ······ 480	완두콩 ······ 128, 427
오스트레일리아 ······ 277	온풍기 ······ 149	완료하다 ······ 539
오스트리아 ······ 277	온화하다 ······ 92	완만하다 ······ 434, 480, 499, 539
오이 ······ 127, 426	올 ······ 452, 465	완벽하다 ······ 499
오이소박이 ······ 127	올— ······ 427	완성 ······ 499
오일장 ······ 55	올라가다 ······ 400, 538	완성품 ······ 344
오전 ······ 465	올라오다 ······ 538	완성하다 ······ 539
오존주의보 ······ 399	올록볼록 ······ 64, 434	완전 ······ 499
오줌 ······ 34	올리다 ······ 149, 538	완전범죄 ······ 304
오줌싸개 ······ 7	올림표 ······ 250	완전하다 ······ 499
오지선다형 ······ 202	올림픽 ······ 271	완제품 ······ 344
오직 ······ 499	올망졸망 ······ 434	완치 ······ 45
오징어 ······ 127, 414	올바르다 ······ 92	왕 ······ 7, 290
오찬 ······ 128	올빼미 ······ 414	왕관 ······ 106
오케스트라 ······ 249	올챙이 ······ 414	왕국 ······ 290
오토바이 ······ 390	올케 ······ 16	왕년 ······ 465
오판하다 ······ 78, 216	올해 ······ 465	왕래하다 ······ 390, 539
오페라 ······ 249	옭다 ······ 539	왕비 ······ 7, 290
오페라가수 ······ 249	옭매다 ······ 539	왕세자 ······ 290
오피스텔 ······ 149	옮기다 ······ 539	왕손 ······ 290
오해하다 ······ 78, 216, 538	옮다 ······ 499, 539	왕왕 ······ 465
오후 ······ 465	옳다 ······ 499	왕자 ······ 7, 290
옥 ······ 375	옷 ······ 106	왕조 ······ 290
옥니 ······ 34	옷가게 ······ 106	왕족 ······ 290
옥상 ······ 149	옷감 ······ 106	왕진 ······ 45
옥색 ······ 442	옷걸이 ······ 106, 149	왕후 ······ 290
옥수수 ······ 128, 427	옷고름 ······ 106	외가 ······ 16
옥수수차 ······ 128	옷매무새 ······ 106	외가집 ······ 16
옥저 ······ 277	옷솔 ······ 106, 149	외계 ······ 480
옥토 ······ 375, 480	옷장 ······ 106, 149	외계인 ······ 480
온기 ······ 399	옷차림 ······ 106	외고 ······ 202
온난전선 ······ 399	옷핀 ······ 106, 149	외과 ······ 45

외교	290
외교관	290, 359
외교통상부	290
외국	290
외국어	171
외국어고등학교	202
외국인	290
외근	359
외다	539
외동딸	16
외래어	171
외롭다	78
외부	480
외사촌	16
외삼촌	16
외상	344
외손녀	16
외손자	16
외손주	16
외숙모	16
외숙부	16
외식	128
외식산업	375
외아들	17
외양간	375
외우다	79, 171, 539
외유내강	92
외장	149
외장재	149
외채	344
외출복	106
외치다	171, 539
외톨이	7
외투	106
외판원	344, 359
외할머니	17
외할아버지	17
외향적이다	92
외화	344
외환	344
외환보유고	344
외환시장	344
왼손잡이	7
왼쪽	480
요	149
요가	271

요구르트	128
요구하다	171, 539
요금	344
요도	34
요도염	45
요란하다	64
요르단	277
요리	128
요리사	128, 359
요리하다	128, 539
요사스럽다	92
요새	314, 466
요술	266
요식업	375
요양원	45
요양하다	45, 539
요일	466
요절	55
요즘	466
요청하다	171, 539
요통	45
요트	271, 390
욕	171
욕구	79
욕망	79
욕설	171
욕실	150
욕심	79
욕심쟁이	7
욕쟁이	7
욕조	150
욕하다	92, 171, 539
용	414
용감무쌍하다	314
용감하다	92
용기	92, 150
용돈	344
용맹하다	314
용사	314
용서하다	79, 539
용암	400
용액	499
용언	171
용역	359, 375
용의자	304
용해	499

용해도	216
우간다	278
우글우글	499
우기다	92, 171, 539
우동	128
우두머리	326
우등고속버스	390
우등상	202
우등생	202
우랄어족	171
우람하다	435, 499
우량계	400, 452
우러러보다	539
우러르다	79, 539
우렁쉥이	414
우렁이	414
우렁차다	64
우레	400
우려하다	79
우롱하다	171, 539
우루과이	278
우르르쾅쾅	400
우리	150, 375, 414
우리나라	290
우리다	128
우물	480
우물우물	128
우박	400
우방	290
우방국	290
우비	107
우산	150
우산꽂이	150
우상숭배	229
우세	499
우세하다	499
우수	466, 499
우수하다	499
우스갯소리	171
우승	271
우시장	375
우엉	427
우울증	45, 79
우울하다	79
우월감	79
우유	128

우유부단하다 … 92	운반 … 390	웃음 … 79
우유빛 … 442	운반비 … 390	웃저고리 … 107
우족탕 … 128	운반선 … 390	웅대하다 … 435, 500
우주 … 480	운석 … 480	웅덩이 … 480
우주개발 … 480	운소 … 172	웅변가 … 172
우주먼지 … 480	운송 … 390	웅성거리다 … 540
우주복 … 480	운송비 … 390	웅장하다 … 435
우주비행사 … 480	운송수단 … 390	웅크리다 … 540
우주선 … 390, 480	운송업 … 375	원 … 344, 435, 452
우주여행 … 480	운송하다 … 539	원가 … 344
우주인 … 480	운수 … 229	원고 … 184, 304
우주정거장 … 480	운수업 … 375, 390	원고료 … 184
우주탐사 … 480	운영하다 … 359, 539	원근법 … 250
우쭐대다 … 92, 539	운율 … 250	원금 … 344
우체국 … 189, 290	운임 … 390	원급 … 172
우체통 … 189	운전 … 390	원기둥 … 435
우측 … 480	운전기사 … 359, 390	원내총무 … 290
우크라이나 … 278	운전면허시험 … 390	원년 … 466
우편물 … 189	운전면허증 … 390	원동력 … 384
우편배달부 … 359	운전병 … 314	원두막 … 150
우편번호 … 150, 190	운전사 … 390	원두커피 … 128
우편엽서 … 190	운전석 … 390	원로가수 … 250
우편집배원 … 190	운전하다 … 390, 539	원로배우 … 250
우편함 … 190	운하 … 480	원료 … 375
우표 … 190	운항하다 … 390, 539	원료시장 … 344
우회전 … 390	운행 … 390	원리 … 216
운동 … 271	울긋불긋 … 442	원만하다 … 92
운동감각 … 271	울다 … 79, 414, 539	원망 … 79
운동경기 … 271	울먹이다 … 539	원망하다 … 79
운동기구 … 271	울보 … 7	원반 … 272
운동량 … 271	울부짖다 … 172, 539	원반던지기 … 272
운동모자 … 271	울음 … 79	원불교 … 229
운동복 … 107, 271	울창하다 … 500	원뿔형 … 435
운동부 … 271	울타리 … 150	원산지 … 375
운동선수 … 271, 359	울퉁불퉁 … 64, 435	원색 … 442
운동신경 … 271	울화통 … 79	원생 … 202
운동장 … 202, 271	움막 … 150	원소 … 216, 452
운동정신 … 272	움직씨 … 172	원소기호 … 216
운동종목 … 272	움직이다 … 539	원수 … 314
운동하다 … 272, 539	움츠리다 … 539	원숙하다 … 500
운동화 … 107, 272	움큼 … 452	원숭이 … 414
운동회 … 272	움트다 … 427	원시 … 34, 45, 64
운량 … 400	움푹하다 … 435, 500	원시사회 … 326
운명 … 55	웃다 … 79, 540	원시시대 … 466
운명하시다 … 539	웃어른 … 7	원시인 … 7, 237
운문 … 250	웃옷 … 107	원앙 … 23, 414

원양어선 375, 390	위법 304	유년기 55
원양어업 375	위산 34	유능하다 500
원어민 172	위생병 314	유달리 500
원예업 359	위성 481	유대교 229
원예학 216	위성방송 184, 190	유도 272
원예학자 216	위성중계 184, 190	유도분만 24
원유 375, 384	위성통신 190	유도신문 304
원인 216	위암 45	유도하다 540
원자 216	위약금 345	유라시아 278
원자력 216, 384	위염 45	유람선 390
원자로 216, 384	위인 7	유람하다 261, 540
원자재 375	위인전 184	유럽 278
원장 202	위자료 345	유력하다 500
원정경기 272	위장 34	유령 229
원주민 7	위조지폐 345	유로화 345
원주율 452	위조하다 540	유료 345
원통하다 79	위쪽 481	유리 150
원통형 435	위치 481	유리수 452
원피스 107	위치하다 481	유림 229
원하다 79, 540	위탁금 345	유망주 8
원형 435, 500	위탁판매 345	유명인 8
원화 344	위통 45	유명인사 8, 326
월 172, 466	위패 55	유목민 8
월간지 184	위헌 304	유물 55, 237
월경 24, 34	위험하다 500	유미주의 250
월계관 107, 272	윗도리 107	유발하다 540
월계수 427	윗목 150	유방 34
월급 344, 359	윗몸일으키기 272	유방암 45
월급쟁이 359	윗배 34	유별나다 500
월드컵축구 272	윗사람 8	유보하다 540
월부 344	윗입술 34	유복자 8
월부금 344	유가공 375	유부남 24
월세 150	유가족 55	유부녀 24
월식 400, 481	유가증권 345	유사품 345
월요일 466	유격대 314	유사하다 435, 500
월척 261, 375	유격전 314	유산 56
월출 400	유고슬라비아 278	유산균 128, 414
웨딩드레스 24, 107	유골 55	유생 229
위 34, 481	유괴 304	유서 56
위경련 45	유괴범 304	유선방송 184, 190
위관 314	유교 229	유성 481
위궤양 45	유권자 290	유세 290
위도 481	유급 202	유세장 290
위령제 55	유기농업 376	유수같다 466
위문품 345	유기정학 202	유식하다 79
위반 304	유난히 500	유신론 229

유아 ·· 8	유해 ······································ 56	웃 ·· 266
유아교육 ································ 202	유행가 ·································· 250	웃놀이 ·································· 266
유아기 ···································· 56	유행병 ···································· 45	으깨다 ························· 128, 540
유아복 ·································· 107	유행성출혈열 ························ 45	으뜸 ···································· 453
유아어 ·································· 172	유행어 ·································· 172	으뜸음 ·································· 250
유아원 ·································· 202	유형 ···································· 435	으름장 ·································· 172
유언 ·· 56	유혹하다 ······························ 540	으리으리 ······························ 150
유언비어 ······························ 172	유화 ···································· 250	으리으리하다 ······················ 435
유연화장수 ·························· 107	유효하다 ······························ 500	윽박지르다 ·························· 540
유원지 ·································· 266	유흥가 ·································· 376	은 ·· 376
유의어 ·································· 172	유흥비 ·································· 261	은광 ···································· 376
유의하다 ······························ 540	유흥업 ·································· 376	은발 ······································ 34
유익하다 ······························ 500	유흥업소 ······························ 376	은방울꽃 ······························ 427
유인원 ·································· 414	육 ·· 453	은빛 ···································· 442
유일신 ·································· 229	육가공 ·································· 376	은사 ···································· 202
유일하다 ······························ 500	육각형 ·································· 435	은색 ···································· 442
유자 ···································· 427	육감 ······································ 64	은어 ··························· 172, 414
유자차 ·································· 128	육감적 ···································· 65	은은하다 ······························ 442
유적 ···································· 237	육개장 ·································· 128	은총 ···································· 229
유전 ···························· 376, 414	육교 ···································· 390	은하계 ·································· 481
유전병 ···································· 45	육군 ···································· 314	은하수 ·································· 481
유전자 ······················· 34, 414	육군사관학교 ·············· 202, 314	은행 ··························· 345, 376
유조선 ·································· 390	육류 ···································· 128	은행가 ·································· 345
유조차 ·································· 390	육면체 ·································· 435	은행나무 ······························ 427
유죄 ···································· 304	육상경기 ······························ 272	은행대출 ······························ 345
유지하다 ······························ 540	육성회비 ······························ 202	은행원 ·························· 345, 359
유채꽃 ·································· 427	육수 ···································· 128	은행장 ·························· 345, 359
유채색 ·································· 442	육식동물 ······························ 414	은혼식 ···································· 24
유추 ·························· 79, 216	육중하다 ······························ 500	은화 ···································· 345
유추하다 ····················· 79, 216	육지 ···································· 481	읊다 ··························· 172, 540
유충 ···································· 414	육체 ······································ 34	음각 ···································· 250
유치 ······································ 34	육탄전 ·································· 314	음경 ······························ 24, 34
유치원 ·································· 202	육포 ···································· 128	음계 ···································· 250
유치원생 ······························ 202	육풍 ···································· 400	음극 ···································· 217
유치장 ·································· 304	육회 ···································· 128	음독 ···································· 172
유쾌하다 ································ 79	윤년 ···································· 466	음란하다 ································ 92
유태교 ·································· 229	윤달 ···································· 466	음력 ···································· 466
유통 ···································· 345	윤리 ·························· 304, 327	음료 ···································· 128
유통경로 ······························ 345	윤일 ···································· 466	음료수 ·································· 128
유통구조 ······························ 345	윤회 ·························· 56, 229	음매 ···································· 414
유통마진 ······························ 345	율무 ···································· 128	음반 ···································· 250
유통망 ·································· 345	율무차 ·································· 128	음색 ···································· 250
유품 ······································ 56	융자 ···································· 345	음성 ···································· 172
유학 ······················· 202, 216, 229	융통성 ···································· 92	음성언어 ······························ 172
유학생 ·································· 202	융해 ···································· 217	음성학 ·································· 172
유학자 ·································· 217	융해열 ·································· 217	음소 ···································· 172

음수 453	응용력 92, 217	의원내각제 291
음식 128	응용미술 251	의자 150, 203
음식문화 237	응용하다 217	의젓하다 92
음식점 128, 345, 376	응원가 272	의존하다 540
음악 250	응원단 272	의지력 92
음악가 250, 360	응원하다 272, 540	의지하다 540
음악감상 261	응접세트 150	의처증 46
음악감상실 250	응접실 150	의태어 172
음악계 250	응하다 172, 540	의학 217
음악관 250	의결기관 291	의학자 217
음악당 251	의과대학 202	의형제 17
음악대학 202	의구심 79	의회 291
음악성 251	의기양양하다 92	의회정치 291
음악실 202, 251	의논하다 172, 540	이 34, 414, 453
음악인 251	의뢰인 8	이감 304
음악제 251	의료기구 45	이곳 481
음악학 217	의료보험 45	이곳저곳 481
음악회 251	의료보험증 45	이글이글 400, 500
음영 442	의료원 45	이기다 272, 315, 540
음운 172	의료진 45	이끌다 540
음운론 172	의류 107	이끼 427
음자리표 251	의무 327	이날이때 466
음절 172	의무경찰 304	이내 466
음정 251	의무병 315	이농 376
음주운전 390	의문대명사 172	이농현상 376
음주측정기 390	의문문 172	이다 540
음지 481	의문사 56	이단 229
음탕하다 92	의미론 172	이동 391
음표 251	의복 107	이동통신 190
음향 65, 251	의부증 45	이동하다 540
음향기기 65	의붓아버지 17	이듬해 466
음화 261	의붓어머니 17	이등변삼각형 435
음흉하다 92	의붓자식 17	이등병 315
읍 150, 290	의사 46, 360	이따가 466
읍내 150	의사소통 172	이따금 466, 500
읍사무소 290	의상 107, 251	이때 466
읍장 291, 360	의생활 56, 107	이라크 278
응고 500	의석 291	이란 278
응고점 217	의석수 291	이랑 376
응고하다 500	의성어 172	이레 466
응급실 45	의심 79	이력서 172, 360
응급환자 45	의심하다 79	이론 217
응달 481	의약품 46	이롭다 500
응답하다 172, 540	의욕 79	이루다 540
응시자 202	의용군 315	이륙하다 391, 540
응시하다 65, 540	의원 46, 291	이르다 172, 466, 540

이름		이십사절기	466	이혼	24
이름	327	이쑤시개	129, 150	이혼소송	305
이름씨	172	이앙기	376	익다	427, 500
이름표	203, 327	이앙법	376	익사	56
이리	414, 481	이야기	172	익숙하다	500
이리저리	481	이야기하다	172, 540	익히다	129, 203, 541
이마	34	이어달리기	272	인	229, 453
이메일	190	이용료	376	인간	8
이명증	46	이용업	376	인간문화재	237
이모	17	이용하다	540	인간미	92
이모부	17	이웃	8, 150, 327, 481	인간성	92
이모작	376	이웃사촌	8	인간적이다	92
이무기	414	이웃집	150	인감도장	150
이미	466	이월금	345	인건비	345, 376
이민	150, 291	이유식	129	인격	93
이민국	291	이윤	345	인공	500
이민족	291	이의신청	305	인공분만	24
이발사	360, 376	이익	345	인공수정	24
이발소	107, 376	이익금	345	인공심장	46
이발하다	107, 540	이인칭	173	인공위성	190, 481
이방인	8	이자	345	인공호흡	34
이번	466	이자율	345	인구	327
이번달	466	이장	291	인구동향	327
이별하다	540	이재민	8	인구문제	327
이복형제	17	이전	466	인구밀도	327
이부자리	150	이제	466	인구분포	327
이불	150	이종사촌	17	인구이동	327
이브	8	이주	150	인구정책	327
이비인후과	46, 65	이중국적	291	인구조사	327
이빨	34	이중언어자	173	인구폭발	327
이사	150, 360	이중창	251	인권	327
이사가다	540	이진법	453	인권변호사	305
이사오다	540	이집트	278	인권보호	327
이사장	203	이집트문명	237	인권선언	327
이삭	376	이쪽	481	인권유린	327
이산가족	17	이쪽저쪽	481	인근	481
이삿짐센터	376	이차산업	376	인기	251
이상	500	이차원	481	인기가수	251
이상하다	500	이체	345	인기배우	251
이성	24, 79, 217	이층집	150	인내	93
이스라엘	278	이탈리아	278	인내력	93
이스트	128	이태리	278	인내심	93
이슬	400	이틀	466	인대	34
이슬람교	229	이하	500	인도	278, 391
이슬비	400	이해력	92	인도네시아	278
이승	56, 229	이해하다	79, 217, 541	인도문명	237
이식수술	46				

인도유럽어족 173
인력 217, 376
인력시장 345
인류 8
인류문명 237
인류문화 237
인류학 217
인류학자 217
인류 305
인맥 327
인명 8, 56
인문과학 217
인문대학 203
인물사진 261
인물화 251
인민 291
인민공화국 291
인분 453
인사 8, 327
인사발령 360
인사성 93
인사이동 360
인사하다 173, 327, 541
인삼 427
인삼차 129
인상 34, 345
인상깊다 79
인상적이다 79
인색하다 93
인생 56
인생관 93
인생살이 56
인성 93
인솔 327
인솔교사 203
인솔하다 541
인쇄 184
인쇄물 184
인쇄소 184
인쇄업 360
인쇄하다 184
인스턴트식품 129
인습 327
인식하다 79, 217, 541
인심 93
인어 414

인연 230
인용 173
인용하다 173, 541
인재 8
인절미 129
인접하다 481, 541
인정 93
인제 466
인조 500
인조인간 8
인종 8
인주 150
인지하다 79, 217
인척 17
인칭 173
인칭대명사 173
인터넷 190
인턴사원 360
인품 93
인하 345
인해전술 315
인형 266
인형극 251
인형놀이 266
인화 261
인화지 262
인화하다 262
일 360, 453, 466
일간 467
일간지 184, 190
일거리 360
일곱 453
일곱째 453
일광절약시간 467
일구다 376, 541
일기 400
일기예보 400
일기장 173
일깨우다 541
일꾼 360
일년생 427
일다 400, 541
일당 305, 345, 360
일등병 315
일러스트레이션 251
일몰 400

일문학 217
일문학자 217
일방통행로 391
일벌 414
일본 278
일본어 173
일부다처제 24
일부일처제 24
일사병 46, 400
일상복 107
일상어 173
일선 315
일시불 346
일식 129, 400
일식집 129
일신교 230
일어나다 541
일어서다 541
일어학 217
일어학자 217
일요일 467
일으키다 541
일인극 251
일인칭 173
일자리 360
일전 467
일직 360
일찌감치 467
일차산업 376
일차원 481
일처다부제 24
일체감 80
일출 400
일치 500
일컫다 173, 541
일터 360
일편단심 80, 93
일품요리 129
일하다 360, 541
일흔 453
읽기 173
읽다 173, 541
잃다 541
잃어버리다 541
임관 315
임금 291, 346

임금 665

임금 … 360	입사하다 … 360	잎새 … 427
임기응변 … 93	입술 … 34	
임대 … 150, 346	입술연지 … 107	
임대가 … 346	입시 … 203	
임대가격 … 346	입시생 … 203	## 자
임대료 … 150, 346	입심 … 173	
임대주택 … 150	입씨름 … 173	
임대하다 … 346	입양아 … 17	자 … 150, 203, 435, 453
임박하다 … 467	입양하다 … 17	자가용 … 391
임부복 … 107	입원 … 46	자갈 … 150, 481
임산물 … 376	입원실 … 46	자격정지 … 305
임산부 … 24	입원하다 … 46	자격증 … 327
임시교사 … 203	입자 … 500	자격지심 … 80, 93
임시국회 … 291	입장하다 … 541	자궁 … 24, 34
임시열차 … 391	입정 … 305	자궁암 … 46
임시직 … 360	입증 … 217	자그마치 … 500
임시직원 … 360	입증하다 … 217	자극 … 217
임신 … 24	입질 … 262	자금 … 346
임신하다 … 24	입질하다 … 262	자긍심 … 80, 93
임야 … 427	입찰 … 346	자기력 … 384
임업 … 360, 376	입천장 … 34	자기앞수표 … 346
임연수어 … 129, 414	입추 … 467	자기장 … 217
임원 … 360	입춘 … 467	자꾸 … 467
임자씨 … 173	입하 … 467	자녀 … 17
임종하다 … 56	입학 … 203	자다 … 541
임질 … 46	입학금 … 203	자당 … 17
임차료 … 346	입학생 … 203	자동사 … 173
임학 … 217	입학시험 … 203	자동차 … 391
입 … 34, 415	입학식 … 203	자동차등록증 … 391
입관 … 56	입학하다 … 203	자동차세 … 346
입구 … 481	입헌 … 305	자동판매기 … 129
입국사증 … 291	입헌군주국 … 291	자동화 … 376
입금 … 346	입헌주의 … 291, 305	자두 … 427
입다 … 107, 541	입후보 … 291	자라 … 415
입대 … 315	입후보자 … 291	자라다 … 427, 541
입대하다 … 315, 541	잇다 … 541	자랑하다 … 93, 541
입덧 … 24	잇몸 … 34	자력 … 384
입동 … 467	있다 … 500	자루 … 151, 453
입력 … 190	잉꼬 … 415	자르다 … 541
입력하다 … 173	잉꼬부부 … 24	자리 … 481
입맛 … 65, 129	잉어 … 129, 415	자막 … 251
입맛다시다 … 129	잉카문명 … 237	자만심 … 80, 93
입방아찧다 … 541	잉태 … 24	자매 … 17
입법기관 … 346	잊다 … 80, 541	자매품 … 346
입법부 … 291, 305	잎 … 427	자메이카 … 278
입병 … 46	잎사귀 … 427	자명종시계 … 151

자몽 427	자영업 346, 360	작물 376
자문기관 291	자외선 401	작별하다 542
자문하다 541	자욱하다 401, 500	작사 251
자물쇠 151	자유기고가 184, 360	작사가 360
자반 129	자유주의 291	작사하다 251, 542
자백 305	자유주의국가 291	작살 377
자백하다 173, 541	자유형 272	작성하다 542
자본 346	자율학습 203	작약 427
자본가 346	자음 173	작업 377
자본금 346	자음동화 173	작업대 377
자본주의 291, 327	자작농 376	작업반장 377
자본주의국가 291	자잘하다 435, 501	작업복 107, 377
자부심 80, 93	자장가 251	작업시간 377
자비 230, 346	자장면 129	작업실 377
자빠지다 541	자재 376	작업장 377
자살 56	자전 481	작용반작용의 법칙 217
자살하다 56	자전거 266, 272, 391	작용하다 217, 542
자서전 184	자정 467	작은곰자리 481
자석 217	자존심 80, 93	작은달 467
자선공연 251	자주 442, 467, 501	작은따옴표 173
자선바자회 346	자주색 442	작은방 151
자세 93	자지 34	작은아버지 17
자손 17	자정하다 173, 541	작은어머니 17
자수 107	자취방 151	작은집 17
자수정 376	자취하다 151	작은창자 34
자습서 203	자치기 266	작전 315
자식 17	자치단체 327	작정하다 80, 542
자신감 80, 93	자치령 291	작품사진 251, 262
자연 400, 500	자치활동 327	작황 377
자연과학 217, 400	자치회 327	잔고 346
자연대학 203	자칭하다 173, 541	잔금 346
자연법칙 400, 415	자퇴 203	잔돈 346
자연보호 400	자판 190	잔디 427
자연분만 24	자판기 129	잔뜩 501
자연사 56	자폐증 46	잔말 173
자연색 442	자화자찬하다 173, 542	잔병치레 46
자연수 453	작가 173, 184, 251, 360	잔소리하다 173, 542
자연숭배 230, 400	작곡 251	잔액 346
자연식품 400	작곡가 251, 360	잔잔하다 401
자연신앙 230	작곡하다 251, 542	잔챙이 262
자연재해 400	작년 467	잔치 327
자연주의 400	작다 435, 453, 501	잘 501
자연파괴 400	작동하다 542	잘다 435, 501
자연현상 401	작두 376	잘록하다 435, 501
자연환경 401	작명하다 327	잘못하다 542
자영농 376	작문 173	잠 34

잠그다 542	장군 315	장식하다 151, 542
잠깐 467	장기 34, 46, 262, 266	장신구 107
잠꾸러기 8	장기자랑 266	장아찌 130
잠들다 542	장기판 262	장애인 8
잠비아 278	장끼 415	장어 415
잠수정 315	장난 266	장염 46
잠수함 315, 391	장난감 151, 266	장음계 251
잠시 467	장난꾸러기 8	장의사 56, 360
잠업 377	장난치다 266	장의차 56, 391
잠옷 107	장남 17	장인 17, 251
잠자리 151, 415	장녀 17	장인어른 18
잠자리채 266	장년 8	장인정신 251
잡곡 377	장년기 56	장작 384
잡귀 230	장님 8, 65	장작개비 384
잡다 377, 542	장단 251, 435	장점 501
잡답하다 173, 542	장담하다 173, 542	장정 8
잡비 346	장대높이뛰기 272	장조 251
잡수시다 129, 542	장도리 151	장조림 130
잡식동물 415	장독 130	장지 34, 56
잡아내다 542	장독대 130	장차 467
잡아매다 542	장려금 346	장치 377
잡역부 360	장례 56	장터 346
잡종 415	장례식 56	장티프스 46
잡지 184, 190	장로 230	장판 151
잡지사 184	장로교 230	장편소설 252
잡채 129	장롱 151	장학관 203
잡초 427	장마 401	장학금 203, 346
잡화상 346	장마전선 401	장학사 203
잡화점 346	장모 17	장학생 203
잣 130	장모님 17	장화 107
잣나무 427	장물 305	잦다 467
잣다 542	장물아비 305	재개발 151
잣죽 130	장미 427	재건축 151
장 151, 346, 453	장방형 435	재고 347
장가 24	장보기 346	재고정리 347
장가가다 24, 542	장본인 327	재고품 347
장갑 107	장부 346	재교육 203
장갑차 315, 391	장사 56, 346	재귀대명사 174
장거리전화 190	장사군 346, 360	재다 107, 130, 453, 542
장관 292, 360	장사하다 346, 542	재단 107
장관급 315	장성 315	재단사 360
장교 315	장소 481	재단하다 107, 542
장구 251	장송곡 56	재두루미 415
장구벌레 415	장수하늘소 415	재떨이 151
장국 130	장식장 151	재래시장 347
장국밥 130	장식품 151	재무 347

재물 ····· 347	잼 ····· 130	적극적이다 ····· 93
재미 ····· 80	잼잼 ····· 266	적금 ····· 347
재미교포 ····· 292	잿빛 ····· 442	적금하다 ····· 347
재미없다 ····· 80	쟁기 ····· 377	적다 ····· 174, 453, 501, 543
재미있다 ····· 80	쟁반 ····· 130	적당하다 ····· 501
재방송 ····· 184	쟁의 ····· 327	적대국 ····· 292
재배 ····· 377	저가 ····· 347	적도 ····· 482
재배하다 ····· 377, 542	저고리 ····· 107	적령기 ····· 56
재벌 ····· 347	저곳 ····· 481	적립 ····· 347
재범 ····· 305	저금 ····· 347	적립금 ····· 347
재봉 ····· 107	저금하다 ····· 347, 542	적막하다 ····· 65, 501
재봉사 ····· 360	저기 ····· 481	적발하다 ····· 543
재봉틀 ····· 107, 151	저기압 ····· 401	적법 ····· 305
재산 ····· 347	저녁 ····· 130, 468	적삼 ····· 107
재산세 ····· 151, 347	저능아 ····· 8	적색 ····· 442
재색 ····· 442	저당 ····· 347	적설량 ····· 401
재선 ····· 292	저렴하다 ····· 347	적성 ····· 93
재선거 ····· 292	저리 ····· 481	적십자사 ····· 327
재수생 ····· 203	저리다 ····· 46, 542	적외선 ····· 401
재일동포 ····· 292	저명인사 ····· 327	적용하다 ····· 217
재작년 ····· 467	저물다 ····· 401, 501	적자 ····· 347
재잘거리다 ····· 174, 542	저미다 ····· 130, 542	적자생존 ····· 415
재적 ····· 203	저번 ····· 468	적적하다 ····· 80
재적생 ····· 203	저서 ····· 184, 217	적지 ····· 315
재정 ····· 347	저소득층 ····· 327	적진 ····· 315
재정경제부 ····· 292	저술하다 ····· 174, 542	적혈구 ····· 35
재주 ····· 93	저승 ····· 56, 230	전 ····· 130, 468
재주넘기 ····· 266	저승사자 ····· 56, 230	전갈자리 ····· 482
재주부리다 ····· 542	저울 ····· 151, 453	전골 ····· 130
재즈 ····· 252	저울자리 ····· 481	전공 ····· 203
재채기 ····· 35	저자 ····· 174	전공하다 ····· 217
재촉하다 ····· 174, 542	저작권 ····· 184	전과 ····· 204
재치 ····· 93	저주하다 ····· 174, 542	전과자 ····· 305
재킷 ····· 107	저지대 ····· 482	전광판 ····· 151
재판 ····· 305	저지르다 ····· 542	전구 ····· 151
재판관 ····· 305	저지하다 ····· 174, 542	전국 ····· 292
재판소 ····· 305	저쪽 ····· 482	전국구 ····· 292
재판정 ····· 305	저축 ····· 347	전국체전 ····· 272
재학 ····· 203	저축하다 ····· 347, 543	전극 ····· 218
재학생 ····· 203	저택 ····· 151	전기 ····· 184, 218, 384
재혼 ····· 24	저항 ····· 315	전기기사 ····· 360
재화 ····· 347	저항하다 ····· 315	전기요금 ····· 347
재활교육 ····· 203	저혈압 ····· 46	전기장판 ····· 151
재활용 ····· 347	적 ····· 315	전나무 ····· 427
재활용품 ····· 347	적국 ····· 292, 315	전단 ····· 190
재활학교 ····· 203	적군 ····· 315	전달하다 ····· 543

전담교사 ········· 204	전시하다 ········· 543	전축 ········· 151, 252
전당대회 ········· 292	전시회 ········· 252	전치 ········· 46
전당포 ········· 347	전압 ········· 218	전통 ········· 327
전도 ········· 230	전업 ········· 361	전통가요 ········· 252
전도사 ········· 230, 361	전역 ········· 316	전통문화 ········· 237
전도하다 ········· 230	전열기 ········· 384	전통사회 ········· 328
전동기 ········· 377, 384	전염 ········· 46	전통혼례 ········· 24
전등 ········· 151	전염병 ········· 46	전투 ········· 316
전등갓 ········· 151	전용강의실 ········· 204	전투경찰 ········· 305
전람회 ········· 252	전용도로 ········· 391	전투기 ········· 316, 391
전래동화 ········· 252	전용차로 ········· 391	전투력 ········· 316
전래문화 ········· 237	전용차선 ········· 391	전투복 ········· 316
전략 ········· 315	전우 ········· 316	전투부대 ········· 316
전략가 ········· 315	전우애 ········· 316	전투적이다 ········· 316
전력 ········· 218, 384	전원주택 ········· 151	전투하다 ········· 316, 543
전류 ········· 218, 384	전위예술 ········· 252	전투함 ········· 316
전망 ········· 151	전인교육 ········· 204	전파 ········· 190
전면 ········· 482	전임강사 ········· 204	전파하다 ········· 237
전문가 ········· 361	전자계산학 ········· 218	전하다 ········· 190, 543
전문용어 ········· 174	전자관 ········· 218	전학 ········· 204
전문직 ········· 361	전자레인지 ········· 130	전학생 ········· 204
전반적 ········· 501	전자석 ········· 218	전해질 ········· 218
전방 ········· 315, 482	전자오락 ········· 266	전화 ········· 190
전범 ········· 315	전자오락실 ········· 266	전화걸다 ········· 174
전병 ········· 130	전자우편 ········· 190	전화국 ········· 190, 292
전보 ········· 190	전자파 ········· 218	전화기 ········· 151, 190
전복 ········· 130, 415	전자회로 ········· 218	전화번호 ········· 151, 190
전복죽 ········· 130	전장 ········· 316	전화번호부 ········· 190
전부 ········· 501	전쟁 ········· 316	전화선 ········· 151, 190
전분 ········· 130	전쟁고아 ········· 316	전화요금 ········· 347
전사 ········· 56, 315	전쟁놀이 ········· 266	전화카드 ········· 190, 347
전사하다 ········· 315	전쟁터 ········· 316	전화하다 ········· 174, 190, 543
전생 ········· 56	전적으로 ········· 501	절 ········· 174, 230
전선 ········· 151, 316	전제 ········· 218	절구 ········· 130
전설 ········· 252	전주 ········· 252	절굿공이 ········· 130
전성기 ········· 468	전지 ········· 218, 384	절기 ········· 468
전성시대 ········· 468	전지훈련 ········· 272	절다 ········· 46, 543
전세 ········· 151	전진 ········· 391	절단하다 ········· 543
전속가수 ········· 252	전진하다 ········· 543	절대 ········· 501
전송 ········· 190	전차 ········· 316, 391	절대값 ········· 453
전술 ········· 316	전채요리 ········· 130	절대자 ········· 230
전술가 ········· 316	전처 ········· 18	절뚝거리다 ········· 543
전승 ········· 316	전철 ········· 391	절름발이 ········· 8
전승문화 ········· 237	전철표 ········· 391	절망 ········· 80
전승하다 ········· 237	전체적 ········· 501	절망감 ········· 80
전시장 ········· 252	전체주의 ········· 292	절벽 ········· 482

절약하다 93, 347, 543	정각 468	정보산업 191
절이다 130, 543	정갈하다 501	정보산업고등학교 204
절친하다 328	정감 80	정보수집 191
절편 130	정강이 35	정보원 191
절하다 328, 543	정거장 391	정보지 191
젊다 501	정견 292	정보처리 191
젊은이 8	정겹다 80, 93	정보처리사 191
점 35, 230, 435, 453	정경 292	정보통 191
점괘 230	정계 292	정보통신부 191, 292
점보다 230	정구 272	정보화 191
점선 435	정권 292	정복하다 543
점성술 230	정권교체 292	정부 8, 292
점수 204	정규군 316	정부간행물 184
점심 130, 468	정근상 204	정부종합청사 292
점원 347, 361	정기간행물 184	정비병 316
점자 65, 174	정기구독 184	정비사 391
점잖다 93	정기국회 292	정사각형 435
점쟁이 230, 361	정기예금 347	정삼각형 435
점집 230	정기적금 347	정상인 8
점치다 230	정년퇴임 361	정서 80
점퍼 108	정답다 93	정서법 174
점포 152, 347	정당 292	정설 218
점화 384	정당하다 501	정성 93
접 453	정독 174	정세 292, 501
접대부 361, 377	정들다 80	정수 453
접대하다 93, 543	정떨어지다 80	정수기 130
접두사 174	정량 453	정수리 35
접미사 174	정류장 391	정식 130
접붙이다 427	정맥 35	정신 80, 218
접사 174	정면 482	정신과 46
접선 190	정문 152	정신력 80, 218
접속 190	정물 252	정신박약아 9, 46
접속사 174	정물화 252	정신병 46
접속하다 543	정미소 348, 377	정신병자 9, 46
접시 130, 453	정미하다 377	정액권 348, 391
접시꽃 427	정밀묘사 252	정어리 130, 415
접시돌리기 266	정밀화 252	정열적이다 94
접영 272	정박아 8, 46	정오 468
접착제 152	정보 190	정원 152, 427
접촉사고 391	정보검색 191	정원사 361
접촉하다 543	정보과학 191, 218	정월 468
젓가락 130	정보교환 191	정월대보름 468
젓갈 130	정보기관 191	정육점 130
젓다 130, 543	정보망 191	정의감 94
정 80, 93, 252, 377	정보비 191	정의롭다 94
정가 347	정보사회 191, 328	정의사회 328

정자　671

정자 …………………………… 24	정황 …………………………… 501	제적 …………………………… 204
정장 ………………………… 108	젖 ……………………………… 35	제조업 ………………………… 361
정전기 ………………………… 218	젖가슴 ………………………… 35	제조하다 ……………… 348, 543
정정하다 ……………………… 543	젖꼭지 ………………………… 35	제주 …………………… 57, 230
정족수 ………………………… 292	젖니 …………………………… 35	제지하다 ……………… 174, 543
정지하다 ……………………… 543	젖다 …………………… 401, 501	제출하다 ……………………… 543
정직하다 ……………………… 94	젖소 …………………………… 415	제트기 ………………………… 391
정진하다 ……………… 218, 543	제 ……………………………… 453	제품 …………………………… 348
정찰 …………………………… 316	제— …………………………… 453	제품디자인 …………………… 252
정찰가 ………………………… 348	제곱 …………………………… 453	제품시장 ……………………… 348
정찰제 ………………………… 348	제과점 ………………… 130, 348	제헌절 ………………… 293, 468
정책 …………………… 292, 328	제국 …………………………… 293	조 ……………… 131, 427, 453
정초 …………………………… 468	제국주의 ……………………… 293	조각 …………………… 252, 501
정치 …………………………… 292	제기 …………………………… 130	조각가 ………………… 252, 361
정치가 ………………………… 292	제기차기 ……………………… 266	조각도 ………………………… 252
정치개혁 ……………………… 292	제끼다 ………………………… 543	조각칼 ………………………… 252
정치계 ………………………… 292	제대 …………………………… 316	조각품 ………………………… 252
정치관 ………………………… 292	제대하다 ……………………… 316	조각하다 ……………… 252, 543
정치구조 ……………………… 292	제도 …………………………… 328	조간 …………………………… 184
정치권 ………………………… 292	제독 …………………………… 316	조감도 ………………………… 152
정치기구 ……………………… 293	제방 …………………………… 482	조감독 ………………………… 252
정치노선 ……………………… 293	제법 …………………………… 501	조강지처 ……………………… 18
정치단체 ……………………… 293	제부 …………………………… 18	조개 …………………… 131, 415
정치도덕 ……………………… 293	제비 …………………………… 415	조개탄 ………………………… 384
정치면 ………………………… 184	제비꽃 ………………………… 427	조건반사 ……………………… 218
정치범 ………………… 293, 305	제사 …………………… 57, 230	조경학 ………………………… 218
정치비리 ……………………… 293	제사상 ………………………… 230	조계종 ………………………… 230
정치사상 ……………………… 293	제사지내다 …………………… 230	조교 …………………………… 204
정치유세 ……………………… 293	제삼자 ………………………… 9	조교수 ………………………… 204
정치윤리 ……………………… 293	제삿날 ………………… 230, 468	조국 …………………………… 293
정치이념 ……………………… 293	제설기 ………………………… 401	조그맣다 ……………… 435, 501
정치인 ………………………… 293	제설작업 ……………………… 401	조금 …………………………… 501
정치일정 ……………………… 293	제수 …………………………… 18	조급하다 ……………………… 94
정치자금 ……………… 293, 348	제습기 ………………………… 152	조기 …………………… 131, 415
정치체제 ……………………… 293	제안하다 ……………… 174, 543	조기교육 ……………………… 204
정치하다 ……………………… 293	제약회사 ……………………… 47	조기졸업 ……………………… 204
정치학 ………………………… 218	제왕절개수술 ………………… 24	조끼 …………………………… 108
정치학자 ……………………… 218	제육볶음 ……………………… 131	조난사고 ……………………… 262
정치협상 ……………………… 293	제의하다 ……………… 174, 543	조달청 ………………………… 293
정통 …………………………… 230	제일 …………………………… 501	조달하다 ……………………… 348
정하다 ………………………… 543	제자 …………………… 9, 204	조도 …………………………… 218
정학 …………………………… 204	제자리표 ……………………… 252	조동사 ………………………… 174
정형 …………………………… 435	제작 …………………………… 377	조랑말 ………………………… 415
정형외과 ……………………… 47	제작사 ………………………… 252	조례 …………………………… 305
정화조 ………………………… 152	제작자 ………………………… 252	조롱하다 ……………… 174, 543
정확성 ………………………… 94	제작하다 ……………… 184, 377, 543	조류 …………………… 401, 415

조르다 174, 543	조직사회 328	종교인 231
조리 131	조찬 131	종교전쟁 231
조리기구 131	조카 18	종교철학 231
조리대 131, 152	조퇴 204, 361	종교탄압 231
조리사 361	조퇴하다 204	종교학 218
조리하다 131, 544	조판하다 184	종기 47
조립 377	조폐공사 348	종달새 415
조립주택 152	조합 348	종례 204
조립하다 152, 377, 544	조합원 348	종묘 377, 428
조명 152, 252, 442	조형예술 253	종사하다 361
조명기구 152	조화 427, 501	종성 174
조명실 252	조회 204	종신형 305
조문객 57	족두리 108	종아리 35
조물주 57	족벌체제 293	종업식 204
조미료 131	족보 18	종업원 361
조밀하다 501	족제비 415	종이 152
조바심 80	족집게 152	종일 468
조부모 18	존경하다 80, 94, 328, 544	종자 377, 428
조사 174	존댓말 174	종족 293
조사하다 544	존재하다 501	종종 468
조상 18, 231	존중하다 94	종지 131
조상신 231	졸다 544	종친회 18
조선 278	졸도 47	종파 231
조선족 293	졸병 316	종합금융사 348
조세 348	졸업 204	종합대학 204
조소 252	졸업생 204	종합병원 47
조식 131	졸업식 204	종합예술 253
조심성 94	졸업여행 204	쫓다 544
조약 293	졸업장 204	좋다 80, 94, 401
조언하다 174, 544	졸업증명서 204	좋아하다 80, 544
조업 377	졸업하다 204	좌석버스 391
조역 252	졸이다 131, 544	좌천 361
조연 252	좀도둑 305	좌천되다 361
조연출 184	좀벌레 415	좌측 482
조용하다 65, 501	좁다 435, 482, 501	좌회전 391
조위금 57	좁히다 544	죄 305
조율 252	종갓집 18	죄다 544
조의금 57	종강 204	죄송하다 80
조이다 544	종교 231	죄수 305
조작하다 544	종교개혁 231	죄수복 305
조절하다 544	종교계 231	죄악 305
조정하다 544	종교관 231	죄인 305
조제실 47	종교단체 231	죄책감 80
조제하다 47	종교서적 231	주 468
조종사 361	종교음악 231, 253	주가 348
조직 328	종교의식 231	주가지수 348

주간 ··· 468	주민등록 ··· 152	주지스님 ··· 231
주간지 ··· 185, 191	주민등록증 ··· 152, 328	주차 ··· 391
주거 ··· 152	주민세 ··· 348	주차관리인 ··· 361, 391
주거비 ··· 348	주발 ··· 131	주차권 ··· 391
주거지 ··· 152	주방 ··· 152	주차기 ··· 391
주거환경 ··· 152	주방기구 ··· 131	주차단속원 ··· 305
주격 ··· 131	주방용품 ··· 131, 152	주차장 ··· 152, 391
주격턱 ··· 35	주방장 ··· 361	주책맞다 ··· 94
주검 ··· 57	주변 ··· 482	주초 ··· 468
주격 ··· 174	주변국 ··· 293	주춤하다 ··· 544
주관성 ··· 80, 218	주부 ··· 9, 361	주춧돌 ··· 152
주관식 ··· 204	주사기 ··· 47	주치의 ··· 47
주교 ··· 231	주사놓다 ··· 47	주택 ··· 152
주권 ··· 293	주사맞다 ··· 47	주택가 ··· 152
주권국가 ··· 293	주사약 ··· 47	주택문제 ··· 328
주근깨 ··· 35	주사위 ··· 266	주택조합 ··· 152
주급 ··· 348, 361	주산 ··· 453	주파수 ··· 185, 218
주기도문 ··· 231	주생활 ··· 57, 152	주판 ··· 453
주눅들다 ··· 94	주석 ··· 174	주홍 ··· 442
주님 ··· 231	주소 ··· 152	주화 ··· 348
주다 ··· 544	주술 ··· 231	주황 ··· 442
주동자 ··· 9	주스 ··· 131	죽 ··· 131
주둔지 ··· 316	주시하다 ··· 65, 544	죽다 ··· 57, 544
주둥이 ··· 415	주식 ··· 131, 348	죽순 ··· 131, 428
주례 ··· 24	주식시장 ··· 348	죽음 ··· 57
주례사 ··· 24	주어 ··· 174	죽이다 ··· 57
주룩주룩 ··· 401	주역 ··· 253	준공 ··· 152
주름 ··· 108	주연 ··· 253	준공검사 ··· 152
주름가다 ··· 108	주요리 ··· 131	준말 ··· 175
주름살 ··· 35	주위 ··· 482	준비운동 ··· 272
주름치마 ··· 108	주유소 ··· 348	준비하다 ··· 544
주말 ··· 468	주유소 ··· 384	준위 ··· 316
주머니 ··· 108, 152	주의주다 ··· 174	준장 ··· 316
주머닛돈 ··· 348	주의하다 ··· 544	줄 ··· 272, 453
주먹 ··· 35	주인공 ··· 253	줄곧 ··· 468
주먹구구 ··· 453	주일 ··· 231, 468	줄기 ··· 428
주먹밥 ··· 131	주임교사 ··· 204	줄넘기 ··· 266, 272
주먹질하다 ··· 544	주장하다 ··· 174, 544	줄다 ··· 501
주먹코 ··· 35	주저앉다 ··· 544	줄다리기 ··· 266
주목하다 ··· 65	주전선수 ··· 272	줄이다 ··· 108, 544
주무르다 ··· 544	주전자 ··· 131	줄임말 ··· 175
주문 ··· 231, 348	주점 ··· 131	줄자 ··· 152, 454
주문생산 ··· 348	주제 ··· 175	줄타기 ··· 266
주문서 ··· 348	주제가 ··· 253	줄표 ··· 175
주문하다 ··· 174, 348, 544	주주 ··· 348	줌 ··· 454
주민 ··· 152, 328	주중 ··· 468	줍다 ··· 544

중 231	중앙시장 349	증권시장 349
중간 482, 502	중앙은행 349	증권회사 349
중간상인 348	중앙집권제 293	증명사진 262
중개업자 348	중어학 218	증명서 328
중개인 348	중얼거리다 175, 544	증명하다 218
중계기 191	중위 316	증발 502
중계무역 348	중이염 47	증발하다 218
중계방송 185, 191	중장 316	증산교 231
중계하다 185, 191	중장비 377	증상 47
중고가구 152	중장비기사 361	증세 47
중고품 348	중저가 349	증손녀 18
중괄호 175	중절모 108	증손자 18
중국 278	중죄 305	증언 175
중국문명 237	중지 35	증언하다 175, 305, 544
중국문학 218	중진국 293	증여세 349
중국어 175	중창 253	증오 81
중국집 131	중창단 253	증오하다 81, 544
중남미 278	중탕하다 131, 544	증인 305
중년 9	중태 47	증조할머니 18
중단하다 544	중턱 482	증조할아버지 18
중독 47	중퇴 204	증편 131
중동 278	중편소설 253	지각 205
중력 218, 482	중학교 205	지각하다 81, 205, 218
중령 316	중학생 205	지갑 108, 152
중류사회 328	중형 435	지게 377
중류층 328	중환자 47	지게차 391
중립국 293	중환자실 47	지겹다 81
중매 24	쥐 415	지관 361
중매결혼 24	쥐다 544	지구 482
중매쟁이 24	쥐불놀이 266	지구당 294
중복 468	쥐색 442	지구력 94
중사 316	쥐치 415	지구본 482
중산층 328	쥐치포 131	지구의 482
중상 47	즈음 468	지구촌 294
중상모략하다 175, 544	즉사 57	지금 468
중생 231	즉석사진 262	지급 349
중성 24, 175, 218	즉시 468	지급하다 349
중성자 218	즉흥곡 253	지긋지긋하다 81
중세 468	즐거움 80	지껄이다 175, 545
중소기업 348, 361	즐겁다 80	지나가다 545
중소기업청 293	즐기다 80, 544	지나다 468, 545
중소기업특별위원회 293	즐비하다 502	지나오다 545
중순 468	즙 131	지나치다 502, 545
중식 131	증거 305	지난날 468
중앙난방 152	증권 349	지난달 468
중앙방송 185	증권거래소 349	지난번 469

지난해	469
지내다	153
지네	415
지느러미	415
지능	81, 218
지능지수	81, 219
지니다	545
지다	272, 316, 401, 428, 502, 545
지대	349, 482
지도	391, 482
지도교수	205
지도력	94
지도자	328
지도층	328
지도층인사	328
지독하다	94
지동설	482
지략	317
지렁이	415
지뢰	317
지루하다	81
지름	454
지름길	482
지리	482
지리다	35, 545
지리학	219
지리학자	219
지린내	65
지면	185
지명	294
지명하다	294
지문	35
지물포	349
지방	57, 131, 153, 231, 482
지방방송	185
지방법원	306
지방세	349
지방자치단체	294, 328
지방자치제	294
지방행정	294
지배인	361
지배자	328
지배하다	294
지병	47
지불	349

지불하다	349
지붕	153
지사제	47
지서	306
지석	57
지석묘	57
지수	454
지시대명사	175
지역	482
지역감정	328
지역구	294
지역사회	328
지역시장	349
지역전	317
지연	328
지열	401
지옥	57, 231
지우개	153, 205
지우다	108
지원군	317
지원병	317
지원부대	317
지원유세	294
지저귀다	415
지저분하다	502
지적하다	545
지점	349
지주	377
지지다	131, 545
지지하다	545
지진	401
지진계	454
지진대	401
지진아	9, 205
지질	402
지질학	219
지질학자	219
지체부자유자	9
지축	482
지출	349
지출하다	349
지치다	502
지침서	205
지켜보다	65, 545
지키다	317, 545
지팡이	153

지퍼	108
지평선	482
지폐	349
지피다	384, 545
지하도	391
지하수	482
지하실	153
지하자원	377
지하철	392
지형	482
지형도	482
지혜	81, 94, 219
지혜롭다	81, 94, 502
지휘	253
지휘관	317, 361
지휘자	253, 361
지휘하다	545
직각	435
직감	65
직거래	349
직계가족	18
직공	361, 377
직관	65
직급	361
직렬	219
직물	108
직불	349
직불카드	349
직사각형	435
직사광선	402
직선	436
직업	361
직업관	361
직업교육	205
직업병	361
직업윤리	361
직업의식	361
직원	349, 361
직장	349, 362
직장동료	9, 362
직장상사	9, 362
직장생활	362
직장인	362
직접세	349
직접인용	175
직접화법	175

직종	362
직진	392
직행버스	392
진	317
진—	442
진갑	57
진격	317
진격하다	317
진공관	219
진급	317
진급하다	317
진눈깨비	402
진단서	47
진단하다	47, 545
진달래	428
진달래색	442
진담	175
진도표	205
진돗개	415
진동	219
진드기	415
진딧물	415
진땀	35
진땀나다	81
진땀난다	545
진료	47
진료하다	47, 545
진리	219
진물	47
진법	306
진보하다	545
진술하다	94
진술	175, 306
진술서	306
진술하다	175, 306, 545
진실	502
진실성	94
진실하다	94, 502
진심	81
진열대	349
진열장	349
진열하다	349, 545
진영	317
진자운동	219
진작	469
진절머리나다	81
진정	306
진정서	306
진정제	47
진정하다	81
진지	131, 317
진지하다	94
진짜	502
진찰실	47
진찰하다	47, 545
진통제	47
진폐증	47
진품	349
진하다	442, 502
진학	205
진한	278
진행자	185
진행하다	545
진행형	175
진혼곡	57
진화	384
진화론	57, 415
진화하다	545
진흙	482
질	24, 454
질겁	81
질겁하다	81
질경이	428
질그릇	131, 153
질기다	502
질녀	18
질다	132, 502
질량	219, 454
질량불변의 법칙	219
질리다	81
질문하다	175, 545
질병	47
질부	18
질산	219
질서	306, 328, 392
질소	219
질식사	57
질의하다	175, 545
질책하다	175, 545
질투	81
질투하다	81, 545
질화로	385
질환	48
짐승	416
짐작하다	81, 219, 545
집	153, 454
집게	153
집게벌레	416
집게손가락	35
집권당	294
집권하다	294
집기	153
집다	545
집단	328
집단생활	328
집단의식	328
집단이기주의	328
집단행동	328
집무실	153
집문서	153
집사	231
집사람	18
집세	153, 349
집안	18
집어넣다	153
집주인	154
집중력	81, 94, 219
집중하다	84, 545
집짐승	416
집짓기	266
집필하다	175, 545
집합	454
집행유예	306
집행하다	306
집회	328
짓다	132, 154, 545
짓밟다	545
짓이기다	546
징	253
징검다리	392, 546
징계	306
징계하다	306, 546
징병	317
징수	349
징수하다	349
징역	306
징역살이	57, 306
징집	317

징집되다 ... 317	찌다 ... 132, 402, 546	차용하다 ... 350, 546
짖다 ... 416	찌들다 ... 502	차원 ... 482
질다 ... 442, 502	찌르다 ... 546	차일피일 ... 469
짚다 ... 546	찌르레기 ... 416	차조 ... 428
짚신 ... 108	찌르르르 ... 416	차주전자 ... 132
짜깁기 ... 108	찌푸리다 ... 546	차지다 ... 132
짜다 ... 65, 108, 132, 502, 546	찍다 ... 185, 262, 294, 546	차표 ... 392
짜증 ... 81	찍찍 ... 416	착각하다 ... 65, 81, 219, 546
짜증나다 ... 81	찐빵 ... 132	착공 ... 154
짝 ... 454	찔레꽃 ... 428	착공하다 ... 154
짝사랑 ... 24, 81	찜 ... 132	착륙하다 ... 392, 546
짝수 ... 454	찜질 ... 48	착복하다 ... 546
짝짜꿍 ... 266	찜긋하다 ... 546	착수하다 ... 547
짤막하다 ... 436, 502	찢다 ... 546	착시 ... 65
짧다 ... 436, 469, 502	찧다 ... 132, 546	착실하다 ... 94
짬 ... 469	―째 ... 454	착용하다 ... 108, 547
짬뽕 ... 132	―쯤 ... 469	착하다 ... 94
짭짤하다 ... 65, 132		찬거리 ... 132
짱구 ... 35		찬란하다 ... 502
째다 ... 546	**차**	찬미 ... 231
째려보다 ... 65, 546		찬밥 ... 132
짹짹 ... 416		찬불가 ... 231
쨍쨍 ... 402	차 ... 132, 392, 454	찬송 ... 231
쩔쩔매다 ... 94, 546	차갑다 ... 65, 94, 402	찬송가 ... 231
쩝쩝 ... 132	차고 ... 154	찬송하다 ... 231
쩨쩨하다 ... 94	차관 ... 294	찬양하다 ... 175, 232, 547
쪼개다 ... 546	차다 ... 108, 402, 482, 502, 546	찬장 ... 154
쪼그리다 ... 546	차단하다 ... 546	찬조금 ... 350
쪼글쪼글 ... 502	차도 ... 392	찬합 ... 132
쪼다 ... 416	차량 ... 392	찰과상 ... 48
쪼들리다 ... 502	차례 ... 57, 175, 231	찰나 ... 469
쪽 ... 454	차례상 ... 231	찰떡 ... 132
쪽빛 ... 442	차례지내다 ... 231	찰흙 ... 482
쪽파 ... 132	차로 ... 392	참 ... 416, 428, 502
쫀득쫀득 ... 132	차리다 ... 546	참가하다 ... 547
쫄깃쫄깃 ... 132	차림 ... 108	참견하다 ... 175, 547
쫄깃쫄깃하다 ... 65	차림새 ... 108	참고문헌 ... 175, 219
쫄바지 ... 108	차림표 ... 132	참고서 ... 205
쫓다 ... 546	차분하다 ... 94	참고인 ... 306
쬐다 ... 546	차비하다 ... 546	참기름 ... 132
쭈글쭈글 ... 35	차석 ... 205	참깨 ... 132
쭉 ... 482	차선 ... 392	참나무 ... 428
쭉정이 ... 377	차용 ... 349	참다 ... 547
찌 ... 262, 377	차용어 ... 175	참되다 ... 502
찌개 ... 132	차용증서 ... 349	참말 ... 175
찌그러지다 ... 546		참모총장 ... 317

참신하다	502
참외	428
참을성	94
참전	317
참전국	294, 317
참전용사	317
참치	132, 416
참하다	94
참호	317
참회하다	81, 547
찹쌀	132
찹쌀떡	132
찻길	392
찻잔	132
찻집	350
창	154, 253, 272, 317
창고	154
창공	483
창구	350
창녀	25, 362
창던지기	272
창문	154
창업	362
창의력	81, 94, 219
창자	35
창작곡	253
창작무용	253
창작예술	253
창작품	253
창작하다	253, 547
창조론	57, 416
창조자	232
창조주	57
창조하다	253, 547
창틀	154
창포	428
창피하다	81
찾다	547
찾아가다	547
찾아보기	175
찾아오다	547
채	154, 454
채광	154
채굴하다	378
채권	350
채권자	350

채널	185, 191
채다	547
채도	253, 442
채무	350
채무자	350
채색	442
채소	132, 378, 428
채송화	428
채식주의자	132
채썰다	133
채용하다	363
채우다	108, 154, 547
채점	205
채점하다	205
채집	219
채취하다	219, 378
채칼	133
책	175, 185, 205, 219
책가방	154, 205
책꽂이	154, 205
책망하다	175, 547
책받침	205
책방	350
책벌레	9, 175
책상	154, 205
책임	328
책임감	81, 94
책임자	328, 363
책장	154, 205
챙기다	547
처가	18
처가살이	25, 57
처남	18
처녀	9, 25
처녀자리	483
처량하다	81
처리하다	547
처마	154
처방	48
처방전	48
처방하다	48, 547
처벌	306
처벌하다	306, 547
처서	469
처신	94
처음	469

처절하다	81
처제	18
처조카	18
처형	18, 57, 306
처형하다	306
척	454
척박하다	378
척추	35, 416
척추동물	416
천	108, 454
천국	232
천당	57, 232
천도교	232
천동설	483
천둥	402
천리교	232
천리안	65
천막	154
천문대	219, 483
천문학	219
천문학자	219
천민	328
천벌	306
천사	232
천성	94
천식	48
천연	502
천연가스	219, 378, 385
천연기념물	416, 428
천연두	48
천연색	442
천연수지	378
천왕성	483
천장	154
천재지변	402
천적	416
천주교	232
천주님	232
천지	483
천진난만하다	502
천천히	469
천체	483
천체망원경	483
천하무적	317
천하장사	272
철	378, 469

철거하다 ·············· 154, 547	청년회 ······················ 329	체납하다 ···················· 350
철광 ························ 378	청동기시대 ·················· 237	체력 ························ 272
철근 ························ 154	청둥오리 ···················· 416	체력단련 ···················· 273
철기시대 ···················· 237	청량음료 ···················· 133	체류하다 ···················· 154
철길 ························ 392	청력 ···················· 35, 65	체면 ···················· 82, 95
철도 ························ 392	청렴결백하다 ················· 95	체벌 ························ 205
철도청 ······················ 294	청록 ························ 442	체신 ························· 95
철들다 ······················· 82	청명 ························ 469	체언 ························ 176
철모 ························ 317	청명하다 ···················· 402	체온 ························· 35
철봉 ·················· 266, 272	청문회 ······················ 294	체위 ························· 25
철사 ························ 154	청바지 ······················ 108	체육 ························ 273
철새 ························ 416	청색 ························ 442	체육관 ············ 154, 205, 273
철야농성 ···················· 329	청소기 ······················ 154	체육대학 ···················· 205
철야작업 ···················· 378	청소년 ························ 9	체육복 ················ 108, 273
철없다 ······················· 95	청소년기 ····················· 57	체육부 ······················ 273
철인 ·························· 9	청소년문제 ·················· 329	체육학 ······················ 219
철자 ························ 175	청소년범죄 ·················· 306	체육회 ······················ 273
철저하다 ····················· 95	청소도구 ················ 154, 205	체조 ························ 273
철쭉 ························ 428	청소부 ················ 363, 378	체중 ························· 35
철철 ························ 502	청소업 ······················ 378	체중계 ·················· 35, 154
철학 ························ 219	청소원 ······················ 378	체증 ···················· 48, 133
철학자 ······················ 219	청순하다 ···················· 502	체질 ························· 35
첩 ·························· 454	청승떨다 ····················· 95	체취 ···················· 35, 65
첩보 ·············· 191, 294, 317	청승맞다 ····················· 95	체코 ························ 278
첩보망 ······················ 191	청신경 ······················· 65	체포 ························ 306
첩보원 ······················ 192	청심환 ······················· 48	체포하다 ·············· 306, 547
첩자 ························ 294	청어 ························ 416	체하다 ············ 48, 133, 503
첫 ·························· 454	청와대 ······················ 294	체형 ························· 35
첫— ························ 454	청원경찰 ···················· 306	첼로 ························ 253
첫날밤 ······················· 25	청음 ···················· 65, 253	쳐다보다 ················ 65, 547
첫눈 ························ 402	청자 ························ 176	쳐들어가다 ·················· 317
첫사랑 ······················· 25	청정해역 ·············· 378, 483	쳐부수다 ···················· 547
첫째 ························ 454	청주 ························ 133	초 ···················· 154, 469
청각 ························· 65	청중 ························ 176	초— ························ 469
청각예술 ···················· 253	청진기 ······················· 48	초가집 ······················ 154
청각장애인 ··················· 65	청첩장 ······················· 25	초과 ························ 503
청각장애자 ··············· 9, 175	청초하다 ···················· 502	초대장 ······················ 329
청개구리 ···················· 416	청춘 ························· 57	초대형 ······················ 436
청결하다 ···················· 502	청취 ························· 65	초등학교 ···················· 205
청과시장 ···················· 350	청취율 ······················ 185	초등학생 ···················· 205
청구 ························ 350	청취자 ······················ 185	초록 ························ 442
청구서 ······················ 350	청취하다 ·············· 65, 185, 547	초록꽃 ······················ 428
청구하다 ············ 175, 350, 547	청하다 ······················ 547	초범 ························ 306
청국장 ······················ 133	청혼하다 ·············· 25, 547	초보운전 ···················· 392
청년 ·························· 9	체 ·························· 133	초보자 ························ 9
청년기 ······················· 57	체감온도 ···················· 402	초복 ························ 469

초상 … 57	총채 … 154	추하다 … 503
초상집 … 57	총천연색 … 442	축 … 454
초상화 … 253	총총 … 402	축가 … 253, 329
초선 … 294	촬영 … 185, 262	축구 … 273
초성 … 176	촬영기사 … 363	축구공 … 273
초소병 … 317	촬영하다 … 253, 262, 547	축농증 … 48
초소형 … 436	최루탄 … 318	축배 … 329
초순 … 469	최면 … 232	축복 … 232
초승달 … 483	최면술 … 232	축사 … 378
초식동물 … 416	최상급 … 176	축산업 … 363, 378
초음파 … 219	최상품 … 350	축산업자 … 378
초인종 … 154	최소공배수 … 454	축산업협동조합 … 378
초저녁 … 469	최소공약수 … 454	축산폐수 … 378
초조하다 … 82	최종 … 469	축산학 … 220
초청장 … 329	최초 … 469	축소하다 … 436, 548
초하루 … 469	최후 … 469	축음기 … 253
초혼 … 25	추곡 … 378	축의금 … 25, 329, 350
촉각 … 65	추곡수매 … 378	축전 … 192
촉감 … 66	추궁하다 … 176, 547	축제 … 329
촉매 … 219	추기경 … 232	축축하다 … 66, 402, 503
촉매제 … 219	추남 … 9	축하하다 … 176, 548
촉박하다 … 469	추녀 … 9	축협 … 378
촉진제 … 48	추다 … 253, 547	춘곤증 … 48
촉촉하다 … 66, 402, 503	추도식 … 58	춘부장 … 18
촌 … 483	추락하다 … 547	춘분 … 469
촌놈 … 9	추론 … 82, 219	춘추 … 58
촌뜨기 … 9	추론하다 … 82, 219, 547	춘하추동 … 469
촌스럽다 … 108	추리 … 82, 220	출가하다 … 232
촐랑거리다 … 547	추리하다 … 82, 220, 547	출간하다 … 185, 548
촘촘하다 … 503	추모식 … 58	출감 … 306
총 … 273, 317	추분 … 469	출구 … 483
총각 … 9, 25	추상화 … 253	출근 … 363
총각김치 … 133	추석 … 469	출금 … 350
총각무 … 133, 428	추석빔 … 108	출납 … 350
총검 … 317	추세 … 503	출렁거리다 … 402
총계 … 454	추수 … 378	출력 … 192
총리 … 294, 363	추수감사절 … 232	출마 … 294
총명하다 … 503	추수하다 … 378, 547	출마자 … 294
총사령관 … 317	추어탕 … 133	출마하다 … 294
총살 … 57	추억 … 82	출발하다 … 548
총선 … 294	추위 … 402	출산 … 25, 58
총선거 … 294	추정 … 82, 220	출산하다 … 548
총알 … 318	추진력 … 95	출생 … 58
총알받이 … 318	추측 … 82, 220	출생률 … 58, 329
총장 … 205	추측하다 … 82, 220, 548	출석 … 205
총재 … 294, 363	추키다 … 548	출석부 … 205

출석하다 548	측면 436, 483	친할머니 19
출세하다 548	측은하다 82	친할아버지 19
출연료 185, 253	측정 454	칠 155, 454
출연자 185	측정하다 454, 548	칠레 278
출연하다 185, 253, 548	층 154, 454	칠면조 133, 416
출옥 306	층계 154	칠부바지 108
출입구 483	치 454	칠순 58
출입하다 548	치과 48	칠판 206
출자 350	치다 254, 350, 378, 402, 548	칠하다 155, 254, 443, 548
출장 363	치렁치렁 108, 503	쥐 428
출전선수 273	치료제 48	침 35, 48
출전하다 273, 548	치료하다 48, 548	침공 318
출제 205	치루 48	침공하다 318
출출하다 66	치르다 350, 548	침구 155
출판 185	치마 108	침대 155
출판사 185	치마바지 108	침대보 155
출판인 363	치맛바람 205	침략 318
출판하다 185, 548	치매 48	침략하다 294
출항하다 392, 548	치밀하다 95	침례 232
출현하다 548	치사량 48	침례교 232
춤 253	치아 35	침몰하다 548
춤곡 253	치안 306	침범하다 294
춤꾼 253	치약 154	침샘 35
춤동작 254	치어 378	침실 155
춤사위 254	치우다 548	침울하다 82
춥다 66, 402	치자나무 428	침전물 220
충고하다 176, 548	치장하다 108	침착성 95
충돌하다 548	치즈 133	침착하다 95
충만하다 503	치질 48	침침하다 66, 503
충실하다 95	치통 48	침투 318
충전기 385	치하하다 176, 548	침팬지 416
충전하다 385	친교 329	칫솔 155
충치 48	친구 9	칭송하다 176, 548
취 133, 428	친목회 329	칭찬하다 95, 176, 548
취급하다 548	친숙하다 503	—초 469
취미 262	친인척 18	
취미생활 262	친자 18	
취미활동 262	친절하다 95	**카**
취사병 318	친정 18	
취재기자 185	친정아버지 18	카나리아 416
취재하다 185, 548	친정어머니 18	카네이션 428
취직 363	친족 18	카누 273
취직하다 363, 548	친족관계 18	카드 350
취하다 503	친지 18	카드놀이 267
측량 454	친척 18	
측량하다 454, 548	친하다 329, 503	

카드빚 350	코란 232	크리스마스 232
카메라맨 363	코미디언 363	크리스트교 232
카메룬 278	코바늘 109	큰곰자리 483
카톨릭교 232	코뿔소 416	큰달 469
카투사 318	코스모스 428	큰따옴표 176
카페 133	코스타리카 278	큰방 155
칵테일 133	코치 273	큰아버지 19
칸 454	코털 36	큰어머니 19
칼 133, 155, 318	코트 109	큰집 19
칼국수 133	콘크리트 155	큰창자 36
칼라사진 262	콜라 133	큼직하다 436, 503
칼륨 220	콜레라 48	킁킁거리다 549
칼슘 133, 220	콜록콜록 48	키 36, 392, 436
칼질하다 133	콜롬비아 278	키다리 9
칼집내다 133	콤바인 378	키스 25
칼춤 254	콧구멍 36	키스하다 25, 549
칼칼하다 66, 133	콧날 36	키우다 416, 549
캄보디아 278	콧노래 254	킬로그램 455
캐나다 278	콧대 36	킬로미터 455
캐내다 548	콧대높다 95	
캐다 378, 548	콧등 36	
캐드 254	콧물 36	## 타
캐묻다 176, 548	콧방울 36	
커다랗다 436, 503	콧수염 36	
커튼 155	콩 133, 428	타계 58
커피 133	콩가루 133	타계하다 58
커피메이커 133	콩고 278	타국 294
커피전문점 133	콩고물 133	타다 134, 392, 503, 549
커피포트 133	콩고민주공화국 278	타동사 176
컴컴하다 443	콩기름 133	타령 254
컴퓨터 155, 192, 206	콩나물 134, 428	타박상 48
컴퓨터공학 220	콩자반 134	타살 58
컴퓨터공학자 220	콩팥 36	타악기 254
컴퓨터그래픽스 254	쾌감 82	타원 436
컴퓨터아트 254	쾌활하다 95	타원형 436
컴퓨터오락실 267	쿠데타 294	타이르다 176, 549
컴퓨터통신 192	쿠바 278	타자 273
컵 133	쿠웨이트 278	타자기 155
컵받침 133	쿵푸 273	타자치다 176
케냐 278	퀴퀴하다 66	타작 378
케이크 133	크기 436, 454	타작하다 378
켜다 254, 385, 549	크낙새 416	타조 416
켤레 109, 454	크다 436, 454, 503	타조알 134, 416
코 35, 66, 416	크레타문명 237	타향살이 58
코끼리 416	크레파스 254	탁구 273
코딱지 36	크로아티아 278	

탁구공	273	탐내다	82	터	155, 483
탁아문제	329	탐독	176	터널	392
탁아소	206	탐미주의	254	터득하다	220
탁자	155, 206	탐사하다	549	터뜨리다	549
탁주	134	탐색하다	549	터미널	392
탁하다	503	탑	155	터울	470
탄광	378	탑승	392	터전	155, 483
탄광촌	378	탑승구	392	터키	279
탄내	66	탑승수속	392	턱	36
탄산음료	134	탑승하다	549	턱걸이	273
탄생	58, 416	탓하다	176, 549	턱수염	36
탄소	220	탕	134	털	36, 416
탄수화물	134	탕수육	134	털다	549
탄원	306	태국	279	털모자	109
탄원서	306	태권도	273	털보	9
탄원하다	176, 549	태극기	294	털신	109
탄자니아	278	태기	25	털실	109
탄전	378	태도	95	털옷	109
탄탄하다	503	태만하다	95	털장갑	109
탄핵	306	태몽	36	텃밭	379
탄환	318	태생	58, 416	텃새	416
탈	254	태아	9, 25	테너	254
탈곡	378	태양	483	테니스	273
탈곡기	378	태양계	483	테두리	483
탈곡하다	379	태양광선	402	텔레비전	155, 185, 192, 206, 254
탈골	48	태양력	469	토끼	417
탈모증	48	태양에너지	385	토끼풀	428
탈상	58	태양열	220, 385, 402	토란	134, 428
탈색	109, 443	태양열주택	385	토론	206
탈색하다	443	태어나다	416	토론하다	176, 549
탈수기	109, 155	태업	363, 379	토마토	134
탈수하다	109, 549	태우다	549	토마토케첩	134
탈영	318	태음력	469	토막	503
탈영병	318	태초	469	토막내다	134
탈영하다	318	태평성대	469	토목공사	155
탈옥	306	태평소	254	토박이말	176
탈옥수	307	태풍	402	토산품	350
탈의실	109	택견	273	토성	483
탈진	48	택배	379	토실토실	36, 436
탈출하다	549	택시	392	토씨	176
탈춤	254	탤런트	254, 363	토양	379
탈취제	66	탯줄	25	토요일	470
탈환	318	탱양열발전	385	토의하다	176, 549
탈환하다	318, 549	탱크	318	토정비결	58, 232
탐구하다	220, 549	탱탱하다	503	토종	417
탐나다	82	탱화	232, 254	토지	483

토지세 350
토질 379
토하다 48, 549
톤 455
톨 455
톱 155
톱밥 220, 385
톳 428, 455
통 134, 155, 294, 455
통계 455
통계청 294
통계학 220
통계학자 220
통고하다 176, 192, 549
통곡하다 549
통과의례 232
통과하다 483, 549
통근버스 392
통꽃 428
통나무집 155
통닭 134
통독 176
통로 483
통보하다 176, 549
통분 455
통사론 176
통상 350
통솔하다 329, 549
통신 192
통신병 318
통신사 185, 192, 363
통신시설 192
통신원 192
통신위성 192
통신판매 192, 350
통역사 176
통역하다 176
통일 295
통일감 82
통일교 232
통일국가 295
통일부 295
통일신라 279
통장 295, 350, 363
통조림 134
통증 49

통지하다 176, 549
통찰력 95, 220
통찰하다 66, 549
통치자 295
통치하다 295
통통배 392
통통하다 503
통풍 402
통화 206
통학버스 392
통학생 206
통합하다 549
통행료 392
통화 192, 350
통화료 192
통화팽창 350
통화하다 192
퇴각 318
퇴각하다 318
퇴근 363
퇴비 379, 428
퇴원 49
퇴원하다 49
퇴장하다 549
퇴정 307
퇴직 363
퇴직금 363
퇴직하다 363
퇴짜놓다 176, 549
퇴출 363
퇴학 206
투고하다 185
투기 350
투기꾼 350
투덜대다 176, 549
투명하다 443, 503
투박하다 503
투병 49
투수 273
투약하다 49
투원반 273
투자 350
투자가 351
투자신탁 351
투자자 351
투쟁 318

투전 267
투정하다 176, 549
투포환 273
투표 295
투표권 295
투표소 295
투표용지 295
투표율 295
투표자 295
투표하다 295
투표함 295
투피스 109
투항 318
투항하다 318
퉁기다 550
퉁명스럽다 95
튀기다 134, 550
튀김 134
튀김옷 134
튀다 550
튤립 428
트다 503
트랙터 379
트럭 392
트로이문명 237
트림 36
트집잡다 95, 550
특강 206
특공대 318
특권층 329
특별사면 307
특별소비세 351
특별수사대 307
특별시 155, 295
특별활동 206
특보 186, 192
특산물 351
특성 503
특송 379
특수교육 206
특수부대 318
특수하다 503
특수학교 206
특용작물 379
특이하다 503
특종 192

특종기사 ······ 186	파벌 ······ 295	팔등신 ······ 36
특질 ······ 503	파산하다 ······ 550	팔뚝 ······ 36
특집 ······ 186	파상풍 ······ 49	팔면체 ······ 436
특징 ······ 503	파생 ······ 176	팔목 ······ 36
특파원 ······ 186	파생어 ······ 176	팔방미인 ······ 9
특허청 ······ 295	파손하다 ······ 550	팔순 ······ 58
튼튼하다 ······ 36, 503	파업 ······ 363, 379	팔씨름 ······ 267
틀 ······ 436	파열하다 ······ 550	팔찌 ······ 109
틀니 ······ 36	파자마 ······ 109	팥 ······ 134, 428
틀다 ······ 550	파출부 ······ 363, 379	팥죽 ······ 134
틀리다 ······ 504	파출소 ······ 295, 307	패다 ······ 428, 504, 550
틀림없이 ······ 504	파충류 ······ 417	패랭이꽃 ······ 429
틈 ······ 470, 483	파키스탄 ······ 279	패류 ······ 379, 417
티끌 ······ 504	파푸아뉴기니 ······ 279	패류아 ······ 307
티내다 ······ 95, 550	판 ······ 455	패배 ······ 318
티눈 ······ 36	판결 ······ 307	패배하다 ······ 318
티브이편성표 ······ 186	판결문 ······ 307	패션 ······ 109
티셔츠 ······ 109	판결하다 ······ 176, 550	패소 ······ 307
(목이) 타다 ······ 134	판단 ······ 82, 220	패스 ······ 392
	판단력 ······ 82, 95, 220	패자부활전 ······ 273
	판단하다 ······ 82, 220, 550	패잔병 ······ 318
	판돈 ······ 351	패전 ······ 318
파	판례 ······ 307	패전국 ······ 318
	판매 ······ 351	패전하다 ······ 318
	판매고 ······ 351	패하다 ······ 273
파 ······ 134, 428	판매액 ······ 351	패혈증 ······ 49
파견하다 ······ 550	판매업자 ······ 351	팩스 ······ 192
파계승 ······ 232	판매원 ······ 351	팩시밀리 ······ 192
파괴하다 ······ 550	판매직 ······ 363	팬티 ······ 109
파김치 ······ 134	판매하다 ······ 351, 550	팽개치다 ······ 550
파나마 ······ 279	판별하다 ······ 82, 220, 550	팽이 ······ 267
파다 ······ 550	판사 ······ 307, 363	팽이버섯 ······ 134, 429
파도 ······ 402	판소리 ······ 254	팽이치기 ······ 267
파라과이 ······ 279	판소리문학 ······ 254	팽창 ······ 220
파란색 ······ 443	판자촌 ······ 155	팽팽하다 ······ 504
파랑 ······ 443	판잣집 ······ 155	퍼붓다 ······ 550
파랗다 ······ 443	판정승 ······ 273	퍼센트 ······ 455
파래 ······ 134, 428	판정하다 ······ 273, 550	퍼지다 ······ 504
파렴치하다 ······ 95	판판하다 ······ 436, 504	퍼포먼스 ······ 254
파릇파릇 ······ 443	판화 ······ 254	퍽 ······ 504
파리 ······ 417	판화가 ······ 254	펄펄 ······ 402
파리채 ······ 155	팔 ······ 36, 455	펑퍼짐하다 ······ 436, 504
파마머리 ······ 36, 109	팔각형 ······ 436	펑펑 ······ 402
파마하다 ······ 109, 550	팔굽혀펴기 ······ 273	페루 ······ 279
파멸하다 ······ 550	팔꿈치 ······ 36	페인트 ······ 155
파발 ······ 192	팔다 ······ 351, 550	펜싱 ······ 273

펀치 155	평상복 109	포로 318
펭귄 417	평생 58	포로수용소 319
펴다 109, 550	평생교육 206	포르투갈 279
편 455, 483	평생교육원 206	포만감 134
편견 82	평수 155	포물선 436
편곡 254	평야 483	포박하다 550
편곡하다 254	평영 273	포병 319
편도선염 49	평온 82	포상금 351
편동풍 402	평온하다 82	포수 274
편두통 49	평원 483	포식 134
편리하다 504	평일 470	포악하다 95
편서풍 402	평점 206	포옹하다 25, 550
편식 134	평평하다 436, 483, 504, 550	포용력 95
편안하다 82, 504	평하다 177, 550	포유류 417
편애하다 82, 95	평행 436	포장마차 134
편육 134	평행봉 273	포진 49
편의점 351	평행사변형 436	포크 134
편입 206	평행선 436	포환 274
편입생 206	평형 155, 504	포환던지기 274
편입하다 550	평화방송 186	폭 436, 455, 504
편지 192	폐 36	폭격 319
편지봉투 192	폐가 155	폭격하다 319
편지지 192	폐결핵 49	폭군 9
편집기자 186	폐광 379	폭동 295, 329
편집인 186, 363	폐교 206	폭력배 307
편집장 186	폐렴 49	폭로하다 177, 550
편집하다 186, 550	폐백 25	폭리 351
편파보도 186	폐쇄하다 550	폭발 319
편하다 82, 504	폐수 402	폭발물 385
편협하다 95	폐암 49	폭발하다 385
평 155, 379, 436, 455	폐업 351, 363, 379	폭설 402
평가 206	폐점 351	폭식 134
평가절상 351	폐품 351	폭약 319
평가절하 351	폐활량 36, 274	폭우 402
평가하다 82, 220	폐회식 329	폭죽놀이 267
평각 436	포 134	폭탄 319
평균 504	포개다 550	폭파 319
평균대 273	포경선 379	폭파하다 550
평균치 455	포고하다 177	폭포 483
평년 470	포교 232	폭풍 402
평년작 379	포교사 232	폭풍경보 402
평론 254	포기 429, 455	폭풍우 402
평론가 254	포기하다 550	폭풍주의보 402
평면도 155	포도 429	폴란드 279
평민 295	포도주 134	표 177
평범하다 504	포동포동 36, 436	표고버섯 134, 429

표구 254	품종개량 379	피난민 319
표기법 177	품질 351	피난살이 58
표기하다 177, 551	품질검사 379	피다 429, 504
표면 483	품질관리 351	피동문 177
표명하다 177, 551	품팔이 351	피라미 417
표밭 295	풋— 429	피로 49
표백제 109, 155	풋고추 135	피로연 25
표백하다 443, 551	풍 417	피뢰침 156
표범 417	풍경 254	피리 255
표본 220, 504	풍경화 254	피부 36
표어 329	풍금 255	피부과 49
표음문자 177	풍기다 504	피부관리 109
표의문자 177	풍년 379, 470	피부관리사 363
표절 186, 254	풍랑 483	피부미용 109
표제 186	풍력 385	피부병 49
표준어 177	풍로 385	피부암 49
푸념하다 177	풍만하다 504	피부염 49
푸다 135, 551	풍부하다 351, 504	피살 58
푸닥거리 232	풍산개 417	피살되다 58
푸대접하다 95	풍선 267	피시통신 192
푸르다 443	풍성하다 504	피아노 255
푸르스름하다 443	풍속 329, 403	피어오르다 403
푸석푸석 66	풍속계 403	피우다 135, 385, 551
푸성귀 429	풍습 237, 329	피의자 307
푸짐하다 504	풍악 255	피임 25
푹 436	풍요롭다 504	피임약 25
푹신푹신 66	풍작 379	피자 135
푹신하다 66, 504	풍족하다 351, 504	피해자 307
푹푹 403	풍진 49	핀 109
푼 455	풍차 220, 385	핀란드 279
푼돈 351	풍토병 49	핀잔주다 177, 551
풀 155, 429	풍향 403	필 455
풀다 109, 551	풍향계 403	필기 177
풀밭 429	프라이팬 135	필기구 156
풀빵 135	프랑스 279	필기도구 156, 177, 206
풀색 443	프로듀서 186, 363	필기하다 177, 551
풀이씨 177	프린터 192	필독 177
품 109	플라타너스 429	필독도서 177
품다 551	플랑크톤 417	필름 262
품목 351	피 36	필리핀 279
품사 177	피고 307	필사본 177, 186
품삯 351	피고인 307	필사하다 177
품성 95	피곤 49	필요하다 504
품앗이 379	피곤하다 504	필통 206
품위 95	피구 274	핏줄 36
품종 379	피난 319	핑계대다 177, 551

하

하강하다 504
하객 25
하관 58
하구 483
하구언 483
하급생 206
하나 455
하나님 232
하느님 232
하늘 483
하늘나라 58
하늘색 443
하늘소 417
하늘하늘 504
하늬바람 403
하다 109, 551
하단 483
하도 504
하드웨어 192
하루 470
하루살이 58, 417
하루종일 470
하마 417
하사 319
하사관 319
하사관학교 319
하산 262
하선하다 392
하소연 177
하소연하다 177, 551
하수구 156
하수도 156
하숙집 156
하숙하다 156
하순 470
하얀색 443
하양 443
하얗다 443
하오 470
하위어 177
하의 109
하지 470

하차 392
하찮다 504
하천 484
하청업자 363
하키 274
하품 36
하품하다 551
하현달 484
학 417
학계 220
학과 206
학과사무실 206
학과장 206
학교 156, 206
학교교육 206
학구적 220
학구파 220
학군 206
학군단 319
학급 206
학급문고 206
학급회의 207
학기 207
학년 207
학대하다 96
학도병 319
학력 207
학령기 207
학문 220
학문적 220
학번 207
학벌 207
학보 207
학보사 207
학부 207
학부사무실 207
학부장 207
학부형 207
학비 207, 351
학사 207
학사경고 207
학사일정 207
학사장교 319
학생 207, 363
학생식당 207
학생증 207

학생회 207, 329
학생회관 207
학생회비 207
학생회장 207
학설 220
학수고대하다 82
학술 220
학술답사 207
학술대회 220
학술용어 177
학술원 221
학술정보 192
학습 207, 233
학습서 207
학습하다 82, 221, 551
학업 207
학연 329
학예회 207
학용품 207
학용품 351
학원 207
학원생 208
학원폭력 208
학위 208
학위논문 208
학위수여식 208
학자 363
학장 208
학적 208
학적부 208
학점 208
학질 49
학파 221
학풍 221
학회 221, 329
한 82, 455
한— 470
한가운데 484
한가하다 504
한결 505
한결같다 96, 505
한과 135
한국 279
한국과학재단 221
한국관광공사 262
한국교육개발원 208

한국도로공사 392	한창 470	합집합 455
한국무용 255	한파 403	합창 255
한국문화예술진흥원 237	한파주의보 403	합창단 255
한국방송공사 186	한학 221	합치다 551
한국어 177	한학자 221	합하다 551
한국은행 351	한해살이 429	합헌 307
한국자수박물관 237	할 455	항고 307
한국정신문화연구원 237	할머니 19	항공권 393
한국학 221	할미꽃 429	항공기 393
한국학술진흥재단 221	할부 351	항공모함 393
한국학자 221	할부금 351	항공사 393
한국화 237	할아버지 19	항공우편 192
한글 177	할인 352	항공운항 393
한글날 177, 470	할인가 352	항구 393
한글문화 237	할인매장 352	항렬 19
한기 403	할인품목 352	항로 393
한나절 470	할증료 352, 392	항만 393
한눈팔다 551	할퀴다 551	항문 36
한더위 403	핥다 135, 551	항변하다 178, 551
한동안 470	함 156	항복 319
한두 455	함락 319	항복하다 319
한들한들 403	함박눈 403	항상 470
한랭전선 403	함정 392	항생제 49
한로 470	합 455	항성 484
한류 379, 403	합격 505	항소 307
한문학 221, 255	합격하다 208, 551	항아리 135, 156
한문학자 221	합계 352, 455	항암제 49
한민족 295	합기도 274	항온동물 417
한반도 279	합동 436	항의하다 178, 551
한밤중 470	합리 221	항해사 364, 393
한방 49	합리적 82	항해지도 393
한복 109	합리주의 221	항해하다 393, 551
한복판 484	합법 307	해 403, 455, 470, 484
한식 135	합병하다 551	해결하다 551
한식집 135	합산 455	해고하다 364, 551
한약 49	합산하다 455, 551	해골 36
한약방 49	합선 385	해군 319
한옥 156	합성수지 379	해군사관학교 208, 319
한의사 49, 364	합성어 177	해녀 379
한의원 49	합숙 156	해달 417
한의학 221	합의하다 177, 551	해당화 429
한자 177	합장 58	해독제 49
한자문화권 237	합장하다 233	해돋이 403
한자어 177	합주 255	해동하다 135, 551
한정식 135	합주단 255	해로 393
한참 470	합중국 295	해롭다 505

해류 379, 403	핸드볼 274	향수병 49
해마 417	햅쌀 135	향신료 135
해명하다 178, 551	햇— 429	향어 135, 417
해몽 233	햇과일 135	향유하다 237
해바라기 429	햇볕 403	허가하다 178, 552
해박하다 82	햇빛 403	허공 484
해변 484	햇살 403	허구 505
해병대 319	행군 319	허기 135
해부하다 551	행군하다 319, 552	허기지다 135, 505
해산 25	행동거지 96	허덕이다 552
해산물 135, 379	행동양식 96	허둥대다 552
해산하다 25, 551	행복 83	허락하다 178, 552
해삼 135, 417	행복하다 83	허름하다 505
해상교통 393	행사란 186	허리 37
해설 178	행성 484	허리띠 109
해설하다 178, 551	행운 233	허무하다 83
해수욕장 484	행운목 429	허물 505
해안 484	행운아 9	허물다 552
해양경찰청 295	행위예술 255	허벅다리 37
해양수산부 295	행정 295	허벅지 37
해역 379	행정가 295	허비하다 352, 552
해열제 49	행정고시 295	허상 505
해오라기 417	행정구역 156	허수 455
해오름 403	행정기관 295	허수아비 379
해왕성 484	행정법 307	허술하다 505
해외 295	행정병 319	허약하다 505
해외관광 262	행정부 295	허여멀겋다 443
해외여행 262	행정소송 295, 307	허영심 83
해이하다 96	행정요원 295	허용하다 178, 552
해일 403	행정자치부 295	허우대 37
해저 484	행정직 364	허우적대다 552
해제하다 403	행정학 221	허전하다 83
해조류 379, 429	행정학자 221	허점 505
해초 379, 429	행주 135, 156	허탈하다 83
해충 417	행주치마 109	허파 37
해치다 552	행진곡 255	허풍쟁이 9
해탈 233	행진하다 552	허허벌판 484
해파리 135	향가 255	헌금 233
해파리 417, 403	향교 233	헌법 307
해협 484	향긋하다 66	헌병 319
핵 221, 385, 417	향기 66	헌병대 319
핵가족 19	향기롭다 66	헌혈 50
핵무기 319	향나무 429	헐겁다 505
핵전쟁 319	향내 66	헐다 156, 552
핵폭탄 319	향년 58	헐뜯다 96, 178, 552
핸드백 109, 156	향수 66, 109	헐렁하다 505

험담하다 ········· 178, 552	현찰 ················· 352	형용사 ············· 178
험상궂다 ············· 505	현충일 ··············· 471	형장 ················· 307
헛간 ··················· 156	현행범 ··············· 307	형제 ··················· 19
헛구역질나다 ······· 552	혈관 ··················· 37	형태 ················· 437
헛기침하다 ·········· 552	혈기 ··················· 37	형태론 ·············· 178
헛소리 ················ 178	혈색 ··················· 37	형태소 ·············· 178
헝가리 ················ 279	혈압 ············· 37, 50	형편 ················· 505
헝겊 ··················· 110	혈압계 ················ 50	형평 ················· 505
헤매다 ················ 552	혈액순환 ············· 37	형형색색 ····· 437, 443
헤아리다 ········ 83, 552	혈액형 ················ 37	혜성 ················· 484
헤엄 ··················· 274	혈연 ··················· 19	혜안 ··················· 66
헤프다 ··········· 96, 505	혈연관계 ············· 19	호감 ··················· 83
헬기 ··················· 319	혐오감 ················ 83	호기심 ················ 83
헬륨 ··················· 221	혐오하다 ············· 83	호다 ············ 110, 552
헬리콥터 ············· 393	혐의 ················· 307	호두나무 ············ 429
헹구다 ····· 110, 135, 552	혐의자 ·············· 307	호떡 ················· 135
혀 ············· 37, 66, 418	협곡 ················· 484	호랑이 ·············· 418
혀끝 ···················· 66	협동하다 ············ 552	호루라기 ············ 156
혀뿌리 ················· 66	협력하다 ············ 552	호미 ················· 379
혁명 ··················· 296	협박하다 ······ 178, 552	호박 ··········· 135, 429
현관 ··················· 156	협상하다 ······ 178, 552	호박꽃 ·············· 429
현금 ··················· 352	협소하다 ······ 437, 505	호박죽 ·············· 135
현금지급기 ·········· 352	협심증 ················ 50	호상 ··················· 58
현금카드 ············· 352	협심하다 ············ 552	호소하다 ······ 178, 552
현기증 ················· 50	협약 ················· 296	호신술 ·············· 274
현대 ··················· 470	협의하다 ······ 178, 552	호언장담하다 · 178, 552
현대무용 ············· 255	협정 ················· 296	호외 ················· 186
현대문명 ············· 237	협주곡 ·············· 255	호우 ················· 403
현대문학 ············· 255	혓바늘 ················ 50	호우경보 ············ 403
현대미술 ············· 255	혓바닥 ················ 66	호우주의보 ········· 403
현대사회 ············· 329	형 ·············· 19, 437	호주 ··········· 156, 279
현대음악 ············· 255	형광 ················· 443	호주머니 ············ 110
현대인 ··················· 9	형광등 ·············· 156	호출기 ·············· 192
현명하다 ············· 505	형광색 ·············· 443	호출하다 ······ 178, 552
현모양처 ·············· 19	형구 ················· 307	호텔 ··········· 156, 379
현미 ··················· 135	형기 ················· 307	호통치다 ······ 178, 552
현미경 ················ 221	형님 ··················· 19	호프집 ·············· 135
현상 ··················· 262	형무소 ·············· 307	호화롭다 ············ 156
현상하다 ······· 262, 552	형벌 ················· 307	호황 ················· 352
현실 ··················· 505	형법 ················· 307	호흡 ··················· 37
현악기 ················ 255	형부 ··················· 19	호흡기관 ············· 37
현장학습 ············· 208	형사 ················· 307	혹 ················ 37, 50
현재 ··················· 471	형사소송 ············ 307	혹평하다 ······ 178, 552
현재시제 ············· 178	형상 ················· 437	혼 ··············· 58, 233
현재완료 ············· 178	형수 ··················· 19	혼담 ··················· 25
현재형 ················ 178	형식 ················· 505	혼동하다 ········ 83, 552

혼령 233	화랑 255	화제 178
혼례 25	화려하다 110	화창하다 403
혼백 58, 233	화력 221, 385	화채 135
혼삿날 471	화로 385	화초 429
혼수 25	화면 186, 255	화투 267
혼수상태 50, 505	화목하다 83, 505	화판 255
혼영 274	화문석 156	화폐 352
혼인 19, 25	화물 393	화폐가치 352
혼인신고 25	화물선 393	화포 320
혼잡통행료 393	화물열차 393	화학 221
혼잡하다 393, 505	화물차 393	화학반응 221
혼잣말 178	화방 255	화학약품 221
혼합하다 552	화백 255	화학조미료 135
혼혈 296	화법 178, 255	화학처리 379
혼혈아 296	화병 50	화학치료 50
홀가분하다 83	화분 429	화해하다 553
홀리다 552	화사하다 443	화혼 25
홀몸 9	화산 403	화환 429
홀소리 178	화산대 403	화훼 429
홀수 455	화살 274	화훼단지 381
홀아비 10, 25	화상 50	화훼시장 352
홀어머니 19	화생방전 319	확고하다 96, 505
홀짝거리다 553	화선지 255	확대사진 262
홀쭉이 10	화성 255, 484	확대하다 437, 553
홀쭉하다 505	화술 178	확률 456
홈드레스 110	화실 255	확성기 66, 192
홉 456	화씨 403	확실하다 505
홍당무 135, 429	화약 319	확실히 505
홍색 443	화염방사기 320	확언하다 178, 553
홍수 403	화요일 471	확연하다 505
홍어 135, 418	화용론 178	확장하다 553
홍역 50	화음 255	환각 66
홍차 135	화자 178	환각제 50
홍학 418	화장 58, 110	환갑 58
홍합 135	화장대 110, 156	환경 296
홍합 418	화장솔 110	환경디자인 255
화 83	화장솜 110	환경문제 329
화가 255, 364	화장수 110	환경미화원 364, 381
화교 296	화장술 110	환경부 296
화끈하다 96	화장실 156	환경오염 329, 403
화나다 83, 553	화장지 110	환기 156, 403
화내다 83, 553	화장터 58	환담하다 178, 553
화농 50	화장품 110	환등기 208
화단 429	화장하다 553, 58, 110	환불 352
화덕 385	화재 385	환산 352
화란 279	화재경보기 156	환상 83

환송하다 ... 553	회갑 ... 58	후미지다 ... 484, 553
환영하다 ... 553	회계사 ... 364	후방 ... 320, 484
환율 ... 352	회고록 ... 186	후배 ... 10
환자 ... 50	회교 ... 233	후보선수 ... 274
환전 ... 352	회교도 ... 233	후보자 ... 10
환절기 ... 404, 471	회담 ... 179, 297, 329	후불 ... 352
환조 ... 255	회답하다 ... 179, 553	후비다 ... 553
환청 ... 66	회복실 ... 50	후손 ... 19
환풍 ... 156	회복하다 ... 50, 553	후식 ... 136
환풍기 ... 156	회비 ... 352	후유증 ... 50
환하다 ... 443	회사 ... 352, 364	후임 ... 364
환호하다 ... 83, 553	회사원 ... 364	후진 ... 393
활 ... 274	회상하다 ... 83, 553	후진국 ... 297
활개치다 ... 553	회색 ... 443	후진하다 ... 553
활기차다 ... 505	회수권 ... 393	후처 ... 19
활달하다 ... 96	회수금 ... 352	후추 ... 136, 429
활동사진 ... 262	회양목 ... 429	후퇴 ... 320
활동하다 ... 553	회오리바람 ... 404	후퇴하다 ... 320, 553
활발하다 ... 96	회원 ... 329	후회 ... 83
활용 ... 178	회의 ... 297, 329	후회하다 ... 83, 553
활용하다 ... 553	회장 ... 352, 364	훈계하다 ... 179, 553
활주로 ... 393	회전 ... 393	훈련 ... 274, 320
활짝 ... 429	회전의자 ... 156	훈련병 ... 320
활화산 ... 404	회진 ... 50	훈련생 ... 320
황 ... 221	회화 ... 179, 255	훈련소 ... 320
황금분할 ... 255	횡단보도 ... 393	훈련조교 ... 320
황금어장 ... 381	효과 ... 255	훈민정음 ... 179
황당하다 ... 83	효녀 ... 19	훈시하다 ... 179, 553
황무지 ... 484	효도 ... 19	훈장 ... 320
황사현상 ... 404	효도관광 ... 262	훌라후프 ... 274
황산 ... 221	효모 ... 136, 429	훌륭하다 ... 505
황새 ... 418	효부 ... 19	훑다 ... 381, 553
황색 ... 443	효율 ... 364	훑어보다 ... 66, 553
황소 ... 418	효자 ... 19	훔치다 ... 307, 553
황소개구리 ... 418	후 ... 471	훗날 ... 471
황소바람 ... 404	후각 ... 66	훤하다 ... 444
황소자리 ... 484	후계자 ... 10	훨씬 ... 505
황야 ... 484	후광 ... 443	훨훨 ... 418
황인종 ... 10	후년 ... 471	훼방놓다 ... 553
황제 ... 296	후대 ... 471	휑하다 ... 506
황태자 ... 296	후덕하다 ... 96	휘감다 ... 553
황토색 ... 443	후라이팬 ... 136	휘다 ... 437, 506
황혼 ... 404	후련하다 ... 83	휘발유 ... 221, 385
황혼기 ... 58	후루룩 ... 136	휘어잡다 ... 553
황후 ... 296	후면 ... 484	휘황찬란하다 ... 444
회 ... 136	후문 ... 156	휴가 ... 364

휴강	208	흘리다	554
휴게실	208	흙	484
휴교	208	흠	506
휴대전화	192	흠잡다	96, 554
휴대폰	192	흠집	506
휴양지	262	흡사하다	437, 506
휴업	352, 364, 381	흡연	136
휴일	471	흡족하다	83
휴전	320	흥건하다	506
휴전선	297, 320	흥겹다	83
휴정	308	흥미	83
휴지통	156	흥미롭다	83
휴직	364	흥분하다	83, 554
휴학	208	흥정	352
휴학생	208	흥정하다	352, 554
휴화산	404	흥청대다	554
흉가	156	흥행사	255
흉기	320	흥행하다	256
흉내내다	553	흩다	554
흉년	381, 471	흩어지다	554
흉보다	96, 553	희곡	256
흉부외과	50	희귀하다	506
흉악범	308	희극	256
흉악하다	506	희극인	256
흉작	381	희끗희끗	444
흉터	37, 50	희노애락	83
흐느끼다	83, 554	희다	444
흐르다	404, 471	희롱하다	96, 554
흐리다	404, 506, 554	희망	83
흐물흐물	66	희망하다	83, 554
흐뭇하다	83	희박하다	506
흑백	444	희생하다	554
흑백사진	262	흰머리	37
흑사병	50	흰색	444
흑색	444	히잉	418
흑색선전	297	힌두교	233
흑연	381	힘	221, 385
흑염소	418	힘들다	506
흑인종	10	힘쓰다	554
흑자	352	힘없다	506
흑점	484	힘있다	506
흔들다	554	힘줄	37
흔들의자	156		
흔하다	506		
흘겨보다	66		
흘기다	554		